PULL OUT for your TIMESAVING blueprint to using this book

SAGE was founded in 1965 by Sara Miller McCune to support the dissemination of usable knowledge by publishing innovative and high-quality research and teaching content. Today, we publish over 900 journals, including those of more than 400 learned societies, more than 800 new books per year, and a growing range of library products including archives, data, case studies, reports, and video. SAGE remains majority-owned by our founder, and after Sara's lifetime will become owned by a charitable trust that secures our continued independence.

Los Angeles | London | New Delhi | Singapore | Washington DC | Melbourne

STRATEGY

Theory and Practice

2nd Edition

Stewart R Clegg
Jochen Schweitzer
Andrea Whittle
Christos Pitelis

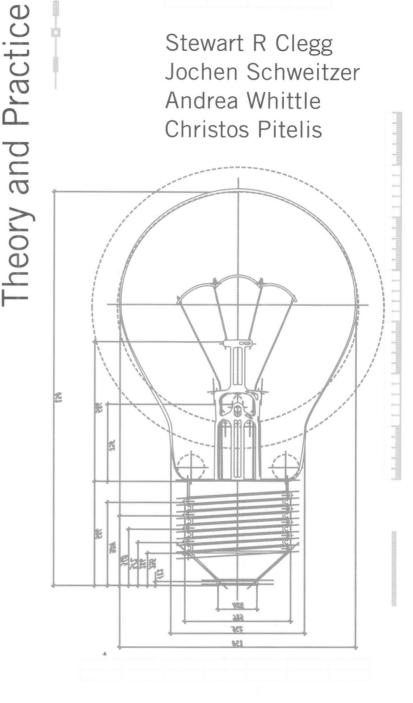

Los Angeles | London | New Delhi
Singapore | Washington DC | Melbourne

Los Angeles | London | New Delhi
Singapore | Washington DC | Melbourne

SAGE Publications Ltd
1 Oliver's Yard
55 City Road
London EC1Y 1SP

SAGE Publications Inc.
2455 Teller Road
Thousand Oaks, California 91320

SAGE Publications India Pvt Ltd
B 1/I 1 Mohan Cooperative Industrial Area
Mathura Road
New Delhi 110 044

SAGE Publications Asia-Pacific Pte Ltd
3 Church Street
#10-04 Samsung Hub
Singapore 049483

Editor: Kirsty Smy
Development editor: Sarah Turpie
Editorial assistant: Lyndsay Aitken
Production editor: Sarah Cooke
Copyeditor: Christine Bitten
Proofreader: Fabienne Pedroletti Gray
Indexer: Silvia Benvenuto
Marketing manager: Alison Borg
Designer: Shaun Mercier
Typeset by: C&M Digitals (P) Ltd, Chennai, India
Printed in the UK by Bell & Bain Ltd, Glasgow

© Stewart R Clegg, Jochen Schweitzer, Andrea Whittle and Christos Pitelis 2017

First edition published 2011
This second edition published 2017

Library of Congress Control Number: 2016942048

British Library Cataloguing in Publication data

A catalogue record for this book is available from the British Library

ISBN 978-1-44629-828-2
ISBN 978-1-44629-829-9 (pbk)
ISBN 978-1-47393-845-8 (pbk & interactive ebk) (IEB)

At SAGE we take sustainability seriously. Most of our products are printed in the UK using FSC papers and boards. When we print overseas we ensure sustainable papers are used as measured by the PREPS grading system. We undertake an annual audit to monitor our sustainability.

BRIEF CONTENTS

DETAILED CONTENTS

COMPANION WEBSITE ⑨SAGE edge™

FOR STUDENTS

A wealth of interactive and informative online content – designed to help you go further in your studies and achieve success in your course – can be found on the book's SAGE edge website. Visit **https://edge.sagepub.com/strategy2e** to find:

- Multiple choice questions
- Flashcards of key terms
- Free access SAGE journal articles discussed in the text
- Interviews with top strategists (linking to In Practice features in the text)
- Links to key websites and online articles
- Links to videos

FOR LECTURERS

A selection of tried and tested teaching resources have been honed and developed to accompany this text and support your course. Visit **https://edge.sagepub.com/strategy2e** to set up or use your instructor login to access:

- Editable and adaptable PowerPoint slides to integrate into your teaching
- A tutor's manual providing ideas and inspiration for seminars and tutorials, and guidance on how you might use the features in the book in your own teaching

ABOUT THE AUTHORS

Stewart Clegg is Professor of Management and Research Director of the Centre for Organization and Management Studies at the University of Technology, Sydney Business School. For over forty years he has been extremely active in teaching and researching organizations and management from a sociological perspective, in both Europe and Australia.

His major research interests have always centered on power relations in organizations and in theory. He is the author of many books, including *Strategy: Theory and Practice* (2011), a further collaboration with Martin Kornberger, amongst others, as well as being the editor of a great many volumes, including the award-winning *Handbook of Organization Studies* (2006). He has published many articles in leading journals such as the *Academy of Management Review, Organization Science, Organization Studies, Administrative Sciences Quarterly, Journal of Political Power, Human Relations, Organization* and the *Journal of Management Studies.*

Stewart seeks to be the embodiment of the potential of the sociological imagination to illuminate social reality. To this end he has tried, with his co-authors, to make understanding management and organizations relevant, accessible and stripped of pretension.

Jochen Schweitzer teaches Strategy, Innovation and Entrepreneurship and is the Director of the MBA Entrepreneurship at the UTS Business School. He is also Research Stream Leader for Strategy and Creativity at the Center for Management and Organisation Studies (CMOS) and Founder/Director of U.lab, a multidisciplinary innovation hub. Previously he has worked as a Design Thinking Coach, Management Consultant, Production-Planning Engineer and Cultural Program Coordinator. His research, teaching and consulting focuses on issues of strategy, collaboration, entrepreneurship and innovation with a special interest in design thinking, urban planning and open innovation.

Andrea Whittle is Professor of Management at Newcastle University Business School and previously Head of the Strategy, Organization and Society Research Group. Before joining Newcastle University in 2013, Andrea held a Chair in Organization Studies at Cardiff University. Andrea started her academic career in Natural Science, then did a PhD in Sociology in the field of Science and Technology Studies and since then has taught Management in Business Schools. Andrea's interest in strategy started without plan or design – much like many strategies themselves emerge. While doing an ethnography of a group of management consultants for her doctoral research, she was fascinated by the social, political, material and discursive processes through which the group tried to shape the firm's strategy agenda, albeit not always successfully. Since then, she has gone on to develop a keen interest in strategy as practice, applying organization theory and social theory to the study of strategizing processes in a range of contexts. Her more recent work has included longitudinal ethnographic research on a strategy project team in a Multinational Corporation and work on how top managers account for their strategic decisions following crises and scandals. Central to all her work is a concern for understanding how discourse and power are implicated in all forms of organization – of which strategy is not an exception but an exemplar.

 **Christos Pitelis** is Head of Brunel Business School and Professor of Strategy and Sustainable Competitiveness. He co-founded, and for twenty years directed the Centre for International Business and Management (CIBAM) at both the University of Cambridge, where he is a Life Fellow of Queens' College, and the University of Bath, where he was also a Professor of Sustainable Global Business. He has held visiting appointments, at the University of California Berkeley; Copenhagen Business School; University of St Petersburg and University of Technology Sydney among others. He has published extensively in leading Strategy, Organization and International Business journals, single-authored and with the leaders in these fields.

ACKNOWLEDGEMENTS

Stewart and Jochen wrote the first edition of the book with Chris Carter and Martin Kornberger. The second edition sees a new authorial team, with Chris and Martin retiring and being replaced by Andrea Whittle and Christos Pitelis. The contribution of Chris and Martin was essential to framing this project in the first instance. In this much-revised second edition, to the best of our knowledge, specific contributions attributable to their input are not present. We acknowledge their past contribution with gratitude.

We also wish to acknowledge the support and encouragement for this project of Kirsty Smy and Sarah Turpie, without whose efforts and encouragement it might never have been accomplished. The reviewers that Sage contacted were also very helpful.

Stewart would like to acknowledge the many helpful comments he received on the draft chapters as they unfolded from colleagues at the Centre for Management and Organization Studies and from the Management Discipline Group at the University of Technology Sydney, including Ace Simpson, Marco Berti, Wal Jarvis, Natalia Nikolova, Danielle Logue and David Bubna-Litic as well as comments from Gerry Davis, J.C. Spender and David Weir.

PUBLISHER'S ACKNOWLEDGEMENTS

We are very grateful to everyone who has granted kind permission to reproduce their material in this book.

We would also like to extend our warmest thanks to the following individuals for their invaluable feedback on the proposal and the draft material for this book:

Lecturer Reviewers

Christos Apostolakis, Bournemouth University

Clive Kerridge, University of Gloucestershire

Dr Kent Springdal, Kingston University

Ehsan Sabet, Loughborough University

Elizabeth Alexander, University of the West of England

Garry Carr, Leeds Beckett University

Ingrid Bonn, Bond University

Keith Halcro, Glasgow Caledonian University

Konstantinos Pitsakis, Kingston University London

Louisa Jones, University of Central Lancashire

Neil Botten, Westminster Business School

Patricia Murtagh, University of Liverpool

Pers Bergfors, Copenhagen Business School

Sheena Davies, University of Portsmouth

Sue Miller, University of Durham

Tahir Rashid, University of Salford

Ted Sarmiento, Leeds Beckett University

Ursula Plesner, Copenhagen Business School

Student reviewers

We are very grateful to the following students for providing invaluable feedback on the text, and helping us to develop the fold-out guided tour document:

Dipti Rohera Khatriya, Aston University

Emma Wilson, Aston University

Nasa Lin, University of Leeds

STRATEGY: THEORY AND PRACTICE – AN INTRODUCTION

ORIGINS, ISSUES, OVERVIEW

Learning objectives

By the end of this chapter you will be able to:

1 Gain an understanding about the origins of contemporary business strategy

2 Grasp the basics of strategy in theory and in practice

3 Appreciate the importance of strategy for management practice

4 Understand recent overviews and current directions in strategy

5 Start to think strategically about different competitive strategies in various sectors

6 Appreciate some of the limits of conventional views of strategy

BEFORE YOU GET STARTED

I think it may be the case that Fortune is the mistress of one half our actions, and yet leaves the control of the other half, or a little less, to ourselves ... Fortune ... displays her might where there is no organized strength to resist her. (Machiavelli, 1909, *The Prince* [Harvard Classics edn]. New York: P.F. Collier & Son. p. 107)

Introduction

In this introductory chapter we will address the organizing themes of the book, which are 'strategy', 'theory' and 'practice'. In this first chapter we will separate them to some extent; as the book unfolds we will integrate them.

What is strategy? Put simply:

Strategy = Knowledge + Capability (or the power to accomplish things)

Knowledge is needed in order to be able to have both the concepts with which to imagine a future state of affairs and the know-how and skills with which to try and get there. Capabilities, as the *power to* get things done, are needed in order to be in a position to implement ideas, visions and plans. Strategy (as capability/power to + knowledge) has a double edge; it is both what is conceivable *and* what is doable – as such it is a practice. Hence strategy is not just concerned with the 'ends' (future desired state) imagined but also with how to turn the ends and visions into 'reality'.

By its nature, strategy involves a paradox: the more the future is like the past the better the strategy will be at articulating ways of potentially dealing with it. The easier it is to imagine the future the better planned the strategy will be. However, the more disjunctive and disruptive the future turns out to be with respect to the past, then the less useful strategy will be because the knowledge it is founded upon will be redundant in the face of a radically discontinuous future. In this sense, and to the extent that the past informs the future, strategy is most *useful* where it is least *needed* while, where it is most *needed*, it will be least *useful*. It is partly for this reason that the original approach to strategy as 'planning' has gradually given way to more sophisticated perceptions, such as a process of 'strategizing', for example, by undertaking actions that place a firm in a better position than competitors. However, in this book, we won't only be looking at firms; we will also be considering the way that strategizing is done in public sector, charitable and other not-for-profit organizations.

The most simplistic understanding of strategy sees it as planning a sequence of actions based on a prediction of what the future will bring. However, a more sophisticated view of strategy, which, as we shall see in Chapter 3, was inspired by Edith Penrose, can revolve around the idea of developing and leveraging resources and capabilities so that we can face *unpredictable* futures. In fact the more unpredictable the future is, the more successful a strategy based on developing flexibility and agility is likely to be.

What does this introductory chapter aim to do? This chapter aims to give the reader an understanding of the dual *military* and *business* history of thinking about strategy. From there we shall consider, briefly, some of the influential strategy thinkers in what we refer to as the 'classical age' of strategy; classical because these early theorists were largely unchallenged in founding the field, becoming revered as pioneers.

Learning about eminent theorists' ideas is one way of understanding strategy. Another, perhaps more useful, way is to relate some central ideas encountered in strategy to something with which the reader is already familiar. We assume a reader that is aware of and interested in fashion and shopping, so we contrast two styles of fashion retail, M&S and Zara, to make some basic points about strategy.

Finally, in this introductory chapter, we survey the contemporary strategy scene to set the stage for the remainder of the book. A number of recent surveys of the strategy field are useful in demonstrating contemporary concerns, which we elaborate towards the end of the chapter.

We conclude the chapter by outlining some limits to overly rationality-based accounts of strategy. Such limits relate to complexity, contradictory interests, the inevitability of surprises, and the so-called 'Red Queen' effect. For those who recall *Alice in Wonderland* by Lewis Carroll (1946), the Red Queen tells Alice that in order to stay in a (competitive) place you have to run very hard, whereas to get anywhere you have to run even harder. Each of the limits considered pose challenges to rationality-based approaches to strategy. Moreover, each is likely to be encountered in practice that is rarely simple, non-contradictory and unsurprising; hence, strategies based on such assumptions will constantly be outpaced or outflanked.

Let us first dip into the wisdom of some selected ancients.

Strategy in theory: Ancient antecedents

Modern notions of business strategy did not just spring into being, fully formed. There are prehistories of thought that shaped the way that more recent business theorists made sense of the term. Business strategy has antecedents in *political* and *military* strategy in particular. These areas represent two major zones of strategy as a 'craft' oriented to 'winning'. We can look at two famous examples drawn from modern strategy's antecedents to explore this aspect of contemporary strategy.

Writing from the perspective of military strategy, both Hart (1982) and Ferrill (1966) stressed the strategic import of Herodotus' account of the battle of Thermopylae in Ancient Greece. The Greeks, led by the Spartans, held the much more numerous Persians at bay through superior military strategy, despite being out-numbered. For these writers warcraft represents the birth of strategy. Similarly, other writers favour Sun-Tzu, the famed Chinese warrior–strategist, as a precursor to modern strategy (Sawyer, 1994).

Certainly, there are ancient writings on strategy that have proven resilient. However, the continuities with contemporary accounts of strategy *per se* are not obvious. Accounts of how to wage warfare and exercise statecraft in ancient times are not always sound strategic guides to the twenty-first century world of modern organizations.

EXTEND YOUR KNOWLEDGE

For a fairly academic yet readable perspective on strategy, you could check out Stephen Cummings' book *Recreating Strategy*. He starts with the ancient Greeks and relates strategy back to the key thinkers of that age.

Cummings, S. (2002) *Recreating Strategy*. SAGE: London.

More recent historical thinkers than the Ancient Greeks or Sun-Tzu have been identified as antecedents of modern thinking about strategy. Some scholars position thinking about strategy as emerging with the discourse of statecraft, that is, the practice of governing a territory and its population. The most notable of these was Niccolò Machiavelli (1469–1527), an Italian Renaissance diplomat and author. Machiavelli was a senior official in the Florentine Republic, responsible for both diplomatic and military affairs, who was also secretary and chief advisor to senior officials and princes. Wolin (1960) notes that modern thinking about political strategy began with Machiavelli. His distinctive contribution, in Wolin's view, was a relentless strategic focus.

Image 1.1   Engraving of philosopher Niccolo Machiavelli from 1870. Copyright: Ralf Hettler

Machiavelli was a political realist and strategic thinker because, in Powell's words:

> He was the first to … consider a world where the natural order was not set down by God but dominated by unchanging human nature. Machiavelli did not contest the rules that had bound those who went before him; he simply ignored them … he was the first to consider power and how it should be used and retained in a utilitarian rather than a utopian way. (Powell, 2010: 4)

Machiavelli's themes have been persistent and popular ideas for contemporary managers and leaders (Jay, 1994; McGuire and Hutchings, 2006). Machiavelli is usually seen as having referred to the effectiveness of power without making reference to ethical and moral standards. The term *Machiavellianism*, used to describe individuals who will behave immorally to achieve their own desired ends, has entered into popular discourse as a word with heavy pejorative baggage. As a dark disposition (Judge et al., 2009: 867), it has been 'used to define a personality trait characterized by cunning, manipulation, and the use of any means necessary to achieve one's political ends'. The adjective thus compresses all that is negative about those in power and chimes with fashionably cynical perspectives on management (Kellaway, 2010: 12).

What did Machiavelli offer to strategy? Machiavelli avoided the ethical issue of constructing ultimate values that should guide conduct. For him, *power* was to be conceived as pure expediency, doing whatever it takes to get what is wanted, while *strategy* involved the understanding of the means necessary to achieve the desired ends of power. Machiavelli's world of power was one of flux, discontinuity, intrigue and illusion that few were able to understand and it was the task of the strategist to master. Power needed strategy as much as strategy needed power. Power was gauged by the effectiveness of strategies for achieving for oneself a greater scope for action than for others – or, to put it simply, getting what you want.

Strategy, for Machiavelli, concerned itself with a political economy of violence; knowing when to be hard and when to be cruel, as well as when to be cruel to be kind, and occasionally, when to be kind – but always with an agenda behind the scenes. On occasion, securing *consent* may be a more effective form of translating power into strategy than always having to *coerce* recalcitrance. The good strategist was, in essence, a good ethnographer (someone who studies other peoples and cultures); someone who is alert to the shifting and seemingly inconsequential details and dramas of everyday politics amongst the elites in society.

In Machiavelli's world, according to Jackson (2000: 434),

> Because of the difficulty of knowing who is virtuous and who is vicious, Machiavelli tells a Prince to act as if most people are vicious ['A man who wants to act virtuously in every way necessarily comes to grief among so many who are not virtuous'; Machiavelli, 1961: 50].

Familiarity with Machiavelli's work can be of great value for any politically competent person, especially those who are managers striving to be strategists. His emphasis on the *realpolitik* of power driving strategy will be relevant to a sophisticated grasp of strategy, as will become apparent in the rest of this book.

As well as Machiavelli, one other figure that has been much studied for his insights into strategy is Carl von Clausewitz (1780–1831). Clausewitz was a Prussian military officer who, in his eight-volume treatise, *On War* (Clausewitz, 1943), argued that

Image 1.2   Stamp printed in GDR (East Germany) showing Carl von Clausewitz. © cityanimal - Fotolia.com

military strategy is not a completely rational process. The passions and emotions are central to engagement in it and its accomplishment (Gardner, 2009: 127). Strategies for the future shape action in the present designed to bring that future to fruition (Kornberger, 2013). The future is always hostage to the present; although not always in the ways one might ordinarily think.

Clausewitz suggests that 'the more we know about the "infinity of petty circumstances", the more information we have at hand, the more our uncertainty will increase' (Kornberger, 2013: 1064). For Clausewitz, if a strategy were useful then all competing parties would use it, thus cancelling out any advantage it might offer. In these circumstances:

> [O]ne could expect both to deviate from the true strategy to reap the bene-fits of surprise. The truth put forward in the theory would defeat itself, so to speak. Its truth would be a function of its dissemination. Hence strategy can-not represent a body of knowledge about how to manage and master future conflicts successfully. (Kornberger, 2013: 1068)

Classic military strategy tends to assume a 'realist' view of the object of strategy, as expressed in the military adage attributed to the Prussian general von Moltke: 'no plan survives contact with the enemy'. Strategic activity *constructs* social worlds. It does not simply alter circumstances but more importantly creates enemies and allies, shapes interests and invents ends, rather than merely serving them. In other words, interests, ends, allies and enemies are never immutably fixed.

Senior executives use strategy to calculate conflicting interests and make intelligible the situations that they face. If a situation is made intelligible as an object of strategic analysis, it becomes something one can attempt to control. However, to the extent that specific theories of strategy are available to competitors, it is more difficult to gain competitive advantage. If everyone has access to the same tools and similar resources with which to implement them, innovative strategy is less likely to occur.

Strategy in theory: The classical age of strategy

As the previous section has established, the forms of capability/power + knowledge that framed strategy historically were closely related to the conduct of warcraft and statecraft. Strategy was concerned with how 'governors' of various kinds defended or expanded their territories and governed their populations. Influential thinking about strategy also emerged from the US military academy at West Point, north of New York, marking a fundamental shift in both US business and military strategy in the mid-nineteenth century.

During the American Civil War (1861–1865), the role of a General Staff, who were separate from direct surveillance of the battlefield but schooled in logistics and planning, was decisive in the industrialized North's victory over the agrarian South. Military strategy learnt from this victory that control of resources was decisive. A modern agenda for military strategy was being formed that broadened the vision from the field of battle to the whole campaign, an influential insight that was later crystalized by Mahan (1890) in his naval warfare book *The Influence of Sea Power upon History*.

Strategy continued to learn about long term planning from warfare. For example, the US planning of the Normandy landings in the Second World War provided many lessons which, according to Hoskin and colleagues (1997), were prefigured by the

Image 1.3   West Point Stamp. Copyright: traveler1116

history of West Point military education from 1817 onwards. These lessons were initially implemented in the American Civil War. Much of this knowledge, based in engineering, was then applied to civilian campaigns, such as building the continental railroad infrastructure. Hence, military strategy and nineteenth century business strategy had common roots in the kinds of military strategy taught at West Point. At their core was a professionalism, based on success in 'written, graded examinations' qualifying personnel as 'successful, disciplinary experts' capable of careful examination of specialist problems. Strategy, in this view, was the joint achievement of the analysis of 'past data to produce a way of seeing the future' (Hoskin et al., 1997: 7). In this view, strategizing (in both the military and in business) required a formalized structure of stable power-relations and a body of codified expert knowledge. In short, those at the top of the chain of command should 'think', 'plan' and 'instruct' and those underneath should 'do'.

The Normandy landings, which assured the defeat of Germany in the Second World War, were planned and strategized with a high degree of secrecy and an enormous attention to detail. The success of the long range planning that was assembled for this campaign became a strong inspiration for the post-war generation of strategic leaders, many of whom had learnt their leadership, management and strategy skills in the war. The importance of context was not as thoroughly learnt. For example, that these landings pitted the cream of US armed forces against weakened German troops, whose strength was shattered by the war on the eastern front, was less the lesson learned than the internal focus on *planning*. Nonetheless, the post-war generation of strategy thinkers gave birth to what we might refer to as the classical age of strategy, tied up with the rise of the multinational corporation designed on the multi-divisional form (MDF) – largely autonomous units (subsidiaries) guided and controlled by a centre (parent) – in the post Second World War period.

The education schooled at West Point proved decisive in the nineteenth century transformation of strategy; a no less decisive break occurred in the context of management education in the twentieth century. As a result of two separate commissions of inquiry into business education in the United States – the Carnegie and Ford commissions both published reports in 1959 (Khurana, 2007) – it was concluded that the majority of US business schools were little more than trade schools with a low level of intellectual legitimacy. The remedy was to import social science, especially quantitatively oriented social scientific theories, such as economics. Behavioural theory was in the ascendancy (Cyert and March, 1963) and widely imported and developed in the reformed business schools. The behavioural perspective on 'bounded rationality' fed into later development of the transaction costs perspective by Williamson (1985). Other strategy scholars adopted the ideas of other economists: imperfect competition from Chamberlin (1933); the idea of the innovative entrepreneur from Schumpeter (1934/2008), as well as the notion of the firm as a collection of resources from Penrose (1959). Of these first generation business strategists, arguably the most influential was Alfred Chandler (1918–2007), one of the first scholars to popularize the use of the term 'strategy' itself.

Alfred Chandler

Early in its life, strategy was not called strategy; it was typically referred to as 'business policy' or 'long range planning', the latter still the title of an influential journal. Chandler's book *Strategy and Structure* (1962), popularized the idea that managers were able to adapt firms' structures to accommodate them to new strategies, linking strategy formulation to the structure of the organization and the processes of its implementation. Chandler brought the language of *strategy* to practitioners and students.

Chandler wrote the history of business in America in terms of strategy, structure, scale and scope, especially focusing on the rise of the multi-divisional firm (MDF). At roughly the same time, Chandler's ideas became a critical input into the European business schools that developed from the late 1960s onwards. He made the idea of strategy tangible for the new scholars and students that were gathered in these institutions.

As a business historian, Chandler (1962) saw changes in the business environment creating a need for new strategies in firms. As new strategies developed, they required a new organizational structure to support them. Strategy, driven by business objectives and changes in the environment, should drive the organization. Thus, Chandler (1962) built on the proposition that strategy drives and determines organizational structure.

Chandler studied nineteenth century pre-industrial, small-scale, family owned and rudimentarily managed enterprises in the United States. He investigated their transformation into large-scale, impersonally owned and bureaucratically managed multi-divisional structures by the early twentieth century. How did this happen?

The end of the nineteenth century saw the emergence of a smaller number of dominant firms that grew by incorporating suppliers, marketing outlets, and so on. What had been distinct businesses were reconstituted under more centralized organizational control (Edwards, 1979: 18). Organizations grew in part as a strategic response to the failure of markets in those situations where contracts tended to be longer rather than shorter term; where the environment was more, rather than less certain; where the barriers to entry for new agents were high. Implicitly, these barriers were frequently *organizational* because they concerned the capacity to hire labour, raise credit and secure supplies. Hence, modern organizational forms were a necessary response to strategies that, in turn, were informed by business objectives and market conditions.

The first significant change occurred as a result of the conquest of US continental space by the railways. To manage and control systems that were now nationwide and covered vast geographic territories, railway companies developed military models of bureaucracy and a modern 'multi-unit' corporate form. The railways adopted strict rules of time-tabling, uniforms for their staff, and many other elements of a military model, especially a linear, hierarchical bureaucracy based on rank, divisions of labour and expertise.

Once railways connected the whole country, local and regional markets became integrated into an emerging national market. The possibilities of a mass market could now be entertained, anticipating the growth of global markets. The railroads made the national market possible and revolutionized logistics because firms could now source and sell beyond local markets. The railways also created opportunities for property speculation to occur around railheads, thus creating new and more concentrated urban markets. The growth of Chicago as the abattoir of the mid-west to which pigs and cattle were shipped is a case in point. Many other secondary industries, such as canneries, food processing and glue factories arose around the stockyards and slaughterhouses that clustered near the railheads.

By the end of the nineteenth century and through the early years of the twentieth century, US businesses were becoming more national as improved communication and transport links forged the national continental market. Businesses found that it was more efficient to incorporate internally the purchase of raw materials, debt financing, marketing, and distribution that had previously been entrusted to regionally specialized agents. Administrative coordination began to replace market exchanges as the major mechanism of control because it was more technically efficient and allowed for a greater volume of business. Productivity and profits were higher and costs were lower where the fragmentation of markets was replaced with rudimentary bureaucratization of organization. The new organization structures better fitted the emergent strategies; hence, structure follows strategy.

Chandler's ideas were enormously influential, in part because in these early days he virtually defined the field. They spread into practice, informing the work of other early scholars such as Andrews (1971). Determining strategy became conceptualized as a rational and objective process, divided into two aspects: strategy formulation and implementation (Andrews, 1971: 68). Researchers isolated these phases for analytic purposes. Andrews' ideas created the basis for the well-known SWOT matrix developed by a consultant, Albert Humphrey, who devised this new form of analysis in the 1960s. It analysed organizations in terms of strengths, weaknesses, opportunities and threats (SWOT). The first two concepts focused on an organization's internal condition, and the latter two analysed its environment. The core strategic assumption concerned the identification of opportunities that an organization could exploit better than its competitors. From this point of view, strategic management involves auditing the environment carefully for opportunities and threats and looking internally for strengths that can be exploited and weaknesses that must be overcome. Once the strengths and weaknesses have been elaborated and the opportunities and threats have been identified, then appropriate strategies can be developed. Due to its simplicity and straightforwardness, this approach became widely recognized in the field and is still in frequent use today (Learned et al., 1969).

Strategy was emerging as a field in its own right, setting the parameters for organizational action. It was Igor Ansoff who saw the implications of this emergence for the stratification of organizational action.

Igor Ansoff

For Ansoff (1965: 123) strategy defined the nature of an organization's business; hence, his focus was more on strategy formulation than implementation. Igor Ansoff made his important contribution to understanding strategy as a planning process in his book, *Corporate Strategy* (1965). Ansoff identified three different levels of action:

- *Operational*: the direct production processes
- *Administrative*: the maximization of efficiency of the direct production processes
- *Strategic*: the concern with the organization's relation with its environment

Ansoff's influence is echoed in management thinking that understands those at the top as the strategic thinkers of the organization. From this perspective, their task is to define the big picture and to steer the organization. Top management is given a role denied to the lower levels of the hierarchy; since the latter lack data and strategic foresight, their role is to support and implement strategy.

Ansoff argued that there are five strategic decisions that a company should make:

1. Scope of the product market
2. Growth vector (the direction in which the scope is changing)
3. Competitive advantage (unique product or market opportunities)
4. Internal synergy generated by a combination of capabilities and competencies
5. Make or buy decisions (Ansoff, 1965: 130).

On the basis of this analysis, the organization can build a strategy.

In his day, Ansoff was a major strategy thinker. But today many strategy scholars would see him only as a historic founder who did not go beyond identifying the key issues and weaving them together. Arguably the first or best to have done this was Edith Penrose.

Edith Penrose

For economists working in the strategy field, one of the most significant foundations is provided by the work of Penrose (1959, 2009) on *The Theory of the Growth of the Firm*. She saw the firm as a collection of productive resources, including people as well as physical resources (e.g. land, equipment, etc.), subject to administrative coordination and authoritative communication. Much as Coase (1937) before her (discussed later in the chapter), Penrose established the firm as an object of specific economic analysis separate from the market.

For Penrose, firms consist of bundles of resources directed and managed to produce goods and services that sell in markets for a profit. The boundaries of the firm are defined by the limits of authoritative coordination and communication. Directing a firm entails making effective use of resources, material and human, most successfully when combined in uniquely innovative ways.

Resources are not finite but created through experience and growth. Managerial numbers, acumen and ability determine the limits to growth because they conceive of possibilities in the external environment that their command of the firms' internal environment can realize. In the long run, profitability, growth and survival of firms depends on establishing 'relatively impregnable "bases"' (Penrose, 1959: 137) – forms of uniqueness and differentiation that mean that others cannot compete with them – from which to adapt and extend their operations in an uncertain, changing world.

Penrose's definition of the firm in terms of resources enabled strategists to conceptualize the uniqueness of the firm in terms of the specific resources that they command. Resources, especially intangible resources such as managerial capabilities or cumulative experience that are not easily copied by competitor organizations, are the real source of differentiation and value for a firm. It is resources, not products, which define firms; realizing this enables a better understanding of growth and evolution, diversification and innovation.

Firms always have more resources than they currently need, that is they have 'excess resources'. This is partly because of the indivisibilities of resources (for example, if you need ten workers and two and a half machines for optimal production, you can only buy three machines, meaning you either under produce or you have excess resources), but mostly because of cumulative *learning* that makes humans more productive.

Building on Penrose's (1959, 2009) resource-based perspective of the firm, Wernerfelt (1984) suggested strategy should be understood in terms of the management of internal resources – a theme picked up in the discussion of the so-called resource-based view (RBV) of strategy in Chapter 3. He thought of a firm as a bundle of resources that represent strengths and weaknesses. These internal resources, and their configuration, would determine firm performance. The strategist's job is to manage these resources, develop them and ensure that the firm has the capabilities to compete. This view focuses on the internal management of the organization. The focus is on the firm and the dynamics of how effectively resources are positioned, exploited and renewed. The knowledge that the firm includes can also be the basis for a knowledge-based view of the firm (see Chapter 3). Essentially, it is a combination of the management of resources, such as knowledge, and the imagination of the entrepreneur in enacting the environment for the firm, which limits its growth.

In this view, sustained competitive advantage – that is, competitive advantage that can be sustained over a period of time rather than lost as competitors quickly 'catch up' – depends on firms developing unique combinations of resources providing competences that allow for flexible development in an uncertain and changing environment. Penrose provided the foundations for the resource, knowledge and dynamic capabilities perspectives discussed in Chapter 3 of this book, approaches that have increasingly been represented in major journals in the field, such as special issues of the *Strategic Management Journal* (Winter 1986), *Organization Science* (September–October 1996), *Journal of Management Studies* (2004) and *Organization Studies* (2008).

Michael Porter

In the 1980s, the dominant theory of strategy became that of Michael Porter, a leading advocate of a rationalist analysis, based on the Industrial Organization (IO) approach. Michael Porter is a Professor at Harvard Business School, where he leads the Institute for Strategy and Competitiveness. Porter (1980) first advanced his ideas in the hugely successful book, *Competitive Strategy.*

Porter offered a highly rational view of competitive strategy, which we explore in more detail in Chapter 2. He introduced key terms that will be discussed in later chapters, such as the 'three generic strategies' and what are commonly referred to as the 'Five Forces framework' for industry strategy. The latter framework suggested that the aim of strategy should be to reduce the power of competitive forces in the industry the firm is competing in (or indeed, exit highly competitive industries in favour of less competitive industries), to position oneself within the industry in terms of the three generic strategies and to align these strategies to the firm's value chain (the set of primary and supporting activities that help generate profit margin).

For Porter, strategy is to be conceived, planned and executed with precision, using data. While he acknowledged the role of surprise (chance factors) and internal structure and of wider institutions such as government, he thought these subsidiary factors. These became themes that the next generations of strategy theory, associated with figures such as Mintzberg and Pettigrew, introduced, drawing on different disciplines from economics, such as anthropology and sociology.

At the height of the post-war era of the 'organization man' (Whyte, 1956) and of modern organizations founded on planning and hierarchy, strategy established itself as a discipline with its own highly regarded specialized journal, the *Strategic Management Journal*. By the 1980s, strategy writers such as Michael Porter and Gary Hamel had become famous not only academically but also as consultants. These authoritative figures, straddling commercial practice and academic life, became known as 'gurus' (Huczynski, 1993; Micklethwaite and Wooldridge, 1996). They had enormous popular legitimacy and were widely read by people in business and other organizations. One particular audience for these more popular books was the rising ranks of MBA students. Hence, the links with practice were well established from these early days, as the students graduated and started to put these ideas into practice in the workplace. Ideas were also translated into practice by large consulting firms (Ghemawat, 2002; Rumelt et al., 1994), such as the Boston Consulting Group, which developed popular notions such as the experience curve and the growth-share matrix, alongside other consultancy firms, such as McKinsey's influential 7s framework (Henderson, 1970, 1973).

Transaction Costs Economics (TCE) – Ronald Coase and Oliver Williamson

At the core of many organizational activities are transactions – transactions with customers, suppliers, regulators and other organizations in general. A focus on transactions defines one of the more successful economic approaches to strategy, known as *Transaction Cost Economics*.

TCE started with the question:

Why do firms exist in a world of markets and exchanges where, at least in theory, everything a firm does could also be done through impersonal market exchanges?

Apparently a simple question, but one to which the answer has seen the development of TCE analysis and has given rise to two 'Nobel' prizes in economics for both Coase and Williamson.

According to Ronald Coase (1937), production is organized in firms when the transaction costs of coordinating production through market exchanges is greater than the costs of internalizing the transaction within a firm. There are many different types of costs that accompany buying from an open market: the costs of searching for suppliers and gathering information about their goods or services, the costs of comparing their various offerings, the costs of bargaining with the chosen supplier and drawing up a contract, and the costs of policing and enforcing the terms of this contract, for example when the goods are faulty or deficient in some way. In short, firms exist when it is deemed more efficient to 'make' something yourself rather than 'buy' it from the marketplace.

Internalizing activities within organizations simplifies the renegotiating and monitoring of the many contracts that would need to be created if only market exchanges were used. Instead, long-term employment contracts can be used to create some degree of certainty about available resources. Such contracts will be issued until that point where costs of intra-firm transactions become equal to the costs of undertaking the same transaction through alternative market arrangements.

Williamson (1981a, 1981b) built on Coase's theoretical framework. According to Williamson, firms exist because all complex contracts are incomplete – they cannot anticipate and cover all possible future contingencies. When the complexity and cost of contracts increases, it makes sense to organize transactions within the firm.

Williamson followed Simon (1972) in claiming that individuals are characterized by bounded rationality (they are not fully rational) as well as opportunism (they act in ways that are self-interested but masked with guile – where diplomatic deceit masks self-interest). Where different firms own specific assets (there exists 'asset specificity'), then market contracts can lead to bilateral dependencies, where each party depends uniquely on the other for access to those assets, hence generating protracted bargaining and coordination costs. In such cases, foresighted agents can internalize the transaction in an organizational hierarchy.

Monteverde and Teece (1982) first operationalized TCE and showed that the degree of asset specificity could help determine the degree of integration. That spearheaded empirical research that ultimately led to Williamson receiving the 'Nobel' Prize in economics. Subsequently, Williamson critiqued other theories, such as market power (as in Porter, 1985) and the so-called resource-based view, for being non-operationalizable, a rather controversial view according to some critics (see Clegg and Pitelis, 2016). In critiquing Michael Porter, Williamson was positioning himself against the leading author of economics-based strategy studies.

Some of the themes that fed into TCE were developed from the behavioural perspectives of Simon (1947) and Cyert and March (1963), which eventually became used in developing the hallmarks of strategy as an emergent process, which we will encounter in Chapter 9 in the form of the emergent school's chief protagonist, Henry Mintzberg. The emergent tradition highlighted the unintended outcomes of the strategic process, suggesting that strategies are mostly rationalized in hindsight through the organization's everyday actions and decisions. In contrast to more rationalist perspectives, emergent strategy considered strategy to be a pattern of decisions taken in response to unfolding events.

By the turn of the century the positioning school launched by Porter had been superseded by a concern with competitive dynamics, responding to rapidly changing competition. Teece et al. (1997: 537) noted the shift in focus was to the firm and its capabilities, rather than industries, as core units of analysis. The central concern was on maintaining fast moving competitive advantage in rapidly changing, even hyper-competitive (D'Aveni, 1994), times.

Strategy in theory: Contemporary perspectives

The academic field of strategy is now well established, albeit highly diverse and differentiated. There is a strategy division at major conferences such as the Academy of Management in the US and a specialist yearly meeting organized by the Strategic Management Society. Strategic management is a pivotal ingredient of business education (that's why you are reading this book!) and many professors in business schools define themselves as strategy scholars. A huge textbook enterprise now supports the discipline. Textbooks have a particular role to play in the philosophy of science – they define the 'normal science' constituting a paradigm. Thomas Kuhn (1962), the famous historian of science, defined a 'normal science' in terms of what he called a 'paradigm' – the relatively unanimous agreement on the central questions in a field that defines what gets into textbooks on the subject. But does strategic management have any such unanimous agreement?

Nag and his colleagues (2007) speculated that strategy scholars might share more implicit than explicit definitions of their field. It is precisely the implicit assumptions characterizing a field that have been seen as paradigmatic by historians of science such as Kuhn (1962).

In order to gather evidence for their hypothesis, Nag and his colleagues (2007) picked 447 journal articles from three major US journals that were published over a time span of 20 years. The three journals that were mined for articles included the *Academy of Management Review, Academy of Management Journal* and *Administrative Science Quarterly* (note the US-centric choice of journals, implying that American scholarship counts most when defining a field). Nag and his colleagues then emailed 585 authors who had presented at the strategy division (more accurately the Business Policy and Strategy Division) of the meetings of the Academy of Management. They asked their respondents to rate whether the articles (presented with titles and abstracts, but no authors) were:

1. *Clearly* a strategic management article

2. *Probably* a strategic management article

3. *Probably not* a strategic management article

4. *Definitely not* a strategic management article.

Surprisingly, the respondents displayed a high level of agreement with regard to what they perceived to be strategic management. Nag et al. then studied the abstracts of articles identified by their respondents. On the basis of the responses that they received, they reduced the list of abstracts to 385 that were definitely about strategy according to the evaluation. From these abstracts they identified the 54 key terms that appeared most often, which they were able to reduce to six categories:

1. Strategy involves *major intended and emergent initiatives* such as innovation, acquisitions and diversification;

2. Strategy is an activity *undertaken by general managers on behalf of owners* concerned with central issues of governance and management;

3. Strategy involves *the utilization of resources* such as the firm's assets, capabilities and competencies;

4. Strategy should enhance *the performance of an organization* in terms of issues such as growth, return on investment and competitive advantage;

5. Strategy, as represented by the literature they covered in their survey, is overwhelmingly *something that is done by firms* – although in this book we do discuss the uses of strategy by other organizations that are not-for-profit;

6. Strategy involves understanding the organizations' *relationship with the external environment* such as the industry, competitors and markets.

Doing so, they arrived at the following paradigmatic definition of key aspects of **strategic management**.

There have been other studies that have sought to provide an overview of the strategy field. Furrer and his colleagues (2008) conducted a painstakingly detailed literature review of the strategic management field. They analysed all the papers dealing with strategy that had been published in the *Academy of Management Review, Academy of Management Journal, Administrative Science Quarterly* and the *Strategic Management Journal* between 1980 and 2005. They chose these four US journals because they are frequently referred to as the most influential journals in the strategy field. (Implying that strategy is primarily a North American phenomenon. With their exclusive choice of journals, Furrer et al. contribute to the continuation of this bias.)

> **Strategic management** involves the 'major intended and emergent initiatives taken by general managers on behalf of owners involving utilization of resources to enhance the performance of firms in their external environments' (Nag et al., 2007: 942–943).

In Furrer et al.'s study, 2,125 articles were identified that engaged with strategy. Unsurprisingly, 65% of the articles were published in the *Strategic Management Journal*. Furrer and his colleagues coded the articles by identifying 26 keywords. One article could contribute to more than one keyword, so some papers counted twice. Here are their findings:

1. The most frequent keyword that was used to describe strategy research from 1980 until 2005 was *performance* (777 papers). Performance includes subtopics such as wealth creation, profitability, risk and return, productivity and others. In short, strategists were occupied with how well a company did.

2. The second most frequently used keyword was *environmental modelling* (534 papers) which included a vast array of topics dealing with the interaction between the firm and its environment.

3. The third most frequently used keyword was *capabilities*, with 518 mentions. Capabilities focused on the resources inside a firm, and how they were deployed strategically.

4. Finally, there was the term *organization* (492 papers), which included issues around implementation, change, learning and structure.

While performance was clearly the most important concept for strategy researchers (with 36.6% of the total), the concepts of environment, capabilities and organization came in close to each other in terms of their importance (25.1%, 24.4% and 23.2% respectively).

During the 26-year period covered in this study (1980–2005 inclusive), some interesting developments and trends occurred. Performance was the constant number one concern. However, interest in the environment (this is interest in what strategists call the environment – an economic term referring to that which is outside the firm – not the natural environment conceived in terms of business' strategic effects on it in terms of carbon footprint, climate change and so on) reduced over time, replaced with an increased concern with capabilities. Other topics closely aligned with capabilities, such as innovation, also increased in frequency of occurrence: while only 4.9% of strategy research focused on innovation between 1980 and 1985, 22.9% researched its relation with strategy between 2001 and 2005.

In another study of the strategy field, Stephen Cummings and Urs Daellenbach (2009) analysed all 2,366 articles published by the end of 2006 in the journal

Long Range Planning. This is particularly significant as *LRP* is by far the longest running academic journal devoted to strategy, publishing its first issue in 1968. The authors start their article with a quote by Benjamin Franklin:

> At twenty years of age, the will reigns; at thirty, the wit; and at forty, the judgment.

Applied to strategy, Cummings and Daellenbach argue that Porter's Five Forces and the BCG Matrix were creatures of the 'will'. They argue that we have entered the period of 'wit', marked by the fact that the 'fields of strategy and organization studies have spilled over into one another, and the focus on the noun strategy has shifted toward an interest in the verb *strategizing*' (2009: 234). The 'wit' in strategy analysis that we have enjoyed over the past years has also a downside: as the '"wit" has gradually obscured the focus prevalent at the outset – there are now so many varied views of strategy it has become hard to be sure of what we mean when we use the term' (2009: 235). Hence, Cummings and Daellenbach suggest a new orientation towards the fourth decade of strategizing – a focus on judgment.

They found six re-occurring themes that represent the baseline of much of strategy research over the past 40 years.

1. First, the notion of 'corporate' has been a key aspect – signifying strategy's interest in the for-profit sector, especially large firms.

2. A second keyword was 'organization', which grew rapidly from 2000 onwards. In line with other research, we can speculate that an interest in the inner workings of firms has started to occupy strategy researchers.

3. Mergers and acquisitions, divestments and joint ventures have always been high on the strategist's agenda.

4. 'Technology' has enjoyed a prominent place in strategy research – but surprisingly it has not increased in importance over 40 years.

5. There has been a steadily growing concern with 'change', identified by Cummings and Daellenbach as one of strategy's master concepts.

6. Recently, notions of 'creativity and innovation' have enjoyed increased attention from strategy scholars, reflecting some of the challenges of management in the knowledge economy.

The authors conclude:

> Combining our key word data from LRP titles and abstracts enables us to interpret strategic management's most constant (and so perhaps its fundamental) themes, as *processes* and *practices* relating to the *corporate* whole, the *organizing* of resources and how the corporation responds to or manages *change*. Thinking more broadly, one could add to this set responses to or *decisions* about *technology* and other related *environmental* issues, and a recognition of the importance of *creative* or *innovative* developments. (Cummings and Daellenbach, 2009: 239)

Cummings and Daellenbach also look to the future as well as assessing the past. They identify five emerging trends for the future of strategic management:

1. Strategic management will become more comfortable with eclectic approaches built on a smaller number of fundamental elements;

2. Strategists are becoming more politically astute in their practice;

3. Strategists are becoming more aesthetically aware, for example, when publishing the results of strategy analysis the presentations will be artfully designed with graphics, images and bullet points rather than dense text and figures;

4. There is increasing recognition that strategy is influenced equally by conceptions of the past and of the future, and should not dismiss strategic management's archive as limited, simplistic and outmoded;

5. Prescriptive tools and models will become less important as scholars increasingly appreciate the uniqueness of organizations. Since a 'focus on particular cultures, practices and processes highlights […] the uniqueness of organizations (and therefore of their strategies), we are less likely to believe in the power of general prescriptions, and be more interested in rich case studies' (2009: 254).

The authors suggest that there will be a diminishing use of tools and models, which will be offset by a rise in frameworks and case studies. Interpreting Cummings and Daellenbach, we can argue that strategy is evolving from a managerial–economistic perspective towards an empirically informed social science that seeks to understand what people do when they do 'strategy' – a shift our book seeks to contribute to. In a nutshell, strategy is a particular form of sensemaking, as we explore in more detail in Chapter 10, when we discuss strategy as practice.

Strategy as practice

A relative newcomer to the field of strategy is a body of work that goes by the name Strategy as Practice (SAP) (Johnson et al., 2007; Golsorkhi et al., 2015). We discuss the SAP approach in more detail in Chapter 10. From the SAP perspective, we should study what it is that strategists actually *do* when they do strategy. SAP's concern is with in-depth analysis of the social practices that produce strategy formulation, planning, implementation and so on. In this respect, SAP research picks up on the earlier focus on real-life organizing processes that once set the agenda for strategy research under Mintzberg but which largely disappeared beneath the quantity of contributions from micro-economic approaches and statistical analysis of variables.

SAP research offers different theories and methodological choices to the mainstream represented by more orthodox work. The new approach is clearly to be understood as a systematic critique of orthodox, hegemonic and mainly North American (or at least North American-inspired) strategy research with the objective being to 'break through the economics-based dominance over strategy research' (Jarzabkowski and Spee, 2009: 70).

The objective of 'breaking through' the dominance of economics approaches to strategy is not easy. The economics profession has become a somewhat inverted paradigm, inwardly focused on its criteria of legitimacy and disdainful of any positions that are outside of its domain assumptions. From this position of intellectual solipsism, it is easy to ignore the babble of voices keyed to a different disciplinary register. Hence, the emergence of SAP has not (yet) breached the barriers of 'normal' strategy research so much as constituted an alternative stream, largely separate from the mainstream.

Strategy in practice

In reality, strategy is rarely as predictable and rational as implied by Porterian, RBV and TCE views. Strategy in practice consists of patterns of actions and decisions, some conscious and explicit and others not, created prospectively and in an ongoing fashion. This pattern, of course, may involve complex operational activities and decision-making leading to tactical execution. For instance, Kodak refused to give up on printed photography, went bankrupt and closed down as a result of their inaction in the face of a changing market. Blockbuster decided to move from video rentals into online downloads – but too late as Netflix and others already occupied the space. The actions and decisions that organizations make translate into routines. Organizations seek to sustain and improvise around these routines, even in the face of unanticipated events. Strategy is not a science of predictive formulas so much as a basis for creative improvization.

Strategists explore, develop and advise how organizations can best define and achieve goals of creating and capturing *value*. The organization might be a large multinational corporation, a political party, or an organization like a charity in the not-for-profit sector.

The creation and capture of value and the pursuit of sustainable competitive advantage (SCA) are widely regarded as two critical concerns of strategic management and organization scholarship (Collis and Montgomery, 1998; Saloner et al., 2001; Ghoshal et al., 2002; MacDonald and Ryall, 2004; Teece, 2007a; Lepak et al., 2007). 'Value' is an elusive term in social science and management scholarship (Dobb, 1973; Ramirez, 1999). Value can be defined in many ways: for instance, in terms of shareholder returns, public utility or political advantage. The value could be a return on investment, share valuation, winning political office, or securing benefits for service users or other stakeholders. What is of value to some stakeholders, such as shareholders, may be gained at a loss to others, such as polluted communities, redundant employees or dissatisfied customers.

If organizations seek to be successful, whether as political parties, businesses, public sector organizations or not-for-profit organizations, they have to improvise and change as the worlds in which they operate change, otherwise they risk inexorable decline. Challenges must be faced, opportunities seized, problems responded to rapidly. To make these points in a way that is understood more easily we can relate these ideas to the world of fashion retailing, in this instance, in Marks & Spencer and Zara. We will contrast their two different approaches to retailing to make some essential points about the role of strategy.

IN PRACTICE

Strategy at Marks & Spencer

A good example of an organization that has found it hard to change and improvise strategies is M&S, the British-based and international retail institution. M&S had a certain ethos that characterized its strategy:

> The brand was a byword for Britishness and British-made quality goods. It was the place where the customer was always, but always, right. If you could produce the receipt you could return the goods, no matter how long ago you

Image 1.4   M&S Store in Westfield Shopping Centre, Stratford, London. Copyright: nicolamargaret

bought them. It took no credit cards. It avoided borrowing! It had nearly 50,000 employees, no trade unions, a workers' profit-sharing scheme, and chiropody as part of the contract.

But M&S created its own force-field so successfully that it failed to notice how fast the world was changing … The world changed, and M&S didn't, or at least not enough. And maybe it can't.

Not that it is all doom and discount sales. Food does brilliantly and home is doing OK. It's the clothes that are the problem. A real problem. Clothes are still almost half the business, and at least three-quarters of the store's identity, but a trip to any M&S clothes department is a magnificent explanation of why they don't make money […]

But now the retail business model is to turn over cheap stock fast to customers with not a lot of cash and a bottomless yearning for something new. The clothes are made in sweatshops in Bangladesh or Mexico, the warehouse staff are on zero-hours contracts, and the shop workers are on the minimum wage. The M&S mid-market recipe of good value and nothing too scary works brilliantly with food, but it's a dud in fashion. (Perkins, 2015)

The generation that defined the M&S customer lived through the post-war era; now they are dying out, literally. M&S built a valid value proposition based on quality, returnability and the Britishness of its brand – St. Michael – with the vast majority of its clothes manufactured in Britain. However, from the 'swinging sixties' onwards it ceased to be a magnet for younger fashion buyers. Initially challenged only by stand-alone boutiques, such as Biba, by the 1970s the competitors were chain stores such as Next. By the 1990s the initiative had been seized by the Spanish retailer Zara and the Swedish firm, H&M.

M&S News Article

In recent times M&S has made many attempts to revamp its fashion business; indeed, in the three years before 2015, no fewer than three executives in succession had been in charge of the fashion business. The head in 2015 had been moved across from the food division, the most successful area of the retailer, to take charge of fashion. Reportedly, he would concentrate on the supply chain, planning a visit to factories in Bangladesh with supply chain experts Mark and Neil Lindsey, whose expertise helped M&S rival Next become a far more profitable business than M&S, on half the turnover.

In addition, M&S has appointed a former Inditex (owners of Zara) executive as its first design director, promoting Queralt Ferrer from the post she had held for the previous two years to become responsible for womenswear, lingerie and beauty design in its Autograph and Limited Edition ranges. Other initiatives, echoing successful food promotion strategies, include recruiting sustainable textiles campaigner Livia Firth to create an exclusive fashion line based on sustainable materials.

M&S CEO Retirement

These strategies to date have not proven particularly successful. Market share for M&S in womenswear has fallen from a peak of around 16% in 1997 to less than 10% in 2015, according to Verdict Research. CEO Marc Bolland 'retired' in 2016 after six years in the job, having presided over 17/18 quarters of declining sales.

IN PRACTICE

Strategy at Zara

Zara introduced the idea of fast fashion some two decades ago, developing a highly centralized design, manufacturing and distribution system for a fashion empire built on the idea that speed and responsiveness to the latest fashion trends from London, Milan or Paris are as important as cost. As Berfield and Bagiorri (2013) explain, Zara delivers new clothes to stores quickly and in small batches. Twice weekly, at precise times, store managers order clothes and new garments arrive on schedule. Zara is able to do this because it controls more of its manufacturing than most retailers: its supply chain provides its competitive advantage, with many of the clothes being made in Spain or nearby countries. Zara's head office, known as The Cube, is situated in Arteixo, a small town on north-western Spain's Atlantic coast.

> Just outside the Cube is the company's 5 million-square-foot main distribution center. The company produces about 450 million items a year for its 1,770 stores in 86 countries. Some 150 million garments pass through the center to be inspected and sorted, according to Zara ... Whether a shirt is made in Portugal or Morocco, in China or Bangladesh, it still goes to Spain before being shipped to a store. Beyond the distribution center are the 11 Zara-owned factories. Every shirt, sweater, and dress made in them is sent directly to the distribution center via an automated underground monorail. There are 124 miles of track. Across the surrounding Galicia region are subcontractors, some of which have worked for the company since Amancio Ortega founded it in 1975. (Berfield and Bagiorri, 2013)

Image 1.5   Zara Store. Copyright: gioadventures

Production of clothes for Zara follows a simple model. The more fashion-conscious clothes – designs that 'interpret' *prêt-à-porter* collections – are mostly produced in Spain or nearby countries. The 'basics' – the T-shirts, sweatshirts and jeans – are produced in larger batches with longer lead times in China and other cheap manufacturing East Asian countries, such as Bangladesh. These goods are very price responsive to the costs of raw materials: for instance, as cotton prices increased up to 2014, production switched to cheaper fabrics. From 2014 on, because the higher prices had attracted more primary production of cotton, the prices slumped to a five-year low and Zara switched back to manufacturing in cotton.

The simple story of relative market success and failure of M&S and Zara tells us a lot about strategy. Retailers such as M&S, to the extent that they focus on their core customers, kill off the customer base – not the existing one but the next generation that does not want to be seen wearing what their mother wears. Instead, they want edgy, current fashion, they want it now and they don't mind if it doesn't last because fashion changes so fast.

Zara clearly understands the essence of fashion retail. Of course, it is much easier for Zara because it does not have a 50-year heritage of clothes retailing based on a national model founded in economically hard times. They did not have to try and reinvent themselves in high street stores that were 'department stores', selling fashion and much else besides. They were not embedded in an essentially national model of retailing and supply. They were able to design an innovative business model from scratch – the IT system, the monorail, the network of suppliers and subcontractors, and the fast model for fashion based on the latest collections.

Strategy clearly works from knowing your customer; M&S knew theirs – but they knew them too well. As the nature of the customer generations changed, M&S failed to change with them. In the 1990s, they sought to make strategic changes within the envelope of customary business practice, introducing more specialist fashion lines, such as Per Una and Limited Edition, but for the younger and more fashion conscious customer these in-store brands hardly competed with the allure of going into Zara and seeing what the latest fashions were. Zara is designed in such a way that the fashions are already on view before the store is entered, as are the crowds of customers creating the buzz and vibe inside the store (see www.telegraph.co.uk/finance/newsbysector/epic/mks/).

M&S vs Zara

Zara also know their customers and they built on the innovations of a previous generation of Italian fashion retailers, such as Benetton (Clegg, 1990), to design their practice. From Benetton they learnt the advantages of IT systems at the point of sale that kept them posted on a daily basis on what lines, in what colours, sizes and style variations were selling where. From Benetton, they also learnt the importance of a regional network of reliable contractors, which they found in northern Spain and in Portugal, in areas where fashion and textile manufacturing was well developed and embedded. These local manufacturers were trusted to make the most fashion-responsive goods.

The following lessons can be gleaned from the above.

- Strategy attends to the *context* of an organization. M&S gained its direction from a prolonged period of limited choice and limited expenditure amongst its key customers in post-war austerity Britain. Zara's context was set in an era of unrivalled prosperity for the Spanish economy as it came out of the relative stupor of the years of the Franco dictatorship and boomed as a member of the EU.

- M&S had a *long-term direction* of seeking to be a generalist. Zara, by contrast, set a specialist direction by being a conduit from the catwalk to the high street through its interpretations of the latest fashions. What the young and fashionable might have seen in *Vogue* would be in store in a matter of two weeks, interpreted for a mass market (but not so "mass" as to lose the cachet of feeling that you needed to buy them there and then because you knew that they would not be there tomorrow).

- *Scope*: M&S was set in a particular national model of retail as a department store, concentrating on many different lines; unlike Zara it was not a dedicated fashion retailer.

- *Long-term competitive advantage*: The setting and accomplishment of *long-term objectives* is a vital aspect of strategy. M&S, as a one-stop shop for basic clothing lines that were stocked in multiple sizes and numbers for the mass market, had effected a very good strategic fit with a particular business environment in which there was little choice, competition or cash. This was the market in which the store was established as a British institution.

Clothes were sold from counters rather than racks, with little in the way of presentation and no sense of in-store experience or excitement. Retail staff wore dowdy uniforms rather than clothes available in store. As the market changed from the sixties onwards, those retailers that learnt from the boutiques, coupled with high-tech supply chain and distribution systems, had a much better fit with a newer generation of customers more knowledgeable about fashion, who were prepared to spend to stand out. Zara, with a number of other retailers, such as H&M, captured this market.

- The *emergent and paradoxical trends*, from a chain store point of view, of a youth-oriented fashion market based on difference and trends, were not really dealt with effectively by M&S. The basic model did not change to meet the emerging market. One reason for this was an unintended and unanticipated aspect of the way M&S organized. It recruited non-graduate entry staff and trained them rigorously in the M&S way. A great deal of individual learning occurred but not much *organizational* learning. In fact, it was very difficult for the organization to learn new ways because its whole system consisted of imprinting a specific way of working on its staff. All staff promotions were internal so there was little opportunity for new ideas to be introduced.

- M&S had a basic management model that reduced *complexity* to M&S systems: routinely, M&S managers were 'grown' in the firm. The upside was tremendous loyalty and deep knowledge of the M&S way of doing things. The downside was a highly restricted capacity to learn different ways of doing either the same or different things. M&S handled the complexity of changing environments through a strong set of organizational routines embedded in a large-scale bureaucratic structure that delivered mass products for mass markets. Zara, by contrast, started from a structure that enabled it to deal with a wide geographical scope and a wide range of fashions.

- The limited size range of Zara's stock was a subtle way of reducing the complexity of the *environment*. Zara's size range focused on smaller sizes while M&S had a full size range. The necessity to create designs that would work across the range from slender body sizes to large body sizes was a restricting factor for M&S. Also, it meant that if you bought an M&S garment and were young and trim you might see someone 'old' and 'fat' wearing it. Instead of retailing clothes for everyone, Zara set market niche parameters.

- Zara's *strategic capability* was to deliver the right clothes, at the right time, at the right price, in the right kind of bright buzzy and airy stores designed to appeal to fashionable young buyers. Its storefronts and windows *narrate possibilitie*s of being attractively dressed in the latest fashions. The savvy shopper knows the stock is frequently changed and up to the minute – a narrative that needs no words or advertisements to communicate because the shopper can construct it for herself from the visual cues and experiences. M&S, by contrast, had much more traditional high street stores, in which fashion was a barely discernible element in clothes retailing, itself only a part of the overall business. These strategic capabilities, in terms of its resources and competences, were very much based on learning existing systems rooted in past experience. By contrast, Zara's strategic capabilities were based in regional networks, in sophisticated use of technology, in cutting edge design interpretation, using the highly centralized rapid distribution system.

- M&S was a paternalist organization: it looked after its people. Its *values* were consistent with this ethos, in as much as it offered value for money. It was also proudly British in design and manufacture, with the expectation that its customers would reward it with loyalty and repeat purchases of a basic repertoire of goods that did not change dramatically. You could rely on M&S for twin-sets, sweaters and what they used to call 'underwear' (before it became 'lingerie') and you could also buy home wares and, increasingly, food as well, if you wanted to. The new generation of younger shoppers, however, were more interested in up to the minute fashion and you didn't expect to find that in M&S. Zara, from the start, knew its values: on-trend styles, two-week 'runway to rack' approach and international reach. When a trend hits the runways of the world's most fashionable cities, Zara positions these looks on its shelves within two weeks, anywhere in the world, at a price you can afford.

Store Wars

Go Online: Retail strategy is a fast moving area. Its earliest analyst was the French novelist Emile Zola (1883) – see 'Doctor Clérambault in Zola's paradise' by Pierre Guillet de Monthoux which you can find by searching on Google Books. Nonetheless, it is surprising how some of the basics of the Department Store have not changed greatly since Zola first analysed them. More recently, 'Store Wars', in various countries, have attracted attention – you might want to relate these debates to what you know of such stores where you live. Go to the book's website at www.edge.sagepub. com/strategy2e to find further articles related to this topic.

Zola Analysis

De Monthoux, G. (1994) 'Doctor Clérambault in Zola's paradise', in *Good Novels, Better Management: Reading Organizational Realities*. Chur, Switzerland: Harwood Academic Publishers.

Fashion is serious business. We have used the comparison of Zara and M&S to make some basic points about strategy as the reader, someone who enjoys shopping, might see its effects. Of course, looking at strategy through the store window only tells us about strategy in practice. We need also, having discussed some of the antecedents of contemporary strategy thinking in theory to supplement this account of contemporary practice, in this case of fashion, with accounts of contemporary theory, which we will return to throughout the book as we weave back and forth between theory and practice.

The comparative example of the two chains, Zara and M&S, also illustrates how 'structure' (the organization, which includes both human actors and non-human actants such as computer systems and supply chains, as well as tangible processes and assets and intangible cultural/identity elements and always, of course, power relationships) is constraining or facilitating strategic choices and also acts as a mechanism for producing the emergence of particular strategies. Structural influences on strategy counterbalance the emphasis on agency of many corporate strategy writers – the idea that a strategist can take the organization anywhere he or she wishes, unconstrained by history, culture or politics. Certain strategies are formulated not because the strategists are intrinsically convinced that they are the 'best' course of action for their company but because they are the only politically feasible alternative for them. In other words, M&S cannot, for all the reasons of its history and its structure, be similar to Zara, or at least not without a major disruption of its history, culture and power relations.

Strategy in theory and practice: The limits of strategy

Complexity

In the past, many companies saw strategic planning as an exercise in modelling and predicting the future. They crunched through data and enjoyed lengthy planning sessions. PowerPoint presentations charted the path to the future, followed by Excel spreadsheets that translated the opportunities along the way into numbers. Camillus (2008) argues that this old-fashioned approach works as long as we are dealing with simple or trivial problems. In a world of increased complexity and **wicked problems**, however, strategy needs to change.

> **A wicked problem** is a problem that is hard to describe, has many interrelated causes, no criteria for evaluating potential solutions, where actions to address the problem tend to cause more unanticipated problems and where defining the problem itself is as difficult as identifying potential solutions.

Global warming, terrorism or poverty, for instance, may all be considered wicked problems. Defining the problem is as hard, if not harder, than finding potential solutions. There are no 'correct' solutions to wicked problems, only better or worse. There is no ultimate test of a solution to a wicked problem; unexpected consequences of solutions make evaluation a tricky task. You can only evaluate whether a solution is working after you have started to do it, after which turning back and trying something else is no longer an option. Moreover, any attempt to 'solve' a wicked problem tends to create more unexpected problems along the way.

Every solution to a wicked problem is a 'one-shot operation' because there is no opportunity to learn by trial and error. Once a potential solution has been tried, there is no way to turn back time to try a different one. Trying out a solution also changes the situation and therefore changes the nature of the problem, sending you right back to the beginning again. Every wicked problem is essentially unique even if it looks familiar: this means past experience does not help you to identify prime causal factors or candidate solutions. How you try to explain the problem determines the nature of the problem's resolution – change the definition and the candidate solution also changes.

For instance, Bill and Linda Gates seem to have learnt some lessons in dealing with wicked problems. They use prizes to foster the development of unexpected developments. The Bill and Linda Gates Foundation uses this strategy extensively to promote and fund the search for solutions to social issues; one good example is their approach to fighting AIDS. Since research shows that the best solution to reducing HIV transmission is protected sex, they have launched a global competition to design new types of condom that people would want to wear because they would make sex *better*, not just safer. This is an interesting example of a strategic approach that is partially rational, partially creative, partially rhetoric, partially emergent and wholly engaged with the complexity of the problems involved.

In organizations, most issues that are truly strategic show strong elements of 'wickedness'. Camillus (2008) use the example of Wal-Mart to illustrate the case. Wal-Mart, the world's largest organization, deals with many different stakeholders with different values and priorities. More than 2 million employees want good working conditions and a reliable pension system; shareholders are more interested in annual dividends and the stock price; suppliers want to establish long-term relationships and struggle over standards and working practices; consumers are keen to pay as little as possible for as much as possible; many non-governmental organizations monitor Wal-Mart's behaviour, especially its environmental record, while unions abhor its anti-union orientation.

Rittel & Webber Article

Go Online: Camillus arrived at the findings discussed above from revisiting the contribution made by two urban planners, Horts Rittel and Melvin Webber, who wrote their 'Dilemmas in a general theory of planning' in 1973. You can download Rittel, H. and Webber, M. (1973) 'Dilemmas in a general theory of planning', *Policy Sciences*, 4: 155–169 via a web link on the book's website at www.edge.sagepub.com/strategy2e.

It's easy to see how these different groups have different demands that Wal-Mart can hardly satisfy with one neat strategy. The matter is further complicated by the fact that the cause of some of the problems is extremely complex. Pressure on lowering prices is handed down by Wal-Mart to its suppliers who might not always adhere to the highest ethical or environmental standards *and* fulfil low cost criteria. When tackling some of these challenges, Wal-Mart experiences another characteristic of wicked problems: they are moving targets. Let's say Wal-Mart decides to put its employees first and promises fair pay, good health care and a decent pension plan. Shareholders would be up in arms as they would not earn the dividend their money could earn elsewhere. Wal-Mart's stock would lose value. Consumers would also be disappointed, as they would face higher prices. They would argue that Wal-Mart is breaking its promise of 'always low prices'. What if Wal-Mart follows the shareholders' interest instead? Unions, employees, local governments and NGOs will start putting pressure on Wal-Mart. Consumers might call for a boycott to punish Wal-Mart and shares will lose value in consequence.

To make wicked problems more complicated, Camillus (2008) adds that they represent new challenges that have not been experienced before. Wal-Mart cannot simply follow someone else who has mastered the wicked problems it finds so challenging. Rather, the problems, their complexity and their configuration are novel, and might not repeat themselves. Even worse, answers to wicked problems are hard to evaluate. Often, one only develops a sense of right or wrong well after a decision has been made and the strategy is being implemented. Usually, this is too late to change the course of action.

Camillus (2008) defines five principles for resolving complex problems.

- Stakeholder involvement is crucial. Strategy becomes a forum in which to work out what the challenges might look like, as well as in what order or priority they should be tackled.

- Making sense of the situation and agreeing the nature of the problem are paramount. Strategic conversations are a communication platform for these discussions.

- While the strategic plans for coping with problems will change, the organization's sense of purpose and identity should not. In other words, the question of 'who we are and what is our purpose' should be clarified before strategic plans are crafted. In this sense, identity precedes strategy. We can't decide what we should *do* before we decide who we *are*.

- Because wicked problems are complex, we cannot think through every permutation and then act on the results of our reasoning. Rather, we have to experiment, put ideas forward, act on them, and then adjust in the light of experience. Trial and error, learning, making experiments, adopting pilot programmes and creating prototypes seem to be better ways forward than following grand plans.

- Feedback is not the best way to learn, as the name suggests, it feeds *back* onto something from the past. A 'feed-forward' orientation would scan the environment for weak signals. Who would have thought that the rise of the Internet would change the music industry? Feedback tells us that it *did*; feed-forward could have told us that it *would*.

Contradictory Interests

Strategists working in real-life organizations, not the imaginary strategy planning scenarios of theorists, must respond to different demands from coalitions of multiple and potentially contradictory interests (Küpers and Paullen, 2013; Saïd Business School and Heidrick and Struggles, 2015). The act of managing *per se*, creates boundaries that foster tension.

- By defining what to do, strategy defines what *not* to do, creating *performative* tensions between, for instance, the global versus the local, or efficiency versus innovation;

- By defining how to operate, it triggers *organizing* tensions, such as decentralized versus centralized designs;

- By defining who does what, *belonging* tensions emerge, such as sharing power versus expressing authority, reflecting contradictions of identity, roles and values;

- Finally, there are tensions between present and future in *learning* from differences that unfold as cognition apprehends the familiar differently and confronts novelty (Smith and Lewis, 2011).

Strategies can also produce unanticipated consequences that sometimes reveal themselves to be diametrically opposed to the intended objectives (Wit and Meyer, 2010), creating new tensions that were not planned or predicted in advance (Clegg et al., 2002a).

Being faced with opposites can trigger a number of reactions: arrogance, paralysis or inertia as well as the potential for strategic wisdom in certain circumstances. For instance, when dualisms create emotional anxiety, individuals activate defence mechanisms to avoid inconsistencies (Vince and Broussine, 1996). Organizational members can revise their beliefs or actions to enable integrative responses (Cialdini et al., 1995) or remain stuck in beliefs or behaviours in order to maintain past–future consistency (Weick, 1993). An organization's strategy can emphasize systematization over creation, power over empowerment, stability in preference to change – or vice-versa.

There are a number of reasons why a strategic orientation to action that feeds forward is increasingly important. Complex systems live on the edge of chaos, having to choose strategically between preserving structure and responding to surprise (Kauffman, 1995). Contrary to the traditional views of strategy, such systems may not tend towards equilibrium. Indeed, they may never pass through the same state more than once (Levy, 1994). Rapid change in the business landscape is now normal. Globalization, deregulation, complex alliances and partnerships, as well as the constant pressure for business innovation all throw up strategic challenges.

Surprises

CEOs sometimes state that they want no surprises. Anyone that does not want to be surprised must vest a great deal of faith in rational planning's capacity to eliminate uncertainty. Of course, surprises need not be unpleasant. The opposite of a planned strategy is one that is serendipitous. Serendipity starts accidentally, when someone is looking for a solution to a given problem (Problem A); in the process, the person notices something that will lead to the solution of a different problem (Problem B) that may be of even greater value. For the discovery of a solution for B while looking for A, a metaphorical leap has to occur: A has to become seen as *an attribute of* or *equal to* B in some way.

Chance, luck and happenstance may be as relevant in strategy as in other domains, however far they may appear to be from the predictable matter of science. The idea that there may be logic in disorder (Warglien and Masuch, 1995) and mess (Abrahamson and Freedman, 2006) is largely excluded from formal strategy theory. That there is logic to disorder does not mean that organizations are irrational or incoherent but rather that there is an element of unpredictability and emergence in the fabric of organizations that needs to be considered and studied. Making something out of the unexpected is not purely a matter of luck.

Merton and Barber (2004: 171) note that luck is not randomly distributed but rather tends to favour prepared minds; those ready to benefit from it. Preparedness itself, they argue, is linked to qualities such as alertness, flexibility, courage and assiduity. There is merit in being able to reap the fruits of serendipity by connecting discoveries and needs and it is in this sense that serendipity may be viewed as capability rather than mere chance. Sometimes both the discovery and the need are new. The process of serendipity thus involves the relational ability to 'see anew'. Attention to ways of *seeing* – and we would add *making sense* of what you see – signifies the importance of cognitive processes for strategy.

As observed by Gonzales (2003: 120):

> The design of the human condition makes it easy for us to conceal the obvious from ourselves, especially under strain and pressure. The (Union Carbide) Bhopal disaster in India, the space shuttle Challenger explosion, the Chernobyl nuclear meltdown, and countless airliner crashes, all happened in part while people were denying the clear warnings before them.

Shrivastava and Schneider (1984) discussed the way managers develop frames of reference, or sets of assumptions that determine their view of business and the organization. These frames prepare managers to attend to some phenomena; equally they prepare them, inadvertently, to not attend to other phenomena – to be surprised. Frames of reference may be helpful because they focus attention on what is important. But they may create patterns of habitual thought – 'as they grow more rigid, managers often force surprising information into existing schema or ignore it altogether' (Sull, 1999: 45). They form a dominant logic in the organization that is widely shared. A dominant logic may impose cognitive blinkers, which prevent the organization from seeing relevant but peripheral information (Prahalad, 2004).

A recent victim of blinker mentality was the record industry, which ignored the Internet and left it to others (including Apple's iTunes) to build new business models around the changing distribution channels. The record industry was surprised by the speed of its demise from dominance as an outlet for music dissemination.

Dell's mail order strategy, introduced as early as 1985, caught the personal computer industry by surprise. The effectiveness of Domino's delivery strategy was a surprise to Pizza Hut. Consumers' reaction to New Coke was surprising, considering the discrepancy between predictions and actual responses by consumers. The George W. Bush administration were surprised that the citizens of Iraq did not greet an invading army as liberators and proceed in an orderly direction towards a liberal democratic market economy.

Clearly, while all these phenomena may be deemed surprises, they are not all cut from the same cloth. The first two cases provided surprises to competitors; the second two cases proved surprising for their progenitors – it was their expectations rather than those of their rivals that were confounded.

Some surprises prefigure themselves in the form of warning signals that, for one reason or another, may go unnoticed (Wissema, 2002), while others apparently arrive without warning (Levy, 1994). Normal accidents, where overly complex and tightly coupled systems pose evident risks, can subsequently be seen as unsurprising accidents waiting to happen (Perrow, 1984). Some surprises, when dissected in retrospect, could have been avoided – such as the loss of life from the Titanic due to an inadequate number of lifeboats (Watkins and Bazerman, 2003).

Every strategist should expect to be surprised. Events undo planned strategies at every turn. Let us use a current affairs example at the time of writing to make the point. Of course, by the time that you read the book the example might no longer be relevant, as it will have been superseded by events, which is exactly the point that we want to make.

Oil is the liquid which fuels the global economy – significant shifts in its price have knock-on effects for almost all business strategies. Few, if any strategists, however, foresaw the strategy that the Saudis developed for beating the competition. At the time of writing the price of Brent crude oil has dropped more than 50% in a fairly short time. Few if any analysts expected this to happen. The implications for strategy are considerable, especially for marginal cost producers in the US, Canada and Russia where profitability depends on a much higher price. Saudi Arabia is driving down prices *below* the costs for others of extraction and treatment of oil. The Saudis can still sell oil profitably even at US$25 a ton.

Saudi Strategy &
Price of Oil

IN PRACTICE

The global oil trade

If there is one industry in which global politics are most complex, it is probably the international oil trade. In recent times, as those who follow the business press will be aware, the price of oil has slumped dramatically. The reason it has slumped is because Saudi Arabia stopped supporting oil prices in November 2014 and flooded the market with oil supplies in order to try and drive out rivals, boosting their own output to 10.6m barrels a day (b/d). The main target was the huge boost in oil reserves that the development of fracking in the United States had unleashed. The Saudi strategy is to drive the price sufficiently low that it will bankrupt US producers so that, having eliminated competition, they can return to business and escalating prices as usual, leveraged through the position of being the major player in the OPEC oligopoly.

This is a risky strategy.

(Continued)

Global Oil
Trade

(Continued)

Go Online: There are a number of web-based resources that could help you build your knowledge about this case and answer the question below. A good place to start any answer would be a careful reading of columns by Ambrose Evans-Pritchard in the *Daily Telegraph*, the UK newspaper. A starting point might be an article published 5 August 2015 titled **'Saudi Arabia may go broke before the US oil industry buckles'**. After this we recommend you also read an article titled **'Saudis are going for the kill but the oil market is turning anyway'** (18 April 2016). Another useful website is 'DRILL OR DROP? Independent journalism on fracking, onshore oil and gas and the reactions to it'. On this website you can find a fracking timeline from November 2014.

Question

Considering changing forms of energy provision, changing automotive technologies and energy technologies as well as exchange rate implications, how would you analyse the strategies and risks that the Saudi oil producers face in terms of long-term competitive strategy?

The Red Queen effect

The Red Queen effect occurs when competitors constantly evolve together to reach what is only ever a provisional and uneasy balance. The Saudi response to the increase in reserves that the US fracking revolution has created is interesting because they have chosen to compete on price alone. It is a strategy of surprising co-evolution. Fracked oil is profitable to extract only at a certain price level and the Saudi strategy has been to destroy that price level and in the process they hope to destroy investment in the US fracking industry, presumably before driving the price up again. Short-term pain for long-term gain. The co-evolution of competitors making moves against each other can give rise to an effect whereby interacting populations alter each other's competitive fitness. Flooding the market with high volumes of cheap oil is a competitive strategy that makes competition harder for competitors like US fracking companies as they co-evolve. Fracking might have looked to be a good investment economically when oil was much more expensive. Strategically, from the vantage point of creating non-dependency, it might still look worthwhile to invest in fracking (if creditors or governments can be convinced to bank-roll it), especially given the volatility of its price. Economically, however, the flooding of the market with cheap oil defies the economic logic of extracting expensive oil.

From the rationalist perspective, being surprised is perceived as the opposite of 'good management' (Pondy and Mitroff, 1979). Traditional organizational wisdom, engineering-based and rationality-oriented, emphasizes objectivity, detachment and control (Shenhav, 2003). As a result, as noted by Tsoukas (1994: 3) 'in our modern societies (...) prevention is deeply valued; we don't like to be taken by surprise'. Organizing is reduced to predictability – to a phenomenon lacking any surprising or non-routine qualities. McDonald's is often seen as the prototype – you should never be surprised by a McDonald's burger (Ritzer, 2004). But while this may be applicable to some products, it is unlikely to be applicable to the field of strategy where surprise is the norm, not the exception.

How to use this book

There are many strategy books that are the equivalent of a McDonald's burger, offering no surprises. We hope that this book is surprising in many respects. We cover much of what these other books would address but we think that we do so in a way that is a little more open to a wider set of ideas; hence, with a little more relevance, and with a cooler attitude towards the affordances of the digital world and the possibilities for strategy's futures (Chapter 13). Table 1.1 gives an overview of the overall structure of the book and the guiding questions that underpin each chapter.

Using a linear, chapter by chapter approach is not the only way to use the book, obviously. Unlike most textbooks, which are highly stipulative and tend to close down options, we have sought not to do so. The idea behind the textbook is to open windows on the world through cases that are vibrant and engaged, through digital links that allow you to explore topics in more detail, through video and other links that allow you to relate theory to practice. We want the book to be a tool that you find easy to use, switching from the Interactive E-Book (IEB) to the print text and back again, an informative, exploratory and introductory device to the important world of strategy.

Please appreciate and enjoy!

No book is produced *de novo*. Our views, in part, are necessarily grounded in the recent surveys considered in this chapter. We have also brought preconceptions already formed in other publications as well as experience from the teaching that we have been engaged in, to this second edition. And of course, although this edition varies considerably from the first edition – it really has been subject to major and significant additions, deletions and revisions – we have still sought to capture what we think important and relevant in strategy scholarship.

There is much in this book that would be familiar to any teacher or reader of strategy texts. As in many contemporary strategy texts you will find discussion of competitive positioning, transaction costs, agency theory, corporate governance, strategic change, strategic alliances and collaboration but these will be discussed in a way that is refreshing, critical and engaged. Notwithstanding familiarity, there are also some surprises, discussions that are less evident in conventional strategy texts: strategy in not-for-profit organizations; strategy and process theories; strategy as practice; strategy and globalization; strategy and organizational politics and decision-making as well as the futures of strategy.

Table 1.1   Overview of book structure

Strategy questions	Chapters
What is strategy?	1
What strategy should we follow?	2, 3, 4
Where should we go?	
What should we do?	
Which activities should we be doing?	5, 6, 7
Who should do these activities?	
Where should we operate?	
How do strategies get formed?	8, 9, 10, 11
How strategic change is implemented?	12
What is the future of strategy?	13

TEST YOURSELF

Want to know more about this chapter? Review what you have learnt by visiting www.edge.sagepub.com/strategy2e.

- Test yourself with multiple choice questions
- Revise key terms with interactive flashcards

EXERCISES

1. Having read this chapter, you should be able to say in your own words what the following key terms mean:

   - Strategy
   - Rational planning
   - Administrative, operational and strategic action
   - Wicked problems
   - Feedback
   - Feed-forward
   - Red Queen hypothesis
   - Serendipity

2. Who are some of the key thinkers who might be cited as antecedents of strategy and what did they have to say?

3. What are some of the key trends in strategy theory?

4. What are the main strategic differences between Zara and M&S?

5. If surprises can always happen what is the point of strategy if it cannot predict the future?

CASE STUDY

Shabby chic

STEWART CLEGG

Shabby: in poor condition through long use or lack of care;

Chic: stylish and elegant.

Shabby chic: at first glance the very idea of shabby chic seems paradoxical, impossible, nonsensical. However, as viewers of her television programmes or readers of her books will know, shabby chic signifies a certain look that is the signature of Rachel Ashwell.

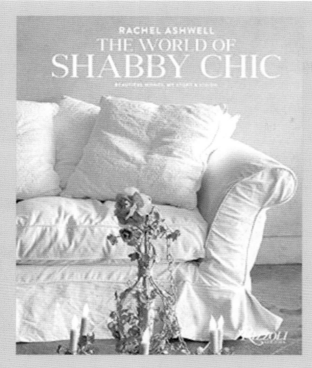

Image 1.6   *The World of Shabby Chic* (2015) by Rachel Ashwell

In her book, *The World of Shabby Chic* (2015), not only does Ms. Ashwell introduce the reader to the style that she has made her own, she also imparts some valuable lessons for any start-up's strategy.

Shabby chic was born of experience. Rachel Ashwell's mother and father were collectors, custodians and caretakers of old things – books and dolls respectively. Her mother repaired broken vintage dolls, restoring them not to complete perfection but to much-loved possessions with a history inscribed in them. The dolls were received and sold through a market stall in London's Camden Passage that the young Rachel assisted her mother in running and in doing so not only learning how to trade and restore dolls but also how to make a profit in the process.

She writes that when she first started to sell 'vintage' furniture her inspiration was her mother, with a handbag full of envelopes and plastic bags for cash and receipts. Her mother was a very capable 'can do' sort of woman, making the children's clothes, doing running repairs on the house, furnishing it with second hand finds that she tastefully restored or renewed. The dolls were restored so as to be usable but to be imperfect; Ms. Ashwell refers to it as an aesthetic that celebrated the 'Beauty of Imperfection'.

Leaving school at 16, she worked in a number of low-level clerical jobs before becoming a junior photographic stylist and at 17 making it to Disney World where she was in charge of a shoot. As her father was American (her mother was a Kiwi) she had relatives there and, as luck would have it, one of them, a cousin, lived in Los Angeles in Beverley Hills. From this base she found, with persistence, a job in styling film sets for a

(Continued)

(Continued)

production company that was in the soft porn magazine business. She fell in with other young Brits in Hollywood, such as Adrian Lynne and Tony Scott, who went on to become successful film directors. From this circle of contacts she was able to network more styling jobs and leave the magazine behind. She not only found work but also romance, marrying the director David Ashwell.

The marriage was not long-lived but enabled her to learn two vital business lessons. The first was, that as a mother of young children, keeping a house picture perfect was a thankless task. Sticky fingers were everywhere! Recalling that slipcovers on the chairs and sofas were a mainstay of English country homes, she started to make slipcovers for her furniture, which could be easily removed and washed in the washing machine as needs be, making the business of maintaining a home that much easier. She designed something that she could not find in the market. She wanted a machine-washable, pre-shrunk slipcover custom made for her sofa. When her friends saw it, they wanted one as well – the birth of what became the founding idea of Shabby Chic. The second business lesson was the importance of storyboarding techniques, notably the importance of narrative. For her husband, these narrative techniques helped plan a movie; for Ms. Ashwell they became the basis for establishing a retail business – more modestly, a shop – that told a story. Initially, the business was called 'Slips', after one of the signature products but after seeing a story in a magazine about a castle that was described as both shabby and chic, it became Shabby Chic.

After she separated from her husband she moved out of Malibu where they had lived and down the Pacific Coast Highway to Santa Monica, where she established Shabby Chic in premises on Montana Avenue. As she says, it was not the best location in which to site a home furnishings business because it was basically a neighbourhood of convenience stores. She had no business experience or knowledge; made no study of the suitability of the neighbourhood in terms of the passing foot traffic or the comparable price points of nearby stores. She had no conception of cash flows or inventory, still adhering to her mother's very basic business model. Basically, this business model was one of arbitrage, where she trusted her aesthetic sense in finding pieces that could then be artfully displayed in a setting designed to project a certain look and be sold to customers striving to emulate that look.

The slipcovers were the basic line complemented by vintage finds, sometimes distressed a little more to make them more interesting; other times left just as they were. These pieces were sourced from flea markets. The overall colour palette of the business was overwhelmingly white on white – exploiting all the different shades – mixed with pale pastels and vintage items such as ornate mirrors, chandeliers and vintage lace. She collected many different kinds of objects such as rugs, lamps, mirrors, furniture and accessories. The garage at her home acted as a storage depot and workshop. She ran the business on a cash basis, buying cheap from people who did not see the aesthetic value in what they had that she could see and selling the goods more expensively to people who could see the value once she had 'storyboarded' the objects in the Shabby Chic collection.

Lacking inventory other than what she could source from flea markets, she had no strategy other than to buy pieces that seemed translatable from the flea market to a shabby chic context. She quickly built a network of craftspeople that she could call on to help her in presenting her finds: furniture makers and repairers, seamstresses and pattern cutters. In her words, she learnt how to run a business one sofa at a time.

Her retail success was based upon a simple innovation for the market she was in – the machine washable slipcovered sofa – and her styling in displaying these amongst the host of shabby chic finds that were also for sale. The slipcover idea was generalized to bed furnishings; old pieces were painted white but with traces of the past left visible, telling a story, hinting at the history of the pieces. The storyboarding concept was crucial – the store was keyed in one harmonious theme, whose dominant tones were various shades of white, set off with faded pastels. No strong colours were evident. (Put 'shabby chic' in the browser, click images and you will see what is meant.)

Working with trusted suppliers, she developed rule of thumb approaches for making her cushions and bedding appear luxuriously soft and squishy, slowly learning about the importance of inventory, cash flow and sales goals.

Six months into the venture of the Santa Monica shop, for which she sourced pieces at the flea markets accompanied by her children (at this stage a baby and a toddler), she was approached to open a store in New York on the east side of the United States. Unable to manage this business herself, she forsook her cash business basis in favour of a bank loan and established store number two, which one of her employees elected to run for her. In her account she states that 'it was a brilliant strategic move to suddenly be a national bicoastal company, although it wasn't strategy on my part' (Ashwell, 2015: 33). She was not educated in business and had no understanding of strategy.

Nonetheless, Ms. Ashwell had a strategy: each time she opened a new store she would borrow $100,000 to buy inventory and to act as security for the lease, providing working capital for about three months. Loans were paid down immediately with cash flow. Ms. Ashwell did this operating from her Santa Monica base; meanwhile, so did the woman whom she had put in charge of the New York store. As often happens they did not share the same vision for their lives or business and, as Ms. Ashwell (2015: 34) narrates it, 'we had neglected to write down legally what our relationship was'. A business divorce followed: Ms Ashwell let the New York and San Francisco stores go to her erstwhile collaborator and kept the Santa Monica and Chicago stores (the latter was the least successful), while retaining the rights to the Shabby Chic brand. As she says,

> By not wanting to confront the situation and negotiate a cleaner split, many years of confusion were caused as to whether the New York or San Francisco stores were the true Shabby Chic or not. (Ashwell, 2015: 34)

From this point Rachel Ashwell's Shabby Chic grew enormously. A TV series of 54 episodes for the Style network were globally syndicated; the author of these words first saw them on Australian TV on the Foxtel channel. Rachel Ashwell books began to appear in the marketplace. Ms. Ashwell was becoming as much a celebrity as some of the famous people who frequented her stores, especially the Santa Monica store, which was close to an area that many movie and music stars were moving into.

Celebrities not only have their own TV shows but also appear on other people's shows; in this case Oprah Winfrey's, on which Ms. Ashworth was promoting her book *Shabby Chic Treasure Hunting*. As a thank you to Ms. Winfrey, she sent her a gift of some newly developed Shabby Chic T-shirt sheets that were shown as coveted items in a part of the show called 'Oprah's 20 Favourite Things'. The store phone lines went crazy with people

(Continued)

(Continued)

wanting to buy them, so much so that the order book was impossible to service. Other, more nimble, opportunistic and better-resourced firms stepped into the gap and started selling 'knock-off' versions of her sheets at a much cheaper price. The business could not meet the demand, leaving many frustrated customers, and opening the brand to dilution through the development of cheaper imitations of the product.

By 2007 Ms. Ashwell's children had left home to go to college. Looking for new challenges, she decided to become more systematically business-oriented rather than relying simply on bank loans to expand the business. She settled on Goode Partners to be her investors:

> They were young but seemingly experienced in the retail world, I felt they understood what I was about, and they were very patient and flexible with me during the process of deciding how much of a percentage I wanted to sell. My priority was to have control, at least what I understood that to mean, so I sold a minority stake. It's what is called a 'debt-equity' deal, where there is cash and also some debt layered in by leveraging against the value of the company. With the cash infusion we were finally able to buy back my beloved New York and San Francisco stores. We then had six stores, some licensing deals, and a small wholesale business: the company was clean and steady. I was ready to surrender the business side of things to those who knew more than I did, so I could focus on the magic of creativity with the security of my little nest egg. (Ashwell, 2015: 39)

Goode Partners' plan was to open 57 stores over five years while still maintaining the Simply Shabby Chic line at Target. As she reports it, when she saw the inventory being taken on, the huge warehouses, the complex computer systems, the array of CEOs and Vice Presidents, she felt scared. Her existing stores were all in typical shabby chic locations, older neighbourhoods, a little faded. Fifty-seven new ones meant expansion into malls with all that implies in terms of overheads and location. As the creative designer Ms. Ashwell felt lost: how could she recreate the air of faded gentility and chic in brightly lit and charmless mall spaces rather than old buildings of character? Moreover, in practical terms, as the buyer how could she keep up with the expansion? She had insufficient time and insufficient flea markets to sustain the product. The solution was compromise: a larger percentage of stock was bought from third party suppliers on the open market, stock that was more mainstream than Shabby Chic. Brand dilution was happening.

On top of these concerns the logistics were not working well; shipments were late or arriving at the wrong store; moreover, from being a hands on business in which she had worked with people she knew she was now working in an environment that she didn't understand with people she didn't know.

There was one other major problem in the wings, of course: this was 2007 and the tsunami of the Global Financial Crisis was about to break. 'In two months, November 2008 to January 2009, Shabby Chic sank like the Titanic.' The market had dried up.

The long-term leases on the malls proved to be the most expensive costs to manage; liquidators were called in and everything that was not part of the building was liquidated to set against the debts, including many of her personal items. The name, Shabby Chic, was also sold under the liquidators' jurisdiction and the new owner was more interested in licensing the name rather than running authentically Shabby Chic stores. Eventually, out of the ashes of Shabby Chic, Ms. Ashwell gained the rights to establish Rachel Ashwell's Shabby Chic Couture and she signed on to support the creative side of the licensing deals.

Under the new name she reopened her Santa Monica store and reopened in New York, just around the corner from the old location, as well as in Notting Hill, in London. Although she was hemmed in by non-compete clauses in the legal settlements, these did not extend to hotels so she started to open these, including one in Texas, The Prairie by Rachel Ashwell, which made it to Condé Nast's list of top hotels.

During this time the retail and licensing sides of the business were pulling in different directions; she wanted to make the company whole again and this time, being unencumbered by investment partners, she was able to buy back the brand.

QUESTIONS

The story is fascinating in itself and the world of Shabby Chic is glamorous and beautiful to explore in its own right; more than this intrinsic interest, however, the story also raises some profound questions for strategy.

1. What were the strategic opportunities and limitations Shabby Chic encountered?
2. What role did serendipity play in the Shabby Chic case?
3. Looking at the story, if you had been running Shabby Chic, *how* would you have done *what* major things differently?
4. What were the major strategic mistakes that characterize the Shabby Chic story?

You can explore the world of Shabby Chic at www.shabbychic.com/. There is a discussion of what went wrong with Shabby Chic at www.masterjules.net/shabbychic.htm as well as a *New York Times* article 'Making Shabby Chic, Again', which looks at the reinvention of the brand (see www.nytimes.com/2009/10/15/garden/15shabby.html).

Shabby Chic

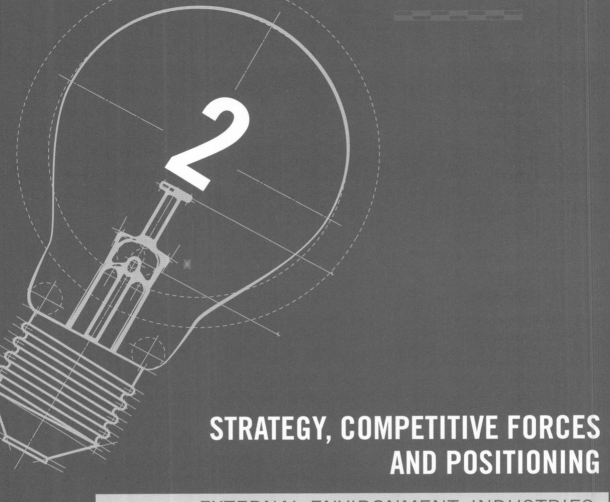

STRATEGY, COMPETITIVE FORCES AND POSITIONING

EXTERNAL ENVIRONMENT, INDUSTRIES, POSITIONING

Learning objectives

By the end of this chapter you will be able to:

1   Understand the importance of differences in competitive environments

2   Explain what competitive advantage is and how it can be achieved

3   Distinguish different types of industries

4   Understand and analyse the role of industry competitive forces and generic strategic positioning

5   Analyse the macro environment and know about how it can affect strategic choices

6   Appreciate the role of strategic groups

BEFORE YOU GET STARTED

- -

The essence of strategy is choosing what not to do. (Michael Porter)

Introduction

Many twentieth century strategy theorists and practitioners focused on an outside–in perspective on strategy, i.e. they gave more attention to the role and importance of the factors that were external to the firm. Strategic managers were encouraged to focus on the analysis, interpretation and the shaping/manipulation of the environment, in particular the industry (or sector) that the firm was operating in. The assumption was that the profitability of a firm is a result of the structure of its industry and the firm's ability to position itself successfully within its (industry) environment. While today we know that there are also many firm-internal aspects that strategists consider when 'doing strategy', the understanding of the business environment that corporations and other organizations compete in remains a central aspect of strategists' work.

This business environment can be conceived of in many ways: as an industry, a business group within the industry, a wider ecosystem, a field of activity and enterprise linking diverse organizations in reciprocal networks, the national and global economy as a whole. Assuming that a firm might be active in several regions and multiple markets, it becomes crucial to understand the environment in terms of the key 'rules of the game', especially those that derive from government regulations that restrict or support the business.

Rules of the game could be, for example, antitrust laws which in the early twentieth century helped avoid monopoly-like domination in the American oil or tobacco industries, or de-regulation laws which had a huge effect on the structure of the energy and telecommunication industries in many European countries, privatizing what had previously been state monopolies.

Rules may also derive from what strategists call overall demand drivers: the factors shaping demand for the organization's goods and services in the environments in which it operates. We will explore various other factors that shape the business environment of an organization in this chapter.

A firm's interactions and relationships with other organizations, individuals, government bodies and many other institutions help shape strategic outcomes. Firms face vigorous competition in most environments but they also have to manage supplier and buyer relationships.

Below we discuss how firms can analyse the external environment, in particular their industry, to shape competitive relationships successfully and how they can respond to competitive forces. We do this at both the business level and the overall corporate strategy level. Before we explore further the frameworks and theories that help us to better understand competitive environments we need to clarify what we mean by business-unit and corporate-level strategy.

Business unit and corporate-level strategy

Strategists operationalize strategy at different levels. Generally, **corporate strategy** deals with overarching matters for organizations that compete in more than one

> **Corporate-level strategy** responds to 'What business should we be in?'

> **Business unit strategies** respond to 'How do we compete in this business?'

line of business, while **business unit strategies** are designed to pursue success in a specific industry in which the organizations compete.

If a company sells toys, for example, its business strategies will be geared toward selling more toys to more people. Business unit strategy concerns the firm's relationship to suppliers, customers and other businesses in the toy industry.

Corporate-level strategy is concerned with the organization as a whole. It examines businesses the firm is currently engaged in and makes decisions relative to those businesses. Corporate-level strategy is concerned with whether the company should be selling toys at all, whether it should diversify in a different activity altogether while remaining in the toys business or even leaving that business altogether. For instance, IBM used to make money by making computers; they divested the manufacture of IBM computers to Lenovo of China and became consultants instead of manufacturers.

Although different, business unit and corporate levels of strategy are closely connected. Corporate-level decisions naturally affect business unit strategy as corporate strategy makes decisions about business to be or not to be in – hence affecting the very existence of the business unit. However, a business unit can also influence decisions about corporate-level strategies depending on its resources and capabilities and how successful and/or influential it is with the top corporate hierarchy. For example, in order to diversify to other business, companies often try to build on existing resources, strengths and capabilities.

> **Functional-level strategies** are concerned with the methods of implementing the decisions that are made at the corporate and/or business-unit strategy.

Another level entails **functional-level strategies**.

Marketing and sales, human resources, as well as financial considerations, are important functional strategies. They focus more on implementing the wider business unit and by extension corporate-level strategy.

Industrial Organization (IO) and the Structure–Conduct–Performance (SCP) approach

The Basics of IO

Industrial organization (IO) is a field of economic theory that helps to explain the interaction between the industry structure and performance and their relationship to the strategic behaviour (conduct) of firms.

Tom Holden Lecture

Go Online: Watch University of Surrey academic Dr Tom Holden give an introductory lecture on industrial organization. You can find the video on YouTube, or a link to it on the companion website for this book. We recommend you skip the first few minutes to find the most relevant material.

The central idea of IO is that the success of an industry in terms of profitability (performance) depends on the conduct of its firms, which in turn depends on the structure of the industry, which is constituted by factors such as barriers to entry and degree of concentration.

Two American economists, Edward S. Mason (1939, 1949) and Joe S. Bain (1956, 1968) contributed significantly to the development of IO and gave the strategy discipline some of the underlying principles and structure that it still retains. The assumption is that a firm's performance is largely a function of the industry environment in which it competes. If that supposition holds the industry structure will largely determine conduct, which in turn determines performance, and therefore performance can

> **Industrial organization (IO)** takes an external perspective, that of the industry or sector, and is concerned with the industry settings within which firms operate and behave as producers, sellers and buyers of goods and services.

be explained in the main by industry structure (as conduct is delineated by structure) – a perspective that has been coined the Structure–Conduct–Performance (SCP) approach. Later variants have however attributed a more important role to conduct and strategic behaviour (Tirole, 1988).

Factors that influence industry structures include the following:

- *Supply conditions*: For instance, technology and cost structures – in a technology-driven industry, such as the computer industry, the average cost of production will tend to fall when there are improvements in the production process or lower material costs.

- *Demand for a product*: Changes in consumer taste and preferences, price, availability of substitute products and the method of purchase can influence overall demand for products or services. If the overall production volume increases because of increased demand, the industry will tend to have only a small number of firms that compete with each other. Hence, the number and size distribution of buyers and sellers indicates the market power that a firm might have in its industry. For example, increasing demand for flights between Australia and the UK is only served by a relatively small number of international airlines.

- *The degree of differentiation of products*: Product differentiation refers to the characteristics of the product and is the way through which firms improve the quality of their offerings over time (usually by means of advertising and/or innovation).

- *Extent of vertical integration and diversification*: Vertically integrated firms, such as the fashion retailer American Apparel or many oil companies, control several steps in the production and/or distribution of their product or service, from raw materials (backward integration) to distribution (forward integration); hence, they can save transaction costs and wield more power in the marketplace. Diversified firms, like the multinational manufacturing company ITT Corporation or General Electric, invest in a variety of different product markets in part in order to reduce exposure to risk in single product markets; hence, in part because of economies of scope (that result when a resource has multiple uses in different sectors).

- *Government policy*: National, regional and local governments as well as economic or political unions such as the European Union (EU) or the North American Free Trade Agreement (NAFTA) enforce regulations that guide and restrict competition, taxes and subsidies, employment, price controls, trade policies or environmental policies for many industries. For example, in early 2010 the EU competition authorities approved a giant merger between France Telecom's Orange UK and Deutsche Telekom's T-Mobile UK to create Britain's largest mobile phone operator. However, The European Commission promoted competition by requiring that the two companies had to agree to amend existing network-sharing agreements with Hutchison 3G UK (3UK).

The two key factors of industry structure are seen to be barriers to entry and industry concentration or consolidation. Michael Porter (1980, 1985), whose contribution to strategy drew on the SCP model, suggested that factors such as initial capital requirements, the threat of price-cutting by established firms, and the level of product differentiation represent 'barriers to entry' for new firm entrants into markets. The issue of barriers has been much discussed in the literature; an excellent account of the state of knowledge with regards to what drives entry is provided by Geroski (1995) while Bunch and Smiley (1992) looks at the ways in which firms actively deter entry.

The degree of concentration among competing players and the extent to which one or a few large producers dominate the market helps determine whether the industry is 'attractive' in terms of being profitable.

A key issue is to define accurately the industry within which one is competing. For instance:

- A narrow definition of an industry might be the one for highly profitable business class air travel on key routes such as that from London to Sydney or Paris to New York.

- A broader definition of the market would be the airline industry as a whole.

A firm that is able to identify and define accurately the industry or industry segment within which it competes is likely also to be in a better position to develop appropriate competitive strategies.

Qualifying the IO Approach

The SCP approach posits that industry characteristics such as those described above influence, indeed actually determine, the behaviour of the firm. However, the distinction between elements of structure and conduct, as well as the direction of causality, is not always clear. For example, product differentiation is a result of conscious strategic choice for a firm. In that sense strategic conduct determines market structure. For instance, IBM used to make computers and then they switched to providing business services. A firm's behaviour is influenced by and influences the structure of its industry; research and development, the development of organizational partnerships, can change markets. Generally, in the last decades the SCP approach has been subjected to criticism and qualifications as follows:

1. *The SCP approach does not always specify precise relationships* between market structures, firm conduct and firm performance and it is not always clear which factors belong to structure, conduct and performance. For example, a firm's effort in regard to strategic initiatives such as advertising, legal tactics, product choice, collusion or major investments in production facilities, act as strategic choices (e.g. Child, 1972; Spence, 1977) that change the market conditions for competitors. Strategic choices are decisions made by the Top Management Team with respect to important factor conditions such as markets, technology and so on.

2. Another example of firm conduct affecting market structure is where there is *asymmetry of information in the market*. Asymmetry of information exists when one party has more or better information than the other, which can influence how the environment is enacted, shaping strategic decision-making and subsequently creating an imbalance of power, as the better-informed party

gains advantage. For example, when a firm supplies competitors with specific information that shapes decision-making, perhaps through an advertising campaign informing potential customers about price and quality, companies can influence the competitive environment through the signals they send and the sense of the environment that they enact.

3. *Firm performance may affect market structure*: the best performing firms can dominate the market in the long term by setting standards for prices, production efficiency and product quality or by having exclusive access to critical resources. Hence, the more firms behave strategically in a given market the more the causal chain of SCP will be broken. Think of the way that clubs such as Bayern Munich, Real Madrid and FC Barcelona have dominated the European football leagues in recent years. Similarly, the opposite can hold, for example, high performance (profitability) can attract new entrants.

The significance of understanding the dynamics of competition between companies within an industry cannot be underestimated. The SCP concept can help identify opportunities for a business, especially if it is planning to enter into an industry as a new player; it helps determine if an industry is attractive, and it can provide a firm with the advantage of ways of differentiating its products or services from similar offerings. Nevertheless, strategic management theorists and practitioners alike have realized that conduct and performance reflect back on industry structures. This led to a shift away from the idea that the industry structure represents the main determinant of competition. Subsequent developments in IO, which are usually referred to as New Industrial Organization (NIO) theories (Schmalensee, 1982), emphasize the influence and importance of a firm's conduct and strategic behaviour. According to these approaches the firm is not seen as a passive participant in markets, but an active player, influencing its industries and competition through strategic decision-making and subsequent actions.

Sustainable competitive advantage

Scholars agree that the primary purpose of strategic management is to guide the organization in achieving superior organizational performance by developing **sustainable competitive advantage** in the environment in which it operates.

While there is no one 'best way' to build competitive advantage, the reality of business success and failure clearly indicates that some strategies work better than others. As a fundamental requirement, an organization will always try and ensure that its financial returns exceed its costs of capital, meaning that the business offers a better return on investment than leaving the money in the bank. For instance, if an organization can get a 5% return on its capital by placing it on deposit with a bank, it will set a significantly higher return for it to achieve through its business activities. SCA enables the organization to make **economic rent**.

While the relative extent of competitive differences may be debatable, there is no doubt that some organizations in an industry will do better than others. From a strategy perspective this suggests that, if such differences are not merely random, then they must be a result of good strategy, including the application of ideas from strategic

> **Sustainable competitive advantage** (SCA) is what allows a business to maintain and improve its competitive position in a market against competitors in the long term. Achieving SCA is the purpose of strategic management since it allows a firm to make a profit in a sustained way. Strategists have diverging ideas about how SCA can best be achieved.

Woltersworld
& Sustainable
Competitive
Advantage

> **Economic rent** may be defined as the situation where an organization earns above average industry returns. It can be a measure of market power or differential efficiency.

management in investigating issues relating to 'competitiveness' at the firm, industry and national level. Given that there are substantial differences between businesses in an industry, competition must be analysed not only at an aggregate industry level but also at the level of the individual firms that compete with each other – the micro-economic level. Indeed, research has shown that the differences in financial returns within an industry are often considerable, and probably exceed the differences that can be seen across industries (Cool et al., 1989; Rumelt, 1991).

What are the factors that might explain variations in organization performance in an industry? Barnett and McKendrick (2004) argue that differences in competitive performance within an industry can be attributed to factors such as firm size. In a study of the global hard disk drive manufacturing industry between 1981 and 1998 they found the ability of large organizations to ameliorate competitive constraints insulated them from an important source of organizational development and protected them from being 'selected out', or disappearing from the market, if they were no longer competitive. On the other hand, while large organizations led the technology race in the hard disk drive market, they have failed to develop into competitors as strong as their smaller counterparts.

Another factor that seems to explain why some organizations do better than others in their industries is related to the firms' interactions and relationships. Horizontal relationships with, for example, competitors, alliance partners, industry bodies or governments and vertical relationships with, for instance, suppliers, customers or communities help shape strategic outcomes. Working out how to manage these relationships successfully, and how to respond to competitive moves, is an important and integral part of successful strategic management.

The theories discussed in this chapter reflect basic economic theory ideas that deal with the strategic implications of such macro and micro environmental factors including industry characteristics, industry structures, organizational attributes, competitive forces, and the horizontal and vertical relationships of the firm. There are many implications of these basic ideas in strategy not only for the innovativeness and ensuing attractiveness of an industry, but for the realization of SCA for the organization in such environments.

IN PRACTICE

Strategy as practised at BCG

James Goth
Interview

Go Online: Visit the book's website at https://edge.sagepub.com/strategy2e to watch an interview with James Goth of the Boston Consulting Group conducted by the author team.

James Goth joined The Boston Consulting Group in 1994 and is a Partner in the Sydney office. He leads the firm's Strategy Practice Area in Australia and New Zealand. At BCG James has worked on projects in a variety of industries in Australia, New Zealand and Europe, with a specialization in consumer goods, airlines and retail. Prior to joining BCG, James worked for the Department of the Prime Minister and Cabinet in Canberra as an Economic Policy Adviser.

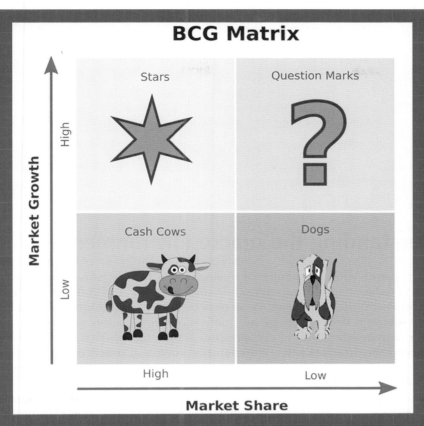

Image 2.1   BCG Matrix: © niki99 - Fotolia.com

As James Goth highlights, BCG are internationally known for their innovative thinking on strategy and competitive advantage. Their famous 'Matrix' was developed in case work to assist clients in defining corporate-level strategy and acquisition strategy to clarify which businesses to obtain in order to further competitive advantage.

Within BCG, strategy is all about the choice of where and how to compete in order to maximize your competitive advantage – that which manifests itself on the profit and loss statement (i.e. is quantifiable) and hence creates shareholder value. James stresses the word 'choice' as it is fundamental to competitive advantage; trade-offs must be made. We interviewed James as a part of the research for this book and made a video with him, which you can find on our website. After you have watched the video and looked at the associated case material we would like you to think in practice about how BCG develops and uses tools to do scenario planning by answering the following questions, for which you will need to utilize the video interview, the Case Study and the listed reading resources.

Questions

1. What is the framework that guides BCG's approach to strategy development based on? How can firms achieve increased shareholder value?

(Continued)

(Continued)

2. What is the role of the strategy consultant? How can consultants help organizations to understand and develop strategic competitive advantage?

3. Over the past decades some very influential strategy concepts emerged from BCG. What are the most important frameworks James talks about and to what extent do they still inform today's thinking on strategy?

4. James refers to the tri-factor of strategy. What does he mean and how does the concept help strategists?

5. What are the various steps, stages and perspective that BCG strategy consultants employ to develop strategies? What kind of data is necessary?

Understanding the macro environment

It doesn't matter what the nature of business is, a firm is embedded in a complex network of relations with various other organizations and individuals. It is these relationships and the strategists' awareness of current and important developments that help shape a firm's strategy and determine its position and competitiveness. The macro environment for an organization is therefore the world in which it operates. Macro influences are often sufficiently complex in practice that strategists will refer to industry associations or external consultants for more detailed information.

Yet, strategists need to build and base strategic decisions on their own perception about key influences in the broader environment. A thorough analysis of the macro environment helps ensure that they have fully addressed the current and future operating environment for the firm. Such analysis is often referred to as PESTEL analysis. PESTEL is an acronym that stands for Political, Economic, Social, Technological, Environmental and Legal influences, factors which are usually beyond the firm's control but must be considered both as sources of competitive advantage (opportunities) and as a potential source of erosion of competitive advantage (threats).

- *Political* influences: governments and other political bodies matter in a number of ways. Government action can foster industry creation and economic development. Mahmood and Rufin (2005), for example, consider the role of government in the process of technological development and show that its role regarding technological development varies during the development process. Other political factors that can be considered when analysing the macro environment of the firm include the impact of corrupt governments on firm-level decision-making by managers of multinational enterprises, the attractiveness of political markets and the impacts they can have on firm-level strategies, and the role of deregulation for the competitive situation of an industry. When a country is far from technological frontiers, government can spur economic development through the centralization of economic and political control but as the economy approaches the technological frontier, government's role usually changes considerably, political and economic freedom being preferred.

- *Economic* influences refer to macro-economic factors such as exchange rates, business cycles and economic growth rates or interest rates in the countries that the firm operates in. For example, higher interest rates may deter investment because it costs more to borrow, while a strong currency may make exporting more difficult because it raises the price in terms of a foreign currency. Other dynamics include that inflation may provoke higher wage demands from employees and raise costs, while higher national income growth may boost demand for a firm's products. At the time of writing commentators are speculating about the economic prospects for the global economy in the medium term.

- *Social* influences incorporate changing cultures and demographics, such as ageing populations or urbanism in many parts of the world. Such changes can have an impact on the market for a firm's products and the availability and willingness of people to buy from or work for companies. In the UK, for example, the ageing population has led to some firms shutting pension funds to new entrants, while at the same time the demand for sheltered accommodation and medicines for elderly people has increased.

- *Technological* influences refer to innovations such as the Internet, biotechnology and nanotechnology or the invention of new materials. Mobile phones, computer games and high definition TVs are new markets due to technological progress. Such technological developments often reduce costs, improve the quality of products and services, and provide benefits for consumers as well as the companies that make use of new technologies.

- *Environmental* influences are important 'green' issues, such as pollution and waste that can affect industries such as farming, tourism, travel, transportation or insurance. With major climate changes occurring created by global warming, greater environmental consciousness and changing policies, environmental factors are becoming a more significant issue for firms to consider. The growing desire to protect the environment is having an impact on consumer buying behaviour, which is affecting demand patterns and business opportunities.

- *Legal* influences concern legislative constraints or changes, such as health and safety legislation, recycling regulations, equal opportunity directives or restrictions on company mergers and acquisitions. Each of these influences can have a considerable impact on a firm's costs and the demand for its products and, therefore, on its future ability to successfully compete in its markets.

The automobile industry is often regarded as a mature industry; indeed, sometimes there have been suggestions that the environment is so over-crowded with firms competing for a diminishing market share because of an over-supply of commodities that the market could rightly be regarded as too overcrowded for innovative strategies to be developed.

If asked whether the automobile industry is a mature industry most people would answer 'yes'. Given that the industry is over 100 years old and has evolved over many years from producing motorized carriages to today's sophisticated high tech automobiles, we might be inclined to argue that the industry is likely to be fully matured, if not in decline, given environmental concerns and the fading availability of oil. Especially with the recent Global Financial Crisis in mind, few people see the auto industry as ready for further growth. Even before the damage of the Global Financial Crisis, motor vehicle manufacturing was considered a mature sector, with static or even eroding markets, and with existing firms subject to intense competition. The crisis has put major manufacturers, such as Ford and GM, under immense pressure,

Table 2.1 PESTEL analysis

POLITICAL	ECONOMIC	SOCIAL	TECHNOLOGICAL	ENVIRONMENTAL	LEGAL
Corporate/consumer taxation	GDP	Demographics, e.g. age, ethnic mix	New discoveries and development	Environmental regulation (e.g. carbon emissions)	Changes in employment law
International trade regulations	Credit availability and interest rates	Education	Speed of technology transfers	Environmental campaign groups (e.g. Greenpeace)	Regulation of competition
Overall government attitude	Foreign exchange rates	Lifestyle changes	Internet and mobile technologies	Climate change	Health and safety regulations
Influence of political alliances	Wage rates	Social mobility	Energy use and cost	Eco-system protection (e.g. endangered species)	Government antitrust regulations
Local inducement policies	Stage of business cycle	Living conditions	Technological obsolescences	Weather conditions (e.g. drought, floods)	Quotas and caps (e.g. fishing quotas)
Political stability	Inflation	Attitudes towards work	Decreases in transportation costs	Natural disasters (floods, earthquakes)	Consumer protection laws
Government spending	Consumer confidence	Consumer fashions, trends and celebrities	Scientific advances	Disease (e.g. bird flu, BSE)	
Trade balances	Unemployment	Health and welfare	Access to raw materials		

leading them to fight for their survival by offering deeply discounted products and requiring billions of taxpayer dollars to secure jobs and stay afloat.

But there are also signals that the industry's decline is very much overstated. In a 2009 report, two management consultants with Booz & Company, Ronald Haddock and John Jullens argued that automakers willing to think anew about their markets and their business models will be in a position to benefit from the greatest wave of expansion that the industry has ever seen. In fact, looking beyond the current challenges, they report increasing levels of productivity and capability, significant innovations in technology and the look and feel of motor vehicles, and – most importantly – a wave of accelerating economic development in countries such as China, India, Brazil or Russia that will, sooner or later, produce enormous new demand for personal mobility.

The 2009 launch of the Nano by the Indian firm, Tata Motors Ltd, a much celebrated US$3,000 microcar, was not only a wake-up call for many traditional car manufacturers but can also be considered the starting point of an era in the automobile industry that will be characterized by significant engineering and supply chain breakthroughs in car production and innovative strategies in approaching market segments that thus far have been largely ignored. A number of other vehicle makers, such as Mahindra & Mahindra and Maruti in India, Chery in China, and some global auto companies such as Renault and Volkswagen have been noted for the inexpensive cars they are designing for new markets.

Another example of potentially disruptive changes occurring in the automobile industry is the recent launch of Tesla Motors' electric vehicles. The Tesla Roadster was the first automobile to use lithium-ion battery cells and the first electric vehicle with a range greater than 320 km per charge. Until 2012 the car was sold more than 2,250 times across 31 countries. The company's second vehicle is the Model S, a fully electric luxury sedan, and its next two vehicles are the Models X and 3[1]. Tesla's strategy has been to rival typical technological-product life cycles and firstly enter the car market with an expensive, high-end product targeted at affluent buyers. As the company, its products and consumer acceptance mature, it is moving into larger, more competitive markets at lower price points.

Malaysia Automobile Industry

Perhaps even more disruptive innovations are on the horizon of mass use: the driverless car and the future of the car in the context of the Internet of things. Companies such as BMW are concerned that unless they master the new technologies, they may end up as suppliers of commodity-type products to the likes of Google and Apple – now that would be disruptive!

The two examples at different ends of the car industry spectrum illustrate how established players in the global automobile industry will have to re-think their strategic position and product offerings in the face of tremendously changing market environments.[2] It is not only established players; there are also problems for some of the newer players on the global scene and, importantly, entrants from different sectors, notably IT.

Far from being 'mature', perhaps the car industry is still a spring chicken …

---

[1]See *The Economist* (2014) 'Tesla's electric man', December. Available at: www.economist.com/news/technology-quarterly/21635332-jb-straubel-charged-more-electrifying-californian-carmaker-he (accessed 16 March 2015).
[2]See *Business Week* (2009) 'What can Tata's Nano teach Detroit?', March. Available at: www.businessweek.com/innovate/content/mar2009/id20090318_012120.htm?campaign_id=rss_daily (accessed 16 March 2015).

IN PRACTICE

Malaysia's automobile strategy

For many years the global automobile industry has been in a situation of oversupply of vehicles on the market.

You are engaged as a strategy consultant to Malaysia, which has been developing a national automotive policy as a part of its 2020 vision. Your task is to review the 2014 statement of its strategy in the context of the global changes to the industry.

You can find links to relevant articles on the book's website at www.edge.sagepub.com/strategy2e.

Questions

1. What do you think are the significant recent changes in the environment of the global automobile industry?

2. What do you think is required from traditional automobile manufacturers today that they seemed to have ignored for too many years?

3. What do you think might be the potential advantages of newcomers such as Tata Motors in India?

4. What do you think might be the advantages of newcomers like Tesla Motors globally?

5. To what extent do you think the onset of the driverless car modifies your conclusions?

6. Given your analysis of the global automobile industry, what strategic advice would you offer, based on what considerations, and drawing on what strategic approaches, to the Malaysian Government with respect to NAP 2014?

Types of markets

Using the PESTEL tool for the analyses of key influences of the macro environment is a first step to understand the organization's current and potential future situation.

> A **market** is the group of buyers and sellers, where buyers determine demand and sellers determine supply, together with the means whereby both exchange their goods or services.

A next important step is an assessment of the prevailing **markets** in which the firm chooses to operate.

In other words, a market describes a firm's target customers or buyers with whom the economic exchange occurs. Most models presented in this chapter are based on the idea of a market as the place of exchange. Market types then describe key characteristics of archetypical markets with respect to the number of players and the intensity of competition. Whether a market is highly competitive or not is the key question.

The concept of the industry refers to the group of companies that are related in terms of their primary business activities, involving the similarity of products and/or the processes surrounding the transformation of inputs to outputs. In modern economies, there are dozens of different industry classifications, which are typically grouped into larger categories called sectors. We will look at industry analysis later, after we have introduced different types of markets.

For an organization it is important to understand how different market types can affect its strategic choices. A central characteristic is the extent to which a market is homogeneous or heterogeneous, that is the extent to which it presents the same or different conditions for every firm that is competing within it. We can consider four basic market types: the perfectly competitive, the monopoly, the oligopoly and the hypercompetitive.

1. In a *perfectly competitive* market it is very easy for a firm to imitate success almost immediately because information about the market, its customers, products or production costs is available to all players. In such situations there is little need for strategy. In addition, firms are assumed to produce homogeneous products while there exists free entry and exit. All these ensure than no firm can charge above the competitive price, a price that just covers a firm's average costs. An example of a perfectly competitive market would be the international currency market. However, one can argue that even currency exchange is an imperfect market since central banks try to influence trade and countries often peg their exchange rates.

2. At the other end of the market spectrum is the *monopoly*. It is, similarly to the perfectly competitive market, a special case with little need for strategy since there are no direct competitors to worry about. If an organization is in the fortunate position of having no competitors, its strategic objective will be to retain full control and protect that position. Classic examples of commercial monopolies used to be national telephone companies such as AT&T in the US, which, until the 1980s, controlled the phone networks for local and long distance services and were the sole provider for telephone equipment. In some countries, such as Australia, national telephone companies that were public monopolies were privatized and effectively remained largely private monopolies. It is not only public sector organizations that have been privatized that can be effective monopolies. Today, Microsoft has often been accused of monopolizing the operating system market for computers and has been sued many times over this issue. Very few companies, however, find themselves in a competitive environment that can be classified as either a monopoly or a pure market.

3. *Oligopoly* is characterized by a limited number of players acting in relatively predictable and coordinated ways to supply products and services. Because there are only a few players in an oligopoly each is generally aware of the actions of the others. Decisions by one firm influence, and are influenced by, the decisions of other firms. Strategic planning in an oligopoly, therefore, involves taking into account the likely moves of the other market participants. Oligopolistic industries are prime candidates for collusion. Such collusion occurs when competitors within an industry cooperate illegally for mutual benefit, for example, to stabilize unstable markets or reduce the risks of these markets for investment or product development. In the US, for instance, in the late nineteenth century, a series of antitrust laws were passed to limit such behaviour, responding to the power of the large, integrated holding companies established by Standard Oil and other companies. While it is possible to regulate nationally it is more difficult to regulate globally. The civil passenger

aircraft industry is a good example of an oligopolistic market, since there are only a small number of manufacturers worldwide including Boeing, Airbus/EADS, Embraer and Bombardier. The oligopoly is a very common market form in developed economies as well as being an emerging market form in many sectors, because globalization allows firms to compete in markets that they did not have access to previously. Other examples of oligopolistic markets are the mobile and wireless network industries, which in many countries are heavily regulated, so that often only two or three providers are licensed to operate in the same region. The Organization of Petroleum Exporting Countries (OPEC) and other producers in the global oil and gas industry are an example of oligopolistic markets. OPEC members benefit from high profits by controlling the amount of oil made available.

4. Finally, *hypercompetition* depicts a market in which the sources of competitive advantage can change quickly, and maintaining above average profits over a long time is difficult. Richard D'Aveni (1994) coined the term hypercompetition and argued that in new markets, or what was called the 'new economy' in the 1990s, technologies such as the Internet and related offerings were so new that standards and rules were not yet developed and competitive advantages could not be sustained in the long term. Hence, long-term sustainable competitive advantage has to come from continually disrupting the status quo, changing the rules of the game, by taking the industry in new directions where competitors' strengths become irrelevant. A firm will, therefore, aim for a sequence of short-term advantages that can span across numerous competitive arenas. For example, firms might compete over price or quality, or innovate in supply chain management, new value creation, or raise enough financial capital to outlast other competitors. Thomas and D'Aveni (2009) link such increase of within-industry heterogeneity of returns in the US manufacturing sector to increases in volatility and find a broad, monotonic shift towards hypercompetition. There are links to be made with earlier work carried out by economists sympathetic to the Austrian view by researchers such as Dennis Mueller, who were grappling with these issues in the late 1970s and early 1980s. A good review of this earlier work can be found in Young et al. (1996).

Thomas & D'Aveni

EXTEND YOUR KNOWLEDGE

You can read a journal article by Thomas and D'Aveni (2009) on the book's website at www.edge.sagepub.com/strategy2e.

Thomas, L.G. and D'Aveni, R. (2009) 'The changing nature of competition in the US manufacturing sector, 1950–2002', *Strategic Organization*, 7(4): 387–431.

Although the above categories are often simplifications of a much more complex reality, these terms help distinguish different market characteristics, requiring different strategies, in which it is possible to realize above-average returns.

Real Market Complexities

Obviously, real markets are much more complex and usually entail a mixture of the characteristics described above. Take the Internet, which is an enabling (infra-) structure for buyers and sellers to exchange information, transact and complete various actions before, during and after the transaction. It is a networked information system. In that sense an online market is not much different to a physical marketplace. Yet, there are some important implications that emerge from the fact that the marketplace is online.

- Typically, private electronic marketplaces serve *multiple buyers and one seller*, for example when you buy a concert ticket directly from the organizers' website, or *multiple sellers and one buyer*, where, for example, a number of builders participate in a live reverse auction in response to a call for bids posted by a city council. While such variations occur in physical markets too, they can be scaled more easily in the context of the Internet.

- Another distinguishing factor is the increasingly important role of participants other than buyers and sellers in the transaction. Third parties can provide value-added services to buyers and/or sellers on the Internet, including, for example, accessing information about product quality and price of competing brands from an infomediary rather than the seller. Infomediaries, such as Autobytel.com, BestBuy.com or BizRate.com offer buyers access to large amounts of data about products and companies before they make a purchasing decision, thereby acting as an intermediary between those who want the information and those who supply the information (Hagel, 1999).

- Buyers can also engage in a conversation about quality and price with past and prospective buyers and sellers. Again, while such interactions can also occur in the physical marketplace, their prevalence and scalability are greater in the electronic marketplace. Hence, online buyers are usually much better informed, resulting in a more competitive environment. Ebay is an example of this.

Let's now look at some of the theories that help us further analyse the different aspects of oligopolies and hypercompetition, since these are the most common types of markets a strategist would have to deal with.

Industry analysis

So far we have looked at the macro environment of the firm and identified different types of markets. We now proceed to further examine what is usually called the industry's micro environment, also termed as industry analysis. Remember, an industry is made up of those companies that are related through their primary business activities, involving the processes surrounding the transformation of inputs to outputs. But it's not always obvious for the strategist to know who is competing in the industry or where competition might come from in the future. This is particularly problematic in times of converging industries and technological developments that affect more than one industry. Consider the possibilities of the Internet of Things (IoT) and how that changes how people interact with everyday objects. Those new products are unlikely to be brought to market by traditional members of specific industries but by new players who breach traditional perceptions of industry boundaries.

Very influential in this context, as we shall see, have been the ideas of Michael Porter. Indeed, for many people, the name Porter is synonymous with the term strategy. Turning the SCP approach and IO logic on its head, Porter (1980, 1985) suggested industry analysis and the Five Forces model to determine the attractiveness of an industry and construct a sustainable competitive position for the firm amongst competitors. The model captures the main idea of Porter's theory of sustainable competitive advantage in that it emphasizes five forces that define the rules of competition within an industry. Given the blurred lines of contemporary industries Five Forces analysis requires scoping of what can be considered within or outside the boundaries of a respective industry based on the question of who is going to or is likely to compete. It is important to define the scope of the industry before attempting to apply the Five Forces model since a scope too narrow might lead to overlooking important players while a scope too broad might render the analysis meaningless.

Porter argued that competitive strategy must emerge from a refined understanding of the rules of competition that determine industry attractiveness. He claimed that the 'ultimate aim of competitive strategy is to cope with and, ideally, to change those rules in the firm's behavior' (1985: 4). The crucial question in determining profitability, from this perspective, is how much value firms are really able to create for their customers, and how much of this value will be captured or competed away by rivals. While the market structure determines which players capture the value, a firm is capable of influencing the five forces that define competition within the industry through its own conduct. In that sense Porter opposes the initial SCP logic suggesting that conduct influences structure as much as structure determines conduct.

Five Forces Model

The model is a practical tool with which to analyse an industry's attractiveness. In particular, it enables a firm to construct a cogent competitor analysis since it specifies the competitive structure of an industry in a more tangible manner. In addition, it recognizes the role of firms in formulating appropriate competitive strategy to achieve superior performance.

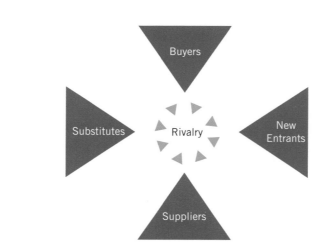

Figure 2.1   Adapted from Porter's Five Forces model

In the model, four forces – the bargaining power of customers, the bargaining power of suppliers, the threat of new entrants and the threat of substitute products – influence a fifth force, the level of competition in an industry. Together these forces are close to a firm and directly affect its capacity to serve its customers and thus make a profit. A change in any of the forces normally requires a firm to re-assess its position in the marketplace. Each of these forces has several determinants:

1. *The bargaining power of customers or buyer power* refers to the immediate buyer in the industry value chain rather than the final consumer or end user. Demand is the main factor that determines the power of buyers. For example, buyer power is strong when there are many firms that compete for few buyers. Think of a retail supermarket chain such as Tesco or Woolworth that has huge buyer power by deciding which supplier to purchase tinned food from to stock all shops in the country. As buyer (customer) Tesco and Woolworth have significant power because they can compare prices and switch easily. This is different to a patient who needs a special drug for a rare disease that is only offered by one pharmaceutical company. In this case, the buyer has little power and will have to accept the price the pharmaceutical company sets. There are various factors that help determine the relative power of customers. These include the degree of buyer concentration in relation to firm concentration within the industry, the typical volume that a buyer demands, the costs of switching to a new producer, the availability of information for buyers about products and services in an industry, the overall price structure and price sensitivity of buyers.

2. *The bargaining power of suppliers.* Supplier relationships can be complex, especially when suppliers, for example, have exclusive access to important inputs such as raw materials, technology or knowledge. Suppliers can be in a very strong position and eventually dictate the quality, volume and, most importantly, prices of goods and services. The factors that help determine supplier power in an industry include the degree of supplier concentration in relation to firm concentration, the supplier's switching costs relative to those of the firm, the degree of differentiation of inputs, the availability and presence of substitute inputs, the threat of forward integration by suppliers relative to the threat of backward integration by firms, the cost of inputs relative to the selling price of the product and the importance of the buyers volume to the supplier. For instance, OPEC states are important suppliers to the airline industry and wield significant power because of the limited number of potential suppliers of oil; also, think of a highly unionized firm in which suppliers (qualified labour) can call for a strike and stop production.

3. *The threat of new entrants.* When new firms enter an existing industry, it will have an impact on competition. Porter suggests that strategists should assess how easy it is for a new company to enter an industry or how easy it is for an existing firm to exit the industry. Obviously, the most attractive segments will have high entry barriers and low exit barriers. Entry barriers might include capital requirements, brand equity, product differentiation, profits based on economies of scale, switching costs for buyers, access to distribution channels, other cost advantages, experience or government policies. Take for instance the pharmaceutical industry: entry barriers are extremely high because it takes many years to research and test drugs before they can be sold for profit. Hence, a new start up would face huge costs and long-term

investment without returns, which is not a very attractive prospect for capital. In each industry, companies and firms that are already established will seek to protect those areas where they are most profitable and attempt to prevent any additional competitors from entering the market. It is not uncommon for rivals to work together temporarily. The motive for creating such barriers is to keep out companies that perform poorly and sustain a situation where all existing competitors have the potential for better profits.

4.   *The threat of substitute products.* Where substitute products are readily available in other industries and have the potential to satisfy a similar need for customers they can shape the strategic context. As more substitutes become available and affordable, the competition is more intense since customers have more alternatives. Substitute products may limit the ability of firms within an industry to raise prices and improve margins. The factors that determine this force include the buyer propensity to substitute, the relative price performance and quality of substitutes, buyer switching costs and the perceived level of product differentiation within an industry. Take the example of CDs as substitute for vinyl, and MP3 technology as substitute for CDs. Or take Skype as an example of a new technology that may displace traditional telephony. In these cases, the new technology does not compete with the old one but substitutes it. The danger is that strategists might benchmark themselves to other firms within their industry without realizing that the real threat emerges from elsewhere. Typewriter companies in the 1970s competed fiercely with each other for better quality typewriters – overlooking that the real threat came from what was the then infant personal computer industry.

5.   *The intensity of competitive rivalry.* At the heart of the Five Forces model is the degree of rivalry amongst firms within the focal industry. The number of players, and their relative size, matters, as do other characteristics of the industry (see the discussion earlier in this chapter). A larger number of firms, for example, will increase rivalry because more firms will be competing for the same customers and resources. The rivalry also intensifies if the firms have a similar market share, leading to a struggle for market leadership. If a market is characterized by slow market growth, firms will compete more intensely for market share, while in a growing market firms are able to improve revenues simply because of the expanding market. Also, if companies are facing a high level of fixed costs in producing goods and services, profits usually stem from an economy of scale effect so that the firms must produce near capacity to attain the lowest unit costs. Given that the firm must now sell large quantities they will have to fight more aggressively to achieve profitable market share. Limiting the ability of a company to leave the market through exit barriers also increases competition. This is because a company that otherwise might prefer to leave is forced to stay in the industry and endure excess capacity and competitive pressures. A common exit barrier occurs in industries with high levels of asset specificity, that is when a firm's assets, like the plant and equipment required for manufacturing a product, are highly specialized and, therefore, cannot easily be sold to other buyers in another industry. Other factors that increase the rivalry in an industry are low switching costs or low levels of product differentiation, whereas brand identification and loyalty tend to constrain rivalry.

Go Online: On *The Conversation* website Don Scott-Kemis makes some interesting observations about industry structure in discussing innovation in an article entitled 'If we want to promote innovation we need to focus on businesses'. He notes, in connection with the Australian mining industry, that it is often 'the quality of demand, which is related to the competency of the users, that enables innovation' in a way that is illustrative of Porter's point about demand conditions. You can read the piece by searching for it on the *Conversation* or via the article web link on the book's website: www.edge.sagepub.com/strategy2e.

Don Scott-Kemis Article

The central idea of Porter's Five Forces model is that the profitability of an organization depends on its bargaining power when negotiating prices with suppliers and customers. Logically, a strong bargaining position means that in relation to its competitors an organization pays less to its suppliers and sells at a higher price to its customers. Hence, economic market structures, such as those characterized by monopoly, oligopoly or hypercompetition, are shaped by the five forces and ultimately determine the bargaining power of the firm. Hence, strategic management, in Porter's sense, means navigating through the web of opportunities and threats framed by external competitive forces.

In a market with low barriers to entry the threat from newly competing rivals is only likely to be high when the level of profitability in this industry is also high. Therefore, the strategy in an industry with a high threat of new entrants might be to limit prices that, although keeping profits low, helps avoid competitors entering the market. The Five Forces model directs the strategist towards some of the most important aspects in achieving long-term competitive advantage; it helps identify the sources of competition and determine their relative strength. In that sense a firm's conduct or strategic behaviour is influenced by its assessment of the five forces.

On the other hand, similar to the SCP approach, Porter's model is in essence static and to some extent underestimates the role and importance of uncertainty and change that can occur in the competitive environment of the firm. The mere analysis of a list of forces in the competitive environment will not advance strategic management efforts until the few driving factors that really define and bring about change within an industry are identified and understood.

Another force?

Recently there have been suggestions that industry analysis should be expanded beyond the five forces that Michael Porter suggested to include one that explores the analysis of additional forces in terms of the relative power of other stakeholders.

One notable school of thought considers the sixth force to be complementors; that is businesses offering complementary products within an industry, an idea credited to Andrew Grove, the former CEO of the Intel Corporation. Grove positioned Intel as a powerful complementor of Microsoft products. Together both companies have dominated the global PC markets through their inseparable Wintel combination of Intel processors and Microsoft software. The relationship with a complementor such as a supplier, however, can also involve elements of rivalry, as suggested by Porter. Brandenburger and Nalebuff (1995) coined a term for such situations – coopetition – which is the pursuit of win–win as much as win–lose opportunities jointly with substitutors or complementors, which we discuss further in Chapter 6. Substitutors are alternative players from whom customers can purchase products. Complementors are players from whom customers can buy complementary products. Both substitutors and complementors affect the industry since their technological advances and strategic moves can significantly change its competitive dynamics. According to Brandenburger and Nalebuff (1995) through coopetition organizations can create and capture value better than through competition alone.

Another contender as a sixth force is the state. At a prosaic level the influence of state regulations, such as network licenses for mobile phone companies or quotas for the fishing industry can enhance and restrict the profitability of an industry. It is crucially important not to neglect the role of the state. Porter maintains that the state can only operate through the five forces and is not a separate sixth force.

Finally, other powerful groups that possess power in Porter's terms include stakeholders such as the general public, shareholders and employees. The role and influence of employees, which is well established in countries that have works councils, such as Germany and the Netherlands, has also increased in many industry sectors of Anglo-Saxon economies. Employees generally now have more demanding requirements in regards to green management practices and corporate social responsibility. In some industries, for example the US automobile sector, employees remain highly unionized, constituting a powerful influence that strategists have to analyse closely in order to understand a firm's competitive position. In Porter's model employees are mere suppliers of factor inputs hence their power needs to be reduced. This ignores the positive role that can be engendered through collaboration.

In response to the various claims of additional forces in the model, Michael Porter (2008) argued that

Andy Cavanagh on Strategic Groups

> Complements can be important when they affect the overall demand for an industry's product. However like government policy, complements are not a sixth force determining industry profitability since the presence of strong complements is not necessarily bad (or good) for industry profitability. Complements affect profitability through the way they influence the five forces [...] The strategist must trace the positive or negative influence of complements on all five forces to ascertain their impact on profitability. (Porter, 2008: 86)

While the specifics of competition may change, the fundamental influence of the five forces changes little. That is, although complementary products, as well as state regulations and the influence of other groups are important phenomena, they are typically looked at as factors that feed into competitive analysis through the five forces (Stonehouse and Snowdon, 2007).

Strategic groups

The presence of **strategic groups** in an industry has a significant effect on the industry's profitability, countering the IO economics' assumption that an industry's members differ only in market share.

Firms can be classified into categories of strategic similarities within, and differences across, groups (Hunt, 1972). For example, in the US automobile industry GM, Ford and Chrysler constitute 'The Big Three', while Toyota, Honda, Nissan and Mazda are 'The Samurai', and Mercedes, Audi and BMW belong

Porter (1980) defined a **strategic group** as a group of firms in the same industry that follow the same or similar strategies.

to the 'Luxury Car' group. While IO economics considers structural aspects of an industry, work on strategic groups is largely focused on firm groupings within an industry. Bauerschmidt and Chrisman (1993), for example, report a reduction in strategic diversity in the global microcomputer industry between 1985 and 1989 due to a consolidation from six to four strategic groups. While many survivors changed strategies, it was those firms with broader-scope strategies that were more likely to be successful.

More recent studies (Porac and Thomas, 1994; Ketchen et al., 1997; Nath and Gruca, 1997; DeSarbo and Grewal, 2008; DeSarbo et al., 2009) confirm that strategic groups exist across various industries and have a distinct role in explaining competitive market structures and firms' strategic postures/recipes. The existence of strategic groups influences competition because firms that utilize similar strategies compete more directly inside their strategic group than outside. As a result, the competitive environment will be more distinctive in regards to the forces that determine each company's position (DeSarbo and Grewal, 2007).

Thinking in terms of strategic groups can change the way executives perceive their business in relation to others (McNamara et al., 2003). For example, managers can see a computer and software store as a meeting point for people interested in gaming or as a provider of IT services for business people. The first strategic group competes with cafes or sports facilities, the second with other more professional IT service providers. Findings in the area of strategic group identity suggest that strategic group membership is stable over time and that firms within a strategic group will co-evolve. Spencer and his colleagues (2003), for example, examine the extent to which consensus exists amongst managers' perception of strategic groups and explore task and institutional factors that might influence such perceptions.

EXTEND YOUR KNOWLEDGE

You can read a journal article by Spencer and his colleagues by going to the book's website www.edge.sagepub.com/strategy2e.

Spencer, B., Peyrefitte, J. and Churchman, R. (2003) 'Consensus and divergence in perceptions of cognitive strategic groups: Evidence from the health care industry', *Strategic Organization*, 1(2): 203–230.

Spencer, Peyrefitte & Churchman

The idea of strategic groups has been incorporated within Michael Porter's general approach to strategic analysis by explaining strategic groups in terms of **mobility barriers** (McGee and Thomas, 1986).

Firm-specific sources of mobility barriers include organizational structure and control systems, management skills and capabilities, the nature and extent of diversification and of vertical integration, and the nature of the firm's ownership and its connections with powerful groups such as unions, consumer groups and state regulators. Mobility barriers can be enhanced by **isolating mechanisms** that allow firms to make it very difficult for other firms to compete with the firm.

Mobility barriers are similar to barriers to entry, but act as barriers for a group within an industry rather than for the industry as a whole.

An **isolating mechanism** is an entry barrier or a mobility barrier to a market that can limit market entry. Unique firm characteristics make competitive positions stable and defensible.

Identification of strategic groups has led to Strategic Group Analysis (SGA) (Fiegenbaum and Thomas, 1990), which is useful because it helps identify direct and indirect competitors and their basis for competitive advantage while also clarifying how likely it is that a firm moves from one strategic group to another, or what general strategic opportunities or problems an industry or strategic group is facing. In analysing strategic groups, you need to identify organizations with similar strategic characteristics that follow similar strategies or compete on similar bases. Strategic groups can be identified by comparing rival firms in terms of the extent of their product diversity, geographic coverage, the amount of customer segments served, the use of distribution channels, the importance of branding and marketing, overall product quality or pricing strategies. The strategic group concept restores strategic decisions to the centre of analysis and re-emphasizes the firm as an important unit of analysis. A detailed understanding of the industry context, the position a firm holds in relation to its competitors, the implications of strategic groups, as well as the power of suppliers and customers can all help the creation of strategies that can lead to competitive advantage for the firm.

Strategic action

Firms position themselves in relation to the forces; at best they will be mastering them to rewrite industry rules in such a way as to amplify the organization's power by diminishing the control of other organizations over these five forces. It is thus a zero sum conception of power. The zero sum probabilities can be changed, however, through strategic action. Organizations can pursue growth and spread risk by diversification and acquisition. Overall, there are three calculations that any organization needs to make in assessing its strategy:

1. *Attractiveness*: what makes an industry attractive to diversify into will be that it has a high return on investment accompanied by high barriers to entry. In such a situation customers' and suppliers' power will be moderated and there will be few substitute products.

2. *Cost of entry*: the cost of entry has to pass the hurdle text; it should not be so high that it will potentially reduce the profitability of entering the industry.

3. *Mutual competitive advantage*: the acquisition must be such that both parties see an advantage in the deal; otherwise it is not likely to be successful.

For Porter these calculations require a seven step strategic analysis.

1. First, be clear about the business units involved: what are the existing interrelationships between them?

2. Second, what is to be the core business – one with assured competitive features in an attractive industry that will be the strategic foundation for the future?

3. Third, what are the horizontal mechanisms that need to be created in order to ensure interrelationship of core businesses?

4. Fourth, what diversification opportunities allow for these interrelationships and that pass the calculations test?

5. Fifth, what synergies offer themselves for a transfer of skills and capabilities if faced with limited opportunities for sharing activities with potential partners?

6. Sixth, if the previous five considerations cannot be met satisfactorily, what opportunities are there for restructuring the existing organization?

7. Seventh, can dividends be paid such that shareholders become portfolio managers?

Porter argues that firm profitability is dependent on industry structure. For instance, if you are in the airline industry, the recent years have been tough as high oil prices, terrorism, environmental concerns, entry of cheap airlines have been amongst a range of factors eroding the profits of most airlines. No matter how good you are in the airline industry, you have to try very hard to make a living. You can only do so at the expense of other competitor firms in the environment; you have to exercise *power over* them.

On the other hand, consider the pharmaceutical industry: higher life expectancy, better medical care for more people and costly R&D means that there are barriers preventing the entry of new firms that enable established players to generate double digit profits. They were able to do so because they controlled the market *power to* innovate. Porter argues that the industry structure matters more than the firm's capabilities; crudely put, the environment determines success, not the resources controlled.

Generic strategies

Yet another influential concept that Michael Porter suggested is the concept of generic strategies. Remember that Porter argues that the primary determinant of a firm's profitability is a combination of its position within the industry that it operates in and the overall attractiveness of that industry. In fact, even if an industry generates below-average profitability, a firm that is positioned well can still generate superior returns. To position a firm successfully, managers have to leverage the company's strength and meet a unique customer need with a uniquely differentiable product or services.

In addition, the organization's activities must link together in terms of the value chain. It is the combinations comprising the value chain that make overall capabilities inimitable. Trade-offs will be necessary; choosing to do some things and striving to do them excellently means that there has to be strategic focus as this may well mean choosing not to do certain things that have been done in the past. The essence of strategy is choosing what not to do.

In his concept of generic strategies (see Figure 2.2), Porter argues that a firm's strengths eventually relate to three basic types of competitive advantage: *cost leadership, differentiation* or *focus*. Managers have to decide which type of competitive advantage they build their strategy on. In short, *cost leadership* concerns striving for efficiencies that make the firm the lowest cost and best value for money provider in the industry – think of WalMart; *differentiation* is about offering something different, extra, distinctively special like M&S' food retailing that is based on convenience and perceived quality, and finally *focus* seeks to achieve dominance in a niche market, such as Wholefoods dominance of the organic food market.

For Porter, each of these is a clear and definite strategy; pursuing one of them provides strategic focus; mixing them produces strategic muddle. Knowing which one to choose depends on the five competitive forces that the organization has to manage. Let's have a closer look at these generic strategic options.

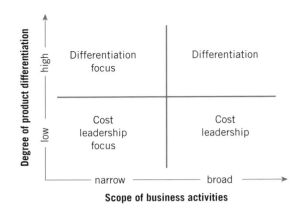

Figure 2.2   Adapted from Porter's generic strategies model

Cost Leadership

> To implement a **cost leadership** strategy successfully a firm has to develop efficiencies in regards to the use of facilities and production processes to create the same benefit for customers at a much lower cost than competitors.

A widely used strategy for achieving competitive advantage is that of **cost leadership**.

The source of cost advantage can vary for different industries but commonly involves the pursuit of economies of scale, proprietary technology, or better access to raw materials and other production factors. A firm following a cost leadership strategy must find and take advantage of all sources of cost advantage to sustain its position. Only then can it command prices at or near the industry average that result in above average returns. Cost leadership strategies can usually be found in broad markets. If, for example, pricing is very competitive or the industry matures and prices decline, the firm that follows a cost leadership strategy is often able to maintain profitability longer while other competitors suffer losses.

Companies that have followed a cost leadership strategy with significant success include Wal-Mart, Aldi, Toyota, Southwest Airlines and IKEA. Typical strengths of a cost leadership strategy include:

- Access to capital that allows significant investment in production assets and, at the same time, represents an entry barrier that other firms may not be able to overcome.

- Ability to develop products very efficiently, for example, by using only a few components or having a short assembly method. IKEA is a good example.

- Access to world-class expertise in manufacturing processes, service delivery or well-organized distribution channels.

To maintain their strength, low-cost operators such as Southwest Airlines know that they must continuously improve productivity and efficiency, which may include substantial investments in, for example, acquiring the newest and youngest fleet in the industry, rather than buying used airplanes. While that is costly, Southwest is able to save on pilot training, maintenance, spare parts inventory, and other activities by volume purchasing only one type of aircraft, the Boeing 737. Yet, maintaining a position of cost leadership in an industry is not easy, especially when other firms are also able to lower their costs. By cost reduction the competition gains improved access to technology, capital and knowledge, enabling them to reproduce strategic production capabilities, thus eliminating competitive advantage.

Differentiation

Another widely used strategy for competitive advantage is that of **differentiation**.

Difference in a firm's offering can come from various sources, including the brand image, technology, superior and additional features, better customer service, dealer networks and outstanding support. In general, products and services can be differentiated on the basis of either tangible or intangible features.

- Tangible features include things such as size, colour, design and weight that are recognizably different and increase the perceived quality of the product. Other tangible differentiators are pre-sales and post-sales services such as payment options, accessories, available upgrades and spare parts that complement a product.

- Intangible differentiators represent unique characteristics that a firm is able to offer buyers, such as exclusiveness, individuality, brand image or security. The crux is to find those attributes of an offer or a combination thereof that a sufficiently large group of buyers within an industry see as important. A firm can then develop the right products and services and thereby obtain a position where it can meet exactly those customers' needs.

Firms that follow a differentiation strategy are usually rewarded for their uniqueness with an ability to charge a premium price, which should cover the extra costs incurred in offering the unique product. Even in cases where suppliers increase their prices a firm may just be able to pass along those costs to its customers for whom it might be difficult to find substitute products.

Companies with successful differentiation strategies include the automobile manufacturer Mercedes, the audio and video equipment manufacturer Bang & Olufsen, the transport and logistics provider FedEx and luxury fashion companies such as Chanel, Gucci and the like. The organizational strengths of these companies include access to leading research and development, highly creative product developers, a smart sales force that can communicate the outstanding qualities of the product and an overall reputation or brand recognition for quality and innovation.

> In a **differentiation** strategy a firm seeks to be unique in its industry by offering products or services that stand out from the competition based on features or components that customers value most and are willing to pay for.

To ensure long-term success these firms have to make sure the combination of factors used to achieve differentiation is difficult, if not impossible, to imitate by rivals. This is often achieved through entry and mobility barriers or building a strong brand and a loyal customer base. At the same time companies that follow a differentiation strategy have to be aware of changes in customer tastes and preferences, since competitive advantage can easily vanish by losing sight of what customers want.

Porter's generic strategies are 'generic' because they are not dependent on the firm or the industry and because they characterize strategic positions at *the simplest and broadest level*. Yet they are useful in that they emphasize the implications of the strategists' decisions about the type and the scope of a firm's competitive advantage. There are different risks inherent in each generic strategy, but, as Michael Porter puts it, being 'all things to all people' is a sure recipe for mediocrity.

Michael Porter said firms that do not follow one of the three generic approaches, or firms attempting to pursue more than one of these strategies, would be 'stuck in the middle', meaning that they would find themselves in a position where they might be unable to realize profits above the industry average. The reason is that a firm's decisions about how to allocate its resources would become unclear, thus not providing competitive advantage in any of the three generic ways. Customers, suppliers and others would receive confusing impressions.

For example, if a firm aims to differentiate its offer by producing high quality products, it might undermine the customers' perception of that quality if it seeks to become a cost leader at the same time. Even if the quality did not suffer, the firm would risk leaving a confusing impression with its customers. In fact, only a few firms have sufficient resources to pursue more than one strategy at a time.

Porter wanted to emphasize the importance of strategic clarity in making these two fundamental strategic decisions: first, about taking a low-cost position or developing uniqueness in buyers' eyes, and, second, whether to attempt to serve the entire market or a smaller segment of buyers. To be successful over the long term, a firm must select only one of these three generic strategies.

Porter (1996) argues that strategy is about doing things differently or doing different things. The strategic advantage of product innovation is that no one else can offer what you offer, as we address further in Chapter 4. Cost leadership via process innovation, on the other hand, focuses on creating new and ultimately more cost effective ways of assembling and/or delivering products and services. Think of Dell computers. Dell did not invent a new product. Rather, the firm thought of a clever way of distributing PCs directly to customers over the phone or the Internet. Cutting out retailers, Dell and its customers shared the savings. Dell's strategy is cost leadership via process innovation because it re-defines the way products are sold. Here, the strategy is based on a new way of delivering a product.

The two strategies cannot always be neatly separated. Consider the example of the online telephone service Skype, founded in 2002 by the Swede Niklas Zennström and his Danish partner Janus Friis. In 2005 they sold Skype to eBay for $2.6 billion and subsequently, Microsoft acquired Skype for $8.5 billion in 2011. Skype's innovation challenged the business model of telephony. Traditional providers try to make their customer speak as much as possible and as long as possible on the phone, maximizing their revenue through usage. Skype, on the hand, is free of charge when used online from computer to computer. So how does Skype earn an income? First, its cost base is very low because its innovative software works with the individual user's hardware to run Skype. Also, Skype does not pay for the network as users are already connected to the Internet anyway. Finally, marketing costs are very low because dedicated users will encourage friends and family to join Skype. Skype's business model relies on additional services that extend beyond free computer-to-computer telephony. For a small fee, you can call mobile phones or landlines via the Internet. For Skype this works: since the cost per user is minimal, a large number of users, each spending a small amount of money on additional services, generates an attractive business. Hence, Skype's innovation is centred on a new business model.

Strategic Focus

The firm's choice of a narrow competitive scope within an industry defines the focus for their generic strategies. Hence, pursuing a focus strategy entails targeting a particular segment to meet its needs, thus achieving high levels of customer loyalty and subsequent above-average returns. The focus strategy has two variants: the differentiation focus and the cost focus. While in a differentiation focus a firm seeks differentiation in its specific target segment, cost focus seeks cost advantage in a target segment. In other words, a differentiation focus exploits the special needs of unique buyers and groups, while the cost focus exploits differences in cost behaviour.

The bottom line for any firm adopting a focus strategy is to make sure that customers really have different needs and wants that it serves. That is to say that firms have to ensure that there is a valid basis for segmentation, that customer needs can be better serviced by entirely focusing on them and that currently available products do not yet sufficiently meet those needs and wants. There are many well-known examples of a differentiation focus strategy:

- *The Body Shop* is an example of a differentiation focus strategy. While an advantage of a differentiation focus strategy is that firms may be able to pass higher costs on to customers since substitute products are hard to find, the trade-off for this strategy is that the market share is usually limited to the size of the specific segment. However, within this limitation, profits can be significant – at least, until there is a plethora of similar competitors offering similar products and promise.

Body Shop was distinctive. It took a basic low value added product, cheap personal care items, branded them and sold them in specialist retail outlets. Previously, prior to the emergence of the Body Shop in the 1970s, you would have bought these items in a pharmacy or department store, choosing from a variety of well-known brands. However, there are now many high street and mall competitors such as Lush that are very similar, having copied the original business model.

A different strategy available to manufacturers and retailers is to promote and market based on a strategy of cost leadership.

- An example of cost leadership focus would be those retailers who sell own-label or discounted label products, often called 'me-toos'. Since a firm following this strategy seeks a lower-cost advantage in one or a few market segments it will usually offer a more basic product, which is still acceptable to a sufficient number of consumers. This can be risky, however, because a broad-market cost leader might be able to adapt its product easily and compete directly. Think of mass retail chain store pharmacy outlets, for instance.

While Porter originally suggested that firms should avoid being unclear about their strategic intention (or being stuck in the middle) with regard to the three generic options, strategists found that various combinations of generic strategies are possible as well as profitable. For example, a single generic strategy might not be the best option when customers seek multi-dimensional satisfactions from a given product in a mixture of quality, style, convenience and price. Hence, a high quality producer might closely follow a differentiation strategy and then suffer when another firm enters the market and offers a lower quality product that better meets the overall needs of customers. It is important to understand exactly which product aspects or combinations customers look for and which they don't look for.

A successful combination of generic strategies is often a result of seeking advantage on the basis of one generic strategy while pursuing parity on the other. The term 'value for money strategy' has been coined to describe this case (Pitelis and Taylor, 1996). Alternatively, firms may pursue multiple strategies by creating separate business units for each strategy. In either case the competition will attend to cost, differentiation and focus to the extent that an industry sometimes becomes characterized by homogenization of strategies, which may trigger that state described earlier as hypercompetition.

Table 2.2 gives an overview of how the three generic strategies affect the Five Forces (see Figure 2.1) of industry competition.

Table 2.2 Strategic implications of generic strategies and industry forces

	Differentiation	**Cost Leadership**	**Focus**
Buyer Power	Buyers have less power to negotiate because of limited alternatives.	Firms may be able to offer discounts or lower price to powerful buyers.	Buyers have less power to negotiate because of limited alternatives.
Supplier Power	Firms may be able to pass on supplier price increases to customers.	Firms are more protected from powerful suppliers.	Low volumes lead to more supplier power; however, a differentiation-focused firm is able to pass on supplier price increases to customers.
Entry Barriers	Firms are better protected because customer loyalty can discourage potential entrants.	The capability to cut prices deters potential entrants.	Unique competence as a result of a focusing strategy can represent an entry barrier.
Threat of Substitutes	Threat of substitutes is reduced since customers become attached to differentiating attributes.	The capability to cut prices can help defend against substitutes.	Specialized products and unique competences protect against substitutes.
Rivalry	Brand loyalty can help keep customers from switching to rivals.	Cost savings and production efficiencies allow competing on price.	Rivals may not be able to meet differentiation-focused customer needs.

IN PRACTICE

IKEA and Dell

IKEA and Dell are two very successful organizations in their industries. What is it that sets them apart from the competition?

IKEA combines stylish furniture with affordable prices. In order to deliver this unique proposition, it innovated how furniture is displayed (in the showroom furniture is shown in mini-room displays, creating ideas about how it could be used, which inspires people); IKEA gave away attractive catalogues full of IKEA products that you could linger over at home and imagine how useful or beautiful they would be in your environment; IKEA saved money on warehousing through flat-packing its furniture; it created an aura of Swedish wholesomeness and practicality by its naming strategy – who had ever thought of calling flat-pack shelves Billy?

Additionally, IKEA makes its customers a partner in the fabrication of the furniture; it is the customers who have to put the flat-pack boxes together at home. It also added some services, such as childcare facilities and the IKEA restaurant where the whole family can relax over a cheap meal and experience a little imagined Sweden with their soused herrings or meat balls. IKEA is an example of what Michael Porter calls strategic positioning, i.e. 'performing different activities from rivals' or 'performing similar activities in different ways' (Porter, 1996: 62).

Positioning concerns the creation of a unique and valuable position, involving a different set of activities, exactly what IKEA does. Could a competitor copy IKEA? Yes, you could build a company from scratch that is modelled on IKEA. But it would be a risky business lacking the learning and experience that IKEA has gained since it opened its first store in 1958 in Sweden. How about companies that are already in the furniture business – could they not simply imitate IKEA? Yes, but this means they would have to give up their current showrooms, their spacious warehouses, break contracts with their suppliers, retrain their staff and so on. They might as well start a business from scratch! The key point that Porter makes is that you cannot have it both ways: you cannot have IKEA's flat-pack system that co-opts customers into being amateur furniture assemblers and offer your customers a premium experience. Strategy, Porter argues, is all about choices and trade-offs. The set of activities that results from these choices creates your unique strategy. The main threat to a successful strategy is compromise – trying to be too many things to too many people.

Dell, on the other hand, is a classic example of a company that produces goods at a low cost, derives profits from economies of scale, and has a distinct competitive advantage because it can undercut its rivals predominantly on price. Dell's success is due to the company's famous build-to-order direct sales business model, which eliminates expensive middlemen, lowers working capital investments and provides real-time market information to management. The direct model also means small overhead costs and allows Dell to undercut rivals without sacrificing features or profitability. The firm has consistently improved margins and increased revenue. At the same time Dell replicated its business model across numerous new markets, most recently by moving into consumer electronics. Meanwhile, Dell's competitive advantage in building computers, servers and notebooks at the lowest possible prices has made life extremely difficult for other manufacturers, such as Gateway GTW and HP Compaq HPQ.

Questions

1. What is IKEA's and Dell's core strategy? Which of Porter's generic strategies do the firms follow?

2. Can a firm follow more than one generic strategy? Discuss the implications of such a strategy.

Another contribution by Porter was the concept of the value chain, the set of primary (such as production) and supporting (such as research and development) activities of the firm. This looks inside the firm and it is more appropriate to discuss in the next chapter where we discuss firms' resources and capabilities. It is worth noting that Porter suggested that in order to succeed, the generic strategies must be aligned to the value chain. For example, in order to differentiate one needs to spend on innovation but to be a cost leader one had better focus on mass-produced non-differentiated products. There is more on value chains in the next chapter.

Problems with Porter's framework

Industry analysis is widely used and can significantly improve the strategic understanding of the competitive environment of a firm. However, there are potential problems with Porter's framework. Perhaps most importantly, the boundaries of an industry are increasingly difficult to identify. Firms behave in ways that are increasingly strategic in their search for competitive advantage. Today's firms link their products and services in new ways that span multiple old and new industries adding to an increasingly blurred picture of industry boundaries. Companies such as eBay, Amazon or Google are re-defining and blurring the differences between the markets for online shopping, news and email services, search engines, advertising, entertainment and communication. Given these dynamics, industry analysis has been criticized because it provides a static picture. It assumes the security of industry distinctions that in reality keeps changing.

While every business possesses capabilities that enable it to position products and services in a market, only a few of these capabilities need to be superior to the competition. These are the distinctive capabilities that support a value proposition that is valuable to customers and hard for competitors to match. Treacy and Wiersema (1995) suggest a generic framework for gaining such a competitive advantage. In their framework a firm typically will choose to emphasize one of three 'value disciplines':

- *Product leadership* is a strategy where a firm continuously improves the performance of its products and services to gain a superior market position. Apple is a leader in personal computer technology while Intel is a product leader in computer chips, as well as Mercedes in the automobile industry or Nike in athletic footwear. These companies achieve superior market positions through major technology advances, rapid product variation and innovation (see Chapter 4), and an ability to create products and services that serve customer needs better than competitors. The strategy is based on a firm's ability to sense market opportunities, fast product development and launch, technology integration and flexible manufacturing.

- *Operational excellence* describes a value discipline that focuses on providing middle-of-market products at the best price with the least inconvenience. Companies such as Aldi in groceries and Matalan in clothing, or food outlets such as McDonald's, Burger King and KFC provide such no-frills mass-market retailing. This strategy requires a firm to achieve operational excellence in the core processes of order fulfilment, supply chain management, logistics, service delivery and transaction processing.

- *Customer intimacy* is a value discipline that focuses on the cultivation of a close customer relationship and the delivery of very specific products and services that exactly match the need of specific customers. An example would be Dell, which produces personal computers to very specific customer specifications. A firm pursuing this strategy has the ability to flexibly incorporate customer needs through maintaining long-term customer relationships while at the same time producing enough volume for the micro-segments of the markets that it is serving.

Finally, the model also assumes that a firm can only profit and grow in a zero-sum game, that is, at the expense of another firm's profit and growth. Such a perspective is limited, since firms are also able to grow their returns by creating win–win relationships with suppliers and competitors alike or by innovating processes and products.

Blue Ocean Strategy

The static nature of Porter's approach has also been criticized by Kim and Mauborgne (2005). The authors observed that while in Porter most industries are taken to exist, in reality entrepreneurs often create industries; for example, Isaacson (2011) claimed that during his life Steve Jobs, the famed founder and CEO of Apple, created five new industries!

For Kim and Mauborgne, the best way to compete is in the way that Jobs did: that is you create an uncontested blue ocean, one with no sharks swimming in it, as opposed to trying to compete within an ocean made red by the competition for resources from sharks, as in Porter. Of course if you are in a red ocean you need to do the best you can but it is best to avoid this altogether and enter a blue one. This view is important in that it emphasizes the role of strategists as creative entrepreneurs not just effective managers. It also highlights that competition involves much more than dealing with the five or six or more forces!

Summary

Competition is a complex matter. While economies globalize and exchanges between different economic systems increases, industry definitions have become blurred by multifaceted activities of increasingly diverse participants. In hypercompetitive environments profits are more difficult to capture and sustain. The most effective competitive strategy is always to create new sources of competitive advantage before a competitor can copy the market leader's position. These activities may allow a firm to preserve sustainable profits, but innovation is risky and failure rates are high. Hence, oligopolistic markets are often much more attractive.

In this chapter we have explored how comprehensive analysis and thorough understanding of macro and micro environments can influence strategic decision-making and help strategists create sustainable competitive advantages for their organizations. Grounded in industrial organization economics and the structure–conduct–performance view we introduced and discussed various concepts and instruments that support the strategic manager. The key lessons for the student of strategy include: different types of markets entail distinct sorts of competition; profitability of an industry can be assessed by analysing five forces that shape the competitive environment; it is important to identify unique capabilities within the firm and amongst competitors; competing within strategic groups requires a more refined unique selling proposition; generic strategies and value creating disciplines enable a firm to focus its strategic direction and avoid being 'stuck in the middle' and macro environmental influences can be better understood using a PESTEL analysis.

TEST YOURSELF

Want to know more about this chapter? Review what you have learnt by visiting www.edge.sagepub.com/strategy2e.

- Test yourself with multiple choice questions
- Revise key terms with interactive flashcards

EXERCISES

1. Having read this chapter, you should be able to say in your own words what the following key terms mean:

   - Competitive strategy
   - Five Forces
   - Sixth force
   - Industrial Organization economics
   - Strategic choice
   - Asymmetry of information
   - SCP model
   - Sustainable competitive advantage
   - Economic rent
   - Homogenous market
   - Monopoly
   - Oligopoly
   - Hypercompetition
   - PESTEL analysis
   - Asset specificity
   - Strategic groups
   - Mobility barriers
   - Isolating mechanisms
   - Generic strategies
   - Cost leadership
   - Differentiation
   - Focus strategies
   - Product innovation
   - Process innovation
   - Blue and red oceans

2. How might we differentiate strategic groups within the airline industry, for example?

3. What are the factors that make it more difficult to achieve competitive advantage within a strategic group rather than outside?

4. Why do firms choose to position themselves within a strategic group even though competition is usually fierce?

CASE STUDY

brandsExclusive

LARS GROEGER

This case describes the market environment challenges brandsExclusive faced, the strategic decisions they took and the value propositions they created to gain a competitive advantage during the first six months of their operation in 2009; followed by a short description of accelerated growth, acquisition and repositioning during Stage II of their launch.

brandsExclusive is an Australian company based in vibrant Darlinghurst, in Sydney, that sources fashion clothing, accessories and shoes directly from fashion brands and organizes online sales events. Their community of shoppers can access sales events online and purchase at significantly reduced prices – up to 70% off normal retail prices. Membership is by invitation only and non-members are not able to access or buy from the website. However, membership is free of charge and there are no further commitments or obligations to buy. Sales events last only several days with limited stock available exclusively for members.

'Every brand wants to sell online, but there are a lot of reasons they can't – protecting the brand and price or existing distribution channels are some of them', says Daniel Jarosch, Co-founder of brandsExclusive. His partner, Rolf Weber adds: 'There is strong consumer demand to buy genuine brands from a trusted online source at an affordable price.' Once you combine the two trends and find a solution to intermediate between brands and consumers, a new distribution channel is created. However, no matter how obvious the market opportunity seems, it was not until May 2009 that brandsExclusive provided a solution to meet the needs of Australian fashion brands and consumers, creating value for both.

STAGE I: THE INITIAL BUSINESS IDEA AND LAUNCH

How did the two entrepreneurs come up with the idea in the first place? Having an international background and extensive e-commerce and fashion industry experience, Daniel and Rolf carefully observed the development of highly successful exclusive shopping clubs in Europe over the past years. Online Private Shopping Clubs began in France with the launch of the vente-privee.com website in 2001. While the first three years of vente-privee.com were characterized by investment and development, an accelerated period of growth started in 2004. By the end of 2008 the company had expanded operations to Spain, Germany, Italy and the UK, with 6.5 million registered members across Europe and estimated revenues of AU$ 1 billion [€ 510 million] for 2009.

The business model has since been adopted by a number of companies globally including GILT.com, BuyVIP.com, hautelook.com or ruelala.com. Succeeding entrants in the European market were able to generate high revenues even within a shorter period of time: German based Brands4friends.de was founded in 2007 and reached

(Continued)

(Continued)

the break-even point within 6 months, generating revenues of AU$ 50 million [€ 30 million] during the first year.

The guiding principle for the different players in the European and American market is the same: fulfil the need of apparel brands to sell excess stock quickly without harming the brand's image or competing with other distribution channels. However, a closer look at their strategic positioning reveals key differences with regards to sourcing strategy, scope of target market, quality and exclusivity of offered goods, as well as the exclusivity of the membership community. Hence, for brandsExclusive the question was whether the Australian market offered the same potential as the international markets; and if so, which particularities had to be considered in order to transfer and realize a proven business model from overseas to the Australian continent?

The Australian apparel industry

'Fashion is made to become unfashionable', said Coco Chanel, and fashion by its very nature is unpredictable. Yet, the Australian apparel retail industry has shown strong rates of growth in recent years and was worth AU$12.8 billion in 2008. In general, clothing retailers purchase a variety of clothing products and accessories from manufacturers and wholesalers and sell these products directly to consumers without developing or changing the products further. Retailers typically have access to both supplier groups. In addition, they also engage in customer service, product merchandising, advertising, inventory control and cash handling. Existing retailers can be grouped into the following categories: department stores (e.g. David Jones, Myers, etc.), major chains (e.g. Just Jeans, Jay Jays, etc.), independent stores, brand stores (e.g. Diesel flagship store, etc.), direct factory outlets, off-price retailers and direct online channel of brand (e.g. skins.net). At the time of brandsExclusive's launch there was one online retailer in the market that followed a similar approach to the Private Shopping Clubs in Europe: ozsale.com.au. Launched in 2007 the company focused at first primarily on children's apparel following a self-registration membership strategy.

It is important to consider that apparel-purchasing decisions are very personal and closely linked to the individuals' feelings of self-esteem, their body image and the image they wish to project. Thus, the importance of brands and the image the brand carries is tremendous. If brand loyalty exists, it is more likely to be loyalty toward the designer than to the retailer, thereby strengthening the position of the fashion manufacturer – usually towards the top end of the brand. Nevertheless, there is a growing industry for 'Apparel Retail' that is affordable and fashionable at the same time, such as Zara or H&M.

While creating and sustaining an exclusive brand is of utmost importance for fashion manufacturers, excess inventory is a major problem. Manufacturers would like to use channels other than their regular ones to clear inventory but the risk of damaging the brand value by finding the premium AU$ 250 designer jeans next to no-name brands in the bargain bin is too high. Consequently, it is common practice for premium brands to destroy their goods rather than jeopardizing the premium image.

E-commerce in Australia in 2008

Adequate online infrastructure is a prerequisite to entering the Australian online apparel industry. Australia is amongst the ranks of the most connected nations, with an Internet penetration rate of almost 80% – that translates to over 17 million Internet users. Australians also make frequent use of the Internet. According to NielsenOnline, in 2008 the amount of time Australians spent online surpassed the amount of time spent watching TV for the first time. Hence, the online infrastructure for adapting the principles of the European exclusive shopping clubs to Australia looked very promising.

Market potential

Defining the market is the first step to forecast sales. In order to define the market in which to compete accurately a number of descriptors are chosen that characterize and set the limits of a market. Rolf and Daniel defined their market in terms of customers' needs as 'anyone who wants to buy genuine branded goods at a high discount from a trusted source online.' Thus, the market opportunity is large and broad; spanning geographic as well as demographic boundaries such as age, gender, family size, income, occupation or education. Internet access and eligibility to engage in legal transactions on the Internet act as the only main constraints to the size of the potential market.

To understand the market potential better one would also need to look at the size of the Australian apparel retail industry (AU\$ 12.8 bn), of which 10–25% represent out of season or overstock (AU\$ 1.28 bn). Assuming that 30% of these goods are sold online (AU\$ 0.384 bn), and that brandsExclusive might gain a market share of 20%, it could result in revenues of AU\$ 77m per year. Yet, Rolf Weber points out that 'the business model doesn't necessarily need to limit itself to overstock products in apparel or the apparel category. It will eventually evolve, as we see overseas. This means the opportunity increases accordingly with more available stock and added categories depending on the preferences and needs of the consumers.'

Challenges

Market opportunities always come with risks. During the past decade numerous e-tailing start-ups have appeared, seeking new market opportunities. But market development had not been as successful and rapid as expected and many players vanished as quickly as they had appeared. For example, after spending \$135 million of venture capitalists' money in just 18 months and attracting few customers, boo.com became what the *Financial Times* referred to as 'the highest profile casualty among European e-tailing start-ups' (2000). While the conditions for e-commerce have changed, it seems that the bad memories still hold back major retailers from going online. Compared to the USA and UK, brandsExclusive, as well as other online channels in Australia, are confronted with consumers who are still wary of online shopping. The number of complaints regarding online transactions is fairly high and has undermined consumer trust and added to the fear of e-consumers of falling prey to online fraud – mostly around credit cards. Furthermore, experts cite the lack of a catalogue shopping culture as another cause for consumer concerns in Australia.

Apparel online shopping is associated with high levels of perceived risk and has to compete with the classical brick and mortar channels. Most importantly, is the difficulty of accurately assessing the product online. Many of the characteristics of a garment that are pivotal to the consumer decision-making process – colour, touch and feel, and fit – are difficult, if not impossible, to communicate virtually. The accuracy of colour on

(Continued)

(Continued)

the web is of particular concern to consumers. Conventional thinking held that shoppers would be reluctant to buy clothes they could not touch, feel and try on. Thus, product presentation and the website atmosphere are critical factors to evoke positive emotion and eventually increase positive shopping responses. Furthermore, consumers do not receive instant gratification for their purchase as they do in a bricks-and-mortar store. The joy of presenting the newly purchased bargain amongst friends and family has to be postponed until the goods finally arrive at home.

Pure e-tailers face relatively few barriers to entry in setting up a shop online. The combination of low capital requirements and the above outlined broad and large market opportunity leads to a high threat of new entrants. With competitors being a click away for consumers, loyalty and trust are even harder to build in the web environment. brandsExclusive needed to quickly establish relationships with exclusive fashion brands, building trust and to overcome any concerns regarding possible channel conflicts or the dilution of the brand image. The market is viewed as having a supply surplus, but it is essential for the start-up to quickly attract a large number of shopping club members by conducting sales events with premium brands. Thus, brandsExclusive had to clearly position itself on two markets: fashion brands as suppliers on one side and the end consumers as buyers on the other side.

Value proposition for fashion brands

The major benefit for the manufacturers is to have access to a proven online retail channel, without any extra costs or risks. This enables the supplier to generate high sales volume through fast clearance of excess inventory. Channel conflict is avoided since the goods are sold to a new, exclusive and closed customer base, maybe even reaching out to previously hard to reach customer segments. Removing a campaign from the site as soon as it is finished with no trace that it existed protects the brand identity; sales also do not show up in Google searches. The brand stays in control and might also benefit from cross selling in other channels; due to the short time period of the sales event and its exclusivity, members might not be able to buy what they wanted. brandsExclusive produces the campaign and executes it as well; thus, there is no effort for the brand. In addition, the fashion brand also receives a detailed sales analysis report, gaining valuable consumer insights from every single campaign.

The delivery of these promises is built on the two fundamental principles of relationship management and trust. While it would be feasible to source the branded goods from China or the US or receivership goods, brandsExclusive only purchases the products directly from the brand itself. This sourcing strategy clearly differentiates them from other players in the market, which purchase the goods in higher volumes from several sources. This allows the competitors to obtain better prices; however they also have to finance and handle the stock. By contrast, brandsExclusive only orders the aggregated consumer demand at the end of the sales event. The following graphic illustrates the key steps in the sales cycle.

Whereas this ordering procedure leads to a longer waiting period for the consumer, it mitigates inventory and cash flow risks as no cash is tied to inventory. The direct brand sourcing strategy differentiates brandsExclusive not only from other online channels in the 'brand market' but also is a prerequisite to fulfil end consumers' needs to buy genuine, authentic brands from a trusted source.

Value proposition for consumers

The supply of genuine brands is guaranteed through the direct sourcing strategy and the resulting continuous high quality of the goods. To overcome consumer concerns regarding the online shopping experience, brandsExclusive acknowledged the high importance of trust and relationship building with each and every consumer. To achieve this, the founders state that there is only one way – 'To constantly deliver our promises'. Besides the authenticity of the goods, the high price discount is the second main promise they need to deliver. brandsExclusive main advantage compared to traditional channels is that they are able to deliver the price promise with every sales campaign. Not holding any inventory leads to no warehousing and personnel costs and the virtual showroom also reduces fixed costs. Furthermore, online marketing costs are kept to a minimum due to the by-invitation-only membership approach. Marketing focuses on email announcements to members and personalized customer relationship management. Satisfied members spread the news about the shopping club on behalf of the firm and provide brandsExclusive with the most powerful marketing tool: word of mouth. To foster member referrals, brandsExclusive provides a range of invitation applications for the members to choose from, such as address book uploads, Facebook integration, or text messages. The highly competitive cost structure enables the start-up to pass the savings on to the fashion manufacturers in terms of attractive margins and to the club members in terms of highly discounted prices.

Department stores and fashion retailers, on the other hand, are trapped in the sales cycle – consumers are increasingly suspicious of special sales and have learned that within short time intervals the next sales will occur – why pay the full price? brandsExclusive creates a limited edition of the brand with every sales event due to exclusivity, the limited time and limited quantity of the merchandise. With a growing sense of haste in people's lives, there is also a passion about things that shout 'act now!' or you will miss out on the fleeting experience. To create a truly inspiring and natural online experience and overcome the limitations of assessing products only online, brandsExclusive pays great importance to the presentation of the product. To create a quasi 3D effect visual product presentation is on human models – instead of laying the goods out flat. Detailed description of the models provides further information for the consumer too, e.g. 'our model is 175cm tall, weighs 57kg and is wearing a size 8 in this product'. Pictures of the models from different angles as well as high-resolution zoom-in features on the merchandise further create an informative visual display. Nevertheless, the consumer is unable to try the goods on and thus might still be afraid of a mispurchase and the following consequences. brandsExclusive's answer: return policy with no questions asked, further underlining the commitment to excellent customer service.

Outlook in 2009

brandsExclusive's target was to build membership to a minimum of 100,000 within the first year and have between 25 and 50 sales campaigns per month by the end of

(Continued)

(Continued)

2009 –while maintaining a high conversion rate. The focus was on two key areas: membership growth and supply of a wide and deep range of products. By the end of 2009, Daniel Jarosch expected to see at least five private shopping club operations in Australia as a result of the success of the business model. In addition, venture investors' habit of chasing the latest trend, driving up valuations and encouraging a glut of copycats, could spoil the party, as the *Wall Street Journal* stated in July 2009. However, the importance of strategic planning for e-commerce firms cannot be overstated and will eventually lead to sustainable competitive advantage.

Before you continue reading about the successful development of brandExclusive, consider the following questions about the situation and strategic choices made by the start-up as they entered the market in early 2009.

STAGE I QUESTIONS

1. Analyse the industry that brandsExclusive operates in by using the models presented in this chapter. What is brandsExclusive's competitive position? Who are their direct and indirect competitors?

2. Which of the generic strategy options is close to the strategy that brands Exclusive follows? What are the possible short-term and long-term implications of this strategy?

3. How should brandsExclusive address the two main challenges of membership growth and the necessary supply of a wide and deep range of exclusive goods?

4. What are the challenges of accelerated growth rates? How should the start-up overcome these challenges?

5. Which Key Performance Indicators (KPI) are of greatest importance for this business model?

STAGE II: CONTINUED GROWTH, ACQUISITION AND DIFFERENTIATION

brandsExclusive's development

By December 2009 brandsExclusive had increased membership to 100,000 and was showcasing 30 sales events a month. Growth accelerated even more during the first half of 2010 and by July membership had reached 500,000, more than 120 sales events a month were showcased and 400 brand suppliers had collaborated with the start-up. By mid-2011 the start-up had surpassed the one million members threshold and drew the attention of multiple investors to their start-up. Throughout 2011 and early 2012 the two founders were managing the challenges of exponential growth as well as negotiating with existing and potential investors. In their annual ranking BRW dubbed brandsExclusive as the No.1 Fast Starters in 2013.

Acquisition

The trans-Tasman media company APN News & Media acquired in June 2012 an 82% stake in brandsExclusive for $36 million, with an additional $30 million due if performance targets were met in 2013. Jarosh and Weber were described as the most successful exiters from the 2011–12 e-commerce boom.

With additional capital brandsExclusive continued on their growth path and reached 2.5 million members by 2013, dispatching more than 16,000 items from its Sydney warehouse every day and generating revenue in excess of $56m. However, just 18 months after brandsExclusive was acquired, APN offloaded the business to Aussie Commerce Group following a competitive process, receiving $2m in cash and 8% of the equity in Aussie Commerce. The site's performance was hampered by management upheaval and a change of strategic direction by its new owners.

The CEO of APN said the company had 'overpaid' for the business under his predecessor and booked an AU$20.5m impairment charge to write down goodwill in the first half of 2013. While sales rose 30% in that period, it recorded a pretax loss of AU$2.6m, citing increased competition in online retailing as the main reason. He further explained that 'the divestment of brandsExclusive is the next important step in our ongoing strategy to consolidate the structure of APN, allowing for greater management focus on our core media and digital businesses.' APN Outdoor was also sold in January of the same year.

Aussie Commerce is one of Australia's leading e-commerce groups, has more than three million members, over 125 employees and operates seven established and successful online shopping brands including The Home, Luxury Escapes and Cudo. The brandsExclusive acquisition is aimed at adding new products to its portfolio and reducing its reliance on group-buying deals. The co-founders both took time off to 'research business models' after leaving their management roles when the site was sold to AussieCommerce Group.

Following the acquisition and turbulent times, brandsExclusive unveiled a new look online channel in early 2015. According to CEO Alexandra Mills the redesign is one aspect of a broader reaching overhaul, intended to bring the online retailer back to its premium fashion roots adding even more luxury to the offering.

Development of Australian e-commerce and apparel industry

The majority of the Australian e-commerce ecosystem was formed between 2006 and 2010. As opposed to creating a social network similar to Facebook, e-commerce requires more trading than coding skills; capital to purchase stock and build a technology platform is also essential. In contrast to 2009, adopting a multichannel retail strategy is now at the centre of every major retailer's strategy, with most of the local major retailers in Australia entering the channel in an attempt to catch up with foreign retailers and pure online retailers. Services like click and collect are being introduced by retailers in an effort to better integrate physical and digital channels along the customer journey.

Australian clothing retailing was under continued pressure over the five years from 2010–2015, with industry revenue expected to contract at a compound annual rate of

(Continued)

(Continued)

0.6% reaching $13.1 billion in 2015. The industry continues to be highly fragmented and market share concentration is low, which has spurred some of the merger and acquisition activities, as major players have sought to capture greater market share and improve economies of scale. On the other hand, apparel and footwear Internet retailing continues to hold the largest share within Internet retailing (13%) and a compound annual growth rate of 22% from 2009–2014, reaching $4.1bn in the year to March 2015 – demonstrating the growth opportunities for the major players.

STAGE II QUESTIONS

1. How has the environment changed between Stage I and Stage II of brands-Exclusive's launch?

2. How have these changes impacted on the competitive positioning of the site?

3. What do you think were the reasons for APN's acquisition of brandsExclusive in 2012? Why did the company sell the start-up again within 18 months?

STRATEGY, RESOURCES AND CAPABILITIES

Learning objectives

By the end of this chapter you will be able to:

1   Understand the origins and assumptions of the resource-based view (RBV) of the firm

2   Appreciate the nature and determinants of value creation and capture

3   Have a critical understanding of the central concepts associated with the RBV

4   Appreciate the role of Dynamic Capabilities (DCs) in building sustainable competitive advantage

5   Explain the link between the RBV, DCs and knowledge-based views of organizations.

6   Relate DCs to entrepreneurship

BEFORE YOU GET STARTED

The greatest achievement of the human spirit is to live up to one's opportunities and make the most of one's resources. (Marquis de Vauvenargues, French moralist and essayist, 1714–1747)

Introduction

All organizations may be thought of as assemblages or bundles of **resources**.

Resources vary: some are human, some technological or natural factor endowments, while others are financial. Many resources are highly tangible such as machines, while others are intangible, such as reputation or knowledge. Intangible resources are of unique value. Any organization with access to financial resources, can discover a rival's technology, clone it through espionage or reverse engineer its products; what such an organization cannot do is replicate the unique use to which non-human resources are put when they are working with human resources and attributes such as specific human ingenuity, social networks, intellectual or reputational capital.

> **Resources** are stocks of tangible and intangible assets that can generate value. There are four major types – capital, labour/human, land and knowledge/organization.

The resource-based view of the firm argues that it is those resources that are unique and inimitable that can really provide competitive advantage. While rival firms can copy products, processes and technologies, they cannot duplicate their unique bundling because human resources – employees, managers and entrepreneurs – are the source of creativity and innovation. In other words, strategic capabilities depend ultimately on human resources. An effective resource and capabilities bundle, one that is fit for purpose, is called the competency of the organization.

Strategy scholars often refer to a **core competency** or, in the plural, core competencies.

> **Prahalad and Hamel (1990)** introduced and popularised the term **core competencies**, which may be defined as an assemblage of multiple resources, skills and capabilities located at the organization level that work together effectively to achieve the collective learning necessary to maintain a competitive edge.

Rarely can the source of this competitive advantage be easily identified; often it is an intangible artefact resulting from a complex assemblage of history, branding, people, technologies, etc. Such assemblages comprise durable **organizational capabilities**, not easily eroded or lost, which competitors find hard to rival.

> An **organizational capability** is an organizationally embedded and firm-specific resource that is hard to transfer and/or imitate.

For instance, in the first chapter we identified a number of features of Zara that contribute to its success. At the core of its capabilities is a highly centralized design, manufacturing and distribution system that serves a fast fashion design model based on interpreting the latest fashion looks from the catwalk into affordable pieces delivered in a timely fashion. The assemblage connects consumers' expectations of affordable and fashionable design with a system for delivering and retailing these. No one element of the assemblage is sufficient to explain the competitive advantage – it is the way the elements are put together, the network of relations that they sustain, as well as the continuous capability for design innovation, manufactured and delivered in a speedy, targeted and affordable fashion that is crucial. Those customers who keep coming into Zara expecting something new, stylish and affordable to wear or outfit their homes must see value as customers in what Zara offers.

For Zara to deliver value requires a system of assemblages – designers, technologies, contracts, suppliers, distribution channels, etc. – that deliver a significantly better value proposition for customers than do rival firms. The assemblage that makes up Zara cannot be easily replicated; hence, imitators cannot easily outflank Zara. Sure, they can copy the same designs but they can hardly imitate Zara's system-wide embedded strategic capabilities, without being Zara themselves.

Go Online: Zara is well served with interesting videos available online. The *Business Insider* website contains a video discussing Zara's customer experience titled 'The one reason Zara is dominating the fashion industry right now'. There are two other videos that can be found on YouTube that are relevant – one is a talk on Zara's history titled 'Zara (retailer)' and the other is a talk by Zara's communications manager titled 'Zara operations'. Finally, you can find an interesting video on the *Bloomberg News* website that talks about how Zara gets customers given that it does no advertising, titled 'How Zara gets shoppers in the door'. Links to all these videos can be found on the book's website at www.edge.sagepub.com/strategy2e.

Zara Videos

In this chapter we will first discuss value creation and sustainable competitive advantage. While in Chapter 2 we paid attention to how created value is captured in the form of profits, the authors that we considered there, such as Porter and related theories, did not delve into how value is initially created. The RBV pays attention to value creation as well as to value capture. Hence below we will also discuss these concepts.

According to contemporary theories of the firm, core competencies and capabilities are essential to value generation and its sustainable maintenance. Some theorists concentrated on what they termed dynamic capabilities and built a theory of the firm from this basis. The resource-based view of the firm argues that resources and capabilities (which some also see as resources), should be *valuable, rare, inimitable* and *non-substitutable* (VRIN). In a development of the resource-based view, some strategists argue that knowledge has a privileged status as a resource, developing the approach known as the knowledge-based view and the practice of knowledge management.

Value and sustainable competitive advantage

Pitelis (2009b) defines **value** in terms that are surpassingly subjective for those of us used to thinking of value as a monetary phenomenon. Value is multifaceted: It is not just a matter of value in monetary terms. Value can be generated because potential users find rarity, use-value or aesthetics inhering in some thing or service, for example. From an organizational strategy perspective, value must inhere in activities, products and services offered for sale in the market to potential beneficiaries, such as consumers. Firms or organizations produce an 'offer' to the market that consumers can either accept or be indifferent towards; it is only when the offer is accepted and the goods or services

> **Value** is perceived worthiness of a subject matter to a socio-economic agent that is exposed to and/or can make use of the subject matter in question.

offered consumed through sales on the market that value is captured. Sale at an agreed price represents the point of exchange at which perceived producer value equals consumer value. Prior to this, however, any producer value that is created is only potential and it can well diverge from perceived consumer value (Kim and Mahoney, 2002). In simpler terms, producers can offer something but it may be the case that consumers are not willing to buy at the price offered.

The word 'perceived' in the definition of value is important here. Value does not *reside in* a particular product or service. Value is not an 'attribute'. A change in perception can quickly change the value of a particular good or service, which can be measured through the price the customer is willing to pay for it – or indeed whether they consider it worth buying at all. For example, a product that was previously highly *valued* by some customers can quickly become *value-less* if it is now perceived as 'unfashionable' or 'out dated' because it is associated with the 'wrong' celebrity, or if the celebrity it is associated with suddenly does something which their social followers disapprove.

Stock markets are a good example of the inherently *social* nature of perceptions. A simple rumour about a firm going into financial difficulty on a web-based investor forum can spread like wildfire, changing the *valuation practices* of investors and traders and immediately hitting the valuation of the firm through the share price.[1] Perceptions are not merely subjective judgments but intersubjectively constituted and shared. In this sense value is co-perceived.

Value is mediated by a variety of social practices, technologies and systems of measurement. Hence, value needs to be understood as a calculative social process, involving social practices and technologies of *valuing* (Kornberger et al., 2015). For example, nowadays, ranking systems play an important role in constructing perceptions of value. Today, rankings are everywhere. Students select the university they want to attend based on university rankings, making universities design their strategies around how to get higher in these rankings (Espelend and Saunder, 2007). Cities around the world are now ranked according to a range of criteria, shaping where people choose to live, work, invest or visit. These rankings also make cities view themselves as 'competing' with each other – creating 'competition' where previously there was none (Kornberger and Carter, 2010). Rankings therefore do not just describe the 'reality' of different types of value (economic, social, cultural, etc.) – they create it or 'perform' value (Kornberger and Clegg, 2011).

Where an agent creates value others can capture it through appropriate strategy (Teece, 1986). Moreover, value creation and value capture by an economic agent such as a firm, need not coincide because value can be co-created by other economic agents, including competitors, suppliers, customers and users (Pitelis and Teece, 2009).

The term 'value added' is frequently used in business to represent what the firm creates. For example, Kay (1995) defines 'value added' as 'the difference between the (comprehensively accounted) value of a firm's output and the (comprehensively accounted) cost of the firm's inputs' (1995: 19). He regards 'value added' as 'the key measure of corporate success' (1995: 19).

---

[1] In an interesting novel about various complex systems of meaning, Sebastian Faulkes explores this phenomena, through the character of a hedge fund billionaire, John Veales, who plants a rumour that will make him even wealthier than he already is at present. The novel is called *A Week in December* (Faulkes, 2009).

As we have already noted, the strategy literature and textbooks have traditionally focused on value capture. More recently, however, the value creation attributes of strategy have been acknowledged and understood. Indeed, Ghoshal et al. (2002) went as far as prescribing that strategy should focus on value creation, not value capture. But what factors determine organizational value creation?

Four Generic Determinants of Value Creation

Creating added value, suggests Pitelis (2009b: 1121), has four generic determinants: human resources and their services; unit cost economies/increasing returns to scale; firm infrastructure and strategy; and innovation.

Human resources play a prominent role both in classical economics and in management. In Adam Smith (1776/1937), labourers are said to engender productivity enhancement through teamwork, learning by doing and inventions. In Karl Marx (1959), the capitalist was the driving force of economic change. The 'entrepreneur' and entrepreneurship played a similar role in Schumpeter (1942) as well as in the recent literature on entrepreneurship (Casson et al., 2006; Alvarez and Barney, 2007; Ireland, 2007; Foss et al., 2008) and in strategic human resource management (Becker and Huselid, 2006; Kang et al., 2007). In Penrose (1959) the focus was on the 'manager' (Pitelis and Wahl, 1998).

More recently, scholars such as Coff (1997) and Pfeffer (1998) have underscored the importance of human resources in organizations. Human resources are unique and individual and their combination and relationships help create the distinct 'personality' of the organization (Peteraf, 2006) and affect the strategy of the organization (Pitelis, 2007). Helfat et al. (2007) and Kang et al.'s (2007) work on how HR architectures structure managerial capabilities link HR specifically to organizational value creation. In all, it can be argued that the quantity, quality and relationship between HR and the services they provide are an important determinant of value creation. Non-human resources can also be important in the RBV especially when they satisfy the conditions of being valuable, rare, inimitable and non-substitutable, thereby facilitating value capture. This is particularly the case when they interact with human resources in inimitable ways.

Reductions in unit costs (unit costs economies thereafter) can be achieved from several factors, including economies of scale and scope (Chandler, 1962), economies of growth (Penrose, 1959), transaction costs economies (Coase, 1937; Williamson, 1975b), economies of learning (Arrow, 1962), economies of joint governance (Williamson, 2005), external and agglomeration economies (Kaldor, 1970; Porter, 1980; Krugman, 1991, 1996; Henderson, 2005) and economies of pluralism and diversity (Mahoney et al., 2009; Pitelis, 2009b). The stronger a firm's unit cost economies are, the lower will tend to be its unit costs and the higher its ability to create value.

Organizational infrastructure refers to a firm's systems, routines and decision-making processes, and internal organization. Cyert and March (1963), Nelson and Winter (1982, 2002), Simon (1995) all explore the role of a firm's systems, routines and internal decision-making processes and dynamic capabilities. In addition, these insights have been developed further by the RBV and the Dynamic Capabilities (DCs) views (Teece et al., 1997; Teece, 2007a, 2007b). These developments have been taken further more recently, as Hedlund (1986) and Birkinshaw and Hood (1998) have discussed the importance of internal organizational forms. These authors consider the choice of a firm's internal structure as an essential aspect of implementation, increasing efficiency and productivity, acquiring and upgrading knowledge. Organizational infrastructure, given its efficiency benefits, is also sensible to include as a determinant of value creation. Strategy is important because it can help create value both through cost efficiencies and differentiation/innovation.

Innovation (see Chapter 4) is the surest way of improving a value proposition. Adam Smith (1776/1937) regarded the benefits of the division of labour, teamwork and 'inventions' by labourers, engendered through learning by doing, as a critical determinant of productivity and wealth creation (Smith, 1776/1937: Chapter 1). Marshall extended Smith's analysis by identifying knowledge as 'our most powerful engine of production' (Marshall, 1920: 138). Schumpeter's (1942) focus on competition and 'creative destruction' highlighted the role of innovation on intertemporal efficiency. Innovation, knowledge and creative destruction are linked directly to value creation (Amit and Zott, 2001; Felin and Hesterly, 2007). Chapter 4 focuses extensively on innovation.

The four generic determinants of value creation depicted in Figure 3.1 interact with each other. Human resources are the source of firms' innovation and strategy. Technology and innovation can help reduce unit cost economies. Innovation and technological accumulation can be explicit elements of strategy (Cantwell, 1989). Firm infrastructure is crucial for the implementation of strategy, the leveraging of human resources and technology (Cyert and March, 1963; Loasby, 1998; Nelson and Winter, 1982). Unit cost economies/increasing returns to scale enable innovation and the leveraging of HR for the undertaking of R&D and innovation (Chandler, 1962).

The four generic determinants have an impact on both cost and perceived utility. For example, a process innovation can reduce unit costs and engender product differentiation. Infrastructure and strategy can reduce costs (for example through integration) and help differentiate the firm through branding and business model innovation (Teece, 2009). Human resources can affect subjective utility through strategy, product differentiation and/or innovation. 'Subjective utility' and cost reductions can feed back to the four generic determinants. For example, a firm's 'brand' can help it receive better terms for advertising and from suppliers, thus engendering unit cost economies.

In all, the four generic determinants of value creation help reduce costs and create a firm's unique 'business model' (Chesbourgh and Rosenbloom, 2002; Teece, 2009)

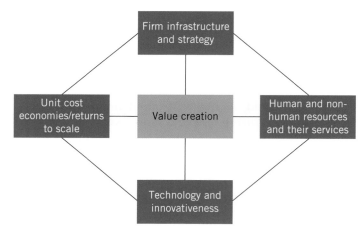

Figure 3.1   Four generic determinants of firm value creation

Source: Authors

that can create 'firm differentiation' and add perceived value to consumers. Business models help firms to capture value (see Chapter 4). In the remainder of this section, we focus on strategies for value capture. First, we look at the value chain, a tool originally proposed by Porter (1985), which allows us to visualize the activities through which value can be created within the organization.

The value chain

The value chain is where a firm would look at activities for improvement as well as for fit with its chosen generic strategy, which we discussed in Chapter 2. As can be seen in Figure 3.2 the value chain has primary activities (those essential for the production and sale of a product or service) and supporting ones (those that supplement and support the primary activities).

> A **value chain** is a set of activities that an organization carries out to create value for its customers by delivering a product or service that the market values and is prepared to buy at a price that affords the organization a profit margin.

Porter (1985) suggested that the value chain is a most useful tool for analysing the added value of processes of production or delivery of services, shifting attention towards internal activities and the question of how, in fact, one 'creates' competitive advantage.

Competitive advantage grows out of the way firms perform discrete activities – conceiving new ways to conduct activities, employing new procedures, new technologies, or different inputs. Hence, as a strategist you would analyse each step in this process that actually adds value to services and products and thereby guides a firm into its strategically relevant activities. The added value is captured as the difference between the cost of production and the revenue realized in the marketplace.

Think, for example, of your favourite restaurant; it transforms fresh produce into great meals. It has to source the produce from quality *providores* – procurement – and it has to set up a reliable and consistent supply of produce – inbound logistics – and then deliver it to the customer's table looking fresh, being ready to eat, and delightful to the senses – the outbound logistics. In between there is the skill of the kitchen staff under the chef's supervision. If the restaurant is to flourish it will need to be marketed and represented in the various marketing channels for

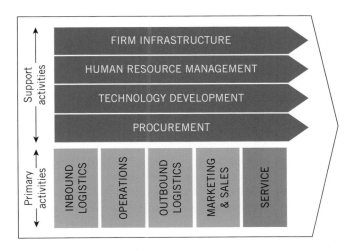

Figure 3.2   The value chain (Porter, 1985)

restaurants. How the restaurant is organized internally, its infrastructure, as well as the way it recruits and trains its staff, the management of human resources, will also be important. The value the restaurant adds consists of the skills of the chef, the friendliness of the waiter, and the overall ambience – in short, the added value is that which exceeds the value of the sum of the parts. And at times the value added is quite amazing. Take, for example, a restaurant that has been voted the best in the world, Restaurant Noma in Copenhagen. Analysing the restaurant's value chain, we can scrutinize each of its activities as a potential source of advantage.

Nordic cuisine, in the past, has not been noted in terms of Michelin star rated restaurants. French cuisine, certainly; maybe Italian or Spanish, yet Nordic cuisine seemed associated in the popular imagination with pickled herrings, reindeer meat, potatoes – in many guises – heavy food accompanied by beer and schnapps.

Restaurant Noma, jointly owned by successful food entrepreneur Claus Meyer, who provided the capital to start the business, and chef, René Redzepi, is situated in an old warehouse building in Copenhagen, once the headquarters of the Royal Greenland Trade enterprises. The building now houses, in addition to Noma, Iceland's embassy and the Home Rule representation for the Faroe Islands and Greenland.

The intention behind Noma was to renovate the reputation of Nordic foods. The first step in doing this was to seek out the very best *providores* (suppliers) of raw materials that were recognizably indigenous to the North Atlantic region. Ingredients such as horse mussels, deep-sea crabs and langoustines are flown in alive from the Faroe Islands to be freshly prepared and cooked immediately prior to serving. Halibut, cod, seaweed and curds are flown in from Iceland. Lamb, musk ox, berries and Greenland water are also sourced. If an ingredient is not in season or cannot be fished out of a nearby sea, fjord, lake or river, it doesn't make it onto the menu. Basic Nordic ingredients such as cereals, hulled grains and legumes are experimented with to make surprising preparations that supplement some of these rare ingredients. Setting up reliable and trusted supply chains was essential.

Second, Noma sought to establish a culture of excellence and a preparedness to experiment. The Noma chef and other joint owner René Redzepi, came to Noma after having served as assistant manager at Kong Hans Restaurant in Copenhagen and had previously worked for extended stints at some of the world's most highly esteemed 3-star Michelin restaurants (French Laundry, El Bulli and Jardin des Sens). He was a craftsman who had served as a fine apprentice and had learnt from master chefs to reinterpret the use of basic materials. At Noma, the potential of milk and cream are explored for modern cuisine. Different cereal grains are used in unfamiliar ways. Berries and herbs are collected on excursions to the countryside, including certain varieties that are rarely gathered; thus, some raw ingredients are used that could not be sourced through the usual *providores*. Traditional methods of preparing Nordic foods are reinterpreted. Smoking, salting, pickling, drying, grilling and baking on slabs of basalt stone are used, as are self-made vinegars and distilled spirits. In the North Atlantic Nordic region's peasant antecedents these were all methods of preserving and cooking foods in the long, cold, dark winters when fresh produce was scarce. Rather than Mediterranean-sourced wines for sauces and soups systematic use is made of beers and ales, fruit juices and fruit-based vinegars as the basis for sauces and seasonings. Vegetables, herbs and spices and wild plants in season play a prominent role. Old manuscripts and recipe collections are scoured for anthropological insight into past traditions that have hardly survived into the modern world. Old ingredients, forgotten traditions and experimental methods are combined in state of the art kitchens, equipped with the most modern kitchen appliances. The watchwords for Noma are purity and simplicity – both in the ingredients and in their transformation. The menu is a rich array of degustation courses, served with style and simplicity.

Third, there is ambience. Restaurant Noma has simple hand crafted cutlery with bone and horn handles, Nordic in style and fabrication. The chairs and tables are plain local timber, beautifully aged, as are the floors and beams, reminders of the old warehouse. Patrons are as likely to turn up on a bicycle as in a taxi or a car and will not feel intimidated by the democratic ethos of the restaurant. (Of course, while the ambience may be elegant, understated and recognizably Nordic so are the prices! But also the quality!)

Fourth, unlike many restaurants, Noma has a full-time business manager, a Copenhagen Business School graduate, who is engaged not only in day-to-day managing but more importantly in articulating a strategic vision and mission designed to gain Noma that third but elusive Michelin star.

Fifth, the wait-staff at Noma are professionals: they are elegant, discrete, attentive and integral to the operations of the business. They are not recruited cheaply from the ranks of students or out-of-work actors or models. Of course, business managers, fresh ingredients, specialist *providores*, and accomplished wait-staff are not cheap.

Sixth, is the role of the state, coordinated through the Nordic Council of Ministers, a collaborative council established by the Nordic states, which launched a New Nordic Food programme to expose the value of Nordic food and its associated culture. René Redzepi was appointed as one of the ambassadors for the programme because of his ongoing efforts to advance and promote the knowledge of Nordic food. The role of New Nordic Food programme should not be underestimated. There is a reciprocal relation between the Nordic Council's efforts and the culture of excellence and experimentation being developed at Noma. Redzepi's rendition of Nordic gourmet cuisine is a response to the 'challenge to play a part in bringing forth a regeneration of Nordic culinary craft, in its capacity to encompass the North Atlantic region and to brighten the world with its distinctive tastiness and special regional character' (Evans, 2000).

IN PRACTICE

Restaurant Noma: the value chain

In April 2010, Noma was declared the best restaurant in the world by acclaimed publication, *Restaurant Magazine*, taking the top spot from Spanish restaurant *El Bulli* and English restaurant *The Fat Duck*. Since that listing, the three-month waiting list increased exponentially as they take a new booking every two minutes. While no longer number 1, they are still one of the most acclaimed restaurants in the world.

(Continued)

(Continued)

Image 3.1   Restaurant Noma

Questions

1. Which industry does Noma operate in?
2. Would you characterize Noma's resources and capabilities as VRIN and why?
3. What is the generic strategy followed by Noma (see Chapter 2) and how is this supported through its value chain activities?

Visit the companion website at www.edge.sagepub.com/strategy2e to find web links offering further information about the Noma organization.

Noma

A firm sustains competitive advantage by performing strategically important activities better than its competitors. The value chain framework emphasizes that competitive advantage can come not just from great products or services but also from activities along the value chain. Several primary activities (from inbound logistics to services) describe the chain of production. Porter would also include support activities that keep the primary activities going.

Decisions about outsourcing can often flow from a value chain analysis, as we shall see in more detail in Chapter 6. Outsourcing means eliminating parts of activities that can be better or more cheaply contracted ('outsourced') to another company that is a specialist in this area but without endangering the organization's competitive position. For instance, instead of having their own accountancy department, companies might outsource the tasks to specialists. They can do it better and cheaper, preserving more value, than if it were internally organized. It is, hence, important to understand how a firm fits into the overall value system, which includes the value chains of its suppliers, distribution channels, outsourcing partners, and buyers.

Although strategy might suggest that outsourcing can cheapen costs and thus add monetary value in an operation, Noma tells us that value is not purely about pecuniary issues: it is also about the value of innovation, quality and culture more generally.

The question, 'should Noma outsource the cooking?' would never make strategic sense because that is the unique element at the heart of the value chain.

Value capture and creation

Many strategy scholars see capturing value from value creating advantages as the main objective of firms (Teece, 1986; Brandenburger and Nalebuff, 1995; Teece et al., 1997; Pitelis and Teece, 2009). Through market power, strategy, ingenuity, imagination and luck, firms try to out-compete rivals in order to capture value. In general, firms can capture less, equal or more value than the one created through their activities (Brandenburger and Nalebuff, 1995). The amount of value captured by a firm depends on factors such as barriers to entry (Bain, 1956; Porter, 1980), firm-level 'generic strategies', namely cost leadership, differentiation and niche strategies (Porter, 1985), integration cooperation and diversification strategies (Penrose, 1959; Chandler, 1962; Williamson, 1981a; Teece, 1986) and firm-wide differentiation strategies.

The literature on barriers to entry goes back to Bain (1956), who identified three main barriers to entry for new firms, which allow incumbents to capture super-normal profits: absolute cost advantages, economies of scale and product differentiation. Bain's empirical work showed that differentiation (or the 'preference barrier') was most important. Subsequent literature focused on pricing (Modigliani, 1958), investments in excess capacity (Spence, 1977), product proliferation and advertising (Scherer and Ross, 1990). Strategy scholars such as Porter (1980) built on Bain and the IO and made explicit the link between barriers to entry and value capture in the form of profit. As we have already noted in Chapter 2, a limitation of this perspective is that it focuses on the level of the industry, not the firm, thus underplaying intra-firm resources and capabilities.

Firm-level 'generic strategies' such as 'cost leadership', 'differentiation', 'focus' or 'niche', as well as 'value for money' (Pitelis and Taylor, 1996) focus on the firm level and have been explicitly couched in terms of value capture (Porter, 1985). They allow firms to position themselves in a sector, so as to capture value by reducing the forces of competition. On the other hand, integration, diversification and cooperation strategies aim to capture value, either through efficiency, as for example occurs in the transaction costs literature or through market power, as for example in Porter (1980). The two are often linked. For example, firms can often obtain market power through the successful implementation of transaction costs reduction-motivated integration strategies (Pitelis, 1991).

Penrose (1959) discussed both Bain-type barriers to entry and intra-firm barriers, which she termed technological or 'relatively impregnable bases' (Penrose, 1959: 137). These are bundles of skills, competences, innovation capabilities and the whole gamut of advantages that distinguish them from other firms and allow them to grow through diversification by building on strength (Pitelis, 2002, 2004a and below).

Hard to imitate intra-firm resources and capabilities, as well as 'relatively impregnable bases', in addition to the overall 'business model' (Chesbourgh and Rosenbloom, 2002; Augier and Teece, 2007), can also help shape a firm's 'distinct identity' (Peteraf and Shanley, 1997; Peteraf, 2006) that can serve as a value capture strategic tool. The four types of value capture strategies interact. From Bain's three barriers, two relate to Porter's generic strategies (cost leadership and differentiation). Integration, cooperation and diversification strategies are often viewed as barriers to entry (Porter, 1980). They also have an impact on 'firm differentiation' because they help determine a firm's 'business model' – its distinct identity.

In their interactions, the four types of strategies for value capture are also linked to value creation. Bain's cost and differentiation barriers and Porter's generic strategies help reduce unit costs and/or increase perceived value. Intra-firm barriers, 'relatively impregnable bases' and the 'business model' help firms create potential value through 'branding'. For example, integration strategies create value by reducing transaction costs (Pitelis, 2009b).

As we have already noted, strategy itself is a potentially value creating 'advantage' from which firms can capture value, so as to obtain SAs. Clearly not all advantages lead to improved performance. In addition to competition, this will depend in part on stakeholder bargaining power (Coff, 1999; Lippman and Rumelt, 2003a, b), the type of human capital and HR practices (Coff, 1997; Bowman and Swart, 2007) and the extent of intra-organizational conflict (Amit and Schoemaker, 1993; Pitelis, 2007), and also the interactions between value creation and capture (Pitelis, 2009b).

Some value-based strategies are almost exclusively concerned with value capture – such as strategic entry deterrence and monopolistic restrictions (Penrose, 1959). Other more explorative innovations (March, 1991), such as EMI's CT scanner, focus more on value creation. In this context there are likely to be trade-offs between value capture and value creation strategies (much as in March's (1991) exploration and exploitation strategies). In particular, it could be argued that resources allocated to pursuing value capture may be taken away from resources required for value creation (for example explorative innovation) and vice versa, as Mizik and Jacobson (2003) suggest. The pursuit of value creation versus capture may also require different types of knowledge and capabilities (Loasby, 1998).

Organizations that build sustainable business models need to be able to assemble heterogeneous skills and capabilities that can be more efficient, effective and innovative than those of rivals. Such differences can be attributed and/or reflected in production and/or transaction costs. For example, firms that are more efficient can capture higher profits than competitors by lowering costs even when charging the average market price (Schumpeter, 1942; Williamson, 1968; Demsetz, 1973). Knowledge, based on core competencies and key capabilities, is essential to these processes.

Assembling core competencies

The theory behind the idea of organizational core competencies has its roots in the work of Simon (1947) and is elaborated further in Nelson and Winter (1982), Winter (1988), Teece et al. (1994) and Dosi et al. (2010).

The assembly of core competencies is dependent not only on the internal capabilities of an organization but also on the ways that it relates to customers and constitutes networks of relations with other organizations such as contractors, suppliers and distributors.

Some competencies result from activities that are performed repetitively, or quasi-repetitively. Organizational competencies enable economic tasks to be performed that require collective effort. Organizational competencies are usually underpinned by organizational processes/routines. Indeed, they represent distinct bundles of organizational routines and problem solving. In short, ordinarily competence defines sufficiency in the performance of a specific organizational task. Competency concerns doing things at least well enough or possibly, very well, without attention to whether the activity is the right thing to do. Learning comes in at this point: we may be doing things very well but are we doing the right things? A competence can be quantified to the extent that performance in it can be measured against particular quasi-stable task requirements. Such benchmarking is good at capturing the formal elements of performance; it is less good at capturing tacit and taken-for-granted elements.

Capabilities, football and strategy

In terms of *internal capabilities,* it is rarely any single competence that is important. The combination of training and skill formation, the human resources system, the affordances of the technologies in use and the creativity and skill of those using them will all play a role. What is coalesced in any assembly of talents in an organization is complex and there is rarely a single factor that dominates all others.

Rather like a football team composed of star players and a star manager, such as Chelsea and the once 'chosen one', José Mourinho, it is difficult to define what it is that leads to competitive success or, in 2015, failure. That the management is held responsible is a norm in football, giving rise to the precariousness of managerial tenure but, in terms of the assemblage that constitutes a football team, it is somewhat simple minded to assign either strategic credit or deficit to a single individual. Great players, such as Lionel Mesi, perform brilliantly in their Barcelona home team context but rarely achieve at the same level in the Argentinian national team. It is not the individual brilliance of a few resources that counts but the whole assemblage, the way that the team is put together, practises and learns.

Even more intangible elements may be embedded in an organization. Competitive advantage may be culturally sustained or diminished; in the 2014 World Cup in Brazil a German team that had a culture less of excessive individualism and more of solid team development roundly defeated the home side of individual stars. At the base of this team culture, as *Newsweek* explained after Germany won the World Cup so convincingly in 2014, was the linkage with the youth programme.

> On selected weekdays during the professional football season, a scattering of fans gathers around the perimeter of the pitch to watch Bayern Munich's senior team practice in the open. In a few months, you'll be able to spot Manuel Neuer, Bastian Schweinsteiger, Jérôme Boateng, Toni Kroos, Mario Götze, Philipp Lahm or Thomas Müller doing squats. From 2007 to 2011, Miroslav Klose would have been there, too.

> But on other days you can catch the youth team, part of a system that most experts credit with Sunday's [2014 World Cup] victory in Brazil. Germany revamped its youth development programme after the national team turned in a dismal performance at the European Championships in 2000. In the following years, the German Football Association invested €1 billion in coaches, facilities and workshops and rethought the German approach to the game – and in doing so created the generation of fit, flexible, creative players who dazzled fans at the World Cup. (Jacobs, 2014)

Jacobs, the author of the *Newsweek* analysis, attributes competitive success not only to a major investment programme but also more intangible *cultural and historical* elements. First, there is a national cultural bias towards problem solving by analysis and design of solutions. Second, there is a strong tradition of cooperation in all walks of life, founded on deep historical roots of local democracy that neither fascism nor communism were able to obliterate. These pragmatic cultural resources were drawn on in the preparation that delivered the German national team's competitive advantage and the World Cup.

Untangling these elements is not easy; they are characterized in their assemblage by a degree of causal ambiguity. The tacit sense of national pride and cooperative spirit drawn on is not easily dissected into components that can be readily replicated. The *Bundesliga,* as the football league with the highest average stadium attendance

**Football &
Germany**

worldwide, in comparison with the English Premier League has far less commercialization and does not regard fans as secondary to sponsors and investors. Managers in post match interviews are less likely to spend time talking about or promoting their sponsors. No English manager could begin to emulate or, perhaps, understand the specific factors at play in Germany. Creating competencies that are complex, ambiguous and embedded in specific assemblages of factors makes it very difficult for competitor organizations to copy them.

In building sustainable competitive advantage managers of football teams and other organizations have to create assemblages of capability that offer value to customers, are rare and not easily replicated – they should be 'inimitable'. As we shall see, in the resource-based view of the firm, they should also be unsubstitutable.

Resource-based view

Origins

The early days of strategy work were dominated by Porter's (1980, 1985) market structure and positioning-based approach. The resource-based view (RBV) emerged in the early 1980s with the works of Teece (1982) and Wernerfelt (1984). Following contributions by Barney (1991), Peteraf (1993), and Mahoney and Pandian (1992) it reached new heights. These, and many other authors, drew on early contributions by Penrose (1959) and Demsetz (1973), in particular, gradually leading to two related variants of the RBV – one that focused on **innovation and resource-value creation**, (notably Teece, 1982), the other that emphasized **value appropriation/capture** (notably Barney, 1991; Peteraf, 1993).

> The **innovation and resource-value creation** variant draws on Penrose's focus on endogenous firm growth through learning and the appropriation of knowledge.

> The **value appropriation/capture** variant emphasizes the ability of firms to capture above-average rents by virtue of differential resource-bases.

According to Penrose, organizations exhibit differential productivity advantages that are embedded in their particular assemblage of resources. These are likely to be engendered through intra-organizational specialization and division of labour, cooperation and learning. For Penrose, cooperation and learning create additional resources and opportunities for endogenous firm growth (where the firm grows without recourse to external mergers and acquisitions), the rate of which is limited by the availability (and quality) of management. 'Penrose argued that one cannot even start to analyse the external environment of the firm (to include the market) without a prior understanding of the nature of the firm, which is its human and nonhuman resources, and their interaction', suggests Pitelis (2007: 479).

For Penrose (1959: 137), building packages of external, internal and explicit and tacit knowledge barriers to mobility helps secure organizationally sustainable advantage. When this situation is achieved it is one of 'relatively impregnable bases' (RIBs) that represent a package of skills, competences, innovation, capabilities and advantages. These distinguish the firm in question from other firms and allow growth through diversification built on these internal strengths (Pitelis 2002, 2004b).

Resources

Resources are firm-specific assets that in the RBV are difficult or impossible to imitate. They are stocks, not flows (although the two can be related – Romme et al., 2010).

Resources tend to be either property-based or knowledge-based.

1. *Property-based resources* are legally defined property rights held by the firm, such as the physical plant, the right to the use of labour, finance, raw material inputs and intellectual property. Other firms are unable to appropriate these rights unless they obtain the owner's permission. Contracts, patents or deeds of ownership protect property-based resources.

2. *Knowledge-based resources*, such as technical expertise or a history of good relationships with trade unions, suppliers, and other stakeholders may be difficult for other firms to access.

While many resources are tangible, especially property-based resources, others are intangible and more difficult to assess. For instance, an organization's culture might be an intangible resource that is crucial to an organization's success (Rindova et al., 2011). Such assets are idiosyncratic in nature, and are difficult to trade because their property rights are likely to have fuzzy boundaries and their value is likely to be context dependent, as would be the case with an organization's culture or its intellectual property, process know-how, customer relationships, and the knowledge possessed by groups of especially skilled employees.

Because the value of a resource/asset is context dependent, the market for such assets is generally thin. Two powerful economic implications follow: when one is able to secure strategic resources/assets through purchase, they can be bought for less than they are worth to the buyer because their value to the buyer is considerably more than it is for the seller (the converse is also true). Put differently, from some perspectives, the market need not fully price strategic resources/assets. Accordingly, 'supernormal' profits can flow, at least for a while, from securing (either by purchase or through 'building' internally) such resources or assets.

- -
Go Online: Jay Barney is the contemporary strategist most associated with the RBV. You can watch him briefly discuss it in a video on YouTube titled 'Resource based view of the firm by Jay Barney'. Also on YouTube, you can see Barney in action giving a lecture on 'Gaining and sustaining competitive advantage'. You can find links to both videos on the book's website at www.edge.sagepub.com/strategy2e.
- -

Jay Barney Videos

The resources that are especially difficult – although not impossible – to trade consist of knowledge assets. Knowledge assets are tacit to varying degrees and costly to transfer (Teece, 1981). The market for know-how is also riddled with imperfections, which favours internalization to capture strategic value in that certain assets are more valuable to one firm than another. Assets that have such special value are referred to as strategic assets.

A firm's resources, which can include knowledge and intellectual property, are significant potential sources of advantage. Because the term 'resources' indicates a stock, not a flow, resources must be constantly renewed as they are depleted (Teece, 2009). The logic of renewal is amplified in fast-moving environments characteristic of high-tech sectors.

Resources, as the productive assets of the firm or organization, are essential elements for business. Particular firms bundle them up in specific ways, as Penrose suggests (Barney, 1995). Entrepreneurship consists of bundling that produces extraordinary returns.

Think of the iPod and its family of related products – these use much the same technologies and offer the same, in some cases less, functionality than their rivals but have been more shrewdly marketed and branded with more complementarities with apps than rivals. Creative produced the Zen, which offered all of the product features of the iPod as well as offering FM radio reception. The iPod was more aesthetically elegant in its design and slightly smaller.

It was not the aesthetics of the iPod that led to its success. With another firm's digital recording device, you could record from yours or your friend's CDs. Only with an iPod could you lock into iTunes and record anything available. The iTunes system was an isolating mechanism (see Chapter 2). When you bought an iPod you accessed a resource much greater than a specific product; you accessed the resources of iTunes through the software that accompanied the product. iTunes proved to be a killer app because it locked you in to a system.

Kor and Mahoney (2004) identify five generic isolating mechanisms that can render a firm's resources particularly valuable.

1. Path dependencies in resource development

2. Firm-specific knowledge possessed by managers

3. Shared team-specific experience of managers

4. Entrepreneurial vision of managers

5. The firm's idiosyncratic capacity to learn and diversify

Valuable, Rare, Inimitable and Non-Substitutable Resources

Even the most specialized and rare of resources can lead to little benefit when managed by individuals unable to appreciate the usefulness and potential services of resources and/or leverage them so as to satisfy their own and/or any organizational objectives. Resources require capabilities to be realized. Capabilities require human agency and implementation.

Relatively, the most impregnable bases of sustainable advantage occur because of a specific pattern of resources, according to the RBV. Barney (1991) argues that for a resource to be a secure basis for competitive advantage, it must display four characteristics that are often referred to as the VRIN model:

1. *Valuable*, in that they enable a firm to produce a good or service in an efficient and/or effective manner to exploit opportunities and counter threats.

2. *Rare*, in that few organizations possess them.

3. *Inimitable*, in that it is difficult for competitors to copy the resource.

4. *Non-substitutable*, meaning that there are no strategically equivalent resources available that can be exploited by a competitor firm. For example, a unique top management team cannot be replicated identically by a competitor and is thus non-substitutable.

Competitive advantage can diminish over time, especially as competitors do imitate its sources and thus the value of the capability lessens. While the erosion of competitive advantage is to be expected, the speed with which this takes place can vary dramatically. There are four central factors determining the sustainability of a firm's competitive advantage. They are:

1. *Durability* – the extent to which a competitive advantage is long lasting depends, in part, on the durability of a firm's capabilities. Technological innovation can often sound the death knell for a capability's capacity to generate competitive advantage. For instance, many high street travel agents have seen their margins slashed and viability threatened by the explosion of web-based travel booking services, such as expedia.com. That is why technology itself is rarely a source of competitive advantage that can be sustained – it is what is assembled in relation to the technology in terms of people, know-how and other elements of the assemblage that is important.

2. *Opacity – or the transparency problem.* If a set of resources and capabilities can be imitated in another context, the source of competitive advantage can be rapidly diminished. Where it is difficult or virtually impossible to identify the resources that are most important in explaining the competitive advantage enjoyed by an organization then its competitive advantage is likely to be more sustained. Those capabilities that require complex coordination between large numbers of diverse resources are the most difficult to copy.

3. *Isolating mechanisms restricting transferability* – the extent to which resources and capabilities can be isolated within the firms or easily transferred will have an impact upon the longevity of a firm's competitive advantage. Once key resources and capabilities are identified, competitive advantage is likely to be short-lived. Isolating mechanisms can be highly variable: they could include factors such as geographic immobility, making it difficult to transfer resources and capabilities from once context to another. Certain resources and capabilities may well be highly firm specific and turn out to be more or less immobile. Often when firms hire talented staff to replicate what they had achieved in another context it ends in failure. Remember Lionel Mesi: a great player for his home team of Barcelona but who never seems to achieve the same levels of performance for the Argentinian national team.

4. *Non-replicability* – where the transferability of resources and capabilities can prove difficult, rival firms may instead attempt to create their own. In some cases, the resources and capabilities that sustain competitive advantage can be easily copied. Where capabilities are particularly complex or locally specific, it will be more difficult to replicate them.

Strategic Architecture

While a particular resource may be acquired, assemblages of resources are the most difficult to imitate. Prahalad and Hamel (1990) refer to these as 'the strategic architecture of the firm'. The architecture is built around the core competencies of the firm and the technologies that are required to support these capabilities. Assembling this strategic architecture involves designing an organizational structure that allows linkages to be made across different competencies, in order to frame, organize and pattern them, as well as a reward system that motivates their continued application and development.

At the core of the assemblage will be people whose expertise interacts with technology in an organizational structure. Their knowledge is always in flux, it is not a tangible item but always in process, always being socially constructed (Sillince, 2006: 802). Entrepreneurs and managers create markets, new assemblages of know-how and resources, and capture value.

Firms must not only decide whether to integrate or outsource to protect value, they must also consider whether to invest in intangibles, to bundle products, to offer complements, how to segment the market and what value propositions to put to the customer. These are not just questions about running the business; they are often questions about creating markets and designing the firm. Solving these questions alone will likely involve creative activity. Certainly more is likely to be involved than selecting from a known set of alternatives. Novel alternatives may need to be created.

The resource-based view (RBV) of the firm regards competitive advantage as residing in the application of a bundle of valuable tangible or intangible resources unique to the firm (Wernerfelt, 1984). Such resources are *valuable* because value-creating strategies can be built using them. Sustained competitive advantage requires these resources to be both heterogeneous in nature and not perfectly mobile; they are valuable because they can neither be imitated easily nor can they be substituted without great effort (Barney, 1991). Where a firm can maintain heterogeneous and inimitable resources within its boundaries, above average returns can be expected.

Key to the value of a resource is its *rarity*; if any firm could easily access these resources then the strategy would easily be copied. Copying is harder still when the resources are *inimitable* because competitors are not able to duplicate the strategic asset perfectly, perhaps because of rarity or perhaps because of causal ambiguity, when the source of competitive advantage is unknown. If the resource in question is knowledge-based or socially embedded, causal ambiguity is more likely to occur where it is not clear what resources or combination of these is the particular source of advantage. Finally, even if a resource is rare, potentially value creating and imperfectly imitable, it should be non-substitutable – the resource should be unique and impervious to substitution with something that can fill the same function (Dierickx and Cool, 1989).

Problems with the RBV

How Useful is the RBV? Does it Explain How Managers can Manage Better?

The RBV has been criticized on numerous grounds, some more serious than others. Kraaijenbrink et al. (2010), for example, cite eight types of criticisms, three of which they consider as serious challenges. The first serious challenge is that VRIN-ness and/or organization are neither necessary nor sufficient for sustainable competitive advantage (SCA); the second refers to the definition of resources, which seems to be all-inclusive and undifferentiated; the third is that VRIN requires that resources are valuable, which supposes that value pre-exists and is known in advance to all.

One major criticism of the RBV frequently made is that it is tautological. Consider Barney's statements of the theory:

> Firm resources include all assets, capabilities, organizational processes, firm attributes, information, knowledge, etc. controlled by a firm that enable the firm to conceive of and implement strategies that improve its efficiency and effectiveness. (Barney, 1991: 101)

> Resources are valuable when they enable a firm to conceive of or implement strategies that improve its efficiency or effectiveness. (ibid.: 105)

> A firm is said to have a competitive advantage when it is implementing a value creating strategy not simultaneously being implemented by any current or potential competitor. (ibid.: 102)

Value and uniqueness appear in both *explanans* and *explanandum*; hence the RBV can be said to be causally ambiguous. The value of a resource and the SCA it generates are defined in identical terms. Additionally, it is difficult to see what would not be a resource – at various stages in different accounts of the RBV the category of a 'resource' seems to be capable of being applied to almost anything (Kraaijenbrink et al., 2010). For instance, if a resource is 'anything which could be thought of as strength or weakness of a given firm' (Wernerfelt, 1984: 172) it is hard to know what the boundary conditions of 'anything' might be.

Go Online: On YouTube you can find a good lecture titled Resource-Based View. The lecture looks at a variant of VRIN, VRIO, by substituting Organization for Non-Substitutability. In the link, none of the cases mentioned are discussed in detail. (If they were, the argument might not be sustainable.) A link to this lecture can be found on the companion website for this book at https://edge.sagepub.com/strategy2e in the list of weblinks for Chapter 3.

Resource-Based View Lecture

There may be a heuristic value in the VRIN in sharpening managerial focus but as a practical tool it leaves a lot to be desired. It is for this reason, perhaps, that there are few convincingly detailed accounts of firms possessing VRIN resources in the literature although many cases of loose description. It is relatively straightforward to identify VRIN resources in terms of monopoly access to natural resources, as in the case of de Beers and diamonds. When the notion of resources is stretched to include almost anything it becomes much more difficult. The concepts of VRIN resources and capabilities as well as Penrose's concept of relatively impregnable bases need to be quantified and tested more extensively in order for further progress to be made. Having said this Mahoney (2005) does find extensive support for the RBV. The debate goes on.

Sometimes a VRIN resource becomes known in most interesting ways. A recent story about a business dispute demonstrated an individual dynamic capability in action very clearly. An employee of BlueScope Steel, a software development manager, Chinnari Sridevi 'Sri' Somanchi was made redundant in June 2015. Before leaving, however, she downloaded a cache of company secrets so financially important to BlueScope that it launched emergency legal action in the Federal Court of Australia as well as in Singapore, where she is now based, to stop the information falling into the hands of its competitors. Allegedly stolen are emails, 13 software packages, and the source code for eight software programs. That the company has gone public and is pursuing the alleged theft through the courts is indication that it treats the software as valuable, rare, inimitable and non-substitutable. Ms Somanchi is now the innovation manager in a 50–50 joint venture between Japanese steel giant Nippon Steel & Sumitomo Metal Corporation and BlueScope in Singapore, known as NS BlueScope which is the major cause of concern. NS BlueScope does not have access to BlueScope's intellectual property and only uses its technology under license.

Ms Somanchi has acquired individual dynamic capabilities through her access to the IP in question.

BlueScope Steel

Dynamic capabilities

Despite Penrose's (1959) reference to capabilities (not just resources), and the use of a capabilities-based perspective by George Richardson (1972) to explain the market–integration–inter-firm cooperation nexus, the early RBV emphasized resources, not individual or organizational capabilities. Even the most specialized and rare of resources can lead to little benefit, however, when managed by individuals unable to appreciate the usefulness and potential services of resources and/or leverage them so as to satisfy their own and/or any organizational objectives. As Kraaijenbrink and colleagues (2010) propose, to create SCA it is necessary not only to have a VRIN bundle of resources but also the managerial capabilities to recognize and exploit them. The competence-dynamic capabilities (DCs) view of Teece (2007a) and Dosi (1982), who built on Nelson and Winter (1982) as well as Penrose (1959) and Richardson (1972), emphasizes the capabilities of organizations to sense, seize and reconfigure resources through learning so as to acquire and maintain SCA. DCs are often seen as higher-order 'routines' that, while they help transform more mundane routines, also involve a high degree of agency, which was arguably underplayed in the canonical earlier contribution of Nelson and Winter (Katkalo et al., 2010).

Teece et al. (1997; Teece, 2007a) developed the idea of **Dynamic Capabilities** (DCs), drawing on earlier literature.

> **Dynamic Capabilities** are the firm's capacities to integrate, build and reconfigure internal and external resources/competencies to address and shape rapidly changing business environments (Teece et al., 1997).

The dynamic capabilities perspective (Teece and Pisano, 1994; Eisenhardt and Martin, 2000; Zollo and Winter, 2002; Helfat et al., 2007; Teece, 2007b) is the most relevant recent development in the theory of the firm. While Penrose (1959) and resource-based scholars used the concept of capabilities to explain the growth, scope and boundaries of firms, as well as the institutional division of labour between market, firm and inter-firm cooperation (Richardson, 1972), they did not go so far as to analyse how firms can leverage these resources and capabilities so as to obtain SCA. Additionally, there has been limited discussion on the nature and types of capabilities that can help engender quasi-SCA. This has been the agenda of the DCs perspective.

Dynamic capabilities may sometimes be rooted in particular change routines (e.g. product development along a known trajectory) and systems of analysis (e.g. of investment choices). However, they are more commonly rooted in creative managerial and entrepreneurial acts, such as pioneering new markets. The DCs view (Teece et al., 1997; Dosi et al., 2000; Teece, 2007a) complements the rather static early focus of the RBV. Barney (1991), Grant (1996) and others argued the importance of addressing issues of agency and implementation in the early RBV (Kraaijenbrink et al., 2010) to which these developments are a response. Capabilities suggest the importance of processes (Dosi et al., 2008) not just resources.

According to the DCs view, a firm's basic competencies, if well honed, will enable it to perform its activities efficiently. However, whether the enterprise is currently making the right products and addressing the right market segment, or whether its future plans are appropriately aligned to consumer needs and technological and competitive opportunities, will be determined by its dynamic rather than basic or ordinary capabilities. Moreover, DCs require the organization and especially its top management to develop conjectures, validate them, and realign assets and competencies for emerging requirements. DCs will enable the enterprise to orchestrate its resources, competences and other assets in a way that engenders SCA and profitability.

According to Katkalo et al. (2010), DCs reflect the speed and degree to which the firm's idiosyncratic resources and competences can be aligned and realigned so as to match the opportunities and requirements of the business environment, while also shaping it. An organization with strong DCs will be able to achieve supernormal returns. Were DCs to be traded, markets would not price them at their value to the seller, because when the seller possesses complementary and, in particular, co-specialized assets, s/he has the opportunity to add value that other market players may not have.

The essence of dynamic capabilities, accordingly, is that they cannot generally be bought or sold but instead they must be built. Sensing, seizing and transforming are particular attributes that firms possess that enable them to evolve and co-evolve with the business environment. Such capabilities are critical to long-term profitability (Teece, 2007b).

Generally, it is necessary to first create or co-create markets before it is possible to capture value. Determining how to profit (or capture value) from intangible assets and other advantages and/or capabilities constitutes an important thread in the business strategy literature (Teece, 1986, 1998, 2006; Winter, 2003). Accordingly, the diagnosis, upgrading and integration of intra-firm resources and organizational capabilities, especially dynamic capabilities, so as to achieve firm-level sustainable competitive advantage (Teece, 2007; Helfat et al., 2007), can be regarded as 'the essence of the firm' (Augier and Teece, 2008). For Pitelis and Teece (2010), creation and co-creation with other economic actors, such as suppliers, customers, the state and even competitors, should be seen as the DC *par excellence*.

The rise of Web 2.0 strategy, new digital, information and network economics and ensuing digital disruption of existing industries, such as the Taxi industry by Uber, are often referred to as a New Dynamic Capabilities framework, one that is global almost from the outset, due to digital affordances that allow the integration of digital design that integrates customer experience and feedback into the organization (see Chapter 7 on 'born global'). On the basis of this continuous feedback loop existing strategic assets can be transformed or reconfigured by organizations that are agile.

> **Agile** organizations have 'the capacity (1) to sense and shape opportunities and threats, (2) to seize opportunities and (3) to maintain competitiveness through enhancing, combining, protecting, and, when necessary, reconfiguring the business enterprise's intangible and tangible assets' (Teece, 2009: 4).

Agility can be built in various ways. One way is through either formal or informal workplace learning of new patterns of activity, new 'routines'. Another way is through collaborations and partnerships that introduce innovations or improve weaknesses. Alliances and acquisitions can introduce new strategic assets from external sources. Changing routines to stay ahead of the competition depends on the ability to scan the environment and to evaluate markets. Sometimes a firm's assets achieve value because they have a unique value when in combination. For example, a particular technology when combined with specific research capabilities can provide a synergistic combination of complementary assets (Teece, 2009).

Sensing, seizing and transforming

Dynamic capabilities involve three main attributes, namely *sensing*, *seizing* and *transforming*.

1. *Sensing* involves grasping opportunities that may have potential in the business environment. For instance, given the technology platform from which the organization operates and the current plant, equipment and likely switching costs, where should the business be heading, given its history and the constraint and opportunity this legacy may pose for its future? Sensing can be a matter of knowing when to let go of a platform. Kodak hung on to print processing of film too long and went out of existence because it did not make the digital switch. Another example is sustainability: in the future there will be decisions to be made around technology choices associated with carbon-based fuels. With the switch in many advanced economies towards a more carbon neutral future what opportunities or threats do these changes pose for present and future business lines? Clearly there will be processes of co-evolution at work: shifts in public policy will help drive shifts towards more carbon neutral futures.

2. *Seizing* means being able to take advantage of sensed opportunities. Opportunities sensed but not seized are opportunities lost. Seizing an opportunity entails designing business models to satisfy customers and capture value; developing proficient investment protocols; gaining access to capital, and showing leadership and commitment in delivering on the capabilities. Business models need to be able to identify which market segments to address; value propositions for customers; appropriate technology and product functions, as well as design a method for capturing value.

3. *Transforming* refers to continuous renewal, aimed at maintaining SCA. Sensing and seizing are similar to two activities discussed in the management literature as potentially problematic within a single organization: exploration and exploitation (March, 1991). Exploration (e.g. research on a potentially disruptive technology) has a longer time horizon and greater uncertainty than exploitation (e.g. selling mature products). The two types of activities require different management styles. One possible solution is an 'ambidextrous organization' where two separate sub-units with different cultures are linked by shared company-wide values and by senior managers with a broad view – and appropriate incentives (O'Reilly and Tushman, 2004). The process of perennially trying to keep DCs as relevant and up to date through continuously developing co-specializations, complementarities and systemically related innovation in collaboration with others (see Chapter 7) entails reconfiguring that which has been seized. Co-specialization requires management of assets and their development in relation to each other in alliances and collaborations; it requires relating strategy to both structure and process so that complementarities are managed as they co-evolve between the different firms involved. Hence sensing and seizing refer to the mobilization of requisite resources and organizational infrastructure and strategy to address an opportunity, namely to capture value from so doing.

As we have seen, DCs can be classified according to whether they support sensing, seizing or transforming. Table 3.1 portrays the activities conducted to create and capture value, organized by clusters of DCs. As the requisite resources and capabilities for the design and building of value creation and value capture architectures can

Table 3.1 Creating and capturing value by combining dynamic capabilities

	Sensing	**Seizing**	**Transforming**
Creating value	Spotting opportunities; identifying opportunities for research and development; conceptualizing new customer needs and new business models	Investment discipline; commitment to research and development; building competencies; achieving new combinations	Achieving recombinations
Capturing value	Positioning for first mover and other advantages; determining desirable entry timing	Intellectual property qualification and enforcement; implementing business models; leveraging complementary assets; Investment or co-investment in 'production' facilities	Managing threats; honing the business model; developing new complements

Source: Katkalo et al. (2010)

differ, it is arguable that the successful inter-temporal management of the trade-offs between value capture and value creation-related capabilities is a critical DC in itself (Pitelis, 2009b; Teece, 2010).

Clearly there are cognitive dimensions to sensing, seizing and transforming. Moreover, in the absence of ubiquitous perfect markets, specialization in one of the three fundamental clusters of DCs is difficult if there is generally not a viable business model to support it, which forces entrepreneurs and entrepreneurial managers to deal simultaneously with the challenging task of bundling and managing many types of DCs (Teece, 2010).

Routines and dynamic capabilities

The capabilities of an organization reside not only in its human resources but also in its organizational routines (Nelson and Winter, 1982; Cohen et al., 1996; Dosi et al., 2000). In this context, the firm is more than the sum of its resources and more than the sum of the capabilities of its individual members (Winter, 2003); indeed, arguably more than the sum of its routines.

Some scholars see DCs as higher order capabilities or meta-routines that help firms deal not only with their operational decisions but also with strategic, long-term ones (Zollo and Winter, 2002). For Katkalo et al. (2010), however, reference to higher order and/or meta-routines, fails to convey fully that the difference between static or ordinary and dynamic capabilities is not just quantitative. DCs are more than routines, whether operational or higher order, in that they embody a qualitative difference, namely conscious human action. Routines partly serve the purpose of minimizing the need for such agency on a continual basis, by providing order and stability. DCs suggest that at a higher level of decision-making, such human action is critical in transforming existing routines and can even disrupt order and stability.

As noted, capabilities can be static (given at a point in time) or dynamic (changing over time). While static capabilities (such as operational routines) are both useful and can, at least for a while, be a source of SCA (Teece, 2009), it is DCs that undergird the sustainability of enterprise-level SCA (Teece, 2007a).

To summarize, dynamic capabilities reflect the capacity a firm has to orchestrate activities and resources within the system of its overall specialization and co-specialization with partners (see Chapter 6). They reflect the firm's efforts to create a market in ways that enable value to be captured. This often requires extending, modifying, or, if necessary, completely revamping what the enterprise is doing so as to maintain a good fit with and sometimes transform the market space that the enterprise occupies.

EXTEND YOUR KNOWLEDGE

The resource-based view and dynamic capabilities are not without their critics: see, for example, Richard J. Arend's (2014) critique in the journal article '**Mobius**' edge: Infinite regress in the resource-based and dynamic capabilities views', which you can read on this book's website at www.edge.sagepub.com/strategy2e.

Arend, R.J. (2014) 'Mobius' edge: Infinite regress in the resource-based and dynamic capabilities views', *Strategic Organization*, 13(1): 75–85.

Richard J. Arend

DCs, value creation and value capture

DCs can be grouped in two essential classes of interrelated activities – those that are mainly intended to create value and those that are mainly intended to capture value. The former relate to the ability of firms to have a positive impact on the determinants of value creation, such as its human resources, technology and innovativeness, unit cost economics and firm infrastructure and strategy. The latter relate to the ability of firms to build value capture architectures that combine value capture strategies, such as strategic entry deterrence, generic strategies, integration, cooperation and diversification strategies (Pitelis, 2009b).

Not infrequently, innovating firms create or co-create a market, such as when an entirely new product is offered to customers, or when new intermediate products must be traded. Dynamic capabilities, particularly the more entrepreneurial competences, are a critical input to the market creating and co-creating processes (Pitelis and Teece, 2009, 2010). Entrepreneurs have to make strategic calculations, take risks, using imagination, creativity, expectation and judgments to build their firms by putting together resources, activities and routines (see Jones and Pitelis 2015: Matthews 2010). Creativity implies that acts of entrepreneurial imagination, coupled with efficient management of the routines that underpin them, are the basis for 'organizational learning' that makes routines more effective. In building these routines managers/entrepreneurs must decide:

1. Whether to invest in new product/process development
2. The activities to be outsourced
3. How should products be priced?
4. What is the value proposition to the customer?
5. Whether the product is to be bundled for sale and if so, who should do the bundling?

These are key top management strategic decisions. They involve questions about finance, resource allocation and choice of business model. Clearly operational decisions need to be understood too. However, the essence of the firm is not just about the operational details of running a business but is also about creating and co-creating markets and designing the business.

The skill of entrepreneurship lies in putting activities together, combining and recombining them in a series of activities that deliver increasing returns. What links resources and activities are the standard operating procedures that firms develop – the routines – that are progressively specialized and recombined to make up specifically and sustainably patterned performance.

The entrepreneurial sensing, seizing and transforming of resources involves both efficiency and market power, particularly when the 'external' environment is seen, at least in part, to be endogenous to organizational strategy and hence, up to a point, malleable. Malleability, in turn, is a function of an organization's ability to achieve desired change through acting on the environment. It is 'the diagnosis, configuration and leveraging of knowledge assets and organization capabilities' (Pitelis and Teece, 2009: 5) that allows the principals of organizations to capture value in the form of profit from both the creative and routine operations of the organization.

A couple of quite concrete examples taken from the experience economy can illustrate these points about malleability. Think of the difference between two tourist activities that are very popular: whale watching and the Sydney Harbour Bridge climb. Whale watching has no barriers to entry and once the technologies (boats, spotting services: see Lawrence et al., 1999) are in place, other entrepreneurs can compete for market share. Climbing the Sydney Harbour Bridge requires using a piece of infrastructure that one entrepreneur gained access to through making an unsolicited and innovative proposal to the government that owns the bridge and from which, in consequence, it enjoys monopoly economic rents.

Of course, it is not just the fact that there is only one Sydney Harbour Bridge that makes BridgeClimb profitable. It was the ingenuity of its founders in seeing a business opportunity in the structure. Ingenuity combined with monopoly access to a facility provides a powerful but rare basis for profit.

BridgeClimb

It is not only a monopoly of a material resource that can be a source of significant VRIN-based SCA. Virtual monopoly helps as well. During 2014, according to Keen (2015), the world's Internet users – all three billion of them – sent 204m emails, uploaded 72m hours of YouTube video, undertook 4m Google searches, shared 2.46m pieces of Facebook content, published 277,000 tweets, posted 216,000 new photos on Instagram and spent $83,000 on Amazon every minute, every day. Google created a VRIN-based competitive advantage through a monopoly based on knowledge generation competences. Google handles 3.5bn searches daily and controls more than 90% of the market in some countries and is worth more than seven times General Motors, which employs nearly four times more people. The digital economy lends itself to monopolies as a global platform for free-market late capitalism as a frictionless, borderless economy. Firms such as Uber, AirBnB and Google may be seen as contemporary exemplars of VRIN and Porter-type barriers to entry and hence monopoly in the making.[2]

While the VRIN approach to resources focuses on those factors that can provide economic rents as a basis for maintaining a privileged market position, however temporary, the resources-based perspective of Penrose differs in emphasis: the focus is on value creation through endogenous knowledge, innovation and growth (Penrose, 1959). Teece (1986) explored conditions under which an innovator (such as the music company EMI which first invented the CT scanner) might fail to profit from its value-creating innovations. He attributed such failures to the lack of strong appropriability through patents as well as firms' lack of complementary skills and capabilities vis-à-vis their competitors. The focus on the nature and wider determinants of appropriability goes far beyond the focus on monopoly rents through barriers to mobility and brings the issues of firm-level capabilities and organizational strategy centre stage.

---

[2] A 2013 survey by the US Institute for Local Self-Reliance found that, on average, a regular bricks-and-mortar store creates jobs for 47 employees to generate $10m in turnover; Amazon achieves the same with 14 employees. In this sense Keen (2015) claims Amazon destroyed roughly 27,000 US jobs in 2012. Hence while as consumers we might welcome the world of Amazon, Facebook and Google in the short run, as taxpayers and citizens we should not. Rather than encouraging creativity, stimulating competition, creating jobs, distributing wealth and promoting equality, Keen argues that the Internet does the reverse. It should be added that in addition, in the long run, when and if they achieve monopoly positions, prices are also likely to go up.

Refining dynamic capabilities

According to some criticisms, the Teece et al. (1997) approach is tautological – you know something is a dynamic capability when it produces SCA! The upshot of this is that many *ad hoc* judgments as cases of SCA were attributed to DCs. In 2000, this unsatisfactory state of affairs led Eisenhardt and Martin to ask 'Dynamic capabilities: What are they?'

Eisenhardt and Martin (2000) suggest that DCs can be understood as a reaction and challenge to static descriptions of the RBV. Many important strategic resources rarely just exist; they are constituted, made up and integrated into processes or routines within firms. A focus on DCs changes analysis from focusing on bundles of resources to asking questions about processes. Processes are what can acquire, secure, configure and renew resources. Eisenhardt and Martin identified a set of specific organizational and strategic processes, such as product innovation, strategic decision-making and alliancing, which managers of firms use to build, create and alter the set of resources available to them. The role of 'best practices' is to capture basic routines from a wide variety of firms over time in order to transfer their dynamic capabilities from the specific cases.

A key distinction is based around the nature of the market in which the firm operates. High velocity markets are the most dynamic. They are characterized by rapid technological change; short product life cycles; rapidly evolving customer expectations; frequent launches of new competitive moves as well as the entry of important new rivals. In these high velocity markets, market boundaries and successful business models are unclear and market players are ambiguous and shifting. Extant routines based on existing knowledge and resources are less useful than the rapid ability to create new situation-specific knowledge. Depending on the velocity of the market, the outcome and pattern of DCs may be very different. What are strategically most important in such high velocity markets may not be a particular resource but the ability to reconfigure resources quickly and to adapt.

IN PRACTICE

David Deverall Interview

Go Online: Visit the book's website at https://edge.sagepub.com/strategy2e to watch an interview with David Deverall talking about the financial service industry.

In 2009 David Deverall was the Managing Director and Chief Executive Officer of Perpetual Limited, Australia. Prior to his appointment he worked at Macquarie Bank Limited, holding several senior management positions. In view of his considerable knowledge and ability within the financial sector, David was selected to lead Perpetual after only two years as head of Macquarie's funds management division. During his time at Perpetual David managed to buck a few industry trends by holding onto Perpetual's key fund managers; those that typically leave to form their own boutique operations and often take with them big institutional clients. This success is credited to the recognition that while he is the CEO, many of the decisions relating to the strategic direction of the business are largely in the hands of the fund managers and, as such, his role is to guide this process.

A high degree of coordination is required for firms to realize sustainable competitive advantage. Aligning core resources – which could include such diverse aspects as capital equipment, employee skills and the brand – and their ultimate capabilities, with the regular routines of the firm and, creating the appropriate network of relationships between these resources requires a shift in operational focus in organizations. As you will see in this Case Study, the business function of Human Resource Management comes to the fore.

The Human Resource department becomes, with the incorporation of HR aspects into the line manager's role, the 'production manager' of knowledge-based firms, nurturing and developing its resource base. 'Resources' can be seen as stocks that depreciate with time and that have to be replaced, augmented and upgraded.

Commenting on the nature of an organization where the main asset and intellectual property is the staff, David introduces himself as a strategist who is the 'Chief Human Resources Manager' of Perpetual Limited; a position that truly reflects the implications of the unique strategies required in knowledge-based organizations. Further, as the process of strategy within Perpetual is uncovered, it becomes clear just how important effectively leveraging each available human resource is to the organization's competitive advantage. From the unique blend of heterogeneous skills and experiences selected for the board, through to the top-down and bottom-up approach of developing strategy, this knowledge-based organization involves staff at all levels. Additionally, once that strategy has been crafted and communicated within the firm, it becomes a multi-level strategy with which tactically to access and engage all relevant stakeholders in order to foster implementation.

By engaging the staff throughout the complete strategy process, Perpetual are tapping into the characteristics synonymous of resource-based theory; value, rareness, inimitability and substitutability.

Questions

1. How do firms build and sustain competitive advantage in dynamic markets?

2. Following the RBV, why do firms perform differently?

3. Reflecting critically on the assumptions that underpin RBV theory, what are its main weaknesses?

4. What do sensing, seizing, reconfiguring and transforming resources entail in the case of services such as in the financial industry?

The knowledge-based view of the firm

For most organizations, a little knowledge can go a long way as they strive for SCA, leading Kogut and Zander (1992) to suggest the creation of a knowledge-based view of the firm. The knowledge-based theory of the firm considers knowledge as the most strategically significant resource because knowledge-based resources are usually difficult to imitate such that socially complex, heterogeneous knowledge bases and capabilities amongst firms are the major determinants of SCA. Corporate interest in knowledge and its management exploded in the late 1990s both in the form of 'knowledge management' and the 'knowledge-based view' of the firm. The knowledge-based view (KBV) of the firm is an extension of the RBV. Grant (1996) initially propounded it in a widely cited article. He began by identifying knowledge as a specific form of resource with a unique potential to create value. Several aspects of knowledge were seen as important:

1. *Transferability*: the transferability of knowledge builds on the tacit/explicit knowledge dichotomy. The KBV privileges codified, explicit knowledge because it is more transferable.

2. *Capacity for aggregation*: knowledge that is easily aggregated is more efficient; hence, the KBV privileges statistical information over idiosyncratic knowledge.

3. *Appropriability*: this is the ability of the owner of a resource to receive a return equal to the value of that resource. Property rights such as patents increase this value.

4. *Specialization in knowledge acquisition*: a knowledge-based division of labour is necessary because of the disciplinary differentiation of knowledge.

5. *Knowledge requirements of production*: all production is seen to be a function of knowledge embodied either in people or embedded in artefacts and devices.

Grant (1996) produces a theory of the firm that is knowledge-based by putting these elements together and this account is updated without major revision in his contribution to Faulkner and Campbell's (2003) *The Oxford Handbook of Strategy*. The disciplinary differentiation of knowledge is key: it takes specialists to produce it even while generalists can utilize it by coordinating many different elements of specialists' knowledge. The firm is a knowledge-integrating institution; rather than seeing the management of transactions as central it regards it as a device for managing team production through *coordination, communication* and *control*.

Coordination occurs through various mechanisms such as markets, bureaucracies and networks. It creates different forms of interdependency. Different forms of interdependency require different forms of coordination. Pooled interdependence relies on rules; sequential interdependence relies on plans; reciprocal interdependence relies on mutual adjustment through routines, while team interdependence relies on group coordination through scheduling meetings. All forms of interdependency are opportunities for sensemaking through language, symbolic systems more generally, translation of specialized knowledge and recognition of individual knowledge domains, the optimal outcome of which is shared meaning.

The achievement of effective *communication* is more pressing the more complex and differentiated are the knowledge domains because as the number and complexity of these increases, the achievement of shared meaning between people with diverse capabilities becomes more problematic.

The role of *control* is vested in hierarchy with delegated decision-making rights. Hierarchy is often argued to be an evolutionary mechanism that is functionally efficient in solving the integration problems of complex coordination.

Takeuchi Paper

Go Online: Takeuchi, one of the founders of contemporary KM, integrates elements of the KBV with KM in a recent paper on a 'Knowledge-based view of strategy'. You can find this paper on the *Harvard Business Review* website, and a link is also hosted on the website for this book: www.edge.sagepub.com/strategy2e.

Knowledge management

An obvious corollary of the knowledge-based view of the firm is that knowledge, if it is so essential, has to be managed: hence, **knowledge management**.

The idea of the **knowledge-based organization**, which initially emerged in the 1980s with the work of people such as Drucker (1988), is a central plank of KM.

In discussions of knowledge-based organizations an important distinction is drawn between **tacit and explicit knowledge**.

A trade secret might be regarded as explicit knowledge. Liebeskind (1996) suggested that firms exist in order to protect explicit knowledge. Employment contracts specify exclusivity and confidentiality clauses, preventing the transfer of economically advantageous knowledge to rival organizations. Firms protect their explicit knowledge by threats of dismissal of staff that pass on information, making their departure costly through the loss of bonuses, pensions, stock options and promotion opportunities. The firm may try to ensure that people have access to no more information than is strictly necessary for them to perform their functions.

In KM the objective is to turn tacit knowledge – knowhow – into explicit knowledge. The influence of Nonaka and Takeuchi's (1995) highly acclaimed account of tacit–explicit knowledge-conversion in Japan's knowledge-creating companies has been instrumental in establishing the importance of the distinction between 'tacit knowledge' and 'explicit knowledge'.

The idea that tacit knowledge is a hidden resource that can be made available to managers is a popular theme. In the industrial era, 'bosses' were expected to tell workers what to do. But, in the so-called knowledge era, knowledge workers are expected both to 'think for themselves' *and* work for the organization. Part of KM's allure seems to stem from the idea that it will make what knowledge workers know explicit and 'empower' managers.

Tsoukas (2003) makes the crucial point that Nonaka and Takeuchi's (1995) book, *The Knowledge-Creating Company*, has helped to institutionalize an erroneous view of tacit knowing. As Tsoukas (2003: 413) noted, Polanyi (1969), who first coined the term tacit knowledge, saw all knowing as personal. The capacity to know is not a transferable commodity: it is inherently personal and inherently tacit.

> A simple definition of **knowledge management (KM)** is that it is a managerial practice that seeks to identify, leverage, control and create knowledge in an organization.

> A **knowledge-based organization** attends to two related processes that underlie its everyday processes: the effective application of existing knowledge and the creation of new knowledge.

> A learner, cannot appropriate **tacit knowledge** immediately because it cannot be explicitly conveyed sufficiently quickly as it is embodied, embrained and taken for granted. A manual for how to ride a bike would not be equivalent to the realization that you *can* do it.

> **Explicit knowledge**, by contrast, is easily absorbed, and can be transferred to various uses immediately by media such as writing or video.

> *All knowledge falls into one of these two classes: it is either tacit or rooted in tacit knowledge* … The ideal of a strictly explicit knowledge is indeed self-contradictory; deprived of their tacit coefficients, all spoken words, all formulae, all maps and graphs, are strictly meaningless. (Polanyi, 1969: 195, original emphasis)

In *The Knowledge-Creating Company*, it is declared that 'The explanation of how Japanese companies create new knowledge boils down to the conversion of tacit knowledge to explicit knowledge' (Nonaka and Takeuchi, 1995: 11).

Tacit knowledge is highly personal and hard to formalize, making it difficult to communicate or to share with others. Subjective insights, intuitions, and hunches fall into this category of knowledge … To be more precise, tacit knowledge can be segmented into two dimensions. The first is the technical dimension, which encompasses the kind of informal and hard-to-pin-down skills or crafts captured in the term 'know-how' … At the same time, tacit knowledge contains an important cognitive dimension. It consists of schemata, mental models, beliefs, and perceptions so ingrained that we take them for granted. The cognitive dimension of tacit knowledge reflects our image of reality (what is) and our vision for the future (what ought to be) …

For tacit knowledge to be communicated and shared within the organization, it has to be converted into words or numbers that anyone can understand. It is precisely during this time that conversion takes place – from tacit to explicit, and, as we shall see, back again into tacit – that organizational knowledge is created. (Nonaka and Takeuchi, 1995: 8–9)

Through tacit–explicit knowledge-conversion it is argued that the inexpressible language associated with an individual's 'cognitive tacit knowledge' can be expressed as explicit knowledge, which is presented as a universally comprehensible language: it can be understood by 'anyone'. Nonaka and Takeuchi (1995) argue that the personal capacity *to know* can be reduced to an object – explicit knowledge – the search for and valorization of which forms the central plank of knowledge management (KM). The core of KM centres on tacit to explicit knowledge-conversion that according to Polanyi (1969), from whom they derived their ideas, is impossible because all knowing is personal and thus cannot be a transferable commodity.

Knowing, no matter how it is defined, resides in the heads and experience of persons. Every person has no alternative other than to construct what they know using their experience (Glasersfeld, 2002: 1). Knowledge may well be embedded in material artefacts, such as organizations, books and laboratories but it is never passively received but always actively constructed by cognizing subjects, who learn how to make sense of their experience.

Polanyi's (1983: 4) observation that 'we can know more than we can tell' is fundamental to his work on the tacit dimension and has become quite well known. It is cited by Nonaka and Takeuchi as part of their claim that, given appropriate effort, cognitive tacit knowledge could be articulated: 'the articulation of tacit mental models, in a kind of "mobilization" process, is a key factor in creating new knowledge' (Nonaka and Takeuchi, 1995: 60).

There are four major mechanisms through which knowledge may be managed, according to Nonaka and Takeuchi:

1. *Socialization (Tacit–Tacit)*: This form of knowledge creation involves the interplay of tacit knowledge creating tacit knowledge. A good example of this is an apprenticeship whereby the apprentice learns through doing, observing and being in the same space as the master crafts-person.

2. *Externalization (Tacit–Explicit)*: According to Nonaka and Takeuchi externalization represents the quintessential form of knowledge creation whereby tacit knowledge is taken from the mind of the worker and transformed into explicit knowledge. This form of knowledge creation has been the driving force behind most contemporary knowledge management programmes. The

premise upon which it is based is far from unproblematic. Many scholars dispute the extent to which tacit knowledge can be translated into explicit knowledge (Cook and Brown, 2002).

3. *Internalization (Explicit–Tacit)*: This form of knowledge production is where someone uses explicit knowledge sufficiently often that it becomes 'second nature'. Often, this happens in professional work where an accountant, doctor or lawyer comes to embody the explicit knowledge.

4. *Combination (Explicit–Explicit)*: This form of knowledge is where two forms of explicit knowledge combine to create a new hybridized form of knowledge. For instance, if a project team contains an accountant and strategist working together, they will be combining two forms of explicit knowledge.

McKinlay (2002) summarized the practical impact KM has had on organizations:

1. KM has acted as a vehicle for an organization to learn about itself by answering questions such as, How do we create knowledge? How, as an organization, do we learn?

2. By attempting to capture knowledge and understand what knowledge the organization possesses, it has served as a brake on corporate forgetting.

3. KM has been an effective means of diffusing small-scale innovations across wider constituencies in the organization.

EXTEND YOUR KNOWLEDGE

Amongst the organizations that have most enthusiastically embraced knowledge management are the major consultancy companies. Andreas Werr and Torbjörn Stjernberg have a most informative paper **'Exploring management consulting firms as knowledge systems'** in the journal *Organization Studies*, based on case studies in Andersen Consulting (now Accenture) and Ernst & Young Management Consulting (now Cap Gemini Ernst & Young). You can read this journal article on the companion website for this book at www.edge.sagepub.com/strategy2e.

Werr, A. and Stjernberg, T. (2003) 'Exploring management consulting firms as knowledge systems', *Organization Studies*, 24(6): 881–908.

Werr & Stjernberg

Knowledge management has been dominated by organizations attempting to codify their knowledge and then 'mine' their knowledge base. The prospect of creating knowledge 'repositories' that can be 'managed' (Durcikova and Gray, 2009) to provide expert knowledge and competitive edge is alluring. With respect to knowledge sharing, for example, such an approach, with its focus on the development of centralized databases that can be used for 'catching', 'storing' and 'transferring' codified forms of knowledge across the organization (Carrillo, 2004), seems a good basis for a 'learning' organization. To achieve this outcome, organizations often implemented **Intranet** systems.

An **Intranet** is a privately controlled and maintained computer system that is very similar to the World Wide Web, except it is normally restricted to use by employees inside the organization. It seeks to store knowledge but also to generate an electronic forum in which knowledge can be shared, communities created and problems solved.

Common problems associated with Intranets include:

1. Not being used but becoming repositories of 'dead' knowledge.

2. Being regarded with suspicion by employees who view what they know as what they know and are reluctant to surrender it and perhaps squander their strategic asset in career terms.

3. Consequently, the Intranet can become a mechanism through which existing rivalries and tensions play out.

4. Being a database, the Intranet is not clearly linked to operational and strategic goals.

5. It imposes centrifugal solutions on centripetal processes rather than stimulating local activity and learning.

6. It can be subject to piracy – as we saw earlier being alleged in the case of BlueScope's actions against its redundant software manager, Ms Somanchi.

An Intranet as a repository of knowledge is much like a traditional library; if organization members don't know what to look for or where to look, chances are they will not retrieve anything useful. Contrast all the dead stories – those not accessed – in a library with the immediacy and powerfulness of oral tradition. Some cultures are defined by their oral traditions, with storytelling a major repository of the wisdom and knowledge of the culture. It is not just cultures, however; organizations are increasingly alert to the insight that a story captured and recounted that passes into the oral traditions of the organization is a most effective way of learning.

The view of knowledge as an entity that people possess, capable of existing independently of them in a codified form (Hislop, 2013), is of limited value. It assumes that knowledge is primarily a cognitive and intellectual entity; something that can be made explicit and be separated from the person who creates, develops and utilizes it (Hislop, 2013). Explicit knowledge is synonymous with a body of scientific facts consistent across varying contexts (McAdam and McCreedy, 2000); most practical strategic knowledge is not of this ilk but far more provisional, far more based on knowing and interpreting than knowledge *per se*. Only individuals do knowing, not databases.

The knowledge-based theory of the firm (Spender, 1996) sees explicit knowledge as enabling power through competitive advantage (Carrillo, 2004). It assumes a docile and compliant workforce happy and able to translate what they know they know into explicit knowledge. What they don't know they know, the tacit, embodied, embrained aspects of knowing, cannot be captured. What they don't want the firm to know they know will not be proffered.

Knowledge as a resource may be less valuable than it might appear to be. Certainly, it has an evident materiality in patents, inventions, and so on but of much more sustained value for commercial organizations are less knowledge *per se* and more the subtle assemblage of valuable and useful know-how. Unsurprisingly then some scholars have argued that a learning-based theory is more important than a knowledge-based one as it is learning that keeps creating and transforming knowledge and even our understanding of what knowledge is and entails (Pitelis, 2007).

Summary

In this chapter we began by reviewing the importance of organizational resources and their link to value creation and capture. We then considered the RBV, identifying its origins in the pioneering work of Edith Penrose. The chapter has considered the development of contemporary RBV theory, looking at some of its key exponents, and raising some critical questions about the framework of assumptions on which it is founded. We introduced some key terms, including resources, capabilities, dynamic capabilities, competency and core competency. These terms were foundations for developing the resource-based and the DCs-based views of the firm. The resource-based view of the firm (Barney, 2001) is closely related to what is known as the knowledge-based view (Kogut and Zander, 1992). Knowledge can be seen as a unique and inimitable resource for creating and capturing value. Building on the resource-based view of the firm, the dynamic capabilities approach attempts to answer the question of how an organization can adapt its pool of resources to stay competitive (Teece et al., 1997). We discussed the growth of knowledge management, or KM. The realization of the importance of knowledge has led many strategists to consider how knowledge is actually shared not just codified. We stressed the importance of knowing rather than of knowledge and of storytelling rather than databases, a theme that we shall return to in Chapter 10.

TEST YOURSELF

Want to know more about this chapter? Review what you have learnt by visiting www.edge.sagepub.com/strategy2e.

- Test yourself with multiple choice questions
- Revise key terms with interactive flashcards

EXERCISES

1. Having read this chapter, you should be able to say in your own words what the following key terms mean:

   - Resource-based view (RBV)
   - Value creation and capture
   - Durability
   - Transparency

   - Transferability
   - Replicability
   - Resources
   - Capabilities

(Continued)

(Continued)

- Isolating mechanisms
- VRIN framework
- Economic rent
- Dynamic capabilities
- Core competencies

- Tacit knowledge
- Explicit knowledge
- Knowledge management
- Intranet

2. What is the significance of Edith Penrose's work to the resource-based view of the firm? How does it extend classical views of the firm?

3. How does the RBV explain value creation and capture?

4. Explain the VRIN framework. Give some examples of firms that have profited from VRIN strategies.

5. What are the implications of the RBV for strategists?

6. Critically assess the relative merits of the RBV and the dynamic capabilites view of strategy.

CASE STUDY

Search engines*

STEWART CLEGG

History of Search Engines

You all use search engines, right? Today they are ubiquitous – or at least the notion of Googling is. A search engine is a program that searches the web for sites based on your keyword search terms. The search engine takes your keyword and returns search engine results pages, with a list of sites it deems relevant or connected to your searched keyword. The early days of the Internet had a number of search engines before Google reigned seemingly supreme in much of the web outside China. Ones that we recall were Ask, Jeeves and Dogpile. Notably, none of these have become household names or verbs in the way that Google has. Its name, incidentally, is a creative spelling of googol, a number equal to 10 to the 100th power, or more colloquially, an unfathomable number.

Today, most people we know use Google but there are still a few Yahoo users out there. However, Yahoo is not doing well: in early February 2016 it announced a major reorganization of its business to cut costs. Of its employees 15% will be made redundant and it is seeking a buyer. Yahoo's slow decline might provide today's Internet entrepreneurs with food for thought; indeed, it could be a test-bed for organizational e-learning.

Yahoo began in 1994 when David Filo and Jerry Yang created it as a directory of sites on the early World Wide Web. It quickly became a portal that people could use to find what they were interested in on the Internet. Up until 2002 they did not have their own search engine but outsourced their search services. Google rapidly emerged as its main competitor using an algorithm-powered search engine that enabled people to find things more easily and quickly on the web.

Yahoo eventually licensed Google's technology before turning to Microsoft's Bing. Doing so was an acknowledgement that it was not a search company in the same way as these companies; instead it was positioning itself as a content provider and destination capable of generating considerable traffic. A great chance was missed: in 2003 Yahoo had the opportunity to buy Google for US$5 billion but turned it down. The then CEO of Yahoo, whose background was in Hollywood would not pay any more than US$3 billion for what was still a start-up, whose future prospects were judged uncertain.

Go Online: An article about Yahoo's decision not to buy Google titled 'How Yahoo blew it' can be found on the online magazine *Wired*, which recounts the effects of the period when Semel ran the company. You can find a web link to the artile on the companion website for this book at www.edge.sagepub.com/strategy2e.

How Yahoo
Blew It

Yahoo has had a number of dominant figures leading it over the years but many did not have a clear understanding of or vision for the business. The co-founder Jerry Yang (who went on to invest in Chinese Internet giant Alibaba) did. It is not clear that Semel did. Scott Thompson was sacked for being economical with the truth about his CV. In 2012, Yahoo's board hired Mayer from Google to turn the company around. Mayer invested heavily in engineering and media talent but there's no sign that these investments are paying off in the form of higher revenue. Frequent leadership changes have meant constant changes to strategy and direction of the business.

Yahoo is different from some other Silicon Valley companies, as Lee (2016) points out:

> The most successful companies in Silicon Valley – including Google, Facebook, and Apple – have an intensely technology-focused culture. These companies are obsessive about hiring the most talented engineers (and in Apple's case, designers) so they can build the best technology products. And this culture tends to be self-perpetuating – very skilled, highly motivated people like to work with other very skilled, highly motivated people. Once you have a critical mass of such people it becomes easy to recruit more of them.

Yahoo has never had the same kind of obsessive focus on recruiting technical talent. Paul Graham, a well-known Silicon Valley investor who sold his company to Yahoo in 1998, has written that even in the late 1990s, Yahoo was ambivalent about its status as a technology company. 'One of the weirdest things about Yahoo when I went to work there was the way they insisted on calling themselves a "media company"', Graham wrote. Yahoo employed a lot of programmers and produced a lot of software, of course — and still does. But it never made software as central to its identity as some of its major competitors.

That's probably because at the time Yahoo was founded, in 1994, no one had ever heard of an ad-supported software company. Back then, software companies sold their

(Continued)

(Continued)

products in shrink-wrapped boxes in computer stores. Yahoo had the same business model as CNN and the *New York Times* – build up a large audience and then make money by selling ads – so it was natural for Yahoo to think of itself as being in the same industry. But one consequence of this was that Yahoo didn't focus as much as it could have on recruiting the best programmers (see www.vox.com/2016/2/1/10862040/yahoo-marissa-mayer-fail).

Postscript: Yahoo sells its core business to Verizon.

http://www.telegraph.co.uk/technology/2016/07/25/yahoo-9-reasons-for-the-internet-icons-decline/

QUESTION

Using the web, compare and contrast Yahoo's strategy with that of Google. Drawing on the resource-based view of the firm and other approaches to strategy with which you are familiar, answer the question what, strategically, went right at Google and what went wrong at Yahoo?

*This case was taken from two news reports:

- www.afr.com/leadership/is-time-running-out-for-yahoos-marissa-mayer-2016 0110-gm33cm

- www.smh.com.au/business/media-and-marketing/yahoo-a-textbook-case-of-how-not-to-run-an-internet-company-20160202-gmk9db.html

4

STRATEGY AND INNOVATION

DIFFERENTIATION, CO-CREATION, CREATIVITY

Learning objectives

By the end of this chapter you will be able to:

1 Understand the importance of innovation for strategic management

2 Appreciate the differences between product, process, service and business model innovation

3 Understand barriers to and drivers of innovation

4 Know about open innovation and open strategy

5 Recognize principles of co-creation and design thinking

6 Understand why larger innovation systems as well as organizational characteristics are important for strategic innovation

BEFORE YOU GET STARTED

We can't solve problems by using the same kind of thinking we used when we created them. (Albert Einstein)

Introduction

Innovation is one of the most strategic of topics. Organizations that master it are usually seen as being on the fast track to achieving competitive advantage. Yet, given the diversity and long history of innovation research, the term remains notoriously ambiguous and often lacks a specific definition or measure (Adams et al., 2006). Nonetheless, innovation is viewed by commercial, non-commercial and government organizations alike as an important approach to improving organizational efficacy and profitability.

If the innovation process is successful, it leads to the emergence and diffusion of new capabilities that could not be achieved previously, or at least not so well and effectively. In the simplest possible terms, innovation involves learning how to do new or different things, or learning to do the same things in a better and more effective way. The links with the previous chapter are obvious: organizations need to be able to develop new assemblages of knowledge, core competencies and dynamic capabilities if they are to innovate. Organizations cannot innovate by repeating existing routines, except by accident rather than design.

In this chapter we will first consider the case of New Product Development as an innovation, choosing a very tasty example from Patak's pickles. Following this we

> **Innovation** refers to the development and introduction of new products, services, processes or business models. In business this means successful commercialization but innovation can also occur in a non-commercial context, when new practices are developed and adopted.

shall ask a fairly important generic question: where does innovation come from? The search for antecedents of innovation has been extensive but largely inconclusive, in part because of a sampling bias towards innovations that are successful. Unsuccessful innovations are legion but rarely legendary. It is important to realize that innovation is not the same thing as invention. Invention refers to a new idea or technology that can reach up to the patenting stage. **Innovation** implies application in practice, which in market economies means commercialization.

Innovation is not necessarily radical or premised on creative destruction; some is but it doesn't have to be. As we will go on to define, distinctions are usually made between product and process innovation and radical and incremental innovation. Being successful at strategic innovation can be a curse as well as a blessing; an organization can become locked in on a particular innovation, overly focused on it and lose sight of threats to its survival.

Although the focus is often on planned innovation, in strategy there are many instances of unplanned innovation, sometimes through accident and sometimes as a result of improvization. Jazz provides many classic examples of improvization and we borrow a famous example from Miles Davis' autobiography.

Service innovation is rapidly growing into a specialist subfield. When the advanced economies are increasingly service-oriented rather than based on manufacturing this sector is of considerable importance. We discuss the emergence of what is known as Service-Dominant logic.

One of the hottest management topics in recent years has been various ideas related to design which we discuss next under the rubric of design thinking, design science and framing, before looking at constraining and enabling innovation. Some views of innovation regard it as more likely to occur in small rather than large firms. Nonetheless, there has been considerable attention paid to how large organizations can be 'ambidextrous' – focused on stable routines that serve existing markets and on innovation simultaneously.

Innovation is considered so nationally important these days that it has become a matter of regional and national policy, often referred to in terms of national or regional innovation (as well as sectoral) systems. We consider the literature on national innovation systems and on the importance of regional clusters of industry as incubators of innovation.

Innovation is not only an organizational affair; it can include customers, clients, suppliers, etc. via co-creation, which is an increasingly fashionable perspective on innovation. Nor is innovation either just service or product innovation; we conclude the chapter with a discussion of social innovation.

Innovation as New Product Development

A common focus of strategy and innovation is new product development, often referred to as NPD in the literature. NPD encompasses the process of bringing a new product to market by transforming a market opportunity into a product (or service). The *PDMA Handbook of New Product Development* (Kahn, 2013) states that the main factors for the success of a new product are sound market research and understanding, analysis of the competitive environment and the market the product or service targets. New products or services should have cost, time and quality benefits prized by customers. Organizations seek to increase their market share by regular NPD innovation.

Organizations don't always get NPD right. That staple of lovers of Indian foods, Patak's Lime Pickle, provides a recent instance. In this case what was claimed to be a new and improved version of an existing product was launched. The reaction in social media to the new formula was so extreme that Patak's ended up reverting to the old product.

Patak News Article

New product development is clearly a process that can extend into the post-launch period if the market reaction is as adverse as it was with Patak's Lime Pickle. Of course, organizations try not to be caught out in this very public way, staging the NPD process from ideation to design, through manufacturing and introduction to the market.

Three main phases have been identified in NPD. First, there is an initial stage of fuzzy ideas, where there is an insight into a potential new product that becomes, if it passes approval processes in the organization, a more detailed product development plan. The second stage is the actual process of designing the product or service delivery so that prototypes are created and tested. The third stage is that of implementation, where detailed design and creation of the launch product or service are finalized. Finally, of course, the launch follows – hopefully not to the dismal reception that Patak's Lime Pickle received!

Where does innovation come from?

There are many answers to that question. However, much of the innovation literature starts by aiming to discover what is called antecedents of innovation, using general holistic approaches such as 'innovation orientation', 'market orientation' or 'entrepreneurial orientation', etc. (see Hurley and Hult, 1998; Hult et al., 2004; Siguaw et al., 2006; Simpson et al., 2006) or focusing on more specific antecedents such as company size or age of business (see Brouwer et al., 1999).

The focus on antecedents of innovation is not surprising since it is well known that innovative firms perform better. Although literature reviews such as Fagerberg (2005: 20) and Hult et al. (2004: 429) show how studies of antecedent factors are inconsistent and/or inconclusive, there is some agreement on innovation factors such as:

> firm culture, experience with innovation, the multidisciplinary character of the R&D team and explicit recognition of the collective character of the innovation process or the advantages of the matrix organization. (van der Panne et al., 2003: 309)

Various antecedent factors need to be critically scrutinized and also compared to other findings before they can be adopted as general predictors of successful innovation. As van der Panne et al. state: 'While some studies claim a certain group of factors being crucial, other studies ignore the very same factors and claim very different factors to be decisive' (2003: 310). Further, there is a 'success bias' in innovation studies: van der Panne et al. note that it is possibly easier to report and take credit for a successful project rather than an unsuccessful one and correspondingly interviewers might not get the 'whole story', leaving them with a fuzzy picture that over-samples 'success' and under-samples 'failure' (2003: 310).

Innovation is often confused with or mistaken for invention: the discovery of something previously not known. The distinguishing feature of innovation from invention is the application in practice of a new process or, in the case of products and services, their commercialization. Inventions can be patented (or not) and stay on a shelf (or remain an idea) while innovation implies further development of the idea to match market requirements and find a willing paying group of customers.

For a long time, innovation was associated purely with science and technology, creating new products that commercialized ideas and inventions. It has also often been viewed as a closed proprietary affair, based on self-reliance in R&D. But organizations trying to do it alone are increasingly seen to be too slow and too costly. The traditional linear perspective that saw invention followed by commercialization is now seen as too simplistic.

Today, innovation encompasses interactions amongst institutional, technological, and human systems, involving a multitude of sources of innovation within and outside the single firm. It entails participating in a complex relational system with concurrent processes of value co-creation including collaboration, design-led approaches and strategic analysis. Increasingly, innovation emerges from systemic interaction amongst markets, research and educational institutions and public funding agencies. At their most successful these evolve into local, national and/or regional systems of innovation (Nelson and Winter, 1982; Malerba, 2002).

Viewed from a strategic management perspective, firms and those responsible for making strategic decisions now engage with many actors in the innovation eco-system that surrounds their organization. Doing so usually goes well beyond the borders of any single industry, since strategic innovation can come from anywhere. Thus, during the past three decades the focus on innovation has broadened to include collaborative innovation and more recently has expanded to open-innovation and co-innovation (Chesbrough, 2006; Lee et al., 2010).

Radical innovation as creative destruction

Joseph Schumpeter (1942) argued that in capitalist market economies innovation usually leads to **creative destruction**. Schumpeter coined the term in his 1942 book *Capitalism, Socialism and Democracy*. Schumpeter defined creative destruc-tion as the 'process of industrial mutation that incessantly revolutionizes the economic structure *from within*, incessantly destroying the old one, incessantly creating a new one.'

> **Creative destruction** involves the replace-ment of older less efficient processes, products, services or organizational prac-tices with newer more efficient ones. It is destruction because it annihilates the old and inefficient but it is creative because it replaces it with the new and more efficient.

Strategically speaking, creative destruction concerns innovation transformations that lead to major challenges for existing companies or opportunities for new organizations. Innovation often happens outside the boundaries of estab-lished firms and sometimes even outside the established industry. For example, digital cameras were not innovated by any of the great camera firms; Kodak did not develop digital imaging; record compa-nies such as EMI did not introduce music streaming.

Image 4.1   Joseph Schumpeter (1883–1950)

Credit line: Image available for free publishing from the Volkswirtschaftliches Institut, Universität Freiburg, Freiburg im Breisgau, Germany. Copyrighted free use

The Netflix Effect

Go Online: In recent times, perhaps one of the best cases of creative destruction is the Netflix Effect. You can find an article on the American Enterprise Institute website titled 'The "Netflix effect": An excellent example of "creative destruction"'. Many of the comments on the article discussing the Netflix effect are revealing – they call for government to 'do something' to stave or salve creative destruction. A link to this article can be found on the companion website for this book: www.edge.sagepub.com/strategy2e.

As consumers favour new technologies and products, some firms will prosper whereas others, locked into past and diminishing preferences, will die. Governments differ markedly in their propensity to do anything about these processes of destruction. Some, usually the more social democratic, have an active labour market policy, where they try to use training and investment schemes to absorb the employment shed by creative destruction. Others, usually on the more liberal democratic end of the spectrum, will leave restructuring entirely to 'market forces' – unless, of course, special interests can prevail, as they so often do in the case of marginal constituencies.

The key role in creative destruction is reserved for technological innovations that can outflank existing products, designs and processes. Over time these form a dominant paradigm within which processes of production become highly efficient and there seem to be few opportunities for radical innovation within the existing paradigm. These industries are most susceptible to creative destruction by incremental innovation, often from competitors elsewhere in the world who have been more attuned to improving the product that they are competing against.

For Schumpeter, innovation can produce any of the following: new production methods, new sources of supply, the creation of new products, the capitalization of new markets and organizing business in new ways. While these are all results of innovation the innovation process must include a cognitive content beforehand: 'each new product or process is the material expression and carrier of new forms of practical knowledge and new capabilities for action' (Lanzara, 2016: 13). Any innovation process will involve the transformation not only of artifacts but also practices and mentalities: people need to see things differently to see the value of different things.

When F.W. Taylor used simple devices, such as a stopwatch and a flowchart, to re-order the factory floor at the beginning of the twentieth century he not only introduced new practices but also transformed cognitive frameworks by introducing new divisions between conceptual and mechanical behaviour, making labour processes more mechanical. Later, of course, robotics did the job even more effectively. Taylor anticipated robotics by trying to eradicate any variation between people and their performance through rigid prescription of workstations and practices.

As the scientific management example provided by Taylor demonstrates, it is not so much material products or techniques alone that are innovated but whole systems of action and knowledge that become embedded in practice. As Lanzara suggests the artefacts and material objects that result from innovation involve change and recombination in 'ideas, social relations, behavioural rules, organizational routines, cognitive assumptions, meanings, learning modes, and even institutional arrangements and normative mechanisms', in ways that are often 'unpredictable and sometimes surprising' (Lanzara, 2016: 13).

Radical versus incremental innovation

Schumpeter's creative destruction defines the epitome of radical innovation. Innovations may be **radical** or **incremental**.

As we have seen in Chapter 2, Porter (1996) defines strategy as being different or doing different things. To be different means finding a set of activities, services or products that set you apart from your rivals: thus, innovation involves knowing either how to make different things or make things differently. Not all such difference is radical, however. When radically different products are introduced, such as streamed music services replacing CDs or CDs replacing vinyl records, then there are system-wide changes created by radical **product innovation**. Plus, there may also be radical **process innovation** at play; for example, with modern recording software every musician can now produce music from his or her bedroom without ever having to enter a costly sound studio.

> **Radical innovation** fundamentally changes what is being offered. **Incremental innovation** makes small or continuous improvements to an existing offering. Introducing difference is the key ingredient.

> While **product innovation** involves creating new things, **process innovation** means making the same product or offering the same service in a different way. Of course, the two are not independent but can be related.

Process innovation tends to be much more usual than product innovation. In part this is because once significant investments have been made in ways of doing things, they tend to stay on the same tracks. Otherwise sunk costs are liquidated, existing systems made redundant and well-honed competencies disabled.

If we think of the relation between process and product innovation as one dimension and the relation between radical and incremental innovation as another dimension there is a strong interaction effect between the two axes of innovation (see Figure 4.1)

Phillips and her colleagues (2006) argue that in 'the steady state' (when 'doing what we do, just better', is fine) good business practices establishing incremental innovation will lead to innovation. Such good practice includes establishing systematic processes for progressing new ideas, utilizing cross-functional teams, continuous learning cycles and good project management.

Good practices can lead to bad results when organizations become too locked in to past routines and their refinement, however. There is little point in incrementally improving a process that has been outflanked by a radical innovation. Once DVDs were invented any continuous improvements to tape-based video became largely irrelevant; a better product had been developed and introduced to the market. In turn, Netflix is making DVDs redundant. Any firms that stayed with the old technology would be faced with a rapidly shrinking market. This is a story repeated everywhere digital disruption happened: cameras and print-based film processing provide a good example. Kodak had become locked in to a model that depended on the sale and processing of film. The use of photographic film to produce negatives was undercut by the market that emerged with new digital cameras and smartphones, which did not need film. Book retailers have been decimated by Amazon, as have CD stores, although sales of books and CDs seem to be surviving well in venues that offer opportunities for second-hand and specialist products.

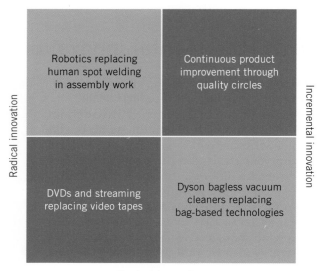

Figure 4.1   Axes of innovation

Source: Authors

Phillips et al. (2006: 181) argue that to avoid lock-in, organizations should adopt the following recommendations:

- High tolerance for ambiguity as rules only emerge over time

- Strategies need to be emergent and the organization needs to adapt and learn quickly

- The culture should support and encourage curiosity-driven behaviour

- Risk taking and tolerance of (fast) failures has to be high

- Developing weak ties and peripheral vision are important to seeing innovation opportunities.

Incremental product and process innovation work best where there is a well-established 'platform' which is not subject to radical innovation.

In addition to radical, incremental and disruptive innovation strategists also discuss architectural innovation. Architectural innovation does not refer to postmodern architecture such as Frank Gehry's designs (Naar and Clegg, 2015); rather architectural innovation changes the nature of interactions between core components, while reinforcing the core design concepts. It refines an existing platform. An architectural innovation modifies an overall system and/or the linkages between different components. For example, an electric vehicle is an architectural innovation because it refines the basic platform of the automobile and innovates a new market for vehicles. Based on distinctions between types of technology and types of market we can distinguish different types of innovation (see Figure 4.2).

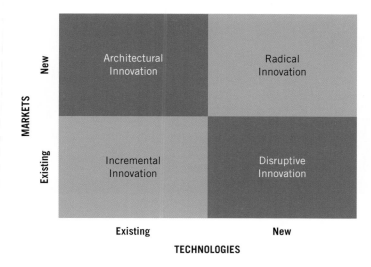

Figure 4.2   Types of innovation: Combining markets and technologies

Source: Authors

IN PRACTICE

How RØDE Microphones stays ahead of its competition

Go Online: Visit the book's website at https://edge.sagepub.com/strategy2e to watch an interview with Peter Freedman conducted by the author team.

Peter Freedman Interview

Peter Freedman is the Founder and Managing Director of RØDE Microphones (http://en.rode.com/). Peter founded RØDE in the early 1990s, creating a new market in high-quality microphones accessible to a mass audience. By creating an infrastructure for design and manufacture of microphones in Australia, RØDE has now become one of the world's largest microphone manufacturers and an internationally recognized name in studio, professional broadcast and consumer electronics.

Peter explains his approach to decision-making and managing RØDE to take the company from a small shop front to a diversified global company with a prestigious brand. Peter shares insights into the tools and strategies he uses to grow the company from the operation and manufacturing facilities based in Sydney, Australia. He describes how automation and new technologies are changing the business processes and reveals how he considers trends and the global business environment to imagine the future of the electronics industry and RØDE's leading position within it. He stresses the importance of a quality product and promoting the brand in target high growth markets. Finally, he describes his personal style to inspire others and provides advice to recent graduates.

(Continued)

(Continued)

Questions

1. What is the role of innovation in the microphone business?

2. What are the types of innovation you can identify when listening to Peter's account of his company's activities?

3. How does RØDE Microphones stay ahead of its competition?

4. What are some innovative technologies that RØDE Microphones is developing?

Innovation platforms

Cusumano and Gawer (2002) argue that strategic and successful firms do not simply develop new products and services and compete with others in open markets. Rather, leading firms establish a **platform** on which new products emerge.

> A **platform** is a base upon which other applications, processes or technologies can be developed. It is an evolving ecosystem that is created from many interconnected pieces.

A good example of a platform can be found in household appliances: consider vacuum cleaners, for instance. Vacuum cleaners have been around since 1908 when the first Hoover was invented (thus giving the product a generic name in its early life). Vacuum cleaners replaced carpet sweepers[1], by adding an electric motor and suction to their design. Basically, the platform of an electric powered dust-collecting device that is manually pushed across a surface has not changed although the product itself has seen much continuous improvement, notably with the introduction of the Dyson range of higher-powered machines without bags.

Automobiles are an example of another everyday product that has been subject to continuous process innovation on the basis of the same platform. Initially, the platform was literally, a platform – the chassis – on which the car was built. From the early 1960s the platform changed from the chassis to monocoque construction. Monocoque means 'single shell' in French and is a construction technique that utilizes the external skin to support some or most of the load, as opposed to using an internal frame or chassis that is then covered with cosmetic body panels. The chassis provided rigidity; in monocoque construction the structural members around the window and doorframes hold the construction rigid and are strengthened by folding the metal several times. In the UK the Triumph Herald platform in the 1960s provided the last chassis used in mass production of automobiles; this enabled Triumph to produce an attractive sports car on the Herald chassis. In this case, the innovation was possible because of a lack of innovation! Had Triumph switched the Herald design to Monocoque construction no chassis would have been available to cut down.

However, the enormous innovation that the automobile offered was mobility. Owning a car freed people from the external contingencies of bus and rail timetables

---

[1]These literally 'swept' the carpet so that any loose matter on it would be pushed by a rotating brush into a dustpan attached behind it, the whole device being mounted on rollers that allowed one to push it across a surface, using a long handle.

Image 4.2   Triumph Spitfire, innovated on the Triumph Herald chassis. Copyright: © neutralgrey1 - Fotolia.com

and the necessity of waiting or going only where the rail or bus routes took us. Cars gave their users freedom, a freedom that car manufacturers still promote heavily in their marketing today, even if the contemporary reality is one of congested traffic, slower speeds and longer journey times. Think of SUV marketing especially: invariably the vehicle is pictured racing though the outback, the countryside, a beach or an alpine scene with no other vehicles or people in sight. A dream of freedom is promoted; the reality of the daily commute, school run and shopping trips is very different however. Cars still have the fascination of cult objects – look at the BBC programme *Top Gear* – but the reality of their ownership rarely matches the mythmaking of the advertisers.

As well as requiring cultural legitimacy to become institutionalized, the car required a huge infrastructure to become useful: roads, highway networks, petrol stations, repair workshops, public licensing authorities, police, legal framework, insurance, and so on.

In the twentieth century, entire cities have been modelled to accommodate the car – Los Angeles is the most often-quoted example. In Los Angeles public transport rapid transit ideas were stymied for decades because of the entrenched power of the petroleum and related products lobby (Whitt, 1982). Thus, a platform producing innovation can lock in strategies to focus on process and incremental innovation – which is the story of the automobile.

Successful strategic innovation is more than just developing an idea; it needs the active shaping of a platform in which the idea can grow and create traction. The platform analogy is often used to describe the ecology of innovative business designs. Managers and organizations increasingly engage in innovation 'ecosystems', investing not only in research and development (R&D) but also in more intangible aspects, such as building social capital, creating and co-creating knowledge and its application and designing integrated systems to disseminate innovations. Iansiti and Levien (2004) suggest that 'a company's performance is increasingly dependent on the firm influencing assets outside its direct control'.

Tesla: Platform Innovation?

Digital platforms

It is not just the automobile that springs to mind as a ubiquitous platform; think of a new application for your iPhone or computer software as examples of complex new products that have to be able to communicate with existing technology. A good example of a platform leader is Microsoft Windows as its ubiquitous operating system forces friends and foes to engage with its technology (Cusumano and Gawer, 2002).

Today, the creation of digital platforms and cloud-based products is a main focus of innovation. The convergence of the computer with the Internet and the development of new communication technologies such as smartphones, tablets and related devices have expanded individual communicative capabilities massively. In consequence, individual behaviour, mundane communication modes, interpersonal relations and social coordination have all changed dramatically in recent years. The emergence of 'hooking-up' apps, the development of virtual markets for accommodation, taxis and dating for instance, have profoundly changed the ways that people live today, in comparison with past generations.

> Fitzgerald and colleagues (2013) define **digital transformation** as 'the use of new digital technologies (social media, mobile, data analytics or embedded devices) to enable *major business improvements* (such as enhancing customer experience, streamlining operations or creating new business models)'.

Digital platforms and cloud-based products can create a competitive advantage for an organization (Porter and Heppelmann, 2014). Digital technologies increasingly cause organizational and market disruptions through **digital transformation**.

Digital Strategy Podcast

Go Online: Digital strategy is now a standard part of strategy consulting. You can listen to how McKinsey sees such strategies developing in a podcast on the McKinsey website (www.mckinsey.com) titled 'Digital strategy: Understanding the economics of disruption'. A link to the podcast can be found on the companion website for this book at www.edge.sagepub.com/strategy2e.

A platform connects an ecosystem of third party applications where the organization that owns the platform does not own the third party applications that connect to the platform. The business model of companies such as Visa, Google, eBay, Amazon, Financial Times or Apple are examples of multi-sided digital platform strategies (Osterwalder and Pigneur, 2010).

John Chambers: Digitization

Go Online: According to Cisco Executive chairman John Chambers, 'If you're a leader in today's world, whether you're a government leader or a business leader, you have to focus on the fact that this (digitization) is the biggest technology transition ever'. You can read the full story in an article on the McKinsey website (www.mckinsey.com). A link to the article can also be found on the companion website for this book at www.edge.sagepub.com/strategy2e.

Tiwana and colleagues (2010) discuss platforms such as those created by Google as ecosystems that evolve in which 'the coevolution of the design, governance, and environmental dynamics of such ecosystems influences how they evolve.' They out-line six reasons why software platforms are both a challenge and an opportunity:

1. 'Competition is increasingly shifting toward platform-centric ecosystems (Katz and Shapiro, 1994)';

2. 'The conventional notion of firm boundaries is expanding to harness outside expertise and ingenuity on an unprecedented scale';

3. 'Technical architectures and organizing principles of these platforms jointly determine their evolutionary trajectories, which in turn influence platform differentiation';

4. 'Governing platforms requires a delicate balance of control by a platform owner and autonomy among independent developers';

5. 'Platforms do not exist in a vacuum, and how well or how poorly they respond to the dynamics of their environment can be influenced by platform designers' technical choices'; and

6. 'The IT artefact has historically tended to disappear from view, treated as a monolithic black box, or become the "omitted" variable (Orlikowski and Iacono, 2001)'.

Most platform strategies are controlled by a single organization. Increasingly, platforms are not static but evolve over time, with both the architecture of the platform and its governance coevolving. Traditional IT Architecture and IT Governance literature, such as Weill and Ross (2013) only focuses on managing IT within the boundary of the organization; in strategy terms we need an inter-organizational perspective to grasp complex platform ecosystems. Just think about Apple – what would its smartphone be without the many companies that develop apps for the device?

Platform Strategy

Innovators' dilemma and sources of discontinuity

Clayton Christensen (1997) focuses on how success in doing things well can create routines that block innovation, which he calls the **innovators' dilemma**.

> The **innovators' dilemma** describes companies whose successes and capabilities can become obstacles in the face of changing markets and technologies.

Most technologies are *sustaining technologies*, meaning that they improve the performance of existing products rather than replace them. Sustaining technologies do not produce innovation. Disruptive technologies, which change the frame of technology, are the key to innovation. Disruptive technologies may result in worse product performance (at least in the short term) for existing products.

Compared to established products, new disruptive technologies often perform at a lower level of perfection. For instance, top-end decks, tone arms and immaculate quality vinyl beat early CDs hands down for tonal warmth and resonance but CDs did not scratch as easily and were easier to use, played more music, and could be used in mobile settings such as automobiles, characteristics valued by markets. Of course, CDs have had their day in the sun: downloads and streaming now beat

CDs! (And once again, the quality of the reproduction has suffered.) The desktop computer was a disruptive technology relative to mainframe computers as was the tablet computer, such as the iPad, compared to desktop computers and laptops.

Established companies generally do not invest in disruptive technologies but keep on perfecting what they do well. Disruption often comes from the margins not the centre of an industry field. Innovation is often bought in from smaller start-up companies, which happens frequently in the bio-pharma sector, or innovative potential is 'spun off' into business units that can be faster and more flexible. Big companies with deep pockets try to buy in innovations and hope for success, something that happened in music in the early days of rock and roll in 1950s' America, when the major labels would buy out the contracts of artists that broke regionally on small labels; Elvis Presley was a case in point when RCA Victor bought him out of his Sun Records contract.

Disruptive innovation requires discontinuity of existing markets. Tidd and Bessant (2009: 32) discuss different sources of discontinuity and disruptive innovation. Most obvious are new markets – take the SMS industry that grew out of nowhere into a billion dollar industry with a profit margin of up to 90%. Originally, SMS was only added to mobile phones as a minor function. It was teenagers who first started using it to avoid the peak tariffs of mobile phone providers. Later services such as Twitter and WhatsApp evolved from this use.

Changing political rules and regulations or trade agreements can be another cause for disruption: take the example of the tobacco industry that has to adapt to a hostile environment that regulates prices, distribution, packaging and promotion as well as law suits from private groups. Finally, there are so called unthinkable events that can prompt discontinuous change: think of terrorist threats and attacks in the past years and the emerging security industry. Through terrorist attack, a whole new business sector has taken shape. Naomi Klein's (2007) book *The Shock Doctrine: The Rise of Disaster Capitalism*, critically scrutinizes this sector.

Business model innovation

New business models introduced by companies such as eBay, Amazon, Spotify, PayPal or Bitcoin are another important source of disruption. These can re-invent whole industries around new ways of creating revenues, serving specific needs or leveraging particular consumer behaviours. Although often used interchangeably with the term strategy, business models differ in that they are predominantly concerned with value creation while strategy itself is more concerned with competition (Magretta, 2002; Baden-Fuller and Morgan, 2010). The strategic analysis and creation of business models has been an important part of economic behaviour for a long time (Teece, 2010), yet the business models of the past have largely followed similar and often industry specific patterns of production, distribution, sales and revenue collection. Only in recent years have firms started to experiment with new models largely influenced and accelerated by the speed, scale and reach that the Internet and digitization provides.

Business models 'provide means to describe and classify businesses; operate as sites for scientific investigation; and act as recipes for creative managers' (Baden-Fuller and Morgan, 2010: 157).

> A **business model** is the complete system that firms use to create, deliver and capture value.

For example, McDonald's uses a very different business model to a high-end á la carte restaurant. The former creates and captures value by providing standardized low-cost products with a fast throughput of customers. The latter creates and captures value by providing specialized and individually designed dishes to discerning diners with low throughput.

Baden-Fuller and Morgan (2010) describe business models as either 'scale models' or 'role models' based on their purpose. The purpose of a 'scale model' is to provide a scaled-down copy of something to be analysed while a 'role model' provides an ideal version of something to be copied from (Baden-Fuller and Morgan, 2010).

From a strategic management perspective, the innovation of business models clearly serves the purpose of finding new or better recipes for doing business. The starting point for business model creation is usually a business idea, an invention, technological advancement and discovery of a market niche or any other knowledge that may promise successful commercialization. Creating a new business model means experimenting with the combination of factors that jointly do not yet exist in a given market context and that together present a unique way of gaining competitive advantage. The starting point of business model innovation can also be an existing business that for some reason has become or is in danger of becoming less viable. For example, this could be the case if competing products and services have taken away market share, due to increased global competition or changing access to key resources. The reasons why an existing business model might weaken are numerous. In any case, such a situation means that strategists can re-position the business or re-think how value can best be created and delivered.

The strategy and innovation methods, tools and techniques being used in either situation are largely the same and focus on examining why and how a business will be viable and valuable in the future. At the core of business model innovation is the simple question of how a business creates and captures value. Other important questions that are being considered include: Where are revenues coming from? What value is delivered to which markets? What costs are involved in delivering that value? Which key activities and key resources are important for gaining revenues?

Osterwalder and Pigneur (2010) state the main purpose of a business model as 'the rationale of how an organization creates, delivers and captures value'. Their framework is the Business Model Canvas (BMC) (see Figure 4.3), which is built up

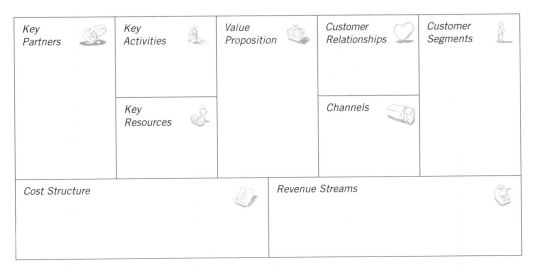

Figure 4.3   Business Model Canvas

Source: BusinessModelGeneration.com

of nine components that together offer a holistic view of a business model and provide a very useful tool to experiment and re-think the role and importance of each component.

As Osterwalder and Pigneur's (2010) BMC method is broadly applied, we outline the model in more detail:

1. A firm's detailed understanding and definition of the *customer segments* it is serving is instrumental for its survival and success.

2. A *value proposition* is the central component of the model and describes the output from the activity system for the customer. It is a bundle of products or services that create value either through price, performance, etc. or satisfaction, user friendliness, design, etc.

3. A *channel* describes the various means used to reach the customer with a value proposition and encompasses how an organization interacts with the customer for distribution, sales, marketing and other forms of communication.

4. *Customer relationships* are the types of relationships a company wants to build with its customers. Several different types of relationship may be present within one customer segment, ranging from personal to automated, self-service to dedicated assistance and individual to communities. Customer relationships can increase the number of customers through customer acquisition, keeping customers through customer retention or moving customers from one of the value propositions to another.

5. *Key resources* are the most important assets needed in order to support the business model; these can be human, intellectual, financial or physical assets, and they support, for example, the value proposition, keeping or building relationships with the selected customer segments and utilizing the channels in the best possible way. Key resources can either be owned by the company or leased or acquired through its strategic partners.

6. *Key activities* describe the most important activities the firm has to perform in order to fulfil the business model. These activities vary based on the kind of business model, but they should all support the other critical building blocks of the model. Examples of such activities may be supply chain management, problem solving, or management of a business platform.

7. *Key partners* are the most important partners in the value network. Partnerships are founded in order to create alliances, optimize the business model or to reduce risks.

8. *Revenue streams* describe how the firm can monetize its product offering and pay for its costs. Innovative business models find a new way to capture value from the value system.

9. *Cost structure* includes all the costs incurred by the business model, broadly distinguished as cost-driven business models – where all costs are minimized – or a value-driven business model – where costs are less important than increasing the value that is delivered to the customer.

The Business Model Canvas as a strategic business model innovation tool focuses on inventing or re-thinking the structure of the business model and business system, and less on the behaviour or dynamics of the market system. Osterwalder and Pigneur (2010) describe business models with similar characteristics, similar arrangements of business model building blocks, or similar behaviours, which they call patterns. The list of innovative business model patterns below is not exhaustive, assuming that new patterns emerge over time.

- *Unbundling*: A concept where corporations who often have different types of businesses within a single corporation can avoid undesirable trade-offs and conflicts by unbundling into separate entities. One example of this is telecommunications companies who divested their network operations either by outsourcing or spin-offs and started focusing on customers, branding and providing content.

- *The long tail*: A concept that was first described by Chris Anderson of *Wired* magazine in 2004, the long tail principle entails selling a small amount of each niche product but offering large amounts of niche products in the inventory, as opposed to only focusing on the bestsellers. Such a model is characterized by low inventory costs and platforms that can make a wide range of niche content available to consumers. An example of a long tail business model is the online self-publishing site lulu.com that allows niche authors and amateur writers to publish their work. The work can either be bought as an electronic version or as a print-on-demand copy. The website features thousands of authors, each selling very small volumes, but the total sales can still be high.

- *Multi-sided platforms*: This model creates value by bringing different customer groups together and facilitating interactions between them. One prominent example of this is Google, which provides consumers with a free online search engine and at the same time offers advertisers advertising space related to specific search terms. This model works best when the number of users is relatively high, given the domain and scope of the model.

- *Freemium*: A pattern where one customer segment benefits from a free-of-charge offer, often financed by other customer segments or other parts of the business model that charges for an up-scaled or premium version of the same offering (Osterwalder and Pigneur, 2010). An example here is Spotify (2011), an online streaming music service where consumers can listen to music for free but are occasionally interrupted by advertising. For added value, consumer can switch to a premium version that requires a monthly paid subscription. The free segment works as both a marketing channel for the premium product and as a revenue stream from advertising.

- *Open*: Open innovation, a term coined by Henry Chesbrough (2003), can be implemented in a business model by systematically collaborating with partners. This collaboration can either take the form of using idle ideas or assets from within the firm (inside–out) or by exploiting ideas from the outside (outside–in) (Osterwalder and Pigneur, 2010). This pattern has been employed by Proctor & Gamble to increase the R&D activities by opening up research and inviting in three innovation sources: researchers at universities, problem-solvers at online platforms and retirees of the company.

Business models are an important source for disruption and offer great potential for creating strategic competitive advantage especially in times of digitization and the ongoing technological advancements including the Internet of Things, robotics and artificial intelligence to just name a few.

Improvisation, trial and error

Kamoche and Cunha (2001: 96) define **organizational improvisation** as 'the conception of action as it unfolds, by an organization and/or its members, drawing on available material, cognitive, affective and social resources'.

Innovative organizations have an ability to practise **organizational improvisation**. Think of lock-in as a matter of sticking to routines and it is easy to see why organizations that encourage improvisation, practice trials on possible new ideas and tolerate error, are likely to have more strategic innovation potential than organizations that just keep on doing what they do, stuck in the grooves of past business models.

According to Rosabeth Moss Kanter (2002), successful and innovative firms do not wait until they have developed big strategic plans that try to second-guess every possible uncertainty the future might hold. Rather, agile companies improvise. Kanter (1992: 76) argues that firms need to act and experiment before they have a completely developed plan.

Firms, perhaps, should be more like a creative jazz group, such as Miles Davis' Quintet, rather than a well-polished orchestra following the score exactly and perfectly.

When Miles and the group recorded the famous album, *Kind of Blue*, he did not allow the musicians to rehearse beforehand but only create and improvise in the studio without any scores. In his own words:

> I didn't write out the music for *Kind of Blue*, but brought in sketches for what everyone was supposed to play because I wanted a lot of spontaneity in the playing, just like I thought was in the interplay between those dancers and those drummers and that finger piano player with the Ballet Africaine. Everything was first take, which indicates the level everyone was playing on. It was beautiful. (Davis with Troupe, 1989: 234)

Of course, the team that Miles Davis assembled was the *crème de la crème* of improvisational players. You wouldn't want to try this unless you were sure you had assembled an outstanding team – in jazz or any other pursuit. Great teamwork depends on great teams.

It is not just musicians like Miles Davis who can teach us a thing or two about strategic improvisation. One of the pioneers of strategic improvisation has been the Grateful Dead, the legendary rock band. Joshua Green (2010) notes how they pioneered ideas that are now par for the course in strategic management. Quoting the band's writer, John Perry Barlow, Green sees that The Grateful Dead, early on, had the emergent Internet economy figured before it existed:

> What people today are beginning to realise is what became obvious to us back then – the important correlation is the one between familiarity and value, not scarcity and value. Adam Smith taught that the scarcer you make something, the more valuable it becomes. In the physical world that works beautifully. But we couldn't regulate [taping] at our shows, and you can't online. The Internet doesn't behave that way. But here's the thing: if I give my song away to 20 people and they give it to 20 people, pretty soon everybody knows me, and my value as a creator is dramatically enhanced. That was the value proposition with the Dead. (Green, 2010: 2)

Strategic improvisation certainly worked for the Grateful Dead – they are widely recognized as creating one of the most loyal fan bases in the music industry. And they built this on the basis of a highly flexible business model: a band democracy that incorporated the whole crew, not just band members, with a revolving chair as well as making special efforts to reward loyal fans with good tickets. The band is often seen as throwbacks to 1960s hippie culture as well as the indulgent purveyors of long meandering guitar solos – but perhaps there are some lessons to be learnt from them. It is noteworthy that it is from music and musicians that business has learnt about strategic improvisation (see also Hill and Rifkin (2000) that also contains a chapter on the Dead).

Improvisation, as 'just in time strategy', as Weick (2001: 352) argues, is 'distinguished by less investment in front-end loading (try to anticipate everything that will happen or that you will need) and more investment in general knowledge, a large skill repertoire, the ability to do a quick study, trust in intuitions, and sophistication in cutting losses.' Such an improvisational approach to strategy making recognizes the need to act and react more quickly than traditional planning.

Because the world is complex and fast changing, the best way to engage in it is to deploy an incremental, step-by-step, or trial and error approach. Tidd and Bessant (2009) propose incremental design as a way of supplementing the problems of a traditional rationalist approach to innovation strategy. They suggest that small steps should be accompanied with frequent and quick feedback loops that constantly evaluate the innovative development of products, services and experiences.

The Japanese auto industry is a perfect case in point of a continuous and incremental effort in innovation. The Japanese auto industry evolved over the post-war years from a perception of Japanese cars as 'Jap Crap' (which they were widely regarded as being when they first entered new markets in the early 1960s) to the quality edge that manufacturers like Toyota, Honda or Nissan now enjoy in many of their global markets. The edge is based on many small incremental process innovations that came from different workplace practices – closer links between R&D and production workers – and a key concern for quality. While the Japanese companies copied European and US manufacturers, they also improved on their processes and products.

In the incremental approach to innovation, mistakes are seen as crucial learning opportunities. Rather than trying to avoid them, mistakes have to be made quickly and cheaply. Obviously, the incremental approach is not irrational: rather, facing a complex environment it can be seen as rational to abandon the Big Plan and substitute it with a more humble step-by-step approach, one that tolerates error and the occasional foolishness, to speak in March's (1976) terms.

EXTEND YOUR KNOWLEDGE

A journal article by M.J. Hatch titled **'Exploring the empty spaces of organizing: How improvisational jazz helps redescribe organizational structure'** discusses how businesses can learn from music. How organizational improvisation can be applied to teamwork is also discussed in Miguel Pina e Cunha and Joao Vieira da Cunha's journal article titled **'Managing improvisation in cross cultural virtual teams'**. Both articles can be read on the companion website for this book at www.edge.sagepub.com/strategy2e.

Hatch / Cunha & Cuhna

(Continued)

(Continued)

Hatch, M.J. (1999) 'Exploring the empty spaces of organizing: How improvisational jazz helps redescribe organizational structure', *Organization Studies*, 20: 75–100.

e Cunha, M.P. and da Cunha, J.V. (2008) 'Managing improvisation in cross cultural virtual teams', *International Journal of Cross Cultural Management*, 1(2): 187–208.

Service innovation

A focus on strategic service innovation is quite recent. Attention has shifted from goods to **services** as the subject of innovation and possibly subsequent competitive advantage (Normann, 2001).

Relatively 'few research articles focus on the strategic management of process innovations, administrative innovations and service innovations' (Keupp et al., 2012: 377). While the work of Gallouj and Weinsten (1997) can be considered an early attempt to explain service innovation theoretically, Tether (2005) outlines descriptive accounts of service innovation in the European Community and there are a small number of publications seeking to synthesize accounts of service and manufacturing innovation (Gallouj and Weinstein, 1997; Coombs and Miles, 2000; Drejer, 2004).

Services are 'the application of specialized competencies (knowledge and skills) through deeds, processes, and performances for the benefit of another entity or the entity itself' (Vargo and Lusch, 2004: 2).

In a service-centred view the role of firms is 'not to make and sell units of output but to provide customized services' (Vargo and Lusch, 2004: 13). For Vargo and Lusch the shift to an increasing component of service in the production and distribution of activities offered for profit in the market means that the Service-Dominant (S-D) logic is replacing the Goods-Dominant (G-D) logic. By defining a service as an interactive process of 'doing something for someone' that is valued, they suggest that goods ultimately are part of service and acquire what they call a 'value-in-use' that complements a more recent focus on service as co-creation (e.g. Bitner et al., 2008).

The central proposition is that all economic exchanges are service exchanges and, even when goods are involved, they are incidental or perhaps simply enablers of the exchange. Hence, S-D logic offers an integrated understanding of the purpose and nature of organizations, markets and society as primarily concerned with exchange of services. Service becomes the common denominator of exchange, where all firms are service providers and service receivers; in which markets focus on the exchange of service, with economies and societies becoming increasingly service based. As a result, a service-based logic should embrace the idea of the value-in-use and co-creation of value rather than the value-in-exchange and embedded-value concepts of traditional G-D logic. Vargo and Lusch (2008) see ten fundamental premises of the Service-Dominant logic:

1. Service is the fundamental basis of exchange.
2. Indirect exchange masks the fundamental basis of exchange.
3. Goods are a distribution mechanism for service provision.
4. Operant resources are the fundamental source of competitive advantage.

5. All economies are service economies.

6. The customer is always a co-creator of value.

7. The enterprise cannot deliver value, but only offer value propositions.

8. A service-centred view is inherently customer oriented and relational.

9. All social and economic actors are resource integrators.

10. The beneficiary always determines value.

Service, when nurtured effectively or as the focus of strategic innovation, can enable or support an organization in outperforming its rivals, an assumption commonly grounded in resource and capability related views (e.g. Wernerfelt, 1984; Barney, 1991; Teece et al., 1997). S-D logic has the ability to explain and unify the service role of interacting partners and boundary objects, such as goods being co-produced, and has already led to new ways of looking at strategic innovation in theoretical as well as practical terms.

Vargo and Lusch have rephrased their original proposition to read 'the customer is always a co-creator of value' (Vargo and Lusch, 2008: 1), a phrase repeated in almost every publication on S-D logic (Sánchez-Fernández et al., 2009; Sánchez-Fernández and Iniesta-Bonillo, 2007; Grönroos, 2008). Empirical evidence within the original article is distinctly lacking (Pels and Saren, 2006) and subsequent discussion has taken place on a conspicuously conceptual plane (Gummesson, 2006) so that overall empirical support for Service-Dominant logic is sparse (Blazevic and Lievens, 2008; Brodie et al., 2006).

Generally, in publications on S-D logic, innovative value creation seems to mean an all-encompassing process. The concept of resources in S-D logic has been shaped by the resource-based view (RBV) of the firm, seen by Vargo and Lusch (2008) as the backbone to their framework. The RBV has more recently begun to stress the importance of having dynamic capabilities that focus on innovation (see Chapter 3).

Innovation in the S-D framework occurs when value is created, a process through which the user becomes better off in some respect (Grönroos, 2008) or which increases the customer's well being (Vargo et al., 2008). Innovation as value creation has elsewhere been researched through the constructs of customer engagement, collaborative agility, entrepreneurial alertness and collaborative innovative capabilities (Agarwal and Selen, 2009).

IN PRACTICE

Gordon Ramsay's food factory

Did Gordon Ramsay get service innovation right? Imagine an established restaurant decided to tweak its business model. The existing core competencies of the business are preparing fresh meals and providing excellent service. Its platform is a celebrity chef and a network of *providores* who could be relied on for supplying high quality ingredients. Such service offering is clearly different to that of a classical fast food or home delivery

(Continued)

(Continued)

operations, which rely on standardization of routines, ingredients and simple menus. If a business wants to enter the market for delivery meals, it must focus on logistics, speed, and know-how about preparing meals that might sit for 30 minutes in a dish before being consumed. Such a business model requires different competencies from the chef, its suppliers and delivery staff. Trouble appears when two so different value propositions and related business models become mixed up – which is what happened to Gordon Ramsay.

As the *Sunday Telegraph* reported 'Gordon Ramsay is serving his pub customers ready-meals prepared in a London "food factory" – and sold with a mark-up of 586 per cent. Dishes are prepared in bulk and then transported in plastic bags by unmarked vans to several of his London restaurants ... The food factory is owned and operated by GR Logistics, the catering production arm of Ramsay's umbrella business, GR Holdings' (see www.dailytelegraph.com.au/news/ramsay-food-cooked-in-factory/story-e6freuy9-1225700066902, accessed 22 April 2016).

Questions

1. Why did Ramsay's innovation strategy fail? What could he have done better?
2. What changes would you make to the way the business is organized?
3. What would a Business Model Canvas for Ramsay's businesses look like?
4. How else could Ramsay leverage the value of his brand without threatening his core business?

Design-led innovation

Design, leading the innovation process, can help to entirely re-engineer products and services. For instance, Apple and earlier BlackBerry, transformed smartphones using design method to outdo products offered by rivals such as Nokia, which lacked the features that made the use of a smartphone intuitive.

In the academic discourse about strategy and innovation there has been increased advocacy for the role of design as an integral capability for strategic firm innovation and adaptation. 'Nobel' Laureate Herbert Simon suggested focusing on the processes that we deploy to *design* the artificial world in which we live: 'Engineering, medicine, business, architecture and painting are concerned not with the necessary but with the contingent – not with how things are but with how they might be – in short, with design' (Simon, 1969: xii). Quite literally, we design interfaces through which we interact with the world. What we see, how we see it, and how we can see things in an innovative way, depends on the design of our interfaces.

Based on these ideas, the management concept of design thinking developed (e.g. Boland and Collopy, 2004; Verganti, 2006; Beckman and Barry, 2007). Business schools all over the world have started to offer courses in design thinking. Even management gurus such as Tom Peters have discovered 'design' as a concept to rethink how companies craft strategies and innovate (Peters, 2005). The assumption behind taking a design-led approach is that companies can learn from creative design practices such as those of architect Frank Gehry (see Yoo et al., 2006).

So what can strategists and business innovators learn from what designers and design firms do? Design firms offer individual, customized products that are complex and not only solve a problem but often also provide an experience. Learning from the architectural design project with Frank Gehry for their new business school – the Weatherhead School of Management at Case Western Reserve University – Boland and Callopy (2004) introduced the notion of design attitude. It is characterized by a continuing search for alternatives. Here is what Boland and Callopy (2004) observed during the design process of their new school: the designers questioned what learning and teaching was, they wondered why academics worked in offices, and why the university was organized in schools and faculties. These disarmingly and ostensibly simple questions are, in reality, complex and deep – and design thinking is a way to deal with these fundamental questions.

What the majority of business schools taught in the past and most executives enact, is a decision attitude that focuses on making the right choices. Strategy, as Michael Porter (1996) reminds us, is about tough choices. It is about analysing the environment. It is about scrutinizing internal resources. But Porter spends little time on imagining possible futures. A design attitude to strategy and innovation does exactly that: it focuses on developing alternatives.

Design Thinking

Design thinking is a new way of combining innovation and strategy.

The promise behind design thinking is that designers routinely develop new ideas and innovate. Applying the principles of their thinking to management could yield a competitive advantage for organizations that fight the innovators' dilemma, which we discuss later in this chapter.

How does design thinking unfold? According to Brown (2008), it is less an orderly step-by-step process than a journey through three different spaces. First, one needs to understand the motivation for the search for a solution. Second, ideation collects ideas for the process of creating, developing and testing ideas; finally, in the implementation phase, the journey to markets is mapped out. Importantly, successful outcomes rely on a movement between these spaces, especially spaces one and two.

> Tim Brown defines **design thinking** as innovation that is 'powered by a thorough understanding, through direct observation, of what people want and need in their lives and what they like or dislike about the way particular products are made, packaged, marketed, sold, and supported' (Brown, 2008: 86).

Go Online: In a delightful TED Talk Tim Brown explores how and why designers can think big. A link to the talk can be found on the companion website for this book: www.edge.sagepub.com/strategy 2e.

**Tim Brown
TED Talk**

Brown (2008) explains how the bicycle component producer Shimano developed a new strategy through design thinking. While sales in the US were declining, Shimano needed to develop a new strategy to increase its business. IDEO applied the principles of design thinking to solve the problem. First, IDEO researchers went out and asked the 90% of people in the US who do not ride a bike what kept them from doing so. Interestingly, most of them had very happy childhood memories of riding bikes but felt uncomfortable buying a bike in a store where only professionals who paid a lot of money seemed to go, where they had to deal with a complicated set-up and endanger their physical safety on the streets.

These insights into motivations came from outside of Shimano's core customer base (the 10% committed bicyclists) and allowed them to re-imagine a new bicycling experience – an experience IDEO labelled 'coasting'. Coasting is done on very simple bikes, with no cables, a back-pedalling brake, and a mini-computer that automatically chooses the best of the three built-in gears. The bike would be comfortable, easy to ride, and low in maintenance. But IDEO went further than that: they also developed a retail strategy and re-invented the consumer experience as non-threatening and fun. Together with local governments, they picked safe places to ride and launched a PR campaign for bike riding. The secret to success, according to Tim Brown, is a human-centred approach to innovation that focuses on the needs of people.

IN PRACTICE[2]

Climate Adapted People Shelter (CAPS)

A competition was developed which asked participants to create an open innovation human-centred design model to develop a new blueprint for eight bus shelters across four municipal council areas. The projection is that by 2031 Sydney Bus customers will make more than 1.3 million journeys per day according to 2013 NSW government estimates. A key motivation for the new shelter design is the effects of heat within the existing shelters. At 32.2 degrees Celsius, the ground surface temperature within the bus shelter itself measures 113.1 degrees Celsius, as the shelter operates as an intense heat island, making it unsuitable for more vulnerable clientele such as the infirm and young children. The usual focus for bus shelter design is utilitarian, focusing on the placement of advertising, some safety considerations and the basic operational needs of transport authorities. The brief for this project identified that the proposed design must meet the criterion of being: Desirable, Smart, Adaptable and Valuable. The research agenda motivating the competition is a focus on resilience, digitization and co-creation with a view to the current project informing future urban design processes and inclusive design practices.

In the current project all of the relevant stakeholders are being consulted and all proposal ideas are being tested with users of the bus shelters as well as experts such as council employees, who are responsible for ongoing maintenance, installation and design components of the existing bus shelters. Contestants are also encouraged to capture the feedback from stakeholders in a variety of formats as evidence-based stakeholder feedback. Finally prototype models will be built and the competitors will present their ideas to the judging panel.

Questions

1. Where else might smart design principles be applied in public infrastructure projects?

---

[2]Written by Daphne Freeder and Lee Wallace, UTS.

2. What are the areas in this example where competing stakeholder interests might require compromise? How would you achieve this with a focus on human centred design?

3. How do you avoid stereotyping of the clientele of bus shelters?

Framing innovation

Kees Dorst (2015) provides a further development of design thinking. In his book, *Frame Innovation*, he argues that when organizations apply old methods of problem solving to new kinds of problems, they usually accomplish only temporary fixes or some ineffectual tinkering around the edges. Today, organizations confront highly complex and interconnected problems – think of the challenge of climate change and the need for political, business and civil responses to the complex set of interrelated questions about how to manage the transition from a carbon to a carbon neutral operating environment – and these types of problems require a radically different response.

What characterize these new types of problems are that they are:

1. *Open* – it is difficult to put a boundary around them.

2. *Complex* – problems that cannot be solved in little pieces and then put back together because there are so many elements and relationships between parts of a problem that it must be tackled as a whole.

3. *Dynamic* – things are always changing and you have to get used to continuous and rapidly evolving dynamics.

4. *Networked* – because there are so many stakeholders involved in every issue, solutions have to be networked and stakeholders managed.

Dorst describes a new, innovation-centred approach to problem solving in organizations, which he calls frame creation. It applies design thinking not to generate solutions but to create new approaches to the problem situation itself.

The strategies Dorst presents are drawn from the unique, sophisticated, multi-layered practices of top designers, and from insights that have emerged from 50 years of design research. Dorst describes nine steps in the frame creation process and illustrates their application to real-world problems with a series of varied case studies. He maps innovative solutions that include rethinking a store layout so retail spaces encourage purchasing rather than stealing, applying the frame of a music festival to understand late-night problems of crime and congestion in a club district, and creative ways to attract young employees to a temporary staffing agency.

Frame Innovation is made up of a nine-step process that consists of asking questions:

1. *Archaeology of the problem*: Why is this a problem? Why has it not been solved? How did it become a problem? Who is the problem owner?

2. *Paradox*: What makes this problem hard to solve? Why is this a hard one? What is it that is really the issue?

3. *Stakeholders*: Who are the stakeholders? What are the stakeholders' values, motives, desires?

4. *Problem Arena*: What is the broad problem space, including which different parties, places, products services and externalities that could be interested and interdependent?

5. *Themes*: What are the main themes that emerge from the problem area?

6. *Frames*: What are the various ways in which the problem is being framed? Can we frame it differently so that we redefine the nature of the problem?

7. *Futures*: What are the future potential solutions and future scenarios for problem resolution?

8. *Transformations*: What needs to be changed for the solution to be implemented?

9. *Connections*: How can the solution be connected to the rest of the world?

Dorst provides tools and methods for implementing frame creation, offering not so much a how-to manual as a do-it-yourself handbook – a guide that will help practitioners develop their own approaches to problem-solving and creating innovation.

Design science

Building on design thinking is a design perspective that focuses on the interaction of theory and practice in design (Romme, 2003; Romme and Endenburg, 2006). Organization theorist Deborah Dougherty, an innovation specialist (see Dougherty, 2006) has developed a 'design science' framework from earlier work by Herbert Simon.

Augier &
Sarasvathy

EXTEND YOUR KNOWLEDGE

You can read a journal article by Mie Augier and Saras D. Sarasvathy titled **'Integrating evolution, cognition and design: Extending Simonian perspectives to strategic organization'** on the companion website for this book: www.edge.sagepub.com/strategy2e.

Augier, M. and Sarasvathy, S.D. (2004) 'Integrating evolution, cognition and design: Extending Simonian perspectives to strategic organization', *Strategic Organization*, 2(2): 169–204.

Dougherty identifies three properties of a large and complex innovative organization: fluidity, integrity and energy.

1. *Fluidity*, according to Dougherty, refers to ongoing, dynamic adaptations in product teams, amongst businesses, and within and across technologies and other capabilities. Fluid organizations will be more loosely rather than tightly coupled. They need to be because, as Danneels (2002) shows, innovations not only draw on but also develop existing organization competencies. New technologies open up previously unthought options; changes in customer expectations privilege different aspects of performance. Innovations must open up prior decisions and routines, must make issues out of what were previously non-issues, if organizations are to realize value. As Dougherty (2006) stresses, an innovative organization is not a bureaucratic organization.

2. *Integrity* means that an organization prizes integration both as a principle structuring thought and action and as an outcome of that thought and action. Product innovation integrates functions because capabilities in technology, manufacturing, marketing, sales, IT (and so on) need to be aligned if innovation is to be organizationally diffused in its effects. Silos restrict alignment, confining innovations to segments. Dougherty (2008: 419) notes Clark and Fujimoto's (1991) argument that firms compete on the 'consistency between the structure and function of the product (i.e. parts fit well, components work well together) and how well a product's function, structure, and semantics fit the customer's objectives, values, production system, and use pattern'.

3. *Energy* means that innovative organizations need continually to energize, enable and motivate people (Amabile and Conti, 1999). Energy is built from power resources, such as information, credibility and alliances (Kanter, 1988), and meaning making (Dougherty and Hardy, 1996). Innovating workers are autonomous workers; not under strict command and control (Damanpour, 1991) and have the opportunity to participate in strategic conversations (Westley, 1990) that energize the organization. Innovation means anticipating problems and constraints and adapting specialized knowledge to those problems that occur *in situ* – not just those that can be solved in theory.

These three core concepts can be thought of in terms of how they relate to both *constraining* and *enabling* factors.

Constraining and enabling innovation

Helping companies to become more strategic and innovative means drawing on rather distinct organizational design principles. For it to occur, companies require governance that both constrains and enables simultaneously.

Strategic innovation is risky and often costly, thus it should be kept separate from more routine activities. As a result, it is often carried out in new project-based organizations. Innovation can also be constrained by the well-known effects of bounded rationality (Simon, 1972), which we discuss in Chapter 5. In addition, a great deal of organizational change occurs at the population level – that is when new entrants come in and change the definition of a field, such as Apple and iTunes did with respect of music consumption – rather than intra-organizationally from amongst firms in the existing field. So much of what organizations do is institutionalized – and to change what is institutionalized threatens legitimacy.

The constraints perspective on innovation is drawn from a specific set of theories, as is the enabling perspective. The constraints approach derives from more structural, functional accounts of organizations while the enabling approach comes from theories that stress the processual nature of organizational life far more than structures that constrain. Organizational designs for innovation should draw on both enabling and constraining perspectives on organizational design. To achieve fluidity, work should be defined and enacted as professional practices of innovation, where the constraints of situated, hands-on practice help to keep people knowledgeable and build stable competencies from which change can evolve. From the enabling perspective we should realize that it is practices that drive behaviour, so the search should always be for better practices. Deborah Dougherty follows up much of the above in more detail in Clegg et al.'s (2006) *The SAGE Handbook of Organization Studies* (Dougherty, 2006).

**Deborah
Dougherty**

EXTEND YOUR KNOWLEDGE

You can read a journal article by Deborah Dougherty titled **'Bridging social constraint and social action to design organizations for innovation'** on the companion website for this book: www.edge.sagepub.com/strategy2e.

Dougherty, D. (2008) 'Bridging social constraint and social action to design organizations for innovation', *Organization Studies*, 29(3): 415–434.

Enabling factors for organizations: Emergence and minimal structuring, minimizing bureaucracy, characterize enabling organizations. Coordination occurs not through detailed rules and prescriptions but through shared practices with which staff can identify and with which they can interact. Projects, where teams dissolve and regroup, are the dominant form for innovation. These enable project management tournaments to be conducted from which the next generation of senior executives can be recruited due to their success in managing the innovation field of battle.

Constraining factors for organizations: These include managers' beliefs that people are intrinsically lazy and opportunistic, keen to transact with guile, as economic theory puts it, as we elaborate in Chapter 5. To the extent that managers believe this and create tight control structures around people and actions then it becomes a self-fulfilling prophecy and will certainly not encourage innovation. In such situations, a structural solution is usually to try to change cultures, promote creativity, reward people for suggestions and innovation and try to recruit innovative-oriented personalities. Focusing less on constraints and more on enabling factors leads to an emphasis on culture in terms of cultural practices that are embedded in everyday organizational life so that people's creativity can be tapped by making workplaces playful, social and enjoyable. Populating them with playful devices, such as game tables, building blocks and drawing materials and structuring play time into work processes (Roos and Victor, 1999; Schrage, 2000) encourages innovation not as a solitary pursuit but a team sport.

Large versus small firm innovation

Some people argue that innovation is more likely to emerge from large corporate organizations; others suggest that most innovative ideas come from small or start-up businesses. The answer is that both can be cradles of innovation – but they do it differently.

Large organizations are able to build vast R&D capacities through the resources they command. Think of the huge laboratories maintained by big pharmaceutical companies. However, such organizations can be notably risk-averse, especially where radical innovation is concerned. Also, they operate in regulatory environments that militate against risk-taking: pharmaceutical product innovation has to undergo years of clinical testing before regulatory authorities can approve it. One way that large well-resourced organizations can innovate is by buying it in; they can simply take over innovative new and small firms in a merger or acquisition and thus incorporate innovations into their product line-up and innovators into their organizations. They have the resources to be constantly environment scanning for opportunities for acquisition or imitation.

The argument for small firm and start-up innovation is simple: small, new knowledge-based technology firms will be better able to take risks, which innovation always entails. Innovation is often easier to manage outside rather than inside established firms. As Pfeffer argues,

> innovation and change in organizations requires more than the ability to solve technical or analytical problems. Innovation almost invariably threatens the status quo, and consequently, innovation is an inherently political activity. (Pfeffer, 1992: 7)

Porter (1996) suggested that innovation means doing things differently or doing different things, implying breaking with the past, with established routines, and old habits which, of course, will rock the boat – and after a course is regained those who were at the helm might no longer be in charge. Hence, innovation is inherently political; it is even more overtly political in established firms than new ones, because there are more vested interests at stake.

Those organizations that most empower their members will tend to be the most energized. Usually they do this through equal rights to returns on innovation through co-ownership or through collective democracy in decision-making (if the organization is small enough for direct democracy to work – usually no more than a handful of people) or through profit-sharing bonus schemes.

Small firms are often closer to their customers as they have to work harder to know them and provide what they want. Customers, along with suppliers and competitors can be the most important sources of learning for innovation. Close relations with customers, as end-users, can lower innovation risks, especially in service innovation. This is especially the case in services firms; services are meant to solve clients' problems, meaning that the service provider has to develop a deep understanding of the client's organization and align its own capabilities to match the current and future problems of the client. While a company such as Apple can choose suppliers for innovative products, a services firm cannot simply decide to offer new solutions. It has to develop internal capabilities, its knowledge base and practices that support learning, especially from customers, as well as engage in environmental scanning for opportunities.

EXTEND YOUR KNOWLEDGE

- -

You can find another journal article by Deborah Dougherty titled **'Organizing practices in services: Capturing practice-based knowledge for innovation'** on the companion website for this book: www.edge.sagepub.com/strategy2e.

Dougherty, D. (2004) 'Organizing practices in services: Capturing practice-based knowledge for innovation', *Strategic Organization*, 2(1): 35–64.

Deborah Dougherty

Ambidextrous organizations

A key strategic issue is how can a firm be successful in the present, and prepare for the future? By being **ambidextrous organizations**, say Tushman and O'Reilly (1996), something that is achieved through growing many small, autonomous units instead of one large organization. These smaller, independent units are more agile and entrepreneurial than the parent company. Managers must create new business units to enable innovation so as not to distract existing managers and units (Christensen, 1997).

> **Ambidextrous organizations** create specialist subunits with unique processes, structures and cultures that are specifically intended to support early stage innovation, comprised of one or more innovation teams *within* the larger parent organization. They are set up to support those unique approaches, activities and behaviours required when launching a new business or product.

The ambidextrous organization characterizes an entity that is capable of simultaneous incremental *and* revolutionary innovation. Successful organizations are obviously good at what they do – so good indeed, that they do not want to change. Success, it seems, breeds failure: the more successful an organization is, the more it adapts to its markets, the more it aligns internal process, the better its strategic fit with its environments, the harder it will be to change and innovate. Success in the short term can breed failure in the long term.

Tushman and O'Reilly (1996: 18) explain that as

> companies grow they develop systems and structures to handle the increased complexity of the work. These structures and systems are interlinked so that proposed changes become more difficult, more costly and require more time to implement.

For managers, the dynamics of innovation represent a huge strategic challenge. While they must increase alignment and fit for short-term survival, they need periodically to destroy what has been created (Tushman and O'Reilly, 1996).

General Motors (GM), for a long time the biggest company in the world, was good at building big cars but was not ambidextrous – it did not build great small cars. When markets changed and it was making more money out of financing the purchase of its cars rather than building and selling them, it was impossible to change the systems and structures fast enough to catch up with new trends for smaller cars. The collapse of the credit market in 2007 in the Global Financial Crisis saw GM, once the proud flagship of American manufacturing, filing for Chapter 11 to emerge from bankruptcy.

Whole industries can lack ambidextrousness but innovation can recover it. Take the Swiss watch industry: it dominated the market for mechanical timepieces but was not immediately able to adjust to the challenges of the new quartz watches that were developed from the mid-1960s onwards until it developed the cheap, disposable and fashionable Swatch watches that won market share by the quality of design and the economy of production, offering watches that were attractive, fashionable, youthful and fun, as well as high quality. Innovative product design reduced production costs: synthetic materials and new technology greatly reduced the number of components.

Backed by the Swiss watch industry and with guarantees, sold in specialist Swatch boutiques and displays, Swatches became a cult item, with clear product differentiation in the lines offered, such as Swatch irony – for the metal cased watches – and Swatch Bijoux – a female-oriented jewellery line. To maintain youth appeal Swatch promote and support sports such as snowboarding and beach volleyball, as official timepieces. And as Theswisscenter's Blog tells us, of 112 Swiss companies, Swatch comes top of the reputational list.

Meanwhile, the traditional Swiss watch industry repositioned itself as a luxury market, selling very expensive timepieces, as potential heirloom and legacy pieces (You never really own a Patek Phillipe but just look after it for the next generation), as expensive gifts, as badges of wealth and subtle signs of success. Pick up any magazine with watch advertisements in it and check out the famous sportsmen and women and actors promoting the products. The adverts are almost identical to the handbag advertisements that often feature in the same edition of *Vogue* or *Marie Claire*. Things that are not usually foregrounded, such as a handbag or a watch, are positioned as the chief figure with the ground being a recognizable celebrity or beautiful model 'wearing' the design.

Velocity and start-up environments

Innovation needs capital; investment is necessary to get an idea commercialized as a start-up company. But how are entrepreneurs to access this investment capital or seed funding? Banks are notoriously conservative.

One route from innovation to start up is to capture network resources. Innovation Bay is a typical venture that seeks to bring together entrepreneurs, investors and business people. Innovation Bay was created in 2003 as an opportunity for capital and creativity to combine. It seeks to enable 'business angels' – potential investors – to meet with innovators and potential entrepreneurs. The networking group holds dinners, breakfasts and other social events at which these different elements of strategic innovation can meet and mingle. Over 300 tech start-ups have raised more than $10 million in

Innovation Bay

seed capital after presenting at these events. Such initiatives are replicated globally in various locales. As well as a chequebook, innovations such as these offer opportunities for mentoring and coaching, creating a focused innovation ecosystem. There is a competitive element to the events that are held; not every proposal makes it to the main event, as the number of innovations being curated is limited to five.

> A **high-velocity environment** is characterized by 'rapid, discontinuous and simultaneous change in demand, competitors, technology and regulation' (Wirtz et al., 2007: 297).

Small firms that are new start-ups based on a radically discontinuous idea are more likely to emerge in what Eisenhardt and Martin (2000) and Wirtz and his colleagues (2007) have described as 'high-velocity environments'.

In a high-velocity environment, innovative strategy requires a continuous process of being alert. Mintzberg (1989: 210) has observed that

> [b]ecause the innovative organization must respond continuously to a complex, unpredictable environment, it cannot rely on deliberate strategy. In other words, it cannot predetermine precise patterns in its activities and then impose them on its work through some kind of formal planning process.

Companies cannot simply rely on planning years ahead: they need experimentation to stay abreast of innovation.

Innovation environments

Institutional entrepreneurs not only play the role of traditional entrepreneurs but also help establish new (and sometimes challenge old) institutions in the process of their activities. They do so by leveraging resources to create new institutions or to transform existing ones (Maguire et al., 2004: 657).

It is sometimes suggested that it is foolish to copy if you want to innovate: the two processes seem counterintuitive to each other. However, in the literature of institutional theory the translation of one practice into another new one that creates a new *field* of enterprise – the whole infrastructure supporting a pattern of organizational activity such as suppliers, consumers, regulators and competitors – is sometimes termed institutional entrepreneurship.

All organizations and their strategies occur within the context of an institutional field. Different institutional fields are bounded by different conceptions of what is normatively ordered and allowed. Organizations' institutional environments are 'characterized by the elaboration of rules and requirements to which individual organizations must conform if they are to receive support and legitimacy' (Scott, 1996: 132).

For Schumpeter (1942), entrepreneurship creates new market opportunities when gales of creative destruction transform economies and societies. To be successful, entrepreneurial efforts have to gain legitimacy if change is to be accepted: thus, entrepreneurs not only need to innovate new things, new goods and new services but sometimes they must also innovate new institutions.

Clusters as a vehicle for innovation

For Porter (1990), a key question is why do some companies achieve consistent improvement by innovating increasingly sophisticated sources of competitive advantage? The answer, he suggests, is to be found in four attributes that effect industries. These are as follows.

1. Factor conditions: the sum and quality of human capital and infrastructure that is capable of enabling a competitive position.

2. Demand conditions: the nature of home market demand – robust home market demand and completion hones international competitive advantage.

3. Related and supporting industry conditions: the density of supplier and related industries.

4. Conditions of firm strategy, structure and rivalry: the national conditions enabling companies to form, grow and diversify.

Clusters are geographical agglomerations of firms in particular, related, and/or complementary, activities, sharing a common vision, and exhibiting horizontal, vertical intra- and/or inter-sectoral linkages, embedded in a supportive socio-institutional setting, and cooperating and competing in national and inter-national markets (Pitelis, 2012: 1361).

According to Porter's theory, firms flourish best in clusters because networks and density create complexity.

Clustering of organizations and people creates more experts and more expertise, a range of more complex approaches to any problem, in close proximity with each other. Agglomeration creates external economies from co-location, concentrating skilled human resources in a region, socially embedding managers and employees in an organizational field. Creating a common organizational field that shares common frames of reference builds trust, reducing transaction costs, creating enhanced opportunities for collaboration and innovation. More complex and sophisticated knowledge can be generated in clusters as an emergent property of interaction, as discussions of the distributed nature of knowledge and the challenges it poses for organizational work indicate (e.g., Orlikowski, 2002).

At the sub-national level, where clusters form in sectorial systems of innovation, organizations belonging to a particular sector engage in innovation through collaborative networks. Regional systems focus on territorial-based innovation systems that seek to ensure the success of specific clusters and industrial districts. Think of Silicon Valley and its digital ecology, or the British Midlands as home to the so-called Motorsport Valley, where many Formula 1 teams and crucial suppliers have development facilities. Such clusters are critical for innovation as they enable learning processes that transcend the capabilities of an isolated firm. Learning usually occurs in regional clusters as a consequence of product development, as in the cases noted.

Regionally clustered innovation systems need not necessarily be hi-tech. Think of the regional systems of innovation that embed furniture design in Northern Italy and outsourcing in Bangalore in India. Bessant et al. (2003) provide another example of a regional innovation system that was not hi-tech. *Saligna* is a species of eucalyptus hardwood that was traditionally used for mining in South Africa that has been re-discovered as an environmentally sustainable raw material for the furniture industry. But in order to realize this opportunity, the whole value chain of the industry needed to learn and innovate. For instance, *saligna* was different to work with and firms had to adapt their operations; furniture production requires consistent quality which means the raw materials have to be improved; new designs that were suitable to *salinga* wood needed to be developed and, finally, new markets from furniture to doors, industrial products, and toys emerged with the new material and competencies (Bessant et al., 2003: 26).

Clusters often enable innovation networks that are regionally situated. Birkinshaw et al. (2007) argue that innovation networks evolve through three steps of *finding*, *forming* and *performing*. An initial challenge that firms face is choosing the right partner (finding) and learning how to work with them (forming). Performing, the third step, follows if one and two have been completed successfully. Birkinshaw et al. (2007) remind us that finding the right partner organization can be as complicated as finding the right partner for life; similarly, it is often easier to search locally when considering where to look for the right partner, how to limit the search and how to conduct due diligence without estranging potential partners. Forming also provides challenges, including how to build relationships, how open your partner might be, how willing to share, risk and explore. Key for the performance of the innovation network are the engagement of partners, trust and reciprocity across the network, a good understanding of one's own position with the network (as opposed to attempting to control it) and, finally, learning when to let go and set your partners (and yourself) free.

Regional innovation systems foster learning networks (Bessant and Tsekouras, 2001) in which organizations conjointly and connectedly learn in a cyclical and social process of experimenting, experiencing, reflecting and conceptualizing. Bessant and Tsekouras (2001: 87) see the advantages of shared learning to be learning and reflecting from different perspectives; shared experimentation at reduced cost; shared experience for more holistic understanding and challenging of business-as-usual approaches through confrontation with other models and ways of doing things.

National innovation systems

> **National innovation systems** are composed of different patterns of institutions and organizational relationships (Coriat and Weinstein, 2002).

The likelihood of innovation emerging increases when there is an appropriate **national innovation system** in place.

Some nations are undoubtedly more innovative than others: the United States and Israel are usually measured as the most innovative. Innovation is inherently difficult to quantify and measure. There are indicators such as the European Community Innovation Survey (ECIS) that measure innovation inputs and outputs and produce national measures that have some degree of international comparability. Major indicators of innovation are usually constructed from data on R&D, patent applications and grants, scientific publications and citations (bibliometric data) and technical performance characteristics (technometric data) as well as input expenditure (Green et al., 2015). These measures are biased towards tangible product innovation. Less tangible elements that might be measured include knowledge management, innovation strategy, organizational culture, portfolio management, project management and commercialization.

The classic comparative text on national innovation systems is Nelson's (1993) edited compilation on *National Innovation Systems: A Comparative Analysis*. As he makes clear, the components of a national innovation system are institutional relations between government, business and research in universities, which can vary from country to country. It is the specific configuration of relations and institutions that are important in framing the national innovation system. What matters are institutions.

- The legal system (especially concerning the ownership and control of intellectual property relations)

- National education and training systems

- Industry structure of competitor, supplier and surrounding organizations

- Efficient capital markets providing venture capital for innovation

- National innovation policies related to science and technology

- Universities and research centres

- Policies related to investments, taxation and other determinants of the 'rules of the game' that shape both public and private sector decision-making (Nelson, 2005; OECD, 1997).

Innovation Websites

Go Online: There are many useful national innovation systems resources available. One of these is the *Australian National Innovation and Science Agenda* website which has a host of innovation resources on it that you can open from downloadable PDFs. Other resources are the *Innovation Tools* website which also has a great many resources, and the *Innovation Exchange* website, where creativity is the currency. Links to all sites can be found on the companion website for this book at www.edge.sagepub.com/strategy2e.

A recent enquiry into a specific national innovation system (in fact, Australia's) is particularly useful in understanding the elements of a functioning system. A number of innovation drivers are identified that are quite generic. What business innovation needs in a national innovation system are the following:

1. Stable, coherent and effective administrative arrangements, a long-term time horizon and a budgeting and resource allocation system that is fit for purpose, investing at least 3% of GDP in science, technology and R&D.

2. Innovation system leadership and coordination through a peak body for science, technology and innovation policy, which engages with key stakeholders to undertake policy foresights, set priorities and develop early responses to challenges and opportunities.

3. Strategic approaches to building innovation capability through improved agility and participation in global value chains, commitment to management capability building and greater collaboration with the research sector.

4. Long-term, predictable and secure funding to support science, research and innovation in alignment with national priorities, as well as research training, researcher mobility and national and landmark research infrastructure.

5. Local and regional innovation ecosystems, as a catalyst and enabler for industry development and transformation through entrepreneurial start-up activities, business and research networks and supportive policies and infrastructure.

6. Tertiary education institutions that are positioned to educate and train future entrepreneurs, employees and managers.

Go Online: Many of these ideas made their way into a 2015 National Innovation policy statement in Australia. Observers and researchers of innovation have welcomed them, but not uncritically. Mark Dodgson makes the important point that 'We mistakenly persevere with the major government support for innovation being directed towards the subsidy of R&D in individual firms, rather than the support for innovation in networks'. You can read in his article titled 'The government's focus on innovation is too narrow' on *The Conversation* website, which you can also access via the companion website for this book: www.edge.sagepub.com/strategy2e.

Mark Dodgson Article

The co-creation of value

The fundamental premise of traditional firm strategizing is that the firm is the locus of active production; what happens outside is passive consumption. Creativity and innovation happen inside the firm, while consumers use products and services. In short, value creation was company-centric. Times are changing, as Prahalad and Ramaswamy (2004) caught on to early. Let's look at a practical example of what we mean.

Essena O'Neill

IN PRACTICE

You don't always want what you get

Essena O'Neill achieved Instafame with more than 500,000 followers on the photo-sharing site Instagram, 250,000 YouTube fans and 60,000 Snapchat followers. She had companies paying her to wear their products. She was a fashion influencer. Then she made a video renouncing the hypocrisy and fakery of her online life. As the *Sydney Morning Herald* (8 November 2015) stated she confirmed what most of us know:

> Most know the world of social media is dubious and that brands have been increasingly willing to pay bloggers and social media celebrities to promote their products. Most social media users surely have a sense that the fabulous lives and bodies of 'influencers' are crafted and curated in some way. Why not? Anyone with a social media account does the same. Very few post their most unflattering photo or write at length about their failures. But we factor some fakery into the medium the way we do with reality TV. We know the contestants are carefully chosen and put in contrived conditions but we accept a level of artifice for our entertainment.

Questions

1. Considering innovations such as Instagram, in what ways have they changed the ways in which fashion can be strategically marketed?

2. In practice, what do you take to be the strengths of the new social media as an innovative vehicle for promotional strategies?

3. What factors would make you trust a social media site?

On the racks (http://www.ontheracks.com/) is an example of a fashion blogger co-creating value. It is not only fashionistas that are able to co-create, however. Increasingly, innovation occurs through the co-creation of value with consumers.

- Consumers are more connected than before; interest groups, communities and other social groupings connect users with each other globally. Social networking sites such as Facebook are a good example of this shift.

- Consumers are more informed; higher connectivity means that information travels faster, with more information being accessible to more people. If you want to find out about anything you go online and find literally hundreds of communities where you can read honest discussions about the pros and cons of your objects of desire or concern.

- Consumers feel more empowered and are more active, creating communities of practice in which expertise is freely shared online. When core competencies cannot be owned within the firm but are distributed it is difficult to profit from them.

In the words of Tapscott and Williams, the '[o]ld "plan and push economy" is giving way to the new "engage and co-create economy"' (Tapscott and Williams, 2008: 31).

Take the example of eBay whose strategy relies on creating interaction and transaction between people, an idea that has made it the second largest retailer in the world. Or think of Wikipedia, the online knowledge bank written by users. Wikipedia's strategy is to provide a genuine co-creation experience for its users. Collaboration with and engagement of consumers with internal production processes are some of the most debated new ideas in strategic innovation. Best-selling books such as *Wikinomics, Wisdom of Crowds*, or *The Long Tail* make the case for a new era of ICT driven collaboration between organizations and their external environments.

Increasingly self-organized, distributed and collaborative human capital networks are augmenting and in some cases displacing the firm as an envelope of competencies. Zander and Zander (2005) argue that customers are strategic resources contributing to company growth, agreeing with Penrose's (1959) notion of customers being an 'insider track' in terms of problem solving. Pitelis and Teece (2009) argued that co-creation concerns not just products and processes but also markets and businesses and their supporting systems and, in the case of MNEs, even institutions (Jones and Pitelis, 2015).[3] Innovative ways of organizing, spearheaded by small and agile consumer incorporating companies, have been seen by some theorists as the likely future after the disastrous effects of the Global Financial Crisis (Davies, 2009). The future, it is predicted, will be one of open innovation and co-creation.

Open innovation and open strategy

Birkinshaw and his colleagues have argued that management innovation is an important yet still relatively unexplored topic (2008; see also Hamel, 2006). Management innovation entails the creation of a new management practice, process or structure that changes the state of the art. An example would be Taylor's scientific management, the divisional M-form or teamwork; they were all, once upon a time, new ways of managing and organizing work.

If we were to think of a recent management innovation that rivalled these earlier examples, such as scientific management, it would probably be open source innovation and its impact on strategic innovation inside organizations. Chesbrough (2006) talks about a paradigm shift from closed to open innovation. The paradigm of closed innovation assumes that successful innovation requires tight organizational control. According to this model, firms must create ideas, develop them, finance them, and bring them all the way to market themselves. In return, they retain the intellectual property rights. Most approaches to strategy are based on a closed model of innovation.

Chesbrough and Appleyard (2007) argue that open innovation poses a challenge to conventional strategy. Strategy used to be about creating defendable positions against competitors and constructing barriers around one's business model. Strategy focused on what the firm owned and controlled. Open source innovation changes the picture markedly. Open innovation is premised on allowing companies and multiple stakeholders to interact and co-create. Innovation networks and communities become important strategic resources because they allow co-creation.

Henry Chesbrough TED Talk

[3]A note on nomenclature: MNC and MNE – respectively, for Multinational Enterprise and Multinational Corporation, are used virtually interchangeably in the literature (see Mayrhofer and Prange, 2015).

Chesbrough and Appleyard (2007: 65–66) differentiate between four 'open strate-gies' that organizations can employ to benefit from open innovation:

- *Deployment*: innovation increases the user experience and they are willing to pay for the enhanced service. IBM, for instance, makes money from training and consulting on open source software applications.

- *Hybridization*: firms invest in add-ons to products developed in the open and remain in control of the IP of the add-on.

- *Complements*: a firm sells a product or service that is related to the use of the open source content. The example in case would be a mobile phone seller who benefits from free software for the mobile.

- *Self-service*: in this model, the community develops a service for its own needs; no one monetizes its value.

Social innovation

How can we solve the great challenges of our time – such as climate change, rad-icalization of cultural identities, poverty, the aging population and rapidly rising health care costs? Doubtless, these challenges need to be addressed in innovative ways. But who could work on holistic, complex solutions for large-scale challenges? Governments and the public sector in general seem to be too thinly resourced and too organized in silos to be able to tackle these challenges. On the other hand, corpo-rations, the drivers of much of innovation in the past two centuries, seem to be more concerned with ensuring the survival of their existing business models and annual (if not quarterly) returns for their shareholders. Neither markets nor government planning provides a satisfying answer. How then can we tackle the big challenges of our time? Who will be the innovators to solve these problems?

Social innovation entails 'new ideas (products, services and models) that simultaneously meet social needs and create new social relationships or col-laborations. In other words, they are innovations that are both good for soci-ety *and* enhance society's capacity to act' (Murray et al., 2010: 3)

One answer that is frequently mentioned in the corridors of power and community movements alike is **social innovation**. Murray and his colleagues define social innovation in their *The Open Book of Social Innovation*.

Social
Innovation

Go Online: You can read *The Open Book of Social Innovation* for free on the NESTA organization website, or by accessing the link on the companion website for this book: www.edge.sagepub.com/strategy2e.

A good example of social innovation is micro-finance. In poor regions, development is often stifled through lack of access to finance, meaning a small amount of money could go a long way. For big banks offering credit to poor people is not an attractive business proposition, especially after the sub-prime fiasco and subsequent Global Financial Crisis of 2007–2009. Banks typically prefer customers with big incomes who use their credit cards frequently and pay back their mortgages on time. The Grameen Bank Project founded by Muhammad Yunus, who was awarded the Nobel Peace Prize in 2006, is a good example of micro-finance. For more details see www. Grameen-info.org.

Two emerging forces shape social innovation. On the one hand, technology as an enabler of social networking, so that people share ideas and solutions. Second, a growing concern with what Robin Murray and his colleagues call the human dimension. How does social innovation work? Murray and his colleagues have devised a six-step process:

1. *Prompts, inspirations and diagnoses.* Every new idea starts with the perception of a problem or a crisis. In the first stage of social innovation, the problem is experienced, framed and turned into a question that tackles the root of the problem.

2. *Proposals and ideas generation.* Initial ideas are developed and proposals discussed. Importantly wide-ranging ideas are taken into account.

3. *Prototyping and pilots.* Talk is cheap – so ideas need to be tested in practice. Trial and error, prototyping and testing are means of refining ideas that cannot be substituted by armchair research. The motto should be *fail often, learn quickly*!

4. *Sustaining.* This step includes the development of structures and sustainable income streams to ensure that the best ideas have a useful vehicle to travel. Resources, networks and practices need to be organized so that innovation can be carried forward.

5. *Scaling and diffusion.* Good ideas have to spread – hence the scaling up of solutions is key. This can happen formally through franchising or licensing, or more informally through inspiration and imitation.

6. *Systemic change* – the ultimate goal of social innovation. This involves change on a big scale driven by social movements, fuelled by new business models, structured by new organizational forms, and regulated by new public institutions and laws.

In a world in which big government and big business are seen as problems there is increasing scope for social innovation to develop new strategies to tackle entrenched problems, empowering ordinary people in the process, rather than making them either clients or customers. Social innovation is not just about creating new products or services, such as new types of condom to help the fight against AIDS or new micro-finance initiatives to help people out of poverty. Social innovation can also be about bringing *existing* resources together in innovative ways. ReSpace Projects is an independent, voluntary and self-funded organization that helps to fight homelessness and provide community facilities in the UK by facilitating rental agreements for community use with landlords of unused buildings. The innovation by ReSpace Projects was not so much *creating* anything new as *connecting* existing resources in new ways. There are an estimated 90,000 empty buildings in London, according to ReSpace Projects, and yet at the same time London was facing an ever-growing homelessness problem. Artists and musicians were also finding themselves charged extortionate rents just for a small studio space in London. Community groups had to pay huge fees for renting space as well. ReSpace Projects helps to negotiate contracts with landlords of unused buildings to provide self-financing rental agreements, with spaces also dedicated to revenue-generating activities such as cafés, community halls for hire, music gigs and artist's studios to generate income. As one of its founding members commented a year on:

When we started this project, on the 30th May 2015, we set out to prove that regenerating an empty building into a useful political, community and social space was really not that difficult and maybe didn't need all the reams of paperwork and applications for funding, all the red-tape and costly admin that eventually sinks most great ideas. We wanted to pioneer a no-nonsense blueprint that made things happen.

We wanted to show that you could solve any number of social issues using space and time creatively. In every area of life we have tried to make sure the building impacts positively … art, culture, music, politics, sport, health, wellbeing, education, environment, economy, etc. And we documented the evidence. We have six small businesses started from the Hive, we have launched art careers and helped train sound and event technicians. We provide courses and classes and fitness clubs as well as alternative health festivals and film screenings, we host meetings and open mics. That's why we called it the Hive: *Human Interest Versatile Environment*.

Hive Dalston

Image 4.3   Blackboard Hive (reproduced with kind permission of HIVE Dalston)

Hive Dalston

Go Online: You can read more about one ReSpace Project initiative, *The Hive* in Hackney, East London, by going to the Hive Dalston website. You can also find a link on our companion website: www.edge.sagepub.com/strategy2e.

Summary

Innovation strategy is a huge and evolving topic. As Jane Marceau (2008: 673) noted, there is still no overall innovation theory. Elements are to be found in different disciplines such as economics, sociology, management, design and organization theory and at different levels, including the firm, region, population of organizations, nation, industry, etc. There is still a great deal of work to do not only in thinking about organization design and innovation but also in conceptualizing how such design articulates with broader questions of the innovation environment in policy, regional, industry and institutional terms.

Innovation is difficult to measure and demands close coordination of adequate technical knowledge and excellent market judgment in order to satisfy economic, technological and other types of constraints – all simultaneously. The process of innovation must be viewed as a series of changes in a complex system comprising the social and economic context of the innovating organization.

TEST YOURSELF

Want to know more about this chapter? Review what you have learnt by visiting www.edge.sagepub.com/strategy2e.

- Test yourself with multiple choice questions
- Revise key terms with interactive flashcards

EXERCISES

1. Having read this chapter, you should be able to say in your own words what the following key terms mean:

   - Product innovation
   - Process innovation
   - Radical innovation
   - Incremental innovation
   - Invention
   - Commercialization
   - Creative destruction
   - Ambidextrous organization
   - Business model innovation
   - Design thinking
   - Frame creation
   - Innovation networks
   - Open innovation
   - Co-creation
   - Disruptive technologies
   - Service-Dominant logic
   - Clusters
   - National innovation systems
   - Social innovation

2. How would you try and design an organization to be innovative?

3. What is creative destruction and what is its role in innovation?

4. What sorts of government policies should be a concern for innovation managers and why?

CASE STUDY

Pixar and Disney

SHAHLA GHOBADI

Who amongst us does not love the incredibly creative artworks of Pixar? Pixar Animation Studios (Pixar) is an American computer animation film studio based in California, United States. The company has produced well-known animation films including *Toy Story*, *Finding Nemo*, *Cars* and *The Incredibles*.

1979–1990

Pixar began in 1979 as the Graphics Group, part of the computer division of Lucasfilm. Initially, its core product was a system primarily sold to government agencies and the medical community, called Pixar Image Computer. In 1986, Steve Jobs, who had recently left Apple Computer, invested in the company. He cofounded Pixar Corporation with another brilliant technologist, Ed Catmull. Although Jobs initially predicted that Pixar would become the HP of imaging, he was aware of Catmull's passion (and that of a few other key people) for making animated films. He allowed the team to make short animated films in order to demonstrate the value of Pixar's hardware. During this time, the Pixar team learnt how to write and narrate animated stories and how to make the technology (hardware and software) that supported making extremely well executed short films. In addition, the Pixar team managed to integrate 'lean concepts' (thanks to its initial hardware production focus) within its collaborative processes. The company designed a rigorous quality control system with a microscopic level of oversight to examine stories, deconstruct and reassemble themes, and tweak and polish animation. Each team had regular meetings to display their work so that any mistakes could be caught early before they mutated into crises; moreover, anyone could make suggestions and express inspirations for creativity. The early years proved to be a difficult journey and cost the cofounders US$ 50 million in personal investment.

In a few years, however, an extraordinary thing happened. Pixar's computers were not selling in the marketplace, threatening to put the company out of business, yet by that time, Pixar had developed its digital animation technology, generated a strong collaborative culture, and had finessed storytelling capabilities to the point that the company won the Academy Award for its short film *Tin Toy* in 1988. Following this success, Jobs and Catmull switched Pixar's vision and focus to let the world know that Pixar was going to be a great animation company.

The strategic collaboration between Jobs and the Pixar team proved to be one of exceptional value. It was a brilliant collaboration, with each person performing the roles best suited to their passion, talents and experiences. While Catmull and a handful of people, including John Lasseter, were visionaries driving Pixar's approach to developing new ideas, Jobs acted as funder, strategist, external negotiator and salesman, in the words of Catmull as '*our protector*'.

1991–2003

By 1991, Pixar was already regarded as a leader in the computer generated animation industry when it established an initial alliance with Walt Disney Corporation to produce its full-length film – *Toy Story*. The alliance was a true triple-win for both Pixar and Disney. Pixar could stay in business by benefiting from Disney's access to funding options, distribution channels and capabilities to produce merchandise. Disney got access to the exceptional creative talent pool of Pixar, minimized the potential threat that Pixar might partner with a competitor and were able to deliver a new animated film segment to the market. Five successful animated films were made in this partnership, most notably *Toy Story*, *Monsters Inc* and *Finding Nemo*, earning more than US$ 3 billion that accounted for more than 25% of Disney's profits. The customers enjoyed the films and the products delivered some of the most beloved characters in film history such as Lightning McQueen from *Cars*, Mike Wazowski from *Monsters, Inc.* and Dory from *Finding Nemo*.

The Pixar team that led and edited production of *Toy Story* were 'funny, focused, smart, and relentlessly candid when arguing with each other. Most crucially, they never allowed themselves to be thwarted by the kinds of structural or personal issues that can render meaningful communication in a group impossible', said Ed Catmull. Out of their working relationship, they developed a collaborative model for highly functional working groups, named the Braintrust: 'The Braintrust meets every few months or so to assess each movie we're making. Its premise is simple: Put smart, passionate people in a room together, charge them with identifying and solving problems, and encourage them to be candid. The Braintrust is not foolproof, but when we get it right, the results are phenomenal', continued Catmull.

2004

Despite this incredible success, the alliance between Pixar and Disney was cancelled in 2004 during the production of *Toy Story 2*. Major disagreements between Steve Jobs and then Disney CEO (Michael Eisner) led Jobs to announce that Pixar would no longer release movies at the Disney-dictated time frame (November), but during the more lucrative summer months. Among the major reasons for the failing alliance were noted differences in cultures, lack of executive commitment and incompatible objectives. As an example, Pixar intended to retain full ownership of its future productions. However, this was not the case; in fact, Pixar and Disney had a 50–50 deal where Pixar was responsible for creation and production and Disney handled marketing and distribution, but Disney exclusively owned all story and sequel rights and also collected a distribution fee. Though the alliance was profitable for both, Pixar later referred to the lack of story and sequel rights and complained that the arrangement was not equitable.

2005–Present

Although it was unthinkable to imagine Disney and Pixar teaming up in 2004, negotiations between the two companies resumed following the departure of Michael Eisner from Disney in 2005. During this time, Pixar delayed the release of *Cars* to extend the time frame remaining on their contract and to see how things would play out between the two companies.

(Continued)

(Continued)

Eventually, Robert Iger (the new CEO of Disney) and Steve Jobs agreed on the acquisition of Pixar by Disney in 2006. Said Disney CEO: 'The addition of Pixar significantly enhances Disney animation, which is a critical creative engine for driving growth across our businesses. This investment significantly advances our strategic priorities, which include – first and foremost – delivering high-quality, compelling creative content to consumers, the application of new technology and global expansion to drive long-term shareholder value.'

Pixar's success justified the price of the deal at a valuation of US\$ 7.4 billion, and Disney safeguarded access to the creative talent of Pixar: 'The question isn't did Disney pay too much but how expensive would it have been for Disney if Pixar fell into someone else's hands', noted Barry Ritholtz, CIO in Ritholtz Capital Partners. Furthermore, Disney and Apple, in which Jobs was CEO by that time, started digital deals. For example, Disney could use the energetic thinking and expertise of Apple in knowing consumer electronics to sell hit ABC prime time shows, such as *Desperate Housewives* and *Lost*, as well as content from ABC Sports and ESPN on Apple's iTunes music and video store.

From Pixar's perspective, the acquisition was a great success as it allowed them to unite and focus on a shared goal. Pixar and Disney were also enjoying a 15-year partnership prior to the time, making it a safe acquisition. Dick Cook, the Chairman of The Walt Disney Studios, said: 'The wonderfully productive 15-year partnership that exists between Disney and Pixar provides a strong foundation that embodies our collective spirit of creativity and imagination. Under this new, strengthened animation unit, we expect to continue to grow and flourish'.

Ed Catmull, now president of both Pixar and Walt Disney Animation, reflected on the importance of the long partnership history in devising collaborative strategies for combining different cultures: 'At the time of the acquisition, we put together a list of things we thought were important to our culture … The agreement was that, though we were wholly owned by Disney, we would still do things in a unique, Pixar way. So we have different systems and policies. Because John [Lasseter] and I were in charge of Disney Animation, we made a clear choice that we would not merge the two studios, nor allow the studios to do any production work for each other at all. We felt this was important culturally, because when a studio solved a problem, then it had the psychological benefit of knowing that it did it on its own. Now people are proud to be part of Disney, but they believe they are Pixar. It's been a model for taking an existing strong culture and letting it thrive.'

Seven years later, in 2013, the deal has accomplished what Steve Jobs had expected: 'Disney and Pixar can now collaborate without the barriers that come from two different companies with two different sets of shareholders. Now, everyone can focus on what is most important, creating innovative stories, characters and films that delight millions of people around the world'. While Pixar has continued to unleash a string of hits, such as *Toy Story 3*, scoring five Oscars, Disney's other animation divisions have been also revitalized. In 2010, Disney released *Tangled*, a musical that grossed almost US\$ 600 million; in 2012, *Wreck-It Ralph* earned an Oscar nomination and grossed more than US\$450 million, and in 2013, *Frozen* was pronounced Disney's best animated musical in two decades.

- -

Pixar Interview

Go Online: You can read an interview from 2016 with Ed Catmull, founder of Pixar, in an article on the McKinsey website (www.mckinsey.com) titled 'Staying one step ahead at Pixar: An interview with Ed Catmull'. You can also find a link to the article on the companion website for this book: www.edge.sagepub.com/strategy2e.

- -

QUESTIONS

1. Explain how Pixar developed competencies and competitive attractiveness in its early years (1979–1990). Reflect on the material in Chapters 2 and 3 (e.g. Five Forces model, Value Change Model, Knowledge Management methods).

2. In light of deliberate versus emergent strategies, discuss Pixar's collaborative strategy (i) within the company during 1979–1990 and (ii) with Disney (1991–present). Draw upon Mintzberg and Waters' articulation of eight types of strategy making (Chapter 9) and types of collaboration (Chapter 6).

3. Using the material on 'open strategies', explore how Pixar practises open innovation at the moment (Chapter 4).

4. What do we learn from the historical decision to cancel the partnership between Pixar and Disney in 2004 and the interactions that followed until its eventual acquisition? Use the material in Chapters 6 and 11 to understand the nature of the political processes that were involved in their interorganizational relations.

STRATEGY: MAKE OR BUY?

TRANSACTIONS, INTERNALIZATION, EXTERNALIZATION

Learning objectives

By the end of this chapter you will be able to:

1   Explain why organizations integrate or outsource and what the advantages and disadvantages of integration and outsourcing are

2   Understand the importance of transaction costs in determining whether to make (integrate) or buy/sell (outsource)

3   Explain the core ideas and understand the limitations of Transaction Cost Economics

4   Distinguish between the different types of uncertainty with which firms have to deal

5   Understand when and why firms integrate horizontally (merge) and the challenges of achieving horizontal integration

BEFORE YOU GET STARTED

For every transaction, there is someone willing to buy and someone willing to sell at an agreed price, both believing that it's good value and that the counterparty is a little crazy. (Sol, 2014: 3)

Introduction

In this chapter we will first consider the broad context that a firm or an organization has to take into consideration in deciding whether to make or buy. To buy (or sell) entails sourcing a good or a service from an outside source (or selling an innovation to a third party), while to make means integrating the sourcing within the organization.

The make or buy decision is a particularly pertinent question for all types of organizations, even a restaurant. For example, in the case of Noma that we examined in Chapter 3, if the restaurant sourced vegetables and other ingredients from the market, this would be a decision to 'buy'. If they grew them, this would be a decision to 'make' their own raw materials (or we could say that they practised backwards vertical integration). Later, they could 'outsource' that activity to an external supplier. Many a relationship changes over time – the key question is why. An answer to this question has been offered by the so-called Transaction Costs Economics (TCE) approach – hence, we next consider TCE, which started life in a 1937 paper by Ronald Coase and was developed further by Sveriges Riksbank 'Nobel' Laureate Oliver Williamson. Drawing on concepts developed by behavioural theorists such as Herbert Simon and Cyert and March, Williamson outlined what he, somewhat restrictively, regarded as *the* alternative models for economic activity: either market (buy) or hierarchy (make). The transactions approach has had a number of applications in the literature, which we consider; it has also been subject to a number of criticisms, also considered.

TCE considers two major forms of governance for integrating (or internalizing) transactions within a firm: through horizontal integration or vertical integration. A third one is diversification, either related or unrelated (conglomerate). We consider each mechanism in detail, outlining when to vertically integrate and when to horizontally integrate. (Diversification is discussed in Chapter 7.)

Finally, we consider outsourcing, which is effectively the opposite of integration – rather than *doing more activities in-house* the firm decides to do *fewer activities in-house.*

Outsourcing as a strategy has been much espoused over the past 40 years not only by private firms but also by governments seeking to contain costs and by large organizations seeking to divest non-core activities that nonetheless require servicing.

Horizontal integration occurs when a firm acquires or merges with another.

Vertical integration involves moving into activities that were previously an input into the firm undertaken by one's suppliers 'downstream' (backward integration) or part of the post-production process undertaken by customers 'upstream' (forward integration).

Outsourcing involves moving activities that were previously undertaken by the organization to outside suppliers as contractors.

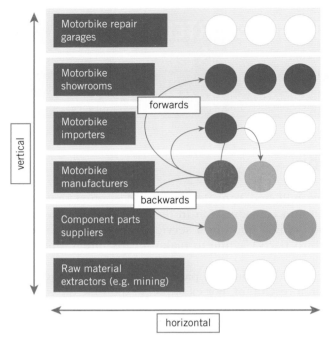

Figure 5.1   Vertical and horizontal integration

Source: Reproduced under the Creative Commons 3.0 Attribustion-ShareAlike License CC BY-SA 3.0. © Martin Sauter, 2010.

To make or buy? That is the question

Whether a firm should make or buy some element of the goods and services it produces is a classic question of strategy that has no easy answer. There are trade-offs between making a product, delivering a service in-house or buying externally.

Internalizing, by adopting the 'make' decision integrates complementary resources and capabilities into the organization. This can occur in one or other of *horizontal integration* (mergers/acquisition), *vertical integration* (backward or forward) or *diversification* intra-country and/or cross-border (multinational).

Madhok and Tallman (1998) suggest four factors to consider in deciding whether to make or buy:

1. Lack of necessary internal capabilities and assets that, with some re-organization, would permit pursuing the new strategic direction without adding new resources.

2. Unavailability of needed resources for purchase in the open marketplace, usually because they are skills and capabilities that are tied to organizations and therefore difficult to transfer.

3. High cost or risk associated with purchasing a firm that has the necessary resources because the actual competency can be hidden by other activities or an outright acquisition might drive off the very human and group assets that are critical for the strategy.

4. Benefits of collaboration, such as evading extensive organizational integration following a merger or acquisition and preservation of critical assets and strategic flexibility.

In one of the most influential works by an economist contributing to the strategy field, Coase (1937) defined the nature of the firm partly in terms of the employment contract between an entrepreneur and labourers. While conceptually it is possible to organize production through the exclusive use of the market mechanism (where relative price changes determine the allocation of resources), Coase observed that the employment contract has advantages in terms of transaction costs. These include not only entering into fewer transactions but also amortizing the cost of the transactions through a time-based contract thus lowering the average cost of transactions. Instead of having to transact with an equal number of independent contractors who may also liaise between themselves. Restaurant Noma, for example, can employ some people as chefs, waiters, etc. An employment contract can replace spot market contracting and thereby obviate the need for continuous renegotiations of contractual terms. Hierarchy and the associated use of the powers of fiat by the entrepreneur and his/her delegates, such as the manager, can lead to less protracted intra-firm negotiations.

Transaction Cost Economics (TCE)

The theoretical arguments about how and why firms have recourse to hierarchy or why exchanges occur in markets largely derive from the TCE perspective, which has become the predominant theoretical framework for explaining **organizational boundary decisions** about what to include in the firms' activities and what to secure from an outsourced third party.

> **Organizational boundary decisions**: According to TCE, the boundary of the firm is a result of economic considerations concerning whether to make or buy, internalize or externalize activities.

As already noted, Ronald Coase (1937) is regarded as the father of TCE. Herbert Simon (1951) joined Coase in identifying the employment relation and the concomitants of hierarchy and authority as defining the essential nature of the firm. Simon, like Coase, saw the employment relationship and discretionary control over employees by the employer as an efficient response to the impossibility of foreseeing the tasks and activities that would be asked of a worker. Bargaining and transactions costs could be too great to negotiate and write a contract for each task. Doing so would lead to market failure, due to high market transaction costs. Arrow (1974) suggested that the reason why markets fail is not simply high transaction costs; rather, in some situations markets simply do not work well. Economic activity should occur within firms where it offers advantages over markets in terms of motivation and coordination. Further development of Coase's framework by Oliver Williamson (1975b, 1985) and Klein et al. (1978) focused on asset specificity as the driver of integration/internalization (Williamson, 1985). High asset specificity implies a lower resale value, as such specificity is a sunk cost: for instance, where a firm has highly specialist equipment that cannot be readily used elsewhere and would have little value if they tried to sell it.

Coase (1991) questioned the importance of asset specificity. Moreover, he expressed regret for almost exclusively focusing on the employment relationship, claiming that one should not just focus on the nature of the firm's assembly but also its essence, what it does, which is 'running a business', something that involves more than the employment contract. In short, Coase seems somewhat dissatisfied with focusing purely on TCE. While offering embellishment of his ideas, TCE does not seem to satisfy Coase's desire for a realistic theory (Coase, 1937).

Williamson and TCE

Williamson's (1981b) development of Transaction Costs Economics (TCE) focuses on efficiency. In Williamson, efficiency is seen primarily in terms of the allocation of scarce resources (allocative efficiency) achieved by minimizing market transaction costs. For Williamson, the emergence of modern firms is said to be an outcome of efficiency in terms of reductions in transaction costs.

Williamson's framework is based on three critical assumptions in regard to the characteristics of economic actors, economic transactions and governance forms.

TCE postulates that human actors are characterized by:

1. Bounded rationality (thus all complex contracts are unavoidably incomplete).
2. Opportunistic behaviour (parties on long-term contracts will breach the spirit of a contract if it is in their self-interest to do so).
3. Feasible foresight (parties to a contract have the capacity to look ahead and to integrate those insights into the *ex-ante* design of governance).

Due to these characteristics, the organization of economic activities involves costs, which are called transaction costs – the costs of running the economic system. Examples include information costs, measurement costs, bargaining and decision costs and contract enforcement costs. A major decision that economic actors need to make is how to reduce transaction costs in order to maximize the outcome of their activities, which is influenced by the characteristics of the particular economic transaction.

The key question TCE raises is whether transactions should be coordinated within a firm or across markets. In asking why things are organized inside a firm, we are also asking why people are employees. That's one part of the question. The central question that TCE addresses is whether a transaction is more efficiently performed within a firm through *vertical integration* inside the firm, or by using *market mechanism*s by buying in goods or services from autonomous third party contractors. Hence, the second part of the question is whether to make or buy. How are those choices made? That's the vertical integration question.

IN PRACTICE

Your university or college, seen from a transactions costs perspective, has internalized in hierarchy a great many activities. For example, it probably employs security officers, IT technicians, cleaners, researchers, etc. You are a consultant, familiar with TCE, who has been asked to investigate ways of diminishing costs and adding value to the activities that the university or college encompasses.

Questions

1. Identify at least two areas of activity that, from a TCE perspective, might be shifted from hierarchy to market.
2. What is the rationale for your analysis and identification?
3. What do you project the benefits to be?
4. What do you project the costs to be?

Contrary to neoclassical IO economics, which postulates that a particular governance structure (perfectly competitive markets) is the most efficient means for organizing exchanges through the price mechanism, competition and contracts, TCE argues that in some cases firms will be a better mechanism.

TCE begins by seeing agents as acting with **bounded rationality**.

> **Bounded rationality**: Taken from March and Simon (1958) this concept captures the fact that we never have perfect knowledge and hence can never be perfectly rational. Because rationality is always bounded it leads to parties not being able to foresee all the possible consequences of a contract.

Bounded rationality refers to 'limitations of information and calculation' (Cyert and March, 1963: 214). It implies the need to set targets and try to satisfy these, as opposed to optimizing the best imaginable solution. For Cyert and March, firms attend to goals sequentially, and follow 'rules of thumb' and 'standard operating procedures'. There exists imperfect environmental matching, meaning that firm performance is not uniquely determined by an exogenously given structure, or 'environment' (as in Porter). Accordingly, history matters, pointing to the importance of organizational adaptation. Unresolved conflict is based on the assumption that in organizations there exist multiple actors, with potentially conflicting interests, that are not entirely alleviated by contracts. Instead, individual and sub-group interests are continuously renegotiated, with consistency being hard to obtain and sustain. The reason is that agents will transact with guile and be open to **opportunism**.

> **Opportunism** prevails when actors try to gain advantage by being economical with, or even distorting, 'the truth'; the possibility of opportunism ensures that there is also the possibility of uncertainty about agreements being maintained.

Not being perfectly rational, actors cannot anticipate all the circumstances that, over time, a contract may be subject to. Negotiation in advance of supply is never perfect. If actors were always truthful they would always deliver on the agreement signed. Because some agents can be opportunistic, seeking their self-interest with guile (on top of boundedly rational), hazards can arise from contracts.

For TCE the replacement of the market by a 'hierarchy' or of voluntary transactions by entrepreneurial 'authority' and 'fiat' helps reduce market transaction costs, also because of the ability of fiat to end prolonged disputes. Transactions differ in regard to three attributes of *asset specificity, unanticipated disturbances* (uncertainty) – which pose the need for adaptations – and the *frequency* with which transactions occur. Asset specificity is the most important of these and refers to the degree to which alternative users can redeploy the asset to alternative uses without loss of value. High asset specificity implies high vulnerability of the party that makes the investment because there is a danger that the other party will try to change the terms of the transaction in its favour once the first party has committed itself. Asset specificity gives rise to contractual hazards. Where there is opportunity for both asset specificity and opportunistic behaviour, transaction costs might be so high that it is more efficient to organize resource allocation within a firm.

Human characteristics of less than perfect rationality and a propensity to cheat on agreements, according to TCE, combine with other factors to make firms – organization by hierarchy rather than markets – a rational choice under specific circumstances. In such circumstances, it is argued, it becomes more efficient to internalize the transactions inside an organization (hierarchy) rather than rely on an imperfect market (see Figure 5.2).

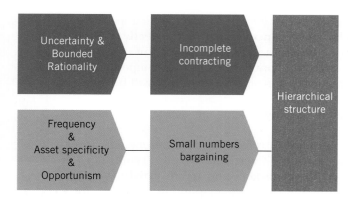

Figure 5.2 Factors predicting firm formation

> **Uncertainty** is associated with the unfolding of events relevant to contracts, the contingencies of which cannot necessarily be controlled. Uncertainty is positively related to hierarchical governance, due to the power of managerial fiat.

A key term in Williamson's vocabulary is **uncertainty** (Williamson, 1975b, 1985)

When the contingencies surrounding an exchange are highly unpredictable such that they cannot be specified in advance in a contract or where the quality of performance cannot be easily verified after the fact, *uncertainty* arises. When contingencies cannot be specified in advance and variations continue to arise that make undertakings more expensive than anticipated, different types of uncertainty might be in play.

First, there is what Walker and Weber (1984) term *volume uncertainty*. Simply put, this arises when the transacting party cannot accurately predict how much of a given material they need. When volume uncertainty is high, buyers may hold excess inventory. TCE suggests that firms, as organizations, ought to be able to coordinate more efficiently than a market the variations that occur through hierarchically organized production schedules and stock holdings. Hence, volume uncertainty should increase the likelihood of hierarchical over market governance.

Second, there is *technological uncertainty*: the inability to forecast technical requirements (Walker and Weber, 1984). Such uncertainty may follow from unpredictable changes in standards or specifications of components or end product, or from general technological developments, as Geyskens and colleagues (2006) suggest. Such uncertainty, they suggest, is best left to market devices. Firms sourcing from markets are able to retain flexibility to switch suppliers as occasion demands. This switching ability avoids the risks of technological lock in (Heide and John, 1990).

Third, *behavioural uncertainty* occurs when there is a problem evaluating performance in terms of contracted outcomes. In these circumstances TCE would predict that vertical integration would be adopted. A further factor increasing the probability of vertical integration in a hierarchy – an organization – rather than purchase on a market, is the frequency with which transactions take place. The more often, and the more routine the transaction, the more sense it makes to absorb the cost in the firm.

When transactions are located in or shifted to market relations, efficiencies are seen to follow. The efficiencies gained through buying from external providers or devolving elements previously integrated to outsourcing contracts derive from a number of factors. First, greater control over costs through new disciplines of centralized data collection. Second, this allows for cost-based accounting and, third, the development of standardized solutions derived from analysis of the data. By creating greater transparency through cost-based accounting, organizations have a better knowledge of the actual costs involved in service delivery.

> **Asset specificity** is the degree to which an asset is specific to a use or user.

The two key terms in Williamson are **asset specificity** and **transaction frequency**.

> **Transaction frequency** refers to the repeatability of transactions.

TCE sees a problem with *transaction-specific assets* that cannot easily be redeployed outside the relationship of the parties to the transaction. Williamson considers asset specificity to be specificity towards a particular customer to serve his/her needs. For example, you invest in a plant or purchase specialized equipment to serve a customer need, and the investment is not redeployable. Most assets are usually somewhat redeployable. Asset specificity is more than a fixed investment. It is a fixed investment that has no other uses and is not redeployable. It leads to high 'sunk' (non-recoverable) costs.

Once a firm has made an asset specific investment, where there are no close alternatives, then the supplier that enjoys asset specificity can try to change the terms of contracts. What starts as essentially a large numbers situation can end up as bilateral trade. In addition, over time, suppliers gain idiosyncratic knowledge about how best to satisfy their customers, knowledge that has asset specificity. Asset specificity can result in hold up costs. Once you get a situation where two parties are stuck to each other, any dispute is going to entail time and money to reach an agreement, and will result in haggling.

Williamson says you solve the market failure problems that result from contracting through vertical integration in three ways:

1. *Information flows.* You can gain access to information more easily if you bring it in-house. By doing so, you can have better auditing capacity to receive critical information and impose controls.

2. *Negotiating costs.* You can also reduce the costs of negotiation. Hierarchy imposes a system of authority that is characterized by a unilateral dispute mechanism. In other words, people in authority positions can say how to do things and get them done.

3. *Incentive alignment.* Through vertical integration, there is no longer any incentive for a firm not to make investments in specialized assets. Once the same firm owns everything, opportunism in the ownership and control of specialized assets will not occur. Vertical integration brings about an incentive realignment.

IN PRACTICE

Vertical integration at Marks & Spencer

During Marc Bolland's tenure as CEO of ailing retailer M&S, described in Chapter 1, one of the many strategic changes he introduced was a change to the firm's integration strategy. When he took the job in 2010, only around 40% of clothing design was done in-house, the rest being undertaken by the firm's many suppliers and other contractors.

(Continued)

(Continued)

By 2015, Bolland had brought 70% of clothing design in-house through vertical integra-tion, by starting to undertake the design activities previously undertaken by other firms.

You can read more about this case in an article by Ashley Armstrong on *The Telegraph* website titled '"Bolland bounce" questions legacy of M&S chief'. Also of interest is an article by Rebecca Gonsalves on *The Independent* website titled 'Marks and Spencer: Can a new team of designers put the spark back into the high-street brand?'

Links to both articles can be found on the companion website for this book: www. edge.sagepub.com/strategy2e.

M&S News Articles

Questions

1. Why did M&S decide to integrate more of the clothing design activities in-house?

2. What are the potential advantages of bringing more of the clothing design in-house?

3. What are the potential risks, dangers or disadvantages of moving more of the clothing design in-house?

When to make *and* buy?

Coase had argued that intra-organizational transaction costs can also be high, hence should only take place when the savings in market transaction costs exceeds the increases in intra-organizational costs. In addition, however, TCE dichotomizes 'make' or 'buy' rather than seeing them as potentially coterminous strategies (Parmigiani, 2007). Firms can and do simultaneously make and buy the same good, using concur-rent sourcing, as Parmigiani (2007) argues. Doing so may seem strange if only because costs are incurred both for internal production (securing capital, allocating plant and equipment capacity, staffing and coordination) and external outsourcing (costs of finding, selecting, negotiating with, and maintaining external suppliers). As she asks, 'Given that concurrent sourcing is more costly to set up and manage, why would firms select this sourcing mode over solely making or solely buying?' (Parmigiani, 2007: 285). Concurrent sourcing involves using both market and hierarchy. The reason may well be that as Bradach and Eccles (1989: 113) stated, 'contracting is problematic without in-house experience ... the simultaneous use of the two mechanisms ... in essence competition between them' (Bradach and Eccles, 1989: 113), offers a solution to the problem. Record companies that use in-house A&R (Artists & Repertoire) to record a song might also invite independent producers to do so as well, sometimes with the same artist, sometimes with different artists. Motown did this frequently.

Concurrent sourcing is more likely to be used to manage:

1. Demand uncertainty, by pushing fluctuations in volume onto suppliers in order to ensure full internal capacity and stable production.

2. The monitoring capacity of suppliers through familiarity with production processes.

3. Situations where uncertainty is high and the potential for synergies significant.

4. Performance uncertainty, market heterogeneity and information asymmetries.

5. Franchising, where the use of both owned and franchised outlets balances incentive and control issues, as well as facilitating learning.

6. Raw materials are abundant or subcontractors are readily available and physical interconnectedness is unnecessary.

7. High economies of scope of both buyer and supplier and diseconomies of scale are insubstantial. In such situations bargaining power is strengthened by the opportunity to benchmark and better evaluate performance of internal and external suppliers.

8. Technological uncertainty, where firms have both a wider range of knowledge sources and adaptive responses by concurrently sourcing internally and externally.

9. Situations with small differences between the supplier's and the firm's expertise.

EXTEND YOUR KNOWLEDGE

Often, driving a country's freeways, motorways, autostrada or autobahns, you will pass or be passed by trucks bearing a haulier's identity; other times they will wear the logo and livery of the company whose goods are being distributed. Like us, you probably have never given much thought to why goods should be trucked in one or the other. Daifeng He and Jack A. Nickerson (2006) have. In a really interesting journal article they ask the basic question 'Why do firms make and buy?' which they answer by looking at 'Efficiency, appropriability and competition in the trucking industry'. One element of their answer is that it is not necessarily an either or answer: firms can pursue concurrent strategies. This journal article can be read on the companion website for this book at www.edge.sagepub.com/strategy2e.

He, D. and Nickerson, J.A. (2006) 'Why do firms make and buy? Efficiency, appropriability and competition in the trucking industry', *Strategic Organization*, 4(1): 43–69.

**He &
Nickerson**

Parmigiani (2007) argues that make-and-buy is likely in TCE terms when there is not a high level of asset specificity. Her research does not support the hypothesis that high levels of specificity lead to higher degrees of internalization, in order to protect the firm from supplier opportunism nor that high volume uncertainty and performance ambiguity favour make-and-buy. Performance ambiguity leads to higher internalization that relies on the domination of authority relations to minimize variance. Make *and* buy is more likely when there is high technological uncertainty, large economies of scope of buyer and supplier as well as specialized expertise on the part of both the buyer and supplier. Accordingly, there is more to integration than TCE.

Applications of TCE

Williamson points out that Chandler's historical account of the problems accompanying firm growth and the structural solution to the problems is consistent with predictions generated by TCE. Williamson argues that the principal problem created by growth through diversification in different activities is that it creates increasing complexity and uncertainty – this time within the organization rather than in the environment – up to a level that exceeds the information-processing and decision-making capacity of the managers. The structural development that occurs through the adoption of the Multi-divisional (M-form) organization simplifies the informational and decision situations by clearly differentiating between the long-range policy decisions to be handled by the general office and the short-term operation decisions to be determined at the divisional level. Business units become profit centres, and the Head Office an internal capital market that receives profits and allocates resources.

From the TCE perspective, the M-form (see Figure 5.3) possesses important advantages over the external capital market:

1. It has easy access to more accurate information about divisions.

2. It can manipulate incentives more easily.

3. It can exercise control over the strategies pursued by divisions (Barney and Hesterly, 1996).

Ouchi (1979, 1980) extended the TCE framework to explain alternative ways of coordinating activities within firms. He argued that firms rely on three basic forms of control: markets, bureaucracies (or what Williamson refers to as 'hierarchies') and clans. Clan control or governance requires intensive people processing, socialization and long-term associations within the firm (Barney and Hesterly, 1996). When performance ambiguity (where it is not easy to make a judgement about how work is done and how it should be valued) reaches very high levels, then neither the measurement of market mechanisms nor bureaucratic monitoring can insure that employees' efforts will be directed towards the organization's goals. Under these circumstances, clan governance is most efficient. Teece (1986) argued that when knowledge is difficult to trade, either because doing so would give away that knowledge or because the necessary infrastructure of capabilities, communication codes or culture is absent, firms will internalize those transactions (Barney and Hesterly, 1996).

Initially, Williamson (1975b) saw hybrid forms of organization as transient and unstable, but later acknowledged that they might be more persistent (Williamson, 1985). Hybrids include governance structures that are neither hierarchy nor market. The most

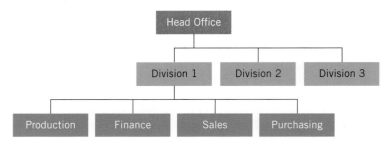

Figure 5.3   M-Form

general answer to why hybrids exist is that they have stronger incentives and adaptive capabilities than hierarchies while offering more administrative control than markets (Williamson, 1991a; Barney and Hesterly, 1996). These administrative controls are enforced in part through the contractual elements of job specifications; TCE suggest that the more specialized the job, the more likely an employment contract will be created.

The major argument for divesting or sourcing transactions on markets rather than integrating them within the firm, the organizational hierarchy, relates to the specificity of the asset in question. Where the asset is non-specific, divestment, outsourcing and securing the asset on the market is recommended (Shelanski and Klein, 1995; Williamson, 1998; David and Han, 2004). The benefits of vertical integration arise from the authority that formal relations of control provide (Weber, 1978).

TCE argues in favour of outsourcing when asset specificity is low. Teece (1984) suggests that outsourcing is most likely to prevail in environments involving mature, autonomous technologies. A strictly technical focus facilitates identification, isolation and solution of independent technical problems. Specialized suppliers will benefit from scale economies by pooling demand from different firms and by focusing on a limited number of well-defined activities to deepen their knowledge of the processes involved (Liebeskind et al., 1996).

TCE has been extremely influential; there have been many empirical applications as well as meta-analysis of much of the research by Geyskens and colleagues (2006).

Problems with TCE

According to TCE, the attempt to minimize transaction costs is the main factor that explains the existence of firms. The trade-off between firm-related transaction costs (coordination costs, costs of monitoring and motivating the workforce) and market-related transaction costs (information costs, negotiation costs and costs associated with the monitoring and enforcing of contracts) helps explain the boundaries of the firm.

The market and hierarchy distinctions that TCE sculpted have become more blurred. Seminal research exploring the paradox of embeddedness in the apparel industry by Uzzi (1997) led to an appreciation of the balance between arm's length (i.e., market-like links) and embedded ties (where economic activity is constrained by non-economic institutions such as ethnic or kinship relations), which foster knowledge transfer (Dyer and Nobeoka, 2000). The assumption of opportunistic behaviour is based on an 'undersocialized' view because it ignores such embedded interpersonal relations and obligations as powerful normative moderators of behaviour. Also, firms may link existing knowledge and make knowledge more valuable through organization learning and assembling different resources as well as through forming networks and alliances (see Chapter 6). Inter-organizational networks (Tsai, 2002) that blend cooperation and competition became seen, in a neologism, as '**coopetition**'.

The work on embeddedness, knowledge networks and 'coopetition' remains firm centric in approach. Latterly, new forms of networks, such as in the field of open-source software or, more recently, in some manifestations of the sharing economy, have emerged. Innovative forms of governance (Demil and Lecocq, 2006) and value appropriation characterize such models, which we explore in Chapter 6. Outsourcing and alliances, as forms of networking, are ways of developing organizations in a globalizing environment (Prahalad and Hamel, 1990). It is, in particular, the development of value chain approaches (Porter, 1985) linking core firms with external partners, which makes networks global.

> **Coopetition** refers to cooperation designed to provide mutual gain between businesses that have previously seen each other as competitors.

Through these inter-organizational networks organizations gain access to external resources and competences that could be combined with their internal capabilities (Foss, 1999; Dyer and Nobeoka, 2000; Kogut, 2000; Acedo et al., 2006; Hagedoorn et al., 2006), which can be captured in the concept of strategic network capabilities (see Chapter 6 on alliances).

One more general criticism is that to show that an institution functions to reduce market transaction costs for individual actors does not explain how that market came into being. It is simply presumed that markets preceded hierarchies. This is a dubious proposition historically, as history teaches us that much pre-modern economic action was organized through monopolies controlled by princely absolutism. TCE starts from the premise that markets pre-exist hierarchy, which is not sustainable historically: Adam Smith (1776/1937), in *The Wealth of Nations*, noted how the state had first to break its state-sanctioned monopolies in order to create markets.

A second criticism is that its view of economic activity remains too rational. Granovetter (1995) argues that conceptual frameworks such as Williamson's underestimate the extent to which economic behaviour is embedded in a matrix of social relations. Neglecting the matrix of social relations surrounding all activities causes the economist to overstate both the extent to which explicit contracts are required to govern economic behaviour in the market and the effectiveness of hierarchical controls and incentive systems within organizations (Scott, 2014).

Among more specific criticisms, three are central:

1. TCE focuses on cost minimization.

2. TCE understates the cost of organizing.

3. TCE neglects the role of social relationships in economic transactions (Barney and Hesterly, 1996).

For example, it is feasible that avoiding opportunism and minimizing governance costs are a secondary consideration. Minimizing transaction costs is of relatively little benefit if a firm has no transaction specific assets (including knowledge) that are highly valuable in the market. Lengthy and costly haggling may often be more severe within a firm than between firms, as Eccles' (1985) study of transfer pricing shows. Indeed, internal organization is often susceptible to costly bargaining and influence behaviour (Milgrom and Roberts, 1988). Granovetter pointed out that contrary to the atomistic view of economic exchange, transactions are embedded within networks of social relationships. These transactions are influenced by expectations formed through the history of the relationship (Barney and Hesterly, 1996).

TCE offers one formalist explanation of why organizations exist. It is an ahistorical argument. TCE also assumes that the existence of an organization means that there must be effective hierarchy and agreement on goals. The assumption in TCE is that agreement is not problematic; reporting in the business press on a daily basis suggests that it is.

Woolworths Shareholders

Go Online: At random, we plucked one news story from *The Sydney Morning Herald* website that appeared on a day this chapter was being written. The story is called 'Long voyage ahead for weary Woolworths shareholders as chairman seeks captain of industry'. The account that the article contains of managerial hubris and lack of agreement concerning goals is a commonplace of accounts in the business press. You can read the article on *The Sydney Morning Herald* website or via a link on the companion website for this book: www.edge.sagepub.com/strategy2e.

Nonetheless, notwithstanding history, markets are seen to have many advantages. You can gather information in the market not only on supply but also on availability. Markets reveal information on the price and quality of goods. Markets provide information on reputation. You can learn information about the actions of actors in the world from other actors. You can find out whether the actor will live up to his/her promises. If there are a lot of suppliers, you can switch suppliers in a relatively costless and easy fashion. Ample choice of suppliers discourages potentially opportunistic suppliers from engaging in such behaviour.

Vertical and horizontal integration

Efficiency will be enhanced, TCE suggests, when a fit exists between the chosen governance arrangement for transactions and the underlying attributes of the transaction and the broader contracting environment (e.g., Williamson, 1985, 1991a). There are two major forms of governance for integrating transactions: through horizontal or vertical integration.

The benefits of either horizontal or vertical integration are strongly dependent upon crucial assumptions regarding the nature of underlying resources, supplementary attributes of the focal firm and other industry conditions.

When to Vertically Integrate?

Vertical integration can enhance performance through effective internal organization within the firm rather than between firms. Common systems, standards and protocols, particularly those related to technological interdependencies that exist between activity stages, aid this. Locating manufacturing outside the firm can make cross-functional coordination much more difficult given the probability that locally differentiated systems will be in use (Griffin and Hauser, 1992; Chesbrough and Teece, 1996; Teece, 1996; Hatch and Mowery, 1998). Vertical integration was a hot topic in the 1990s but it declined in popularity only to become hot again in the current century.

Integration into hierarchy can provide enhanced information transfer and coordination across activities; hence, when dealing with technologies that require a great deal of coordination (Langlois, 1992; Chesbrough and Teece, 1996; Teece, 1996) it makes sense to try and secure these inside the organization. That is one reason why it is currently fashionable to integrate vertically in the tech sector.

Vertical
Integration in the
1990s

Vertical
Integration Now

When to Horizontally Integrate?

According to Vossoughi in the 2012 *Harvard Business Review*, 'Todays best companies are horizontally integrated'.

Why would firms want to buy their competitors? The usual arguments are that horizontal integration:

*Harvard Business
Review* Article

1. Reduces competitive intensity

2. Lowers production costs through scale

3. Boosts differentiation by eliminating similar products or services in the market

4. Provides access to new markets and distribution channels.

Reducing competitive intensity can change the underlying industry structure by taking out excessive capacity from rivals and increasing industry consolidation. A major aim of such acquisitions is to increase bargaining power vis-à-vis suppliers and buyers in pursuit of dominance that can deliver more profits. As well as eliminating competition, more profits can also be delivered through lowering costs. Such moves are often to be found in industries with high fixed costs, such as the pharmaceutical industry. Development and approval periods for new drugs are lengthy and the innovation process uncertain; nonetheless, there are substantial fixed costs of a large sales force to promote the products to medical practitioners.

As the discerning student will have already noted, the arguments for horizontal integration are more reminiscent of Porter than TCE because TCE is mostly silent on mergers. Competitors do not usually cooperate before a merger, something that makes application of TCE ideas less clear than in the case of vertical integration.

It is in part because of the above that horizontal integration can frequently destroy, rather than add, value. The pages of business history are replete with stories of horizontal integrations that did not deliver the value intended and anticipated; they were value destroying rather than value enhancing. Porter (1987) found that more than half of the acquisitions made by US companies were value destroying rather than enhancing. Ravenscraft and Scherer (1987) estimated a divestiture rate of one in three following acquisitions.

There is a greater probability of success if the acquisition is in a related rather than unrelated business. One reason is that it minimizes the probability of integration failure but it can increase the costs of flexibility: taking over and integrating a business means trying to achieve some basic things successfully, things that are not always easy to achieve, such as integrating different IT systems, organization cultures and personnel practices. Especially if the merger creates something that looks suspiciously similar to a monopoly it may invoke legal antitrust implications.

The importance of culture in horizontal integration

If the decision to horizontally integrate through merger with another firm were simply a case of transactional efficiency, the annals of the business press would not be replete with stories of wasted value, bankruptcy and loss of value.

Horizontal Integration

Go Online: In an article on his website (www.joe-cullen.com), Joe Cullen analyses two examples of horizontal integration, one an infamously bad case, the other a good case. The bad case is the Time Warner/AOL merger while the good case is Google/YouTube. You can find a link to this article on the companion website for this book at www.edge. sagepub.com/strategy2e.

Simply put, merging with or acquiring another firm entails major and often indeterminate transaction costs associated with intangibles, such as 'culture'.

While mergers and acquisitions (M&A) studies frequently note that acquisitions will entail the integration of diverse cultures (Nahavandi and Malekzadeh, 1988;

Cartwright and Cooper, 1993; Weber, 1996; Weber et al., 1996; Larsson and Lubatkin, 2001; Sarala, 2010) they often assume that organizations have a homogeneous culture (e.g. Cartwright and Cooper, 1993; Weber, 1996). While this is one step better than TCE, which assumes culture away in the quest for efficiency, it is hardly satisfactory and not at all representative of sophisticated organization theory views of organization cultures and the role that they can play in any transactions striving for efficiency, as we shall see later in the chapter.

In organization theory cultures are understood as complex, heterogeneous and dynamic. They are rarely if ever expected to be unitary; rarely would any organization be expected to have a single culture that all its members shared. Fissiparousness, differentiation and division would be seen as much more probable states of organizational culture (Clegg et al., 2015). Employees are constantly constructing their own subcultures in interaction with whatever is posited as being the formal culture of the organization (Smircich, 1983; Frost et al., 1991; Hatch, 1993; Martin, 2002).

Acquired and acquiring firms can be perceived as cultures made up of how organizational members perceive and understand the realities around them (Vaara, 2000). When culture is conceptualized and interpreted in this way, organizations can be regarded as consisting of multiple cultures (Trice and Beyer, 1993). It is precisely these non-economic aspects of being a person in a social world rather than being exclusively transactional that points out further limits of TCE. When mergers and acquisitions fail to work out it is not just because *individuals* may be transacting with guile; it may well be that different *social* worlds are colliding. Merging and acquiring a business is a modern form of conquest; just as one would not expect colonized, defeated or subjugated subjects to be guileless in their transactions with the victors one should not expect anything different in the business world.

> **Cultural integration** is said to occur when changes are made in two different cultural systems because particular elements of culture have spread from one system to the other, in both directions (Berry, 1980: 215).

Mergers and acquisitions presume that **cultural integration** will and can occur through acculturation.

Van Marrewijk (2016) notes that Nahavandi and Malekzadeh (1988) have drawn on Berry (1983) to identify four strategies for acculturation:

1. *Integration*, when the two cultures are integrated each retains their individual identity; Buono and Bowditch (1989) have defined four strategies for integrating cultures in M&A: taking over, blending, pluralism and resistance.

2. *Assimilation*, which occurs when one culture absorbs the other.

3. *Separation*, when the two cultures are entirely separate.

4. *Deculturation* or marginalization, when a culture disintegrates.

Assimilation rarely occurs unless there have been prolonged collaborations or alliances between organizations over a lengthy period (see Chapter 6 on alliances and collaboration). Separation is a viable strategy but can be costly; it often entails different and incompatible IT, HR and other systems. It can produce resource-based turf wars between constituent entities – this often happens when tertiary education organizations are merged, frequently for externally mandated political or administrative reasons, yet retain the same differentiated staff, location and loyalties. Deculturation or marginalization occurs when a subordinated culture is stigmatized, under-resourced or in some other way denigrated. Most mergers and acquisitions strive to achieve integration.

Integrating cultures after horizontal integration

As van Marrewijk (2016: 2) argues, 'there have been few very fine-grained interpretive and critical studies of how organizational cultures and subcultures interact and affect cultural integration (Teerikangas and Véry, 2012)'. He goes on to note that there is a post-acquisition integration literature in strategy that has tended to see all types of acquisitions in undifferentiated terms (e.g. Teerikangas and Véry, 2006), an approach that risks overgeneralization and oversimplification (Schweizer, 2005).

van Marrewijk's (2016) focus on acquisitions is currently the most sophisticated approach to how organizational integration fares subsequent to merger and acquisition; for this reason, we shall summarize his argument. The focus of his research has been on the media and telecommunications sector. The sector was dramatically transformed in the 1990s. Ill-starred mergers occurred such as that of Time Warner and AOL.

Image 5.1   AOL. Copyright: Jason Doiy

At the height of the dot com boom of the early 2000s two media companies merged together to form (what was seen as) a revolutionary move to fuse the old with the new media. In 2001, old-school media giant Time Warner consolidated with American Online (AOL), an Internet and email provider at a cost of $164 billion. Though the merger occurred as a transaction, the cultures of the two dynamically different companies never gelled. When the dot com bubble burst in 2002 the price paid was revealed as wildly over-valued and when the decline of dial-up Internet access developed in the wake of broadband, the merger became even more dysfunctional. In 2003, AOL/Time Warner reported a $45bn write-down that lead to a $100bn yearly loss until, in 2009, the two companies finally split in a corporate divorce.

- -

Go Online: The AOL/Time Warner story is one of a number of mergers discussed by Megan Ruesnik on the Rasmussen College website (www.rasmussen.edu) in an interesting and informative short article on the facts of 'Top corporate mergers: The good, bad and the ugly'. You can find a link to this article on the companion website for this book at www. edge.sagepub.com/strategy2e.

- -

Top Corporate Mergers

AOL and Time Warner were just the most spectacular of a number of acquisitions that occurred in the new space of the digital media (Ranft and Lord, 2002). The emergence of mobile technology together with changing consumer behaviour encouraged media and telecommunications firms to acquire Internet firms (Uhlenbruck et al., 2006a). As van Marrewijk (2016) notes, many of the firms taken over in this way were rooted in hacker culture (Jordan and Taylor, 1998). They were not occupied by corporate, buttoned up types in suits so much as what we could today call 'hipsters'. They were the diametrical opposite of corporate firms, the firms that were doing the acquiring.

The Dutch Case: Telcom and iPioneer

Van Marrewijk has a background in Telcos, as well as being a cultural anthropologist, so it is no surprise that he chose to conduct longitudinal research into a Telco merger in his native Netherlands. He is not the first researcher to make a longitudinal analysis of mergers but he belongs to a select band of earlier research on post-acquisition integration by Vaara (2003) and Zueva-Owens et al. (2012).

As a part of the privatization fashion that spread like wildfire as a governmental strategy from the 1980s onwards, a number of European governments opened up competition within what had previously been a public sector monopoly industry. Former government-owned telecoms companies were forced to restructure their organizational hierarchies, internationalize their business, rethink their bureaucratic cultures and update their technologies (Steinfield et al., 1994). Rodrigues (2006) described the slow transformation of the Brazilian Telco, Telemig, for example. At the same time in the United States the government restructured the US telecoms market, breaking down the divisions between telephone companies, cable television companies, media enterprises and publishers (Steinfield et al., 1994). A new field of convergent technologies was opening.

Digitalization was the catalyst for the convergence. Digitalization of communication and the development of mobile telephony networks and intelligent communication networks forced the pace of standardization of technology across sectors (Wirtz, 2001). Telephony and media networks converged into a multimedia telecommunications network, stimulating new value chains (Estabrooks, 1995). Organizations that had previously comprised mostly engineers looking after a network of copper wire connections for the terrestrial telephone network that they worked for were radically and swiftly changed; privatization, competition, new product launches, mergers and acquisitions were all part of a brave new world. The acquisitions were intended to create value by integrating acquired technology, innovations and talented employees (Haspeslagh and Jemison, 1991; Puranam et al., 2006) from the Internet world of hipsters, hackers and geeks.

Two worlds, whose integration on paper looked like a great deal for creating value and reducing transaction costs, were set to collide. On the one hand, there were the survivors of the old public sector management engineering culture as well as the newer more market-oriented hires contracted after privatization; on the other hand, there were the mostly male community of hipsters, hackers and geeks who shared a fascination for computer technology, secrecy and anonymity (Jordan and Taylor, 1998). With a hero from an earlier age they seemed to share the conviction that 'to live outside the law you must be honest' (Bob Dylan, 1966). Used to rule breaking, in conventional terms, they shared an ethos of informal illegality and enquiry.

Thus, not surprisingly van Marrewijk (2016: 4) defines the central M&A dilemma for the Telcos as 'how to integrate newly acquired radical Internet firms but at the same time preserve the acquired firms' organizational autonomy so that their capacity for continued innovation is not disrupted (Haspeslagh and Jemison, 1991; Puranam et al., 2006; Ranft and Lord, 2002)'. The Dutch Telecom acquired iPioneer, an Internet service provider that grew out of the cyber-punk hacker community, in 1998. As van Marrewijk (2016: 7) researched the process over a sustained period of 12 years, he identified four phases in the process of integration: inertia (1998–2003), domination (2003–2007), revitalization (2005–2007) and absorption (2007–2010).

In the initial phase of inertia, the iPioneer culture remained much as it had been, despite the takeover: loose, informal, independent, even trading with competitors to its new parent company. After the dot com bubble burst in 2002 things changed. Telcom hired new financial managers more focused on the transactions; pressure was applied to iPioneers to generate additional value; increasing restrictions were placed on the iPioneer culture and a process of infiltration by Telecom staff launched. The result was the emergence of three distinct identities in iPioneer based on organizational generations: the 'Real iPioneers', 'Dogmatic iPioneers' and 'ex-Telcoms'. It is pretty obvious what the Real and the ex-Telcom's identity would be while the Dogmatics were not the first generation iPioneers but second generation followers, not perceived as 'real' by the Real iPioneers. The ex-Telcoms regarded both groups with scant regard, as in breach of every principle of management structure, process and practice to which they genuflected.

In this second phase the ex-Telcom sense of identity and culture had assumed dominance as a result of head office sponsorship. In the third phase, the phase of revitalization, from 2005 to 2007, there was a realization from head office that the very things that Telcom wanted to acquire in the merger were at risk due to the bureaucratic dispositions of the ex-Telcom staffers and the resistance that was being generated amongst the iPioneers. Neither the ex-Telcom nor the iPioneers respected each other; each thought the other cultural identity wrong and theirs right. The head office, realizing this, encouraged employees to actively recreate and re-form the innovative (sub)culture by resynthesizing elements of their cultural framework within the overall culture. Revitalization saw the Real iPioneers try to crystallize previous iPioneer cultural values into a new pattern and reject Telcom cultural values that did not fit and with which they could not identify. As we shall see, this strategy failed.

By the time of the absorption phase, from 2007 to 2010, Telcom's dominance was assured by some decisive decisions to quit from amongst the ranks of the iPioneers who, with many opportunities in the start-up world, saw no reason to be stuck in a bureaucracy. Collaboration intensified, systems, work practices and culture were more closely integrated; only the technology department seemed to hold out. The iPioneers were moved into corporate headquarters in Amsterdam, from the old start-up and improvisational physical spaces and culture into one of clean desks, neat structures and clear rules. Not surprisingly, full integration was unsuccessful: the innovative capabilities had left the firm by this stage, and as van Marrewijk (2016: 13) noted: 'While Telcom acquired iPioneer as a means of incorporating this radical Internet firm's capacity for continued innovation, what remained after full integration was in fact an "empty" brand.'

Lessons from Van Marrewijk's Dutch Case

There are some very valuable lessons to be gleaned from Van Marrewijk's account. We shall enumerate them.

1. A transaction is an event while strategy is a process. A contract establishes a merger through a specific transaction but that is not the end of the event; in this case the event unfolded over a process that lasted 12 years. The iPioneer case demonstrates the long time frame needed to understand the outcomes of a post-acquisition integration process.

2. The assumption that a sound strategy depends on cultural integration is incorrect; striving for cultural integration emptied the merger of the very capabilities that had animated the strategic decision to merge in the first place.

3. Previous M&A research has assumed that organizational cultures are homogeneous and unified (Larsson and Lubatkin, 2001; Sarala, 2010). However, the iPioneer case shows how polar opposite subcultures interact, conflict and change over time, giving voice to different interpretations of the cultural integration process.

4. Revitalization, as a phase in the process of integration, is an opposite strategy to that of deculturation (Nahavandi and Malekzadeh, 1988). In the latter, employees lose interest in their cultural roots while in a revitalization strategy they seek to restore the cultural values of the past and eliminate cultural elements that do not 'fit' anymore. Revitalization is much more than resistance (Trice and Beyer, 1993) or a countercultural phenomenon (Buono et al., 1985).

5. Revitalization might have saved the innovation capability of the iPioneers but it did not, because of unexpected contingencies in the environment in which they operated: the emergence of new forms of post dot com boom start-ups, bubbling with creativity, flexibility and opportunity.

6. Strategists need more organization theory and less economics. Large organizations will always tend to be more formalized, centralized, rationalized and routinized into a bureaucratic configuration. Acquiring dynamic capabilities from smaller firms by taking them over and seeking culturally to integrate these with a dominant bureaucratic culture is unlikely to succeed.

University Mergers in Europe

Outsourcing

Another option, apart from either vertical or horizontal integration, is to outsource those elements that have grown up and remained within the organization but which are not integral to its central production of value. It is a form of regulated contractually bound buying for a specified period of time rather than opportunistic purchase on spot markets.

Outsourcing is the mirror image of integration and internalization. It involves externalizing or disintegrating an activity: hence, the question is why would a firm want to outsource a value-chain activity? In the majority of cases, when organizations move a business function from intra-organizational to third party control, significant efficiency gains can be expected through specialization of the outsourcer, provided the activities outsourced are non-core. In such cases, one can expect 'time, effort and capital on value-creating activities that yield a competitive advantage, an improved overall performance, and security for the organizations' long-term survival' (Hunter and Cooksey, 2004: 27).

Outsourcing is not a new phenomenon: in major production industries such as automotives, the outsourcing of initially non-core and latterly core functions and services has been progressively used since the 1930s (Macaulay, 1966). However, services outsourcing, although common for some time in specialist areas such as advertising and legal services, increased dramatically from the mid-1990s.

The means for organizations to outsource service functions were made possible in the mid-1990s with the commercialization of the web and the development of advanced cost effective digital telecommunications services. At the same time, other digital age developments occurred which created the need. These include the growth of global competition, an increase in productivity and the need for new skills (Brynjolffson, 2004; Holmes et al., 2003). The companies that switched to outsourcing moved away from a vertically integrated into a co-dependent outsourcing model to develop competitive advantage. In one sense, this change of management practice is a change of fashion but it is also a development of a more efficient model for dealing with the changing environmental factors of the marketplace. In other words, outsourcing might be a fashion, but a fashion that can bring about positive effects for the outsourcing organizations.

The outsourcing of sectors such as IT and Telecommunications and Business Processing occurred with the dawning of advanced digital telecommunications services that facilitated the availability of this option. The imperative to outsource – as distinct from the opportunity to do so – was a result of other dynamics of the digital age, primarily globalization and increased competition, leading to a continual need to improve efficiency from productivity and to increase service levels. Vertically integrated services were no longer seen as the best organizational arrangements for gaining competitive advantage.

The idea of extending the organization's capabilities, whether core or non-core, to a third party, is confirmed in research by Gottfredson and colleagues (2005). Gottfredson et al.'s (2005) framework suggests that competitive advantage can be gained by optimizing uniqueness of function versus the proprietary nature of the organization's capabilities.

In contrast to TCE, institutional theory suggests firms can choose a design, such as outsourcing, hierarchy, for reasons of institutional isomorphism – organizations, particularly in the public sector, go to the market because it is politically and ideologically fashionable for them to do so. The institutional argument stresses the pressures of deregulation as a politically fashionable and expedient activity.

EXTEND YOUR KNOWLEDGE

An outsourcing provider typically bases outsourcing decisions on the potential to realize cost savings through economies of scale and specialization. Markets with significant scale economies frequently generate concentrated market structures with a dominant outsourcing supplier. These markets are less attractive for the outsourcing client due to the loss of bargaining power that they enjoy vis-à-vis the concentrated domination. Using a simple analytical model, Achim Hecker and Tobias Kretschmer derive implications for empirical work and formalize some of the practitioner literature on outsourcing in an article titled '**Outsourcing decisions: The effect of scale economies and market structure**', which you can read on the companion website for this book at www.edge.sagepub.com/strategy2e.

Hecker, A. and Kretschmer, T. (2010) 'Outsourcing decisions: The effect of scale economies and market structure', *Strategic Organization*, 8(2): 155–175.

Hecker &
Kretschmer

Outsourcing through hybrid temporary contracting

One area in which outsourcing has grown substantially in recent years is television production, which offers an exemplar of how organization strategy has moved from an essentially bureaucratic internalization of the majority of functions to one in which they are largely contracted out. Historically, national broadcasting systems such as the BBC in the UK or ABC in Australia were characterized by hierarchy and vertical integration of programme production. When commercial television operators appeared they followed the same model: it was the institutional model in the early days of broadcasting. In the past 30 years or so new strategies have evolved that have seen digitalization, globalization and deregulation fuse new organizational structures following shifts in strategy.

The TV industry, dominated by a few large network organizations, often has extremely short term arrangements of informal contracting out for programme production that can be for very short periods of time, sometimes as little as a few days or a week (Bechky, 2006). The form of contracting out is based on personal knowledge, informal ties and shared social capital (Adler and Kwon, 2002). Key people in the large organizations will have networks of trusted operators and suppliers, such as camera crew, scriptwriters, directors and presenters, with whom they will frequently and informally collaborate on project-specific programme production. One consequence of this is that dense networks of independent producers and freelancers exist in the industry, often centred on areas such as Soho in London or Ultimo in Sydney.

Networks are not a new phenomenon – they were the norm in early forms of pre-modern industry such as the jewellery and metal working industries centred on areas such as Handsworth in Birmingham in the eighteenth century. These forms survived well into modern times and still characterize specialist work in the jewellery industry, for example. Elsewhere, in industries such as construction, the network form has been the normal method for accomplishing projects. More recently, however, high technology sectors such as biotechnology and software engineering (Barley and Kunda, 2004) and media production (Bechky, 2006) have seen the emergence of innovative forms of project organization.

The new forms of project organization emerging from what were previously integrated bureaucracies in fields such as media production have seen the emergence of forms of hybrid strategy and organization (Clegg, 2011; Courpasson and Clegg, 2012). These result from the deconstruction and decomposition of what were once classic bureaucracies into new hybrid forms under the pressures of interrelated technological (digitalization), political (deregulation and privatization) and cultural (shifts to portfolio careers and project organization) changes, creating new types of economic organization.

Bureaucracies are based on standardization, formalization, routinization, centralization and a highly integrated configuration in which strategy flowed from the apex throughout the organization. The newer patterns of organizing, while still retaining the strategic cores of bureaucracy in organizations such as the BBC and ABC, are networked into hybrid forms of collaborative, flexible and self-managed modes of working in which improvisation, risk-taking and creativity are at a premium. In the hybrid forms of organizing prevalent in the networks surrounding and supplying the bureaucracies, 'concertive' modes of work regulation typical of high skill, expert-dependent and 'knowledge-intensive' working environments proliferate (Courpasson, 2000; Ezzamel and Burns, 2005; Sewell and Barker, 2006).

There is a symbiotic relation between the bureaucracies at the core of the networks and the creative elements comprising the hybrid organizations. The strategy at the centre is to contract out but to do so along channels composed largely from shared social capital, social relations and the trust these engender. The collaborative environment is constituted by a culture in which individual and collective learning from mistakes and failures is encouraged (Fleming and Spicer, 2007) and in which professional and craft-based modes of working in creative industry encourage highly autonomous technical and creative workers to organize their own strategies for flourishing (Townley et al., 2009).

Flourishing means being able to cope with high levels of uncertainty and instability at the margins of a vertically disintegrated and horizontally coordinated industry subject to rapid technological and regulatory change. The still large bureaucratic organizations at the core of the system facilitate the development and legitimation of 'polyarchic' governance regimes (Clegg et al., 2006; Courpasson and Clegg, 2012) combining 'soft' power relations premised on informality in the networks with 'hard' power mechanisms in terms of deadlines and budgets imposed on the creativity and innovation of those in the network. The creative workers have a relatively high degree of autonomy but work within strategic guidelines determined by the administrative elites in the bureaucratic cores. Polyarchic governance regimes balance elite strategic control and professional operational autonomy. Transactions are often focused on intermittent projects, delivered by temporary teams of autonomous workers that are composed and recomposed as occasion demands (Bechky, 2006; Jones and Litchenstein, 2008).

Media production is a special and specific case of the shift from bureaucratic integration to market hybridization.

Problems with outsourcing

Walker and Walker (2000: 156) suggest that outsourcing may be a modish fad, something that organizations might claim to do for efficiency reasons but which in practice deliver far less efficiency than is often claimed: '… the claim "20 per cent savings from contracting out" became part of the repertoire of catchphrases favoured by privatization advocates'. A study that examined the impact of outsourcing on both organization and employees in large Australian organizations in all industrial sectors covering public and private organizations supported the view that outsourcing has been promoted as a fashionable movement (Benson and Littler, 2002). One of Benson and Littler's findings was that outsourcing did not have a significant impact on performance, compared to other forms of restructuring. Also, in the context of IT, Fischli (1996) wondered whether outsourcing really was a new management tool; a question reiterated a number of times since (Hunter and Gates, 1998; Lonsdale and Cox, 2000).

Critics of outsourcing base their arguments more or less implicitly on institutional theory (Abrahamson, 1991). For instance, Walker and Walker (2000) and Quiggin (1994, 1996) make strong claims that outsourcing in the public sector is the result of public organizations seeking to copy private companies to demonstrate conformity with modern management thought and to show that they are at least trying to improve their services, rather than the result of evidence on the efficiency gains of contracting out. Quiggin (1996: 49) argues 'some moves towards contracting out of public sector activities may be seen primarily as bringing the public sector into line with the standard practices of large private business enterprises', arguing, implicitly, a case for mimetic isomorphism (DiMaggio and Powell, 1983). Hodge (1999: 466) pointed out that in the public sector 'the drive to contract out government services was often heavily founded on the privatization ideology'. Walker and Walker (2000: 153) claim, referring to the reform of the public sector, 'it was simply assumed that the private sector was more efficient than the public sector, so that outsourcing would mean cost-savings'.

Outsourcing and Natural Disasters

Go Online: Many local authorities in the UK adopted outsourcing during the 1980s and 1990s but some, in the twenty-first century, are going back to in-house provision. In some cases, it has taken natural disasters to alert the authorities to the real costs of the contracts that they had entered into, something explored in a story in *The Guardian*, written in the aftermath of severe flooding in the north west of England at the end of 2015 titled 'Why have councils fallen out of love with outsourcing vital services?' You can find a link to this article on the companion website for this book: www.edge.sagepub.com/strategy2e.

From an institutional perspective, efficiency arguments are of less consequence than those that stress mimetic isomorphism, which is adoption based on mimesis or copying (DiMaggio and Powell, 1983). Public sector organizations favour outsourcing practice in part because they became widely institutionalized as a part of the 'privatization package' premised on the contracting out of government services.

Although it is undoubtedly fashionable there is a substantive ignorance of what are the specifics of outsourcing with Top Management Teams often unsure about what it entails (Rothery and Roberts, 1995). Such relative lack of understanding might be a reason for the significant rates of failure to deliver benefits in the terms that contract managers anticipated, as reported by Doig and colleagues (2001), as well as the widespread dissatisfaction reported from Dunn and Bradstreet surveys of outsourcing initiatives. In line with the expectations of institutional theory (DiMaggio and Powell, 1983), outsourcing adoption may occur because it is a culturally valued phenomenon.

In contrast to the institutional perspective, a large number of studies seek to establish empirically that outsourcing should be adopted for the compelling reason that it produces cost efficiencies. Of course, there may well be other compelling reasons, such as diluting union power, facilitating innovation, and transfer of best practices but the promise of cost efficiencies is a potent tool for the promotion of outsourcing services in highly competitive cost-conscious organizations.

The critics of outsourcing argue that efficiency gains are not only much smaller than are claimed in advance but that *costs increase rather than reduce after services are contracted out* (Ganley and Grahl, 1988; Holcombe, 1991; Paddon, 1991, 1993; Walker and Walker, 2000). Some of the main critical arguments include:

1. Cost reductions are often over-estimated because of a poorly specified cost equation. Also, important losses that occur as a result of contracting out are ignored, as has often been the case in the UK public sector (Ganley and Grahl, 1988).

2. Outsourcing causes additional costs (for example management costs in examining and deciding on tenders), which can outweigh the savings from contracting out. These costs amount to an average of 6% of the contract value, suggests Paddon (1991) after study of the British and Australian public sectors.

3. The additional costs associated with outsourcing mean that companies need several years to realize the financial benefits, suggest Benson and Ieronimo (1996; see also Barthelemy, 2001; Gilley and Rasheed, 2000).

4. Cost savings often occur at the expense of quality reductions, deterioration in work conditions and employment reductions suggest a number of authors who have investigated public sector outsourcing (McEntee, 1985; Ganley and Grahl, 1988; Paddon, 1991, 1993; Quiggin, 1994, 1996; Paddon and Thanki, 1995; Walker and Walker, 2000).

The critics' main argument is that the realized savings do not generate a net economic benefit; they are, in fact, illusory, when properly accounted for. In general, these authors conclude that outsourcing is not only a fashion but also a fashion that does not enhance the performance of the adopting organizations. It has, rather, a negative impact on organizations, as Hunter and Cooksey (2004) argue.

IN PRACTICE

Sendle challenging traditional door-to-door parcel delivery

Go Online: Visit the book's website at https://edge.sagepub.com/strategy2e to watch an interview with James Bradfield Moody.

James Bradfield Moody Interview

James Bradfield Moody is the CEO and founder of Sendle, a company that unlocks and makes available the idle back haul in courier vehicles. Prior to this, from 2004 to 2009, Moody held various roles at the Commonwealth Scientific and Industrial Research Organization (CSIRO) including General Manager, Government and International, General Manager, International and Director, Divisional Business Strategy for the Division of Land and Water.

Sendle is taking on the ambitious task of going toe-to-toe with Australia's national Post service, announcing a partnership with one of Australia's largest delivery networks, Toll. The company offers door-to-door parcel delivery for small businesses and delivery partners now include Toll, in addition to local courier services, Fastway and Couriers Please. Sendle harnesses over 3,000 delivery vehicles that deliver over 70 million packages a year with prices for small business for 25kg door-to-door for $9.75 in the same city and $24.75 nationally. Sendle, which launched in November 2014, is backed by a number of investors. In this video James talks about how to grow and gain traction as a start-up business within a segment of the parcel delivery market that is traditionally dominated by monopolies. James explains how the business concept was inspired by the principles of the Circular Economy and the Sharing Economy and he identifies the key trends that will influence the potential for future growth.

Questions

1. Why would a firm outsource its services to Sendle?
2. Which difficulties can you foresee that a company like Sendle has to look out for when providing its services?
3. In Sendle's business model, which activities could be outsourced?

The political economy of outsourcing

It may not just be fashion at work with outsourcing. The decades of the 1950s and 1960s were the decades of heightened vertical integration, especially in the US.

The corporate sector offered secure jobs with rising real wages and career opportunities in firms that were largely nationally oriented, such as the automobile industry, which experienced little foreign competition at this time. Corporate strategists balanced shareholder value with increasing sales growth and market share. Using vertical integration strategies meant internalizing employment in the corporate hierarchy. Internal labour markets resulted, which, to a certain extent, protected the workers employed from market forces. These were not too severe anyway, because until the early 1970s the US economy was running at levels approximating full employment. 'As a result, many low-skill jobs in large manufacturing corporations provided security, opportunities for training and promotion, and decent pay through administratively-determined wages (patterned on union contracts in the auto sector)' (Vidal, 2016).

When industries vertically integrate there are high levels of industry concentration and less in the way of competitive markets for labour; markets tend to be determined administratively in the vertically integrated organization. Vertical integration and administered wages had a long-term effect on the rate of profit. As capital intensity increased the profit rate declined; as administered wages secured industrial peace through steady wage increases the share of value going to profits declined in favour of that going to wages. In other words, capital's loss was partially a consequence of labour's gains. As Vidal (2016) notes the profit rate had fallen from a post-war high of 26.8% in 1951 to a low of 9.4% in 1982.

Meanwhile, by the late 1970s competition in the US market had intensified with the major competitive threat coming initially from Japan. Areas that the US had innovated such as videos and TVs were now effectively destroyed as domestic industries by Japanese competition; Japanese automobiles were making substantial inroads into the US market. Inward Japanese investment in areas such as automobiles showed the future for US producers. They invested in areas where there were weak union traditions, such as Kentucky. A process of de-unionization was initiated in response. As unionization was avoided or declined so wages fell.

New ideologies began to emerge to shape corporate strategies. The most significant of these was 'shareholder value', first articulated by GE's Jack Welch in 1981. In practice this meant adopting policies of divestment of areas of business not returning whatever was defined as shareholder value, the outsourcing of those areas that were not central to the core business and the adoption of lean staffing structures, which restricted opportunities for developing career structures and increased the precariousness of the labour market through part-time and temporary employment, the latter being lessons learned from Japan (Kono and Clegg, 1998, 2001).

> Most important was a return to the market-determination of wages even for full-time, long-term jobs. This provides an explanation for the increase in low-wage work despite a decrease in low-skill work: under the class compromise, low-skill jobs provided decent wages because they were shielded from market forces. Under the ideology of shareholder value and the logic of employment externalization, market competition now forces the wages of low-skill workers down as far as possible. (Vidal, 2016)

The consequences were a greater share of value going to capital and a lesser share to labour. As we shall see in Chapter 13, these shifts in value were most acute at the upper and lower ends of income inequality. Specific strategy theories, notably agency theory, were to play a key role in producing and legitimating this revaluing of the contributions of capital and labour. Pioneered in the US, the fashions for shareholder value, divestment, outsourcing and lean staffing spread throughout the liberal market economies. A consensus was emerging that corporations existed primarily to create shareholder value.

Technology assisted de-structuring, restructuring and outsourcing. The development of the Web during the 1990s made it easier to outsource. Initially, peripheral activities such as catering, cleaning and payroll were spun off and outsourced. Later, even the most central aspects of the business became eligible for outsourcing as firms became more design centres than manufacturers: the actual manufacturing could be outsourced, together with the responsibility for the workforce, to sweatshops in the third world, that offered the peasantry a better deal than life in the fields. 'China's growth as a manufacturing powerhouse made it feasible to outsource many of the lower-value-added tasks of production. Outsourcing firms ultimately came to encompass full-scale assembly and supplier management. The Web made the make-or-buy decision subject to continuous revision because prices were readily available' (Davis, 2016a: 509).

Business organization became a global game of Lego, putting pieces of infrastructure together, contracted at the best rates available. The vanguard was charted by Nike's organizational separation of design and production. Davis (2016a) refers to it as 'Nikefication', increasingly the model for post-industrial organization – Apple, with its subcontracted production by Foxconn in China, is the most famous example. Corporations were increasingly fulfilling the imaginaries of the nexus-of-contracts described by financial economists such as Jensen and Meckling (1976). Access to a global pool of outside contractors made organizing by hiring actual employees largely unnecessary. Why build an organization when you could contract one for a specific period, design what it should do, fix the costs through contract, absolve the company of any responsibility for whatever exploitation of people, communities and the environment? The contemporary Silicon Valley model was created.

Summary

The chapter has traversed a lot of ground. Theoretically, contemporary economics sees decisions about whether to work through markets or hierarchies as a matter of transactional cost efficiency. The latter view, encapsulated in TCE, remains a dominant view. Hence, we spent a good part of the chapter discussing the development of this approach and defining some of its key terms. We explained some basic points about market and hierarchy, two key categories of the theory. TCE argues very much from the efficiency perspective and so we considered the contributions of TCE to understanding make or buy decisions. One thing that TCE has not done is to consider make and buy not as opposite but as joint choices. There are circumstances in which firms might want to make *and* buy.

A major decision that firms have to make as they evolve and grow is whether to pursue vertical or horizontal integration. We looked at both strategies and discussed their advantages and disadvantages of mergers and acquisitions. The TCE literature rarely acknowledges that TCE has little to say on horizontal integration. In addition, conventional strategy approaches underplay the non-economic aspects of mergers and acquisitions even though these are essential to the success or failure of the transaction. To illustrate this, we dealt at length with an exemplary study of a Dutch acquisition and merger in the media/Internet field. It was not a success and there is a great deal to be learnt from its failure.

We also looked at outsourcing and contracting out, contrasting divergent views of the practice. One stresses that it is a management fashion, ideologically promoted; the other sees it a rational transactional view of the organization. We see outsourcing as something that is both a recent fashion in some cases, but also efficient, albeit that any efficiency benefits are being captured by capital at the expense of labour.

TEST YOURSELF

Want to know more about this chapter? Review what you have learnt by visiting www.edge.sagepub.com/strategy2e.

- Test yourself with multiple choice questions
- Revise key terms with interactive flashcards

EXERCISES

1. Having read this chapter, you should be able to say in your own words what the following key terms mean:

   - Vertical integration
   - Horizontal integration
   - Make *or* buy
   - Make *and* buy
   - TCE
   - Asset specificity
   - Bounded rationality
   - Opportunism

   - Organizational boundary decisions
   - M-form
   - Coopetition
   - Forward and backward integration
   - Embedded ties
   - Outsourcing
   - Cultural integration

2. How efficient is outsourcing? Why? For whose interests?

3. Why have outsourcing ideas become fashionable in strategy circles?

4. In what circumstances would you recommend strategies of make *or* buy to a firm?

5. Why might a firm want to both make *and* buy?

6. What are the major issues to be managed in an M&A? How would you manage them?

CASE STUDY

Big data

STEWART CLEGG

Radically changing your business due to disruptive innovation requires a different change process than the standard change processes, because an organization needs new processes, values and new capabilities. When dealing with disruptive innovation, the alignment and/or realignment of an organization's assets might not be enough to sustain competitive advantage. When newcomers use the latest technology to disrupt an entire industry, the incumbents will need to take drastic measures to change their organization.

The emergence of strategies driven by Big Data means a transition to a data-driven, information-centric organization consisting of dynamic capabilities that involve using and applying such data in every aspect of the organization, thereby changing long-standing ideas on management, value and expertise.

Facebook and Google are the epitome of Big Data. One tells you what to know; the other connects you with who you want to know. They have very similar strategies based upon their command of huge sources of data about you and millions of other people.

Facebook is investing heavily in Artificial Intelligence (AI) for 'machine learning' whereby software can, for instance, identify people in photos, and determine which status updates and ads should be shown to each user. Facebook is also using AI-powered digital assistants and chatbot programs to interact with users via short messages. Its Messenger service can be used to do things such as ordering an Uber car. It is investing heavily in Voice Recognition (VR) having bought Oculus for $2 billion in 2014 in anticipation of keyboardless computing.

Google is also using AI techniques to guide self-driving cars. Facebook and Google can attract the best researchers and most promising start-ups, given the vast resources they can command from their enormous profit stream. As *The Economist* says

> Facebook lags behind Amazon, Apple, Google and Microsoft when it comes to voice-driven personal assistants; when it comes to chatbots, it faces competition from Microsoft and a host of startups eager to prove that bots are the new apps ... Microsoft has jumped straight to AR with its HoloLens headset, its most impressive product in years, and Google, already active in VR, has invested in Magic Leap, a little-known AR startup.

These technologies are transforming how people interact with each other, with data and with their organizations and their environments. AI will create devices and services that anticipate your needs (Google's Inbox app already suggests replies to your emails). Conversational interfaces will allow for keyless search and enquiry. Wearable devices, cars and goggles for Virtual and Augmented Reality (AR) are already here. The future of

(Continued)

(Continued)

computing is likely to be AR interfaces mediated by AI, using gestures and speech for inputs with information easily projected within the organization, making possible new forms of communication, creativity and collaboration.

It is not all a techies' utopia, however. There are certain to be privacy and security concerns. Personalized services based on Big Data are highly panoptical, based on digital surveillance. Apple, for instance, placed the privacy of people's personal data above the security of the nation state in a recent case of Californian terrorism (see www.wired.com/2016/02/forcing-apple-hack-iphone-sets-dangerous-precedent/).   Will   consumers be happy to have everything about them that is codified used as personal details to sell them stuff or invade their privacy? Do we trust private sector monopolies to accrue even more information about us than the state? Intimately entwined in billions of peoples' lives and making huge profits from their surveillance, can we trust these new behemoths of the digital age?

Read *The Economist* lead article on 'Imperial ambitions' (9 April 2016: 9; available   at   www.economist.com/news/leaders/21696521-mark-zuckerberg-prepares-fight-dominance-next-era-computing-imperial-ambitions) and answer the following questions.

**Imperial
Ambitions
Article**

QUESTIONS

1. Why does Facebook develop capabilities (Make) and/or acquire companies (Buy) in artificial intelligence, virtual and augmented reality?

2. Why do you think so many tech giants, such as Facebook and Google, choose to buy start-ups for innovation rather than develop the capacities internally?

3. What are some of the issues of cultural integration that might occur when large corporations such as Facebook buy start-ups?

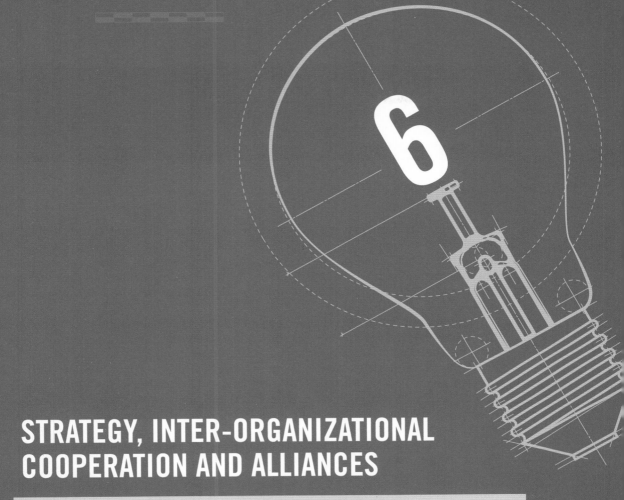

STRATEGY, INTER-ORGANIZATIONAL COOPERATION AND ALLIANCES

STRATEGIC PARTNERS, COLLABORATION AND NETWORKS

Learning objectives

By the end of this chapter you will be able to:

1   Define collaborative strategies and understand their importance

2   Discuss advantages and disadvantages of collaborative strategies

3   Distinguish different types of collaboration and understand their nature

4   Explain why collaboration and competition sometimes go hand in hand

5   Realize the critical role of partner selection, contracting and governance for collaboration in strategic alliances

BEFORE YOU GET STARTED

Alliances and partnerships produce stability when they reflect realities and interests. (Stephen Kinzer, 2011)

Introduction

The world that pioneers of strategy such as Chandler and Penrose described was largely one of standalone organizations. These organizations were growing larger through various forms of 'integration', such as horizontal, vertical or diversified. The organizations that ensued were vast bureaucracies, whose strategic decisions involving other firms were often no more demanding than the decision to make or buy.

Increasingly, however firms are engaged in types of cooperation with each other that transcend the make or buy question. They collaborate and cooperate. One reason that organizations seek inter-organizational cooperation, such as alliances, includes accessing resources, for example, knowledge for product and service innovation (Powell et al., 1996). Firms such as IBM and Cisco collaborate by combining their specific expertise and creating new products and services that offer more integrated IT network solutions for corporate clients by forming an alliance. So to 'ally' can often serve as a viable strategic alternative to make or buy. Three key types of inter-firm cooperation to be examined here are strategic alliances, joint ventures and networks. These are preceded by a discussion of theories of inter-firm cooperation.

Inter-Firm Cooperation (IFC) – Definition and Theories

Inter-firm Cooperation can be defined in the following terms.

> **Inter-firm Cooperation (IFC)** is quasi-stable and durable, formal or informal arrangement between two or more independent firms, aiming to further the perceived interests of the parties involved (Pitelis, 2012).

In this generic definition, IFC involves independent firms (hierarchies) that pursue their interests, without resorting to full integration but in a way that involves more stable relationships than a spot-market contract. IFC is thus situated 'between market and hierarchy' (Williamson, 1996a; Ménard, 2004).

IFC can take various forms (Child and Yan, 1999; Dussauge and Garrette, 1999; Gulati et al., 2000; Ménard, 2004; Nooteboom, 2008):

1. Subcontracting/outsourcing

2. Equity joint ventures (EJVs)

3. Strategic alliances

An important characteristic of IFC arrangements is that, to varying degrees, cooperation can co-exist with competition between firms, especially when co-operating firms are involved in similar activities. In cases such as strategic alliances or alliance portfolios, for example, cooperation can occur in one activity while firms compete in other areas (de Rond, 2003; Child et al., 2005; Ozcan and Eisenhardt, 2009). The apparently paradoxical and often ambiguous power relationships within inter-organizational networks (Tsai, 2002) that are a blend of cooperation and competition became seen, in a neologism, as *coopetition*.

The literature on IFC is voluminous. Forms of IFC, such as EJVs and strategic alliances became so topical in the 1990s that John Dunning (1997) defined the whole era as one of 'alliance capitalism'.[1]

We can distinguish three major analytical perspectives on IFC, although there are variants within each perspective. Given extensive coverage, for example in Faulkner (1988), Child and Faulkner (1998), Mockler (1999), Gomes-Casseres (2001), de Rond (2003), Williamson (2008), Pitelis (2012), we provide a bird eye's view of the following perspectives, which we have already visited in Chapters 2, 5 and 3, but now apply to the case of organizational cooperation:

1. The 'industrial organization' (IO) approach

2. The transaction costs approach

3. The resource-knowledge-capabilities-based approach

The 'Industrial Organization' (IO) Approach

From the IO perspective, IFC is seen partly in terms of price collusion. Firms have an incentive to collude so as to raise price-cost margins, by influencing the structure of the industry (Cowling and Waterson, 1976). Porter's (see Chapter 2) application of the IO approach to strategy, for example, does not recognize any reasons for cooperation other than collusion over prices. The central argument of the Five Forces approach is to reduce the power of competitors and other forces such as suppliers.

Game theoretic work on IFC, such as Axelrod's (1984, 1997), provides additional important reasons and evidence as to why firms may have an incentive to cooperate, for example, in terms of retaliatory 'tit-for-tat' strategies on the part of economic agents (Child and Faulkner, 1988; Parkhe, 1993). Other, efficiency-based, arguments within IO, such as Demsetz's (1973), can also be used to explain IFC in terms of production-side, synergy-related efficiency gains. Within IO and in Porter, however, there was no comparative governance-based analysis of different modes of organizing economic activity, either in terms of market-power in the form of collusion or for efficiency reasons.

The Transaction Costs Approach

The transaction costs approach provides a comparative governance framework. The origins of the transaction costs explanation of IFC go back to Coase's (1937) classic article on why firms (or hierarchies) exist in market economies, where voluntary exchanges rule, there being no apparent reason for hierarchical relations. Coase focused on the nature, or existence, of the firm, vis-à-vis the market and attributed integration by firms to high market transaction costs. He said that the number

---

[1] The literature is extensive: amongst the most important indicative contributions are, for example, Kogut (1988), Lorenzoni and Ornati (1988), Hamel (1991), Hennart (1991), Parkhe (1991), Nohria and Eccles (1992), Locke (1995), Oxley (1997), Child and Faulkner (1998), Gulati (1998), Dyer and Singh (1998), Gulati and Singh (1998), Dyer et al. (2001), Kale et al. (2002), Reuer et al. (2002), Zollo et al. (2002), de Rond (2003), Ménard (2004), Zollo and Singh (2004), Nooteboom (2004, 2008).

and length of transactions, hence their cost, can be very high in voluntary market exchanges and can be reduced if the number and length of transactions can be reduced through a hierarchy.

Following the emergence of debates on cooperation, Oliver Williamson (1985, 1996a) originally viewed such cooperation (and what he called hybrids) as a transient phenomenon, a progression from market to hierarchy. In this perspective, there can be transaction costs benefits of cooperation vis-à-vis markets but generally not vis-à-vis hierarchy, which is regarded as superior in terms of transaction costs reduction. That this is the case is not surprising, given, for example, that as the quantity of transactions increases so do the number of transacting parties. Moreover, for Williamson (1985), hierarchy could also alleviate transaction costs, even given the number of transactions, by reducing negotiation costs through authority.

Important contributions in the transaction costs tradition involve Hennart's (1991) analysis of joint ventures, Oxley's (1997) analysis of alliances and Williamson's (2008) analysis of outsourcing. An implication of the transaction costs perspective is that *ceteris paribus*, in transactional terms (and subject to increases in organizational costs not fully offsetting any transaction costs saving), IFC is an inferior form of organizing economic activity in terms of economizing behaviour than integration by firms; that is, by hierarchy.

The transaction costs analysis is predicated, however, on the assumption that the different modes of the organization of economic activity are essentially the same (Williamson, 1985). This need not and realistically cannot be the case (Langlois and Robertson, 1995; Aoki, 2004). Different organizations are likely to possess different capabilities, advantages and disadvantages, as we saw in Chapter 3.

The Resource-Knowledge-Capabilities-Based Approach

The resource-knowledge-capabilities-based perspective is based on the explicit observation that institutions and organizations differ in terms of their value-creation and capture capabilities (Gulati and Singh, 1998). For Penrose (1959), firms are superior to markets in terms of their endogenous creation of knowledge, innovation and value. For other 'resource-based' and capabilities scholars, each firm is unique in its ability to create and appropriate value (Eisenhardt and Schoonhoven, 1996).[2]

It is important to analyse the differential advantages and disadvantages of organizations both in terms of their costs and value-creation and capture benefits. For example, even if IFC is inferior to integration in terms of transactions cost, it may be superior in terms of value creation benefits (Kale et al., 2001). The cost-benefits calculation is more complex than one based on transactions costs alone.

Markets can be seen as institutions that serve the objectives of economic agents (Greif, 2008) including the reduction of transaction costs (Ménard, 1995, 2004). Firms and markets can be complementary (Marshall, 1920; Simon, 1995); each can have characteristics of both market and hierarchy (Alchian and Demsetz, 1972; Dosi, 1995; Marshall, 1920) and firms can create (Casson, 2005) and co-create markets (Pitelis and Teece, 2010).

Penrose (1959), the originator of the resources/capabilities view, did not originally deal with intra-firm cooperation. Later, she recognized its importance

---

[2]These issues are discussed in more length in, for example, Peteraf and Barney (2003); Mahoney and Pandian (1992); Kor and Mahoney (2000), Dosi et al. (2000); Teece et al. (1997); Foss and Loasby (1998); Teece (2007a, 2007b) and Loasby (1999, 2010).

(Penrose, 1995) and her last published paper focused on networking and IFC (Penrose, 2008). Building on Penrose (1959), Richardson (1972) produced a template, or 'good practice', for the choice of mode of organizing economic activity, in terms of concepts of similarity and complementarity of activities. In Richardson's schema, similar and complementary activities are best integrated in a single firm. Dissimilar yet complementary activities are best undertaken through cooperative arrangements. Markets work best when activities are both dissimilar and non-complementary.

Richardson's contribution was arguably the first conceptual framework that explicitly dealt with IFC, vis-à-vis both market and integration. It preceded Williamson's (1975b) classic book; importantly, it employed the now popular capabilities lens (Hamel, 1991; Parkhe, 1991; Teece et al., 1997; Inkpen, 1998; Loasby, 1999; Dosi et al., 2000, 2008; Dosi and Marengo, 2007; Teece, 2007b) and the concept of activities (Porter, 2008).

> **Strategic alliances** are commonly defined as purposive linkages between organizations that cover collaborations involving an exchange, a co-development or a sharing relationship (Gulati, 1995).

Strategic alliances

One of the most prevalent forms of IFC involves **strategic alliances.**

Strategic alliances have a number of defining features:

1. An alliance brings two or more individual organizations together.

2. An alliance requires these parties to be interconnected in some way.

3. Interconnectedness involves reciprocal relations.

4. An alliance strives to define itself through shared goals, interests or values.

5. In an alliance there is a presumption that the individual parties maintain at least some level of autonomy.

Types of Alliances and Partnerships

There are a number of distinct types of strategic partnerships in which a firm might choose to engage.

1. *Comprehensive alliances* involve the participants' agreeing to perform different stages of the process by which goods and services are brought to market. Because this type of alliance requires that firms engage across multiple functional areas, such as finance, production and marketing, comprehensive alliances are often based on complex contractual agreements or structured as joint ventures. While comprehensive alliance agreements are probably the fastest growing form of strategic alliances, they can be difficult to arrange.

2. *Functional alliances* are less complex and have a narrower scope involving collaboration, for example, in single functional areas of the business. Typically, functional strategic alliances include production alliances, marketing alliances, financial alliances and R&D alliances.

3. In a *production alliance* two or more firms each manufacture products or provide services in a shared facility. Production alliances can also occur as technology *cross-licensing* agreements where trademarks, intellectual property and trade secrets are licensed to a partner firm. While this is a low cost strategy to enter foreign markets, the downside of cross licensing is the potential loss of control over the technology, as well as possible exploitation by the partner of the initiating firm's know-how.

4. Firms may agree on *production licensing*, which only allows a partner to manufacture and sell a certain product. Usually each licensee will be given an exclusive geographic area. Compared to building their own manufacturing facilities and distribution networks, production alliances are a lower-risk strategy to expand the reach of a firm's products and services.

5. In a *marketing alliance* several firms share marketing or services. In such cases, for example, we might see one partner introducing its products or services into a market that another partner already operates in. Affiliate online marketing, for example, has grown over recent years, with the most successful online retailers such as Amazon using it to great effect.

6. An *investment alliance* involves firms that collaborate to reduce the financial risks associated with a project. One way of reducing risk is for both firms to provide the up-front capital investment. Another way is for one partner to provide special expertise that the other lacks in return for financial investment.

7. A *Research and Development* (R&D) alliance occurs when two or more organizations join together to conduct joint research or produce products jointly. The emergence of rapid changes in technology life cycles together with high costs for R&D make this attractive.

8. A *public–private partnership* (PPPs) is a special type of alliance that involves one or more privately owned firms and a government organization. This type of collaboration occurs, for example, because a firm may enter into an alliance with a government if the country in question does not permit wholly owned foreign operations or is a centrally planned economy. Another important motivation for PPPs is their potential to achieve significant cost reductions in the delivery of services for governments (e.g., Worenklein, 2003). In fact, government contracting with the private (or non-profit) sector is now regarded as the second most common form of public service delivery (Brown and Pitoski, 2003). PPPs have spread globally, and many governments now use them to deliver services, as an important strategy in both developed and developing economies, sponsored both by regional and national governments, as well as supra-national organizations, including the International Monetary Fund and the World Bank. In a context where international financial ratings agencies assess national and sub-national governments' economic performance, and influence resulting investment decisions on the basis of governments' capacity to maintain a balanced budget, PPPs are attractive because they deliver services while minimizing public indebtedness. PPPs, as a preferred strategy towards this end, potentially enhance governments' international and domestic standing.

IN PRACTICE

United Parcel Service

Image 6.1   UPS. Copyright: SeanShot

In September 2009, UPS, the worldwide delivery service and the UPS Foundation announced that they would jointly support a multi-year, multi-million-dollar initiative to improve the capabilities of relief organizations to respond to global emergencies. The effort involves a commitment of up to US$9 million in the form of substantial financial grants, in-kind services and the deployment of logistics expertise supporting some of the world's most respected relief organizations, including the American Red Cross, UNICEF, the World Food Programme, CARE and the Aidmatrix Foundation.

'This broad strategy for global disaster preparedness and response extends well beyond traditional financial support,' said Ken Sternad, president of The UPS Foundation. 'We are combining our supply chain expertise, our assets and linking our key partners to enable more effective response to global emergencies.'

Hundreds of millions of lives are affected daily by natural disasters and humanitarian emergencies. According to UNICEF at the time of the cooperative arrangement, in the last decade an estimated 20 million children have been forced to flee their homes and more than 1 million have been orphaned or separated from their families as a result of these tragedies. These numbers can only have been inflated significantly by recent events in the Middle East and elsewhere. 'If UPS can impact even a small percentage of these disasters that are happening daily somewhere around the world, this initiative will have been a success,' added Sternad.

In launching the initiative, UPS and The UPS Foundation announced major donations to organizations committed to disaster preparedness and relief. They include:

- A US$500,000 cash and in-kind donation to the American Red Cross to provide logistics, shipping and warehouse support, enabling the Red Cross to strategically preposition supplies to more effectively respond to the needs of those affected by disasters.

(Continued)

(Continued)

- A two-year, US$1 million commitment to the U.S. Fund for UNICEF, including a grant to strengthen UNICEF's emergency response capacity for its disaster preparedness programme in the Asia-Pacific region.

- Collaboration support for CARE and Aidmatrix to establish integrated and standardized supply chain management systems.

- Expansion of the UPS commitment to the Logistics Emergency Teams (LETs) initiative that provides logistics experts to the World Food Programme. LETs operate in support of the United Nations Logistics cluster following natural disasters and consist of logistics experts who deploy within 48 to 72 hours for three to six weeks in the aftermath of major natural disasters. Twenty UPS employees will be trained and available globally as LETs responders.

- A US$250,000 grant to Aidmatrix to help fund the international expansion of the organization's transportation aid relief programme. UPS is matching this grant with US$250,000 in donated transportation.

Founded in 1951 and based in Atlanta, GA, The UPS Foundation's major initiatives include programmes that support community safety, non-profit effectiveness, economic and global literacy, environmental sustainability and diversity. The UPS Foundation pursues these initiatives by identifying specific projects where its support can help produce a measurable social impact. In 2008, The UPS Foundation donated $46.9 million to charitable organizations worldwide (see www.businesswire.com/news/home/20090924005530/en).

Questions

1. What type of collaboration is described in the case?

2. How is this collaboration different to more straightforward business collaborations?

3. What are the strategic advantages of this type of alliance?

Factors to consider in constituting collaborative strategies are speed, risk and access to capital. Forming an alliance is likely to be faster than establishing a fully owned start-up organization and less expensive and risky than an acquisition. A firm that collaborates may also be able to leave assets and capital available for other purposes, while at the same time alliances may reduce exposure of capital and assets to risk of loss, for example when investing in unpredictable markets. The decision regarding the choice of an alliance strategy focuses on gaining access to tacit organizational knowledge and capabilities rather than simple commodities or hard assets that can be found in the marketplace. Typically, the latter do not offer significant advantage, because they are available to anyone else who can afford to buy them.

The decision to collaborate can be even more significant in the international context. The global environment contains a diversity of knowledge embedded in national systems of innovation. Firms can face disadvantages from lack of local knowledge relating to social, political and economic conditions in foreign markets (Beamish, 1994). Hence, collaboration has increasingly been a preferred way for many organizations to deal with the lack of knowledge about foreign local environments and entry into such markets (Dunning, 1997).

One of the most important reasons for firms to form strategic alliances has been to gain access to important markets. Foreign market entry strategies can be achieved through absorption strategies of mergers and acquisitions (Casciaro and Piskorski 2005). In other words, when deciding to 'buy' and not to 'make', one firm is absorbed through a merger or acquisition and the external environmental boundaries within which the acquiring firm operates change by gaining direct control over the resources held by the other organization (Hillman et al., 2009). However, gaining access to and control over critical resources may also be achieved by forging partnerships. In fact, to 'ally' can be less expensive and less risky than an acquisition and, in many situations, much faster than buying another business or establishing a fully owned start-up organization. A firm that collaborates may also be able to leave assets and capital available for other purposes, while at the same time alliances may reduce exposure of capital and assets to risk of loss, for example, when investing in emerging and less predictable markets.

Collaboration can also help overcome trade barriers. For example, many Western companies that sought to enter the Chinese market in the early 1990s were only able to do so by finding local partners and setting up a joint venture that was located in China and use this to produce goods and services by making substantial use of local resources and suppliers. While foreign companies invested capital and supplied the technology, they gained local knowledge and, more important, the ability to get around import quotas. Hence, some of the key benefits a firm may seek to realize from strategic partnerships include reducing risk, entering new markets more easily, obtaining new knowledge and realizing operational synergies.

- *Reducing risk.* Alliances can help partners minimize or control risk because they imply that two or more organizations work together and share, for example, investment in crucial technologies, knowledge and production facilities.

- *Entering markets.* Alliances are a way for firms to overcome obstacles that restrict entry to new markets, thereby expanding faster, globally, while keeping costs down. Collaborating with local partners can help surmount regulations regarding entry modes that are imposed by the host government. It can also be a means of obtaining essential information about local customers, distribution networks and suppliers.

- *Gaining knowledge.* A firm may be able to gain access to knowledge and expertise that it lacks via a strategic alliance. Learning from alliance partners can help build capabilities within the alliance and be transferred to other parts of the organization.

- *Achieving synergy.* The complementary strength of alliance partners, combined with the above advantages, can result in synergies that allow for more efficient and effective use of resources, thereby providing a source of competitive advantage.

Barney and Hesterly (1996) suggest that global strategic alliances are motivated by the partnering firms' intent to focus on exploiting economies of scale; gaining low-cost entry into new markets; learning to enhance a firm's knowledge base; managing uncertainty, costs and risks; or facilitating tacit collusion. The most relevant motivation from a global management perspective is to form a *geographic alliance*, where two or more companies come together jointly to market or co-brand their products and services in a specific geographic region.

Other kinds of alliance might be motivated by joint products and services or just sales objectives, when partners agree to go to market together either to develop and sell a specific marketplace solution jointly or sell complementary products and services. These are perhaps the most common forms of alliance. In many cases, alliances between companies involve two or more of the above reasons for partnering.

Where alliances are between firms that might also be competitors in some other spheres, they are referred to as examples of coopetition. Joint ventures in the past between General Motors and Toyota or Apple and Sony are examples.

Gnyawali, He &
Madhavan

EXTEND YOUR KNOWLEDGE

In Devi R. Gnyawali, Jinyu He and Ravindranath ('Ravi') Madhavan's journal article, **'Impact of coopetition on firm competitive behavior: An empirical examination'**, the authors examine how coopetition affects firms' competitive behaviour. You can read the article on the book's companion website: www.edge.sagepub.com/strategy2e.

Gnyawali, D.R., He, J. and Madhavan, R. (2006), 'Impact of coopetition on firm competitive behavior: An empirical examination', *Journal of Management*, 32: 507–530.

Creating value through partnerships

It has previously been noted that alliances may involve higher transaction costs, hence a company would need to compare costs and benefits before deciding what is best overall. An error in factoring in transaction costs or other factors can affect the performance and viability of the alliance.

Strategically speaking, the success of a partnership and subsequent alliance performance is a function of the partner's ability to create added value and share it in a mutually satisfactory way. The ability to create value rests on the set of unique resources and capabilities of the alliance. Two distinct mechanisms – resource-picking and capability-building – are important in how firms create value (Barney, 1986).

Resource picking means that managers gather information and analysis to pick resources, similar to the way that a fund manager picks stocks – seeking the best buys and prospects for future gain. Capability-building means managers design and construct organizational systems to enhance the productivity of resources that the firm acquires. The two mechanisms are not mutually exclusive; that is, firms usually apply both of them (Makadok, 2001). Taken into the alliance context, value similarly results from the partners' search and selection processes (picking the winning resources) and the innovative configuration and deployment of new resource combinations (jointly building new capabilities).

Capabilities reside within the relationships, structures, mechanisms, processes and procedures that enable the leverage of pooled resources and their innovative re-combination. These contribute collectively to the performance of collaborative ventures and ultimately the creation of superior rents. Accordingly, the two value-creating mechanisms can lead to additional sources of competitive advantage, increased efficiency and the leverage of new business opportunities.

One alliance that many people will be aware of is in the airline industry. In 1997, a group of five world-class airlines got together to create something never seen before – the Star Alliance that brought together networks, lounge access, check-in services, ticketing and dozens of other services to improve the travel experience for passengers. As one of the first major strategic partnerships of various airlines the Star Alliance creates value for its partners.

IN PRACTICE

Star Alliance: A global partnership of airlines

Star Alliance is a truly global network of airlines; it was the first airline alliance to offer its customers worldwide reach and a superior travel experience. Its members in 2016 are 28 airlines including Air Canada, Air China, Air India, Air New Zealand, ANA, AEGEAN, Asiana Airlines, Austrian, Avianca, Ethiopian, Egyptair, LOT Polish Airlines, Lufthansa, Scandinavian Airlines, Shanghai Airlines, Singapore Airlines, Shenzhen Airlines, South African Airways, SWISS, TAP Portugal, Turkish Airlines, THAI and United. Regional member carriers enhance the global network, including Adria Airways, Brussels Airlines, Eva Air, Copa Airlines and Croatia Airlines. Overall, the Star Alliance network offers more than 18,500 daily flights to 1,330 destinations in 192 countries, which means easier travel and quicker connections.

While Star Alliance was the first multi-partner alliance in the airline industry, it did not remain the only one for very long. Rivalry among large constellations took off when American Airlines and British Airways launched the Oneworld alliance in February 1999. Amongst the founding members of this group were Canadian Airlines, Cathay Pacific and Qantas. Later, Finnair and Iberia joined, as well as Japan Airlines, LAN, Malev and Royal Jordanian, resulting today in an overall 15 airlines and 30 affiliated carriers covering more than 14,000 daily flights to over 1,000 destinations.

The overall strategy for Star Alliance, as much as for Oneworld, is to make the travel experience smoother, with access to more airport departure lounges, joint frequent flyer benefits, products and other corporate solutions. Member airlines are located closer together in airports, and share technologies and common facilities at airports, coordinating schedules and installing connection teams for faster transfers.

Most alliance activities of Star Alliance are coordinated through Star Alliance Services GmbH, a jointly managed organization based in Frankfurt, Germany. The operational team of about 65 employees from more than 25 different countries manages a portfolio of alliance products and services, and develops new offerings for the partners and manages the Star Alliance brand. Managing this complex alliance is all about enabling connectivity, collaboration and coordination – creating and managing the products and services that make the flying experience as comfortable and seamless as possible for member airlines' customers.

(Continued)

(Continued)

The benefits for partners of the Star Alliance are many. For example, partners are able to optimize their network through an extended 'hub and spoke' system, in which the main airports in a country serve as hubs through which passengers are channeled from and to various spokes that connect the hub to the final destinations. For example, Lufthansa passengers have access to Honolulu, Atlanta, Seattle and other US cities by flying United via the Chicago hub. Similarly, United does not fly from Munich to Frankfurt, but Lufthansa does. Hence, alliance partners have access to millions of new customers and are able to increase sales and subsequent load factors while at the same time building customer loyalty through a smoother transfer.

Another major benefit for alliance partners is to combine purchases and increase buyer power. Star Alliance partners combined purchase of goods and services – excluding aircrafts – amounts to about US$15 billion annually. By jointly sourcing fuel, IT hardware, advertising media, network bandwidth, telecommunications, aircraft parts, in-flight service material and tyres, partners can realize enormous efficiencies.

In 2015 Star Alliance announced that it was to expand its network reach even further with the launch of its Connecting Partner Model. Under this new concept, routes operated by 'low-cost' and 'hybrid' airlines will be able to connect to the network. This will allow customers to select from an even wider choice of destinations and flights.

Connecting Partners will be assessed for their fit into the existing Star Alliance network. While these selected airlines need to comply and adhere to the high operating standard required by the Alliance, they will not become a member of the Alliance itself.

Customers travelling on an itinerary that includes a transfer between a Star Alliance member airline and a Connecting Partner will be offered benefits such as passenger and baggage through check-in. Frequent travellers will enjoy privileges.

Connecting Partners will enter into bilateral commercial agreements with selected Star Alliance member airlines, which may include additional Frequent Flyer Programme based privileges.

Overall, in its 18 years of existence Star Alliance has matured. Over 600 million passengers travel with Star Alliance airlines every year.

Clearly managing these relationships involve very high coordination and other transaction costs such as negotiations. But in this case it seems that these are less than the benefits to all parties involved. In many other cases this is not the case, which is not unusual, implying that care with selection and implementation is of the essence.

Questions

1. What are the advantages of collaborating in the airline industry and what are the disadvantages?

2. How can a partnership such as the Star Alliance be managed effectively?

3. How do the two main competing airline alliances Start Alliance and Oneworld differ? Go to www.staralliance.com and www.oneworld.com and compare the two.

4. Is the Star Alliance resource picking or capability-building? Explain why.

Difficulties with strategic partnerships

Despite the potential benefits and the evident and increasing importance of alliances, their outcome has not always been satisfactory. Many alliances have not accomplished their objectives (Ellis, 1996; Hennart et al., 1998; Parkhe, 1991; Pearce, 1997). Alliance partners can end up wasting valuable time and resources trying to understand each other, even before the actual collaboration starts.

Difficulties with strategic alliances arise as a result of various issues, all of which are exacerbated in global contexts in which there is often not a high degree of mutual understanding:

- When partners are unable to match resources and align cultures, decision-making processes and systems in the alliance team (Kale et al., 2000)

- When they are unable to create trusting relationships (Ariño et al., 2001)

- When they have to manage conflict (Doz and Hamel, 1998)

- When inter-personal ties need to be cultivated (Hutt et al., 2000)

- When there is a need to handle rivalry and managerial complexity (Park and Ungson, 2001; Sampson, 2005)

- When methods of dealing with environmental change differ (Mitchell and Singh, 1996).

These challenges and the failures of strategic partnerships, which are often closely related phenomena, are also a reminder that strategy should always be regarded as being in process: partnership strategy has to deal with emergent issues and new sources of complexity rather than being an unchanging plan of campaign. These aspects of inter-organizational collaboration, and many other strategic as well as practical issues, are important for partners to consider when entering strategic alliances or getting involved with networks. To begin with, firms have to assess whether or not collaboration is a viable strategy. They then have to find suitable partners, negotiate terms and conditions, implement governance structures, processes and policies and choose and integrate the alliance management team and team members. They need to weigh up advantages and disadvantages vis-à-vis alternatives, such as acquisitions, and ultimately know when best to exit the partnership. In what follows we will look closer at different aspects of collaborative strategies, explore various types of alliances and the means that firms can use to govern and manage their sometimes multiple relationships with different strategic partners.

IN PRACTICE

An alliance between Ford and Fiat in the 1990s failed due to managerial complexities that neither partner was able to overcome. After more than a year of discussing a wide range of proposals, they realized that they could not agree on the management structure necessary to launch the alliance. The differences in management and operational

(Continued)

(Continued)

structures were so big that Ford and Fiat decided it was impractical to enter into a cooperative relationship.

In 1992 IBM, Toshiba and Siemens announced an alliance to design and manufacture 256-megabit chips, which required a high level of interaction amongst the partners. Despite the strong economic interest of the partners, the alliance was unsuccessful, due to high coordination costs. The economic potential was overshadowed by difficulties in coordinating the three culturally very distinctive firms; IBM perceived Toshiba as excessively group-oriented and Siemens as overly concerned with costs and details of financial planning.

In fact, in the last decade there have been repeated reports suggesting up to 50% of alliances fail to satisfy the set objectives of collaborating partners. A study by the management consulting firm PricewaterhouseCoopers (Rea, 2004) revealed that half of the senior executives who were interviewed considered alliances vital to their business and that the number of alliances they engage in is growing substantially. However, while the understanding and use of alliances has clearly improved, executing a successful alliance is not without difficulties. Over half of the survey respondents either didn't know whether their organization's alliances were meeting their performance goals, or admitted that fewer than 50% succeed.

Question

You are working as a strategic advisor to a firm that is contemplating a strategic alliance with another firm in the same industry. You have been asked to provide a generic briefing note on the likely advantages and probable pitfalls of strategic alliances. Drawing on theories that you have encountered in the book thus far, what would your table of pros, cons and reasons include?

EXTEND YOUR KNOWLEDGE

Heimeriks
et al

In Koen Heimeriks, Geert Duysters and Wim Vanhaverbeke's 2007 journal article, '**Learning mechanisms and differential performance in alliance portfolios**', you can read about the differential performance effects of learning mechanisms in alliance portfolios. The article is available on the companion website for this book: www.edge.sagepub.com/strategy2e.

Heimeriks, K.H., Duysters, G. and Vanhaverbeke, W. (2007) 'Learning mechanisms and differential performance in alliance portfolios', *Strategic Organization*, 5: 373–408.

Alliance organization – contractual agreements and governance

The mechanisms, structures and practices of **alliance governance** that partners establish to direct the alliance are at the core of successful partnership strategies. Especially given the different nature of various types of partnerships it is important to choose governance wisely so that strategic performance of alliances is enhanced.

Ariño and Reuer (2006) stress the distinct differences of contracting and governance in alliances. While the contract is concerned with the allocation of risks and trading gains resulting from exchanges between cooperating partners, governance refers to the institutional context in which the collaboration takes place. Research on governance for alliances has largely been based on a distinction between equity and non-equity arrangements. A number of authors argue that equity alliances provide partners with more managerial control than non-equity alliances by virtue of the establishment of an administrative hierarchy that allows partners to exercise a right of control (Hennart, 1988; Pisano, 1989).

> **Alliance governance** concerns the way an alliance is co-governed by the partners, in particular with regard to the integration of their interests, the use of combined resources and their relationship.

- *Equity alliances*, such as joint ventures, involve the creation of a separate, new organizational entity. Joint venture partners provide financial capital and other resources to the newly created firm, which typically has its own management team reporting to a board composed of representatives from the joint venture partners. Equity ownership is associated with greater control under the assumption that owning more equity provides a partner with more voting power. Shared equity ownership might also be expected to align the incentives of partners, thereby creating mutual interests that reduce the need for control (Oxley, 1997).

- *Non-equity alliances* are based on contractual agreements and entail any form of cooperative relationship between two or more firms. The agreement can be more or less formalized and either emerges from the interactions of two or more firms or is the result of purposefully establishing a collaborative organizational relationship. Non-equity alliances are seen as more akin to arm's-length transactions (Contractor and Lorange, 1988) and include, for example, long-term supply relationships, licensing arrangements and distribution agreements.

The distinction between equity vs. non-equity alliances does not, on its own, account for the many different types of alliance governance that firms employ to manage their partnerships. For example, Reuer and Ariño (2002) suggest that contractual agreements can change extensively with different forms of governance. Contractual arrangements differ in respect of their trust or relational quality (Wang and Nicholas, 2005), the specificity of alliance related investments (Reuer, 2005) and the purpose and type of alliance (Lui and Ngo, 2005).

EXTEND YOUR KNOWLEDGE

In Jeffrey Reuer and Africa Ariño's 2002 journal article '**Contractual renegotiations in strategic alliances**', there is an empirical investigation of the incidence and antecedents of contractual renegotiations in strategic alliances. You can find this article on the companion website at www.edge.sagepub.com/strategy2e.

Reuer & Arino

Reuer, J.J. and Ariño, A. (2002) 'Contractual renegotiations in strategic alliances', *Journal of Management*, 28: 47–68.

To manage alliances jointly, firms usually agree on a shared structure, an assigned management or a delegated arrangement. *Shared management agreements* are ones in which each of the partners have a full role in managing the alliance. High levels of coordination are required to make this work as well as detailed agreements. Where one party assumes primary responsibility for the alliance, in order to minimize conflicts and misunderstandings, this is called an *assigned arrangement*. Where operations and management control are delegated to the legally constituted joint venture, something that typically occurs in equity alliances or joint ventures, the partners agree not to get involved in day-to-day management control issues, leaving the exercise of such discretion to the joint venture vehicle.

Joint ventures

In the last two decades, **joint ventures** have been a popular type of equity-based partnership despite the relatively high failure rate of such efforts (Park and Ungson, 2001). While some small business owners have been able to use this business strategy to good advantage over the years, the practice is usually one associated with larger corporations.

> A **joint venture** is an entity owned by multiple parent firms that is legally distinct from the parent firms. The joint venture is undertaken to share the cost and profit of a specific business project.

While joint ventures can be operational and informal, such as an agreement by two companies to share a stand at a trade show, they represent a very useful strategic choice. A strategic joint venture, such as a number of major car manufactures joining to develop new technology, involves much more complex governance agreements. An example is the recent joint venture between Daimler and BYD Auto to meet demands by the Chinese Government for a massive increase in electric cars to fight air pollution (*Wall Street Journal*, 2014). In the past, joint ventures have also been a very common and effective structure to enter new markets where barriers to entry and cross-cultural difficulties can make entry by foreign firms difficult and costly.

A joint venture is not an organization in the sense of a proprietorship or corporation; it entails a contractual agreement between parties that is tied to a particular purpose and time frame. More broadly, it is an entity formed by independent firms that choose to carry out an activity jointly rather than pursuing the project individually or by merging or acquiring entire business units.

Joint ventures differ from mergers and acquisitions in that the entity has access to only a limited set of each partner's activities or operations, and there is no change in the control of the parent firms, which remain as independent firms with their own strategic goals and business interests. Executives may be hired from outside the operations to run the joint venture, or may be transferred from the parent company, but in both cases have real power and autonomy in decision-making.

While non-equity strategic alliances require no financial stake by participants and are in general a less rigid agreement, a joint venture encompasses a broad range of operations, which could in fact lead to and ultimately include a merger. Other operations include cooperation for particular functions, such as research and development, production or distribution. The focus is generally upon the purpose of the entity and not the type of entity, meaning that a joint venture may be a corporation, a limited liability company, a partnership or other legal structure depending on a number of constraints such as tax and liability regulations.

Another commonly cited motive for the formation of a joint venture is knowledge acquisition. A joint venture can be a vehicle to acquire specialized knowledge that would otherwise be very costly to acquire in a market-based transaction. Companies also use joint ventures to pool together resources to obtain synergies in production or marketing, or gain efficiencies through vertical relationships.

A joint venture can be managed in three ways: parent companies can jointly manage the venture, one parent can manage the venture alone, or an independent team of managers can be hired to run it. Particularly when partners choose an equal ownership and management structure a joint venture can be unstable. When, for example, two partners each hold a 50% interest in equity and the cash flow that is generated by the joint venture, subsequent shared decision-making and the possibility of frequent negotiation or bargaining, can make the locus of control elusive in a joint venture.

Joint ventures are typically broader in scope and have a longer duration than other types of strategic alliances. The duration of a joint venture is, on average, five years, with the most frequent reason for termination being the acquisition of the joint venture by one of the partners, or the failure of the joint venture. Joint ventures involving government partners are seen as particularly risky, showing a higher incidence of failure than their private sector counterparts, and overall, any joint venture faced with a situation of highly volatile demand or rapid change has a very low chance of success.

EXTEND YOUR KNOWLEDGE

In an excellent journal article by Hong Ren, Barbara Gray and Kwangho Kim called **'Performance of international joint ventures: What factors really make a difference and how?'** the authors present an in-depth review and critique of research on international joint venture (IJV) performance. This article can be found on the companion website for this book at www.edge.sagepub.com/strategy2e.

Ren, H., Gray, B. and Kim, K. (2009) 'Performance of international joint ventures: What factors really make a difference and how?', *Journal of Management*, 35: 805–883.

Ren, Gray &
Kim

Managing strategic alliances through different stages

The process of forming an alliance is complex, involving at least two, and perhaps many more, already complex organizations, as partners or owners. In reality, the process of collaboration is likely to be compressed in some stages, extended in others, simultaneous when predicted to be sequential, and otherwise unwilling to be placed on a neat timeline.

In an idealized model we can talk about an alliance life cycle. The idea of the alliance life cycle makes reference to separate stages of collaboration, and the role of the partners and alliance managers at each stage. These life cycle stages can be defined ranging from two stages of pre-incorporation and post-incorporation for joint ventures

Table 6.1   Alliance life cycle stages

Foundation		Development		Maturity		Termination	
The alliance is in the formative stage – partners are just beginning to understand each other's needs and objectives		The alliance is growing closer – partners have developed mechanisms to coordinate efforts and align goals and objectives		The alliance is strong – partners have a common view of business and are managing joint affairs to mutual satisfaction		The alliance is mature – it is beginning to show some signs of strain due to changes in goals and/ or market conditions	
Anticipation	Engagement	Valuation	Coordination	Investment	Stabilization	Decision	End
Pre-alliance competitive needs and motivation emerge	High-energy, strategic potential, goal congruence	Focus on analysis, financial issues, business case	Focus on operations, division of work and parallel activities	Commitment and reallocation of resources, broadening of scope	Focus on maintenance, assessment of value and partner contribution	Strategic evaluation and decision of future direction	The alliance has ended
Business Case	Selection	Negotiation and Governance	Alliance Management		Alliance Assessment and Termination		

Source: adapted from Dyer et al., 2001 and Spekman et al., 1998

(Newbury and Zeira, 1997) to an eleven-stage model (Parkhe, 1996). Dyer and his colleagues (2001) discuss five alliance phases: alliance business case development, partner assessment and selection, alliance negotiation and governance, alliance management, and alliance assessment and termination. Spekman and co-authors (1998) captured the emergence, growth and dissolution of alliances in seven stages; anticipation, engagement, valuation, coordination, investment, stabilization and decision.

From a strategic perspective, global alliance formation stages (including, e.g. anticipation, engagement and valuation) represent the partnering firms' resource picking, whereas alliance management stages (including, e.g. coordination, investment and stabilization) represent capability-building within the alliance. Alliance life cycles, whether they consist of two, four, five or eleven stages, reflect managerial processes that account for differences in managerial behaviour and the changing role and influence of the alliance manager over time. Accordingly, the successful functioning of alliances has different requirements during different evolutionary stages. We can highlight three main stages: foundation, development and maturity, and termination.

Foundation

Once the decision to collaborate is made, a firm starts to consider partners. Michael Geringer (1991) suggests that the alliance foundation stage is critical since partner choice influences resource availability and the viability of the alliance. At this stage real costs begin to be incurred, as the focal firm approaches potential partners to evaluate their true value and mutual fit. Hence, search costs can vary widely, depending on the experience of the firm, the complexity and specificity of the assets that are involved, the number of possible partners and related concerns.

A number of factors influence the firms' choice for or against a potential partner. Das and Teng (1999) suggest that fit between partners can be either complementary or supplementary. Complementary fit implies sharing of distinct resources, for example in alliances between large firms with access to capital and market know-how and small innovative firms with entry to new markets. Supplementary fit, on the other hand, implies pooling of matching resources to reduce costs and improve efficiencies. In another study on partner search and selection criteria, Michael Hitt and co-authors (2000) find that firms in developed markets often emphasize unique competencies and local market knowledge as criteria for partner choice. Hence, the selection of an unskilled partner, or a partner with incompatible systems, or a partner that is unwilling to expose its critical assets, will not add value to the alliance but will still be costly. Other studies also suggest that alliances between strong firms are likely to be successful, while alliances between strong and weak firms, or between weak firms, tend to fail (Bleeke and Ernst, 1991). Thus, identification of strong and capable partners is critical.

Another important aspect in the alliance foundation stage is the assessment of the integrity of a potential partner. Gathering information about partner integrity is important since 'moral hazard' can arise from opportunistic behaviour by a partner leading to unforeseen costs and alliance failure (Balakrishnan and Koza, 1993). A related aspect is the extent to which the partner's goals are compatible (Das and Teng, 1999). Difficulties in identifying genuine strategic objectives increase due to their changing nature over time. Hence, the network of prior alliances often serves as an information guide in the choice of potential partners (Gulati, 1995). A partner may, therefore, be preferred due to prior relationships or ties that have demonstrated both strategic and operational fit. In global operations these issues and the attendant risks are especially acute.

When a partner is selected the subsequent negotiation of contractual agreements and governance models (see earlier in this chapter) must balance the inherent requirement for control with the advantages of flexibility in order to take full advantage of collaboration and its anticipated strategic benefits. The more organizationally embedded and tacit are the resources that the partners hope to share, the greater the potential value of the alliance but the more difficult it will be to negotiate a complete contract. Prior ties can mean that there is a degree of trust between the partners; however, the ambiguity that is part of sharing complex resources also makes contractual negotiations difficult and the agreement of coordinating mechanisms more complex. The successful final outcome of the foundation stages is the choice of an appropriate partner and an agreed alliance contract that in some way determines the governance of the partnership.

Development and Maturity

The next stage of the alliance process involves developing, monitoring and managing the ongoing partnership. This operational stage eventually determines the success or failure of the partnership. Given the high failure rate of alliances, reported in the management literature as being up to 50%, this stage is without doubt the most difficult to master. However, there are many organizations that collaborate successfully. Researchers who studied both alliance failures and successes suggest that experience and dedicated alliance management functions within the parent firms (Kale et al., 2002), comprehensive contracts and good governance (Poppo and Zenger, 2002), a suitable contribution of resources (Robins et al., 2002), the right balance of control and ownership, compatible organizational cultures, as well as mutual knowledge exchange and learning, enhance the chances of successful and long-lasting collaboration.

Further aspects that alliance partners should consider include the agreement of procedure to explicitly deal with conflict between partners (Doz, 1996) and cross-cultural differences (Kale et al., 2000). Bruce Kogut, for example, suggests that greater cultural distance increases the propensity for alliance formation since in global joint ventures cultural differences between a firm's home country and the foreign location in which it is operating leads to a greater rate of contractual governance modes, as opposed to equity ownership (Kogut, 1988). While in such contexts a non-equity alliance is generally more difficult to operate (Almeida et al., 2002), the required local knowledge might be found only in the country's context and can only be accessed through a partner who is also embedded in the context.

In addition, relying on the local context, alliance partners can develop important skills, including staffing, trust building, resolving conflicts, transferring resource and know-how, training and renegotiating agreements that are part of managing the partnership at this stage (Simonin, 1999). Moreover, to build cohesive and high performing alliances, dedicated alliance management teams responsible for creating strategic alignment, a shared governance system and managing interdependencies between the firms are required (Bamford et al., 2004). A dedicated strategic alliance function that coordinates all alliance-related activity within each partner organization helps in institutionalizing processes and systems. It can teach, share and leverage prior alliance-management experience and know-how throughout the company across countries (Dyer et al., 2001).

Overall, agreeing a good contract and building superior alliance management skills can help avoid considerable losses through alliance strategies. Contracts need not be comprehensive, especially if previous relationships and related levels of inter-organizational trust compensate for more complex agreements; however, alliance management capabilities at both the alliance level and the organizational level are the key to successfully implementing alliance strategies.

During the development and maturity stages of the alliance life cycle alliance partners generally seek longevity and stability, in order to fulfil the objectives of the original alliance strategy. However, even successful alliances may need to undergo changes as the relationship evolves, which leads to the last stage, the termination of the alliance.

Termination

Serapio and Cascio (1996) suggest that knowing when and how to exit an alliance is critical to a firm's achieving collaborative objectives without compromising other competitive aspects of its operations. Hence, alliance termination usually occurs due to achievement of the alliance objectives but it may also occur because partners realize that they were not able to manage vital aspects. For instance, these could include complementary resources, anticipated synergies, changing circumstances, evolving roles or changing inter-firm relationships. Other authors (Simonin, 1999) also assert that organizations that do not prepare exit strategies in time may either fall into **competency traps** or find that their collaborators are ready to exit when they are not.

Competency traps occur when firms unconsciously adhere to routines and deny the need for change. They lead them to rely on past successful processes that may no longer be optimal.

It is, hence, important to understand how the alliance evolves over time, how the partners' relative contribution changes, and how the original deal, even if profitable, might no longer work (Zajac and Olsen, 1993). Alternatively, the re-evaluation of the collaboration and adjustments in its structure and objectives by renegotiating the agreement, can lead to new and better results. Some authors suggest that a repetitive sequence of negotiation, commitment and execution stages (Ring and Van de Ven, 1994) and associated learning and subsequent adjustments (Doz, 1996), advances collaboration through alterations of contracts, governance structures and monitoring mechanisms (Reuer et al., 2002).

Another option is the acquisition of the alliance partner (Vanhaverbeke and Noorderhaven, 2002). In this case one partner clearly considers full control of alliance assets and know-how by integrating the alliance into the organization as the best way to achieving strategic advantage.

Alliance termination does not mean that the alliance failed to deliver its outcome; if the objectives of the alliance are accomplished or a changing market or evolving capabilities have made the venture no longer make sense, then termination is the preferred outcome. Similarly, if the alliance has greater value for one partner than the other, for example, due to differential learning, changing strategies, new opportunities or simply different assessments of value, then acquisition is a good outcome as well.

It is only when an economically viable partnership is terminated because of distrust, disagreements, impatience or other relational issues that it can be considered an alliance failure. Firms that build their partnerships on experience, contractual mechanisms for renegotiation, mediation or arbitration, organizational units with specific responsibilities for maintaining relationships and the like contribute to a better understanding of potential and actual alliance issues and more effective solutions. While the termination of a particular contractual agreement may not mean the end of the alliance, renegotiation, termination and acquisition must be recognized as logical steps in the life cycle of collaborative strategies.

IN PRACTICE

Hazel Dooney – Not a hard sell

Hazel Dooney is one of the Asia-Pacific region's most controversial young female artists. According to the *Australian Financial Review*, she 'walks the razor's edge between respect and celebrity in today's artworld' (September 2006). Her work has been exhibited at shows in Australia, the USA, the UK and Japan and is included in private, corporate and institutional collections around the world. At www.hazeldooney.com, Hazel writes thought-provokingly and provides further information about her work and the market dynamics in the arts industry. In a comment on her involvement with auction houses she gives a great example of informal, but very valuable collaboration in the arts.

Hazel has written that

My independence from the traditional primary market has had only positive effects on the regard for my work – and me – in the secondary market, where the financial value of even the most famous artists' works and reputations are tested in public. The idea that artists who manage themselves aren't taken seriously in this market is as dead as the Dodo. No matter what old-school commercial galleries keep telling us, contact between independent artists and even the largest auction houses is not just accepted – it's welcomed. Auction houses

(Continued)

Image 6.2   'Sex, Drugs, Whatever'. Copyright: Hazel Dooney

recognize that artists who understand the function of auctions and who care not only about the condition of work offered for sale but also about contributing to its long-term value are a resource that enhances their efforts.

Remember, too, artists don't make any money on the sale of work through the auction house, which is usually acting on behalf of collectors who insist on anonymity even from the artist. However, we work together on the basis that the interests of the auction house, the collector and the artist are parallel. Commercial galleries do their damnedest to discredit artists who work outside the traditional system – the so-called primary market – because they believe a lack of complete control will undermine the influence (such as it is) they exert on their collector base and their income. It's a shortsighted and stupid attitude. As collaborations between artists and auction houses are demonstrating – look at Damien Hirst's incredible pre-crash marketing and sales coup with Sotheby's – the benefits for galleries who work with artists on equal terms far outweigh the meagre risks.

Questions

1. How would you characterize the type of collaboration described in this case?

2. What are the benefits for the artist, owners, collectors and auction houses by collaborating in the way described?

3. How is value created through collaboration in this case?

Strategic networks

The emergence and proliferation of **network forms of organization** has sparked interest and debate in organization studies. We have learned much about the effects of networks but our understanding of how they are formed, how they change and how networks can themselves possess agential properties that make them complex social actors is limited.

Once scattered across the landscape of the social sciences, social network analysis has coalesced into a vibrant programme of research, one with enviable inter-disciplinary reach, ranging from physics and biology to economics and criminology (for reviews see Borgatti et al., 2009; Freeman, 2011). This explosion in the popularity of network research is readily discernible in the field of management where network research has already generated significant research that has analysed relationships within and across organizations (Brass et al., 2004: 809; Kilduff and Brass, 2010; Ahuja et al., 2012).

> The **network form of organization** can be defined as a collection of two or more actors engaged in repeated and enduring exchange relations with one another but that lacks a legitimate organizational authority to resolve disputes that may arise during exchange (Podolny and Page, 1998: 59).

With the emergence of online social networking services, such as Twitter and Facebook, as well as the rise of networked forms of organization around the globe, it is not hyperbolic to argue that 'the network has become the dominant metaphor of our time' (Scott and Davis, 2007: 278; cf. Wellman and Berkowitz, 1988). In the increasingly global and technologically connected world in which we live, networks can be considered the basic fabric of society. Sociologically oriented organizational theorists have noted the proliferation of networks, organizational configurations that are dissimilar from both markets and hierarchies. Networks are not a new form of organization but they have in recent years become 'a key feature of social morphology' (Castells, 2000: 5).

Scholars have argued that the networked form of organization possesses its own logic (e.g. Powell, 1990; Hamel, 1991) and is becoming more prevalent because it offers efficiency advantages – e.g. in learning – afforded by neither markets nor hierarchies (Podolny and Page, 1998). The progressive emergence of the network society has been captured in the field of strategy across at least three broad streams of research.

Hierarchy After Bureaucracy

First, a succession of scholars since the early 1980s have described the emergence of internal network forms that contributed to the establishment of the post-bureaucratic era. Criticisms of bureaucracy were associated with the questioning of control mechanisms, such as strategic planning or input controls (Lenz and Lyles, 1985; Huber, 1991; Marx, 1991). Critics such as Mintzberg and Waters (1985), who we will encounter in more detail in Chapter 9, argued that strategy was emergent rather than planned and that strategic planning was of limited value (Mintzberg, 1993). The classic tools of bureaucratic controls, it appeared, were less appropriate when confronted with unstable, unpredictable environments (Pascale, 1990; Daft and Lewin, 1993; Victor and Stephens, 1994).

Bureaucracies, by definition, tended to be set in their routines; hence, one important criticism of bureaucracy was that it hampered organizational learning (Argyris and Schön, 1978; Fiol and Lyles, 1985; Senge, 1990; Argyris, 1991; Quinn Mills and Friesen, 1992; Mintzberg, 1993). Inspired by the post-bureaucratic/network organization perspective, various scholars pointed to seemingly new organizational forms characterized by autonomous connections between decentralized units and empowered individuals that stimulated collaboration, knowledge sharing and learning (Josserand, 2004). These new organizational forms included the adhocracy (Mintzberg, 1980), Silicon Valley organizations (Rahrami, 1992), the N-form (Hedlund, 1994) and the model of

British Petroleum (Quinn Mills and Friesen, 1992). Increasingly, research stressed the collaborative and knowledge-sharing capabilities of these new organizations (Kogut and Zander, 1992; Winter, 1993; Ghoshal and Moran, 1996; Nahapiet and Ghoshal, 1998; Zack, 1999; Merali, 2000).

Rather than a pure form premised solely on networks, post-bureaucracies appear as hybrids (Josserand et al., 2006), located between a network logic (Eccles and Crane, 1987; Jarillo, 1988; Bradach and Eccles, 1989; Powell, 1990) and the remnants of bureaucratic controls (Josserand, 2004). Post-bureaucracy may not signal the end of bureaucracy so much as its refurbishment (Clegg and Courpasson, 2004). These new forms are not ideal structures free from domination, the hallmark of bureaucratic relations as Weber (1978) defined them. Orientations structuring goal attainment are internalized in terms of market norms, performance targets and other forms of discipline, rather than being bureaucratically imposed by regulation (Foucault, 1991).

Resource-Based Views of Networks

Inter-organizational networks and collaborations have gained increasing attention over the last decade, with one central theoretical foundation being the resource-based view of the firm (Barney, 2001), developed into the knowledge-based view (Kogut and Zander, 1992). Building on the resource-based view of the firm, the dynamic capabilities approach attempts to answer the question of how an organization can adapt its pool of resources to stay competitive (Teece et al., 1997). A practical translation of such theoretical development was the interest in the 1980s not only in core competencies but also in outsourcing and alliances – forms of networking – as ways of developing organizations in a globalizing environment (Prahalad and Hamel, 1990).

The development of value chain approaches (Porter, 1985) linking core firms with external partners made networks global. Through these inter-organizational networks organizations gained access to external resources and competences that could be combined with their internal capabilities (Foss, 1999; Dyer and Nobeoka, 2000; Kogut, 2000; Acedo et al., 2006; Hagedoorn et al., 2006), captured in the concept of strategic network capabilities. External networks for accessing resources to develop new competencies, expanding capabilities, in terms of strategies, became a central focus of analysis (Borys and Jemison, 1989; Dyer and Nobeoka, 2000; Kogut, 2000; Hagedoorn et al., 2006).

The shift to a focus on networks blurred the market and hierarchy distinctions that TCE sculpted. Seminal research exploring the paradox of embeddedness in the apparel industry by Uzzi (1997) led to an appreciation of the balance between arm's length (i.e. market-like links) and embedded ties, where embedded ties foster knowledge transfer (Dyer and Nobeoka, 2000).

Work on embeddedness, knowledge networks and, as we discussed earlier, coopetition, remain firm-centric approaches: latterly, these have been challenged by emergent forms of networks, such as in the field of open-source software or, more recently, in manifestations of the sharing economy. Innovative forms of governance (Demil and Lecocq, 2006) and value appropriation characterize such models.

Networks as Strategic Devices

Networks have been studied as an intermediary level of structure between fields and actors – individual or collective – as the structures holding institutional fields together

(Meyer and Rowan, 1983) and influencing their evolution (Powell and DiMaggio, 1983). Networks can be powerful carriers of new social norms, values and practices – think of social media networks that emerge through shared interests. Numerous studies have shown the contribution of networks to the diffusion of practices (see Fligstein, 1985; Mizruchi, 1992; Westphal and Zajac, 1997). The diffusion of practices often depends on the socio-metric position of specific actors in a field (Burns and Wholey, 1993) as well as the proximity between actors (Davis, 1991). For instance, the network that follows Taylor Swift is different in kind from a network that connects people in a community of practice that is locally focused. The former is not face-to-face; the latter is more likely to be so. Networks are tools that shape contexts through the practices of network entrepreneurs (see, for example, Leblebici et al., 1991). The website, http://www.mamamia.com.au/, for instance, developed from the entrepreneurship of a young mother and onetime *Cosmopolitan* editor, Mia Freedman. Despite their agency, networks are still often considered as inert and invariant diffusion channels (Owen-Smith and Powell, 2008) rather than as devices for translation (Czarniawska and Sevón, 2005).

A few studies adopt a co-evolution perspective in which it is accepted that 'networks shape institutions but institutions sculpt networks and direct their growth' (Owen-Smith and Powell, 2008: 605). Powell and DiMaggio (1983) discussed how network development was crucial in structuring a field. Such process is not straightforward. While networks are inherently dynamic, their connections are not always positive – they can become a liability, due to shifts in the environment; conversely, they can show unexpected relevance, leading to innovation and transformations, be it organizational, inter-organizational or social, as events shape their relevance and acuity. Transformation initially encouraged by an actor or actors through networks can become a threat, creating resistance and counter-resistance.

Digital Networks and Digital Strategies

With advances in technologies, networks are constantly changing and co-evolving, making them significant social actors. Communication networks, including digital mass self-communication networks, are core to the networked economy. These channels present a paradox as they are increasingly plural in their messages, customers and products but increasingly concentrated in their ownership, as we elaborated in Chapter 3.

At present there are widely disparate forecasts about the future promise of a networked economy. On the one hand, there is the prospect of intensified monopoly capitalism as Internet-based digital business normalizes around monopoly capital models; on the other hand, in their affordances, such as the sharing economy, those less inclined to focus on ownership and control of the means of production might see a post-capitalist future of interdependent entrepreneurs.

Some observers do see the future as post-capitalist, stressing, as does Mason (2015), the mass commercialization of everyday life and desires by applications such as Facebook. For Mason, abundant information is currently both too valuable and too cheap for an economic model based on private property to endure, creating a tension between knowledge (which is limitless) and ownership (which is limited), representing the basic contradiction of capitalism. Mason's unifying idea is 'networks versus hierarchies', such that the central challenge of contemporary politics is to discover new ways to reconcile networks with hierarchies through the institutions of representative democracy.

Communication flows in ways that have been revolutionized since the development of digital technologies, creating the global network society in its interactions and exchanges with, as well as its marginalization of, already existing societal sites, cultures, organizations and institutions of various types.

The network economy lends itself to monopolies as a global platform for free-market late capitalism as a frictionless, borderless economy. The Internet concentrates wealth on the one hand and on the other empowers and promotes a democracy of prejudice and ignorance. While it may also foster a commonwealth of knowledge, as it transcends the boundedness of international relations, the discrimination required to make essential judgments remains tied up in professional codes rather than the democracy of the commons.

Castells (1996) concluded that the network society is one in which capitalism 'shapes social relationships over the entire planet.' (1996: 502). Networks are evolving and dynamic structures. In what has become an increasingly information-based economy, there may be substance to Castells' claim that 'the power of flows takes precedence over the flows of power' (Castells, 1996: 500). Organizations often fail in network transformations because they tend to stick to the illusion that networks are instrumental webs that provide reliable and stable access to resources and manageable and predictable innovations. They thus neglect the power of networks and their transformative force as social actors.

IN PRACTICE

Strategy and the City

Alan Cadogan Interview

Go Online: Visit the book's website at https://edge.sagepub.com/strategy2e to watch an interview with Alan Cadogan conducted by the author team.

Alan Cadogan says, 'the consultation never stops'. Alan led the City of Sydney's Strategy Unit and led the Sustainable Sydney 2030 project – Sydney's long-term vision for a sustainable future. What he refers to is the continuous practice of collaborating and interacting with multiple stakeholders in the strategy formulation process.

When defining Sydney's vision for the future the council engaged in a process of intense consultation with the people of Sydney and included a range of other agencies, partners, consultants as well as the neighbouring councils and a team of Sydney's best minds in urban planning, architecture and design.

During 12 months the internal strategy team and an expert consortium hosted more than 30 community forums, round-table discussions, business forums and City Talks; received more than 15,000 website visitors, and more than 2,000 comments over the phone. People of all ages and backgrounds expressed that they wanted an environmentally sustainable city, one in which people can feel at home and yet connected to the world; a city whose thriving economy positions it as a global centre of excellence, while supporting a rich and creative culture. People want a city that continues to respond, adapt to and manage the issues and challenges of climate change and a global economy.

Further down the track, when implementing strategy, the collaboration continues. Alan emphasizes that coordinating and managing collaboration is at times difficult but more effective in the long term. A key to success is to build trustful personal relationships.

Since many activities within a city are different to what business organizations deal with it is at times a challenging entity to organize. The City of Sydney's internal strategy team had to gain expert knowledge in areas such as sustainable energy supplies to enable and encourage implementation at all levels.

Questions

1. What are typical reasons to engage in collaborative strategies and why does collaboration seem to be the better option?

2. The City of Sydney claims to pursue a collaborative approach for designing and implementing the city's vision for the future. What are the roles of stakeholder consultation and involvement for the development and the success of collaborative strategies?

3. Collaboration can take many different forms ranging from loose information sharing to joint organizations with equity stakes and formal contracting. Discuss different forms of collaborating and their advantages and disadvantages for the partnering organizations.

4. The ongoing management of alliance relationships is key to successful collaboration. What are some elements of successful alliance management that are mentioned above? What other elements can you think of?

EXTEND YOUR KNOWLEDGE

Read the account of the Sydney 2030 strategy by Martin Kornberger and Stewart Clegg **'Strategy as performative practice: The case study of Sydney 2030'** – also available at www. edge.sagepub.com/strategy2e.

Kornberger, M. and Clegg, S. (2011) 'Strategy as performative practice: The case study of Sydney 2030', *Strategic Organization*, 9: 136–162.

Kornberger & Clegg

Alliancing[3]

One form of alliance that has rapidly developed in recent years is known as alliancing. Here the stress is less on the governance structure and more on the creation of appropriate processes.

---

[3]We have drawn the material in this section from research that Stewart Clegg published with colleagues: Pitsis, T., Clegg, S.R, Marosszeky, M., and Rura-Polley, T. (2003) 'Constructing the Olympic Dream: Managing innovation through the future perfect', *Organization Science*, 14(5): 574–590 and Clegg, S.R., Pitsis, T., Rura-Polley, T. and Marosszeky, M. (2002) 'Governmentality matters: Designing an alliance culture of inter-organizational collaboration for managing projects', *Organization Studies*, 23(3): 317–337.

Stewart Clegg, one of the book's authors, first came to know about alliancing in the context of preparations for the Sydney 2000 Olympics (Pitsis et al., 2003, from which the following account is taken). A decision to undertake a major project in the run up to the Sydney 2000 Olympics was taken as a part of the NSW Government Waterways Project in May 1997, designed to clean up NSW rivers, beaches and waterways. Cleaning up the waters of Sydney Harbour was seen as a priority for the Olympics in 2000 given that the 'eyes' of the world would be on the city in just over three years. The proposal sought to capture sewerage overflows that occurred during Sydney's sub-tropical storms, when storm water backs up the sewage system, and overflows into the harbour, bringing in not only raw sewage but also street detritus such as litter, syringes and dog faeces. The main detail of the project was to build approximately 20km of tunnel in the sandstone under very affluent areas north of Sydney Harbour.

At the time of commencement, relatively little was known about the ground conditions and the tunnel had not been designed. Given the tight time frame the availability of Tunnel Boring Machines (TBMs) was critical, as these had to be sourced on subcontract from elsewhere in the world. The first stage of the project, of about 18 months, involved a detailed exploration and design phase. Without this, the contractual risks arising from latent conditions would have been unacceptable to any government client. That made completion in an extraordinarily short period of time vital, obviating against a conventional strategic planning process; instead, a constant process of thinking through the future perfect was implemented. The process comprised imagining a future and then seeking to realize it, subject to constant revision, an approach that seemed inductively to fit Schütz's (1967) conception of the future perfect.

The degrees of ambiguity and uncertainty inherent in the project were high because of the deadline, the lack of engineering information, the lack of information about the characteristics of major pieces of technology (the TBMs), and also the characteristics of the communities affected by the project. Because of the higher than usual degree of uncertainty the project was to be managed in a unique way. Instead of a tender process, where the entire project has to be specified in advance and those specifications made public for community comment, Sydney Water invited expressions of interest from companies willing to enter an alliance to deliver the project. The specifications were only 28 pages in length (unheard of in conventional construction where the bill of works and associated contractual documents can run into many thousands of sheets). As the project would involve concurrent engineering much of the design was unspecified. Specified in detail were the agreed principles that the partners were to commit to as the means for resolving issues within the alliance. These differed markedly from traditional detailed construction contracts with the prospect of arbitration when agreement broke down. A typical approach to selecting partners for the alliance was followed (cf. Stiles and Oliver, 1998), choosing the partners on the basis of their commitment to the envisaged process.

Having thought of the usual way of doing things, with the usual problems that this might entail, with worst and best case parameters, they then set about trying to think of unconventional ways of creating the desired outcome. The outcome was easily encapsulated colloquially: 'a lot less shit and rubbish in the harbour' and sparkling blue water for the TV cameras covering Olympic sailing and swimming events, as well as, in the long term, less pollution generally for residents and tourists. The detailed design of the tunnel was commenced by the alliance once it was established in early 1998 through first defining a Business As Usual (BAU) case, using conventional scenario planning approaches; the outcome that would be most likely to occur with the project if they designed and constructed it through traditional planning methods, such as reverse scheduling. But the project partners wanted to do much better than this – they wanted breakthrough innovations. The alliance partners sought to imagine the project, in terms of outcomes that were so good that everyone benefited: the marine life in the harbour (who were a potent symbol in the project iconography); the residents around the foreshore and above the tunnel route; the local communities with whom they would interact in the process; the Olympics organizers; public works contractors throughout the State of New South Wales and the employees, contractors and client themselves – the members of the alliance. An innovative approach to organizational collaboration framed their thinking and action.

Management consultants experienced in large-scale construction projects helped design a project culture. The consultancy assumed that the alliance would only achieve its objectives if staff at all levels shared the same values, believed that the project was 'something special', and had only its ultimate success in mind – rather than sectional strategic interests. They recommended that cohesiveness could be fostered through creating a project culture that was explicitly designed and crafted to encourage shared behaviours, decision-making and values. (The design and functioning of this culture is addressed at greater length in Clegg et al. (2002a).) A list of value statements was produced by the PALT (Project Alliance Leadership Team), which comprised the formal statement of the culture: the two core values were striving to produce solutions that were 'best for project' and having a 'no-blame' culture:

1. Build and maintain a champion team, with champion leadership, which is integrated across all disciplines and organizations;

2. Commit corporately and individually to openness, integrity, trust, cooperation, mutual support and respect, flexibility, honesty and loyalty to the project;

3. Honour our commitments to one another;

4. Commit to a no-blame culture;

5. Use breakthroughs and the free flow of ideas to achieve exceptional results in all project objectives;

6. Outstanding results provide outstanding rewards;

7. Deal with and resolve all issues from within the alliance;

8. Act in a way that is 'best for project';

9. Encourage challenging BAU behaviours;

10. Spread the alliance culture to all stakeholders.

The project sought to exceed BAU expectations and achieve outstanding results. In order to do this, they were constantly thinking in the future perfect: what would they have to have done to achieve the outstanding performance across the demanding range of indicators to which they had committed? When contrasted with the more traditional construction methods of adversarial exploitation of contractual details for profitable advantage – which are not at all oriented to the future perfect; rather more the future imperfect – and the prospect of their ultimate resolution in arbitration then the uniqueness of the project approach can be grasped.

The basis for the contractors and client benefit was a risk/reward calculation. The project agreement provided for a risk/reward regime based on performance compared to project objectives defined in terms of five key performance indicators (KPIs): cost and schedule – no surprises there – but also safety, community and environment – which are not usually part of construction KPIs. There was one non-negotiable performance criterion, the completion of the project for use by the Olympics. While the alliance had the responsibility of defining BAU objectives in terms of suitable criteria, there was no precedent for a construction project being assessed against such parameters. To ensure independence, external consultants were engaged to review the benchmarks for the non-cost/schedule criteria that had been developed by the alliance. For each area, performance levels, ranging from poor to outstanding, were defined – with the brief being simply to define outstanding through the future perfect – what would an absolutely spotless report card and review of the project require? The specialist consultants also assessed and reported performance against all criteria regularly throughout the project. Success against the non-cost/schedule criteria was critical for project success both in commercial and overall terms and, as such, this area presented the alliance team with significant risks.

There were positive and negative financial outcomes for performance on each of the objectives in the risk/reward process. Financial rewards were payable on a sliding scale for performance above BAU to Outstanding. All objectives, except cost, had a maximum amount. Financial penalties accrued when performance was below BAU and, most importantly, performance in any one area could not be traded-off against any other area that was represented by the KPIs. Only outstanding performance against all five KPIs would yield the maximum return; less than this in any one area would diminish that return and adverse performance would put the reward at risk as penalty clauses began to bite. To make the future perfect concrete meant constructing something that could be imagined as already complete and subject to audit. Thus, in each area performance processes and outcomes were constructed on which the project would be assessed.

The discipline of collective imagination of a future perfect, framed by the designer culture and bound by the governmental strategies of the KPIs and the risk/reward scheme, tied the loose coupling of the collaboration together, as regularly reported in the monthly PALT meetings. In addition, specific future perfect strategies were routinely used as management devices throughout the project. Three specific means of managing through the future perfect strategy were identified. These means included the creative use of strange conversations; the rehearsal of end games and the practice of workshopping and the projecting of feelings, concerns and issues. Each of these adds to our knowledge of how the future perfect strategy is possible, and so we elaborate them here.

Strange Conversations

Karl Weick (1979: 200) introduced the notion of strange conversations to the management literature. Weick defined strange conversations as ones where the agenda, process and outcomes were unclear. A great many community meetings were associated with the project: in each of these, the agenda was unclear, the process highly emergent and the outcomes unknown. In these meetings community members were invited to surface anxieties and make suggestions in relation to the project (almost all of which took place beneath the surface, of which they had little knowledge). What they proposed was often a surprise that, in terms of the rationality of the engineers involved in the project, made little sense: for instance, they were concerned about the visual obtrusiveness of the above-ground works; the noise; mud on the roads; potential loss of access to walk their dogs or for children to play. These were all secondary considerations for the engineers, intent on building the project.

Often, in initial meetings, it was unclear what it was that was being discussed, as talk ranged so widely, in terms of the community members' emotional and aesthetic response to the engineering works. In fact, it was often the case that the eventual outcome informed what it was that the conversations had been about: for instance, once the proposal for the concealment and beautification of one of the sites had emerged, then it crystallized as what had been wanted all along, even though, at the outset, this was not clear at all. Later in the project community liaison officers found themselves organizing BBQs between community and project members, where more such intriguing conversations occurred.

End Games and the Practice of Workshopping

End games helped concentrate minds on the future perfect strategy in the project. End games occurred frequently, as project completion was enacted in the future perfect. Here is an example that occurred at the January 2000 meeting, when a project leader reminded everybody of the objectives. He said:

> We know where we want to be, where we want to go, and where we want to finish up. We need to plan the end and work out each step to get there so everything is synchronized. We need ownership over the deliverables at the end of the project. The ultimate project is the built product.

The significance of end games was that they worked as aids for visualization of the future perfect and enabled the PALT to focus on the future perfect they were seeking to construct. One of the key techniques used to maintain future perfect focus on the end game was workshopping. When it looked as if the project might run over schedule, the PALT agreed to have a workshop to address the alignment of the five key objectives between headquarters and construction sites (PALT meeting, June 1999). They agreed that by the time of the workshop, one of the project leaders would have met with the programme managers responsible for the key objectives. He would have discussed the alignment of the overall objectives with those of the particular construction sites. Additionally, he would have codified the learning breakthroughs at each construction site, so that they could identify how they had reached their outstanding achievements. Further, he would have discussed the workshop agenda with management consultants and would have arranged a workshop venue. Once again, the PALT engaged in future perfect strategy.

Projecting Feelings, Concerns and Issues

Although the PALT team were almost all engineers, people with a technical background who were more professionally versed in technical than social construction, there was some explicit recognition of the importance of social construction in one aspect of the PALT meetings. The agenda for each meeting originally contained a section titled 'Projecting Feelings, Concerns and Issues'. We were rather surprised when we first saw this in action: we had not expected such empathetic and social maintenance work from highly professional engineers. Any member could raise anything under this recurring agenda item, with the issue remaining on the agenda until 'it was no longer important or was addressed to the satisfaction of the person who raised the issue in the first place.' The inclusion of this clause was supposed to ensure that future perfect thinking maintained a reality check: if an issue had been constructed in regard to any aspect of the project that was causing concern, then it was reiterated monthly, until it was no longer a matter for concern. While some of these feelings, concerns and issues were quite technical – about scheduling and such like – others concerned more complex community relations.

The technique was significant – it ensured that the future perfect agenda was open and democratic in its projections amongst the top leadership team. It managed polyphony. It created a space in which emotional aspects of the project could be discussed (Fineman, 1996; Albrow, 1997). Increasingly, the routinized use of the item, which, after a while, became merely a matter for noting rather than action, and was then later abandoned, signalled the limits of future perfect thinking when confronted by community matters that were outside of project control.

The project occurred despite the absence of strategic planning decisions made early on, based on minimal information, that lock the process into an inevitable and unquestioned future. Instead, the people who had the greatest opportunity to alter the outcomes were the people who made the strategy up as they went along; normally they would be locked into protecting decisions already made for them through tactics that invariably lead to litigation. Rather than using detailed project scoping and planning to reduce high ambiguity, as is typical of construction (Stinchcombe, 1985), the PALT project leaders sought to reduce it through creating a shared culture that enabled future perfect thinking to flourish in an imaginative process oriented to a broad range of imagined outcomes by which they would hold themselves accountable.

Future perfect thinking worked most smoothly where the planners had most control – that is, control of the technological and material context for future action. When external actors were empowered to question, achieving the future became more difficult. There were pitfalls in allowing for voice but not providing accompanying responsibility that increased the potential for a project to become hijacked. While project managers may adumbrate a strong culture they need to avoid being sucked in by its rhetoric and realize that it does not necessarily incorporate all stakeholders.

The project grew from just 28 pages, with no design and no clauses, other than an injunction to think in the future perfect and create a much cleaner Sydney Harbour, to a project that delivered what it set out to do: on time, only slightly over budget, it made Sydney Harbour sufficiently clear that in July 2002, in an ecologically symbolic representation of the success of the project, three 80 ton whales came into the harbour to frolic under the famous Sydney Harbour Bridge, with the equally famous Opera House behind them, although cynics might remark on the clarity of the water due to extensive drought. In living memory whales had never been this far into the Harbour before – the Olympic dream appeared to have been spectacularly realized.

Summary

There are various underlying motivations for why organizations might engage in collaborative strategies. Firms use alliances to reduce risks, enter new markets, gain knowledge or achieve synergies. Most importantly firms seek partnerships because they want access to resources that they deem important in creating competitive advantage. Rather than organically growing capabilities a partnership with another firm promises quick access to such needed factors as knowledge, technology or local markets.

The benefit of having quick access to resources usually comes with an increased need for coordination. The issues and implications of contractual agreements and subsequent governance for alliance have been discussed in detail and point out how different types of alliances including equity or non-equity alliances, functional alliances, or public–private partnership have different advantages and disadvantages. A firm has to be aware of such structural and contractual choices before entering into negotiations with potential partners. The concept of the alliance life cycle finally emphasizes the importance of a stepwise approach and re-occurring negotiations for agreeing the optimal alliance contract, the ongoing operations of alliance management, and finally the partner's awareness of when to exit the partnership.

Networks, especially those that are digitally enabled, are an increasing form of collaboration in the contemporary age. Indeed, some writers suggest that we are now living in the era of a 'networked society'.

We have included a number of practical examples of collaboration in alliances, with the City of Sydney 2030 strategy, as well as the example of alliancing that produced some of the Sydney Olympics infrastructure. Although each of these cases draw on the city in which Stewart and Jochen live and work the examples are quite easily generalizable.

TEST YOURSELF

Want to know more about this chapter? Review what you have learnt by visiting www.edge.sagepub.com/strategy2e.

- Test yourself with multiple choice questions
- Revise key terms with interactive flashcards

EXERCISES

1. Having read this chapter, you should be able to say in your own words what the following key terms mean:

    - Inter-firm Cooperation
    - Strategic alliance
    - Alliance governance
    - Equity alliances
    - Non-equity alliances
    - Alliance governance

    - Public–private partnerships
    - Joint ventures
    - Alliance life cycle
    - Competency traps
    - Networks
    - Alliancing

2. What are some of the major issues that require managing in an alliance?

3. What are the distinctive features of 'alliancing'?

4. What are the main drawbacks of alliances?

(Continued)

(Continued)

5. To what extent and in what ways can it be said that we live in a 'network society'? Illustrate your answer with examples.

6. In your view, in what situations would a dissolved alliance signal success and not failure?

7. In what ways does the digital environment afford opportunities for collaboration?

8. What are the stages in alliance formation?

9. What major theoretical approaches in strategy have been used to talk about alliances? Outline their key assumptions and strengths and weakness.

CASE STUDY

Menagerie

MEGHAN HAY

Menagerie is a collaborative arts project between Object – the Australian Centre for Craft and Design – and the Australian Museum. Throughout 2008 and 2009 these two Sydney-based organizations developed a major touring exhibition of animal form sculptural works by Aboriginal and Torres Strait Islander artists from across Australia. The resulting exhibition, Menagerie – Contemporary Indigenous Sculpture, featured more than 50 outstanding new works by 34 prominent artists, demonstrating the breadth of contemporary Indigenous sculptural practice.

The exhibition was presented in Sydney from September to November 2009 in both Object and the Australian Museum's exhibition spaces. 'We had to think about what it might mean for the two spaces. Does one space get all the lizards? Do we go by state? We really wanted a more equitable division, knowing that some visitors may see one space and not the other, and that's what we've tried to achieve', says Bliss Jensen, from the Australian Museum.[4] After its Sydney presentation, the exhibition embarked on a two-and-a-half-year tour to nine cities around Australia.

Although in the past there has been a sustained public interest in the contemporary paintings of Aboriginal and Torres Strait Islander artists, sculptural works have often taken a back seat. The exhibition put together by Object and the Australian Museum has marked the beginning of a significant new emphasis of current trends within the medium of sculpture. The works are created from a range of materials including fibre, ceramics and wood carving along with some bronze and aluminium casts, and all of the artists selected cover a broad geographical spectrum. 'This significant exhibition

---

[4,5] Interview by Joanna Lowry. Available at: www.timeoutsydney.com.au/museums/event/12985/menagerie-contemporary-indigenous-sculpture.aspx.

is the most extensive survey of contemporary Indigenous sculpture to tour Australia. Menagerie celebrates the art and culture of Aboriginal and Torres Strait Islander people and demonstrates the sophistication and diversity of Indigenous art, craft and design in Australia', says Object director, Steven Pozel.[5]

Not long after its success in Sydney the Australian Museum Foundation announced that it considers Menagerie so important that the foundation decided to purchase the entire collection to ensure that the works remain together permanently and thereby accessible to the public. Such acquisition not only sends a very positive message to the artists but also generates significant income directly to artists contributing both to individual communities and the sustainability of the sector generally.

Why has this collaborative effort been so successful? One reason clearly lies within the overall strategic significance of the project and its objectives. Menagerie is important because it is one of only a very few exhibitions of this scale to exclusively focus on Indigenous contemporary sculptural practices when formerly other forms of Indigenous artistic expression like paintings, dance and storytelling had been more commonly featured. Given this gap in the market of exhibition and the strategic opportunity, Object and the Australian Museum aimed to showcase the significance of sculpture within contemporary Indigenous art, craft and design.

Other objectives included the celebration of the diversity that Australia's Indigenous cultures have to offer by showcasing the work and personal stories of a selection of outstanding artists, the acknowledgment of the importance of people's relationship with animals and the unique and diverse environments that we share with them, to promote greater understanding of Aboriginal art and culture through integrated educational programmes, and, finally, to create opportunities for Indigenous people.

The initiative for Menagerie came from Steven Pozel and Brian Parkes – the Director and Associate Director of Object – who knew that Object had the knowledge and ability to conduct the project research, select the artists and the works, produce the publication that would accompany the exhibition and manage a national touring programme. However, the organization was facing organizational limitations: Object's exhibition space was not large enough to accommodate the expected size of the show, nor did Object have the conservation experience that would be necessary to catalogue and protect the anticipated works. Knowing that they would need a partner to turn an inspiring idea into reality, Steven and Brian started looking out for potential candidates to collaborate with. With its focus on nature and culture, the availability of significant exhibition space in Sydney in close proximity to Object's location, as well as its significant expertise both in cultural object conservation and in putting together large-scale projects, the Australian Museum was the perfect organization to approach with the Menagerie proposal. However, despite a history of cross-promoting shows and co-presenting public programmes, the two arts organizations had never collaborated on a project before.

In 2008, a memorandum of understanding was signed outlining the way in which both organizations would bring their respective strengths to the project. This comprehensive agreement outlined crucial relationship parameters such as the legal structure of the venture, the process for decision-making, the division of project management responsibilities and cost responsibility as well as specific allocation of duties relating to

(Continued)

(Continued)

the development, design, production and presentation of the exhibition. Subsequently, during the two-year project development period, other key partnerships developed that supported the dynamic between Object and the Australian Museum.

One example of such a partnership was the one forged with Sydney's Taronga Zoo, which became involved with the creation of an engaging and inspiring children's education programme, one of the key initiatives for the project. While Object and the Australian Museum worked together to create an education kit for primary school students and teachers that would help communicate the skill of the artists, their cultural heritage, and their passion for the natural environment, it was the partnership with the famous Sydney-based zoo that brought the learning programme alive. Through this collaboration, primary school students visiting the exhibition at Object would first meet zoo staff outside the gallery who would introduce the students to living native animals. The children would get to touch the animals and learn about their habitats and their relationship with humans. The students would then spend some time in the gallery, viewing the Indigenous sculptural interpretations of similar animals to the ones they had just met, to then have the opportunity to create their own animal sculptures in the gallery space, surrounded by the artists' sculptures. During the two-month exhibition period, over 800 children were able to share this experience in Object's modest, inner-city gallery space.

Overall, audience responses recorded through visitor evaluation surveys in both venues indicated very high levels of visitor satisfaction with the content and nature of the exhibition. More than 100,000 people saw the exhibition while it was in Sydney.

The exhibition has received significant media coverage in each of the cities in which it has been presented thus far. Critical reviews of the show have been overwhelmingly positive. Moreover, through the project, numerous Indigenous artists found their work promoted to a national audience, and received income in the form of artist and photographic reproduction fees.

QUESTIONS

1. Thinking of this collaboration in terms of the types of inter-firm cooperation covered this chapter, how would you classify it? Why?

2. All alliances involve stakeholders: who were the stakeholders in this case and how did they each receive value from the alliance?

3. What potential downside for the future do you see arising from the alliance for the Indigenous stakeholders? How might this be rectified? What difference would you suggest making to the alliance to protect the future interests of the Indigenous stakeholders?

STRATEGY: GOING GLOBAL

CONVERGENCE, DIVERGENCE, HYBRIDIZATION

Learning objectives

By the end of this chapter you will be able to:

1   Define globalization and identify several misconceptions about it

2   Understand theories of the Multinational Enterprise (MNE)

3   Grasp different approaches to how multinational enterprises internationalize

4   Understand the phenomenon of being 'born global'

5   Explain the strengths and weaknesses of different multinational global strategies

6   Understand supply chains and their political dimensions

7   Understand the specificities of the BRICs and their strategies

BEFORE YOU GET STARTED

[W]e are in the epoch of simultaneity; we are in the epoch of juxtaposition, the epoch of the near and far, of the side-by-side, of the dispersed. We are at a moment, I believe, when our experience of the world is less that of a long life developing through time than that of a network that connects points and intersections with its own skein. (Michel Foucault, 1986: 22)

Introduction

Today, with the right digital devices and technology, anywhere can be connected almost everywhere. The powers of connectivity are not, however, evenly distributed. It is evident that there are global nodal points that concentrate the flows through which capital and investment move. These are centred regionally in the global economy: cities in the developed world, notably New York, Tokyo and London, channel many of these capital flows. The International Monetary Fund (IMF), in defining globalization, pays particular attention to trade and financial flows, as well as the movements of people and technologies across international borders. Trade is usually thought of as entailing the physical transfer of goods from one place to another in a very material sense (on ships, trains, trucks and planes). As steamships, railways, trucks, automobiles and jet airplanes gave way to the Internet as the major communication device, its distinctive modes of communication make the present wave of globalization different from the past because information now travels at the speed of light. Today, globalization also refers to the movement of immaterial things in the form of downloads, capital and culture, with financial flows being the most immediate, liquid and virtual manifestation of globalization.

In this chapter we will first discuss globalization as a complex of historical, cultural and economic phenomena. While contemporary forms of globalization might be based on new technologies there are plenty of precedents for the processes under consideration. Globalization is one of the most contested concepts of current times; the Occupy movement and protestors at Davos and World Trade meetings bitterly oppose it while politicians and captains of industry extol its virtues of free trade and liberal markets. Critics and fans of globalization are to be found in the ranks of scholarship as well; meanwhile, in the real world, things become mashed up – glocalization prevails as a strategy of making the local global.

Multinational enterprises (MNEs), defined as companies with facilities and other assets in at least one country other than its home country, own and control production facilities in different countries and usually have a centralized head office where they coordinate their global operations.

Multinational enterprises (MNEs) have long been a staple of the International Business (IB) literature and we outline some of the central arguments and models to be found there; later, we shall suggest these models are being superseded by emerging markets' multinationals.

The key element in developing a global strategy is often regarded as arbitrage. Arbitrage can be leveraged over many markets; of particular interest is the labour market. Inescapable aspects of multinationals' operations are issues centred on complex and frequently contested employee relations. On the one hand, multinationals can afford generous terms and conditions in terms of local norms in their subsidiaries and branch plant operations. On the other hand, they often engineer supply chains at whose extremities there are practices that they might not want their customers and publics to know about.

Multinational–politics – the politics associated with multinational operations in terms of both centre – periphery relations between head office and subsidiaries as well as with national governments – are also an inescapable fact of multinational strategies. Typically, multinationals use mandates as tasks assigned to subsidiaries by headquarters or that are acquired independently by the subsidiary, with a specific time and content limitation placed on them, to frame the internal division of labour within a MNE. Framing a mandate does not mean that it necessarily is implemented: there is many an opportunity for translations of ideas to go awry as they move from inception at the centre to reception in the periphery of a multinational. To be implemented, a mandated change needs to accrue legitimacy, something that cannot be established by central fiat.

One commentator, *New York Times* journalist, Thomas Friedman, has regarded multinationals as making the earth flat. Others like Harvard Professor Ghemawat question this claim, insisting that the world is actually more spiky than flat; it is at best 'semi-globalized'. Why Friedman is wrong takes us into debates about convergence, divergence and hybridity, debates that come to life when we look at the cases of the so-called BRIC economies – Brazil, Russia, India and China. These economies have a lot less in common than the BRIC label assumes. In particular, we focus on China, now the world's largest economy. China has been at the centre of some important debates about innovative capacity and political structure, which we address. We discuss current trends in China, looking at strategies in the context of Chinese family businesses as well as the phenomenon of *Shanzai*, the local name for piracy and counterfeiting, which prompts us to ask: how innovative are Chinese enterprises? On this question, the answer to which is not yet apparent, much will depend for the future of globalization.

Globalization

Globalization as Historical Phenomena

Contemporary commercial globalization is usually seen as a late twentieth century phenomenon, although there is an argument that says that the world economy in the early twentieth century was almost as globalized as it is now. Hirst and Thompson (1996) suggest that the currently intensely interconnected economy is not unprecedented historically, albeit that the mechanisms of globalization differed – the telegraph instead of the Internet, for instance. From this perspective, globalization is just internationalization speeded up and in no way differs from processes that have been characteristic of trade in much of past human history. For instance, the age of colonialism by the end of the nineteenth century had produced a remarkably globalized world; one in which global trade flowed through schemes of imperial preference with currencies readily exchangeable because of the gold standard. This era of globalization ended in carnage and autarchy with the First World War and the Depression of the 1930s, giving rise to the Second World War.

In the past, steamships, railways, trucks, automobiles and jet airplanes spread global ideas, trades and peoples.

Globalization can be thought of as worldwide integration in virtually every sphere, achieved principally through international movement of diverse goods, services and processes across the borders of global regions and countries into different geographic locations or markets.

Today these forms of communication have given way to the Internet as the major communication device, making the present wave of globalization different from the past because information now travels at the speed of light. Globalization existed long before the Internet, however.

There are historically unique features that constitute globalization (Darwin, 2007: 7–8). Enumerated, they are the following:

1. The emergence of a single global market for most widely used products; especially for the supply of capital, credit and financial services.

2. Increased political intensity of interaction between states: with the exception of North Korea there are few states preferring autarchy.

3. The deep penetration of almost all cultures by global media, especially through the Internet and the ubiquity of leading brands promoted through these media.

4. Huge scale migrations and diaspora creating global networks and connections as a result of economic migrations and the effects of wars. Most refugees today are from Africa and the Middle East and, given their youthful demographics, the flows are not likely to diminish.

5. The dominance of the United States as a hyper-power after the bipolar arrangement of the Cold War era (1945–1989).

6. The dramatic resurgence of China and India as manufacturing powers, with deep reserves of population to draw on as consumers and producers in a domestic market (about 1.3 billion and 1 billion respectively).

The translation of historical imperialism into contemporary commercial globalization is usually seen as a late twentieth century phenomenon, although, as we have discussed, there is an argument that says that the world economy in the late nineteenth and early twentieth century was almost as globalized as it is now.

Globalization as Cultural Phenomena

Globalization intensifies social relations over ever-greater distances; it links different and previously separated peoples and places; it transforms spatial and temporal organization of global flows of power, people, ideas and things. Globalization is a relational process better thought of as globalizing, as a verb, rather than as a noun, because there may be nothing that corresponds to it; simply, it is a process rather than a thing.

In globalizing, flows and values of key resources, such as commodities as well as currencies, are subject to continuous change, such that flux seems the apparent norm. Although all senses of time are always relative and plural, not absolute, dominant contemporary flows of time associated with digital immediacy have become pervasive. Presence and immediacy hasten the adoption of dominant discourses as they can flow anywhere and everywhere simultaneously. Globalizing modernity is thus more than merely a globalization of economic forms but is a globalization of whole forms of life (Ibarra-Colado, 2008). Globalization transforms social as well as economic relations.

Almost all the basic strategy models for thinking about globalization derive from North American and European assumptions about the internationalization of business.

Hence, they tend to be rather ethnocentric, seeing globalization as a western 'conquering' of the world. These frameworks have historical roots in modernization theory, which was itself rooted in older notions of progress and evolution. European expansionism and the growth of trade and long-distance travel, as a force for globalization, may be said to have developed from early national trading companies, such as the East India Company. Indeed, much of what we later have come to think of as multinational global strategies were already prefigured in such companies. Seeing the world as something to conquer has been a part of the North's dominant myth-making ever since the Euro-Asian world expanded greatly as a result of the voyages of discovery in the fifteenth century, of which Columbus' is best known. The idea that the world 'out there' was waiting to be conquered has been both instrumental in developing imperial worldviews in Europe and America and latterly in European and American business, as a constitutive part of competitive strategy.

Globalization as Economic Phenomenon

To the extent that globalization flows through multinational organizations it does so in two ways: through the export of their products and through the investment decisions that they make outside the home country – **Foreign Direct Investments (FDI)**.

> **Foreign Direct Investment (FDI)** involves ownership and/or control of production capabilities and facilities cross-border. It often involves participation in management, joint venturing and transfer of technology, branding and expertise. It can take place through mergers and acquisitions, building new facilities, reinvesting profits earned from overseas operations and intra-company loans.

Global products require a process whereby the products or services are accommodated to local tastes or local tastes become accommodated to global products. The former strategy is that of MacDonald's where significant local variations in the basic product may be found globally. The latter strategy is that of Coca-Cola – a coke is a coke everywhere – there are no local variations. Of course, to deliver either local variations or a universal product or service the organizations in question have to engage in FDI. Globalization occurs through the spread of global products and services through exports, licensing and franchising and, notably, through the mechanisms of FDI.

Globalization is carried in part by organizations that open up new markets and capture geographically unevenly distributed resources (Dicken, 2007b), including skills that emerge as a result of global domination by transnational organizations as well as from institutional entrepreneurship. Multinational corporations do not penetrate everywhere equally, in part because massive amounts of capital concentration are not pouring into the least developed countries. In fact, developed countries continue to be the bedrock of capital investment. It is only in recent years that FDI into developing and emerging economies has surpassed that flowing into developed ones, according to the annual reports of the United Nations Conference on Trade and Development (see the UNCTAD Annual Report 2014, https://unctad.org).

UNCTAD

The role of the Internet in contemporary globalization is Janus-faced. On the one hand it enables many small companies to be born global, as we shall discuss; on the other hand, it enables some to become virtual monopolies straddling the globe, such as Amazon. The Internet has always been a highly political arena. In the early days of its development the Internet was seen as a great liberator, a power for empowerment, for democratization. Economically, its capabilities create rational individuals armed with perfect information acquired from the Internet able to pursue their interests relatively free of governments and geographical obstacles; people whose interest was primarily in getting what they wanted for the cheapest price possible. Micklethwaite

Bruce Schneier TED Talk

and Wooldridge (2000) saw this version of contemporary digital globalization as an unfettered freedom, working not just for multinationals but also for people more generally; globalization, they suggest, produces an economy close to a liberal's utopia.

Today, virtually the whole world economy as a market is incorporated into a world system dominated by capitalism. Mediated by money, exchange can be subject to impersonal and precise division and manipulation and measurement of equivalents. Flows of capital promote seemingly rational calculation, furthering the rationalization that is characteristic of modern society. Contemporary flows of capital are increasingly digitally mediated, creating and extending immaterial capacities for the global translation of invention and innovation.

Glocalization

While globalization increases the ubiquity of objects, practices and experiences in increasingly homogenized, standardized and convergent modes, not everyone around the globe eats the same industrially produced foods, watches the same movies, and wears the same global chain store produced clothes. Globalization does not mean that local cultural differences are obliterated. The persistence and the wider dissemination of local products and tastes into ubiquitously global products, such as the translation of sushi from a Japanese delicacy to a global fast food or vodka from a northern European drink to a global taste, offer opportunities for strategic management. Often these processes are referred to as 'glocalization'. Emerging markets' local products can become global: think of *guaraná*, a fizzy and very sweet Brazilian drink made out of Amazonian berries. Once a specialty only to be found in Brazil it is increasingly available as a sports drink globally and, as such, it is an example of **glocalization**, a neologism coined by sociologist Roland Robertson (1982).

> **Glocalization** as a term is a hybridization of the global and the local, of globalization and localization. It is intended to describe how regional tendencies and local cultures intersect with the proliferation of global corporations. Glocalization means the simultaneous presence of both universalizing and particularizing tendencies.

Glocalization is not just a cultural and consumer phenomenon. Multinational firms face disadvantages from lack of local knowledge relating to social, political and economic conditions in foreign markets (Beamish, 1994). In recent decades a preferred way for many organizations to deal with the lack of knowledge about foreign local environments and entry into such markets is to collaborate with firms already there: they go 'glocal'. Glocal strategies are followed by organizations that seek to go global by entering into some form of local relationship with organizations in another country.

For instance, components for the iPhone are variously assembled in China, Korea, Taipei, Germany and the US, involving almost a dozen companies that are hard to pigeonhole with any national label. Sylvia Yanagisako (2002), in studying the Italian textile and fashion trade, noted that so many of the key processes had moved to China that she had to shift her research to Shanghai. If globalizing means that things that are quintessentially Italian are, in fact, produced by Chinese workers and managers, in China, then we can hardly be sure about the bounded and bordered provenance of anything organizational that we consume in the contemporary world. It is, truly, a hybridizing and glocalizing world in which hybrid strategies are emergent.

New hybrid models of 'integrated networks' (Dicken, 2007a: 301) are emerging that are post-national and that allow new forms of geographical advantage: managers speculate in London or Tokyo, manufacture in the PRC, move the headquarters to the benign fiscal system of the Netherlands, do Corporate Social Responsibility in Uganda and launder money in Zurich or the Bahamas. Different countries position themselves on the basis of their valuable, rare, inimitable and non-substitutable national resources (Barney, 1991) and firms disintegrate their activities to take advantage of this specialization. In consequence, they globalize, decompose and re-compose (Clegg, 2011).

Globalization: Critics and fans

Pro-globalizers argue that the best chance of diminishing immiseration is through the incorporation of more spaces and peoples into processes of globalization.

Globalists argue that as a result of vastly more efficient agro-businesses, the planet is able to sustain a population of six and a half billion, which has doubled in the last 30 years, and that the huge growth in business has in part contributed to this increased population by providing more and better jobs and improved availability of foodstuffs. However, more does not mean equal shares; the benefits are hardly distributed evenly. For instance, the US consumes nearly 40% of the planet's resources such as food, oil and timber – but contains only 6% of the global population, of whom 30% are obese from consuming too much. This degree of concentration is one reason why many critics of globalization claim that it is really 'Americanization'.

OECD Health
Data 2005

Critics of globalization point to the fact that not only are great swathes of the world's population barely incorporated into the global arena but that there are many obstacles and barriers to globalization erected by various interests. Amongst these are states and their governments; domestic industrial players, keen to protect themselves from global competition; trade unions, equally keen to ensure that the price of labour in the labour market is not cheapened and weakened by too global a flow of poor people who will enable employers to cut labour costs. Global society spreads with no regard for borders; the carbon footprint of the most globally advanced nations is warming the planet for even the poorest people on it, who barely contribute to warming.

- -

Go Online: There are many barriers to globalization in practice in a word of nation states and trade blocs such as the EU and ASEAN. Some of these are discussed on the website www.hubpages.com. For a much fuller and more detailed discussion you can consult the 2011 Aarhus University PhD thesis by Christian Gormsen Schmidt, which is available online on the www.pure.au.dk website. An interesting video discussion of 'Globalization – opportunity or risk?' is available on the Deutsche Welles Global Talks webpage. Finally, there is a balanced discussion from a World Bank perspective on 'Globalization and international trade' which is available on the website www.worldbank.org.

Links to all these resources can be found on the companion website for this book at www.edge.sagepub.com/strategy2e.

- -

Barriers to
Globalization

Businesses born global

Businesses that are **born global** are companies that expand into foreign markets and exhibit international business prowess and superior performance, from or very near their founding. The affordances and opportunities offered by the Internet make it

> **Born global** businesses may be defined as organizations that, from or near their founding, seek superior international business performance from the application of knowledge-based resources to the sale of outputs in multiple countries (Knight and Cavusgil, 2005: 24).

quite possible for a small business to become a global business quite quickly.

Very early multinational organizations, such as the East India Company (founded in 1601), were global organizations from their inception. They were 'born global' as international trading ventures. In the past the international business strategy literature suggested that internationalization occurred as a result of an evolutionary model, in which internationalization was the outcome of a move from exports, to joint ventures, to fully owned operations (Johanson and Vahlne, 1977). Most of this literature focused on large and multinational organizations, as we shall see.

By contrast, born global firms begin with a global view of their markets, and develop the capabilities needed to achieve their international goals at or near the firm's founding. Today, the most likely candidate firms for being born global are not the major national trading companies of the past but digital enterprises defining the present and the future.

Many companies in the digital economy have been global virtually from the outset. Facebook is a good example, as the film, *The Social Network* (Fincher, 2010), makes clear. More recently you might think of Airbnb or Uber. The point is, Internet start-ups are replete with born global firms: Atlassian in Australia, Skype in Denmark and Amazon in the United States are all examples that are quite familiar.

The concept 'born global' was first used in Rennie's (1993) Australian report for McKinsey and Co, and it has been widely used and discussed together with similar concepts, such as, for example, International New Ventures (McDougall et al., 1994; Oviatt and McDougall, 1994; Knight and Cavusgil, 2005). The basic point is that it is not necessary to have evolved into a large firm to internationalize. E-commerce companies operating in a virtual domain overcome spatial and temporal barriers to undertake international operations quickly and cheaply.

A number of factors can be identified as contributing to the phenomenon of firms being 'born global', including more global market conditions, new developments in transportation and communication technologies, especially the Internet, and an increase in the available numbers of people with international experience. Additionally, born-global firms may produce standardized products but operate in a highly specialized niche.

Distinctive Characteristics of Born-Global Firms

Born-global firms possess the following distinctive characteristics, according to Tanev (2012):

1. High activity in international markets from or near the founding, with the founder's vision playing an important role.

2. Limited financial and tangible resources.

3. Present across most industries, but mostly tech firms.

4. Managers have a strong international outlook and international entrepreneurial orientation.

5. Emphasis on differentiation strategy targeting niche markets.

6.   Emphasis on superior product quality.

7.   Leveraging advanced information and communications technology (ICT).

8.   Using external, independent intermediaries for distribution in foreign markets or engaging in direct sales.

There are a number of contextual factors that encourage born-global organizations. Fertile ground is provided by universities as anchor points as is the clustering of firms operating in the same industry. Dense flows of technological knowledge, experienced people and contacts with local venture capitalists follow. Having a small home market obliges firms to go global; in such cases the customers will often already be global multinationals. Being able to tap into global know-how through strong relations between the firms and foreign sales subsidiaries is also significant. It helps greatly if the product or service is easily accessed through digital delivery. Demanding local clients that will not settle for less than high-quality service are also important; beating the best in a demanding local market prepares an enterprise for going global. Having managers that already have global experience is also important as a lot less learning is required (see Tanev, 2012 for elaboration).

A born-global business is, of course, multinational by definition.

Multinationals – the agents of globalization

Globalists argue that globalization has created the liberalization of global markets and the design of a 'flat' or 'borderless' world – where flat and borderless are metaphors for an open market, conceived as a levelling of opportunities for all who compete in it. Yet, as critics are quick to point out, there is no inevitability about liberalization – it can as easily go into reverse as forward motion, and many of the elements of national responses to the Global Financial Crisis of 2008 suggest that we are currently in reverse with the emergence of austerity politics in many economies.

Economic liberalization and financialization were key elements in the models for globalization that prevailed until the Global Financial Crisis. In the light of that crisis, and the highly uneven world economy that has emerged subsequently, with the Eurozone and the UK in austerity politics, the United States recovering and the East Asian economies booming, we need to address globalization as a long-term process of transformation that is contradictory, uneven and eventful; likely to be as resisted as celebrated (Morgan, 2009: 557).

The main organizers of globalizing, above all, are the multinational corporations that own and control assets in more than one country, many of which have been in business for a long time in fields such as mining, retail, transport and property. It is their strategies of investment, production, marketing, contracting and employment that frame globalization. There are about 80,000 such firms in the world today, accounting for over 70% of world trade.

A few companies are truly global – they span the globe with a presence virtually everywhere. They are an important part of the effective infrastructure of globalization. They are centres of world trade and global communication and serve as conduits of cultural transfer, in which institutions and practices for dealing with global connectedness have been developed. Often they do so not as independent entities but through a strategy of broad-based alliances and networks.

Multinational organizations leverage localization from their globalization, in a synergy some analysts refer to as *glocalization,* as we have seen, doing so through cross-investments and partnerships with national, regional and local companies that deliver deeper penetration of global markets. Strategies for glocalization constantly have to steer between a tendency to play to a set of values and beliefs that are believed to be widely shared around the world – the traditional basis for economies of scope and scale – but also have to be alert to the existence of highly specific values and beliefs that differentiate particular identities globally and regionally. For instance, the burgers sold by McDonalds in Israel are kosher, in India they are not made of beef and in Muslim countries they are certified Halal. After Qantas joined an alliance with Emirates airways to fly the London route through Dubai it changed all of its foodstuffs so that they contained neither alcohol nor pork in deference to the sensibilities of their new partner airline and its co-shared passengers. Meanwhile, Emirates airlines do serve alcohol on their planes in deference to the sensibilities of their non-Muslim and non-teetotal customers. In each case, local sensibilities rooted in a specific religious culture shape and are accommodated to the service offerings in question, demonstrating how local cultures frame global offerings, glocally.

Multinational organizations are usually seen as strategically premised on producing goods and services that can be readily implanted in new contexts. Multinational organizations are conduits through which economic, military and cultural flows and global networks are created. Multinational organizations' global connectedness sees their elites try to channel and therefore control the effects of their global connectivity, reconfiguring spatial organization of the global economy and culture, disorganizing as well as organizing what might have seemed previously settled modes of life.

Theory of the MNE and FDI

The origins of the modern theory of the MNE are usually traced to Stephen Hymer's (1960/1976) PhD thesis. Hymer had asked the question 'why do MNEs exist?', meaning why is integration through Foreign Direct Investment (FDI) often selected by firms over potentially less hierarchical alternatives for cross-border business, such as exports and/or licensing of a technology or other advantage to foreign firms? Hymer felt that for a number of reasons FDI afforded better returns to firms on the basis of reasons mostly related to market power and monopolistic advantages. In addition, he had argued that FDI helped reduce cross-border inter-firm rivalry and served as a means of international risk diversification.

The major post-Hymer contributions have been the theory of 'internalization' of markets by MNEs as a result of high market transaction costs and, more recently, the evolutionary, resource-based and/or dynamic capabilities (DCs) views. Unlike Hymer's focus on power and monopoly, both of these major perspectives focus on mostly efficiency-related reasons for 'internalization'.

Classic contributions on 'internalization' included Buckley and Casson (1976), who emphasized the role of intermediate product market failures (such as markets for technology and innovation which are notoriously flawed) and Williamson (1981b) who emphasized bilateral interdependencies and hold-ups (hence protracted negotiations) induced by asset specificity. These were said to increase market transaction costs, hence making it more efficient for firms to internalize the cross-border transaction and therefore become MNEs.

Teece (1976) focused on differential cross-border resource-transfer costs, while Hennart (1982) suggested that the MNE could be seen as an organization that coordinates cross-border interdependencies more efficiently through employment relationships than through output markets. These interdependencies involved knowledge and reputation, intermediate products (such as raw materials, agricultural inputs, parts and components), as well as distribution and even financial capital (Hennart, 1982).

The evolutionary, resource-based and learning-dynamic-capabilities perspective drew on works by Penrose (1959, 2009) and developed and integrated these with transaction costs arguments (Teece, 1981, 1982) as well as the partly Penrose-inspired work of the Scandinavian school (Johanson and Vahlne, 2009) that emphasized learning and the role of 'psychic distance' – this refers to the distance in mentalities between different cultures in terms of their world views. In addition, the 'evolutionary theory' of Kogut and Zander (1993) emphasized the importance of knowledge and the advantages of its intra-organizational versus inter-organizational transfer.

The resource-based and learning-dynamic-capabilities perspectives – discussed in Chapter 3 – emphasizes the role of history and path dependence in the derivation of advantages, as well as the capabilities of entrepreneurial management in creating and leveraging cross-border resources, which, in Barney's (1991) terms are Valuable, Rare, Inimitable and Non-substitutable (VRIN). John Dunning's (1980, 2001) classic 'Ownership, Location, Internalization' (OLI) framework also stressed the important role of location (Dunning and Lundan, 2009). For Dunning all three aspects of the triad must be present for an MNE to appear. A firm must have the following characteristics:

1. Ownership: Own an advantage

2. Location: Identify a foreign location with suitable locational advantages

3. Internalization: Find it more profitable to internalize production than undertake an arms length transaction, such as licensing, franchising, or using a distributor (see the 'make or buy' discussion in Chapter 5)

The OLI triad, according to Dunning, explains *why* and *where* a firm will become an MNE.

More recent theories such as Pitelis and Teece (2010) question the emphasis of some internalization theories on market failures, stating that in many cases MNEs create and often co-create markets and supporting business ecosystems with other actors, such as suppliers, buyers, the government and, indeed, with competitors. They named this co-creation capability as the Dynamic Capability *par excellence*. The business and institutional context within which OLI related decisions are taken as well as the need to bring into the analysis of the MNE the role of demand, such as that of consumers but also the total demand in an economy and its fluctuations, has been stressed by Jones and Pitelis (2015).

Multinational strategies

Buckley (2003) sees the advantages of multinational strategies in terms of their ability to deviate from models of perfect competition in goods markets through product differentiation, marketing skills and administered pricing. Additionally, MNEs have access to factors such as knowledge, capital and skill, especially as these are embodied in managerial expertise. They enjoy economies of scale due to vertical integration that enable unit costs to be dramatically reduced and standardization to be practised, further driving down costs. By moving inside national territories they are able to accord with local laws that might limit their capacity to trade as outsiders.

There are at least five different models of global strategy promulgated in the international business literature:

1. *Decentralized federation; multinational strategy.* According to Bartlett and Ghoshal (1995), this is the typical European model that developed between the wars, although to characterize a single European model is perhaps a little too coarse-grained. The decentralized federation was seen to characterize an era of tariff protection and quotas; to get round these, firms would establish different national subsidiaries to produce inside the protectionist regimes. These flows of trade, people and capital were basically devised to get around the obstacles to more global flows that states erected. In an era of primitive communications technologies, subsidiaries thrived with a great deal of autonomy, constrained largely by personal relations and financial controls. The end result was a portfolio of different national subsidiaries, within which local learning was largely contained. Moreover, due to constrained resources sourced locally, the ability to respond to local markets may be limited. Responding, decisions may be made wholly in terms of local relevancies, which may not always serve the interests of the centre. For instance, there may be duplication of effort as each periphery replicates functions locally, on a small and more costly scale, with a degree of resistance to innovations from rival centres in the federation.

2. *Coordinated federation; international strategy.* The post-Second World War era was characterized by widespread US penetration of European and other markets with technologically more sophisticated products than were available elsewhere. Typically, these companies were professionally managed by trained MBAs using sophisticated management control systems. The result was highly centralized management. The flow was largely one way, of Americanization as globalization. Centralist assumptions about where innovation and ideas came from and went to became widespread. While this model might advance efficiency, in terms of standardization, it limited the opportunities for local learning to feed back into the parent organization. Also, functional management becomes dominant at the local level because of their key transmission role in translating central company skills, knowledge and capabilities.

3. *Centralized hubs; global strategy.* For Japanese firms that internationalized from the 1970s onwards the idea of continuous improvement was at the heart of strategy. Japanese firms emphasized quality, cost and feature advantages. They were able to offer more features, at better quality, for less cost, due to tight central control of product development, procurement and manufacturing. In addition, they made extensive use of new managerial approaches, such as just-in-time manufacturing, delegated *ringi-ko* decision-making and an innovation culture closely tied to the shop-floor and to a management highly loyal to the company that employed it (Clegg, 1990). At least initially, an export-based model of growth led this strategy, although by the 1980s, many Japanese firms were establishing overseas subsidiaries in countries such as India, the UK and the US, giving rise to a whole literature on Japanese inward investment, especially in the UK (Elger and Smith, 1994). Knowledge and learning tended to be tightly coupled in Japanese core organizations. In the case of Japanese organizations, centralization is reinforced by culture, as it is rare for non-Japanese managers to move from the peripheries and gain positions in the core. Local managers are pressured to conform to the expectations of their home context while also being subjected to the transfer

of practices from the multinational organization. The head office managers transfer practices, people and resources to subsidiaries in order to try and maintain control and achieve objectives while local subsidiaries may resist these transfers or develop them in their own interests.

4. *Matrix organizations; binary strategy.* The matrix organization attempts to achieve the benefits of both project and functional forms of organization (Galbraith, 1971). Davis and Lawrence (1977) define a matrix as any organization that employs a multiple command system that includes related support mechanisms and associated organizational culture and behaviour patterns. The principles of matrix structures have been applied widely in organizations, such as engineering-oriented firms that do business through a number of distinctive projects (Khandwalla, 1977). Many organizations have adopted various types of matrix structures (Sayles, 1976). By definition, the matrix is a grid-like organizational structure that allows a company to address multiple business dimensions using multiple command structures. In order to ensure that people focus simultaneously on two or more organizational forces a system of dual reporting relationships is put in place. It is an attempt to structure flows where they are directed within the organization as a global enterprise. Kotter (1996) researched more than 100 matrix organizations in the 1980s and found that few were successful. Minor disagreements could blow up into major turf wars, characterized by conflict and confusion over who should be responsible for what; information log jams occurred, because of the multiple reporting channels, and a loss of accountability due to international barriers of time, distance, language and culture.

5. *Integrated network; transnational strategy.* A fully transnational organization has developed multidimensional perspectives, distributed, interdependent capabilities and flexible integrative processes. Each individual centre might be a champion for a particular global competence, process, product or knowledge within the overall network. Relatively autonomous centres are able to translate local issues and concerns into flows of information around the network; having a high degree of standardization of business models connecting the different elements in the network ensures a coordinative capacity for managing system-wide responses with local calibrations. Top management needs to be focused on centralization, formalization and socialization as three interdependent management processes. Centralization will require strategically managed interventions from time-to-time; formalization will mean developing a procedural mechanism that must evolve with individual national and management roles; while socialization means that the organization must constantly be aware that it is managing a complex multiculturalism, both in terms of national and intra-organizational differences. Clearly, there is ample room for political misadventure in such a complex balancing of powers, cultures and management devices.

Based on developmental models such as the above, there is a pronounced tendency in the international business literature to see the world as increasingly homogenous. According to Buckley (2003: 699), multinationals

> are perfectly placed to exploit the differences in international integration of markets. The existence of regional goods and services markets enables firms

to exploit economies of scale across several economies. Differential labour markets enable costs to be reduced by locating the labour-intensive stages of production in cheap labour economies.

The result is that horizontal integration is assisted by

regional goods and services markets, vertical integration by differentiated labour markets and distribution of key raw materials. Strategic trade and foreign direct investment can be seen to take place within this framework. (2003: 699)

Top-level strategic managers of global organizations typically seek to have:

- Unrestricted access to resources and markets throughout the world
- Freedom to integrate manufacturing with other operations across national boundaries
- Coordination and control of all aspects of the company on a worldwide basis
- Maximization of shareholder value
- Minimization of tax liabilities by establishing corporate headquarters in low tax regimes, such as Dutch Antilles or the Cayman Islands
- Low levels of government regulation in the markets in which they operate

To have a successful strategy for entry into a foreign market – one that is not in the home territory of the business in question – means that the enterprise must be better at doing what it is doing than other businesses that already do what it does and that are domiciled in the country in question. Moreover, it must be the case that they can so do profitably.

The key element in developing a global strategy is often regarded as **arbitrage**.

Sometimes arbitrage entails a strategy of transfer pricing. Arbitrage can also occur when multinational organizations are able to exploit exchange rate movements profitably by switching production into cheaper currencies. To be able to exploit the global opportunities for profit that arbitrage offers, a multinational organization needs strategies that enable it to have maximum flexibility in locating production, know-how and knowledge, as well as the ability to react rapidly to threats and opportunities. Reactive ability will be limited by the necessity of abiding by the rules of the states in which they invest, if only because firms are not always so liquid that they can easily move. Arbitrage is also facilitated by different state administrations competing for foreign direct investment. If the local state does not provide what the global investor requires, mobile capitalism can threaten simply to exit the scene and set up where the benefits sought can be ensured.

> **Arbitrage** is the practice of profiting from differences in costs and processes across borders – basically buying where prices are lowest, selling where prices are greatest, and using international operations as a means of reducing tax liabilities in countries with high tax regimes and concentrating profits in low tax regimes and losses in high tax regimes.

The national diversity of operations has become a source of advantage, an advantage that Kogut (2002: 265) refers to in terms of 'embedded options'. A further distinction can be made between 'across-country' and 'within-country' options. Across-country options refer to arbitraging of borders, such as shifting production, arranging tax accountabilities, utilizing lower cost labour or transferring innovation from one country to another. How economically successful these across-country strategies are is highly variable since the conditions of arbitrage that prevail at a decision-point may not prevail when the strategy comes to maturity. Within-country options, on the other hand, refer to establishing a platform, such as brand-recognition, from which later investment strategies can develop.

Multinationals and the politics of employment

Cheap labour markets do not tell us all we need to know about multinationals but they are certainly an important political consideration. Over the past 30 years, globalization has had profound effects on international power structures and the strategies of business organizations, consequently influencing the political organization of work by corporations and resistance by collectivized labour. Of particular significance has been the expansion of multinational corporations whose influence has extended beyond their immediate activities through the proliferation of complex production networks spanning national boundaries (Josserand, 2004; Parker and Clegg, 2006; Banerjee et al., 2009; Clegg and Carter, 2009; Clegg, 2011). Millions of workers today, working at the end of multinational supply chain strategies in the 'Third World', are at risk of labour and human rights violations ranging from poor working conditions to human trafficking and slavery (ILO, 2008).

In Asia, supply chain networks associate multinationals with local small and medium enterprises, as well as a mix of government agencies belonging to countries characterized by various levels of democracy and authoritarianism, resulting in malpractices that range from unacceptable working conditions to practices such as human trafficking (ILO, 2008). The regulation of labour standards in global supply chains (James et al., 2007; Lakhani et al., 2011; Lee, 2016) through international labour movements and activist networks is receiving increasing attention (Riisgaard and Hammer, 2011; Kaine and Wright, 2013). However, existing mechanisms that seek to deprive unethical businesses of patronage, such as consumer pressure and activist networks (Wright, 2011; Donaghey et al., 2013), fail to address some of the most unacceptable labour issues. Company audits can assist in identifying unethical practices but do not consistently produce timely or lasting results, especially as many companies do not cooperate with audit. Diplomatic efforts on the part of governments and the International Labour Organization (ILO) are often counter-balanced by trade agreements that largely focus on goods, services and investment to the exclusion of labour standards.

Alongside workplace-based strategies, unions have developed a renewed focus on international collaborations through a range of global strategies involving the Internet (Carter et al., 2003) but such efforts are difficult to conduct in the absence of a local representative base. While making a contribution, these actions have not achieved a fundamental improvement of labour conditions in the region or globally.

Due to the fragmentation of production, neither state action, labour power, nor consumer action match the power of capital (Donaghey et al., 2013). Multiple

Exploitation in Electronics

Image 7.1   International Labour Organization (ILO). Copyright: chelovek

jurisdictions, the prevalence of migrant workers, geographically fixed represent-ative institutions and the proliferation of non-standard employment relationships combine to create a challenging regulatory environment. Different types of regu-latory attempts have sought to improve labour standards ranging from activities of international institutions such as the ILO, international framework agreements, social movement activities, private initiatives of MNEs and labour clauses in multilateral trade agreements (Meardi and Marginson, 2013; Berliner et al., 2015; Marx et al., 2015).

Efforts so far have been unsuccessful in triggering expected improvements (Clarke and Boersma, 2015). While the proliferation of global supply chains has been blamed for the multiplication of malpractices in non-democratic countries (Fisher et al., 2010), they may, conversely, provide new opportunities for the organization of labour resistance. Resistance seeks to force authorities to listen to the voicing of what are largely considered non-issues (see Chapter 11).

According to the code of Social Accountability (based on ILO core standards), there exists a 'requirement to facilitate parallel means of independent and free asso-ciation and bargaining' (O'Rourke, 2006: 903) in countries where it is not possible to form free trade unions. However, 'this provision remains highly controversial as it is not clear exactly what qualifies as effective parallel means of representation in countries such as China' (O'Rourke, 2006: 903). Repertoires of collective resistance to global capital face difficulties in scaling up from local struggles to have an interna-tional impact (Heery, 2009).

The embedded nature of labour systems in non-democratic and authoritarian regimes limits the capacity of external efforts to trigger change. Improvements to working conditions are difficult to effect from the outside, necessitating interventions from within, interventions that can then be supported by outside networks and skilful collaboration, particularly using social media to organize boycotts of multinational organizations implicated in scandals. Informal structures and networks enabled by widespread information technology can perform communication functions without traditional formal organizations and may even be more effective in some situations (Diani, 2000).

Multinationals and centre–periphery power dynamics

The balance of power does not always lie with the centre, with the MNE headquarters. As Dörrenbächer and Gamelgaard (2006: 209) suggest, 'a career-oriented subsidiary manager', especially an expatriate, may well manage to decline mandate requests from headquarters where they calculate that there is a career advantage in doing so. The loyalties of expatriates will usually differ from those of host country nationals or third country nationals, with the assumption usually being made that expatriates are more loyal to headquarters (Harzing, 1999).

Host country nationals' loyalties tend to be regarded as allying more with the fortunes of the subsidiary. Consequently, it has been argued that third country nationals will be more balanced in their outlook on the micro-politics of subsidiary/headquarters relations. These dynamics have a significant qualifying effect on more structural and deterministic explanations: actors' micro-strategies can accelerate or impede central projects and their reasons for pursuing those strategies they choose may not align at all with the assumptions made at headquarters.

Dörrenbächer and Gamelgaard (2006: 210–212) provide a short story that nicely illuminates micro-political dynamics. A German engineer managed a German automobile company's French subsidiary. He greatly expanded its technical expertise and sought to utilize the expanded knowledge resources through additional financial investment. The request was blocked at headquarters because the company was increasingly focusing on short-term increases in shareholder value that additional investment would jeopardize. The engineer's approach was based on technical improvement to a flexible manufacturing system through R&D that both added and cost value. However, the company was moving from its roots in German engineering excellence and closer to a shareholder value model: they had different rationalities and their clash produced considerable conflict. The engineer did not lose totally and was able to maintain the flexible production system.

The strategy of imposing conformance with a central financial performance-related strategy is often used by headquarters to discipline subsidiaries; depending on the degree of development of locally embedded resources and networks, such as technical expertise and R&D, subsidiaries may follow a successful subversive strategy and create a space for more autonomous and local strategy (Morgan and Kristensen, 2006).

In MNEs the majority of politics around the strategy process relate to mandated change in headquarters/subsidiary relations (Crozier and Friedberg, 1980; Dörrenbächer and Gamelgaard 2006: 206). Typically, at headquarters level, one would expect board members, the strategy team, and selected functional managers to be involved; as adversaries to the changes being mandated one would expect to find subsidiary managing directors and their appropriate functional managers.

Other parties will surround subsidiary managers with strategic interests:

- Significant shareholders seeking more efficient exploitation of their assets in the business through changing international cost, service and regulatory environments

- Trade unions, who resist measures that run against the strategic interests of those members that they represent

- Governmental agencies seeking to secure investment opportunities

- Non-governmental agencies with a remit to protect specific strategic interests, such as the environment or child labour

- Suppliers, for whom the changes represent hard-to-comply-with specifications

- Customers who may be dissatisfied with the changes made to a favourite brand, product or service.

How subsidiary managers might manage or ignore these local pressures may not be a matter for calculation at the supra-local level of the corporate centre but it can pose real struggles and challenges for local actors. Often these struggles and challenges are not recognized at the centre and an inability to manage them conveniently is seen as a sign of local failure rather than of the complexity of local environments.

All large organizations are complex by definition. They have more extensive divisions of labour, a greater number of reports to authorities, and are often structured as complex divisional structures. Complexity is multiplied when the organization in question works across national boundaries.

Think of international business operations where there is significant spatial separation of core from peripheral business units. There will be geographical, political, socio-economic, cultural and religious boundaries separating the core from the peripheral actors and action. Not only will there be extensive politics around who controls and has access to what resources but there will probably be quite different understandings of the rules of the games to be negotiated between participants, especially host governments and MNEs. Boddewyn and Brewer (1994) argue that host governments represent both strategic risks and opportunities: governments may appropriate value from MNEs but they can also protect them (e.g., Boddewyn, 1975, 1988, 1993; Moran, 1985; Rugman and Verbeke, 1993; Eden and Molot, 2002). What they cannot always do, or choose to do, is to protect their citizens from multinationals.

Multinational mandates

Mandates are tasks that are assigned to subsidiaries by headquarters or that are acquired independently by the subsidiary, which have a specific time and content limitation placed on them, and which frame the internal division of labour within a MNE.

Any MNE comprises a highly complex configuration of ongoing micro-political power conflicts at different levels. Social actors and groups inside and outside the firm interact with each other and create temporary balances of power. Sometimes external organizations can succeed in changing organizational **mandates**. Think of the role of activist civil society organizations shaping pharmaceutical company testing procedures on animals, or their impact on mining companies' interactions with indigenous communities (Morgan and Kristensen, 2006: 1473).

IN PRACTICE

Mandate change: Who wins when good intentions prevail? The soccer ball case

A story of an interesting soccer ball (or football) case can be found in the downloadable journal article by Farzad R. Khan, Kamal A. Munir and Hugh Willmott (2007) 'A dark side of institutional entrepreneurship: Soccer balls, child labour and postcolonial impoverishment', *Organization Studies*, 28: 1055; available at www.edge.sagepub.com/strategy2e.

Khan, Munir & Willmott

The link takes you to a seemingly 'feel-good' story about a major mandate change wrought in an industry by media, NGO and industry stakeholders. It concerns the basic tool of the world's most popular game: the soccer ball. The majority of the world's hand-stitched soccer balls are produced in Sialkot, Pakistan (Cummins, 2000: 4, 27). Until relatively recently, most of these balls were hand-stitched by child labour. On 6 April 1995, a CBS news documentary showed that the soccer ball suppliers employed child labour in dark and dank one-room workshops. The CBS report was picked up by other mass media around the world. In 1996, a campaign against the exploitation of child labour was launched. By 1997 manufacturers in the global soccer ball industry announced a project to eliminate child labour in collaboration with carefully selected civil society NGO partners. The industry successfully positioned itself, in the eyes of the western media and consumers at least, as a constructive actor working to remove the bane of child labour while preserving the Sialkot soccer ball-manufacturing cluster. However, the benefits for children were questionable and the majority of women had to drop out of the workforce. The unintended consequences of removing child labour from the manufacture of these balls and thus preserving the brand value of the global business names that marketed the balls was a loss of income, disruption to family life and withdrawal from work of women, effects that were never given significance by NGOs, the industry or the western media. The child labour was reduced – but at what cost?

Questions

1. Analyse the case, focusing on its politics in various locales.
2. Who do you think were the winners?
3. Who do you think were the losers?
4. Elaborate the evidence and the analysis that enables you to draw these conclusions.

Mandates relate directly to the control of resources and the steering of potential actions; hence, mandates bestow different propensities for exercising power in internal relations within MNEs (Cyert and March, 1963; Pfeffer and Salancik, 1974; Birkinshaw and Ridderstråle, 1999). When mandates change there is immense potential for conflict within MNEs because the relative power relations of the different subsidiaries and the *centre* change in consequence. Any change can be simultaneously a process of downgrading and upgrading: as one subsidiary shifts to a more or less demanding task all others change relatively in their relations with each other and the *centre*

(Dörrenbächer and Gamelgaard, 2006). Shifts in these relativities can translate directly into changes in status, careers and incomes – things often hard fought for.

The politics of mandates

MNEs are inherently political entities in terms of their relations not only with competitors and in the way that they organize themselves; they cannot avoid having political relations with the governments and civil society organizations that interface with them.

Governments in both host and home countries want to accrue as much value as they can from MNEs in terms of tax, investments, employment, knowledge production and minimize as much as possible any disutility that the MNE activities might create, such as pollution, despoliation or social upheaval. As resources with which to bargain they can use whatever location specific resources they have available, such as talent pools, natural resources or infrastructure.

External stakeholders, such as civil society bodies and NGOs, usually want to ensure that local resources are not unduly exploited, whether labour, the environment, or political and social capital. They can mobilize public opinion and communicate specific messages about specific firms and their legitimacy.

Multinational mandates and the problem of implementation

Implementation is complex and difficult in any MNE because it is an internally differentiated set of intra-organizational and extra-organizational linkages in which resources are constantly being exchanged. The complexity of the networks makes it difficult for any nodal point in the network to know where the most critical resources reside. As Bouquet and Birkinshaw (2008: 485) note

> new technology can bring power to its inventor, but only to the extent that it can be brought to the attention of people who, through their direct and indirect connections, can facilitate its identification and deployment to other parts of the corporation (Andersson et al., 2007; Andersson and Pahlberg, 1997).

Those closer to the centre are more readily able to achieve such a bringing to attention compared to those further out in the periphery (Prahalad and Doz, 1987).

The greater the degree of both corporate embeddedness of a subsidiary, as well as its degree of external embeddedness in its host nation, the more probable it will be that it has a more advanced mandate within a MNE.

The fact that a strategic mandate may be set centrally does not necessarily minimize the creative and positive resistance of the margins suggest Bouquet and Birkinshaw (2008: 491). Subsidiaries can:

- Develop new products or bid for new corporate investments.
- Build profile through stronger relationships with other parts of the global company.
- Most radically, subsidiaries can seek to 'break the rules of the game' (Markides, 2000).

The capacity for subsidiaries to break the rules of the game depends on the structural relations that prevail within corporate empires. A great deal of corporate action in an MNE is simultaneously decentralized *and* linked to corporate strategy. Local actors will use the resources the MNE provides to seek local advantages over local rivals while the MNE will use the locals to tap into networks and mobilize resources that they would not otherwise access.

Implementing alliances between local and supra-local actors will often be difficult to accomplish, Bouquet and Birkinshaw (2008: 481) note because:

1. Some countries have levels of corruption that clash with norms of acceptable behaviour in the larger MNE system (Alvaro, 2006; Doh et al., 2003; Rodriguez et al., 2005; Uhlenbruck et al., 2006b).

2. Other countries have an investment climate that is unattractive to foreign investors (Kessing et al., 2007); for instance, where there are unstable political conditions (Henisz, 2000), such as many of the countries in Africa (Harbeson, 1995) and other resource-poor countries that struggle to attract investments, let alone value-added activities, from multinationals.

3. Where subsidiaries operate at the periphery of the world economy (Harzing and Noorderhaven, 2006), subsidiary activities can easily be misunderstood or perceived to be of little significance (Galunic and Eisenhardt, 1996; Brown, 2004; Prahalad, 2004); for instance, they have few location-specific advantages (Dunning, 1981) or can be located in relatively depressed industrial areas (Dawley, 2007).

4. Small or youthful operations can rarely demonstrate a proper track record (Birkinshaw, 1999), or are constrained by relatively small market sizes, limited purchasing capacities, inadequate infrastructures.

Subsidiaries that seek to improve their local standing in the MNE and host nation will need to be able to demonstrate that they can deliver corporate objectives and plans; provide strategic information and knowledge on local competitive developments; and generate innovations that can be spread through the global corporate empire. Subsidiaries that cannot exploit these sorts of resources will be unlikely to exercise much power in the web of MNE relations.

EXTEND YOUR KNOWLEDGE

The full story on subsidiary and multinational power relations can be found in the downloadable journal article by Cyril Bouquet and Julian Birkinshaw (2008) **'Managing power in the multinational corporation: How low-power actors gain influence'**, which you can read on the companion website for this book at www.edge.sagepub. co.uk/strategy.

Bouquet & Birkinshaw

Bouquet, C. and Birkinshaw, J. (2008) 'Managing power in the multinational corporation: How low-power actors gain influence', *Journal of Management*, 34(3): 477–508.

IN PRACTICE

Norsk Hydro – a truly multinational firm

Image 7.2   Norsk Hydro. Copyright: theplatypuus

Go Online: Visit the book's website at https://edge.sagepub.com/strategy2e to watch an interview with Svein Richard Brandtzæg conducted by the author team.

Svein Richard
Brandtzæg
Interview

Norsk Hydro Asa is a Norwegian aluminium and renewable energy company, headquartered in Oslo. Hydro is one of the largest aluminium companies worldwide. It has operations in some 50 countries around the world and is active on all continents.

Svein Richard Brandtzæg is the CEO Norsk Hydro Asa. Previously Svein has held several international leadership positions within Norsk and he is now responsible for a business area with more than 12,000 employees in the sectors Rolled Products, Extrusion Eurasia, Extrusion Americas, Precision Tubing and the business unit Automotive Structures.

For Norsk Hydro multinational operation is embedded in the organization, the staff and processes. They see it as an inevitable aspect of business. Svein links strategy very closely with organizational change on a global scale; for Hydro strategy is the constant process of having to adapt to the continual changes that occur in the external environment.

From the top management down, where a Strategy Team exists in this centralized organization, through to the active involvement of line managers, Hydro utilize those leaders who can exercise strong decision-making, influence and communication skills, and have the ability to execute and implement strategy. Nowhere was this need for communication and understanding more important than when Norsk decided they had to exit the magnesium market despite being the industry leaders; a bold change for any organization but one that was absolutely necessary.

Questions

1. Which of Norsk Hydro's characteristics make it a truly global and multinational organization?

2. According to Svein Richard Brandtzæg, how do you go about constructing and implementing a global strategy?

3. What is Hydro's competitive position in the different markets it is operating in?

4. What were the reasons for changing Hydro's global strategy? Why did the management decide to exit the global magnesium industry?

5. What are the implications and consequences of leaving an industry in a global competitive market environment?

6. How can multinational organizations achieve a continuous responsiveness to changes in their environments?

7. How does Svein Brandtzaeg see the future of strategy making? What is Hydro doing today to be prepared for future?

All models of the MNE (Hedlund, 1986; Ghoshal and Bartlett, 1990; Forsgren et al., 1995) suggest that the practices of foreign subsidiaries are constrained by different contextual rationalities to those of the supra-local MNE (Geppert, 2002; Geppert et al., 2003):

- Subsidiaries have to adapt to the institutional factors and national business systems characterizing the markets in which they operate (Geppert and Matten, 2006; Geppert and Williams, 2006; Rosenzweig and Nohria, 1994)

- Subsidiaries have to find ways to translate corporate ideals into a tangible set of local practices that effectively bridge the expectations of the head office, if they are to exert any influence on MNE decisions.

- Without legitimacy, subsidiaries will have little influence on corporate decisions (Westney, 1993; Kostova and Zaheer, 1999; Tempel et al., 2006).

- Not only must subsidiary managers seeking to engage in the MNEs have legitimacy, they must, according to the VRIN model, also have some control over resources that are scarce, not substitutable, in demand in the centre and competitively sought elsewhere.

Subsidiaries and legitimacy in strategy

In order to be implemented, any mandated change must accrue **legitimacy**.

The process of legitimization involves far more than merely developing an agreed strategy at the top level of the organization that the strategy team regards as appropriate or desirable: it also means implementing it, even against resistance from stakeholders.

MNEs often seek to legitimate mandate changes by making a competition of them; bids framed in terms of a change mandate are invited from subsidiaries within

Legitimacy has been defined as 'a recognized perception or assumption that the actions of an entity are desirable, proper, or appropriate within some socially constructed system of norms, values, beliefs and definitions' (Suchman, 1995: 574).

the MNE as well as from organizations outside (Birkinshaw and Lingblad, 2005). Competition to deliver on the decisions made legitimates the outcomes. To justify such MNE testing of options it can be claimed that open competition offers the best chance of adapting to market pressures, meeting emergent standards or enhancing shareholder value. All these legitimating claims work well – even when there may be other reasons at work, such as whittling a subsidiary down or obtaining greater control over it. Mandate changes offer subsidiaries an opportunity to enhance their strategic importance for the MNE. Subsidiaries are not just passive receivers of such mandate changes. Claims for mandate change can be made equally from subsidiaries as from the centre, perhaps in response to claims of changing market imperatives or customer relations, while the covert agenda may be to secure and improve their relative position.

The strategic options open to an MNE are always framed within specific contextual factors that affect how best to pursue legitimation:

- Host country contextual factors: determined by the national institutions, economic structures, resources and foreign investment policies of the country that is host to the investments made.

- Subsidiary contextual factors: determined by the resources and capabilities at a subsidiary's disposal. The crucial element, according to the resource-based view of the firm (Barney, 1991), is the extent to which the subsidiary controls inimitable resources that bring added value and are hard to substitute.

- Headquarter contextual factors: in dealing with any specific subsidiary what are the headquarters' options? If the subsidiary is inimitable, they may be few; dealing with substitutable subsidiaries or outsource companies swings the balance of power in mandated change towards the MNE.

The more legitimacy subsidiary powers can accrue to their actions the greater the probability of their being engaged in corporate decisions (Mitchell et al., 1997). However, their very distance from strategic centres makes this difficult. MNE strategic managers are often far removed from subsidiaries, culturally, geographically and in terms of time zones.

What is a clear strategic plan at headquarters becomes much more confusing if the specificity of all the national regulations, policies, norms and infrastructure systems that the firm is engaged in have to be factored in. Where subsidiaries are only loosely committed to the firm or where practices are believed to deviate from parent company objectives, they will often fail to secure legitimacy.

Where subsidiary companies can develop unique bundles of resources and capabilities that are particularly in demand, according to the VRIN model, (Birkinshaw and Hood, 1998) they can enter into significant positions in MNE circuits of power. To do so they make themselves more central by becoming more interlinked in MNE networks, because it is centrality that makes resources valuable, not just having them.

Multinational diversification and competitive advantage

As noted earlier, diversification was one of the main factors originally employed by Hymer (1960/1976) to explicate the MNE. From a strategic point of view diversification into new territories is principally a means for gaining competitive advantage and is more likely to occur when:

- Firms possess high endowments of intangible resources such as knowledge (Delgado-Gomez et al., 2004; Nachum and Zaheer, 2005)

- Firms are in information-intensive industries seeking intangible resources such as knowledge, for example, when western technology firms enter places such as Bangalore, India (Hitt et al., 2006)

- Firms' Top Management Teams have an elite education, lower average age and greater international experience (Sambharya, 1996; Tihanyi et al., 2000; Wally and Becerra, 2001; Herrmann and Datta, 2005)

- Firms are owned by institutional investors, professional investment funds and pension funds.

Oligopolistic positioning of multinationals in advanced economies enables the development of sophisticated product-improvement cycles, through economies of scale, research and development, and innovation, competitive pricing and branding (Bartlett and Ghoshal, 1987, 1989). Together with the ability to exploit supply chains, these are seen to reduce transaction costs (Williamson, 1975b, 1981a, 1985). The combination of cheaper transaction costs and sophisticated innovation is what provides multinationals with their competitive edge.

The contemporary scene: Flat horizons or differentiated vistas?

Thomas Friedman (2005), celebrated *New York Times* writer, has proclaimed that the world is 'flat'! In his book *The World is Flat: A Brief History of the Twenty-first Century* he analyses globalization in the early twenty-first century. The title alludes to what he sees as the eclipse of historical and geographical divisions that are becoming increasingly irrelevant in a world of increasingly free trade, enabled by the Internet. In such views, the multi-divisional, increasingly multinational, organization becomes seen as the pinnacle of a universal model of corporate evolution for all advanced economies based on Chandler's (1962) initial framework. As Spicer (2006: 1467) notes, 'The debate about organizational globalization is split between those who argue that organizational logics *converge* on a single Anglo-American model, and those who contend that organizational logics continue to *diverge* into national types'. To models of converging and diverging organizations we will add the possibility of hybridizing. We shall look at how each approach understands the global economy, beginning with those arguments that emphasize convergence.

Thomas Friedman

Image 7.3   Thomas Friedman (right), author of *The World is Flat*, in conversation with Paul Krugman (left) of the *New York Times*. Copyright: 2009 Getty Images

Friedman's flat earth view is old hat. *The Economist*, ever alert to potential trends, suggests that the best days of the multinationals, when strategies were relatively easy and relatively similar, are behind them. In the past, multinationals benefited from rising consumption and industrial investment, the availability of low-cost labour and more globalized supply chains. These are of declining competitive advantage. Discussing a McKinsey Global Institute (MGI) report (Dobbs et al., 2015) *The Economist* (2015) notes the following:

1. Corporate profits more than tripled in 1980–2013, rising from 7.6% of global GDP to 10%, of which Western companies captured more than two-thirds.

2. The after-tax profits of American firms are at their highest level as a share of national income since 1929.

3. More than twice as many multinationals are operating today as in 1990, making for more competition.

4. Margins are being squeezed and the volatility of profits is growing. The average variance in returns to capital for North American firms is more than 60% higher today than it was in 1965–1980.

5. Corporate profits, on present projections, may fall from 10% of global GDP to about 8% in a decade's time.

6. The number of American firms listed on stock exchanges has fallen from 8,025 in 1996 to about half that number now: businesses are becoming more concentrated in ownership and less likely to be publically listed.

What are the reasons for these transformations? A major reason is the rise of emerging-market competitors in the *Fortune 500*. In 1980–2000 they comprised 5% of the list;

today they represent 26% of the list. The 50 largest emerging-world firms have doubled the proportion of their revenues coming from abroad to 40% in the most recent decade. Second, the rise of high-tech companies has seen China's e-commerce giants Alibaba, Tencent and JD.com rapidly raised to global prominence. Powerful digital platforms such as Alibaba, in turn, serve as a launching pad for thousands of small and midsize 'born-global' enterprises, giving them the reach and resources to challenge larger companies.

The most prosperous national sectors and survivors are those focused on 'idea work' (Carlsen et al., 2012). Labour- and capital-intensive industries offer little competitive advantage against emerging-market rivals whereas idea-intensive firms in media, finance and pharmaceuticals as well as logistics and luxury cars, continue to flourish. The 'idea sector', as MGI defines it, accounts for 31% of profits generated by Western companies, compared with 17% in 1999.

> Profits are shifting from heavy industry to idea-intensive sectors that revolve around R&D, brands, software, and algorithms. Sectors such as finance, information technology, media, and pharmaceuticals – which have the highest margins – are developing a winner-take-all dynamic, with a wide gap between the most profitable companies and everyone else. Meanwhile, margins are being squeezed in capital-intensive industries, where operational efficiency has become critical.
>
> New competitors are becoming more numerous, more formidable, and more global – and some destroy more value for incumbents than they create for themselves. Meanwhile, some of the external factors that helped to drive profit growth in the past three decades, such as global labor arbitrage and falling interest rates, are reaching their limits.
>
> As profit growth slows, there will be more companies fighting for a smaller slice of the pie, and incumbent industry leaders cannot focus simply on defending their market niche. Our analysis of thousands of companies around the world shows that the top performers share three traits: they invest in intellectual assets, they play in fast-growing markets, and they have the most efficient operations (Dobbs et al., 2015).

Increasingly, old advantages will not secure new futures. The rise and rise of emergent markets' multinationals, although these may have setbacks from time to time, is likely to continue. Brazil, for instance, is not often thought of as a highly innovative economy but in its São Paulo based core regional economy it clearly is. Brazil is a major industrial innovator with firms such as *Empressa Braziliera de Aeronáutica* (Embraer), the third largest aircraft company globally.

Globalization: Hybridization or convergence?

Globalization mingles and mashes up cultures, with hybrids being the result; it makes curry the English national dish, and sees the *niqab* become a garment of affirmation – or protest and subjection, depending on perspective and politics – worn around the world (Clegg et al., 2014). It sees young people from global cities fly to the Middle East to become a part of Isis' jihad, courtesy of global airlines and airports. Anti-globalization groups are just as likely to use the technologies of globalization, such as the Internet and mobile phones, to articulate protests against it, as are the proponents. Islamic State, for instance, shows a high degree of digital capability.

For some observers, globalization signals convergence. We are sceptical. The world is not converging, as we shall argue in this chapter. The present epoch of global integration is one in which there is an entanglement of disparate trajectories that irreversibly dissolve any autonomous entities such as specific societies, cultures or civilizations. Globalization involves permanent struggles over identity, sovereignty and autonomy. Islamic State is as much a force of and for trajectories of globalization as is Coca-Cola. We are not seeing a homogenization of the world or a sharp opposition between the 'global' and the 'local'. While there are dynamics that are integrating the world there are others that simultaneously fragment, differentiate and stratify the world as radically unequal and decentred (Middell and Nauman, 2010).

IN PRACTICE

Global investments

Global Investments

Image 7.4   London city skyline. Copyright: Starcevic

London is now one of the most expensive cities to live in, to buy or rent property, in the world. There are a number of factors that have produced this situation, with one of them being the explosion in property prices in the city. One reason for this is the fact that property in global cities such as London has become a way of channelling global wealth into investments that are increasing at an exponential rate (see www.businessinsider. com.au/london-property-market-and-home-prices-analysis-rics-cml-cab-data-and-interest-rate-rises-2015-11?r=UK&IR=T). The fact that London property prices are increasing so rapidly is seen by many observers as one of the effects of globalization as wealthy people from overseas with considerable capital bid up the prices of even quite ordinary accommodation (see www.thestandrewseconomist.com/2015/12/07/is-foreign-investment-in-london-to-blame-for-property-prices/). Clearly, as the revelations of the 'Panama papers' reveal, many tycoons and world leaders have built substantial property portfolios in London property (see www.theguardian.com/news/2016/apr/05/panama-papers-world-leaders-tycoons-secret-property-empires). The impact of globalization on London property is dramatic – but there are many less dramatic ways in which globalization makes itself felt.

Questions

1. Think about the region that you live in. Are there any signs of the impact of globalization in that region?

2. Looking at the impact of globalization, has the impact been largely positive or negative do you think?

3. For whom do you think, and in what ways, has the impact been largely positive?

4. For whom do you think, and in what ways, has the impact been largely negative?

Globalization: Convergence

The 'universalistic' theories of strategy and organization associated with Chandler (1962), Channon (1973) and Dyas and Thanheiser (1976) apply to Europe, according to Mayer and Whittington (1999) and Whittington and Mayer (2000). The convergence theorists stress the emergence of dominant models of divisional structure based on financial markets and professional management in Anglo-Saxon contexts. If we focus only on large-scale quantitative-based research work that deals in *Fortune 500* type companies we will tend to see convergence, in part, as an effect of the standardized data sets used.

Convergence theorists argue that organizational logics are becoming increasingly similar. Organizational logics are the outcome of different strategies; they are sense-making frames that provide understandings concerning what is legitimate, reasonable and effective in a given context (Guillén, 2001a: 14; see also Biggart, 1991: 222–224; MacDuffie, 1995; Biggart and Guillén, 1999). When strategy is aligned with action it produces a shared organizational logic. Typically, organizational logics are thought of in terms of an implicit business systems model, because, suggests Spicer (2006), they tend to be embedded in shared spaces, such as the nation state (Granovetter, 1985). Some argue that this is because of the functional efficiency of certain strategy/structure models (Donaldson, 1999, 2000, 2001); others argue that it is because of processes of institutional isomorphism, where, because dominant and prestigious models are dominant and prestigious, they are widely imitated – not because they are necessarily efficient but because they are held in high regard.

The factors that are seen to be leading to convergence are creating a 'disembedding' of multinational organizations from national space and seeing them re-embedded into a global space (Giddens, 1990). A number of factors are seen to be driving this disembedding:

1. Real-time technology (Castells, 1996).

2. Volatile capital flows that circumvent the reach of nation regulation (Strange, 1996).

3. Geographically homogeneous consumer demand across the globe.

4. Pressures from international standards (Brunsson and Jacobsson, 2001) on how an enterprise should be managed to ensure 'quality'; how enterprises should deal with the environmental impact of their operations; how they should manage their risks, knowledge and complaints made against them; how they should keep their accounts and ensure regulatory compliance and probity in other ways (Higgins and Hallström, 2007).

5. Increasing homogeneity of the nation state form, the professions and scientific reason (Meyer et al., 1997).

Because they are subject to these convergent pressures firms become increasingly disconnected from national economies (Ohmae, 1990, 1995) and a largely American-inspired model organization that legitimates shareholder governance, short-term antagonistic employment relationships, short-term price-driven buyer-supplier relations and individual training (Hall and Soskice, 2001) is adopted. The strategy/structure researchers seem to favour this model, drawing equally on cultural learning as the decisive factor in divergence, in which unique institutional advantages assert themselves, and a form of determinism in which the functional efficiencies of US models see them emerging as dominant.

Multinational organizations need to be able to do what they do more efficiently and effectively than local organizations; otherwise, local firms would always be winners due to their deep immersion in local laws, institutions, cultures, norms, etc. Local embeddedness is something that every transnational has to overcome because, at least initially, it is this that has produced the customer preferences of their prospective consumers.

Kogut (2002: 266) suggests that expanding internationally improves firm performance by providing an enhanced incentive for firms to invest in intangible assets, such as copyrights, patents, trademarks and brand loyalty, as well as intellectual property intangibles such as know-how and knowledge. Perhaps most important of all is the accrual of human capital – experienced personnel familiar with local ways of doing business in the multinational who can translate this knowledge globally and learn while doing so. The contemporary multinational is best seen as a network of subsidiaries (Kogut, 2002), linked through networks and global collaborative initiatives that provide global competitive advantage.

Globalization: Divergence

Kostova and Zaheer (1999) argue that establishing multinational subsidiaries opens up the possibility of 'institutional duality'. On the one hand, headquarters pressure them to adopt their desired practices while the subsidiary is pressurized by its host context to follow local practices. Thus, it has to deal with a double and conflicting set of legitimation expectations about strategy. The greater the 'institutional distance' between the home and host countries, the more dualism will be experienced (Xu and Shenkar, 2002), and the more likely host influences will prevail (Morgan and Kristensen, 2006).

Recent studies, especially in what is known as the business systems literature (Whitley, 1991, 1992, 1994a, 1999) and related theory (Djelic, 1998; Hall and Soskice, 2001), argue for more than institutional duality, noting that economic transactions are always locally embedded (Granovetter, 1985), shaped by nationally specific factors, such as structures of ownership, buyer–supplier relations, labour relations and legal infrastructure (Hall and Soskice, 1999). Moreover, divergent state institutions, such as national industrial relations and tax systems, the financial system, skill development and control, and culturally specific values such as trust and authority relations, produce divergent, nationally specific organizational logics (Whitley, 1999). Many empirical studies document that organizational logics differ markedly across advanced capitalist economies (Wade, 1990a; Whitley, 1992; Fligstein and Freeland, 1995; Storper and Salais, 1997; Fligstein, 2001; Gullién, 2001).

National differences in terms of business practices are seen to influence how firms develop with respect to strategy and structure. Nationally embedded business systems (Whitley, 1999: 117–136) have specific features that globalization can exacerbate (e.g. Hall and Soskice, 1999) because these function as unique competencies in the global market (Biggart and Guillén, 1999). The fact that most Japanese people live in small apartments meant that when it came to the miniaturization of domestic electronic components, such as hi-fi systems, firms had a considerable advantage over those in cultures such as the United States, in which suburban sprawl and larger dwellings were the norm. When Apple needed to learn about miniaturization early in its career it formed an alliance with Sony to do so.

Not all national business models are equal. Capelli (2009) noted the ascendance and dominance of the US business model for most of the twentieth century. At its core were a number of assumptions: corporate ownership and managerial control as opposed to family ownership, more often found in Europe and in Chinese family businesses, for instance; large-scale mass production methods, rather than more flexible production; open markets and informal oligopolies in contrast to the more formal cartels that were common in Europe and to a lesser extent in Asia; multi-divisional form structures, compared with more informal organizational family-based business; a form of workplace-based collective bargaining with largely instrumental – rather than political – trade unions. As Capelli notes, these business arrangements were both imposed on the defeated powers after the war (although with strong national characters, we might say) and spread through example and learning.

While the decade of the 1980s may be said to have been the decade of learning from Japan (Kono and Clegg, 1998, 2001), in the 1990s and the new century US models were reinvented in terms of 'financialization' of value and 'flexibility'. The former meant the ascendancy of models of shareholder value and 'incentivization' of executives through stock options and other financial packaging; the latter the 'network' model that emerged from California's Silicon Valley from the 1980s onwards, seen by many commentators as indicative of future strategy. If one compares it with the corporate American model whose heyday flourished in the 1950s and the 1960s, they are sharp contrasts with each other (See Table 7.1).

The core of the Silicon Valley model is its project basis that depends for its success on a ready pool of known, mobile and highly technologically qualified labour that can learn and move fast (Saxenian, 1994; Bahrami and Evans, 1995; Casper, 2007). The project form also encouraged the roles that venture capital plays; risks could be spread and realized with relatively low transaction costs. The strategy is one of backing ideas that will disrupt, reconfigure or create markets, forming projects to develop them and rapidly realizing gains or moving on quickly. These project-based knowledge networks seem to be quite specific to certain sectors of business activity, such as highly knowledge specific and highly trained technological expertise in areas such as information technology, biotechnology and nanotechnology. Moreover, they rely on a specific kind of infrastructure of defence contracting, large pharmaceuticals or a sophisticated health-based industry ready to buy-in innovation, and research-based universities with

Table 7.1   Contemporary US project-based versus corporate models

Silicon Valley model	Corporate US model
• Highly flexible small-firm start-ups able to reconfigure rapidly the nature and organization of core activities and skills	• Large size
• Limited diversification	• Diversified divisions
• Rapid commercialization and speed to market of new products and services, exploiting niches and discontinuous innovations, with strategic competition against existing capabilities – including those of the innovating organization	• The mass production of standardized goods, mass marketed and distributed to largely homogeneous mass markets
• Shallow hierarchies	• An extensive hierarchy of managerial controls
• Extensive network linkages externally	• Systematic centralized managerial coordination and control of the disaggregated elements of development, production and marketing
• Knowledge workers and creative industry employees controlled by culture rather more than structure with the culture being focused on 'can-do' and 'change', not unionized	• A largely proletarianized and relatively deskilled workforce, unionized
• Highly responsive to rapid changes in markets and technologies with highly skilled knowledge workers and knowledge networks focused on particular projects that can be rapidly developed and terminated	• High development of mechanization limiting flexibility and favouring long production cycles
• Value delivered through start-up focus so that those who are on the ground floor can get rich quick with initial public offerings (IPOs) that deliver equity ownership, with informed venture capital supporting start-ups	• Value delivered through a strong focus on cost reductions through capital intensity (downwardly), flexible labour markets and outsourcing to suppliers who could be beaten down on price
• Workers who move fluidly from project to project rather than building organizational careers, who are able to operate in highly dynamic and uncertain environments	• Lifetime employment in the model of the 'organization man'
• Clustering of related industries and firms in ecological proximity to one another, and to major technology-based universities, creating a 'hot-house' talent pool	• Extensive supply chains and subcontracting with contracting largely based on 'at-length' hard-money contracts

either private, state or a mix of funding, to supply the knowledge-based personnel in a national innovation system (see Chapter 4).

Globalization: Hybridization

Knowledge and innovation are increasingly being outsourced internationally; moreover, new firms from emerging-market countries are increasingly diversifying into international markets. Companies such as the Indian conglomerate Tata, through their subsidiary Corus, owned and controlled significant overseas assets, such as British steel mills, which they are presently divesting at the time of writing.

EXTEND YOUR KNOWLEDGE

- -

You can read Michael A. Hitt, Laszlo Tihanyi, Toyah Miller and Brian Connelly's 2006 journal article '**International diversification: Antecedents, outcomes, and moderators**', on the companion website for this book: www.edge.sagepub.com/strategy2e.

Hitt, M.A., Tihanyi, L., Miller, T. and Connelly, B. (2006) 'International diversification: Antecedents, outcomes, and moderators', *Journal of Management*, 32: 831–867.

Hitt, Tihanyi, Miller & Connelly

Global investments and the learning that accompanies them can produce cross-fertilization and hybridization (Abo, 1994), with a translation of practices occurring from one place to another (Czarniawska-Joerges and Sevón, 1996). Spicer (2006) notes such translations occurred when Japanese total quality management moved into the USA (Abo, 1994), when North American scientific management and British human relations moved into Israel (Frenkel and Shenhav, 2004; Frenkel, 2005) and when North American corporate governance moved into Germany (Buck and Shahrim, 2005). In each case what was being globalized changed as it was adopted *in situ*. Recently, the focus on translation of business practices has been on what a consultant termed the BRICs – newly emerging economies, in this case, Brazil, Russia, India and China, although sometimes other emerging economies such as South Africa, are spotlighted.

The BRICs and strategy

The collective term BRIC was developed, as we have said, to describe the 'emerging economies' of Brazil, Russia, India and China, all of which departed in various ways from a convergence in their business models with those dominant in the US, with the central government controlled China doing so most evidently. When Jim O'Neill, the Chief Economist for Goldman Sachs coined the term in 2001, he bundled these countries together as large emerging economies that he anticipated would become increasingly important in redefining the global economy. With new players came new approaches to strategy, translating the terms of existing models.

The BRICs have not evolved similarly. Brazil and Russia are in deep economic crisis, in part due to their mutual resource dependence and in Russia's case, the effects of sanctions imposed as a result of its recklessly nationalistic foreign policy adventures. China's economy is slowing while India's still maintains momentum but is hindered by major legacy issues in terms of infrastructure, posing massive opportunities for reform of sclerotic institutions.

The collective categorization device of BRIC might lead one to suppose that these countries are likely to demonstrate increasingly convergent organizational forms; overall, the soubriquet of the BRIC countries constitutes a meaningless category, precisely because the category encapsulates four vastly different countries, Brazil, Russia, China, and India, which share, at best, only a tendency for their largest domestic organizations to adopt a common conglomerate form. Each has distinct institutional histories and trajectories, just as was the case for the established global powers.

Image 7.5   BRIC countries. Copyright: TinaFields

All transitions from pre-modernity to modernity, from a society dominated by feudal agrarianism to one dominated by industry, have been based on historical access to massive resources at minimal cost to the state.

1. **Brazil** was the last state in the Americas to abolish slavery and in its early plantation economy and long history of protectionism it followed the early US model.

2. **Russia**: The Soviet Union gained control of resources of labour and nature through collectivization and state capitalism. Modern Russia inherited the legacies of the Soviet Union, which in some respects, regarding collectivization, were a model for China.

3. **India** retained many of the elements of a colonial state bureaucratic superstructure that it inherited from British institutions.

4. **China** initially followed a Soviet model but with disastrous demographic and economic consequences in the 1950s and 1960s. After 1979 it became more open to controlled foreign investment and developed a globally export-oriented economy in parallel with the state-owned enterprises sector.

BRIC: A Useful Category?

- There are considerable differences between the BRIC countries. India has a dynamic market economy and democracy emerging from a Soviet-style planned economy, with a strong and globally represented manufacturing base; it is politically stable; it enjoys democratic government; it represents huge regional diversity and strong regional identities. It has a youthful and fast growing population. Russia, by contrast, is a far more corrupted state with the semblance of democracy dominated by the executive and by politically favoured oligarchs that are largely resource-based; while it is politically stable it has dangerous undercurrents of Russian nationalist neo-fascism. It is also suffering a demographic collapse constituting an increasingly ageing population that is distinct from the other BRIC countries, one for which, short of pandemic conditions, there is no historical precedent (Jackson and Howe, 2008: 10).

- Brazil was until relatively recently a military dictatorship, albeit one that has succeeded in democratization and a relative defeat of runaway inflation, once the scourge of Brazil; corruption, which was the hallmark of the Fernando Collor de Mello presidency in the early 1990s, remains a major problem, especially in the political systems of the national government and the states (Brum, 2016). It has large and dynamic internal markets, huge regional diversity and resources aplenty. Its government is social democratic. Communication infrastructure is better in Brazil than in India, Russia or China.

- Each of these BRIC countries has seen the state promote imperfectly competitive markets to achieve growth simultaneously with protectionist policies, which has created a characteristic conglomerate organization of business groups that has evolved to serve many markets and offer a diversity of unrelated markets, such as the Votorantim Group in Brazil, Haier in China, Alfa Group Consortium in Russia and Tata in India. Each of these conglomerates share common structural elements. Within each there exists a core group of manufacturing and banking enterprises surrounded by a wide web of financial institutions, and manufacturing and distribution across a broad basket of unrelated products. In each case, this structure is a reaction to the context of centralized economic planning from which these conglomerates emerged. These conglomerates developed to deal with less than wholly competent governments and problems arising from hopelessly underdeveloped markets. The organizational forms of these dominant groups look more like the Korean *Chaebol* than they do recent dominant US models.

The changing reality of BRIC investment globally limits the applicability of much of what we accept as knowledge about globalization strategies because so much of this knowledge has been based on large manufacturing firms based in the United States. We don't know if this knowledge is applicable everywhere where there is high institutional distance between home and host countries. Recent work by Cappelli and his colleagues (2011) suggests that there are now opportunities for the United States and other major developed economies to learn from innovations in countries such as India.

Both India and China have institutional contexts in which government and its agencies have been important in steering development (Dunning and Narula, 1996). Being foreign in these strongly nationalist contexts can be a liability, especially when the institutional distance between home and host country institutions is large; where languages, religions, laws, cultures, folkways, norms and mores all differ sharply. For instance, in situations where political imperatives dominate all other institutions, including legal processes, there are widespread opportunities for foreign businesses to land in trouble. Where there is a huge and impenetrable bureaucracy to circumnavigate in order to do business the risk of taking short cuts that line some importuning official or middleman's pockets is always present. Local practices and governance standards in the home base do not necessarily coincide (see van Iterson and Clegg, 2008 for the case of the Australian Wheat Board and Saddam's Iraq); the same provisos hold for high profile cases in China (Rio Tinto) and India (Lockheed), while the problems of an absence of due process and natural justice are legion in Russia where out of political favour plutocrats can be easily imprisoned if the state deems it necessary. In Brazil, allegations of corruption have recently rocked the political elite with charges of corruption being laid against past presidents Lula (Simoes, 2016) and Rousseff.

China and India are the strongest emerging markets; consequently, both outward/inward foreign direct investments (FDI) from/to them are significantly on the rise. Recently, in both India and China, a number of firms have begun to internationalize; as global players in international markets they are developing the capacity to organize their overseas operations systematically and seeking to integrate their existing practices into new acquisitions (Hansen, 2005). Both Indian and Chinese capitalism display elements of what has been referred to in the literature as 'late development', an argument initially applied to Japan and subsequently to the emergent economies of East Asia, notably Taiwan, South Korea, Hong Kong and Singapore. Late coming firms within these countries engaged in outward investment to gain knowledge of practices in technology and business in the more developed economies (Matthews, 2002: 471).

Building on initial competitive advantages, such as low labour costs, East Asian firms developed higher-value products to move into more sophisticated markets – classic cases being Korean firms such as LG and Samsung. International investment is a means of addressing initial competitive disadvantages for firms in such economies. In the case of Haier, in China, the firm began to go global because the municipality in which it was located promoted its conglomeration of other firms; once established, the firm learnt managerial methods from a combination of German engineering principles and textbook knowledge of Japanese and American management. The emergence of the firm, now a major player in the global white goods industry, was a story of hybridity.

A similar hybridization appears to be at work in India. Cappelli et al. (2011) note that many Indian managers have been trained in Western business schools and took back the ideas that they had learnt. As they returned they developed a different way, partly similar but also partly different, of organizing and doing business. Indian managers, they suggest, are more holistically engaged with their employees than in the west; they innovate in and out of adversity and, because of the context of relative poverty, they are able to develop 'out of the box' value propositions. They do so by placing their emphasis not so much on shareholder value but on community, country and family.

China – organizations and global strategies

Some western commentators, such as Jacques (2009), see China as a harbinger for modernity's global future. Jacques (2009: 29) argues that the proposition that 'there is only one modernity and it is western' is fallacious. As he puts it, 'Far from western universalism we are entering the age of contested modernity.' China's modernity helps constitute many of the possibilities of contemporary global flows of goods, credit and commodities. He sees this as presaging a new divergence rather than it being a convergence on already existing business systems.

Some other western observers, such as Hutton, remain sceptical about the strategic innovative potential of Chinese enterprise. As Hutton (2007b: 4) states:

China must become a more normal economy, but the party stands in the way. Chinese consumers need to save less and spend more, but consumers with no property rights or welfare system are highly cautious. To give them more confidence means taxing to fund a welfare system and conceding property rights. That will mean creating an empowered middle class who will ask how their tax renminbi are spent. Companies need to be subject to independent accountability if they are to become more efficient, but that means creating independent centers of power. The political implications are obvious.

Hutton's (2007b) view is that if the Chinese middle class is to develop more confidence and entrepreneurial energies, developing new organizational forms, it will mean greater taxing of incomes and profits to fund a welfare system as well as concessions on property rights. That will mean companies being subject to independent accountability as centres of business power and more efficient markets. For Hutton (2007a; Jacques and Hutton, 2009) 'China's economic and social model is dysfunctional. It is not just corrupt and environmentally dangerous. It is wildly unbalanced and lacking in innovation.'

- -

Go Online: The potential for corruption in the People's Republic of China is clearly signalled in the revelations about China in the Panama Papers. You can read more about this in an article by Juliette Garside and David Pegg on *The Guardian* website titled 'Panama Papers reveal offshore secrets of China's red nobility'.

Panama Papers & China

You can find a link to this article on the companion website for this book: www.edge. sagepub.com/strategy2e.
- -

In China four factors have combined to create the conditions of the current national business strategy:

1. The state owns all the land.

2. China has easy access to global raw materials both from foreign direct investments in Africa and through open markets in Australia and Latin America.

3. The Chinese government controls an endless supply of cheap and highly exploitable labour.[1]

4. China, as the most significant creditor state, is the source of massive capital inflows into the US, servicing its indebtedness, in part to consume the global flow of commodities that are produced in China under authoritarian developmental state conditions readily available and exploited by foreign capital.

It is China that exercises centrifugal force in the contemporary world economy and China cannot be assumed to be converging with dominant Western organizational forms, despite the extensive trade, tourist, investment and educational links that exist. Huge regional variations make the notion of 'China' as a unitary state deeply problematic. It is characterized by demography that makes the absorption of a surplus, rural and youthful population in large-scale organizations (in which its military bureaucracies are at the forefront) an absolute imperative. Its provinces are larger than most European countries and its large cities are much larger than their European counterparts. The regions are more important than the whole.

Translation of ideas about organization flow into China through two main conduits: the state and foreign direct investment. China is a corrupt state subject to absolutist party domination with no real semblance of democracy. Recent anti-corruption campaigns have been designed by central political figures in part to disgrace political opponents within the Communist party as well as to weed out corruption. These campaigns are having unintended consequences for entrepreneurship. Much of the entrepreneurship occurring in areas such as construction was linked to the bribing of public officials for permissions. With the crackdown, housing investment is falling and large numbers of speculatively built apartments remain empty, with sales slow. Real estate decline has translated into substantial decreased demand for commodities and energy.

In many Chinese industries, particularly in the state sector, there are high levels of underutilized capacity that a hesitant government, fearing a loss of legitimacy and aggravation of a slowing economy, is reluctant to act on. These problems are feeding into economic activity more broadly: steel is massively overproduced as are coal, ships, cement and energy generation – both carbon and clean.

The capacity usage rate in the power, metals and mining sectors has fallen to around 70% or less and in the beleaguered shipbuilding industry, it is even lower, at about 60%. Up to three-quarters of China's coal mining companies are losing money, and painful as it will be, many mines will be closed, entailing the loss of hundreds of thousands of jobs. (Magnus, 2016)

Under these conditions a great deal of what passes for strategy in Chinese state-owned enterprises occurs not so much at the corporate level but at the levels of national and regional politics.

---

[1]In addition to well-publicized resistance such as Tiananmen Square in 1989, there are considerable subordinated ethnic, religious and local contestations, often condensing around peasant resistance to local bureaucracy, taxation and corruption. Individual resistance also occurs; local riots, often over local corruptions and taxes, are not uncommon. The state in China is not as monolithic as it sometimes appears to be to outside observers; much local resistance occurs. Scandals often are associated with supply chain subcontracting. The practices of Apple's subcontractor, Foxconn, in Shenzen, reveal extreme cases of child labour, excessive overtime, authoritarian management, sexual harassment, falsified records and suppression of rights (Hickman, 2010; Yinan, 2010).

It is the state, since the late 1970s that has orchestrated translation of market ideas and in doing so freed up the resource capabilities that underlie China's dynamic organizations. The state has built an export-oriented economy largely dependent on foreign investment, which is, in turn, often implicated in local corruptions; it is politically unstable, with government by the Communist Party and many of its leading state-owned enterprises closely linked with high officials in the People's Liberation Army. The energy requirements of its rapid modernization have led to widespread pollution, which a substantial rise in the use of green technologies will not quickly abate.

The Chinese state is marked by strongly regionally regressive tax policies of the central state as well as a low level of official tolerance for various forms of regional autonomy. The Chinese state is 'a loose system of bureaucratic institutions and practices … an imaginary of legitimate power, an ideological construct that is an historical product of discourses that shape perceptions of domination and coercion', as Pieke (2004: 518) suggests. One corollary of this is that there is little in the way of robust civil society outside the state.

Facing an extremely weak development of civil society, including a weak system of NGOs, or of democratic decision-making outside the Communist Party (which actually is internally very competitive), the Chinese Central Government sees the free flow of information as the biggest threat to the legitimation of their power. Giving up attempts at domestic control of media communication is one of the last things the Chinese government would compromise. Google was eventually persuaded to move out of China as a result of the contradictions of both 'doing no evil' and accommodating with the Chinese government's control of communication flows.

Current Trends in China

Chinese family businesses

Domestically owned industry tends to be dominated by Chinese family businesses. These were in the recent past characterized by owner control and relatively simple hierarchies, primarily financed from reinvestment of profit, lacking professional management, with low capital intensity, not fully functionally integrated, with little or no product and market development (Carney, 1998: 156). Carney (1998: 157) saw the 'desire for family control and income … [as] likely [to] inhibit the development of organizational capabilities since it deprives the firm of the research, marketing and human resources assets needed to compete in technologically advanced markets'. An indigenous organizational ecology based on firms that are 'highly diversified and are organizationally segmented into separately managed units' (Hamilton, 1996: 291–292) premised on webs of countless personal relationships (Fei, 1992: 32; see also Yeung, 2000) developed from this domestic industry.

Today, many firms are evolving from a simple familial model in which they were subcontractors, to more complex network modes of organization. The familial form is being transformed by the employment of a growing stratum of professional middle managers. University graduates are being employed in larger numbers than hitherto, mainly in product development and design departments and in technical positions. Liaison with universities is being cultivated to access research and development facilities and to ensure access to the best and brightest technical graduates. In consequence, day-to-day control of manufacturing operations is being delegated (Chan and Ng, 2000). With day-to-day operations under the control of professional managers, the owners are able to focus their attention on business development opportunities either independently or with US, European and Japanese partners whose branded goods they have been manufacturing for several years. New business development opportunities include the key long-term objective of developing own branded products not only for the Chinese but also the US and European markets. With few exceptions, however, Chinese brands are at present globally unknown: they are sustained by an enormous domestic market and so are barely visible overseas. Despite the organizational network innovations that may be producing them, Chinese brands are not known globally for their uniquely innovative or creative content; largely they are 'me too' brands or have been bought in, such as Lenovo.

One form of innovation in China that is widespread is the copying or plagiarism of overseas brands for local consumption.

Shanzai

Copying other firms' products and brands is a well-known business strategy. In China it is elevated to new heights and goes by the name of **Shanzhai**.

> **Shanzhai** refers to a part of China's informal industry that is known for fast product cycles as well as the tendency to seek inspiration in, or simply copy, successful products.

Basically, the Shanzhai economy is a pirate economy in which ideas are stolen and things copied. While premised on imitation as theft, however, the imitation can lead to innovation. Technologies and customer expectations co-evolve in an innovation network; for example, mobile phones have features built into them to suit local conditions such as the lack of reliable electricity supply: solution – put a torch in the mobile.

Although every Shanzhai company differs, they have a number of features in common. Their focus is on the domestic market and adapting ideas for the market. Because they do not have to innovate the basic product or respect licensing laws they are able to achieve very short cycle times in introducing products. Costs are kept low for this reason although quality is often not as good as the originals that are copied.

Shanzai Web Links

How Innovative are China's Businesses?

The major actor in China's globalization, apart from the state and a very loose network of provinces, regions, counties, cities, towns and villages, is foreign direct investment (FDI). In terms of FDI, a large part of China's attractiveness is its low labour costs as well as close access to suppliers, customers and markets. Essentially, most firms from outside China are there to access these factors. In such a state-society constituted as a very loose network of relations it is FDI that connects China with globalization.

Globalizing investment strategies in search of low labour costs as well as close access to suppliers, customers and markets means that a great deal of what global consumers purchase today is made in China. Its manufacture has meant an unparalleled boom in resource-based economies elsewhere and increasing levels of domestic saving in the PRC. Hutton (2007b: 4) sees this saving as in part a response by highly cautious consumers with no property rights or welfare system. Low interest rates in the core economies of the world economy have helped push consumer demand for Chinese manufactured goods, creating a more empowered Chinese middle class whose surplus wealth has created a highly speculative market in shares and property.

China's globally oriented economy is materialized in what Gallagher (2007) terms 'market nationalism' and is fuelled by strictly regulated FDI. Many of its state-owned enterprises represent forms of state capitalism more befitting of fascism than an ideal communist society, yet in its interstices entrepreneurial strategic interest groups of differing normative hues and characteristics populate niche spaces (Heberer, 2003).

The business systems that are developing in China are not yet innovative for the world in a similar way to the systems that emerged from early twentieth century America. China's state enterprises and PLA-owned firms are dominated by coercive management systems and exploitative labour relations premised on basic US models, with strong state direction in economic development, mobilization of resources and the picking of winners in industry. Nonetheless, China over the past 30 years has seen considerable functional, political and social pressure (Oliver, 1992) for the deinstitutionalization of Maoist norms, aiding the development of a new hybridity (Gamble, 2010).

One endogenous element in Chinese hybridity has been the development of an indigenous organizational ecology based in part on firms that are 'highly diversified and are organizationally segmented into separately managed units' (Hamilton, 1996: 291–292) based on webs of countless personal relationships, rather than a framework of organizations (Fei, 1992: 32; see also Yeung, 2000). In rural areas this Chinese network model of social relations, *chaxegeju*, has proven to be dynamic in terms of business development and, contra Hutton, innovation (at least organizational innovation).

Innovation in China

Innovation in China can be seen in various ways. For one thing, a Chinese company, Huawei Technologies, is now the number one filer of patents under the Patent Cooperation Treaty. There are a number of ways in which innovation is occurring, although one should express a caution: in a country whose provinces are larger than most European countries, and whose large cities are much larger than their European counterparts, it is virtually impossible to generalize.

1. *Endogenous innovation*: Firms are evolving from a simple familial model in which they were subcontractors, to more complex network modes of organization. The familial form is being transformed by the employment of a growing stratum of professional middle managers. As noted university graduates are being employed in larger numbers than hitherto, mainly in product development and design departments and in technical positions. In Wenzhou, by 1990 more than 3,000 families were involved in producing lighters through more than 700 private family businesses, with a division of labour between them. Their costs diminished and they entered the world market, to outcompete Japanese and South Korean firms. There are numerous such highly competitive, family-based networks, usually clustered in a geographical area, with high flexibility and low costs, and also, increasingly, high levels of knowledge and technology. In the rural area of Shengzhou by 2002 more than 1,000 family-based firms made 250 million neckties a year. In two years they invested about AUD$ 25 million in new technologies and collaborated with European designers and quality experts enabling them to deliver ties to the big fashion houses, such as Armani. They collaborate with the fashion industry on design via software over the Internet and make new products from new designs in 24 hours.

2. *Exogenously introduced innovation*: As well as endogenous sources of institutional innovation, exogenous innovation translated through strategic alliances with Western multinational firms are crucial sources of technology, capital and market resources for the transformation of Chinese family enterprises into more open structures integrated into the production networks of MNE countries (Zhang and Van Den Bulcke, 2000: 142). It is joint ventures that are doing most global product research in China, with local firms more engaged in product development or adjustment for local

markets, while the state-owned enterprises are hardly innovative at all (van der Windt et al., 2009). Exogenous innovation translated through strategic alliances with Western multinational firms are crucial sources of technology, capital and market resources for the transformation of Chinese family enterprises into more open structures integrated into the production networks of major MNE countries (Zhang and Van Den Bulcke, 2000: 142).

3. *Institutional innovation*: Liaison with universities is being cultivated to access research and development facilities and to ensure access to the best and brightest technical graduates. In consequence, day-to-day control of manufacturing operations is being delegated (Chan and Ng, 2000). With day-to-day operations under the control of professional managers, the owners are able to focus their attention on strategic opportunities. These opportunities might be explored independently in the domestic market or be born in association with overseas partners, usually from the major MNE regions of Japan, the US or Europe. Locally developed brands, often shanzai in origin, will be unlikely to go global unlike joint ventures.

4. *Patents*: Zhang and colleagues (2010) present data showing that the amount of IP registered through patents is both changing in form and increasing in number in China. It is becoming less a matter of imitation and more genuinely innovative.

Typically, researchers of China follow what Tsui (2006: 2) calls the 'outside in' approach that seeks to apply existing theories in the Chinese context. The assumption is that while management and organizations are universal phenomena the general theory can be informed by the specificity of political, cultural or other contexts (Whetten, 2009: 49). As an approach this is limited, especially with respect to China and its ubiquity. As Child (2009: 64) suggests,

> The problem with much of the research that has been conducted in this vein so far is that the theories applied are a-contextual and, therefore, inherently insensitive to context. As a result, empirical research comparing China with other countries has not generally incorporated measurements of the respective contexts in its a priori design but, rather, has brought in context as a post hoc explanation for differences that are found.

In contrast to 'outside in' Tsui (2006) identifies the 'inside out' approaches. As Child (2009: 65) says, to do such research requires a

> [D]eep knowledge of China and the subtleties of its norms and institutions. It calls for time to be spent in the country, ideally using a grounded approach through observation within organizations and discourse with their members … [that] … is resource- and time-consuming, even applied to only one country. An even greater challenge comes from the fact that the outward intention of the 'inside out' approach also requires some comparison outside China, aimed at confirming or refuting the proposition that the Chinese context is different from that found elsewhere. The extent and nature of any such differences can also contribute to an assessment of how far the concepts and explanations offered by foreign theories can encompass Chinese management. Organizations having units both in China and elsewhere may provide appropriate settings for this

kind of enquiry because they should allow both for close and detailed understanding and for cross-national comparison while keeping other contingent factors relatively constant.

Summary

The twentieth century was the American century in many ways, not least in terms of the development of dominant models of global strategy, which we have reviewed in this chapter. The dominance of North American theories, models and practices of strategy has given rise to a significant degree of debate about whether or not these are culturally embedded and politically dominant models or really the best way of organizing global business. The jury is still out on this but it is notable that the business systems literature would seem to suggest that the US models have a fairly limited remit and that, in the wake of the Global Financial Crisis, US models will be likely to have diminished legitimacy especially in so far as they have elements of financialization implicit in them. While US models work well for Anglo-Saxon liberal market economies their purchase is far weaker when applied to emerging nations with coordinated market economies. On balance the trends in strategy appear to be neither processes of convergence nor divergence but rather ones of hybridization. Hybridization develops where firms follow glocal strategies – that is they try to go global by entering into some form of local relationship with organizations in another country.

TEST YOURSELF

Want to know more about this chapter? Review what you have learnt by visiting www.edge.sagepub.com/strategy2e.

- Test yourself with multiple choice questions
- Revise key terms with interactive flashcards

EXERCISES

1. Having read this chapter, you should be able to say in your own words what the following key terms mean:

   - MNE
   - Globalization
   - Glocalization
   - Hybridization
   - Multi-divisional form

   - Arbitrage
   - Multinational corporations
   - Decentralized federation
   - Centralized hubs
   - Matrix organizations

   (Continued)

(Continued)

- Integrated network
- Project-based knowledge networks
- BRICs
- Chinese family businesses

2. Why is investment in another country likely to be more difficult than investing at home? What are some of the models that can be used to make such investments?

3. How meaningful is it to talk of the BRICs?

4. What models of global strategy are available to multinationals?

CASE STUDY

Infomedia

STEWART CLEGG

Infomedia Ltd is a publicly listed Australian company that has become a leading supplier of electronic parts catalogues for the global automotive industry. The company is headquartered in Sydney and has support centres in Melbourne, Europe, Japan, Latin and North America. While not 'born global', it quite rapidly became so.

The company first expanded into international markets by partnering with other businesses, before distributing more of its product itself through wholly owned subsidiaries. As is typical in many such enterprises, its customers dragged Infomedia into the world market. Infomedia was founded in January 1990 and initially distributed other parties' software under the name of Infomagic but later transformed into a software development company. Today, Infomedia's electronic parts catalogues have become the global standard for the automotive industry, shipping to more than 50,000 dealers in over 160 countries and 25 languages.

The seed of Infomedia was the purchase of the intellectual property for Apple software that enabled the conversion of automotive microfiche and books into user-friendly, digitized catalogues for electronic parts. The inventor of this software, Wayne Sinclair, joined Infomedia as its lead program engineer. Infomedia soon secured its first client, Ford Motor Company Australia, and by December 1990 had developed its first product: Microcat. While others in the market were selling hardware and software packages on five-year contracts, Infomedia offered monthly subscriptions with no obligation to continue purchasing. Subsequent Australian clients were acquired through Nissan and Daihatsu.

Infomedia's first export opportunity arose in 1996, when Ford invited the company to attend a meeting with Ford Europe. The challenge for Infomedia was quickly to produce a catalogue in 17 languages and to beat large competitors. Infomedia's founder, Richard Graham, decided to show Ford Europe what Infomedia could do, so he flew part of his team to Europe, where working from different countries they pulled the product together and made their first export sale in September 1997.

Infomedia's first international success was critical in several respects. First, it marked the beginning of the company's profitability. Secondly, it vindicated the generous and crucial assistance that Infomedia had been receiving from Austrade. Thirdly, it initiated Infomedia's partnering with distributors (Clifford Thames in Europe and the USA, DHL in Europe). Fourthly, the company's relationship with Ford propelled it in succeeding years into Japan, Canada, the USA, and then all of Ford's emerging markets.

Infomedia's rapid international expansion meant that it went from having a distribution of 19 markets, mainly in Europe, to over 100 worldwide. In 2002, Infomedia completed its first foreign acquisition: a division of US technology services company EDS. This acquisition gave Infomedia a license to serve General Motors, which it combined with its previously obtained license to serve Toyota.

By 2004, Infomedia's growth and development was prompting it to shift away from its original business model of third party distribution towards direct dealings with original equipment manufacturers (OEMs). Infomedia was increasingly finding that automobile manufacturers wanted to talk to them directly.

In July 2004 Infomedia established a new entity in Europe to directly manage its in-country relationships with the OEMs. In September 2005 the company also established an entity in North America to do the same. All European customer service is performed in Sydney headquarters, which operates two shifts in a call centre that covers business hours across all international time zones.

So what have been the key determinants of Infomedia's international success? According to CEO Gary Martin, Infomedia's competitive edge can be attributed to its superior technology, its low-cost and agile production and its Australian foundation.

While competitors produced on PCs, Infomedia made use of Apple Macintoshes. These allowed for better catalogue design and search capacity, as well as language switching without rebooting.

Additionally, Infomedia demonstrated that it could operate at a lower cost and faster turnaround of product than competitors. Indeed, Infomedia has had to educate one of its major distributors, who was used to a much more leisurely turnaround. In Martin's words: 'Distributor education is always a big one'.

Finally, Infomedia has taken advantage of its Australian origin. On the one hand, Infomedia can draw on Australian businesses' reputation of being somewhat rough but highly effective. On the other hand, being based in Australia's time zone and in multicultural Sydney enables Infomedia to employ a multilingual workforce that operates globally tomorrow, today.

Source: www.nswbusinesschamber.com.au/?content=/channels/International_trade/Import_Export_assistance/Growing_exporters/casestudy_infomedia.xml

QUESTION

Identify a case of a company such as Infomedia from your own country from any sectors. What key factors in the case have enabled it to become an MNE?

STRATEGY AND CORPORATE GOVERNANCE

GOVERNANCE, STAKEHOLDERS, CODES

Learning objectives

By the end of this chapter you will be able to:

1   Be familiar with the implications of the separation of ownership and management and/or control

2   Explain agency, transaction and stewardship approaches to governance

3   Explain the role of the Top Management Team and boards in strategy formulation

4   Understand significant comparative variations in corporate governance

5   Understand the use of codes in governance and some of the problems associated with them

6   Make reasoned argument about the importance of sustainability.

BEFORE YOU GET STARTED

It is clear that good corporate governance makes good sense. The name of the game for a company in the 21st Century will be to conform while it performs. (Mervyn King, Chairman, King Report)

Introduction

Who controls the corporation, how they do so to set its strategic direction, as well as the context in which these activities take place, is usually referred to as **corporate governance**.

Cioffi's definition is valuable because it recognizes the way in which corporate governance is not readily subsumed within any disciplinary ambit. While being essential to strategy, it is also embedded in law, economics, sociology, accounting, industrial relations legislation and finance. In a narrow sense, corporate governance means what is dealt with in annual reports under that heading; typically, how the board operates and functions, the way it is managed and the information that it communicates to shareholders. Doing this is a statutory obligation. With good corporate governance in place, senior executive members comprising the Top Management Team, under the direction of the board, should be able to shape the vision and mobilize the ranks, making the difference between success and failure, say Tichy (1997) and Charan and Tichy (1998).

> Cioffi (2000: 574) sees the context of **corporate governance** as including a 'nexus of institutions defined by company law, financial market regulation, and labor law'.

In this chapter we begin by discussing the origins of corporate governance in debates about the corporation initiated in discussions in the 1930s about shareholding distribution. From the 1990s onwards a series of national reports revitalized discussion of corporate governance, of which the best known is probably the UK's Cadbury Report. Contemporary interest in corporate governance has been associated with the rise of agency theory, which has dominated the field of corporate governance. Agency theory is not without its problems, including short-termism in practice and excessive abstraction in theory.

Corporate governance includes issues relating to the processes and relationships that affect how corporations are administered and controlled by boards of directors, including the incentives, safeguards and dispute-resolution processes used to order the activities of the various stakeholders recognized by the corporation, such as owners, managers, employees, creditors, suppliers, customers and communities within which business is done. There are both broad and narrow accounts of stakeholders. Broadly, any group or individual affected by the organization's objectives can be considered a stakeholder (Freeman, 1984, 2004). Stakeholder approaches may be descriptive, where only the stakeholders that are formally recognized are considered. We shall spend some time discussing the most usual of these: directors, boards, elites and top management.

There is considerably less research on the powerful people that occupy boardrooms than there is on those who are their delegates. Nonetheless, a number of problems have been identified as typically occurring in board functioning, which we discuss. There are a small number of detailed research reports into what actually occurs in boardrooms and the few we discuss provide a degree of detail that is extremely informative. Board research is developing and it is now possible to highlight a number of problematic issues in practice, which we do.

Issues in board governance are not *sui generis*; they vary greatly with national systems. We discuss four major types of corporate governance system to be found cross-nationally: the US system of shareholder capitalism that characterizes the English-speaking liberal democracies, with some slight variations; stakeholder capitalism; state capitalism; and familial capitalism. We investigate four varieties of regulation in slightly more detail: those of shareholder, stakeholder and familial capitalism (in the guise of the German *Mittelstand*) as well as the hybrid capitalism of East Asia.

Corporate governance, as a legal and binding framework, is only one part of the governance of organizations. Another part is the code of ethics that they espouse. In the final part of the chapter we review the literature on corporate codes of ethics in general and codes of corporate social responsibility in particular.

Origins of corporate governance

Corporate governance is one of those areas that emerged out of an academic debate that was sparked by Berle and Means' (1932) work about ownership and control. Berle and Means (1932) wrote about the decline of the dominance of the great 'robber barons' who commanded US business at the turn of the nineteenth century. It was evident that, as early as the 1920s, control was becoming less fused in a few dominant individuals, as had been the case at the turn of the century and its early years. In part this was a result of the increasing size of the corporations, as discussed by Chandler (1962: see Chapter 1), which made it impossible for individuals and their families to occupy all important management positions – hence the need to appoint professional managers. In part it was due to a changing legislative environment that sought to enforce competitive and antitrust behaviour, as well as the natural wastage of the robber barons as they grew old and died. Moreover, property rights were increasingly being dissolved into a form of nominal ownership to which revenue rights were attached through share ownership. Real ownership was increasingly disconnected from real control.

Berle and Means (1932) were addressing the widespread separation of ownership and control that characterized American business by the 1920s. In the wake of the 1929 Wall Street Crash, they were intrigued by why millions of people were prepared to entrust their life-savings to businesses run by unaccountable managers over whom they had virtually no control. In the 1930s, as Roe (1994) narrates, the US government passed a series of laws forbidding banks and other financial institutions from controlling industrial corporations. At a time when capitalism was not well regarded and there was a popular social movement aligned with the 'New Deal', there was great suspicion about Wall Street's control of the economy.

Bank control of shares in the US remains low, in terms of comparative institutional perspectives. There is a high degree of fragmentation of share ownership, with two groups, in particular, having identifiable blocks of shares: institutional investors such as pension funds, and top managers, as a part of their remuneration package. Given the high degree of fragmentation of shareholding it is apparent that the control of corporations can be achieved with quite small concentrations of shareholding. Opinions have differed about the size of the percentage, with around 4% usually being sufficient to render control in the United States, if the majority of the other shares are either fragmented or held by non-interventionist institutions, such as pension funds (Davis and Useem, 2002: 242).

Where there are significant stockholdings by executives they may well be both agents and effective principals, to use some terms to be introduced shortly. In essence, if the stockholdings are largely passively owned by non-interventionist financial institutions, that merely seek a certain rate of return, as well as by small shareholders, then quite small bundles of concentrated shareholding in the hands of senior executives can combine ownership and control.

Berle and Means, back in the 1930s, maintained that the separation of ownership and control would mean that the managers controlled the corporation and would use its resources to pursue 'prestige, power, or the gratification of professional zeal' (1932: 122). Berle and Means (1932) identified a number of trends:

1. A significant concentration of capital in enterprises of larger scale.

2. Managerial rather than owner control of the assets thus concentrated.

3. Weakening of the discipline of the capital market as a constraint on managerial action as a result of the separation of ownership of assets and their day-to-day control.

4. The development of goals other than that of pure profit maximization as salient for managerial action.

The implications of their analysis pointed to the fact that the 'separation of ownership and control implies an inability on the part of the owners effectively to check the management of the corporation and threatens economic efficiency' (Gomez and Korine, 2008: 233). The problematic of corporate governance – *who controls the corporation and how* – flows directly from Berle and Means' (1932) work. In terms of asking the question, '*how control of the corporation is best regulated*', the answer will have a strongly normative flavour in terms of its balance of regulation and *laissez-faire*.

Contemporary corporate governance

In recent years the normative element in corporate governance has been uppermost in a number of official reports. Amongst these is the Organization for Economic Cooperation and Development's Principles of Corporate Governance, the Cadbury Report in the UK, as well as the California Public Employees Retirement System's Global Principles for Corporate Governance and the Viénot Report in France. In the United States, the Sarbanes-Oxley Act was introduced in an attempt to improve corporate governance in the wake of the collapse of Enron. The Cadbury Report has probably been the most influential of these, in focusing analysts' and investors' attention on matters of regulation, responsibility and reporting to shareholders; the effectiveness of boards in terms of oversight, structures and processes; as well as the requirements of accounting, auditing and accountability.

Company law defines the legal vehicles by which property rights are organized; the legal standing of publicly and privately held corporations, and the legal liability of owners as well as the relationships amongst owners, boards of directors, managers and workers in publically listed corporations. As Fligstein and Choo (2005: 63) suggest, 'the degree to which there is a separation of ownership from control

Image 8.1   Corporate governance. Copyright: Warchi

in publicly held corporations', the extent to which shareholding of firms is wide-spread or concentrated (either in banks, other financial institutions, or families), is the major issue of analytic interest.

Fligstein and Choo (2005) place corporate governance in its regulatory legal and comparative political framework. Financial market regulation regulates how firms obtain capital for their operations, their relationships to banks, other financial institutions, and public equity and debt markets. Where firms sell additional stock in the firm they create an equity market; borrowing money and issuing bonds creates a bond market, where the bonds will eventually be paid out, according to the financial regulations in place.

Laws governing how employees are treated are known as industrial relations law defining the legal parameters of employee's rights as they are constituted in the administrative legal entity, usually the state or sub-state government. In some states these rights include a role in governance; in others they will not. In Anglo-Saxon societies such as the United States, where shareholder primacy is the norm, industrial relations law provides few institutional supports for organized labour and corporate boards maximize shareholder value without regard for labour. In Germany, where stakeholder primacy is the norm, unions have representatives on boards of directors and partners in business decision-making.

There is little need for an explicit governance theory where there is a unity of ownership, control and governance, as would be the case, for instance, where a small business proprietor runs her own business. The need for such theory derives from a situation where ownership and control do not necessarily coincide, as is the case with almost all stock exchange listed companies. However, the questions associated with corporate governance have not been framed in either historical or comparative institutional terms by the discipline that has done most to answer them: economics, particularly the neoclassical branch of the discipline. Here the questions have been posed largely in terms of an approach known as agency theory.

More recently, agency theory has ceded some space to a more pluralist range of research approaches that have flourished with an increasing interest in *how* boards participate in strategy. With the emergence of theoretical pluralism some contours of the field become more evident. US-based scholars are more likely to address issues such as the determinants and consequences of a board's involvement in strategy and to use agency theory, while Europeans focus more on board process and utilize a wider range of theories.

Pugliese and colleagues (2009) reviewed the literature on corporate governance from 1972 to 2007. From the data, the authors derived three distinct research periods which they suggest were demarcated by two principal factors: the quantum of publications and an identified shift in the theoretical and methodological approaches of researchers (2009: 293). Durisin and Puzone (2009) analysed a similar literature comprising over 1,000 articles relating to corporate governance, finding that empirical studies were generally characterized by the use of agency theory as the dominant theoretical framework.

Agency theory

Contemporary treatment of corporate governance is marked by three distinct periods denoted by the quantum of publications and dominant theoretical and methodological approaches (Pugliese et al., 2009). An initial period extended from 1972 to 1989, characterized by an emerging interest in the role of corporate governance in achieving board involvement in strategy. Two landmark studies were published in this period that proved influential in shaping the field. These were a literature review by Zahra and Pearce (1989) and Fama and Jensen's (1983a) use of agency theory.

> **Agency theory** is concerned with resolving problems that can exist in relationships between principals (such as shareholders) and agents of the principals (for example, senior executives and top managers).

According to Fama and Jensen (1983a), problems arise when the goals of the principal and agent are in conflict, when the principal and agent have different attitudes towards risk, and the principal is unable to verify (because it is difficult and/or expensive to do so) what the agent is actually doing. Because of different tolerance of risk, the principal and agent may each be inclined to take different action, with each having different criteria of efficiency.

Some economists have suggested that managerial control leads firms to make investments in size or growth rather than profits (i.e., managers pursued less risky investments to preserve their jobs: Penrose, 1959; Marris, 1968). The economists' focus has been on the minimization of transaction costs (Williamson, 1975b, 1985) and the minimization of agency costs (Jensen and Meckling, 1976). To assess efficiency empirically, economists study the performance of firms (profits, return on capital) or whole national economies (where the dependent variable is frequently measured by changes in GDP). While traditionally the focus of economics has been on the efficient allocation of resources according to price signals, interpreted by rational actors, increasingly they recognize that factors such as law, trust and good government might affect allocative decisions (Berkowitz et al., 2003; Carlin and Mayer, 2003; La Porta et al., 1997a, 1997b, 1998, 1999; North, 1990).

As we have seen, the separation between ownership and control is a staple topic for business students. The basic idea of a separation of ownership and control is that corporate strategy should align top managers' interests with those of shareholders, by making significant stock options available to senior management as a part of their remuneration package. The basic idea is that these managers will then share a common set of interests with shareholders and so manage effectively in terms of these interests.

At the core of the corporate governance approach is a simple question; if the owners of a company do not have charge of its day-to-day business how can they be sure that their interests are being served? Shareholders are the principals in a business; they own capital that they place at the disposal of the business in return for an entitlement to any profits or losses accruing to the shareholders who risk their capital. As the shareholders are many and varied and are generally not engaged in the running of the business, agents manage the business, acting on behalf of the principals.

Now the problem can be phrased quite simply: what mechanisms can be designed to induce managers to maximize stock, and thus shareholder, value? The answer to this question seemed simple – link CEO and Top Management Team pay closely to the company's performance in the stock market. That way the interests of principals, the shareholders, and the agents, the CEO and managers, would be closely aligned. CEOs and Top Management Teams became remunerated in part – indeed, in large part in many cases – through the mechanism of stock options or through performance related pay which tracks share prices. The reasoning is that it is in the interests of stockholders as the principals – the owners of the shares – that the stewards of their capital – the agents – be stockholders having a significant part of their earnings aligned with stock valuations.

The branch of economics known as agency theory considers the shareholders as the principals of the firm for whom managers act as agents who cannot be trusted, unless their interests are closely aligned with those of shareholders in order to maximize shareholder value, according to leading theorists such as Fama (1980) and Jensen and Meckling (1976). In this view, the firm is a bundle of assets whose value is given solely by the shareholders' return on investment. It is argued by agency theory that transparency and accountability are important; however, when firms improve their disclosure quality they tend to attract more transient institutional investors, which, in turn, increase the volatility of share prices in a result exactly the opposite of what the theory predicts. Consider the well-known case of Lehman Brothers, a model for agency theory, having adopted all of its corporate governance principles:

> In most (if not all) the companies that failed in 2008 financial crisis, the majority of executive compensation packages were provided in the form of a variable, performance-based annual incentive delivered in both cash and equity awards. According to the last proxy statement presented by Lehman Brothers, its CEO received over $34 million as his annual compensation and 85% of it was in the form of stock and options ... And this is customary in the industry. Similar compensation practices have long been the norm in large financial services firms. (Berrone, 2008: 2)

The Global Financial Crisis of 2008 revealed widespread lack of accountability and management of risk in the financial industry. To some extent this might be surprising – it is not as if these companies did not employ risk governance procedures: the evidence is that they did; however, these were to a large extent a form of ceremonial and reputational management, as Power (2009) attests, especially in the face of regulatory capture and executive malfeasance, as Perrow (2011) analyses. Indeed, risk is a Janus-faced concept. On the one hand, it is something to be managed, kept at bay; on the other hand, it presents an entrepreneurial opportunity. Managing risk as a paradox, as both threat and opportunity, is never likely to be easy (Vitt, 2013).

Many large financial services firms, such as Lehman Brothers and Bear Stearns, did not survive 2008 and many other firms that did are deeply constrained by debt and government loans that bailed them out. Although advocates of agency theory might argue that, in the long term, weak agency controls will result in poor stock valuations and thus takeover, so that more efficient agency can be exercised and the underlying value of the assets realized, this is hardly adequate as a perspective on the excesses culminating in the events of 2008.

Agency theory starts from the fact that firms need capital. Without capital products cannot be innovated and economies of scale and scope cannot be achieved. Owners of capital do not necessarily have the skills and know-how to run a firm. Managers, who are hired by (the owners of) capital, lack capital. To solve this problem, principals (i.e., the investors) pay agents (the managers) in order for those managers to make profits and assure maximum returns on their investments.

Owners of capital, agency theory suggests, fear being potentially subordinated to managers' interests in the security and growth of the firm rather than in profit maximization. Owners of capital, as absentee shareholders, can hardly monitor management's actions. There is always a temptation for management to keep expectations rising, perhaps by taking big gambles that might well pay off, or by practising increasingly creative approaches to accounting, in order to keep valuations rising. What started out as simply a way of aligning principal and agent interests can too easily end up being dysfunctional for all parties. Top management can favour their short-term interests in inflated share prices rather than a long-term interest in the sustainability of the business. When this occurs **agency cost** may be incurred.

> Where owners of capital lack information about how the organization in which they have invested is organized, they are potentially at the mercy of the managers (the agents), leading to the problem of monitoring those agents. The cost of this monitoring is called **agency cost.**

Governance is supposed to solve the monitoring problem. Boards of directors are charged with a fiduciary duty (an obligation to the owners of the assets with which one is entrusted) to shareholders to monitor the managers; one of the ways that they do so, using the precepts of agency theory, is to tie the remuneration of the Top Management Team to firm performance, thereby aligning their interests with the interests of owners. This linkage is supposed to occur in a context that encourages transparency, in which disclosure laws require timely filing of operational and performance results to current and prospective investors. Agency theory also posits that if managers and boards of directors underperform, despite governance requirements, the existence of a market for corporate control will provide a final check on managerial opportunism (Fama and Jensen, 1983a, 1983b).

In the business world, top managerial pay is closely linked to the company's performance in terms of expectations expressed through the stock market. Executives can make decisions that increase the next quarter's stock price. There is nothing wrong with that, of course – except where the values are based on unrealizable expectations, or where investment decisions are not made because they might have a negative impact on short-term share prices or dividends. Therefore it is in the short-term interests of the Top Management Team to put off costly investments for the future in preference for strategies that shore up or do not dilute present value.

Managers have increasingly been encouraged by analysts to put shareholder value above all other interests. A strategic focus on the short term is reflected in an increased emphasis on cost management, increasing asset churn (think mergers, acquisitions, buyouts and demergers). Instead of a 'retain and reinvest' investment strategy, we get a 'downsize and distribute' regime that rewards shareholders as it sweats assets and shrinks the labour force.

Corporate Capitalism

It is corporate law and financial market regulation that enables performance to be judged by shareholders and potential investors or business analysts. From this perspective the agency problem is resolved through the existence of rules surrounding public corporations. These are supposed to ensure a degree of transparency in accounting for managerial actions, subject to audit. Corporate governance thus consists of 'legitimating mechanisms, processes and codes through which power and authority are exercised by business elites' (Maclean et al., 2006: 2).

Legitimacy is vital for business: most essentially, it is necessary to be able to raise capital. No lender of repute would willingly support a corporate enterprise in which the Top Management Team was unwilling to make information available to the public, or which was clearly being misgoverned by a board of directors (Hansmann, 1996). Clear signals about the importance of corporate governance are signs of legitimacy; hence, effective corporate governance is a major factor in building legitimacy.

Problems with Agency Theory

Agency theory is not overly useful for thinking about strategy. Businesses may produce valuations on the stock exchange but this is not their prime activity. It is a side effect of the way that they are capitalized. Their prime activity is to deliver goods and services, such as automobiles or mortgages. A company might develop a very successful product, raising the stock value. Once that product is launched, and the stock adjusts upwards, the success of that product, while it may be profitable and stable over the long term, may not necessarily be sufficient to drive the stock up further. So other strategies are needed to maintain growth in the share price and keep on delivering returns to existing and new shareholders. As a result, executives can be tempted (or pressured) to make decisions that aren't necessarily good for long-term stability or profitability but which increase the next quarter's stock price, which is known as 'short-termism'.

Maclean et al. (2006: 15) identify three major problems with agency theory in relation to boards:

1. Agency theory fails to confront the social realities of the boardroom and business milieu; it is a set of abstractions with little empirical content.

2. Agency theory fails to recognize that ownership and control are not sharply separated. In part this is a recursive effect of the theory. Cognizant of agency theory, many corporations have sought to make their agents – the Top Management Team – principals through the granting of stock options. Where shareholding is highly fragmented personally and institutionally held, relatively small bundles of shares provide effective control.

3. Not all actors make rational choices: deficient boardroom cultures and practices may encourage abuses of power and recklessness in action as the many corporate scandals of recent years attest. As is evident from the pages of the financial press, business elites command vast resources with which they can both create and destroy value. Destruction can take many forms: an ill-judged mega-merger, a speculative gamble in terms of investments, or corrupt behaviour on a mega-scale. Think of Marconi and its mergers, Vivendi and its takeover of Seagrams, Enron and its corrupt accounting, or the involvement of global companies in the web of bribery and corruption allegedly spun, very profitably, by Monaco-based Unaoil.

Go Online: Unaoil, the company that bribed the world, can be read about on the *Huffington Post* website in a set of articles called 'World's biggest bribe scandal: The company that bribed the world'.

You can find the links to these articles on the companion website for this book: www.edge.sagepub.com/strategy2e.

Unaoil News
Article

Discussion of the problems with agency theory recurs in the context of Chapter 13, near the beginning, and the interested reader might want to skip to that section at this point, although it is not necessary to do so.

Problems with corporate governance and the shareholder/stakeholder value debate

As we have noted, extant economic debates on corporate governance emphasize the need for incentive alignment between shareholders and managers in the context of the debate about the separation of ownership from management and/or control (Jensen and Meckling, 1976). Management-oriented theories, such as 'stakeholder' and 'stewardship' theories on the other hand (see Clarke, 2007; Klein et al., 2012), deal with a broader set of issues as well as with multiple stakeholders other than just shareholders.

Both shareholder and stakeholder approaches have problems explaining why shareholder or stakeholder value deserves such pre-eminence. The transaction costs and resource-capability-based theories of the firm (Coase, 1937; Penrose, 1959; Teece et al., 1997) can help explain value generation by firms by emphasizing efficiencies in transaction and production costs and revenues respectively. What they cannot explain is why there should be a focus on the pursuit of *shareholder* value.

Alchian and Demsetz (1972) justified the focus on shareholder value by saying that in any team effort, where individual output is hard to measure, team members may 'shirk'. Avoiding this requires a monitor, who should also be self-monitored (so as to avoid the infinite regress problem of 'who monitors the monitor'). To achieve this, the monitor becomes a residual claimant on profits, thereby being 'incentivized' to eliminate inefficiencies. Owners (shareholders) are best suited for this purpose, it is argued, as they have invested in firm-specific assets. Therefore, shareholder value is critical. However, the theory suggests that shareholder value can be prejudiced by the pursuit of goals other than profit; for instance, the pursuit of managerial objectives such as sales revenue, discretionary expenditures and non-profit maximizing growth. Hence, it is important to align incentives between owner–shareholders and managers. Subsequent contributions by Grossman and Hart (1986) and Hart and Moore (1990) provided support to the shareholder value maximization idea by showing that, under certain rather restrictive assumptions, maximizing shareholder value equals the maximization of the net present value (NPV) of the corporation as a whole (see Klein et al., 2012).

That owners, separated from control, should be the 'residual claimants' on profits (those who can claim the amount left after all others, such as suppliers, etc., have received their remuneration) is a dubious proposition (Pitelis, 2004b; Klein et al., 2012). Indicatively, workers and other stakeholders also invest their time and skills in firm-specific assets. In knowledge-based activities, for instance, monitoring costs are likely low. Knowledge workers will typically be allowed largesse in self-monitoring. Indeed, the essence of 'professional indetermination' is premised on being an autonomous practitioner, for whom the rules and ethics of the profession are encoded and embrained.

That there is a separation between ownership and management is not in doubt. However, one needs to question what ownership percentage suffices to give control to a cohesive group and how such groups can be identified. In addition, how dispersed does the ownership have to be for shareholder remunerated Top Management Teams to achieve control, with what percentage of share-ownership? In a world created by agency theory, in which elite managers have extensive stock options to align their interests with those of shareholders, these managers' small percentage holdings might well be the most cohesive because the remaining shareholdings are either extremely fragmented individually or the shares are held by institutional investors that do not tend to be 'active', other than through divestment. Such considerations raise doubts as to the importance and extent of management control as something distinct and separate from shareholding (Scott, 1986; Pitelis and Sugden, 1986).

Additional problems refer to the constraints managers face in pursuing their aims, such as the role of equity markets in facilitating corporate takeovers, thus limiting previously existing managerial power and control (Manne, 1965); the role of markets for managerial compensation in framing remuneration packages (Fama, 1980); as well as the role of monitoring and bonding by shareholders and debt-holders. The M-form organization (Williamson, 1991b) can also limit managerial power. So can institutional shareholdings by pension fund managers, who may divest and send share prices plummeting when management pursues what are perceived to be recklessly self-interested policies (Pitelis, 1991). All these considerations suggest that managers' interests will tend to be closely aligned with those of the larger shareholders, hence a focus on a corporate 'controlling group' that comprises top management *and* large shareholders better approximates the issue of who controls today's big corporation (Pitelis and Sugden, 1986).

Importantly, a focus on 'agency' between only 'owners' and 'managers' is overly narrow. In particular, the 'agency' between 'employers' and 'employees', which was critical for Alchian and Demsetz (1972) and at the heart of Coase's (1937) transaction cost theory (not to mention classics such as Adam Smith and Karl Marx), has been all but forgotten. The relation between employers and employees is likely to be more important than the relations between owners and managers, given the more sharply divergent objectives between employers' interests (high profits) and employees' interests (high wages) that can engender intra-firm struggles (Marx, 1959; Cyert and March, 1963; Pitelis, 2007). Given today's extensive discussions about the importance of human resources and their relationship for value creation (see, for example, Pfeffer, 1998, 2010 and Becker and Huselid, 2006), ignoring employees is unsatisfactory.

In addition to the above, the link between corporate governance and shareholder value is predicated on an assumption that all owner shareholders share the objective of profit maximization. Included in this assumption are small shareholders whose investment occurs through their pension funds. Often they are unaware of where their funds are invested. Such unaware shareholders are assumed to be residual claimants; that their interests are reflected in achieving sustainable share price and dividend growth is a somewhat heroic assumption (Pitelis, 2004b; Lazonick and O'Sullivan, 2000), given the lack of awareness.

Klein et al. (2012) suggest that contributions by Rajan and Zingales (1998) and Blair and Stout (1999), question the shareholder supremacy perspective from a stakeholder position. These contributions point to the possibility of a third party (the Board) functioning as a guardian of the wider corporate interest, as opposed to the interests of particular groups, such as the shareholders, seeking to ensure continuing investments by co-specialized and complementary human resources–stakeholders. In a similar vein, Porter and Kramer (2011) propose a focus on shared value, as opposed to shareholder value. However, the stakeholder view has troubles in identifying whom the stakeholders are (everyone? Only key ones? On what basis?), so the debate is likely to continue. Stakeholder theories are accused of being too broad without a clear demarcation criterion of who are the relevant or eligible stakeholders (see Klein et al., 2012).

Pitelis (2013) claimed that there are at least three major relations to be considered and they are layered hierarchically: relations between the company and its stakeholders, between the company and the nation state and between the nation state and the globe – the world as a whole. In this context the shareholder/management agency is merely a sub part of the first of these agencies – very narrow indeed.

- -

Go Online: Corporate governance remains a very hot topic in the wake of the Global Financial Crisis. At the time of writing a most valuable critical resource has become available online – the *Ephemera Journal* website. *Ephemera* is a free online journal and of particular interest is Vol. 16, no. 1, which focuses on themes in contemporary corporate governance, including discussions of the political economy of corporate governance; its comparative diversity – which we address later in the chapter; governance in family firms; corporate social responsibility as a part of governance, which we also address later in the chapter; and the limits of contractual views of governance.

Ephemera
Journal

You can find a link to this issue on the companion website for this book: www.edge. sagepub.com/strategy2e.

- -

Corporate governance, the boardroom and strategy making

The boardroom is the arena in which the managerial elite practises strategy making; where Chairs, Presidents, Chief Executives and Non-Executive Directors meet and mingle purposefully in order to make decisions and manage risk, operating as boards, executive committees and Top Management Teams.

A boardroom is a space in which ambitious egos strive to direct the action, sometimes for matters of purely personal interest, more often than not expressing interests in terms of the rationalities of strategy (Baunsgaard and Clegg, 2013). What corporate governance regulation strives to achieve is the establishment of some rules for the games that are played. As Maclean et al. (2006: 259) write, however, a 'boardroom is more than a place where the agents of shareholders take decisions within a carefully specified set of rules and regulations. They are in essence small, elite communities that function in accordance with established cultural norms and standards'.

These cultural norms and standards are highly variable because no single system of corporate governance exists globally. Some broad comparisons can be drawn. Parker (2002) suggests that there is considerable evidence that boards dominated by

Image 8.2   Boardroom. Copyright: RonTech2000

their CEOs will be weaker and more ineffectual with a greater chance of strategic error that lowers efficiency. The reasons should be evident: where there is a lack of polyphony, of multiple voices joining in a strategic conversation, there will be a disinclination for robust debate and discussion. Matters of judgment can become concentrated in a single point of decision. Putting decision choices in one *supremo* may not always be the wisest course of action. The risk seems greatest, perhaps not surprisingly, in the United States, the country that celebrates leadership and individualism most enthusiastically.

In most companies in the United States the CEO tends to enjoy a considerable imbalance of power compared to the nominal authority of the board that appoints the CEO and to which they are legally accountable. Although in principle, the board delegates power to the CEO, in practice, the CEO has day-to-day discharge of these delegated powers. Boards in the US are usually a non-executive body, with weak ties to operational parts of the business being mediated through just the president and the CEO.

Problems with Boards

1. *Ritualism*: Where authority is vested in a board that meets rarely and is disengaged from operational matters, for all intents and purposes these board meetings will be routine rituals led by the CEO. The CEO controls access to considerable current information, has inside knowledge and extensive staff support, such that they can, and generally do, control the board agenda. While the board has legal authority, it is the CEO that has effective power because they are able to set the agenda. By contrast, the board members will have a lack of relevant information.

2. *Concentration of powers*: Where the CEO is also the chair of the board it is a virtual guarantee that the board will be ineffectual. Given the constraints attached to agenda setting, a board can only be as independent and as effective as its CEO chair wants it to be and is capable of making it, says Parker (2002: 239). It is for this reason that best practice recommends that boards should have an

independent chair that can stand up to the CEO when there is a difference of opinion. It is important to realize that where the CEO is the chair of the board, the board will only get to know what the chair wants them to know, filtered from what management and support staff allow to be known. Often outside directors can only learn that there are serious problems when they blow up: at this stage it is often too late to resolve them, other than by dismissal of the existing CEO and searching for a new incumbent to clean up the mess.

3. *Training*: Being a board member requires training. Most nations have an Institute of Directors that offer programmes of training for board members. It is important that independent directors are qualified to do the job that they have been appointed to do. It is even better if they already have some experience of the role. Better still if they are not nominated and selected by the CEO on a nepotistic basis.

4. *Board size*: Parker suggests that a board of about seven or eight members is likely to be more effective than one that is much bigger. In US research it has been established that companies with smaller boards had stronger incentives for their chief executive, were more likely to dismiss an under-performing CEO, and achieved larger market share and superior financial performance (Davis and Useem, 2002). Perhaps not surprisingly, CEOs prefer a large board as it makes the board less cohesive and less effective in monitoring the CEO's performance. The larger the board, the less likely it will be effective in monitoring and controlling CEO performance and the more likely it is to become factionalized in times of conflict.

A major constraint on board effectiveness is the amount of time that board members devote to their board responsibilities. Often this is limited (Lorsch, 1997). Better boards practise self-management – that is they seek to manage how they perform as a board by instituting processes of assessment. They should decide, collectively, what are the behaviours that they want to encourage in the board and decide these in advance and monitor ongoing meetings for the performance of these. They need to arrange a formal assessment of their performance on an annual basis. Such an assessment can be done independently of the chair by executive recruitment firms that sit in on board meetings to test the development of competencies by board members in their duties. Also, they can aid in the selection of board members, to ensure a degree of broad-based experience and representation in terms of gender and other markers of identity. They also can advise members of the board on the best way of being thoroughly prepared and briefed for board meetings.

- -

Go Online: There is ample evidence that, 23 years after the recommendations of the Cadbury Report in the UK, there are still major problems of corporate malfeasance occurring in boardrooms. Jeroen Veldman and Hugh Willmott explore these in a recent article in *The Conversation* called 'Britain's broken corporate governance regime', prompted by revelations about the lack of corporate control at board level in the UK supermarket company Tesco (see www.theconversation.com/britains-broken-corporate-governance-regime-38239). The lack of control by corporate governance is hardly surprising, as the system in place has no regulatory bite: it is, as they say, a system of private, voluntary regulation. How effective is governance that is almost entirely voluntary, as is the case with most current corporate governance regimes? Even where there is a clear structure of corporate governance, how it is enacted depends very much on local struggles that take place in and around specific organizations.

- -

IN PRACTICE

Woolworths, The Fresh Food People

Go Online: Visit the book's website at https://edge.sagepub.com/strategy2e to watch an interview with Roger Corbett conducted by the author team.

Roger Corbett Interview

Roger Corbett is truly able to comment on the importance of governance. From his initial role in the warehouse loading trucks and sweeping floors, Roger seized the opportunities presented to him to climb the corporate ladder to become CEO of one of Australia's largest organizations. Such a unique career path has provided Roger with unique advice. When he discusses governance and leadership issues, he reflects on the importance of building empathy and relationships with staff. Relationships were leveraged in order to push through the organization's growth and change strategies; the only objectives worth considering when developing a strategy. Emphasis is made on the importance of the relationship between governance structures, Top Management Teams and the employees as it is through the employees that governance and leadership derives legitimacy.

Since beginning his career in the early 1960s on the dock of a Grace Bros' department store, Roger Corbett AO has risen to become one of Australia's most influential figures in the retail sector. After becoming the youngest ever full Director at Grace Bros, Roger joined the Board of David Jones in 1984, then, in 1990 was appointed to the Board of Woolworths Limited. For the next decade, Roger's hands-on experience and understanding of the unique Australian retail sector and changing consumer needs would define his career with Woolworths Limited, one of the two largests grocery chains in Australia.

Roger was appointed Managing Director – Retail in 1997, responsible for all trading divisions, and eventually appointed COO in 1998 and CEO in 1999. In that time, Roger had overseen Woolworths continued market dominance and was directly responsible for the development and implementation of some of the country's most successful new business acquisitions and strategic alliances. He retired as CEO and a Director of Woolworths in 2006 but continued to consult until 2011, in addition to maintaining executive and board responsibilities with several leading corporations and public bodies.

Questions

1. Board composition is a key governance mechanism. What does Roger Corbett look for in a board and how does this view correspond with extant theories of governance?

2. What is Roger's view on leadership and how can you explain his successful approach using the concepts provided by management theories?

3. A leader's role is to provide and explore opportunities for organizational growth and personal growth for subordinates. But, in Roger's view, what can the individual member of the organization do to fully benefit from given opportunities?

4. Different governance theories emphasize different control mechanisms to guide executives and management teams. Discuss the advantages and disadvantages of combining control-based mechanisms with trust-based governance mechanisms.

Strategy in practice in the boardroom

Huse and colleagues (2011) suggest that more research is required to understand *how* boards work. Recently Pugliese and colleagues (2015) conducted an observational study of selected board meetings, leading them to suggest that board dynamics remains an area warranting further investigation. There are notable contributions, however.

Andrew Pettigrew and Terry McNulty (1995: 847) have made a significant empirical contribution to understanding strategy processes in the boardroom. Stakeholders, creditors and outside members of the board all wield influence on strategy making. With the exception of creditors, whose influence is often not invited, these stakeholders are chosen by the senior management as board members. Part-time board members only have a limited commitment of time and discretion to their board activities. Management is infinitely better informed and has access to more information and data than these external influences. Moreover, norms of board conduct often limit the influence of outsiders to little more than an advisory role (Pettigrew and McNulty, 1995: 849), despite their legal mandate.

When they assume board membership, part-time members of boards enter into power relations that are constrained by structural factors shaping the decision-making context, such as shareholder value expectations, as well as by institutionalized expectations and legal frameworks, such as tax laws. In moments of crisis they may well be able to act outside of the 'normal' constraints and oppose executive actions but in other circumstances they are less likely do so. The ability to influence increases with factors such as relevant experience and expertise (the usefulness of which is always contextually framed); the power that can be derived from relations with powerful external agencies; the representational role played on board committees; and, most significantly, the flows of information that come from embeddedness in networks and interlocking directorships.

In a later article, McNulty and Pettigrew (1999) researched a larger sample of part-time board members than the 20 directors investigated in the previous study. Potentially, such directors have a role in exercising strategic control and making strategic choices and changes. Not all directors have the same say: it all depends on context, say McNulty and Pettigrew (1999: 48). The important elements of this context are 'public debate and policy making about corporate governance, the history and performance of the company, the conduct and process of a board and informal relations between board members'. Unfortunately, as they argue, the area of board behaviour has been subject to much abstract theorizing in both agency theory and in resource dependence theory. The former stresses boards as potential arenas for conflicts between owners and managers (principals and agents) while the latter stresses the role that boards play in reducing uncertainty about the environment (Pfeffer, 1972; Pearce and Zahra, 1991). While earlier research tended not to say much about the role of boards in making strategy, it is now widely recognized that boards do set strategic direction through 'mission' and 'vision' statements.

As McNulty and Pettigrew (1999) note, earlier work by Eisenhardt and Zbaracki (1992) summarizes much of what we know about choice behaviour: it is boundedly rational, non-linear, emotional and political in character. McNulty and Pettigrew's (1999) research suggested that part-time board members exercise some control over management with respect to strategy. Some of this involves making strategic decisions on capital investment proposals that come from management. Mostly, boards agree with the proposals put forward – which of course does not mean that they are rubber stamped because the rule of anticipated reaction could well be in play. Only proposals carefully vetted and considered will be likely to be proposed. Skilled executives can anticipate the reaction to those that are not well prepared. Hence, proposals are designed on the basis of what is considered 'rational' in the local context prior to being placed before the board.

Part-time directors shape discussions about strategic decisions in subtle ways, suggest McNulty and Pettigrew (1999), especially in the early stages of formulation. They do so in ways that are episodic, reactive and intermittent, as they respond to the agendas and papers that are tabled. Hence, their role is more one of checking than initiating actions. McNulty and Pettigrew (1999) find that part-time directors often frame strategy discussions through questioning unfolding strategy discussions: for instance, a director might point out the gender or tax implications of a policy that have not been aired. In this way they contribute to the overall normative environment of what constitutes legitimate questioning.

The sample that Pettigrew and McNulty (1995, 1999) interviewed was well sprinkled with titled people. Certainly, the upper echelons of companies will be graced by an elite, which may not necessarily enjoy noble titles, depending on the democratic tenor of the country in question. For instance, Davis and colleagues (2003) found that the American corporate elite was indeed a 'small world', showing remarkable coherence and consistency in its relations and ranks. Davis and Useem (2002) note that, where a US CEO has an elite MBA degree, it accelerates their rise to the top; the more elite the background from which they come, the more likely they are to attract high quality external directorships, while to the extent that they hand-pick their board, it enhances their pay and perquisites (Useem and Karabel, 1986; Belliveau et al., 1996). Overall, they note that when we extend the focus from the chief strategists to the Top Management Team we find that companies with greater diversity at the top gain greater market share and operating profits (Davis and Useem, 2002).

Emergent topics in board research

Recent directions in corporate governance research identify a number of emergent topics that bear on boards. These include the following:

1. The impact of independent members on boards (Woods et al., 2012; Bezemer et al., 2014). Independence promotes the potential for productive conflicts.

2. The role of women and board diversity (Nielsen and Huse, 2010; Torchia et al., 2011; Rao and Tilt, 2015). Diversity introduces more perspectives; this might lead to more conflict but also to the canvassing of a broader range of options.

3. The links between boards and organizational performance (Zhang, 2010; Machold and Farquhar, 2013); boards are ultimately responsible for organizational performance, so they become the site of conflict when performance is failing. Diversity and independence enhance the likelihood of failing performance not being tolerated.

4. The role of boards in major corporate change (Gnan et al., 2013). It is boards that are responsible for strategic – long-term – decision-making.

5. The impact on boards of their operating context, such as the size, location and history of the company (Vaccaro et al., 2012; Gutierrez and Surroca, 2014). Boards are the repository of both history and renewal: the former should not overwhelm the possibilities of the latter. The nature of board dynamics (Hendry et al., 2010; Bailey and Peck, 2011; Bezemer and Nicholson, 2014) between tradition and innovation are vital.

6. The relation between boards and management (Kim et al., 2009; Crombie and Geekie, 2010; Garg and Eisenhardt, 2014). Boards and management need to be able to work with each other effectively.

7. Boards are the ultimate locus of responsibility for ethics, reporting and transparency (Nordberg, 2010). Non-executive directors have a particular role in ensuring that standards are met as they can exercise a checking and balancing function on organizationally internal board members.

Boards and their corporate governance are empirically variable with different national institutions, especially legal requirements. Next we shall look at some of the features that comparative corporate governance alerts us to.

Comparative corporate governance

Given the empirical diversity of systems of governance a key issue is which is the most efficient? Given a question that invites comparative analysis, as you might expect, the answer to the question of which systems of governance are most efficient and effective is best resolved by comparative historical and institutional analysis.

The governance systems in place in the major OECD countries have evolved according to the history, culture, economics, social values and legal systems in each country. One metric that can be used to describe the range of variation is the degree of shareholder primacy; that is, the extent to which shareholders' interests are paramount. In the United States the extent is very high; it is more moderate in Germany, low in France, and lower still in Japan. The top management looks very different in different countries: Japanese boards rarely have outsiders on them; US boards typically have two or three outsiders, while in German and Dutch two-tier co-determination systems, employees hold half of the upper tier seats, while in the UK and Switzerland it is management that dominates the board. Stable and long-term networks of influence largely govern the Japanese *keiretsu*. The People's Republic of China's state-owned enterprises are subject to the China Securities and Regulatory Commission (CSRC) and the State-owned Assets Supervision and Administration Commission (SASAC), statutes that can override economic objectives, acting in the interests of the people, the party and the state, to influence strategies, determine prices and appoint chief executives. Throughout Southeast Asia the norm is paternalistic familial leadership in Chinese family businesses while in South Korean *chaebol* dominant families also enjoy governance powers over massive conglomerate enterprises.

In Fligstein and Choo's (2005: 66–67) terms,

[S]ystems of corporate governance result from political and historical processes rather than from efficient solutions to the functional needs of the owners of capital who seek to maximize profits for themselves … the fact that many societies appear to have experienced comparable economic growth without converging on a single form of corporate governance (i.e., that of the United States) suggests that there is no set of best practices of corporate governance but rather many sets of best practices, and that the relationship linking these institutions to good societal outcomes like economic growth is more complex than agency theory would allow.

Fligstein and Choo (2005) do not stress that micro-economic variables determine the regime of corporate governance strategies. Instead, they stress that corporate governance strategies are best seen as embedded in national trajectories shaped by the outcomes of war, revolution, invasion, colonization, class struggle and politics. Ethnic and religious differences frame governmental approaches; according to some observers, these account for differences in governments' efficiency legitimacy and corporate governance (Coffee, 2001a; Easterly and Levine 1997; La Porta et al., 1997b, 1999b; Stulz and Williamson, 2003).

In many contexts, there will not be a single system of corporate governance. In the state sector of public utilities, at least prior to privatization, there might be a form of state capitalism. In the small business sector, there will be a dominance of familial capitalism. Large private corporations will vary between more or less stakeholder and shareholder capitalism, with the balance varying between countries.

English-language contributors, usually located in Anglo-Saxon countries such as the United States or United Kingdom, dominate corporate governance debates and discussion. You might surmise from this that there is no need to think about comparative variations in corporate governance because the debates are universal, the systems the same everywhere. That this might appear to be the case is an effect of the dominance of neoclassical micro-economics in corporate governance discussion in English. If we look comparatively at how business arrangements are patterned, we find that this presumed universalism is by no means an accurate representation of the situation.

Corporate governance differs from country to country. Agency theory, largely a creation of US neoclassical economists, has been somewhat blind, traditionally, to comparative variation. Proceeding from a theoretical question about the relations of power between principals and agents, it tends to answer the question in terms of building agency theory into a coherent theory. Recall the context in which the issues of ownership and control and the relations between principals and agents arose. It was the New Deal era in the United States. Laws were passed 'to prevent the concentration of economic power in the hands of a few powerful financial institutions. They were not passed to produce efficient capital markets or to solve agency problems of firms' (Fligstein and Choo, 2005: 66).

Moreover, the institutions of governance that emerged in the United States are not apparent anywhere else in the developed world, with the exception of Great Britain and other Anglo-Saxon jurisdictions, which began to model themselves on US modes of governance during the 1980s (Vitols, 2001). Elsewhere, in Japan, Germany, France, Italy, Scandinavia, Taiwan, Singapore, South Korea and China, high levels of industrial development have been achieved without producing American-style institutions or deep capital markets (La Porta et al., 1998; Hall and Soskice, 2001). Fligstein and Choo (2005: 66) suggest that models of governance generated to solve issues surrounding agency cost have a very specific historical provenance.

Go Online: For people who are really interested in corporate governance as a topic then the European Corporate Governance Institute website (see www.ecgi.org), which is an index to many different countries' codes, might be useful.

A link to these codes can be found on the companion website for this book at www.edge.sagepub.com/strategy2e.

ECGI Website

Four Major Variants of Corporate Governance

Fligstein and Choo (2005) identify four major variants of corporate governance in the literature.

1. *Shareholder capitalism*: The US model of shareholder capitalism contains dispersed shareholders who provide the bulk of the financing to large, public firms. Boards of Directors monitor management teams. Workers have few rights and no representation on boards. Audit, through large-scale accounting firms, securities analysts and bond-rating agencies, is integral to legitimation. National government authorities, such as the Securities and Exchange Commission seek to make information available and transparent. Agency approaches determine top management remuneration in a competitive market context in which takeovers and proxy fights also provide competitive market mechanisms designed to align management interests more closely to those of the shareholders. The US model is one in which corporations rely on corporate equity (i.e., stock markets) and debt (i.e., bond markets) for most of their financing.

    The model of shareholder capitalism also characterizes corporate governance in Great Britain, as well as Canada, Australia and New Zealand, countries in which dominion or settler capitalism established institutions based on British

Image 8.3   Shareholders. Copyright: Pali Rao

norms and rules (Acemoglu et al., 2001), although the systems of governance at the firm level tend to differ.

2. *Social democratic stakeholder capitalism*: The German model of social democratic stakeholder capitalism has large stock shareholders, often composed of founding families, banks, insurance companies or other financial institutions who own the bulk of the shares. Close ownership enables large shareholders to monitor day-to-day organization. This close ownership structure enables large shareholders to internally monitor the day-to-day operation of the firm. Insiders often hold shares in other companies, which enables them to have access to opaque information. Organized labour is a significant stakeholder with a key role to play in the governance of corporate firms through the system of codetermination, that sees representation of workers on boards of directors (Roe, 2003). The German model (or variants of it) dominates continental Europe and parts of Asia, including Japan.

    In the German and Japanese models, banks own shares in firms and tend to loan those same firms money. Shareholder primacy is much lower in countries such as Japan and Germany because the focus of strategy is much less on the short-term performance of share values in the market, as predominates in shareholder primacy models. In Germany, where the constitution states that 'Property imposes duties. Its use should also serve the private weal' (Charkham, 1994: 30), corporate governance focuses ultimately on the long-term sustainability of the company from the perspective not just of its owners, the shareholders, but also other stakeholders such as suppliers, creditors, customers and especially employees. Shareholder value does not necessarily override the interests of other stakeholders.

3. *State capitalism* occurs where government has majority ownership of firms. Large firms and the financial sector are owned and operated by the government. Employees are government regulated directly, tending to have careers guided by bureaucratic rules and fixed benefits. State capitalism has been the dominant model in the state-owned enterprises of the People's Republic of China (see Chapter 7 for the relevant discussion, which we eschew repeating here). Finance, other than foreign direct investment, which is tightly regulated, is controlled by state-owned banks. Government ownership of banks has been seen by some observers to be detrimental to growth (La Porta et al., 2002) but there is evidence that such support played an important role in the development of Korea, Taiwan and perhaps China (Wade, 1990a; Amsden, 2001).

4. *Familial capitalism*: In most of the developing world the dominant model is one of family-owned business, familial capitalism (La Porta et al., 1999), where owners are managers, firms are private, and equity and debt markets tend to play minor roles in the provision of capital. Capital is largely drawn from familial networks and assets. Workers generally have little power.

We shall look at three models in a little more detail: US style shareholder capitalism, German stakeholder capitalism and the hybrid forms characterizing East Asian capitalism. Studies of transnational development and diffusion of industrial organization and management demonstrate the importance of examining the historical, political and social construction of seemingly rational economic models and ways of organizing, stressing the historical role of business' relationships with state and society (Blasco and Zølner, 2010). Guillén described how managers use new organizational models to address the ideological and technical problems that appear whenever changes in the scale and complexity of the firm, the international competitive environment, or working-class unrest challenge current practices. (1994: 1)

Models can only ever be broadly descriptive of complex realities.

Shareholder Capitalism

Debates around the US model of corporate governance premised on shareholder value and its associated model of capitalism have been paramount in the literature. In the post-war era, the Unites States or 'American' model travelled to Europe where it was met with resistance: nationally influential commentators, such as Servan-Schreiber (1967) in France, saw the American model of industrial organization as a form of cultural and business imperialism. The core component of the American model, defined against the command economies that emerged in the east of Europe after the Second World War (Judt, 2005), comprised free markets, albeit overshadowed by US corporations that were giant bureaucracies.

Dispersed stock ownership and deep equity and bond markets have been seen as essential for efficient investment (Hansmann, 1996; Hansmann and Kraakman, 2001) but as Fligstein and Choo (2005) suggest, the empirical evidence is more mixed (Levine, 1997). Banks and financial markets produce economic growth independently, serving different functions in the economy. Indeed, during the Global Financial Crisis that burst on the scene in 2008, and which had been quietly maturing prior to that, the financial markets became arenas of increasingly speculative trades in synthetic financial products that created the crisis. Once the crisis was underway, the reluctance of the banks to lend because of the need to trim bad debts from their balance sheets and curtail risk-taking activity saw the crisis deepen, as liquidity dried up and governments pursued austerity politics.

Ideas, beliefs, values and assumptions, organized in more or less cohesive ideologies, always underpin particular models and their preferred ways of organizing, whether the American idea of sacrosanct freedoms or the French idea of a distinct national cultural difference (Maclean et al., 2006). Partly for these reasons, American organizational know-how did not easily or immediately translate into Europe, despite the geo-political balance of power that pertained after the Second World War. European firms were, on average, much smaller, weaker in the global market and more fragmented than the behemoths of US corporate capitalism. In addition, industrial activity in France, Germany and Italy was organized differently, often in smaller, family-owned enterprises and had a greater role for the state. Traditionally, the firm had an important social function, with a main priority being the survival of the firm (and protection of family control).

Social Democratic Stakeholder Capitalism

Industrial relations systems are often seen, especially by employer organizations, as the crucial variable affecting economic outcomes. The result of social democratic parties and industrial relations struggles in advanced industrial societies has been broad welfare state policies that cushion workers from unemployment (Garrett, 1998a; 1998b; Hicks, 1999). In the Scandinavian countries where the rights of labour are most embedded (Abrahamsson and Broström, 1980; Garrett, 1998a;

Hicks, 1999; Rodrik, 2003) there is no systematic evidence to suggest that workers' organizations, workers' rights and welfare state expansion have adversely influenced long-run economic growth. The higher taxing and higher welfare countries of social democratic Western Europe offer more social protection and higher benefits than the Anglo-American countries (the United States, Great Britain, Australia, New Zealand, Canada). Income inequality has been reduced in these countries through higher unionization and more coordinated bargaining but there is, according to the OECD, no 'consistent and clear relationships between those key characteristics of collective bargaining systems and aggregate employment, unemployment, or economic growth' (OECD, 1997: 2). Corporate governance that has stakeholder representation on the board and certain rights of labour embedded in law does not seem to have diluted the entrepreneurial spirits of capitalism.

Familial Capitalism in the *Mittelstand*

In recent times, one approach that has been perceived as superior by elite opinion makers is that of the *Mittelstand* (see Logue et al., 2015). The Institute for Mittelstand Research (IfM) in Bonn defines the contemporary *Mittelstand* organization in terms of 'small and medium-sized enterprises' (SMEs), based on number of employees and/or annual turnover. In Germany that means enterprises up to 500 employees and turnover up to 50 million Euros. The definition of *Mittelstand* is somewhat flexible however; a firm with a workforce of over 1,000 can be considered part of the *Mittelstand* if it is owned and run by a family and if its business culture has retained aspects of the original economic and cultural arrangements, such as family control and management, strong family values, a patriarchal culture, an emphasis on continuity.

The family firm form ensures generational continuity and focused, long-term strategies that are innovation and customer oriented. *Mittelstand* are embedded in laws such as *Mitbestimmung* (codetermination). Codetermination 'ranks among the foundation pillars of the German economic order' and is widely seen as 'the trademark of a socially regulated, tamed, "Renish capitalism"' (Silvia, 2013: 51). Post-war codetermination practices consist of two distinct components: employee representation on supervisory boards and works councils. More broadly, the term captures the relationship between German business and labour as, although the two parties regularly engage in serious conflict, they share an acceptance of each other as legitimate partners, as well as a commitment to the rule of law (Silvia, 2013: 51). Public support in Germany for codetermination is strong, despite recent media campaigns highlighting *Mittelstand* scandals (Kühne and Sadowski, 2011).

The agency problem of split ownership and control and the need for firms to obtain capital are solved differently in different societies because of the differing evolution of the institutional frameworks of law and politics. The *Mittelstand* is one evolution that is particularly admired, especially as it interacts with the national system of codetermination and the German system of bank ownership, where German banks own large blocks of company stocks in their own names. The banks tend not to sell these shares and hold them for the long term.

Political, cultural and legal systems interact with firms over time to produce national systems shaped by national factors and local political, social and economic struggles. What is important is the stability and predictability of institutions rather than their substantive form. Investors need to know that their returns are not subject to arbitrary seizure, that property rights are secure, that their rivals will not profit from bribery and corruption and that the state strives to be a neutral arbiter rather than a sponsor of particular business interests (Wade, 1990a; Wade 1990b; Evans, 1995; Weiss, 1998; Evans and Rauch, 1999). General, contextual factors of politics and culture shape and produce the legal institutions of corporate governance in a given society and, by implication, firm practices.

East Asian Hybrid Capitalism

In addition to the spread of the American model, scholars have also examined East Asian business models, inspired in large part by work that draws from Bendix (1956). East Asian corporate governance combines, in different parts, in different countries, a combination of economic, cultural and authority relations that shape the growth of similar forms of organization across South Korea, Japan and Taiwan. In examining how these industrial arrangements emerged, Hamilton and Biggart (1988) demonstrated the role that market, cultural and structural explanations played in shaping organizational models and practices in each of these countries. For example, the following quote illustrates the complexity of the different national models of organizing, with cultural, market and structural influences:

> South Korean firms draw their managerial culture from the same source, the state, and from state-promoted management policies; they do not have the local character of the corporate culture of Japanese firms. Instead, they have developed an ideology of administration, an updated counterpart to the traditional Confucian ideology of the scholar-official. For this reason, American business ideology has had an important effect in South Korea, far more than in either Japan or Taiwan. (Hamilton and Biggart, 1988: 82)

The stakeholders comprise an extensive network of cross-shareholdings that generally include banks, suppliers, subcontractors and customers, clustered as a *keiretsu*, an industrial group, which characterizes distinctive Japanese ownership patterns. These *keiretsu* make up half of all listed Japanese companies, in which, typically, banks own a third of the company and related corporations own another third. These shareholders comprise long-term stable stakeholder investors who do not trade in the shares. In the event of a crisis, it is often the case that the core bank will intervene and assume direction of the troubled enterprise.

In Japan, corporate governance is oriented to ensuring long-term growth of the assets held by the *keiretsu*. The board in Japanese companies has minimal power, with real corporate governance occurring within the *keiretsu*. The boards tend to be rather large, often comprising 20 to 30 members, most of whom are present or former senior managers of the company. The vast majority of Japanese boards have no outside directors, or very few. The company president chooses the directors who tend to follow whatever the president's strategy might be. The president is extremely powerful and manages in concert with a small and select management committee. The president will not usually be the chair of the board; this role is largely ceremonial and is filled by a retired company president or politician or government official. Rarely will lower level board members challenge strategy (Charkham, 1994: 86). On average, there are only about four meetings a year where they might do so, anyway.

Analyses that stress only state policies or economic accounts focused only on entrepreneurial action do not capture what is specific to East Asian industrialization. Culture is important. Hamilton and Biggart indicate that 'generalized expressions of beliefs in the relative importance of such social factors as belongingness, loyalty, and submission to hierarchical authority' (1988: 53) play an important role, in addition to political and economic factors. Culture shapes ethical conceptions of what should and should not be done to whom by corporate agents. What is permissible depends on the 'moral compass' being used to steer the organization, itself an ethical site of struggle between different stakeholder interests. In the past, these interests were notably factions of labour and capital but more recently ecological interests in corporate social responsibility have emerged. Typically, the moral compass is embedded in corporate codes of ethics.

Corporate codes of ethics[1]

Image 8.4   Code of Ethics. Copyright: IvelinRadkov

Codes of ethics often have an ambiguous status in organizations. Are they legally binding or simply preferential rules?

Law and Codes

Some elements of codes have the force of national regulation and law behind them. Such is the case with occupational health and safety legislation, equal employment opportunity and other areas where the state mandates acceptable behaviours. There is a difference between legal compliance (in areas such as diversity, health and safety, and the environment) and self-governance strictures (in areas such as quality, customer service, professionalism, corporate culture, reputation, corporate identity, etc.). Being locally preferential rules, the latter are not legally constitutive as would be the case of those mandated by juridical decree, with legislative authority. These rules, or structured 'guiding principles' (Paine, 2003: 111), are expressed in codes of ethics as a key part of a top-down strategy. Codes of ethics express strategic preferences with respect to areas of behaviour deemed significant.

> A major aspect of governance is the rules and norms through which governance occurs. These are usually referred to as **'codes of ethics'**.

---

[1]This section is adapted from Adelstein and Clegg (2015).

Increasingly, the extent to which an organization adopts a regulatory compliance system can influence its legal liability for any breaches of law for which it may be held responsible, as Parker and Nielsen (2009) suggest. Despite, or perhaps because of, the recent waves of corporate scandals, increasingly boards have adopted codes of corporate ethics that their organization members should comply with, as an integral part of their corporate governance. Such codes have obvious legitimation functions; in addition, they help frame the way that the Top Management Team, in particular, is expected to behave (Trevino et al., 1999; Thomsen, 2006).

Codes and standards are, in principle, forms of social contract supposed to engender better organizational behaviour. Such codes are expected not only to increase commitment to compliance with the law but also to build a strategic frame that acts as an insurance policy, identifying, correcting and preventing misdemeanours throughout the organization and helping support a corporate culture of ethical compliance.

Corporate codes are not static documents and their sense is never guaranteed by what they state: they have to be interpreted (Jensen et al., 2009) and are subject to constant interpretation in use. On occasions they will be used as accounts to legitimate actions; on other occasions they will be used to try and shape actions and attitudes proactively; on other occasions, they may be used retrospectively to define and sometimes elide responsibilities.

Codes and Compliance

Kjonstad and Willmott (1995: 449) argue that 'instead of acting to encourage and facilitate the development of moral learning and the exercise of moral judgment, codes operate to promote routinized compliance'. A 'compliance mode' of ethics runs the risk of resulting in disempowerment, bureaucratization and feelings of individual irresponsibility. As Kjonstad and Willmott (1995: 446) suggest, 'the provision of codes of conduct is an insufficient, and possibly a perverse, means of recognizing the significance, and promoting the development, of ethical corporate behavior'. Ethical compliance is not guaranteed through rule-based codes (Jackall, 1988; Victor and Cullen, 1988; Andrews, 1989; Warren, 1993; Paine, 1994; Stevens, 1994; Kjonstad and Willmott, 1995; ten Bos, 1997; Weaver et al., 1999a, 1999b).

Barker studied the standards expressed in codes of conduct at General Dynamics and found that these did not induce any fundamental change in regard to organizational ethics. Jackson (2000: 349) showed in his study of 200 companies in the UK, US, France, Spain and Germany that the

> clarity of corporate policy has little influence on managers' reported ethical decision-making. The perceived behavior of managers' colleagues is far more important in predicting attitudes towards decision making or managers across the nationalities surveyed.

The use of rules differs according to local culture-specific and industry-specific practices, interpreted in context (Donaldson and Dunfee, 1995; Spicer et al., 2004). Gouldner (1954) found that what rules mean varies with the context of enactment. As the philosopher Wittgenstein (1968) argued, rules don't do anything by themselves but need to be interpreted and enacted situationally. It is rule *use*, not rule *existence*, which determines ethical conduct (Andrews, 1989).

Jackall (1988) researched the 'moral rules-in-use that managers construct to guide their behavior at work' and found that 'actual organizational moralities are … contextual, situational, highly specific, and, most often, unarticulated' (Jackall, 1988: 4, 6; also see Munro, 1992). Codes depend on the context of their interpretation and their interpreters. Moreover, because of this, codes do not achieve the expressed intentions of their purpose: they do not provide an effective standardizing frame for strategic behaviour. By all means have codes, suggest Jensen et al. (2009) but don't expect too much of them. Sometimes organizational members will choose strategies that are ethically dubious, despite codes. We need to be continually exposed to moral dilemmas if we are not to lose touch with their morality, suggest Jensen et al. (2009), in line with Giddens (1991). Rules and practices do not automatically align.

Several seminal contributions explore the gap between rules and practice. Gouldner (1954) analysed an organization in which the difference between interpretation of rules by the book and their actual interpretation in practice led to an 'indulgency pattern'. The rules were known but no one took them seriously. For Meyer and Rowan (1977), rules are ceremonial façades to be contrasted with the reality of day-to-day organizational life, while Brunsson (1994) finds that public sector organizations maintain and capitalize on the gaps between talk, action and decision. In his words, organized hypocrisy is normal.

In the private sector, there is an explicit set of power relations framing contracts of employment and the submission of the contracting agent to all that they imply corporately. In the private sector Capital hires Labour and, for the time the capabilities of the person are rented, those employed are expected to respect Capital's preferences, as expressed in a code of ethics. If there is a conflict between the ethics of the individual and those of the code, then the common assumption is that the individual's preferences must be secondary and subordinate. Individual employees cannot have ethical autonomy where their preferences, values and interests conflict with those of the employing organization. Whatever ethical autonomy they exercise will be constrained by the implicit framework of their contract of employment. Such contracts are a strategy for organizational risk management.

Corporate governance and codes of ethics are intended to discipline organizational members. Intertwining of corporate governance with member compliance, signified by doing 'what is right', is becoming a normal feature of many organizations' assumptions about how to manage. There is an assumption that the ethics of individual employees need to align with what management elites define as the organization's interests. Tacitly, by extension, management's interests are taken to be definitive of the 'real interests' (Lukes, 1974) of those subject to these codes. A corollary of the premise that management is entitled to define real interests is that if the ethics of individuals and the organization do not align, whatever the distance between an organizational member's moral integrity and that of the organization, then it is the individuals who need to abandon (or at least modify) personal ethical choices for what management deems ought to be done. At critical times, when personal ethics and the need for compliance clash, organizational members may see few options for themselves other than to *exit* (by leaving the organization), give *voice* (by speaking out, perhaps becoming 'whistleblowers') or show *loyalty* (by abiding by management's declarations) in Hirschman's (1970) terms.

Acquiescence is often judged to be a sign of loyalty but it could just as easily be a sign of subordination. An absence of dissent may signal either authentic consensus or one that is more apparent than real. The conditions for democratic consensus are rarely encountered in the normal conditions of organizational life; more likely, preferences will be compromised in the interests of established authority and its power relations. The simple management response often is that if you don't like the way we operate, you can work somewhere else.

Codes and Legitimation

Codes play a strong role in legitimation (Long and Driscoll, 2008). Analytically, a corporation's code of ethics is the documented, formal and legal manifestation of that organization's expectations of ethical behaviours by its employees. It is the visibility that a code offers that enables an organization to be judged as ethical. Indeed, one institution, Ethisphere, benchmarks codes of ethics, scoring organizations' performances against this benchmark and encouraging them to broadcast the results. Doing so, it is claimed, is the criteria for consideration as an ethical company. Such criteria include having an 'ethics and compliance program, governance and corporate responsibility' (Ethisphere, 2014). That the organization has the ability to manage any allegedly 'deviant' behaviour by organizational members is implicit in such corporate prescription of employees' ethical behaviours (Trevino, 1986). There is a strong normalizing function in having codes that suggest strategic risk is being managed (Fombrun et al., 2000; Husted, 2005) because they afford legitimation.

Increasingly, in the wake of contemporary scandals from Barings Bank (1995) onwards, including Enron (2000), Lehman Bros. (2008) and Barclays (2012) and continuing in the ongoing Global Financial Crisis, many organizations have sought to link business interests, employee ethics, and legal compliance in formal codes as legitimation devices. The motivation is to ensure that an organization's code of ethics has high visibility (Basu and Palazzo, 2008: 126) enabling enhancement of corporate reputation (Fombrun, 2005) or, as Milton Friedman (1970) described it, 'hypocritical window dressing' (Bartlett and Preston, 2000).

Since the 1990s, the formulation of codes of business ethics has been seen as a restraint on misconduct and unethical behaviour. In effect, such codes are represented as tools for risk management, limiting opportunities for ethical malfeasance. Codes of ethics both protect an organization from the actions of its members and provide a public declaration of its ethical practices in documented form, closely tied to organizational objectives. As Rasche and Esser (2007) argue, these objectives have a relation to matters of compliance both externally (compliance with the law) and internally (compliance with organizational regulations) (Rasche and Esser, 2007: 109). Christensen (2008) argues that while models of ethical decision-making typically do not include the law, legal norms are implicit even if they are exogenous to moral thinking. Corporate governance and legal compliance are entwined within the code of ethics. While law and ethics may be related, they are not the same (Christensen, 2008: 451).

Codes and Conflict

Codes of ethics *per se* are not legally binding enactments but attempts to construct local social contracts, in a Hobbesian, sense.[2] Many ethnographic studies detail the considerable cynicism and distance found in 'the ranks' about presumed social

---

[2]Thomas Hobbes (1651/1968), in a famous work of political philosophy, written after the English Civil War between monarchists and republicans in England's seventeenth century, argued that there should be a 'social contract' between a sovereign power and its subjects, expressed in terms of reciprocal obligations, if there was to be social peace.

contracts (see, for example: Fleming and Spicer, 2002, 2003, 2007; Collinson, 2003; Collinson and Ackroyd, 2005; Mumby, 2005; Collier and Esteban, 2007; Trevino and Nelson, 2011). In context, ethics do not exist on paper or in a virtual space but in concrete practices; it is not what the rules stipulate but what the actors do that is important (Gordon et al., 2009a, 2009b). Daily practices by organizational members rather than executive management's dictates frame mundane organizational behaviour in which the practice of ethics resides.

Any code ideally elicits an emotional response in employees so that they can feel 'that's right!' For this to happen, organizational members need the opportunity to participate directly in formulating the code, such that it is not only management's preferences that are embedded but also those of the ordinary member. Organizationally, a code will be less effective in all respects (legal and governance) if organizational members are not encouraged to participate in its development and if discussions about ethics are not at the forefront of decisions made by all organizational members. By making management intentions about the code transparent and opening up communication amongst all levels of the organization about different decisions that could be made, there is likely to be far greater 'buy-in' and commitment by members to the organization, going well beyond the formal contract of employment.

Creating Robust Codes of Ethics

So, what can management do apart from recognizing the necessity of compliance by members to corporate values, both legal and non-legal, to ensure that members are committed to them in practice? Here, we offer some resolutions that could be implemented by organizations concurrently.

1. Rules of practice within a code of ethics can result from democratic participation by organizational members in their formulation and evolution rather than being administered from 'on high', by the legal or risk management departments. In this way, a code of ethics can align with the pragmatically and discursively framed moral integrity of employees' agreement; it can be seen as a reciprocal obligation between the organization and its members. The process of consultation cannot be one of permanent negotiation: understandings that are binding need to be enacted on the basis of premises that are acceptable to all, even if ideal for none. At the same time, the statements need to be couched in appropriate terms that are clear and unambiguous, obfuscated neither by legal jargon nor effusive and vague language.

2. In order to guard against ossification and changing contextual circumstances (think of the problems that a code of ethics from 25 years ago would have with anti-corporate webpages), there would need to be provision for periodic review and assent.

3. Ethics, corporate governance and legal compliance should be clearly separate. Ethics do not enjoy the force of law but are norms. Corporate governance requirements may not be mandated legally.

4. Broader conversations about ethics and ethical decision-making need to be part of organizational training and continuing professional development, not just to serve corporate interests but also to address issues of corporate sustainability relating to the environment and social equity. As Clegg et al. (2007: 107) argue, organizations can try to influence the ethical subjectivity

of their members and persuade them to act in particular ways to protect the interests of the organization. Such influence can only be successful if employees' ethical views are acknowledged.

5. Employees can develop an understanding of moral learning and the exercise of moral judgment through education by ethicists rather than corporate lawyers. Management can assist in this. Legal and Corporate Affairs should be involved in educating employees about the legal ramifications of their ethical decisions since that is its area of expertise. No doubt, in most socially responsible corporations this is a necessary adjunct to the preparation of legally binding texts.

6. Individuals should be empowered to act according to personal ethical choices and make moral judgments within the governance strictures of the organization. If Google's ethics are 'To do no evil' it is imperative that nothing that could be construed as evil should be done, which may entail periodic training and explanation by management. Provided that conversations about ethical decision-making are at the forefront of professional development activities, employees are more likely to discuss questionable ethical decisions before implementing them. In many respects, Habermas' (1971) ideas of the conditions of an ideal speech situation would fit the bill: people should feel free to express their concerns, doubts and reservations.

7. A code of ethics should not be subject to stratification according to organizational role. It should apply universally. When rational consensus over vexed issues breaks down amongst different institutional parties such as management and unions, ethicists can be hired, with the fees jointly paid by these parties. The nature of joint cost and responsibility is likely to assure the minimization of vexatious claims.

IN PRACTICE

Run a tight ship? Lessons for managers from a shipwreck

(Edited media interview with Stewart Clegg by Lesley Parker, Media Officer, UTS)

On 13 January 2012, the Italian cruise ship *Costa Concordia* hit a rock close by Isola del Giglio, Tuscany and floundered, with the loss of 32 lives.

The sinking was not just bad luck, bad design or bad behaviour but the result of tensions that exist in many industries – especially those where strict regulation is required but leaders also have a degree of autonomy, where authority is not counterbalanced by a culture that allows questioning of 'captain's calls'.

The sinking illustrates 'the dark side' of improvisation within organizations at the senior level, says Professor Stewart Clegg of UTS Business School, co-author of two just-released papers on the *Costa Concordia* sinking.

(Continued)

(Continued)

Image 8.5   Costa Concordia. Copyright: reeixit

Professor Clegg and his fellow researchers delved into evidence from the trial of the captain of the *Costa Concordia*. The court heard that Captain Francesco Schettino issued an order to 'salute' an island on the western coast of Italy by sailing close to the coastline, providing a spectacle for passengers and onlookers. It was an out-of-route manoeuvre but something captains do from time to time.

According to the trial transcripts, the captain made a last-minute decision to go even closer to the island than planned, with the result that the ship hit a rock, tearing a huge gash in the hull, flooding the engine room and disabling the vessel.

The order to abandon ship was not given until over an hour after the impact.

None of the crew questioned the captain's decisions, the court heard.

'A superficial analysis ... could lead to the conclusion that the captain was simply violating the maritime safety rules', the researchers say of the case. 'However we argue that Captain Schettino's decision and actions ... were not just mere disobedience'.

The researchers say the captain's 'improvisation' took place under the cover of two legitimate standards: the commander's autonomy to determine the route of the cruise and to switch to manual navigation, along with the maritime tradition of tolerating – even praising the bravery of – such salutes.

The existence of multiple standards created the opportunity to 'juggle' compliance – choosing which standard with which to comply, the researchers add.

An attitude of 'organizational subordination' meant no one was prepared to speak out on the *Costa Concordia*, the researchers say.

'If you run a "tight ship", where you have an organization based upon hierarchy and deference to office holders, you don't have any potential checks over the dispositions of those in command', says Professor Clegg, a world leader in the study of organizations.

In his view: 'The only defence against arbitrary authority is democracy. This is true of business organizations, military organizations – and cruise ships'.

A key lesson is to build in the opportunity for people to have a voice, he says.

'In a world where we have so many digital devices it's not difficult to give people the opportunity to give voice to their concerns', he says. 'We have the technologies that would enable it to happen. Now we need the institutional conviction'.

Questions

What lessons can be learnt from the *Costa Concordia* case in relation to:

1. Managerial prerogative, in terms of the managers' right to decide, command and be obeyed?
2. Subordinates' right to question 'captain's choices'?
3. The assumption that highly trained professionals are also 'wise'?
4. The role of 'compliance' as a shelter for arbitrary rules?
5. The role of values and culture in relation to rules and standards?

Go Online: Read the research – Giustiniano, L., Pina e Cunha, M. and Clegg, S. (2015) 'The dark side of organizational improvisation: Lessons from the sinking of the Costa Concordia', *Business Horizons*. Available at: http://dx.doi.org/10.1016/j.bushor.2015.11.007; Giustiniano, L., Pina e Cunha, M. and Clegg, S. (2016) 'Organisational zemblanity', *European Management Journal*. Available at: http://dx.doi.org/10.1016/j.emj.2015.12.001.

Costa
Concordia
Articles

Corporate Social Responsibility (CSR) and corporate governance

In the recent past, since the emergence of a concern with climate change as a political phenomenon in the late 1980s, a discourse of Corporate Social Responsibility (CSR) has emerged. CSR seeks to demonstrate the ways in which particular companies are responding to issues such as carbon emissions by being good corporate citizens. Strategically, CSR has developed in recognition of the fact that business enterprises are both the responsible agents for the promotion of environmental reform and are sufficiently powerful to be able to make such promotion (Hawken, 1993; Hawken et al., 1999). It is this realization that has seen a substantial literature develop on corporate social responsibility and strategy.

Adopting **corporate social responsibility** (CSR) as an explicit code implies that an organization is ecologically reflexive; that it cares about phenomena such as its carbon footprint; strives to measure it, and seeks to minimize it strategically.

Many large corporations have signed up to global citizenship initiatives such as the United Nations Global Compact and the Global Reporting Initiative. The majority of organizations today

> **Corporate social responsibility (CSR)** has been defined by the European Commission (2005) as existing when companies integrate 'social and environmental concerns in their business operations and in their interactions with their stakeholders on a voluntary basis'.

have a strategy for CSR as a part of their overall approach. Sometimes, this is more a case of 'looking good' than making substantial changes to their behaviours. Looking good is typically referred to as 'greenwashing' – as a pun on 'whitewashing' in relation to 'green' issues.

Not all CSR strategies are a greenwash but a great many are more concerned with appearances than with real social change. Real social change entails a change in deep cultural values embedded in organizations. It is for this reason, for instance, that the climate change 'debate' has become so political and so partisan, despite the overwhelming scientific evidence for the reality of climate change. Responding effectively to the threat to the planet and all it contains is not likely to be possible within 'business as usual' approaches (see the extensive argument of Wright and Nyberg, 2015). These business as usual approaches include joining and/or funding lobbying organizations opposed to climate change amelioration and other green issues.

Corporate organizations that seek to promote their legitimacy as socially responsible through self-regulation, marketing and public relations engage in a practice that Wright and Nyberg (2015: 85) term 'exemplifying'. Often this takes the form of sustainability reporting. The investigative journalist and activist, Naomi Klein (2014), writes extensively about strategies of legitimation of corporate interests and the delegitimation of climate change concerns by business in her book about the politics of climate change, titled *This Changes Everything*.

Ecological Modernization

Early sustainable organizational practices were characterized by their appeal to ethical principles by which organizations should guide their ecological actions (Newton, 2002). Until the 1990s, empirical examples of pro-active environmental practices in firms were extremely scarce (Fischer and Schot, 1993). The necessity of incrementally incorporating bio-centric values over time, it was argued, would result in better environmental practices in organizations. Such approaches have been characterized as **ecological modernization strategies**.

> **Ecological modernization strategies** suggest that economic and technological win–win solutions – gaining less pollution and more profits through more efficient use of resources – can ameliorate harmful environmental effects.

From an ecological modernization perspective, all strategy should be oriented to seeing that current modes of production and consumption are redesigned along ecological principles (Spaargaren and Mol, 1992; Mol and Spaargaren, 1993; Mol, 1995; Yearley, 2007). Weizsäcker et al. (1997) propose that in many industrial sectors it is possible to double wealth at the same time as the use of resources could be halved – in mathematical terms, by a factor of four. Because these achievements would be based on the incorporation of ecological principles into current industrial practices, such as resource efficiency and de-materialization, they would represent processes of ecological modernization.

CSR has become a global phenomenon in recent times. Progressive and values-based organizations are now embracing the notion of CSR by considering the concerns of stakeholders other than shareholders by publishing corporate social reports, in order to legitimize business operations with various constituents in society (Deegan, 2002; Deegan et al., 2002), to enhance corporate reputation (Owen et al., 2000, 2001) and reduce corporate risks. It is not only in the west that CSR is fashionable; it is also being introduced with increased frequency in non-western countries. India is the first country in the world to mandate a minimum spend on CSR initiatives, mandating that large companies should allocate 2% of net profits to charitable causes. Elsewhere, social reporting in developing countries is mainly driven by 'outside' forces. Such forces include instructions from head office based in western developed countries, influence of international agencies such as the ILO and World Bank and coercive conditions from international buyers imposed on the developing country companies supplying goods and services to the western market. Social accounting practices are being exported to the developing countries via multinational companies based in western developed countries.

Organizations such as Greenpeace clearly seek to make a difference to corporate practice by drawing attention to corporate misbehaviour – corporate behaviour that is undesirable. They can engage firms in dialogue and enter into partnerships, help frame codes of conduct. These often legitimate the companies as much as they change their behaviour, such that the activist organizations runs the risk of being co-opted. Meanwhile, companies may gain credence for being corporately socially responsible while not being required to document the basis on which these claims are made; their good reputational management might even help them avoid effective legislation.

Problems with CSR

While companies might make their profit-making more sustainable their efforts may have little or no, or even an adverse, impact on the communities whose resources they mine, farm, fish and manufacture, or to whom they market (Banerjee, 2007: 145–147). Banerjee (2007: 149), drawing from the framework Convention on Corporate Accountability prepared for the Johannesburg Earth Summit (Bruno and Karliner, 2002), suggests that if firms are to become really corporately socially responsible then their codes must entail:

- *Mandatory corporate reporting* requirements on environmental and social impacts, and a process for prior consultation with affected communities including environmental and social impact assessment and complete access to information.

- *Extended liability* to directors for corporate breaches of environmental and social laws and corporate liability for breaches of international laws and agreements.

- *Rights of redress* for citizens, including access for affected people anywhere in the world to pursue litigation, provisions for stakeholders to legally challenge corporate decisions and legal aid mechanisms to provide public funds to support such challenges.

- *Community rights* to resources, including indigenous peoples' rights over common property such as forests, fisheries and minerals.

- *Veto rights* over developmental projects and against displacement and rights to compensation for resources expropriated by corporations.

- *Sanctions* against corporations for breaching these duties including suspending stock exchange listings, fines and (in extreme cases) revoking the corporation's charter or withdrawal of limited liability status.

Banerjee (2007: 16–18) sees the following elements as implicit in firms that commit to CSR in other than tokenistic ways:

- A commitment to reporting a firm's social performance, through audit, social impact analysis and social reporting. Often what are measured are perceptions rather than actual performance.

- Exceeding expectations of minimal obligations, that is, going above and beyond what is legally required in positive ways, in terms of worker and community welfare.

- Discretionary behaviour constituted by codes of conduct that are not legally binding but statements of policy and intent in regard to various nominated categories of stakeholders.

There have been recent discussions of the development of strategic CSR (Martinuzzi and Krumay, 2013). The aim of strategic CSR, according to these authors, is to integrate CSR in the four central business decisions of *what, where, how* and *for whom* the company is producing its goods and services. It seeks to ally innovation capacity with the target of social problems and their solutions and to marry business success with social responsibility. The examples that are cited include:

- Grameen bank in Bangladesh and its role in funding micro-businesses in developing countries that can reduce poverty.

- Betapharm, the pharmaceutical company, which has founded a network of facilities for seriously and chronically ill children and their families that offer a broad variety of prevention care and post rehabilitation support.

- Employment of people with Asperger's syndrome by software companies such as Specialisterne and Aspiritech to check coding errors. Rather than seeing such people as handicapped these companies recognize that the attention to detail of those that they employ with this condition makes them highly suitable for highly specialized, highly qualified and highly paid jobs.

At its best, CSR becomes fully integrated into the business of the business – rather than being an afterthought or an addition. Ideally, strategic CSR links socially and ecologically responsible goals with competitiveness, enhances stakeholder relations and creates shared value. It is a long-term developmental strategy, not without its risks to focus and partnerships.

Strategic CSR is a penultimate stage in the strategy journey envisaged by Martinuzzi and Krumay (2013). The destination is 'transformational CSR' in which learning from customers and other stakeholders is embedded in a flexibly democratic and dialogical relationship that evolves as a key driver for sustainable business practices that effect changes in deep cultural values and innovate new standards for enterprise.

Summary

The separation of ownership and control in the United States by the 1930s gave rise to a long-running debate about corporate governance. The major perspective deployed in discussions of corporate governance is that of agency theory. In agency perspectives, a fundamental problem that has to be addressed is that the owners of capital invested in shares cannot necessarily trust those to whom its day-to-day management is delegated to serve their interests. In other words, principals might not trust agents. A large literature has developed to address what is seen as this fundamental problem of trust, which we have reviewed in this chapter. In corporate governance terms, the resolution is seen to reside in a combination of regulation in the governmental, financial and legal spheres, together with oversight by a board of directors. We discussed some of the factors that make boards more or less effective. Whatever strategies are developed and however they are developed, it is widely assumed that they will be accepted and implemented under the direction of the board of directors. Contributors such as McNulty and Pettigrew (1995, 1999) have conducted research into boards and how they shape strategy.

Boards represent the ranks of the business elites. If we are fully to understand corporate governance, then we need to understand the role that business elites and Top Management Teams play in organizations and how they follow different routes into the elite ranks.

Corporate governance, as it is usually discussed, is seen largely through neoclassical and micro-economic terms. These terms are not adequate for detailing the variety of actually existing capitalism and the different systems of governance that have evolved. There is a central axis of differentiation in the OECD societies, ranging from shareholder capitalism to stakeholder capitalism. There are large areas of the economy in these countries in which familial capitalism is dominant, with quite distinct norms of governance. Different societies are marked by different degrees of state capitalism, with a country such as China being dominated by it, with privatization reducing it vastly in countries such as the UK and Australia, while it hardly secured a major foothold in the United States.

Finally, the chapter considered the question of corporate codes and the extent to which they can determine compliant behaviour. One might ask whether ethical principles can be rationalized and whether codes of ethics are merely window dressing for strategies of risk management? Compliance with the law is expected for all employees, regardless of their seniority, their moral intuition or their ethical preferences, since the intent of the laws of the land is for the greater good. Organizations need standards of practice and governance but they need to be recognized as distinct and separate from legal compliance. We suggest several ways in which codes might encourage compliance.

Finally, we addressed the rapidly evolving field of CSR, considering a range of strategy and policy proposals that have arise to deal with the social responsibilities of the corporation.

TEST YOURSELF

Want to know more about this chapter? Review what you have learnt by visiting www.edge.sagepub.com/strategy2e.

- Test yourself with multiple choice questions
- Revise key terms with interactive flashcards

EXERCISES

1. Having read this chapter, you should be able to say in your own words what the following key terms mean:

   - Corporate governance
   - Ownership and management
   - Ownership and control
   - Corporate governance
   - Agency theory
   - Principals and agents
   - Agency costs

   - Shareholders
   - Stakeholders
   - Shareholder capitalism
   - Social democratic stakeholder capitalism
   - State capitalism
   - Familial capitalism

(Continued)

(Continued)

- Corporate codes of ethics
- Agency costs
- CSR

- Strategic CSR
- Greenwashing
- Ecological modernization strategies

2. What's useful and what is limiting in agency theory?

3. What are the four major comparative variants of corporate governance systems and how do they differ?

4. How useful are codes of ethics in general? Provide an example of an excellent code of ethics and explain the reasons that you deem it excellent as well as how it might be improved.

5. What are some of the main issues with the design and use of corporate codes in practice?

6. What is corporate social responsibility (CSR)? What two organizations would you select as having best practice CSR? Explain the reasons for your choice.

CASE STUDY

Microsoft's ethics

JENNIFER ADELSTEIN[3]

Microsoft is named by Ethisphere Institute as 'one of the world's most ethical companies' (Ethisphere, 2014). Microsoft's code of ethics is contained in the Microsoft Finance Code of Professional Conduct (2014a), Microsoft Values (2014b), and Microsoft's Standards of Business Conduct (2014c). Microsoft describes its Standards of Business Conduct as an extension of its Values (Microsoft, 2014b) and its 'commitment to ethical business practices and regulatory compliance' (Microsoft, 2014c) and its Finance Code of Professional Conduct as 'principles of ethical business conduct' (Microsoft, 2014a). The code has not been updated since 2010 (as stated on the website – except for the removal of any reference to former-CEO Steve Ballmer who was signatory on a personalized letter to Microsoft employees. The substance of his letter is now incorporated in a generalized section on Microsoft values.)

Microsoft's code of ethics aims to ensure compliance not only with the law but also its own corporate rules; given that this is the case, how does the code frame intentions in such a way that subjects (employees) will be governable, ethical and biddable? First, according to Microsoft's Code of Professional Conduct (Microsoft, 2014a), the intertwining

---

[3]This case study is drawn from Adelstein and Clegg (2015).

of legal compliance and Microsoft's corporate issues are such that any violations of Microsoft's ethical codes 'may result in disciplinary action, up to and including termination of employment' (Microsoft, 2014a, 2014b, 2014c). The edict includes such activities as to 'share knowledge and maintain professional skills important and relevant to stakeholders' needs' (Microsoft, 2014a). Interpreting this edict clearly requires an identification of stakeholders, their needs, and what is important and relevant to them. For instance, would it be considered in accord with the code to share knowledge with labour organizers in supply chain plants or with the media in an attempt to improve conditions therein? In all probability, no: the interpretation of even a simple matter such as what is a (legitimate) stakeholder is itself ethically contested.

What appears to be neutral and apolitical is capable of being enacted in such a way as to be an imposition on the integrity and autonomy of organizational members through enforcement and management of organizational risk enhancing the interests of the organization but not necessarily its employees. For example, employees are not given a choice whether to share their knowledge or to be supported by Microsoft to develop skills that they, rather than Microsoft, may consider worthwhile. Microsoft states in its policy that it will make these decisions for employees and employees must abide by them or possibly suffer the consequences, that is, discipline or termination. Thus, Microsoft formulates what intentions are readily available and manages them punitively.

Second, and perhaps a little confusing, Microsoft employees are also exhorted to be 'self-critical, questioning, and committed to personal excellence and self-improvement' (Microsoft, 2014c), to self-analyse and effect change in their behaviours. Yet, any such changes will subsequently be open to judgment by management. Microsoft's policies have the practical effect of making it the sole arbiter of any possible infringement of its rules. The corporation holds its rules to be of similar status to that of a country's laws. One might be forgiven for thinking that it is ethically questionable for Microsoft to not only try to frame the ethical subjectivity of its employees in order to protect its interests but also to regard those interests and its recipes for ethicality as equal to the law. It is as if Microsoft sees a potential conflict between performing an act that is virtuous and one that is a moral obligation and takes the choice away from its employees in favour of its own prescribed rules.

Third, employees are to be held accountable for 'commitments, results, and quality to customers, shareholders, partners, and employees' (Microsoft, 2014b) even when such things are outside of the control of specific individuals. So, we have an ethical dilemma in that if organizational members think differently to Microsoft, they are discouraged from exercising moral autonomy or intuition to do what they consider to be the right thing, other than to be ventriloquist's puppets for approved Microsoft behaviours. Yet they are to be held accountable for the outcomes. In the Microsoft codes, moral rules are imposed by a commercial entity for its own interests and the exercise of moral judgment by employees in any other terms is denied. Because the employee's free will to choose an ethical path is disallowed by the organization, one would be hard pressed to designate such codes as ethical.

Fourth, Microsoft's code advises that, before any action is taken, an employee should consult with those in positions of authority, including the compliance and legal departments (Microsoft, 2014c). By closing off alternative interpretations of the code, the argument for inhibiting risk through organizational practice is established. While this closure aims to protect both employees and the company from legal ramifications, the law does not necessarily relate to ethics.

(Continued)

(Continued)

Fifth, Microsoft not only limits its employees' moral intuition but it also restricts their capacity to perform actions with which they, the employees, feel most ethically satisfied. Where individuals are not permitted any choice, there is potential for conflict. One's sense of duty and commitment may act against one's interests, as Microsoft would define them. From this perspective, Microsoft, similarly to other corporations, effectively assumes the right to set organizational citizenship rights in relation to what is probably the most central life-interest: employment and the security it generates. Whatever framing of citizenship rights there may be in the wider state and civil society that are not enshrined in law, are not necessarily relevant to practice. Should moral obligation be the reason for our intentional action, we could regard it as important to maintain a relationship of relative equity between or amongst parties to the actions.

Microsoft's position concerning the consultation an employee is required to have with those in authority, specifies that the 'manager, Legal and Corporate Affairs, or the Director of Compliance' (Microsoft, 2014c) must be consulted 'before taking any action' and that employees 'also have a responsibility to raise compliance and ethics concerns through our established channels' (Microsoft, 2014c). Only those authorities designated by Microsoft as the arbiters of ethics – the manager, Legal and Corporate Affairs or the Director of Compliance – can decide on a course of action. Thus, not only is an employee's moral intuition seen to be a risky basis for making a decision but the employee is also perceived as insufficiently knowledgeable to ascertain the level of risk. Microsoft stipulates that only those with sufficient legal (rather than moral) knowledge can decide ethical action. Ethical domination occurs through the specific strategy of making the discourse a technical instrument dependent on legal training.

At Microsoft, ethics are constrained by the overarching authoritatively determined and thus dominant code. Equally constrained is the possibility of invoking alternative standards that might be implied by the moral intuition of employees. Not all employees are equal though; some are more equal than others. Microsoft favours some employees over others in their capacity to adjudge whether those others are abiding by its corporate ethical policies as part and parcel of the stratification of ethics.

Microsoft's finance employees, plus CEO, CFO and its Corporate Controller, hold what Microsoft describes as

> an important and elevated role in corporate governance (that is Microsoft's policies rather than legal compliance) in that they are uniquely capable and empowered to ensure that all stakeholders' interests are appropriately balanced, protected, and preserved. (Microsoft, 2014a)

Serving and balancing stakeholder interests does not necessarily serve ethics for pragmatic reasons; the balancing of sometimes opposing interests by a commercial organization's Top Management Team would be unlikely to ignore commercial economic outcomes.

Microsoft explains its values in the following way,

> As a company, and as individuals, we value integrity, honesty, openness, personal excellence, constructive self-criticism, continual self-improvement, and mutual respect. We are committed to our customers and partners and have a passion for technology. We take on big challenges, and pride ourselves on seeing them through. We hold ourselves accountable to our customers, shareholders,

partners, and employees by honoring our commitments, providing results, and striving for the highest quality. (Microsoft, 2014b)

When we analyse the above statement, we can see subtlety in the way Microsoft strategizes risk management as integral to its past, present and future values, through the use of the present tense. Inclusiveness is fundamental. These things, they say, 'we' value and 'we' continually modify 'our' behaviours through self-criticism and self-improvement to ensure that 'we' maintain such values. Continually refreshed values feed into commitments, passions, pride and, above all, accountability for all things Microsoft, such as technology, customers, shareholders, partners and other organizational members. Risk management, the Microsoft way, underlies such unarguably beneficent traits such as integrity, honesty, openness, personal excellence and respect.

Microsoft positions its values as being the same for both the company and those individuals employed by it. Given the long history of antitrust violations pursued against it, both globally and in the United States, as well as the frequent claims of patent infringement, it would seem that the corporate personality does not take seriously its own injunctions to act ethically, or at best, disclose its ethics as contested and contestable. For example, in July 2013, the European Commission launched another antitrust action against Microsoft, this time for the practice of linking its Internet web browser with its operating system because it 'harms competition between web browsers, undermines product innovation and ultimately reduces consumer choice' (*USA Today*, 2013).

Despite the fact that the characteristics of integrity, honesty, openness, personal excellence, and so on, are personal virtues, Microsoft intends that all its employees will manifest these virtues and in so doing, these characteristics will be adopted and embodied as company culture. Arguably they are not, as indicated by the 4,810 hits (at the time of writing) that 'legal action against Microsoft' yields on Google. However, the company publicly states its intentions as ethical and therefore, cannot be denoted as intentionally unethical because it has codes in place. However, through their interpretation and practices, Microsoft employees may be at times unethical. This limits the legal liability of Microsoft and may be considered to fit its risk management profile. It provides Microsoft with potential refutation for those myriad Google hits.

Analysis of the first two sentences of its values statement (Microsoft, 2014b), quoted above, show that Microsoft primarily incorporates management intentions for doing the 'right thing' by customers and business partners. It explains that, by valuing certain characteristics as a company and as individuals, good intentions will come to fruition and the company will be doing its duty with respect to its customers and business partners. The other two sentences address consequences. The third sentence describes taking on challenges and seeing them through, which is implicit to planning and strategizing courses of action. However, the final sentence regarding accountability, honouring commitments, providing results and striving for quality, embodies acknowledging outcomes, whether favourable or otherwise. Not only does it entail committing to the rationales of planning for specific outcomes but also learning from experiences. These are clear indications of Microsoft's risk management strategy.

An overarching theme is that Microsoft, both as an organization and through the individuals it employs, professes values about which they are reflective. It is for this reason that they can be used as references for 'constructive self-criticism' and 'continual self-improvement' (Microsoft, 2014b) such that the claim can be made

(Continued)

(Continued)

that the guiding light for actions is moral intuition. Further, because the organization and its individual members 'take on big challenges' (Microsoft, 2014b), they perform actions for which they may have no prior experiences and therefore, no specific contextual reference points. Employees' basic beliefs are presumed to be concomitant with Microsoft values. By applying them to unfamiliar situations, such as 'big challenges', the code suggests that until there is proof that such big challenges cannot be achieved, the company and its employees will see challenges through to completion.

Microsoft's values are stated on the company website: it and its employees embody values not only of 'integrity and honesty' but also take on a missionary zeal to make others better. In other words, there ought to be a singularity of purpose for the Microsoft family and such prescription should be adopted by others, as Microsoft family members help these others to improve and to do things in 'the right way' (Microsoft, 2014c). The reasons why Microsoft has standards of business conduct are, it states:

> *As responsible business leaders, it is not enough to intend to do things right, we must also do them in the right way. That means making business decisions and taking appropriate actions that are ethical and in compliance with applicable legal requirements. As we make these decisions, the Microsoft values must shine through in all our interactions. The Standards of Business Conduct are an extension of the Microsoft values and reflect our continued commitment to ethical business practices and regulatory compliance. (Microsoft, 2014c)*

The statement adds an additional layer of regulatory compliance to the company values as a rationale of its ethical code. The webpage containing the Microsoft Standards of Business Conduct (Microsoft, 2014c) is navigated from the Microsoft *home page/about/ legal and corporate affairs*. While it is obvious that one rationale for Microsoft's standards is the legality of Microsoft actions, it may also be seen as a way of addressing legal requirements by addressing ethics not only as intentions and consequences but also as a way of pre-empting possible legal consequences, if the company or its employees are suspected or charged with illegal actions; in other words, to manage potential risk.

QUESTIONS

1. To what extent do Microsoft's codes of ethics compare with Microsoft's practices? Discuss specifically with respect to various legal cases such as the US antitrust law case of *United States v. Microsoft Corporation* 253 F.3d 34 (D.C. Cir. 2001), ultimately settled by the Department of Justice, where Microsoft Corporation was accused of becoming a monopoly and engaging in abusive practices contrary to the Sherman Antitrust Act 1890 sections 1 and 2. The United States Department of Justice (DOJ) and 20 states initiated the case on 18 May 1998.

2. To what extent are Microsoft's ethics' statements a risk management exercise as a governance device? Is this what codes typically do, in your view?

STRATEGY PROCESSES

EMERGENCE, CONTEXT, STORIES

Learning objectives

By the end of this chapter you will be able to:

1   Understand the limitations of a rational top down approach to strategic planning

2   Understand the ideas of Henry Mintzberg, Andrew Pettigrew and Karl Weick as important process thinkers in the field of strategy

3   Relate strategy to learning

4   Relate strategy to culture

5   Understand the importance of stories for strategy

BEFORE YOU GET STARTED

A good decision is based on knowledge and not on numbers. (Plato)

Introduction

In previous chapters – especially when we discussed Michael Porter's competitive positioning perspective and where we looked at the resource-based view of the firm – we have discussed strategy as a rationalistic undertaking. Remember Michael Porter's theory: he argues that firms should study the structure of the industry they're in and then position themselves within that environment. The resource-based view (RBV) offered an inverse explanation: the firm should identify its unique resources and then develop a strategy that optimizes and leverages these strengths. Transaction costs approaches in turn submitted that one should aim to minimize the sum of inter- and intra-organizational transaction costs.

Whether the strategist crafts her strategy from the inside out, or the outside in, in both instances she relies on one basic assumption: that the world exists objectively out there, waiting to be analysed. When analysed there is faith that a plan will result that, in turn, will inform action. The premise is simple: first, you think, then analyse and action follows: think, plan, do, change is the rational strategist's mantra. The focus is on what should rationally happen, rather more than it is on what actually occurs in practice.

We begin this chapter by considering views that from the 1970s onwards increasingly came to criticize the rationalist agenda of prior strategy thinking. These thinkers were not arguing for irrationality but they were pointing out the irrationality of building neat, tidy models on rational assumptions that everyday experience constantly confounded. The first to make an impact on the scene was the Canadian strategy thinker, Henry Mintzberg, who developed his ideas in opposition to those of more prescriptive theory, based initially on fieldwork that followed five managers in their everyday work and appointments. For Mintzberg strategy was emergent from the flow of events rather than remaining in the direction fixed by strategic deliberation. From this simple observation, based on empirical analysis of what strategists actually do when they do strategy, he developed an entirely different and influential approach to strategy.

Henry Mintzberg was not the only influential strategy scholar making dissonant waves in the fields of rational planning. On the other side of the Atlantic, a British scholar, Andrew Pettigrew, was also developing a process perspective on strategy, with a particular emphasis on politics and context.

Any process perspective is open to the influence of learning. The process perspective allies itself with an approach to organizational analysis that stresses the capabilities of learning organizations. In this context it is perhaps not surprising that Penrose's (1959) resource-based view, which emphasized learning and innovation, was the first process-based view. Subsequent RBV scholars have interpreted Penrose in a more rational, content-based light, as explained above, but her theory of firm growth was primarily an evolutionary, learning-based process theory. In its emphasis on the idea that managers perceive the external environment in terms of an 'image' that is unique to them, it connects with sensemaking perspectives, which we discuss below. We will review some of the more important concepts in the process/learning organization literature.

The extent to which organizations have a capability to learn is in large part cultural. Organizations that prize routines and rational plans will find it much harder to develop emergent strategies, to attend to the flow of process, to be able to improvise as events require. Where organizational elites assume an integrated culture to the organization, usually one that is integrated in their terms, they are less likely to be alert to these opportunities to learn. They are making a restricted sense of the organization and its realities.

There is a vibrant current to contemporary organization theory that is called **sensemaking**, developed by Karl Weick.

> **Sensemaking** is the subjective and inter-subjective process through which people give meaning to their experiences.

While Weick is not usually thought of as a strategy scholar his ideas align remarkably well with those of the process thinkers. Weick (2007) defines sensemaking as the ongoing retrospective development of plausible images that rationalize what people are doing. It is not something done just once but is constantly being done in process. It characterizes emergent strategy and is inherently political as different sense is made by different people of ostensibly the same events, strategy or situation.

Managers not only practise sensemaking; they are also engaged in **sensegiving** to significant stakeholders, such as employees, shareholders and others. That is, they try to make *their sense* the sense that others make. Such sensemaking, when accepted by others as the sense that they should make, when sensegiving works effectively, can work to make processes seem far less paradoxical than they might actually be. Appreciation of paradox is difficult to present as a neat formula; hence, the conclusion of this chapter is that if process is as important as we and schol-

> **Sensegiving** involves the attempt to influence the sensemaking of others towards the preferred version of reality of the sensegiver.

ars such as Mintzberg and Pettigrew think it is, then its appreciation may be best enhanced through storytelling. It is for this reason that we conclude with a brief outline of organizational storytelling as a strategic approach, one that companies such as IBM have used.

Against rational planning: Strategy as emergent and grounded

The study and practice of strategic management has followed a simple logic for most of its career. From the outset, founding fathers of the discipline, such as Igor Ansoff (1965), defined strategy as a planning exercise conducted by top managers. The metaphor that comes to mind is that of the head (Top Management Team) that thinks, and the body (the organization) that follows. In fact, Chandler's (1962) argument that structure should follow strategy made the point succinctly: once strategy is set, and the Top Management Team has decided on where to go, the organization has to be designed, if necessary with a sharp scalpel, to follow suit. In Chandler's (1962: 314) words: 'Unless structure follows strategy, inefficiency rules'. Strategy is the corporation's *cogito ergo sum*: I think therefore I am. Top management plans; therefore the organization is.

tional approach to decision-making came out of the discipline of economics,
-fold process as its central premise:

...al actors access as complete information as is possible pertaining to all
...e available alternatives.

2. All possible consequences of each of the alternatives are mapped out.

3. A comparison of different alternatives, normally done by using a cost-benefit
    analysis, is undertaken.

According to this rational view, after the three-fold process has been followed, strategists are equipped with all the information they require to make a rational decision,
one that will maximize their returns. Rational choice models – many of which the
American military developed – diffused widely by the 1950s.

Starbuck (1983) has argued against overly rationalist views that organizations
are action-generators that think, plan, do and then review; rather, in Starbuck's view,
organizations act and do what they are good at, and then search for problems that look
like a justification for their action. One writer who has taken this insight to heart is
Henry Mintzberg, who sees strategic planning as part of the problem, not the solution.

Mintzberg and Managerial Behaviour

Henry Mintzberg shot to fame in 1973 when he conducted a meticulous recording
of the daily life of five executives in different organizations, by asking them to keep
a diary of their doings. His suspicion was that what managers think they do would
differ radically from what they actually did.

Mintzberg realized that interviewing managers about what they do would not be
a reliable methodology: asking them about their jobs would elicit standard, almost
textbook answers stressing that managing is about planning, controlling, organizing
and keeping an eye on the big picture. In this view, with which managers seem only
too keen to conform, the manager can be seen as a rational planner.

Mintzberg's research told him a different story to that which managers seemed to
believe about themselves: the five executives spent most of their time on mundane
issues, dashing from one conversation to the next, and hardly focusing on any one
issue for a long period of time; most interaction occurred on an *ad hoc* basis, dealing
with problems as they arose, switching focus every ten minutes or so. Management
was based on judgment and intuition. In short, managers did not behave as if they
were rational engineers but played diverse roles and often improvised.

Equipped with thought-provoking ideas, together with an engaging writing style,
Mintzberg remains one of the most outspoken voices in the field of strategic management. In a series of contributions Mintzberg has attacked orthodox strategy thinking.
In 1990 Mintzberg published a critique of the basic assumptions of strategy in the
influential *Strategic Management Journal*, provoking Igor Ansoff (1991) to reply.

Mintzberg turned Chandler's dictum, that structure followed strategy, on its head.
The organization, its design, its culture, and its power games – these all co-shape its
strategy – not the other way round. Organizations should be thought of primarily as
arenas of local politics and disputes, creating cleavages and conflicts. Strategy then
becomes something that local interests seek to articulate and mobilize to further
whatever they desire. Often such desires are quite parochial: to gain influence, belittle

enemies in the organization, forge alliances with preferred friends or the enemies of their enemies. Strategy becomes useful for doing these things because it provides a legitimating rationale, a kind of camouflage. If you are able to justify your actions in terms of 'the strategy' they have a better chance of being viewed as legitimate, even if the actions may have a covert agenda.

Mintzberg argued that strategic planning had become a Taylorized and mechanical exercise where planning systems churned through data and set the future path. A paradox ensued: while planning involved analysing data, emergent strategy was based on synthesis, on thinking creatively and laterally, bringing things together, using the grand plans of strategy as camouflage in doing so. Mintzberg (1994: 333) went so far as to say that planning was the opposite of strategy. Planners and their tools were badly equipped to do the job of being strategic. Being strategic would often mean acting in ways quite antithetical to the formal plans.

Mintzberg further argued that virtually all texts about strategy-making depict it as a deliberate process in which we first think and subsequently act. 'We formulate, then we implement. The progression seems so perfectly sensible' (Mintzberg, 1989: 29). Thinking is reserved as a special task for the Top Management Team. Again, in the words of Mintzberg:

> The notion that strategy is something that should happen way up there, far removed from the details of running an organization on a daily basis, is one of the great fallacies of conventional management. And it explains a good many of the most dramatic failures in business and public policy today. (Mintzberg, 1989: 31)

What matters for strategy is not something static, such as the resources or knowledge possessed by an organization. What is important are the uses to which resources and knowledge are put, something that evolves not only in formal meetings but also in informal arenas and accidental collaborations in the organization. In Mintzberg's view, the distinction between strategy formulation and strategy implementation no longer makes sense: doing strategy does not follow strategy formulation in a linear fashion. In fact, sometimes strategy might follow action, rather than produce it, and strategy would often be formulated as an afterthought to a *fait accompli*. Richard Pascale's (1984) account of the introduction of Honda into the US motorcycle industry is often held up as an exemplar of this process. Strategy in such situations best functions as a story that can be made to fit whatever the facts are represented as being. Strategy is thus used to legitimate how and where an organization has got to rather than showing it how to get there.

Mintzberg, Opponent of Strategic Planning

Mintzberg distinguished between **deliberate** and **emergent strategy**. Most previous strategy theory he sees as having been overly focused on the deliberate aspects of strategy; instead, he wants to reorient attention to the emergent properties.

Deliberate strategy may be what the strategy team intentionally designs as they integrate data and scan the environment.

Strategy, according to Mintzberg, is best characterized as a stream of decisions made over time. Deliberative strategies are fairly straightforward: they are carefully articulated, then communicated widely through an organization, before being implemented with an express outcome in mind. A strategy analyst can then assess whether the objectives of a deliberate strategy are actually achieved.

Emergent strategy originates in the interaction of the organization with its environment. As events unfold and ideas about them coalesce, emergent strategies tend to converge, as ideas and actions from multiple sources are formed into a pattern.

In contrast to a deliberately designed strategy, one that is emergent occurs where an outcome is realized 'despite, or in the absence of, intentions' (Mintzberg and Waters, 1985). The crucial difference between the two types of strategy rests on the *intent* that underpins them: a deliberate strategy is precise and pre-ordained, whereas an emergent strategy lacks express intent. While it is comparatively straightforward to envisage what constitutes a deliberate strategy, one could be forgiven for thinking that emergent strategy is little more than free-wheeling anarchy that denotes a total lack of strategy! What strategy does not derive from intent? On this point Mintzberg and Waters (1985) have the following to say:

> Emergent strategy does not mean management is out of control, only – in some cases at least – that it is open, flexible and responsive, in other words, willing to learn. Such behaviour is especially important when an environment is too unstable or complex to comprehend, or too imposing to defy. Openness to such emergent strategy enables management to act before everything is fully understood – to respond to an evolving reality rather than having to focus on a stable fantasy. (Mintzberg and Waters, 1985: 271)

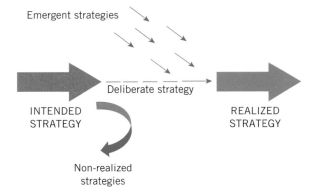

Figure 9.1   Emergent strategy

(Adapted from Mintzberg and McHugh, 1985: 162)

Mintzberg cautions that few strategies, if any, are purely deliberate or exclusively emergent. Instead, strategies are likely to bear the traces of both tendencies. To elaborate this further, Mintzberg and Waters (1985) construct a taxonomy based on the respective degree of deliberation and emergence contained in a strategy. Mintzberg is especially fond of constructing taxonomies!

1. *Planned Strategy* – this is characterized by formal planning with explicit objectives. The strategy is communicated widely by senior executives and is carefully implemented. It is a 'deliberate' strategy. The classical approaches to Strategic Management, such as an Ansoffian approach to strategy, would follow this approach. In this approach strategy making is tightly controlled.

2. *Entrepreneurial Strategy* – where the entrepreneur formulates the strategic vision. It has express intentions and a vision of the future, though it is prone to being halted or altered according to the entrepreneur's whim. It is broadly a 'deliberate' strategy and is tightly controlled by the entrepreneur.

3. *Ideological Strategy* – an ideological organization – such as an extremist political organization, a church or a terrorist group – will often have a very strong culture, which socializes organizational actors into subscribing to a particular set of goals. The goals are often utopian and inspirational for members of the organization. An ideological strategy is broadly deliberate, often determining methods as well as objectives.

4. *Umbrella Strategy* – can be seen where an organization comprises a range of different interest groups and exists in an environment of uncertainty. The senior strategists will define broad boundaries allowing others discretion to adopt strategies within those boundaries. An umbrella strategy is at once deliberate – setting broad goals – and emergent – allowing experimentation to realize those goals. In the process of implementation the goals can often change. Mintzberg and Waters cite the example of NASA in 1960s, as it attempted to 'put a man on the moon' as an example of an umbrella strategy. As a strategy it is far less controlling than the previous three examples.

5. *Process Strategy* – in this case the central leadership of an organization control the process through which a strategy is formulated and the people charged with making the strategy. The content of the strategy is, however, at the discretion of those making the strategy. An example of this might be in a multi-divisional organization where individual subunits are allowed to formulate their own strategies, albeit using an established process for arriving at their strategy.

6. *Unconnected Strategy* – this is where a part of an organization, enjoying considerable autonomy is able to develop its own strategy. From the vantage point of the group making the strategy it might be deliberate or emergent, though from the perspective of the organization such strategy making is always emergent.

7. *Consensus Strategy* – this form of strategy making is generally emergent; an agreed consensus emerges from discussions between different interest groups in an organization. Such a form of strategy making entails negotiation and an organization reaching a 'feel' for a particular issue.

8. *Imposed Strategy* – this is when a powerful group or an event from outside an organization determines a strategy for an organization. An example would be the International Monetary Fund imposing budget cuts on a national government. For the government concerned, an imposed strategy is emergent in nature, although it might subsequently become the subject of deliberate intent by the organization.

Mintzberg and Waters' (1985) articulation of eight types of strategy making is not meant to be exhaustive so much as illustrative of the distinctions between deliberate and emergent strategy. Deliberate strategy is focused on pursuing a particular direction and tightly controlling the implementation of a strategy, whereas emergent strategy is more concerned with adaptation to circumstances and strategic learning. As Mintzberg and Waters' (1985) suggest, strategies are likely to combine both deliberate and emergent features, although some, such as the planned strategy, are more overtly deliberate, while others, such as imposed strategy, are irredeemably emergent.

The logic of emergence and disorder may be found in many instances of organizational life, ranging from strategy making to product innovation to management learning. Cohen and colleagues (1972) suggested that the role of chance, luck and timing in organizational choice through the accidental confluence of problems, solutions, participants and problems is important: decision-making consists of various solutions looking for problems to attach themselves to. For this reason, March and Olsen (1976) referred to organizations characterized by a lack of shared and consistent goals, clear technology and member participation, as 'organized anarchies'. Thus, those strategies that emerge will depend on what specialists, with what knowledge, tools and ways of making sense, were involved in the strategy's formulation.

Chia & McKay

EXTEND YOUR KNOWLEDGE

An interesting paper by Robert Chia and Brad McKay (2007) updates the emergence approach that you read about in the previous paragraph by connecting it to the strategy-as-practice perspective (which you will find in the next chapter). The paper is called '**Post-processual challenges for the emerging strategy as practice perspective: Discovering strategy in the logic of practice**' and can be found on the companion website for this book: www.edge.sagepub.com/strategy2e.

Chia, R. and McKay, B. (2007) 'Post-processual challenges for the emerging strategy-as-practice perspective: Discovering strategy in the logic of practice', *Human Relations*, 60(1): 217–242.

Mintzberg and McHugh (1985) suggest that strategy formation is to some extent the result of spontaneous convergence by a variety of actors. Burgelman (1991) suggests that strategy that benefits from strategic conversations that enable internal experimentation travelling from bottom to top will be better strategy.

Five errors of strategic management, according to Mintzberg

Mintzberg's (1994: 222) critical view of deliberate strategic planning unearths five key assumptions that are routinely made in its name. He seizes on these five assumptions because they are widely promulgated but also, he will argue, deeply erroneous:

1. *Formalization*: strategic finding must be translated into formal concepts. The processes that will lead to strategy's success can be clearly identified, anticipated and must be unambiguously communicated.

2. *Detachment*: the system does the thinking and produces strategies, which 'only' have to be implemented. A divide is presupposed between thinking and action, between strategy and implementation, between strategic planning and operational business. Management acts from a distance, based on remote control, displacement and abbreviation.

3. *Division of labour*: management (the head) thinks, while the organization (the body), has to be either formed or informed of the strategic plans as a corporate body. Once a plan is formulated, the supplementary problem is one of implementation or pure execution.

4. *Quantification*: the strategy-making process is driven by 'hard facts', comprising quantitative representations of the organization and its environment. Knowledge of these is and must be 'objective'.

5. *Predetermination*: the context for strategy making is stable, relies on hard data and predictable states of affairs. The strategic plan is a means to anticipate future developments and forecast coming changes.

For Mintzberg these five aspects of traditional strategy approaches are deeply problematic because they over-rationalize the strategy process. He has a different approach to strategy, one that builds on a tradition of analysis that researchers such as Lindblom (1959) and Cohen and colleagues (1972) pioneered.

In this alternative perspective, strategy making is seen as less a rationally ordered and more a fragmented process; one that takes place over time, in different venues with different participants, in a series of serial and incremental decisions. It involves a great many informal processes, including negotiation and a certain randomness, as problems become defined in terms of the solutions that are at hand.

Quinn (1978) saw strategy making as a process of 'logical incrementalism'. Actions and events move step-wise and a conscious strategy slowly emerges and changes in a fluid but controllable process. Mintzberg (1978) held views closely related to those of Quinn. Mintzberg (1990) pointed out that in turbulent environments with high uncertainty, the process of defining a strategy is most likely to become a messy and experimental process. It will be driven from the bottom up, seeking to capture valuable insights for strategy formulation that reside in the heads of the employees. The myth may be that strategy flows from the head; the reality will be that the body is not an inert relay but an active agency. The implementation and the shortcomings and insights that emerge can be the basis for tomorrow's strategy. In fact, implementation becomes a part of the strategy formulation process.

Most managers are not strategists, suggests Mintzberg (1973). They are stuck in the moment, seeking tangibility and immediacy rather than thinking abstractly or in the longer term. Mostly, they end up being generalists, even if they start out as specialists. As generalists they rely heavily on what they hear from those with whom they communicate, as they work at various fragmented and discontinuous tasks that the moment brings.

Strategy is rarely accomplished as the rational planned process it sometimes aspires to be. Where it is rationally planned, it fosters bureaucratization rather than innovation. Innovation, the essence of strategy, flows from immersion in the messy detail of everyday organizational life and the ability to reflect on process, *in process*, crafting emergent strategies that are shaped around the real rather than the planned contingencies of organizational action.

Mintzberg's five Ps of strategy

Mintzberg is nothing if not a good marketer. In 1994 he suggested replacing *formalization*, *detachment*, *division of labour*, *quantification* and *predetermination* with what he called the five Ps of strategy:

1. *Planning* strategy is formulated prior to the actions to which it applies and it is developed intentionally, with a purpose: it is teleological in that it seeks to bring some defined end into being. While generals usually have plans for a battle they rarely stick to them as the battle ebbs and flows; they modify their actions, as their plan, through emergent strategies, is shaped as much by the enemy as by the planners. Unfortunately, many organizations are not as flexible as many generals – they stick to the plan because it is the plan long after it should have been emergently reshaped. One reason why this is so is because many plans are formulated at a great distance, literally and metaphorically, from arenas of action. The plan is supposed to be conceived on high and unfold down and through the organization to all fields of operations. High and mighty conceptions often make nice fantasies of control and prediction but rarely survive the rough and tumble of operations on the ground in some far-flung corner of the corporate empire.

2. *Pattern* making is often a form of retrospective discovery where the journey that has been unfolding, perhaps somewhat randomly or with some confusion, becomes a recognizable path followed whether consciously or not. The path is defined by the consistency with which it emerges and it has been followed. Not for nothing do social scientists refer to path dependency; the best predictor of direction for the future is the direction in the past. When IKEA stumbled on the idea of flat-packing furniture it initiated a pattern that defines the company.

3. *Position* refers to the place of an organization within its environment. Think of a battlefield and the troops commanding a position – a ridge, fortification or landing beach. If you have a commanding position it is that much harder for the competition (or enemy) to defeat you. Position not only has martial referents: it can also refer to context in ecological or economic terms. A firm may occupy a niche position in a business environment, for instance, as a boutique label or producer of goods or services, such as a small, intimate and distinctive hotel or a boutique fashion shop with distinctive and individual designs unavailable in the malls and high streets. Or, conceived in economic terms, a position may be an ideal niche because it allows the company to make a profit by positioning a specific product in a specific market for which it is ideally suited. For instance, although there will be a limited market for a Maserati or Bentley amongst the Indian elite there will be a far larger market for a Tata Nano amongst the masses.

4. *Perspective* concerns ingrained 'ways of seeing', such as the engineering culture of Hewlett-Packard or the focus on production efficiency of McDonald's. The gaze through which something is seen defines the essence of that thing that is seen, rather than any objective qualities of the thing in itself. If the gaze is fixed on the known numbers, on rational analysis, and on extrapolating the future from the past, it is not likely to see far into the future. To see into the future requires an imaginative gaze. Evidence-based strategy is all very well but it will rarely lead to breakthrough innovation, for instance. The mental models that frame and shape the ways in which we gaze at a phenomenon will define the nature of the phenomenon – they do more than just reveal it as it is – they constitute it as being what it is taken to be. Perspective makes things seem natural and correct. It provides a literal representation of the ways in which we conventionally see things. Thus, by extension, perspective in strategy provides a mental frame or cognitive structuring for the ways in which we apprehend

what we take to be the real. Taking a perspective on things often means that we are applying a paradigm – a conventionally accepted and legitimate way of seeing – to the matter at hand.

5. As a *ploy*, strategy may be thought of as a move designed to beat an opponent: often it is something unexpected or unanticipated, such as the Saudi Arabian ploy to undercut oil prices to discourage investment in the US oil fracking industry.

Mintzberg favours a grassroots model of strategy making. Initially, he suggests, strategies grow 'like weeds in a garden, they are not cultivated like tomatoes in a hothouse' (Mintzberg, 1989: 214). There is an Italian fable in which a peasant patriarch, on his deathbed, tells his indolent sons that there is treasure buried in his land. On his death they begin to dig the soil everywhere, searching for it. They do not find treasure but indirectly create it because they have prepared the ground for sowing and growing crops. Mintzberg suggests that this is how strategies might emerge. Strategy can take root in all kinds of places, with new ideas able to start anywhere in the organization if there are favourable resources. Once these strategies spread organically throughout the organization, they become collective patterns of behaviour. Management's job is to nurture and ensure fertile soil for ideas.

To think of strategy this way is to see it emerging from the roots rather than to go searching for it in the highest echelons of the organization. Strategy starts from the bottom up and gains support and energy from the everyday work of the members of the organization – as opposed to those lofty plans written by top executives during a retreat in a fancy off-site location. It is pretty hard for these documents not to feed the vanities of those participating while simultaneously demonstrating that they are often out of touch with more mundane concerns of the business or organization.

Not surprisingly, Mintzberg's ideas created quite a stir in the world of strategy theory. Some interpreted them as 'humanization' of the field of strategy (e.g. Pettigrew et al., 2002); suddenly, human actors were important again, and the way they made sense of complex environments was important. Strategy was no longer a calculation but a kind of team sport in which the basic rules of the game regulated individual players' moves as they tried to out-manoeuvre their opponents.

Mintzberg's methods

Mintzberg closely observed how managers did what they did and how they accounted for what they were doing. It seems evident that Mintzberg's ideas were influenced by the research approach popularised by Glaser and Strauss (1967) who first coined the idea of emergent theory. In emergent theory understanding is not shaped a priori by a plan. Instead, the researcher seeks to grasp the everyday terms and theories in use in a setting. Discovery proceeds through making direct contact with the subjects' understandings of the situations they are in: hence, the sense that you make of the situation is emergent (Human, 2009: 425).

Strategists may think that strategy follows from the plans and models that they create but, in reality it is being constantly interpreted and negotiated, made and remade sense of through everyday actions. Not just the strategists but also those who resist the strategy shape the strategic outcomes. The plans can rarely predict these inflections.

Mintzberg suggested that to understand strategy we need to understand the categories and concepts that strategists are using to make it up and negotiate its interpretation in subsequent scenes and settings. Some of these categories and concepts might, for instance, come from the strategists' MBA education in rational planning models, Porterian analysis or the RBV. We should bracket any a priori assumption we might have about these being literal or empirically realistic models; instead, we should look at how they become used in practice by those who deploy them. What are important are the values of these in use and the effects they create. We should not assume that these models correspond with reality or any existing state of affairs. However, they can help create 'truths' that correspond to them.

Mintzberg's approach suggests that strategists make up strategy from strategic thinking tools with which they work. If we want to understand the strategy, then we should understand the tools with which it is made up or fabricated. However, as sense is made of complex unfolding realities, strategy emerges not just from the underlying set of theories and tools, but also from the sense made of them because it is constantly being redefined, reconfigured and renegotiated in practice. Strategy is a form of negotiated order or better, negotiated order*ing*, to stress the active aspect.

Mintzberg's grounded theory began its career in close observation and ethnographic analysis of managers at work. Unlike almost all prior strategy thinkers he was not prescribing what strategy should be but describing how it actually emerged in practice. Mintzberg is not the only significant strategy theorist to stress process and emergence; Andrew Pettigrew also stressed process and the way that strategy depended upon its implementation rather more than its design. To the language of process, Pettigrew added a focus on context.

Andrew Pettigrew and process approaches

One of the most important contributors to the theory of strategy as a process came from the UK – Andrew Pettigrew, now at Oxford University Said School of Business. Pettigrew wrote an influential book in 1985 called *The Awakening Giant: Continuity and Change at ICI*. Pettigrew introduced the processual school of organizational change that has been evolving for over 30 years. Pettigrew's framework, which is used extensively, focuses on three key dimensions of strategic change. The first refers to the *content* of the chosen strategy (the 'what' of change); the second is the *process* and management of change (the 'how') and finally, the *context* in which the strategy unfolds (the 'why'). A simple figure illustrates the approach (see Figure 9.2).

For Pettigrew, the process dimension (the how) is not only concerned with the formal procedures, practices and activities that unfold to enable strategic change but also the impact of politics and power relations that ultimately shape the overall process. For Pettigrew, it is not just the strategy that is formulated that makes things change over time, it is also the power and politics that deploy and resist strategy (see Chapter 11). The link between formulation and implementation is their interrelation through time.

Pettigrew directed a whole team of British strategy academics who worked in the 1980s at Warwick Business School's Centre for Corporate Strategy and Change (CCSC), a centre that focused on combining the fine-grained study of specific organizational contexts with an account of the strategy process (e.g. Johnson, 1987). It focused on change that occurred within ICI over long periods of time. Pettigrew was curious to understand why quite similar change initiatives had different outcomes in the organization. Pettigrew found answers to his question by looking at the history, the context and the processes of ICI.

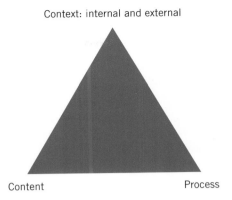

Context: internal and external

Content   Process

Figure 9.2   The processual framework of Pettigrew (1987)

Pettigrew's stress on process was a critique of more static approaches. For Pettigrew and his colleagues, the content of a specific strategy was the result of the strategy-making process. The process determined the outcome through the patterns of domination, the legitimization of cognitive maps, and the organization of interaction in a particular way. Hence, to produce better strategies one had to be able to create a better strategy-making process. Focusing on the strategy process meant abandoning a linear, rationalistic template for strategy and instead following the complex and dynamic evolution of strategic thoughts and how they change the organization.

Pettigrew stressed time. Over time, organizations that do not learn and evolve die. Change is a necessary aspect of organization. No organization stays the same and strategy serves as a way of trying to organize the changes in a desired direction. Pettigrew saw an organization's strategy as the result of a *process* embedded in a *context* developing over *time*. In this context the link between formulation and implementation is not a linear process of *think, plan, act, review* but is conditioned by a complex and emergent temporality which is constantly refining the activities being undertaken as well as the stage of the process in which they are being undertaken. Hence, understanding strategic change means understanding its changing meaning as it emerges and is defined and redefined by various actors and stakeholders over time. Whose definitions of the situation prevail is always an effect of organizational power and politics. Only detailed ethnographic case studies and specific business histories, combined with the eye for detail of an anthropologist, can really grasp strategy as a flow and a process. Pettigrew is an important precursor of the strategy-as-practice perspective, which we will discuss in Chapter 10.

IN PRACTICE

Greenpeace campaigning

Go Online: Visit the book's website at https://edge.sagepub.com/strategy2e to watch an interview with Greenpeace CEO Steve Shallhorn conducted by the author team.

(Continued)

Steve Shallhorn Interview

(Continued)

Image 9.1   Greenpeace. Copyright: Lepro

Steve Shallhorn has an extensive career with Greenpeace, both as a campaigner and senior manager. From his first action as a campaigner for Greenpeace Canada in 1987, to his role as Chief Executive Officer of Greenpeace Australia Pacific, Steve's passion for the environment has seen him become a perceptive strategic manager. Steve led the Australia Pacific operations of Greenpeace from 2005 till 2009 and has previously held the position of Executive Director in Japan and Campaign Director for both USA and Canada.

Steve's Greenpeace career began in 1987, leading a successful campaign to prevent the Canadian Government purchasing nuclear powered submarines. In 1990, Steve famously led a ship expedition to a secret Soviet nuclear weapons test site where he was detained dramatically, at gunpoint. The Soviets went ahead with the nuclear tests but the events were broadcast around the world and it was the last test they ever did.

As you will note from the video, Steve has considerable experience in both developing and implementing strategy. From his time as a student activist through to his position as CEO, he identifies himself as a strategist from the 'school of hard knocks' who believes that strategy is about achieving goals and, importantly, winning.

Greenpeace defines strategy as a process that integrates goals, policies and actions into a cohesive campaign. It gathers and allocates resources for the campaign; it takes advantage of organizational strengths while minimizing organizational weaknesses; it anticipates changes in the political environment, and it takes into account the counter-moves by the opponent.

There are two aspects of strategy making in Greenpeace that are key to the organization; a 'power analysis' to identify who holds the power you want in order to effect change and, by extension, an inclusion of your opponent's strategies in your own strategic thinking.

Perhaps reflective of the values-based nature of Greenpeace and other non-government organizations, is the notion that strategy development is both a top-down and bottom-up process. As Steve states in the video, this required alignment, at both an international and organizational level, is one of the main reasons why organizations need strategies.

Questions

1. To what extent is there competition in the 'markets' that Greenpeace operates in? Who are their competitors and what is Greenpeace competing on?

2. What are Greenpeace's preferred ways for developing strategy and conveying its messages to the public?

3. What are the components of Steve's definition of a successful process for strategy? Are these ingredients different to what a strategist in a for-profit organization would look at?

4. The notion of 'campaigning to win' emphasizes a critical element of passion and commitment to the strategic process and objectives of an organization. How does Greenpeace ensure this commitment reaches throughout the organization and what can for-profit organizations learn from that?

5. Who are the players (stakeholders) in the political environment that Greenpeace engages with when campaigning and implementing its strategies?

6. Overall, what are the main differences of developing a strategy and metrics in a non-profit compared to a for-profit? Do you think one is more difficult than the other? Give reasons for your judgment.

7. You have been recruited by Greenpeace to work with and to develop a strategy for a neighbourhood group that is opposed to plans by the authority responsible for roads and travel planning in your region. They are pushing ahead with building a major freeway intersection, one that will see homes subject to compulsory purchase in the areas it traverses. What would be the key elements that you propose in the strategy of resistance to the government's proposals?

Strategy and learning processes

Change is pervasive, according to both Mintzberg and Pettigrew, occurring through shifts in ideas, personnel, markets and context generally. Rapidly changing technologies, hyper-competition and globalization accelerate change: they leave organizations with little chance but to be learning organizations that are resilient and strive to manage change. Rather than just having a strategy unit or a strategically minded leader at the top, **learning organizations** behave, *as a whole*, strategically. Rather than trying to predict the future, learning organizations are preparing for future challenges that cannot be summarized in neat strategy reports. Preparedness replaces predictability as the strategic imperative.

> **Learning organizations** facilitate learning by all their members in order to improve continuously and transform *what* they do, *how* they do it and *why* it is done.

A learning organization has the ability to manage knowledge. Knowledge is hard to centralize: for instance, Orr's (1996) excellent study of photocopier repairmen illustrated that local knowing, collaboration and improvisation were necessary to fix broken machines. The simple error message that the machines flashed on their display, which distressed the user and greeted the repairman, did not convey enough information to allow quick and simple problem solving. Rather, the repairman had to draw on collectively built experiences and narratives to know how to fix faults. The knowledge that the repairmen shared was distributed across the entire organization, lodged in implicit knowing rather than formal codification. Think of all those Microsoft 'help' options: do you really understand most of them? We don't.

When a research and development team improves the functioning of a given approach or technique it engages in **single loop learning**:

> **Single loop learning** optimizes its knowledge of a given problem by using skills, refining abilities and acquiring knowledge that is necessary to achieve resolution of that problem.

> **Double loop learning** means changing the frame of reference that normally guides behaviour, teaching you how to change the rules of the game. It implies rethinking the task at hand and considering whether its accomplishment is beneficial or not.

While important, knowledge from single loop learning is not necessarily strategic. It might be more focused on efficiency gains and achieving operational effectiveness, a kind of learning that occurs within a given framework, where the parameters are pre-defined and the learning activity focuses on how to optimize (or maximize or increase) your capacity within this frame.

Double loop learning is more strategic.

To put it metaphorically, single loop learning involves learning the competencies necessary to play a certain game successfully, whereas double loop learning requires thinking and learning about what is the most valuable game to play. Single loop learning concerns acting according to the rules of a certain game; in contrast, double loop learning involves learning what the actual rules of the game are and how they could be changed to modify the game or play a different game altogether. Single loop learning focuses on optimizing problem-solving behaviour in a given context, whereas double loop learning challenges the core assumptions, beliefs and values that frame the context. In the words of Argyris and Schön (1978):

> When the error detected and corrected permits the organization to carry on its present policies or achieve its present objectives, then that error-and-correction process is *single-loop* learning. Single-loop learning is like a thermostat that learns when it is too hot or too cold and turns the heat on or off. The thermostat can perform this task because it can receive information (the temperature of the room) and take corrective action. *Double-loop* learning occurs when error is detected and corrected in ways that involve the modification of an organization's underlying norms, policies and objectives. (Argyris and Schön, 1978: 2)

Double loop learning is a core organizational capability for creating an emergent strategy. Double loop learning requires strategic changes: it challenges the core assumptions and beliefs that organizations hold dear. As such, the appetite for learning creates an ability that enables strategies to emerge and shape the organization.

The renowned anthropologist, Gregory Bateson (1958, 1972), conceived of another specific type of learning that he called **deutero-learning**.

Deutero-learning occurs through interaction: in interaction it is impossible not to communicate (Bateson, 1972; Watzlawick et al., 1967). Deutero-learning does not necessarily lead to organizational or individual improvement because adaptation may sometimes be pathological. Largely unconscious habits can be formed that act as if future contexts will exhibit the same patterns, in a self-validating and self-fulfilling prophecy (Bateson, 1958, 1963). It is this kind of deutero-learning that can characterize traditional planning approaches; the assumption is that the past will form the basis for the future.

> **Deutero-learning** is continuous, behavioural-communicative and largely unconscious learning that is a form of triple loop learning. It encompasses and transcends both single and double loop learning by focusing on transforming organizational members by helping them learn how to learn and when to recognize that learning is needed.

In their interactions with other persons and physical objects, individuals experience numerous reinforcing or punishing consequences. *Deutero-learning* implies that they learn about the context in which these consequences are formed, maintained, and altered. Through their repeated experience with contingencies of reinforcement, individuals learn to discern characteristic patterns of conditioning in the various relationships between themselves and someone or something else, and they learn to adapt their behavior in response to those patterns. (Visser, 2007: 660)

Deutero-learning that seeks to disrupt assumptions will be discontinuous, explicitly cognitive and conscious. Such learning, often referred to as meta-learning, will seek to steer and organize a specific direction of organizational and individual improvement. Such learning may be accompanied by processes of *planned learning* that creates and maintains organizational systems, routines, procedures and structures through which organizational members update their knowledge on a regular basis, in part by embedding the results of meta-learning for future application.

Emerging strategists not only foster learning in their organization. They also nurture, and where possible, manage, the culture of an organization. In fact, emerging strategies rely on organizational cultures in which curiosity and innovation are valued and practised.

Strategy and cultural processes

Edgar Schein (1997) defines **culture** as the deep, basic assumptions and beliefs that are shared by organizational members.

Culture is typically plural, often fragmentary and usually emergent around the irruption and condensation of specific issues, so it is usually the case that there is a plurality of organizational cultures in any one context.

> **Culture** represents the taken for granted ways an organization perceives its environment and itself.

The strategic importance of cultures resides in their pervasive impact on how organizational members make sense of opportunities and challenges, how they deal with problems, and how they discuss them. Schein differentiates between three levels of culture:

1. The first level represents the level of artefacts, including visible organizational features such as the physical structure of buildings, their architecture, uniforms, interior design and logos for instance. The playful Google logo that changes on important dates, the iconic architecture and design of the Googleplex, and the campus-like furniture that adorns its interior are good examples of artefacts. One could argue that they are of strategic importance as they help to create a relaxed and playful cultural context conducive to the encouragement of fruitful conversations and new ideas.

2. Schein's second level refers to expressed values. These represent the non-visible facets of cultures, as they express the norms and beliefs that employees express when they discuss organizational issues. Mission statements and espoused values, such as Google's *Don't Be Evil*, are examples in case. Obviously, this level is the strategist's preferred playground when she is working on the strategic mission, vision and values of the organization. Strategists work to create a privileged space around an organization's preferred statements of these to solidify and make them concrete.

3. The third level of culture is the most influential one. This is where the basic assumptions of the organization are hidden beneath artefacts and expressed values. In the language of Karl E. Weick, this level includes the cognitive maps that structure the way we interpret the world. Level 3 is where we store what we take for granted, and don't want to, can't or don't know how, to question. Without being explicitly expressed, this level shapes decision-making and behaviour implicitly. These deep structures of culture are the hardest to articulate and the most influential in practice.[1]

Emerging strategies depend on all three levels, especially the third one. From a cultural perspective, to manage strategy means understanding, and if possible, managing deeply held assumptions about the nature of the organization.

Given that culture is deeply rooted in an organization, the question is: can the strategist manage it to the advantage of the organization? Two McKinsey consultants, Peters and Waterman, wrote a definitive 'Yes' in answer to this question in their book *In Search of Excellence* (1982), which propelled culture to centre stage in corporate analysis. Their message was simple – great companies have excellent cultures. Excellent cultures deliver outstanding financial success. What makes a culture excellent is agreement around its core values and presuppositions and that these are widely shared and acted on.

With the publication of *In Search of Excellence* the idea of culture became seen as a master concept for organization analysis. Indeed, this book, along with one or two other not quite as influential, although still important books, including Deal and Kennedy (1982) and Schein (1997), are often seen as the innovations that made culture a popular and acceptable topic for consultants and managers alike, lifting it out of the relative business obscurity of anthropology, where it had previously been largely located.

---

[1]A good example of how values drive strategy can be drawn from classic literature, in George Orwell's (2003) book, *Homage to Catalonia*, where he describes the ways in which the deep assumptions of the various political factions in Barcelona during the Spanish Civil War drove their strategies (see especially Appendix II).

It was presumed that if you forged a strong culture – one that incorporates all organization members in shared beliefs and commitments – then everything else – good morale, performance and results – should follow strategically. In this view, the strategist's main task was to shape a strong culture that would align all organizational members. A flood of papers in strategic management resulted that argued for the link between strong culture and superior performance (e.g. Hall, 1993). Strong cultures, so the story went, offered the competitive advantage that makes organizations unique and successful.

Relatively early in the RBV debate, as we have seen in Chapter 3, Barney (1986) raised a question: 'Organizational culture: Can it be a source of sustained competitive advantage?' His answer was that firms whose culture displayed three distinct characteristics (being valuable, being rare and being imperfectly imitable) could achieve superior financial performance. However, Barney was less optimistic that management could engineer such a culture. With Socratic grace, he argued that only if the culture of a firm cannot be engineered could it be a source of truly sustainable competitive advantage. If it could be engineered, it would be easily imitable, and hence every organization would 'have' a superior culture. Of course, there would be no competitive advantage in such a scenario. Put simply, culture did matter but it was beyond the influence of strategists that were in search of excellence.

While Barney's critique followed the logic of the RBV view of strategy, the Stanford Professor Joanne Martin (2001) redefined the understanding of culture. In her seminal book on culture, she argued that culture might be more differentiated and fragmented than the functional perspective *à la* Peters and Waterman suggested. In their view, strong cultures are shared cultures – and what is not shared is not part of culture.

Deviations from the cultural ideal of a shared set of beliefs and values are seen as unfortunate, yet exceptional, shortcomings. Often, this approach results in culture being represented as the reflection of an organization elite's preferences as to what this shared set of beliefs and values should be. Such a shared understanding hardly comprises everyday organizational life, with its mundane routines and its vernacular senses of understanding that flourish in different folds of the organization over time – the everyday cultures of the organization. Note the plural once again: it is rarely the case that everyone will share the same understandings and sense of the organization and undesirable that they should because, as we have argued, there would be no impetus for innovation if everyone thought the same way!

Martin (2001) argued that homogeneity is problematic and that in reality organizations are more differentiated, on gender, divisional or national lines, for instance than the strategic culture theorists assumed. While these sorts of differentiation are relatively timeless and slow moving, she also suggests that culture may form in ways that are more transitory, a view she calls 'fragmentation'. According to the fragmentation view, culture is neither clearly consistent nor clearly contested. As issues arise, cultural focus emerges around them and dissolves as the issues recede in importance; new issues engender new cultural formations. Contradictory and confusing cultures battle for the soul of the organization. Individuals are likely to exist in a state where there are competing cultural scripts – where they are constantly under competing pressures to identify themselves and their organization with rival conceptions of what is an appropriate cultural identity. To make things more complicated, this does not mean that fragmented cultures replace one strong integrated culture. As Martin has argued, cultures always contain elements of integration, differentiation and fragmentation at the same time.

Where does this leave the strategist? While culture is a pivotal concept in the emergence strategy perspective, the means to manage it are limited. Culture does matter, but it is hard, if not impossible, to engineer. The critique of this perspective is similar to one that can be raised in relation to Mintzberg's writing: it leaves the eager strategist with little room for action and reduces her task to creating a framework in which a viable strategy might emerge. At least in an organization that has taken the cultures of excellence ideas on board, she can watch the spectacle from the comfort of some beanbags placed in the spaces for mingling and socializing that represent, and hopefully create, an informal learning culture.

Mintzberg and Pettigrew shift the axis of strategy theory away from economics and quantitative analyses towards more ethnographic and qualitative analysis. Each of them registers strategy as a future-oriented way of making sense of the world. Each stresses the role of everyday knowledge: Mintzberg regards the everyday life experiences of being a manager as essential to the task of learning from management theories; Pettigrew regards immersion in the cultures of management as essential for understanding how strategy emerges from local politics. Implicitly, each is stressing the importance of what has become known as 'sensemaking'.

Sensemaking

Many of the conceptions of strategy that we have encountered earlier in the book tend to be rather top-down. The strategy team use an approach such as competitive positioning or a resources-based view, for instance, to design a strategy. The strategy is then 'rolled out'. Ideally, middle management and the rest of the organization should fall in line with whatever changes are proposed in the new strategy. After all the strategy is the result of experts who know best, right?

Expert strategy might have its limits; there is no monopoly of wisdom contained in the sensemaking that occurs in the upper echelons of an organization. Indeed, the sensemaking that occurs, to the extent that it does not take account of the many diverse other ways of making sense in the organization, will more likely be resisted rather than rolled out. Such a view is implicit in both Pettigrew's and Mintzberg's approach to strategy. Both of them stress the centrality of power and politicking to implementation of strategy (see Chapter 11).

People make sense and they make it as they go about doing things. Their doings and their sensemaking are inexorably entangled up with each other. Overall, one function of strategy as an important discourse is to legitimate certain sorts of managerial actions, particularly planning and prediction, which is a mainstay of strategic concerns. Assumptions of rationality and planning act as a talisman, warding off the unexpected, the surprising and the eventful, through providing routine incantations with which to orient action. Such planning helps organizations and strategists to make sense, or as it is called in the literature, it enables them to accomplish sensemaking.

Much of what happens in organizations entails a constant process of sensemaking, especially when it comes to strategy. There are environmental cues to be registered, enacted and reacted to; streams of data and information to interpret; politics to untangle and negotiate; complex bodies of different knowledge to mediate.

Sense is always made in the moment, looking both backwards as well as projecting forwards. In terms of strategy the most significant element of sensemaking is that it should produce a plausible narrative, a storyline that key people can buy into. All strategic sense, as we have seen, is influenced by the social context.

Meanings that are held to be sensible tend to be those for which there is social support, consensual validation and shared relevance. If other people think that a particular interpretation is sensible, then you are more likely to do so as well. Given that disciplinary formation, gender and experience will pattern people's sensemaking, sensemaking differs with the identities of those doing the sensemaking. Different identities in organizations, in terms of regional, professional or divisional characteristics, for instance, will be important in forming different patterns of sensemaking.

Sensemaking concerns the elaboration of traces into full-blown stories, typically in ways that selectively shore up an initial hunch. An initial linkage between a particular experience and a category that is used to make sense of it is elaborated into a more confident diagnosis through successive rounds of selective search for confirming evidence. Strategists will use cognitive maps – their sketches of what's going on and who's who – in making sense, which they have derived from their past experiences; thus they project their pasts onto their futures. Sensemaking involves bracketing, framing, isolating cues, associating and creating new events and labels as it tries to provide an answer to the key question of what the strategic intent should be (Weick, 1995b, 2007).

The human mind interacts with its social and natural environment through communication, in which metaphors play a key role. Metaphors are the building blocks that frame the narratives we use to make such connections. Narratives are composed of metaphorical frames.

> Framing results from the sets of correspondences between roles organized in narratives, narratives structures in frames, simple frames combined in complex narratives, semantic fields (related words) in the language connected to conceptual frames, and the mapping of frames in the brain by the action of neural networks constructed on the basis of experience (evolutionary and personal, past and present). (Castells, 2009: 143)

Familiar metaphors help us in constructing socially available narrative frames that others can relate to; metaphors thus play a key role in strategy.

Managers' interpretations of external complex environments – their sensemaking – may amplify, rather than control, the potential for strategic uncertainty (Starbuck, 1993). Think of a football team with ageing but costly stars and a board that does not realize that the players who attract the crowds' loyalty and support are blocking the opportunities for team renewal in the future.

In a complex world of many cues it is often difficult to isolate what is significant and important; indeed, the status of events and stimuli often only becomes clear in retrospect – which is not much use for a prospective strategy! Much as might the archetypal reader of a thrilling suspense novel be insufficiently attentive to clues, managers may fail to attend to relevant cues and thus be caught out, figuratively losing the plot.

Every one of us is doing sensemaking all the time, using different schemas and experiential repertoires to make sense of what is going on around us. Strategists use different ways of sensemaking, such as SWOT or PESTEL analysis, the BCG matrix or competitive positioning. Unless these ways of making sense take into account the likely sensemaking that others in the organization and the market will make of the sense being made using them, it is probable that the processes of strategy implementation will be more than usually protracted and contested.

For Weick et al. (2005b: 409) 'sensemaking is an issue of language, talk and communication: situations, organizations, and environments are talked into existence'. Weick has used the notion of enactment to stress the fact 'in organizational life, people often produce part of the environment they face' (Weick, 1995b: 30). Organizational members organize themselves through working out the local stories in which they find themselves (Weick, 1979, 1995b). In many ways, especially as they are inducted, new members of organizations are characters in search of a frame with which to guide their perception and representation of reality. Actors adopt frames for making sense in the course of communicative processes (Weick, 1995b). In turn, their sensemaking becomes a 'springboard for action' (Taylor and Van Every, 1999).

Writers on sensemaking argue that there are no pure 'facts' – only interpretations of facts, and precisely these interpretations, these ways of making sense, form the basis for decisions and actions. For instance, Porac and his colleagues analysed the Scottish knitwear industry and found that notions of strategy and competition were constituted by individuals' attempts to make sense of their environment. In the words of Porac et al. (1995: 224), 'market structures are constraints only because managers believe they exist. Rather than being an exogenous force acting *on* managerial minds, market structure is an endogenous product *of* managerial minds.' What managers perceive as their markets is a matter of cognition – and not a given 'fact'.

Following Weick et al. (2005: 41), strategy emerges from *local* acts of sensemaking:

> Students of sensemaking understand that the order in organizational life comes just as much from the subtle, the small, the relational, the oral, the particular, and the momentary as it does from the conspicuous, the large, the substantive, the written, the general, and the sustained.

From Weick's perspective, strategy is as likely to emerge from the tacit and taken-for-granted assumptions that are shared by strategists as from the data they process, if only because the data has to be made meaningful. If there is a great deal of homogeneity between strategic actors, they are likely to make similar sense – when what might actually be required is a radically different interpretation – but there is no one to provide such an interpretation.

Sensemaking is an inherently *political* activity because interpretations, framing and the production of meaning are powerful forms of control (see Chapter 11). And finally, sensemaking is an *ongoing* accomplishment that is particularly important when contradicting or ambiguous events occur that question established routines (Weick, 1995b). Weick (1979: 188) says, '[o]rganizations formulate strategy after they implement it, not before. Having implemented something – anything – people can then look back over it and conclude that what they have implemented is a strategy.'

If we think of strategies as symbolic devices that are effective because their sense is shared, then strategy becomes more of a social organizing device than a tool to forecast the future. Karl Weick (1995a: 54) popularized the story of a map used by soldiers lost in the Swiss Alps to make the point:

> … I can best show what I think strategy is by describing an incident that happened during military manoeuvres in Switzerland. The young lieutenant of a small Hungarian detachment in the Alps sent a reconnaissance unit out into the icy wilderness. It began to snow immediately, snowed for two days, and the unit did not return. The lieutenant suffered, fearing that he had dispatched his own people to death. But the third day the unit came back. Where had they been? How had they made their way? Yes, they said, we considered ourselves lost and waited for the end. And then one of us found a map in his pocket. That calmed us down. We pitched camp, lasted out the snowstorm, and then with the map we discovered our bearings. And here we are. The lieutenant borrowed this remarkable map and had a good look at it. He discovered to his astonishment that it was not a map of the Alps but of the Pyrenees.

In this story, strategy is not a precise roadmap to the future – in fact, if soldiers followed the map in detail, they would have most certainly been lost on the mountains in ice and snow. The map had another, more important function: it gave people hope that their leader could deliver them out of a dangerous situation. Most importantly, it equipped the leader with faith in the situation.

Internally, strategies change reality not because they are implemented but because they are communicated. Planning implies an implicit theory of the organization, thinking of and picking out certain things as a central theme. Plans are maps that create the terrain they pretend to describe (Weick, 1979) – you cannot orientate yourself just through reading a map, because every attempt to understand the terrain through the map changes the sense of the map and the terrain (Clegg and Hardy, 1996). Through the creation of new maps an organization creates new terrain, new possibilities and new realities: far from being out there, waiting patiently to be discovered, 'reality' is the product of our mental constructions.

Generally speaking, managers act on the basis of the mental models that shape their mundane worldview of their work – what Edith Penrose had called an 'image' and 'productive opportunity' – that is the perceived interaction between the internal and external environments. These mental models influence what we believe is relevant, how we think of it, and how we act on it. Mental models can be imagined as 'cognitive maps' that enable organizational employees to orient themselves, decide where to go next, and discuss how to get there. Cognitive maps highlight, simplify and frame what strategists perceive as strategic issues, strategic problems or strategic solutions.

A major problem with much of the mainstream strategy literature is that it encourages cognitive maps that iron out the complex realities of process. Time is a major factor in making things complex because what we understand, what we have designed and what we have planned never stands still. Strategic management is always in motion. A constant interplay between looking backward and looking forward, framing and reframing, allows managers to test past experience under new circumstances (Cunha, 2004). Usually, there is a lack of time to conduct detailed analyses or to listen to everyone's perspectives. There is no guarantee that the general rules applied in the past remain valid now or for the future (Nonaka and Toyama, 2007). The balance between perception and imagination, framing and reframing, looking backward and looking forward, enables integrative approaches that increase the chance of achieving wiser outcomes.

People are not 'moved to act' on the basis of rationality only. Communicating a vision and moving others to action requires the ability to create emotional rapport. Building a shared vision requires working together towards a common purpose, engaging people in a process of alignment of their ethical models, detaching themselves from their personal goals, and balancing the interests of multiple stakeholders (Rowley and Gibbs, 2008).

Processes and wisdom

The tendency of most people, trained in the elimination of doubt and uncertainty, trained to be 'rational', is to discount dissonance in data, seeking for the least equivocal interpretation, drawing on the past to make sense of the present and project the future. Creating comfort with dissonance may reverse the tendency to make contradictions familiar by resorting to past practices and perceptions. As Weick (1993, 1995a) pointed out, wisdom is the attitude of respect towards that which is known *and that which is unknown*. It is not a skill or a bundle of information. Wisdom is simultaneously knowing and doubting. Meacham (1983) states that to know something is also to doubt it, claiming that since the more one knows the more one finds one does not know, learning and development necessarily evolve together.

Simplicity can be deceptive as the more we learn about a particular domain, the greater the complexity, the number of questions, uncertainties and doubts that such learning stimulates. 'Each bit of knowledge serves as the thesis from which additional questions or antithesis arise' (Meacham, 1983: 120).

Understanding why a situation is as it is entails that one sees 'beyond isolated facts, think beyond linear logic and appreciate the whole' (Bourantas, 2008: 5). It requires the ability to frame the concrete situation in 'the larger context (political-economical-social)' (Bourantas, 2008: 10). Since context influences not only how and what a problem is constituted to be but also its interpretation (Shotter and Tsoukas, 2014; Cunha et al., 2015), it is important to frame contradictions positively, to sometimes embrace paradox rather than try to resolve them in favour of one or other element.

Paradox is an essential tool for the strategist – not so much as something to be resolved but as something that can be used generatively. When paradoxes are evident the tendency is to opt for either/or solutions in an attempt to 'solve' the problem. If, by contrast, paradox serves to cultivate doubt, it stimulates the search for new alternatives and fosters new interpretations. It requires imagination to discover and evaluate new possibilities beyond what was experienced or previously known. Closing off paradox by sticking to the view that there must be a 'right' answer means a strategy or problem solution in such situations cannot address the conflicting needs and interests that make a situation paradoxical in the first place. Moreover, it probably means that the decision will be made in a degree of indifference or ignorance of the interests and needs being favoured and slighted. Process is essential to the emergence of paradox; making decisive decisions and sticking to plans, even as events unfold in unanticipated and unacknowledged ways, is not a good strategy but a recipe for rigidity and failure.

Strategy stories

We have argued that strategy is linked to sensemaking. Sensemaking happens through conversations. Hence, strategy emerges out of conversations amongst whatever range of stakeholders are engaged in the strategic conversation. Often these can be quite restricted conversations between like-minded experts, recruited and raised in the cultural homogeneity of the Top Management Team.

Strategic conversations do not always occur only amongst those that share the same worldviews, whose assumptions constrain and confine debate. In fact, where everyone is metaphorically 'on the same page' the least productive strategic conversations occur. It can be more interesting and innovative when they are not in agreement. Sometimes strategic conversations are heated, shouted, and accusatory or finger pointing, involving adversaries such as NGOs, community groups or local political actors. Strategy can emerge from the whole range of conversations; once sense is made out of the positions staked out strategy will be created, negotiated and discussed until the dominant group in an organization (normally management) agrees with its content.

Strategy can be analysed as a form of storytelling. Powerful stories are usually constructed in prestigious environments such as corporate HQ, banks and Treasury buildings. Other times the important conversations are more *sotto voce* and take place

Image 9.2   Powerful buildings (Photo by Stewart Clegg)

in discrete clubs and restaurants, amongst friends or at least people who share certain understandings, style and background, people who belong to the business elite, who often share similar social capital built through social networking on the boards of prestigious institutions, such as galleries, opera houses, cultural centres and charities.

Organizational storytelling

Storytelling approaches began with the work of Boje (1991, 1996), who developed the most widely known academic approach to studying stories in organizations.

Strategy guru, Dave Snowdon, writing in a blog called the *Cognitive Edge*, discusses improved decision-making and innovation being achieved throughout the organization through the effective management of human intuition and experience, augmented by the provision of information, processes and technology, together with training and mentoring programmes. He has become an advocate and consultant for the importance of storytelling in organizations.

Storytelling
Organization

The central premise of the storytelling approach is that the stories that circulate around organizations can perpetuate and create the very reality they seek to describe. It is fruitful to study organizations in and through their stories and narratives because, amongst other things, doing so sheds light on the knowledges that exist in an organization. As Barbara Czarniawska puts it: 'Stories capture

Image 9.3   Storytelling. Copyright: airdone

organizational life in a way that no compilation of facts ever can. This is because they are carriers of life itself, not just reports on it' (Czarniawska, 1997: 21).

**Whittle,
Mueller &
Mangan**

EXTEND YOUR KNOWLEDGE

Andrea Whittle, one of the authors of this book, together with Frank Mueller and Anita Mangan, discuss the role of stories in the temporal development of images of the self at work, in which they draw on an in-depth Case Study of technological change in a UK public–private partnership. They look at how stories position 'characters' in organizations, especially in stressful times of change. The paper is entitled **'Storytelling and "character": Victims, villains and heroes in a case of technological change'**. The journal article can be found on the companion website for this book: www.edge.sagepub.com/strategy2e.

Whittle, A., Mueller, F. and Mangan, A. (2009) 'Storytelling and "character": Victims, villains and heroes in a case of technological change', *Organization*, 16(3): 425–442.

It is often said that academic research has little impact on the real world. Storytelling approaches are definitely an exception.

**Ideal
Wordsmiths**

Go Online: Storytelling is now a business. If you visit www.idealwordsmiths.com and search for easyJet, for example, you will find a company, Ideal Worldsmiths, which produces 'storytelling' corporate histories, in this case for easyJet, as a client. A link to this site can be found on the companion website for this book: www.edge.sagepub.com/strategy2e.

In terms of widely known business cases, it was probably Orr's (1996) study of Xerox photocopy machine repairmen that best communicated the commercial significance of organization storytelling. He told a story about how new communication technology changed the way Xerox repairmen worked. It was no longer necessary for the repairmen to report to the depot each morning to pick up their jobs for the day. Not doing so, they lost the opportunity to spend time chatting, gossiping and generally hanging out with other repairmen. Under the new regime of work, productivity actually fell rather than improved. Why was this?

Detailed investigations revealed that in the coffee time in the depot the repairmen gave over a good deal of time to discussing how they dealt with particular problems: the reason being that the repair manual – while comprehensive – failed to take into account many of the local contingencies encountered by repairmen (such as climatic conditions, inclines on office floors, etc.). Much of the tacit knowledge – the knowing through doing – was shared through these morning coffee breaks. For our purposes, the central point to Orr's study is that knowledge is contained within stories.

IN PRACTICE

Knowledge Cafés

Image 9.4   Knowledge cafés. Copyright: funstock

Stories that work effectively are those that focus on learning and stress the lessons learned from sharing stories. One initiative that has gained traction is the idea of Knowledge Cafés: for instance, see the website maintained by one well-known exponent, David Gurteen – www.gurteen.co. The idea of Knowledge Cafés was behind the creation of a Café Society initiative in a major multinational pharmaceutical company. It was a series of linked websites

(Continued)

(Continued)

comprised of transcribed interviews with employees. A photo of the interviewee was super-imposed on the interview. The interviews opened up a chat-room that aimed to provide a space for debate and dialogue in an imaginative attempt to create a community of practice whereby new knowledge was created through dialogue and critique. Through stories, as they were shared, affordances occurred which vented ideas for radical innovation.

Questions

1. Think about how a Knowledge Café, real or virtual, might help your organization share knowledge.
2. What would be critical knowledge to share?
3. What makes this knowledge critical?

In an important paper entitled 'Strategy retold: Toward a narrative view of strategic discourse', David Barry and Michael Elmes (1997) suggested that a particularly good way to understand strategy is to see it in narrative terms, as a way of constructing a likely story about an organization. Barry and Elmes note the contemporary importance of strategy, suggesting that 'strategy must rank as one of the most prominent, influential, and costly stories told in organizations' (Barry and Elmes, 1997: 430). They analyse strategy as narratives or stories told in organization about the past, the present and the future.

Thinking of strategy as a series of likely stories sounds weirder than it is – think of the notion of 'blue' and 'red ocean' strategy (see Kim and Mauborgne, 2004); of course, no organization is sailing on two differently coloured oceans. Kim and Mauborgne use these coloured oceans as metaphors, encouraging us to assume that whatever lies hidden in the 'blue ocean' is advantageous for an organization, whereas 'red oceans' should be avoided. Through linking experiences and opportunities that we encounter in the world to coloured oceans (clearly a fiction) we automatically attach a negative or positive value to them. The colours red, denoting shark-filled waters devouring their prey, compared with empty blue oceans devoid of predators, make it easy to categorize things as 'good' or 'bad'. But they also shape our mental maps of the world and have an impact on what we consider to be possible actions. The metaphor gives rise to a new way of thinking about the future – a way of thinking that is deeply framed by the metaphor itself. Understanding strategy as narrative focuses on analysing how stakeholders create meaning and make sense of their environment.

IN PRACTICE

Strategic planning as storytelling at 3M

Gordon Shaw, executive director of planning at 3M, and his two co-authors (Shaw et al., 1998) argue that their company has abandoned the bullet-point report and the PowerPoint presentation, and replaced them with stories. According to them, stories not only clarify one's thinking, they also capture the imagination and create excitement within 3M. Bullet points, on the other hand, make us 'intellectually lazy', they argue. Here are the reasons why (of course, in bullet points!)

- Bullet points are too generic and refer to things that could apply to a whole range of projects or organizations. For instance, to say 'engage stakeholders' is important yet the bullet point does not reveal much about the how and why.

- Bullet points leave relationships unspecified: bullet points present the world as a sea of unconnected dots. According to Shaw and his colleagues, they allow only three generic relationships: hierarchy of what is important; sequence of what comes first, second, third, etc.; and defining an element as belonging to a group (e.g. within the European Union there are 28 countries: Austria, Belgium ...). Much as a Pointillist painting, bullet points break up the flow of experience into little apparently unrelated units. However, relationships are crucial and have a complex make-up that bullet points don't allow you to see.

- Bullet points leave important background and contextual information unmentioned: again, to say 'engage stakeholders' reveals little about historical connections, political issues and potential future hurdles in the collaboration.

To fight intellectual laziness, 3M encourages employees to tell strategic stories. Stories have a stage, characters, some sort of conflict or drama that has to be resolved, and some kind of end. This basic structure allows communicating complex messages in an emotional way that touches people's hearts and minds. A strategy that does that is the best pre-condition to motivate people and coordinate action.

Questions

1. What are the stories that best tell the strategy of your organization?
2. Why these stories and not others?
3. Why are they significant?
4. How are they reproduced and known?
5. Compare the stories of men and women in your class – do they differ at all in what they emphasize and if so, in what ways?

Stories as formal narratives

Porter's notion of competitive strategy is one narrative that has become manifest as a widely used idea in strategy texts. In this section we engage in an initial discussion of narrative, which we return to in Chapter 10, looking at it from a practice perspective. Competitive strategy has taken on a materiality and concreteness that makes it utterly apparent (Ezzamel and Willmott, 2008: 197). The idea of competitive strategy is something that has become taken for granted as something real, despite it being ideational, a device for thinking and strategizing.

Rose and Miller (1992: 175) emphasize how specific narratives connect rationalities with 'programmes, calculations, techniques, apparatuses, documents, and procedures' through which strategic ambitions are embodied and given effect. From the perspective of rationalities being connected to techniques the success of a strategy resides in its performative power. Simply put, how persuasive is the strategy for its intended audience? Does it resonate with their sympathies and interest? Does it meet their concerns as they express these as analysts, bankers, employees, customers, or is the strategy that has been laboriously constructed wasted by the indifference or hostility of key constituencies?

Analysing strategies as stories means analysing them as narratives with structuring powers: they frame, anticipate and cast realities. As such, strategy does not differ from other stories, such as autobiographies, biblical stories, novels or movies; they are all ways of making sense of the world, offering solutions to commonly experienced problems. They are scripts we can use to organize our lives. Often, as we have seen, these scripts of strategy are characterized by a high degree of rationalism constituting their deep assumptions.

Ezzamel and Willmott (2008: 192) suggest that the strategy debate has increasingly come to centre on whether literally 'objective' or 'subjective' approaches best capture the essence of strategic management. Mintzberg, together with other contributors such as Pettigrew (1987), shifted focus from the one perspective to the other: from rationalist objectivism to a search for emergent intersubjective interpretivism. Others interested in phenomena such as sensemaking, identity and narrative have taken up the interpretive approach enthusiastically. But is this enough? What is left out? What remains to be addressed?

Discourses as storying

From a discursive perspective, strategy, at its best, *constitutes* a world taken-for-granted. The world of the strategist becomes populated by the taken-for-granted materialities that strategists produce such as competitive environments, markets, segments positioning – all the matter we have covered thus far.

Building on the work of David Knights (Knights and Morgan, 1991; Knights, 1992), which draws heavily on the French historian of ideas, Michel Foucault, Ezzamel and Willmott seek to demonstrate that analysis needs to do more than merely contrast opposites assumed to really characterize strategy. Instead, one should look at how these opposing positions are made up. It doesn't matter, they suggest, whether a term such as 'competitive advantage' implies 'the effective control of some key variable(s) or … the views or meanings attributed to entrepreneurs and/or executives' (2008: 193).

We should see strategy terms as elements in what Wittgenstein (1968) referred to as an evolving language game. For instance, from a narrative or story perspective you might want to study 'competitive advantage' as part of an evolving 'language game through which strategy researchers and managers presently solve their problems' (Powell, 2001: 886). It is through specific discursive practices of strategizing (Knights and Morgan, 1991) that the objects that define a specific strategy are made up. Competitive advantage becomes a handy term with which to gloss corporate success or failure.

To adopt Foucault's (1972) perspective, we need to understand strategy as a practice that constructs its own objects of analysis and thus materializes them through its discourse. In other words, whether viewed through Porter or Mintzberg, strategy terms are talked into being. The stories of strategy that circulate locally in organizations are but instantiations of more overarching discourses. Different theories merely talk different emphases and terms into being as a result of the conventional arrangements relating power and knowledge in that discourse.

> Discourses are inscribed in power-knowledge relations where power is understood to operate through a plurality of relationships to form and institutionalize knowledge claims — claims, for example, about 'organization', 'strategy', 'knowledge' and 'power' ... reality is understood to be do-able and knowable only through the development of diverse, partial and ultimately *politically conditioned* discourses. Foucauldian analysis does not claim that the practices comprising the *social world* are reducible to discourse. Rather, *knowledge* of 'strategy' or 'experts' is understood to be constituted through discursive practices. (Ezzamel and Willmott, 2008: 193, 194)

The discourses of strategy are not imperfect representations of some external reality. Thought of this way we might be utterly confused about what the correct strategy is or what is the best approach to strategy, when there are so many options. Instead, we should think of them as differently staged performances, different ways of doing strategy.

The interpretivist focus on cognitive mapping in theorists such as Mintzberg predisposes analysts to construct cognitive maps that are recursively constituted by the theory itself. That strategists can produce cognitive maps is an effect of the theory that postulates them as possible artefacts. Once accepted as a viable way of seeing the world, these maps will always be found, as the frame of cognitive mapping organizes, politically, the construction of reality.

> There is no appreciation of how interpretivist analysis is inescapably constitutive of what it claims to capture or reflect ... in order to study a social object, such as 'strategy', as a discursive practice, it is necessary to proceed as if our knowledge of this object exists independently of the discourses that enable us to identify and explore it. (Ezzamel and Willmott, 2008: 197, 198)

EXTEND YOUR KNOWLEDGE

You can read Mahmoud Ezzamel and Hugh Willmott's 2008 journal article on '**Strategy as discourse in a global retailer: A supplement to rationalist and interpretive accounts**' on the companion website for this book: www.edge.sagepub.com/strategy2e.

Ezzamel, M. and Willmott, H. (2008) 'Strategy as discourse in a global retailer: A supplement to rationalist and interpretive accounts', *Organization Studies*, 29(2): 191–217.

Ezzamel &
Willmott

Summary

In this chapter we have introduced an emergent perspective on strategy making. Championed by Henry Mintzberg and other process theorists, this approach to strategy critically distances itself from the rational planning approach by arguing that strategy is an emergent phenomenon. Rather than trying to predict the future, the emergent approach depicts strategy as a contested and constantly evolving outcome of the interaction between formal plans and organizational sensemaking. The corollary of this insight is that strategy cannot be planned top-down but relies on bottom-up (emerging) processes that introduce new ideas and unexpected views into strategy. Key concepts that become pivotal to strategy making are organizational sensegiving, sensemaking, learning and culture as these aspects frame the capability to think and act reflexively.

The underlying hypothesis of much of the literature that we have addressed in this chapter is that cognitive maps frame the ways organizational members perceive themselves, their environments, and opportunities and threats they identify within it. These cognitive maps legitimate certain views while discrediting others. The task of the strategist is to shape the canvas on which an organization projects its cognitive maps; by doing so, the strategist has to reflect on self-perception, the taken-for-granted assumptions that are embedded in the organizational culture, fostering an appetite for learning and change. She has to accept that the future is unpredictable; hence, the goal is to create preparedness and agility that will enable the organization to adapt as changes unfold. And the role of researchers is to study how and in what ways she and her colleagues do strategy in practice – rather than normatively stipulating what it should be a priori. Strategy discourses depend on the ways that strategists make strategic sense, the devices they use, the decisions they make. In most organizations the key process in strategy is decision-making. Making decisions is not necessarily a matter of an either/or logic; closing off options stunts possibilities for future processes. Sometimes processes are paradoxical and have to be managed as such.

Engaging with paradox is an exercise in learning and unlearning, acting and reflecting, doubting and being confident, gaining comfort with contradiction, understanding and influencing. We discussed why and how managers and organizations might cultivate wisdom by exposing themselves to paradox, by synthesizing knowledge and ignorance. Engagement with paradox in the search for solutions that transcend habitual dichotomies offers a fertile ground to acquire knowledge and to gain awareness about the limits of the knowledge acquired. Engagement in strategy as a process is best circulated through stories. We considered stories in terms of their narratives and the discourses that constitute the terms that managers use to populate the stories.

TEST YOURSELF

Want to know more about this chapter? Review what you have learnt by visiting www.edge.sagepub.com/strategy2e.

- Test yourself with multiple choice questions
- Revise key terms with interactive flashcards

EXERCISES

1. Having read this chapter, you should be able to say in your own words what the following key terms mean:

   - Deliberate strategy
   - Emergent strategy
   - Process

   - Mintzberg's 5 Ps of strategy
   - Single loop learning
   - Double loop learning

- Deutero-learning
- Sensemaking
- Sensegiving
- Cognitive maps
- Organizational storytelling
- Strategy as narrative
- Strategy as discourse

2. Who are the most influential protagonists of the emergent view on strategy and how do their ideas differ from other strategy schools?

3. According to the *emergence* perspective, what are the means by which strategy can be influenced?

4. Why are strategy *processes* important?

5. How does *sensemaking* influence the way that strategy unfolds?

6. Why does strategy assume a *narrative* form?

7. How does a *discourse* of strategy differ from specific narratives of strategy?

CASE STUDY

HS2

REBECCA O'NEILL[2]

The recent publication of the government's strategic case for HS2 has added to mounting concerns about the strength and validity of evidence put forward to support the project.

Previously, the business case report written by KPMG stated that the high-speed rail link could benefit the UK by £15 billion a year – a claim made just days before a critical vote in parliament that secured further funding.

The KPMG report's authors have been accused of 'cherry-picking' the evidence to exclude any that did not support the project. It listed, for example, the areas that would benefit – such as Greater London by £2.8 billion and the West Midlands by £1.5 billion – but omitted details of those that would end up worse off. This was discovered in response to a Freedom of Information request.

A panel of academic experts subsequently told the Treasury select committee that the KMPG report overstated the HS2's regional economic benefits by six to eight times. Dan Graham, Professor of statistical modelling at Imperial College London, told the committee of MPs: 'I don't think the statistical work is reliable'. The findings were widely cited by the government, including in its new strategic case document, yet used a procedure that was 'essentially made-up", according Henry Overman, Professor of

(Continued)

---

[2]University of Birmingham, Inlogov

(Continued)

economic geography at LSE. It seems critics have every reason to be sceptical about the evidence being presented.

THE WIDER PICTURE

There are few relevant studies that can provide statistically significant evidence of cost performance in transport infrastructure projects. But one that does is by Flyvbjerg et al. (2003). The sample used is the largest of its kind, covering 258 projects in 20 nations worth approximately US$90 billion (at 1995 prices). The findings from the study were as shown in Figure 9.3 below.

Type of project	Number of cases (*n*)	Average cost of escalation (%)
Rail	58	44.7
Fixed links	33	33.8
Road	167	20.4
All projects	258	27.6

Figure 9.3

It shows rail projects incur the highest difference between estimated and actual costs, no less than 44.7% on average. Based on the available evidence it seems rail projects are particularly prone to cost escalation, followed by fixed links such as bridges and tunnels. Road projects seem to suffer this relatively less, although actual costs are still higher than forecast costs much more often than not.

Flyvbjerg and his colleagues then subdivided rail projects into high-speed rail (the study included HS1, the Channel Tunnel Rail Link), urban rail and conventional rail, finding that

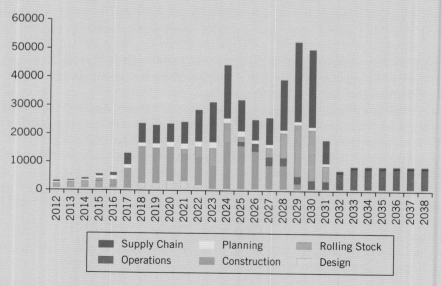

Figure 9.4   Full HS2 job projections

DfT, Strategic Case for HS2.

high-speed rail tops the list of cost escalation at on average 52%, followed by urban rail at 45% and conventional rail at 30%. According to Ricard Anguera's 2006 study, 'the British economy would have been better off had the tunnel never been constructed'. For all three project types, the evidence shows that it is sound advice for policy and decision-makers as well as investors, stakeholders, media and the public to take any estimate of construction costs with a pinch of salt, and especially for rail projects and fixed links.

Be wary of long-term estimates like these.

Cost escalation and benefit shortfalls

Cost performance has not improved over time. The tendency for costs to escalate today is the same as it was 10, 30 or 70 years ago. If our ability to estimate and forecast the costs of infrastructure projects has improved over time, this does not show in the data. In other words, no one seems to have learnt from past experience.

Is this due to the influence of pressure groups, which seem to have some influence over the decision-making process? For example, environmentalists' desire to safeguard the natural environment demands that roads or railways are buried in expensive tunnels, rather than above ground. The historical period that Flyvbjerg draws his data from goes back long enough to include projects from before pressure groups could wield influence over decision-making and costs. Then, as now, cost estimates were as inaccurate and cost escalation as large.

Costs shrunk or inflated to order

Another explanation is that cost underestimations and escalations are intentional. They are part of power games played by project promoters and consultants aimed at getting projects started. Cost underestimation is used strategically to make projects appear less expensive than they really are in order to gain approval from decision-makers. Such behaviour best explains why cost escalations are so consistent over time, space and project type, as Flyvbjerg and Martin Wachs have described extensively.

One of the reasons that the evidence is so easily contested is due to its nature. The data presented in the Strategic Case for HS2 is predominantly predictive. How are we to know in 20 years' time what the expected rail demand will be? Or how commuters will behave? The evidence is a forecast which leaves it open to much criticism and debate.

Those campaigning for the project need to accept that their data will be questioned and look at other ways to justify HS2. It is unlikely that someone whose home must be destroyed to make way for the new high-speed network is going to be sympathetic to evidence that suggests large cities will benefit by billions of pounds. Perhaps a new approach to justifying these large transport infrastructure projects is needed.

QUESTION

Evaluate the evidence for making a decision either to proceed or not proceed with the HS2 decision. What does the case tell us about the processes of strategic decision-making in light of the discussion in this chapter?

STRATEGY PRACTICE

ACTIVITY, DOING, STRATEGIZING

Learning objectives

By the end of this chapter you will be able to:

1   Explain the skills and practices that compose strategy

2   Appreciate how strategy is accomplished in practice

3   Understand the discursive effects strategy produces

4   Identify where and how and what ways strategy is conceived and practised

5   Review the strengths and weaknesses of Strategy as Practice as an approach

6   Understand the central role of business elites and business celebrity in strategy

BEFORE YOU GET STARTED

It takes a lot of work to make a strategy or design an organization. (Richard Whittington, 2003)

Introduction

Save for a few exceptions, increasing in frequency in recent times, the dominant strands within strategic management have been based on economic ideas, as earlier chapters have developed. The theoretical context provided by an economist's approach to strategy engenders a reality in which numbers, equations, models, abstract frameworks and macro-analysis of industry dynamics are dominant representations. What is left out of the economist's picture is the *work* of strategy – work done by the people whose task it is to produce strategy, the tools they use, the workshops in which strategic ideas are born, the language they deploy to make strategic sense of the world and to legitimate their views as strategic.

Research into *strategy* and *strategy practice* are different things (Grand et al., 2010). It is important to focus on strategy practice, how strategy is actually made up, because beneath the surface of a great strategy document or plan there is a considerable amount of hard work expended in gathering data, building support, taking different views into account, designing the strategy and polishing it to a form that invites support. In many ways, this is just the beginning: after all the preparatory work comes the hard slog of trying to enrol support for the strategy, translating others to the understanding of which accords with the strategists' sensegiving rather than adversarial sensemaking.

By engaging with practice, the strategy-as-practice approach strives to be both theoretically coherent and empirically useful. Theoretically, it seeks to explain how and in what ways the doing of strategy is rooted in practical reasoning. It seeks to do so through keen observation of strategy and strategists at work; empirically, the approach generates a portfolio of observations of what strategists actually do in practice.

We begin the chapter by noting that many orthodox approaches to strategy are formulated as practices, such as SWOT, the Five Forces or the BCG growth matrix. These practices produce devices with which to make sense of the organization and its opportunities. We then move, a little bit more theoretically, to reviewing three different conceptions of practice: as phenomenon, perspective and philosophy.

The essence of the practice approach is to study what strategists do when they are strategizing. To organize our discussion of this, we break the topic down into a number of more explicit questions: How is strategy conceived? How is strategy communicated? What are the skills needed to be able to do strategy. Building on the previous chapter, with its emphasis on stories and storytelling in its concluding pages, we ask what role narratives play in the practice of strategy. Mindful of our earlier comments about strategy tools such as SWOT we then ask what are typical tools that strategists use? Moreover, how do they bring these tools off; that is, how do they secure their legitimacy? A corollary of that question is to consider the toolmakers. In the case of strategy, these are overwhelmingly consultants (including academic consultants) – hence, we ask how consultants figure in strategy?

One form of strategy that leaders have recourse to is celebrity. Just as there is celebrity in politics and show business so there is in business. We consider celebrity CEOs and personal brand identity as strategy, looking at the rise of the celebrity CEO and of celebrity firms, such as Apple. Celebrity is a social construct and key channels of communication, in this case the business press, play a crucial role in the social construction of celebrity.

Strategy as practice

Knights and Morgan (1991) wrote an influential study that discussed strategy as a powerful device that creates those problems for which it offers itself as solution. As Knights and Morgan posit, strategy constitutes subject positions. The stories that it tells in its discourse delineate the manager as a strategic actor. Being strategic is a new form of subjectivity that stands in contrast to that of the bureaucrat, the planner and other much criticized embodiments of the 'organization man' (Whyte, 2013). Some authors (Knights and Morgan, 1991; Alvesson and Willmott, 1995; Ezzamel and Willmott, 2004; Grandy and Mills, 2004) see the practice of strategy as always in flux. In some respects what is conceived as a strategy depends on *who* makes *what* salience of specific issues. Strategy thus conceived is the outcome of whoever has the power to impose their version of reality and advance their interests over those of others. It is this that defines the strategic terrain: whether an issue is, for example, seen as one of investment or cost, skill formation or technological substitution, market entry or exit.

What is Practice?

Practice – what people do when working, when engaged in professional practice – mediates individual agency and social institutions.[1] Obviously, it is individuals who construct strategy; equally as obviously, they rely on institutionalized methods, data and approaches to do so. What individuals are able to do is made possible in and through the materials they use. Many elements enter into the material aspects of strategy work: the language in use in a given situation as well as the tools used, such as academic and consulting tools (Porterian analysis, hypothesis testing, etc.), artefacts such as PowerPoint (Kaplan, 2011), the framing role of visual artefacts such as 2 x 2 matrices (Jarzabkowski et al., 2013a) or orienting devices such as SWOT analysis, which urges us to define what we think of as strengths, weaknesses, opportunities and threats to the competitive performance of a firm.

SWOT is a pretty standard strategic practice. Mindtools have a figure that demonstrates SWOT quite clearly and we urge you to look at it. Thinking about the strengths, weaknesses, opportunities and threats to an organization is a way of

Mindtools
Website

---

[1]Practice theories first emerged in sociology with scholars such as Bourdieu (2002), Foucault (1979), Garfinkel (1967), Giddens (1984) and Turner (1994). A philosopher, Schatzki (2001: 2) has defined practices as 'embodied, materially mediated arrays of human activity centrally organized around shared practical understandings' (also see Schatzki, 2002). While it is not necessary for a student to have read these authors to grasp strategy as practice perspectives some material may be clearer if you have done so; see, for instance, Feldman and Orlikowski (2011) and Nicolini (2012).

Image 10.1   SWOT. Copyright: annatodica

categorizing the world it faces. In practice, asking questions such as the following, they suggest, aids strategic focus:

1. Strengths

    i. What do you do well?

    ii. What unique resources can you draw on?

    iii. What do others see as your strengths?

2. Weaknesses

    i. What could you improve?

    ii. Where do you have fewer resources than others?

    iii. What are others likely to see as weaknesses?

3. Opportunities

    i. What opportunities are open to you?

    ii. What trends could you take advantage of?

    iii. How can you turn your strengths into opportunities?

4. Threats

    i. What threats could harm you?

    ii. What is your competition doing?

    iii. What threats do your weaknesses expose you to?

A SWOT analysis is a device for categorizing the options open to an organization. Organizations use many specific categorization devices (Whittle et al., 2015), not only SWOT but also devices such as the BCG matrix.

The BGC Matrix

Image 10.2   Strategy meeting. Copyright: Yuri_Arcurs

Strategy-as-practice's concern is with in-depth analysis of what strategists do when they actually do strategy, the processes that produce strategy formulation, planning, implementation and so on. In this respect, strategy-as-practice research picks up on the earlier focus on process that once set the agenda for research but which largely disappeared beneath the quantity of contributions from scholars more oriented to economics.

Strategy as practice research offers different theories and methodological choices to the mainstream represented by more orthodox work. The new approach is clearly to be understood as a systematic critique of orthodox, hegemonic (mainly North American, or North American-inspired) strategy research with the objective being to 'break through the economics-based dominance over strategy research' (Jarzabkowski and Spee, 2009: 70).

Three ways of viewing practice

Orlikowski (2015) suggests seeing practice through three lenses:

1. *Practice as a phenomenon* – the notion that what is most important in organization research is understanding what happens 'in practice' as opposed to what is derived or expected from 'theory'

2. *Practice as a perspective* – a distinct way of looking at the world

3. *Practice as a philosophy* – seeing what we take for granted as social reality as something that depends on our habitual ways of seeing.

Practice as a Phenomenon

Studying practice as a phenomenon shows that the actual practices that create a strategy matter. We need to understand these empirically. We need to understand the messy, everyday realities of deadlines, late night sessions, away days and so on, which members of organizations experience in doing strategy. Jarzabkowski and Spee (2009: 70) have observed that there 'appears to be little room in mainstream strategy research for living beings whose emotions, motivations and actions shape strategy'. Politics and emotions surround the strategy process (Brundin and Melin, 2006). Emotions can either support or weaken strategic intents. They are gendered (talk of penetrating markets) and culturally and institutionally embedded, often in norms of warfare or manly competition. Strategy, they suggest, is similar to an elaborate dance in which the moves are part crafted and part improvised from the resources and skills that the players can contribute. The metaphor of the tango suggests itself: choreographed, spontaneous, emotional and formalistic all at the same time, something that takes practice and mastery to perform elegantly.

EXTEND YOUR KNOWLEDGE

The role of emotions in strategy is discussed by Quy Nguyen Huy in the 2012 journal article '**Emotions in strategic organization: Opportunities for impactful research**', where he explains how individual-level emotions can explain collective, organization-level outcomes, which represent the central interest of strategy research, that is, firm-level processes and performance. You can download the article from the book's website www.edge.sagepub.com/strategy2e.

Huy, Q.N. (2012) 'Emotions in strategic organization: Opportunities for impactful research', *Strategic Organization*, 10(2): 240–247.

Quy Nguyen Huy

Practice as a Perspective

How we understand a phenomenon depends on the lens or perspective that we adopt. Practice as a perspective entails examining what strategists do when they do strategy and how it is both shaped by and shapes organizational conditions and consequences. The specifics of emergent and contingent aspects of everyday activity, its embodiment, embraining and organizing, as well as its material mediation and embeddedness are considered important. A practice perspective shifts attention to the mundane, the routine everyday experiential world. The role of material things – devices, tools and techniques – is regarded as particularly important. Material elements of strategy include things such as SWOT analysis, the Porter Five Forces, and so on. Practices such as these shape the realities that are experienced as objects of strategy. Strategy represents neither a neutral tool nor a mere technique; rather, strategy in practice constructs that which is its object through means of accounting for, normalizing and representing phenomena as objects of strategy.

Practice as a Philosophy

A practice philosophy, as Tsoukas (1998: 792, emphasis in original) notes, is one in which 'the models through which we view the world are not mere mirrors upon which the world is passively reflected but, in an important sense, our models also help *constitute* the world we experience'. The methods of strategy are productive of that to which they then attend. They do not correspond to a pre-existing reality; instead, they constitute a reality. Rather than a camera capturing what is already there in frame, strategies may be more accurately likened to a generator: they produce the energy of the organization, oriented to the goals of strategy, producing its drive and direction.

Behind the idea of a practice philosophy is the idea that 'social science is performative. It *produces* realities' (Law and Urry, 2004: 395, emphasis in original). Strategy, from this perspective, is a combination of social practices and the material devices that enable these. The conjunction of social practices and material devices is referred to as socio-materiality. Socio-materiality is made up by the practices that involve particular subjects, skills, situations, devices, interactions, texts and so on.

Strategic Organization Special Collection

EXTEND YOUR KNOWLEDGE

There is a special collection of papers published in the journal, *Strategic Organization*, as a *Virtual Special Issue: SO! Strategy Process and Practice Collection*, which is well worth browsing to extend your knowledge of the strategy-as-practice approach. The collection includes a contribution from Chris Carter, Stewart Clegg and Martin Kornberger (2007) called '**Strategy as practice?**' This paper sparked a debate; for the response see P. Jarzabkowski and R. Whittington's 2008 paper '**Hard to disagree, mostly**'; and for the rejoinder read C. Carter, S. Clegg and M. Kornberger's 2007 article '**S-A-P zapping the field**', all of which you can find on the companion website for this book: www.edge.sagepub.com/strategy2e.

Carter, C., Clegg, S. and Kornberger, M. (2007) 'Strategy as practice?' *Strategic Organization*, 6(1): 83–100.

Jarzabkowski, P. and Whittington, R. (2008) 'Hard to disagree, mostly', *Strategic Organization*, 6(1): 101–106.

Carter, C., Clegg, S. and Kornberger, M. (2007) 'S-A-P zapping the field', *Strategic Organization*, 6(1): 107–112.

What do strategists do?

Recent years have seen an increasing interest in the strategy as practice perspective (e.g. Whittington, 1993, 2003; Johnson et al., 2003; Jarzabkowski, 2005) focused on the microanalysis of strategy. Often the approach taken is discursive, capturing strategy as it is talked into practice, an approach that builds on the seminal article by Knights and Morgan (1991: 252; also see Knights and Morgan, 1996; Vaara, 2002; Laine and Vaara, 2007). The focus is on strategizing – the active process of making and enacting strategy. The importance of attending to the structures and contexts through which the processes of enacting strategy – strategizing – are accomplished (Jarzabkowski, 2003, 2004, 2005; Balogun and Johnson, 2004, 2005; Mantere, 2005) is stressed.

Reacting against the often-prescriptive nature of much of the strategy field, this approach seeks to investigate strategy and strategists anthropologically and sociologically, through an ethnographic enquiry into what strategists doing strategy actually do. The focus of this perspective is on cultural contexts, discursive habits and the ways in which managers construct networks of action that lace strategies and practices together. It seeks to follow the actors, study their texts and capture their discourse, so as to observe how strategy is made up and describe what strategists do.

Go Online: Strategy as practice is so popular that it even has its own dedicated website – 'Strategy as Practice International Network'. You can find a link to the site on the companion website for this book: www.edge.sagepub.com/strategy2e.

Strategy as
Practice

At the core of the strategy as practice perspective is the premise that strategy analysis has to take social practices 'seriously' (Vaara and Whittington, 2012). It assumes that strategy work 'relies on organizational and other practices that significantly affect both the process and the outcome of resulting strategies' (Vaara and Whittington, 2012: 2). Using such an approach, Vaara and his colleagues (2010) analyse how strategy discourse shaped the city administration of Lahti, Finland. They argue that strategy documents serve several purposes:

> they communicate negotiated meanings, legitimate ways of thinking and action and de-legitimate others, produce consent but may also trigger resistance, and have all kinds of political and ideological effects, some more apparent than others. (Vaara et al., 2010: 686)

Likewise, Eriksson and Lehtimäki (2001: 202) suggest understanding

> strategy rhetoric as a cultural product on which the strategy-makers draw, because the rhetoric is regarded as effective and convincing [… it] is taken as self-evident and legitimate, and is used without questioning the presumptions on which it is built.

In sum, these and related discourse studies scrutinize strategy's rhetoric and how it legitimizes decisions and justifies actions. As a linguistic genre (see Pälli et al., 2009) strategy becomes institutionalized through textbooks, research programmes, consultancies, etc. In other words, what is taken to be strategy is a 'convention' (Boltanski and Thevénot, 1991); hence, it is powerful because it has become taken-for-granted as a way of framing the world in which we live.

It is not only discourse that makes strategy a powerful force; inextricably intertwined with it are practices, routines and rituals that perform strategy. In a study of strategy making in the City of Sydney Kornberger and Clegg (2011) illustrated how the seemingly mundane practices of strategizing constitute the space, time, objects and subjects of strategy. For instance, through minute organization of interaction with external

Image 10.3   Sydney skyline. Copyright: Leonardo Patrizi

stakeholders, the strategists attempted to 'lift stakeholders' thinking', which resulted in a depoliticized discourse recast as focused on the 'big picture', a literal projection of the future that bracketed interests and concerns expressed in the here and now.

Strategy as practice, in questions and answers

According to Whittington (2004) the key innovation of the strategy-as-practice framework is to treat strategy as an important social practice – as something that organization members do – that requires serious analysis. Strategy is depicted as an activity; 'strategy' is not only an attribute of firms but also an activity undertaken by people. To cover the literature on strategy as practice we have organized it according to a series of important questions that it addresses. We shall start by asking, how is strategy conceived?

How is Strategy Conceived?

Strategy is a process whereby immediate, particular practical concerns are bracketed and relatively abstract organizational properties focused on, in order to try and produce a strategy that is sustainably differentiating. The top management in an organization is expected to *lead* strategy and they do so precisely through the use of such devices as rhetoric, representational techniques, models and other devices, emotions and meetings.

One way of thinking about how strategy is conceived and practised is to concentrate on its performative elements. Strategy as practice offers a distinct perspective on how a frame is constituted in which specific problems and solutions can be identified. Strategizing means developing a (usually big) picture of the future that will frame immediate courses of action. In this sense, strategy turns time around: the future desired becomes the condition for the possibility of action in the present. Hence strategy, in terms of strategizing, is a performative practice. The concept of performativity directs our attention to the circumstance that strategizing is an activity that does something. Strategy's performative effects result from the forms of discursive structure and rationality that strategists draw upon as a resource to justify and legitimize their practice. Flyvbjerg (1998) demonstrated how, in the context of urban planning in the Danish city of Aalborg, the different agencies and authorities involved in the planning arena sought to rationalize their particular versions of rationality as the strategy to be followed. He analysed strategic situations in which power was exercised through the collective rationality deployed by different groups of people with common vested interests. Those who were in positions of dominance in the arena paid least heed to the rationality of their arguments and were less inclined to rationalize their positions and more to advance them as if they were just common sense. Many instances of this phenomenon can be seen in everyday life: for instance, the rationality of an economic argument (e.g. 'a strong economy will offer opportunities for everyone, especially those who are socially disenfranchised now, hence economic growth is the solution for social ills') that encapsulates the interest of certain groups and frames reality in a particular way by identifying causes and effects, hence constituting specific power relations.

EXTEND YOUR KNOWLEDGE

Martin Kornberger and Stewart Clegg wrote a paper about the performativity approach that you have just read about in the previous paragraph, connecting it to the strategy-as-practice perspective. The paper is called '**Strategy as performative practice: The case study of Sydney 2030**'. One of the things that is interesting about the paper is the way it shows that strategy discourses have spread from the commercial sphere to applications such as developing strategies for cities. In a related vein we have also made a paper available online by Earo Vaara, Virpi Sorsa and Pekka Pälli (2010) '**On the force potential of strategy texts: A critical discourse analysis of a strategic plan and its power effects in a city organization**', which also addresses strategy in the city. In doing so they identify distinctive discursive features of the strategy genre that have important implications for the textual agency of strategic plans, their performative effects, impact on power relations and ideological implications. These journal articles can both be found on the companion website for this book at www.edge.sagepub.com/strategy2e.

Kornberger, M. and Clegg, S. R. (2011) 'Strategy as performative practice: The case study of Sydney 2030', *Strategic Organization*, 9: 136–162.

Vaara, E., Sorsa, V. and Pälli, P. (2010) 'On the force potential of strategy texts: A critical discourse analysis of a strategic plan and its power effects in a city organization', *Organization*, 17(6): 685–702.

Kornberger & Clegg / Vaara et al

How is Strategy Communicated?

Samra-Fredericks (2005) identifies four central characteristics for strategists to communicate on public occasions:

1. A concern with *truth*, considered in a factual way

2. An ability to convince an audience of the *correctness* of what is said

3. An ability to expresses the *sincerity* of the claims made

4. An ability to make the claims *intelligible*.

The pragmatic validity claims of *truth*, *correctness* and *sincerity* are normal and constitutive features of almost all interaction settings in which we take for granted that the other is committed to these protocols. *Intelligibility* is different: while claims regarding truth, correctness and sincerity draw on quite generic social skills, intelligibility in strategy terms is quite specific:

1. Intelligibility draws on an ability to speak managerially and strategically.

2. Intelligibility requires mastery in the doing of strategy. It entails being able to speak fluently using terms that are recognizably 'strategic'.

3. The trick is to bring off strategy talk as an argument made in the *organization's* interests.

Making a performance intelligible entails not only use of appropriate strategy categories but also subtle positioning of dominant and subordinate speakers through the use of pronouns. Strategy talk positions the speaker as 'I' in relation to others who are 'you', 'us', 'we' and 'they'. Intelligibility also requires a gendered performance. A successful strategist is confident, assertive, a little emphatic and perhaps even aggressive. Emotions are registered and displayed in the appropriate keys of deference and domination, aggression and appeasement, depending on the status ordering of speakers and hearers.

Certain terms have a rhetorical and representational role in positioning intelligibility and these are learnt, largely, in Business Schools and especially in MBAs. Hence, intelligibility entails learning a facility with strategy as it is taught in Business Schools. Strategy has become the Esperanto of the Business Schools (Vaara and Faÿ, 2012). In practice, technically specific vocabularies intersect with authority relations. One instance would be when a CEO stresses those scenarios regarded as viable (Hodgkinson and Wright, 2002) s/he frames *what is acceptable* from the range of *what is possible*.

What are the Skills Needed to be Able to do Strategy?

The most basic ability required is the capacity to maintain a strategic conversation, steering it, retaining its detail in memory and developing its shape and thrust. Samra-Fredericks (2003) analysed the interactions of strategists and found how their linguistic skills construct strategic realities, including a shared definition of the future. She starts from the observation of Barry and Elmes (1997: 430) that what is needed is a study of how language is used by strategists to establish meanings and create a 'discourse of direction'. As Samra-Fredricks states, much strategy work is accomplished through talk. Samra-Fredericks builds a new direction for strategy research that analyses how strategizing is accomplished during 'real-time' talk-based interaction:

> [I]t is through talking that strategists negotiate over and establish meanings, express cognition, articulate their perceptions of the environment (etc.) and from this basis, legitimate their individual and collective judgements. Even knowledge, know-how and expertise must be expressed in some way and thus, 'made to count'. As Tsoukas (1996, p. 23) also suggests, knowledge such as 'industry recipes' (Spender, 1989) are 'embedded in conversations and social interactions'. It is through speaking these forms of knowledge, the competitive landscape and possibilities for one's own organization are made sense of and realized. Similarly, physical entities such as written reports and flip-chart 'musings' are always talked about and in this way, strategists *breathe life* into

them and make them meaningful for their present purposes. Given this, studies of strategists' naturally occurring talk-based routines are important for understanding how they develop strategic direction and project a viable sense of the 'organization' into the future. (Samra-Fredericks, 2003: 143)

Analysing naturally occurring conversations, she demonstrates the ways in which the opening remarks of one strategist set the scene for what subsequently unfolded. Skilled talk sets the scene.[2]

Strategy talk seeks to create 'objective facts': *this is the competitive threat; these are the strategic opportunities; these are the desired innovations*. Words and images create a strategic world that those privy to the strategic conversations need to understand, using legitimate categories and social constructions. The strategist's role is to introduce these terms and pitch them convincingly. Attending to subtle flows of interaction enables us to see how convincingly they are able to do this.

Samra-Fredericks (2003) identifies six factors defining interpersonal competence in strategy. These are the ability to:

1. *Speak forms of knowledge* – to draw on a tacit competence in using locally and situationally meaningful and typical categories to construct a compelling story of the organization.

2. *Mitigate and observe the protocols of human interaction* (respecting and observing the moral order). This involves achieving political positioning of preferred analyses and doing so while respecting the 'face' of significant others. The skilled use of pronouns that collect or divide – 'we', 'us', the 'organization', the 'team' as opposed to 'them', the 'competition', people who are not 'team players', etc., is particularly important.

3. *Questioning and querying*: skilled strategists are able to construct what is 'reasonableness' in such a way as to simultaneously curb possibilities for counter moves by others (because they would be outside the bounds of being reasonable), often leaving these others wondering how they have been out-manoeuvred.

4. *Displaying appropriate emotion*: strategizing is often emotional work, as signs of frustration, enthusiasm and energy are communicated in words and gestures, looks and embodiment.

5. *Deploying metaphors*: the use of appropriate and gripping metaphors, metaphors that subsequently frame discussion, is a vital skill of the successful strategist.

6. *Putting history 'to work'*: being able to weave past, present and future together from discursively available characterizations, plot lines and themes, and to be able to do this improvisationally, in action, in talk.

---

[2]The analysis of naturally occurring conversations marks off Samra-Frederick's work, in general, from that of other researchers who rely on more conventional interview data and who often elide the substantive display of strategic competencies in situated actions, preferring instead more abstracted and generalized reports, such as one finds in Hardy et al. (2000) and Vaara (2002). Against these less field-based and interpretive accounts she uses ideas from Garfinkel (1967) and conversation analysis (Sacks and Jefferson, 1992) to undertake systematic fine-grained analysis of strategists' linguistic skills and forms of knowledge in practice.

In addition, the art of knowing *when* to do this (the 'right time') is also vital. Above all, the skills required are politically, culturally, and situationally relevant – they work to make and constrain sense in specific strategic situations. They demonstrate you are able to do serious and respectable strategy talk in specific settings.

Maitlis and Lawrence conducted one study that is interestingly non-conventional (2003). They studied the attempt of a British symphony orchestra to develop a strategy. For some members of the organization the strategy was not sufficiently commercial; for others the problem was that it created 'incoherent artistic product' while for the musicians 'the artistic strategy had neither coherence nor commercial viability' (Maitlis and Lawrence, 2003: 125). The strategic issue to be addressed differed with the insight of who was addressing and framing the issue.

What Tools do Strategists Use?

How language is used frames issues (Mantere, 2013). Strategists do not just talk, however. Heracleous and Jacobs (2008) discuss the role of material artifacts in change interventions that are used in order to stimulate particular sensemaking processes. Videos, dramas or staged performances by senior strategists can be used in this way. Carlsen and colleagues (2012) discuss activities such as drama, model building and prototyping in strategy. Whittington et al. (2006) discuss physical objects as particular means of communication.

How events, actors and materials are mobilized and rhetorically brought 'into' the organization is important (Sillince and Jarzabkowski, 2012), as is the way in which relevant meetings are conducted (Hodgkinson and Wright, 2002), how objects and artifacts (e.g. PowerPoint presentations, flip charts, etc.) are used (Kaplan, 2011), how emotions are handled (Huy, 2012), and what forms of knowledge are mobilized.

Kaplan (2011) poses the question, 'How is PowerPoint engaged in the discursive practices that make up the epistemic culture of strategy making?' Her answer is that PowerPoint is a privileged strategy-making support tool that may usefully be analysed as a genre. Why something seemingly as mundane as PowerPoint might matter for strategy making, is suggested in this key passage in the paper:

> [T]he affordances of PowerPoint enabled the difficult task of collaborating to negotiate meaning in a highly uncertain environment, creating a space for discussion, making combinations and recombinations possible, allowing for rapid adjustments as ideas evolved and providing access to a wide range of actors, no matter how dispersed over space or time. Yet, I found, these affordances also supported cartographic efforts to draw boundaries around the scope of a strategy, certifying certain ideas and not others, and allowing document owners to include or exclude certain slides or participants and control access to information. Cartography in the world of ideas is similar to cartography of the physical landscape: drawing maps and defining boundaries help people navigate otherwise uncertain terrain. These collaborative and cartographic practices shaped the strategic choices and actions taken in the organization. (Kaplan, 2011: 320)

Kaplan (2011: 320) conceptualizes strategy making as a practical knowledge production process. Its practices are both discursively and materially mediated. The material mediation afforded by PowerPoint is highly significant. In the process of strategy formulation, it can make strategic ideas that are not yet real appear as real (Stark and Paravel, 2008), making abstract knowledge *material*. However, because PowerPoint documents and presentations are incomplete realizations of the proposed strategies, they are also *mutable* (Geisler, 2001). Users can change the documents and the ideas represented within them because the slide system is *modular* – elements can be easily moved or removed; ideas can travel easily, because PowerPoint as a medium is *digital*. PowerPoint's role in strategy making enables the assembly, interpretation, representation, and sharing of information; it facilitates communication and collaboration – albeit in terms of the logic embedded and expressed in the linear flow of the presentation. The latter aspect is what Kaplan (2011) refers to as the *cartographic* element of PowerPoint. By designing a strategy into PowerPoint and presenting it to gatherings of significant members of the organization attention is seized and focused on those elements displayed. Legitimacy is subtly created for the favoured strategy; what is not included cannot easily enter into a strategic conversation that centres on the graphical presentation. Information can be selectively included and excluded; different members of the organization can be selectively included and excluded from different briefing. The strategy team can choreograph cartography and collaborative inclusion in an example of subtle power at work:

> Its use enables actors to sort through and decipher complex and conflicting information, but in doing so, these actors might simplify the data beyond usefulness or shape the information to suit a personal agenda. Some individuals' voices might be excluded, whereas others' might be amplified. (Kaplan, 2011: 344)

Seidl (2007) and Jarzabkowski and Wilson (2006) also study the ways in which tools and techniques are used differently in different contexts. Such strategy tools function as potential 'boundary objects' that relate different organizational contexts (Spee and Jarzabkowski, 2009). A boundary object is something that allows communication across the boundaries of organizations, between different divisions, disciplines and departments.

Some strategy making is a highly abstract and abstracted process, often done in secret strategy sessions, thus limiting participation in its formation (Mantere and Vaara, 2008). By contrast, some strategy-making processes occur through meetings that promote self-actualization, dialogue and concreteness, enabling greater participation (Jarzabkowski and Seidl, 2008). Often secrecy attends the earliest stages of strategy formation by elites while the public pronouncement follows much later when the contours of the strategy have been shaped. It is at this stage that the meeting becomes a key tool of strategy: in meetings, strategies can be unveiled, resistance sniffed out, support garnered or opposition incubate.

EXTEND YOUR KNOWLEDGE

In P. Jarzabkowski and D. Seidl's 2008 paper '**The role of meetings in the social practice of strategy**', you will find an analysis of how strategy meetings either stabilize existing strategic orientations or propose variations that cumulatively generate change in these. The journal article can be found on the book's website at www.sagepub.co.uk/strategy2e.

Jarzabkowski & Seidl

Jarzabkowski, P. and Seidl, D. (2008) 'The role of meetings in the social practice of strategy', *Organization Studies*, 29(11): 1391–1426.

Spee and Jarzabkowski (2009) suggest that strategic tools such as SWOT analysis or scenario planning work in practice both instrumentally, as means to a desired end, as well as symbolically. Such tools are useful for Top Management Team strategy discussions, for example during workshops (Hodgkinson et al., 2006). They provide a common language with which to have a strategy conversation (Barry and Elmes, 1997; van der Heijden, 2005). Tools enable politics to be played by other means, by hampering shared meaning, particularly across hierarchical levels, by structuring and shaping information (Grant, 2003) and legitimating powerful interests (Hill and Westbrook, 1997). The tools and devices used in strategy are many, as we have seen in earlier chapters. Routines are also important, such as strategy meetings, away-days, corporate dinners, annual planning cycles and other events that recur with cyclical frequency and become key occasions for the public display of these tools.

How is Strategy Legitimated?

In strategy making you struggle for legitimacy by connecting action with structures of social meaning (Vaara and Whittington, 2012). Practices such as the bracketing of issues, turn-taking protocols, voting and stage-managing can be used to legitimate or delegitimate strategies and contributions. Hardy and Thomas (2014) show how strategy discourses construct objects and subjects while Spee and Jarzabkowski (2011) and Vaara et al. (2010) focus on strategic plans.

In highly professionalized organizations, such as hospitals and universities, disciplines are deeply institutionalized, leading to highly specialist language in use; in less professionalized organizations, disciplinary formations will be more locally constructed and much less institutionalized. Where there is deep institutionalization, professional practice is a source of legitimation. In less professionalized contexts, more locally based and less cosmopolitan approaches to strategy may succeed.

> The idea of **institutional logic** is quite simple. Organizations are arenas in which there are many different kinds of members and stakeholders. People draw on well-regarded ideas from professional experts, consultants and so on to try and make their sense of the situations they are in. Highly legitimated sensemaking forms an institutional logic.

Strategy is related to institutional logics, especially in highly professionalized contexts. **Institutional logics** provide discursive props for legitimating strategy. When you use Porter's Five Forces to plot a strategy you are drawing on the legitimacy that Porter's approach has as a widely institutionalized way of understanding strategy.

Most empirical settings are riven with different institutional logics with 'jurisdictional overlap' of competing logics (Thornton et al., 2012: 57). You draw on engineering logics; she draws on design; he draws on finance. Normally, in for-profit organizations, these logics can be reduced to the 'bottom line' and the most profitable will usually win the day. For an organization oriented to making a return on investment as a profit for owners of capital the institutional logic is quite clear: it is to do everything to try and make a profit and not a loss. Formulating a strategy with a simple narrative and consistent direction is relatively easy if this is the clear and consistent goal.

Things can be more complicated elsewhere. Think of complex organizations that are not readily reducible to a more easily managed bottom line, such as hospitals (Denis et al., 2001; Reay and Hinings, 2009), universities (Townley, 1997; Sauermann and Stephan, 2013), or social enterprises (Battilana and Dorado, 2010; Tracey et al., 2011; Jay, 2013; Pache and Santos, 2013). Managing a firm is so much easier than managing a not-for-profit organization – in a firm there is always a 'bottom line'; in a hospital the 'bottom line' probably means some people will die, some illnesses will not be treated because the patient is too old, the drugs are too expensive, other patients have more pressing problems, and so on. Some patients will be less valuable than others, especially in for-profit hospitals.

In complex not-for-profit organizations strategy formulation has to contend with 'constellations' of two or more competing logics (Goodrick and Reay, 2011). Different institutional logics represent different ways of formulating the rules of the game. In these cases, strategy making becomes a much more political process. There are far more professionalized interests to reconcile; there are customers whose diffuse preferences cannot easily be quantified at a price point. Indeed, even thinking of sick people in hospitals as customers rather than as patients seems wrong. Dealing with interests as diffuse and difficult to quantify as life, health and wellbeing or with learning and research is a bit more complicated than selling groceries, as Offe and Wiesenthal (1985) make clear.

Logics define the identities of those who hold strongly to them. They matter in everyday life and practice (Lounsbury, 2007; Zietsma and Lawrence, 2010; Smets et al., 2012; Lounsbury and Boxenbaum, 2013; McPherson and Sauder, 2013). As Thornton (2004: 69) suggests, different logics are expressed through the ways in which 'practices, assumptions, values, beliefs and rules' are enacted and staged as legitimate ways of being and doing. In pluralistic settings competing demands from upholders and embodiments of different logics, embodied in identities such as Doctors or Administrators, Professors or Students, Fundraisers or Activists, need to be managed or accommodated (Denis et al., 2007; Chia and Holt, 2009; Jarzabkowski et al., 2009, 2013b; Zilber, 2011).

It is not only that there are conflicts between professionals of various stripes: practitioners increasingly work at the interface of different institutional logics. Such situations can be the source of strategic creativity, innovation, 'institutional entrepreneurship' where practices or concepts from one field are brought into another.

How is Strategy Narrated?

From the 1990s onwards, a steadily growing body of literature focused on the practices of strategy narration, using discourse analysis to dissect its power effect. For instance, Oakes and colleagues (1998) studied business plans as pedagogic devices that, through their language, formatted how organizations are imagined, what their key properties are, and how they should be managed. In the words of the authors, the 'power of business plans lies in their monopoly of legitimate naming' (Oakes et al., 1998: 273). Plans, and by extension, strategies, categorize actions and by doing so, legitimate them. Strategy exercises what Bourdieu (1977) labelled symbolic power.

Barry and Elmes (1997), as we have seen in Chapter 9, emphasized the fictive nature of strategic narratives as well as the 'multiple realities' constructed through narration. Other authors have made related analyses. Hardy et al. (2000) illustrate the strategy process through analysis of the ways in which those who are strategizing use discursive resources involving circuits of activity, performativity and connectivity. In this way they analyse the micro-processes through which specific strategy statements gain acceptance or not.

Narrative framing is important for the practice of strategy. Fenton and Langley (2011), Brown and Thompson (2013), and Vaara and Pedersen (2014) stress the role of narratives and storytelling. However, it is Nancy Duarte who shows how stories that succeed in stirring up strong emotions of possibility with their listeners are effective. She shows how both Martin Luther King Jr. and Steve Jobs used a similar storytelling format, one that contrasted the status quo (or 'What is') with the future as they envisaged it ('What could be'). Throughout their stories, they used rhythm and repetition to stress the huge gap between the two ideas, using poetics and emotional descriptions of a new world that will be thriving, living in the lofty new idea of 'What could be'. Both King and Jobs use the narrative structure described by Campbell (1988) as the hero's journey, in which the hero battles against adversity, is cast into darkness and despair, and finally overcomes – albeit, in practice, dying tragically.

Storytelling

Go Online: Martin Luther King envisaged a world with freedom for all; for Steve Jobs, this was a world with iPhones for all. You can watch Nancy Duarte stressing the powers of storytelling in an article called '3 TED Talks that uncover the secrets of storytelling' on the Convince & Convert website. You can find a link to the article on the companion website for this book: www.edge.sagepub.com/satretgy2e.

Vaara and his colleagues examine how discursive practices can be used to legitimate and de-legitimate strategic options (Vaara et al., 2005), how strategy discourse is appropriated and resisted (Laine and Vaara, 2007) and how discourses effect participation in strategic decision-making (Mantere and Vaara, 2008). A great deal depends on the stories that are told about strategy as well as the narrative embedded in the strategy documents. Storytelling is a tool that strategists use and the adversaries of particular strategies will use against them. Stories take their form and shape from the discourses and assumptions in which they are embedded.

Simon Sinek
TED Talk

Go Online: Another TED Talk presenter who latches onto the theme of storytelling is Simon Sinek who talks about 'How great leaders inspire action'. The video can be found on the TED Talk website, or via a link on the companion website for this book: www.edge.sagepub.com/strategy2e.

EXTEND YOUR KNOWLEDGE

Storytelling is an important aspect of successful strategy as practice. David Boje's (2008) entry, 'Storytelling', in Clegg and Bailey's Volume 4 of the *International Encyclopedia of Organization Studies* provides a quick guide to the fascinating literature in this area. At greater length you could consult Yiannis Gabriel's (2000) *Storytelling in Organizations: Facts, Fictions and Fantasies*.

Strategy as it is narrated formally has to be flexible in order to accommodate changing circumstances. For instance, the narrative of strategy is often adjusted and reformulated in order to make the strategic framework look – *a posteriori* – even more successful, farsighted and flawless than it actually was. Successful strategists typically exalt the strategic capabilities of their winning formulae, usually ignoring other structural factors.

Chia and MacKay (2007) suggest that strategic practices tend to be marked by unreflective acceptance of certain leading narratives and concepts driven by deeply held – but often unconscious – assumptions and beliefs. These are culturally acquired and unconsciously absorbed. They are soaked up from the milieu within which strategy making occurs. When, as occurs from time to time, strategies come unstuck and organizations have to retreat from them, a narrative has to be produced that situates retreat from strategic objectives as something other than a failure. Politicians, to be successful, have to be particularly adept at this strategy but so do CEOs.

Fenton & Langley

EXTEND YOUR KNOWLEDGE

The importance of a concern with narrative for strategy analysis has been discussed by Christopher Fenton and Ann Langley in their 2011 paper '**Strategy as Practice and the narrative turn**'. Overall, narrative is seen as a way of giving meaning to the practice that emerges from micro-sensemaking activities, of constituting an overall sense of direction or purpose, of refocusing organizational identity, and of enabling and constraining the ongoing activities of actors. This journal article can be found on the companion website for this book: www.edge.sagepub.com/strategy2e.

Fenton, C. and Langley, A. (2011) 'Strategy as Practice and the narrative turn', *Organization Studies*, 32(9): 1171–1196.

Eriksson and Lehtimäki (2001) explored strategy documents to demonstrate how the practice of using rhetoric in strategy texts often reproduces specific and problematic assumptions concerning strategy and the role of specific actors. Samra-Fredericks (2003, 2004a, 2004b) focuses on the rhetorical skills that strategists use to persuade and convince others. Ezzamel and Willmott (2004) show how the reading of strategy statements provides the basis for organizational power relationships. All of these approaches suggest that understanding strategy entails close accounting of the processes of its constitution and deployment.

Phillips et al. (2008: 772) argued that the discourse of strategy is 'continually and recursively acting on individual meaning making through the operation of text'. When strategists write or speak as strategists they engage in a narrative activity that is political. They are seeking to determine how organization members, customers and stakeholders understand the organization. They are seeking to persuade people in and around the organization to see it in the terms in which the strategists want them to use (Phillips et al., 2008; see also Hardy and Thomas, 2014). Fenton and Langley (2011: 3) argue that

> [s]trategy narratives select and prioritize – indeed, this is their ostensible managerial purpose. However, as they achieve this, they also implicitly express, construct and reproduce legitimate power structures, organizational roles, and ideologies. (Mumby, 1987)

Laine and Vaara (2007: 33) note that if we are to understand specific strategy texts and the discourses they are embedded within we need to consider the social context in question. In addition, all such strategy texts will display important ritual elements of strategy making, such as stipulating a 'mission' and a 'vision': these have become staple characteristics of strategy.

EXTEND YOUR KNOWLEDGE

You can read Laine and Vaara's 2007 journal article 'Struggling over subjectivity: A discursive analysis of strategic development in an engineering group', in which they report research using a SAP methodology, on the companion website for this book: www.edge.sagepub.com/strategy2e.

Laine, P-M. and Vaara, E. (2007) 'Struggling over subjectivity: A discursive analysis of strategic development in an engineering group', *Human Relations*, 60(1): 29–58.

Laine & Vaara

Other rituals might include routinized sensemaking patterns and behaviours used for organizational decision-making as well as explicit traditions and methods organizationally specific to particular strategy processes (e.g. Jarzabkowski, 2005). Strategy should be seen as something struggled over by competing groups within the organization as they seek to make their definitions of it dominant. They do so by attempting to fix meaning in ways that represent what they take to be their strategic interests. The result of these struggles, suggest Laine and Vaara (2007: 36) is often a dynamic relation 'between control (using a specific discourse as a means of control) and resistance (trying to cope with or directly resist specific discourses and their implications, e.g. for subjectivity)'. These 'discursive struggles' are concerned 'with competing views concerning organizational strategies' as well as articulating 'more fundamental questions related to the subjectivity of the actors involved' (Laine and Vaara, 2007: 36).

It is evident that the power of a strategy resides not only in what it does, or what it seeks to do; it also inheres in the ways in which specific strategic discourses narrate a sense of ordering of the organization and its relations, both internally and externally, narrations that have the talisman of corporate legitimacy attached to them. This is one reason why discursive struggles over strategy can be so acute: whoever 'owns' the strategy has considerable legitimacy.

Go Online: Someone who expounds and criticizes quite clearly the view that there are a privileged few with an exclusive understanding of the bigger picture is Martin Reeves, of BCG, in a strategic TED Talk. The video can be found on the TED Talk website, or via a direct link on the companion website for this book: www.edge.sagepub.com/strategy2e.

Martin Reeves TED Talk

Much of strategic thinking is designed to make issues and problems routine, to provide narratives linking past and future in which present interests are embedded. In practice, this might mean a degree of staying on message that entails a high degree of redundancy and a high tolerance for repetition.

Go Online: You can find an interview with David Deverall on the website for this book at www.edge.sagepub.com/strategy2e. There is a section where David talks about telling stories, mostly in the sense of communicating strategy as a means of implementing it – 'Only when you are utterly sick of communicating the strategy and when you see first behavioural changes in the organization you know that you have started to implement the strategy'.

David Deverall Interview

How do Consultants Figure in Strategy?

Strategy, if it is to garner support, needs to produce an abstract but well-defined object, embodied in a set of statements and depictions. Typically, these are developed by a small number of highly trained and empowered individuals, who may be either a part of the senior managers of the organization or they may be consultants hired to help develop a strategy, people who are assumed to possess an exclusive understanding of the bigger picture. It has been argued that the success of many strategy devices is due to their simplicity: everyday managers can understand them quickly and their ease of use provides legitimacy. However, when existing legitimacies are eroding, existing routines seem no longer the appropriate ones to be designed, where there is a paucity of emergent adaptive thinking, or there is a new CEO who wants to make a big splash, then the consultants can be very useful.

Consultants are a key player in the production of strategy discourse, alongside other players such as business schools and gurus (see Figure 10.1).

Consultants offer numerous techniques, tools, methods, models, frameworks, approaches and methodologies to support strategic management (Clark, 1997). Consulting companies both produce and use these tools widely; the specific intellectual property embedded in particular tools and the discontinuity between the products creates a turnover in approaches as a more or less coordinated construction. Tools have a season and are regularly superseded.

Consulting has been addressed by a number of organization and management theorists. Researchers have analysed consultants and their methods (e.g. Nordqvist and Melin, 2008) as well as their relationships to organizations (e.g. Sturdy, 1997a, 1997b;

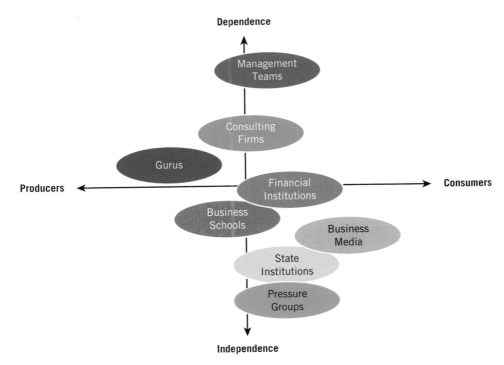

Figure 10.1   The organizational field of strategy: Producers and consumers of strategy discourse

Adapted from Whittington, R., Jarzabkowski, P., Mayer, M., Mounoud, E., Nahapiet, J. and Rouleau, L. (2003). 'Taking strategy seriously: Responsibility and reform for an important social practice', *Journal of Management Inquiry*, 12(4), 396-40.

Fincham, 1999) and the process of consulting more generally (e.g. Schein, 1988, 1999). Consulting has come under scrutiny in its relation to managerial power and control (e.g. Grint and Case, 1998; Clark and Fincham, 2002; Berglund and Werr, 2000; Sturdy et al., 2004). The role of strategy gurus, the super-consultants of strategy, has also been analysed (Hendry, 2000; Whittington et al., 2003).

In practice, in strategy consulting there occurs at least partly a translation from the insights generated by strategy researchers to the organizations that the consultants serve. According to Jarzabkowski and Wilson (2006), theoretical knowledge is initially simplified into strategy tools, such as Porter's Five Forces, the BCG portfolio matrix or the RBV framework and the concept of dynamic capabilities. Translation is never immaculate – changes occur in the process, as strategy practitioners experiment, modify and apply tools in use in a translation process, one often referred to as *bricolage*, so that the tools accord with their own notions of practice (Wright et al., 2013). Such use then becomes material for further analysis of strategy as practice in a recursive loop whose potential is always open.

The consultant acts, in some respects, as a therapist to an organization through introducing strategic conversations that might not otherwise occur. They introduce new conversations and tools into practice with which the organization members can re-form themselves, structurally or processually, or both. Schein (1988, 1999) suggests that consulting interventions can be functional or dysfunctional and elicit positive or negative outcomes. The more functional is the cognition, the more positive the outcomes for the organization and its actors, conceived as an organic entity.

Consultants use strategy tools as artefacts that enable and constrain knowledge sharing across syntactic, semantic, pragmatic and metaphysical boundaries (Carlile, 2002, 2004; Bechky, 2003). Syntactic boundaries assume that knowledge can be translated if there is a common syntax. A semantic boundary exists where common meanings still need to be developed for translation to occur. Pragmatic boundaries are more socially and politically complex, because common interests need to be developed for translation. Metaphysical boundaries are the most complex because they assume the most simplicity: they assume that a universe of meaning is possible and that all can share in it, with no tendencies to Babel-like fragmentation on the grounds of pragmatic, political interests. The transition through the four stages of boundary spanning can be thought of as ever more ambitious consulting. Given that consulting contains no 'necessary structures' (Fincham, 1999: 225), in practice we can differentiate between four types of consulting (see Table 10.1).

Organizational surgery: The prevalence of consultant-driven downsizing, outsourcing or rightsizing – or what Eisenberg (1997) referred to as 'dumbsizing'– is perhaps the most common means through which organizational surgery is deployed by consultants. It causes lesions as it cuts out what are being targeted as redundant organs of the corporate body. Indeed, some forms of consulting advice lead to widespread cutting practices, such as 'delayering' and 'business process reengineering'. It is a moot case how skilled such surgery is: sometimes it is portrayed as the work of 'axemen' (Sturdy, 1997b). Amputating parts of the organization can provide a seemingly quick solution to endemic organizational problems. Practices of portfolio management that segment the organization, for instance, enable its constituent organs to be more easily augmented or divested. The trouble is that sometimes the elements excised turn out to have been valuable in ways that had not been accounted for, because their value resided in tacit rather than explicit knowledge, in terms of Chapter 3.

Consulting, conducted in terms of an organization's 'pathologies' or 'psychoses', sees these as the result of structural causes that work on the structure can cure. When

Table 10.1   Four types of consulting

Type of strategy	Application to organizations	Examples of tools and methods
Organizational surgery	Organizational problems can be solved by physically altering the organization's structure independent of its cognition	• Tight fiscal control • Downsizing • Outsourcing • Radical reengineering
Organizational retooling	Specific consulting processes can be correctly applied to an organization resulting in improved functioning and more independent cognition, through the intervention of technology – usually IT systems	• Employee surveillance through IT • Total quality management premised on a rigorous sampling regime • Organizational restructuring around structure-shaping systems • Employee retraining to create better expressiveness in terms of the new regime of structure and technology
Organizational therapy	Organizations are complex and can only be changed and improved through processes of self-reflection and image recreation directly involving the thinking and acting of the people in the organization	• Cultural change programmes • Strategic change programmes • Organization identity redesigned
Organizational metaphysics	The organization should have a higher purpose to which members should aspire and conform – those who fail to do so should be changed or removed	• Development of vision and mission statements • Transformational leadership • Social and corporate citizenship

the organization fails to behave in ways consistent with its structural contingencies it must be 'restructured' to regain fit (Donaldson, 1987, 1999, 2000). The role of the consultant is thus to identify the problem, isolate the part of the system where the problem lies, and then perform the necessary surgery to fix it. Non-essential elements of design, in terms of present contingencies, are divested.

Organizational retooling: An organization's ills might emerge because of a problem in the 'physiology' of the organization. Just as an anti-depressant medication of the central nervous system can restore a sense of wellbeing to a depressed patient, consultants can introduce innovations to the organization's central systems, such as accounting and management controls. Consultants offer 'expertise' that client organization members may not be able to understand fully, to reform its systems (Starbuck, 1992). Most people within an organization will have little knowledge or understanding of how technologies of accounting, ERP and business software systems work and what they mean in technical terms.

Quality auditing and the adoption of standards such as the ISO9000 series, business excellence frameworks, world's best practice and so on, are technologies that require constant auditing, consulting and administration in their enactment. They help organizations function through creating common systems that enable translation to occur easily. At the simplest, a manager does not need to understand ISO, all she needs to know is if she can tick a box, or answer the question 'Today is Monday, did I do Monday's routines, yes or no?'

Organizational therapy: A therapeutic approach regards an organization's dysfunctions as being rooted not in the body of the organization but in its collective mind. As Kets De Vries (1991) would have it, such approaches seek to put 'organizations on the couch'. One application of this in consulting is to engage an organization in a therapeutic process involving processes of reflection and the development of self-knowledge that cuts through an organization's defence mechanisms – or 'defensive routines' to use Argyris' (1990) terms – in order that the organization builds a healthy self-awareness that enables it to function in a more well-adjusted manner (Brown and Starkey, 2000).

In Nonaka and Takeuchi's (1995) terms, the goal is to make tacit knowledge explicit in a similar fashion to the way a psychotherapist might seek to bring the subconscious to the scrutiny of the ego. Consulting in this tradition is process driven – it emphasizes learning and active participation of the client through the change process (Werr et al., 1997). Therapeutically, the ability to reduce managerial and organizational anxiety and replace it with reassurance, control and order is sought (Sturdy, 1997a, 1997b). Cultural change programmes can seek to modify both employee and organizational identity in the service of improved organizational functioning (Chappell et al., 2003), often in association with coaching.

Organizational metaphysics: Metaphysics deal with those principles of reality transcending any particular science. An organization, it is argued, should have a 'higher' purpose. Charismatic and transformational leaders will propose a combination of visions, missions and values to guide the organization in its spiritual quest. The consultant advises leadership on how to define and achieve its 'true' purpose, one in which the individual is subordinated to the collective organization's total control. Managerially, the striving for such strategic utopias is often obsessed with purity and a strong urge for hygiene, in which everything should be productive (ten Bos, 2000).

Strategy consultants enact possible organizational realities. Pathologies are contrasted with a healthy future paved with myriad obstacles as well as good intentions. The experienced guide – the consultant – knows how to see the hidden dangers and lead the organization into the 'Promised Land'. Metaphysical consultants deal with extremes: they make reality worse than it might be in order to make the future even sunnier, brighter and more appealing. They draw a dark picture of an organization's past and a bright one of an organization's future. The difference between the present and the future may well involve the exorcizing of specific individuals who do not conform to the dominant notions of worthiness needed to reach the future. (This was a political ploy used extensively in the 2016 US Presidential campaign by Donald Trump.)

Alternatively, scenario planning is a widely used visioning strategic tool used to provide direction to the future. The planners begin by enquiring into four environmental factors that they see as framing an organization's future. These include scanning likely social dynamics, economic, technological and political issues that might have a future impact on the organization. Essentially, scenario planners seek to build up a composite answer to a series of questions, answers to which will frame the imaginable boundaries for future action. The actual questions that scenario planners will use vary, creatively, from case to case as they explore each case's specificities; typically, they seek insight into the kinds of areas shown in Table 10.2.

These questions are used to frame a series of interviews with the Top Management Team and any other members of the organization thought appropriate. The data collected is used as a mirror on the organization and its themes, which becomes the focus for discussion with the management team at a subsequent meeting. Working with the members at that meeting, the scenario planners identify critical uncertainties and what members think should be done about them.

Table 10.2   Scenario planning questions (adapted from Ringland, 1998)

Themes	Questions	Rationale
The vital issues	*Would you identify what you see as the critical issues for the future? If the conversation slows, continue with the follow-up question: Suppose I was a clairvoyant and had full knowledge of the outcome, what would you want to know from me? (Strategic Drivers)*	Here the scenario planner is searching for data on where an industry or organization is going; what events might influence it and force the organization to change.
A favourable outcome	*If things were to turn out really well for the organization, being optimistic but realistic, talk about what you see as a desirable outcome. (Positive Scenario Factors)*	Here the scenario planner is searching for data on what really might make the organization successful.
An unfavourable outcome	*If things went really badly, what would be the key factors that you would need to manage to try and prevent this happening? (Negative Scenario Factors)*	Here the scenario planner seeks out information on what threatens the organization, what is putting it at risk?
Internal systems	*Where culture, structure or processes will need to change: What do you think the organization would have to do to achieve the desired future? (Preferable Actions)*	With these questions the scenario researcher is trying to find out what the organization members know about what they will have to do.
Lessons from past successes and failures	*Looking back, what would you identify as the significant events that have produced the current situation? (Critical Pathways)*	Here the analyst is seeking to identify what have been the key drivers for the construction of the present reality.
Decisions that have to be faced	*Looking forward, what would you see as the priority actions that should be carried out soon? (Strategic Priorities)*	With this question the scenario researcher seeks to isolate those factors necessary for the change scenario to be implemented.
If you were responsible	*If all constraints were removed and you could direct what is done, what more would you wish to include? (The 'Epitaph' Question)*	Here the scenario planner thinks beyond the constraints of 'business as usual' and explores the future.

The key factors then form the basis for different scenarios. These scenarios describe how the driving forces might plausibly behave, based on the assumption of the predetermined elements and critical uncertainties. To create the scenario stories the planner leads the members of the organization to determine which of the driving forces are most important. What is most uncertain and what seems inevitable? The idea is to develop narratives that best capture the dynamics of the situation. Once three scenarios have been developed in some detail then it is time to identify what decisions need to be made. If a decision works only for one of several scenarios, then it is risky. The question that should be discussed by management is how the strategy should be adapted to make it more robust if the desired scenario doesn't pan out as predicted. As soon as the different scenarios have been defined, then a few indicators should be selected with which to monitor emergent strategy. If the scenarios have been carefully developed they will identify and translate movements on some key indicators into an orderly set of implications, rather like a game of chess where the opponents are constantly seeking to out-manoeuvre the other player's potential moves – just as their opponents are doing to them.

IN PRACTICE

Oliver Freeman – scenario planning

Oliver Freeman Interview

Go Online: Visit the book's website at https://edge.sagepub.com/strategy2e to watch an interview with Oliver Freeman conducted by the author team.

Oliver Freeman is recognized as one of the leading global proponents of scenario planning. Having guided many international organizations through the scenario planning programmes of Global Business Network, Oliver is acknowledged as a truly innovative thinker at the forefront of strategy.

With an extensive background in publishing, Oliver has conducted a multitude of conferences, seminars and training programmes in strategy and scenario planning. With an increasing focus on workshop facilitation and consulting, Oliver has developed an intensive two-day course on Scenario Planning and Strategic Leadership to assist organizations in realigning their long-term vision with current strategy theory and scenario planning principles.

Oliver says 'The future does not lie at the end of a trend line … We use a definition of strategy as a pathway to the future by helping us to achieve sustainable congruence between our organization and the environments in which it may have to operate'.

In this video Oliver proposes the Q.U.E.S.T tool as a structured practice to uncover future scenarios. The primary task in this approach is to determine the scope and frame the issues or QUestions for which scenarios are to be created. Next is the broad future Environment where the scenario questions are to occur. At this stage it is essential to challenge existing thought paradigms and consider alternative yet plausible situations that recognize the likely pressures acting on the organization. Here the method seeks to explore factors such as Ideas, Nature, Society, Politics, Economics, Culture and Technology. With a strong understanding of the questions to be faced and the issues and influences likely, build the Scenarios of your alternative futures. Create rich storyboards; narratives that help you understand 'what if?' Then, finally, begin to understand the implications for current strategy that these Transformative scenarios identify. Are you heading in the right direction? Have you considered all options?

Questions

1. How is scenario planning as a strategic practice different to other approaches of strategy development?

2. 'Scenarios can't predict the future, so what's the point?' Critically evaluate this statement.

3. How can external advisors help to create scenarios? What is the advantage of having external perspectives included in the practice of scenario planning?

4. Why is the practice of developing scenarios often more important than the actual outcome?

5. Pick an industry context and discuss the major trends and forces that would drive the future of business in that industry.

6. Discuss the issue of availability and quality of the information that you base scenarios on.

7. Discuss whether scenario planning is suitable for any kind of organization. Can you think of organizations that are more likely to benefit from scenario planning than others?

8. How would you explain scenario planning as a different kind of tool to other approaches of strategy development?

Sometimes metaphysics for future directions become explicitly religious. For instance, Bolman and Deal (2001), no longer reframing organizations through just four frames, have discovered the overarching importance of the spiritual frame through a dialogue between two fictional characters, a business leader and his spiritual guide. Others see Jesus as the explicit answer – Jones (1996) applies Jesus' CEO wisdom to more modern and mundane situations. Mitroff and Denton (1999) conclude that most organizations are spiritually impoverished and that real change and improvement in performance will come only when organizations find ways to integrate their stakeholder's personal beliefs with organizational values. Based on their 'spiritual audit' survey of 131 organizations, they identified those beliefs to which employees are most committed and present five models for harnessing the power of spiritual energy. Having God on your side, of whatever faith, as a guide for strategic leadership, is not unusual (see Cunha, et al., 2016).

Who are the champions of strategy?

Intentionally or not, some approaches that use strategy as practice position it as a problem-solving tool for managerial elites. The presumption is that strategy is carried out – for the most part – by those in senior positions. In line with most conventional strategy research, non-executives are usually written out of the picture. When questions such as 'just what do managers have to do to make a difference and what is their impact? What works for them and what does not work?' (Johnson et al., 2003: 16) are asked, the strategy as practice approach remains close to the tradition of mainstream, functional research. It does not emphasize the ways in which outsiders, renegades and strangers might influence strategy in practice.

Finnish researcher Saku Mantere (2005) looked at who champions strategy. By a champion of strategy, he means individuals who try to:

1. Influence strategic issues beyond their immediate operational responsibilities.

2. Influence the organization to affect strategically important issues crucial for the organization's success, survival or completion of its mission.

One might think such a role would be exclusively reserved for those within the corporate elite – senior executives and their advisors. What Mantere's research highlighted was that strategic champions often came from outwith the senior stratum of the organization and, as Whittle et al. (2015) demonstrate, can sometimes try, if not always successfully, to redraw strategy's boundaries.

Strategy may often be taught and thought of as an elite practice but Mantere's (2005) data suggests that strategic champions may be found at various levels of the organization hierarchy: they are not just confined to the upper echelons. He draws these conclusions based on substantial empirical evidence collected across 301 interviews within 12 medium sized organizations in the 100–500 employee range.

Mantere's study not only establishes where strategic champions reside but also proceeds to describe how they work, influencing the strategy process by 'seeking to affect the opinions or activities of superiors, peers and subordinates, seeking to change the organization or its systems, seeking to secure resources and so on' (Mantere, 2005: 157). Such activity can be oriented as much to strategy formulation as implementation.

Strategy making is a major arena in which power relations are played out. Simultaneously, managers have to be able to:

1. Bring off their actions as being in accord with the strategic objectives of the organization that employs them

2. Do so while maximizing their ability to gain access to organizational resources in order to further their own interests

3. Enhance their power relations and the prestige of their office and its contribution to the strategy-making process.

Managers who can play these politics successfully go far in the 'turf wars' that characterize complex organizations (Buchanan and Badham, 2008), in which, according to an important US study of corporate acquisitions in the 1960s, 'top managers are actors, corporations are instruments, and top managers use these instruments to pursue their interests in proportion to their capacities' (Palmer and Barber, 2001: 110). Doing so entails that managers can articulate legitimate narratives in which they situate themselves as champions.

According to Mantere, champions can face conditions that can both enable their efforts to influence the strategy process or disable them, thus producing 'enabled' or 'thwarted' champions. To be enabled is to be in a power relation that allows one to do some strategic things – this might mean having the ear of the chief executive and being able to influence strategy decisively while to be thwarted is to lack access to such power relations; that is, to be in the wilderness and not have one's ideas listened to. The key questions are:

- Determining *what*, *how* and *who* is involved in strategy entails making powerful decisions. Power relations are central to strategy making in a complex way. At a simple episodic level, if you cannot make happen what you have said will happen, you are not much of a strategist.

- More subtly, if you cannot *shape the agenda* from which issues emerge or through which change is implemented, or control the necessary resources, or ensure that the right people are in place to make things happen or, equally, make things not happen, then this is strategic dereliction of duty.

- More subtly still, *strategy is about shaping and framing vocabularies of motive*, those things rationalized as needing to be done in order to achieve strategic goals; it concerns the discursive staking out of legitimated terms, phrases and reasoning that are tightly tied to actions that are intended to achieve strategic objectives (Balogun and Johnson, 2005; Lukes, 1974, 2005).

Linking back to Mintzberg in Chapter 9, emergent approaches are based on *adaptive* practices, allowing space for individual interpretations of strategy, 'achieved through impromptu discussions between strategists and implementers' (Mantere, 2005: 169). In contrast, recursive approaches to strategy stress rational planning 'through the dissemination of information, i.e. objective knowledge, through pre-defined methods of giving feedback and through the operationalization of strategy into explicit targets' (Mantere, 2005: 169). As Mantere (2005: 169) suggests, the two approaches 'are clearly distinct ideals and may often be incompatible, since there is little room for individual interpretation of strategy if it is regarded as an objective phenomenon, existing as pre-explicated targets.' The stress is on introducing episodes of change and seeing it implemented. Table 10.3 summarizes the differences between recursive and adaptive strategy practices.

Strategy that favours recursive approaches stresses order and preplanning in strategy championing:

> Formal channels for information dissemination and feedback enable a wide audience for strategy-related matters and provide an equal opportunity to voice opinions. Operationalized targets and associated measures enable an individual to be an active player in creating strategic performance, as well as reap rewards from it. Explicit task designs and macro-structures, coupled with personnel development practices, create a sense that strategy is a legitimate practice. Official participation practices and channels of mobilizing resources empower championing. But lack of explicitness, an oblique sense of legitimate organizing and unexplicated forms of control, the enemies of the recursive standpoint, lead to confusion, powerlessness, demotivation and cynicism. (Mantere, 2005: 171, 175)

Table 10.3   Recursive and adaptive strategy practices

	Key practices in a recursively-driven strategy process	Key practices in an adaptively-driven strategy process
Strategy formation	Explicit operationalization of targets, mechanisms of information dissemination and feedback	Sensegiving as purpose creation hospitable to interpretation and improvisation, interactive discussions
Organizing	Explicit task definition	Continuous negotiation of responsibility
Control	Explicit practices for performance evaluation, resource mobilization, rewarding and participation	Influence practice through social networks

Source: Mantere, 2005: 179

Recursive practices draw on the champion's sense of control through predictability. Where these practices can become disabling for champions is where they lack the ability to use the tools they have been given predictively, when they are not sure what the outcomes will be. The individual strategy champion has to have *power over* the right tools and levers to make things happen and what is disabling for champions is when they do not have this control.

Adaptive practices are much more a matter of *power to* rather than *power over*.

> Adaptive practices such as interactive impromptu discussions concerning strategy, continuous negotiation of responsibility and exerting influence through social networks enabled champions to express their ideas and create a feeling of ownership about their work. Adaptive practices, through which organizational strategy adapts to internal and external pressures, also seem to be a source of creative freedom and joy in the work of individuals interested in strategy. (Mantere, 2005: 175)

A lack of access to the formal tools and levers of recursive power disables many employees from participating in strategy making. At higher levels, the emphasis is on being adaptive. Hence, strategy in practice translates as relative freedom and power for the elites and relative powerlessness and lack of access to the tools capable of making things happen to those over whom they exercise power. The latter's role is largely to fulfil rational plans and targets and to be rewarded and punished on this basis.

Middle managers, in particular, lack control of issues such as rewarding, performance evaluation, resource mobilization and participation (Balogun and Johnson, 2004, 2005; Mantere, 2005; Rouleau, 2005; Sillince and Mueller, 2007; Fauré and Rouleau, 2011; Rouleau and Balogun, 2011; Thomas et al., 2011). These men and women in the middle thus make recourse to adaptive strategies as ways to 'make do' and 'work round' their lack of *power to* make things happen, using the tools available to them.

EXTEND YOUR KNOWLEDGE

Saku
Mantere

The discussion of strategy and its leaders and champions is informed by Saku Mantere's 2005 journal article **'strategic practices as enablers and disablers of championing activity'**, and, if you want to extend your knowledge further, you can read the paper in its entirety by reading it on the companion website for this book: www.edge. sagepub.com/strategy2e.

Mantere, S. (2005) 'Strategic practices as enablers and disablers of championing activity', *Strategic Organization*, 3: 157–284.

Summing up Mantere's (2005: 178) argument, he suggests:

> [T]op managers seem to be enabled by many things, especially adaptive formation practices, and disabled by few. For middle managers, control is the key issue both as an enabler and disabler, while formation is a close second. The biggest obstacle for middle management championing seems to be a

lack of proper control practices. Organizing seems to be a special concern for middle managers. The operative personnel are in a similar position as the middle management in terms of control, yet their greatest concern is a lack of an explicit and predictable position in strategy formation. They do not know where to get their information, where to voice their feedback and where to get clarification for objectives.

Champions are enabled because they are in a position to be able to use power creatively and innovatively to make things happen; they have a sense of psychological ownership of the agenda for these reasons. The presence or the absence of recursive and adaptive strategies can aid championing or hinder it, as Table 10.4 demonstrates.

What do Strategic Leaders do in Practice?

One article on leadership in practice stands out (Carroll et al., 2008). In this research the idea that there are specific practices of leadership that can be acquired as competencies is discussed critically. The leadership competency literature stresses a number of objective and acquirable features of leadership, conceptualized at the individual level of analysis, that are quantifiable and measurable, embedded in the individual not the relational context in which s/he operates, conceived of in highly rationalistic terms. In contrast, a leadership as practice perspective would stress less objectivist and more social constructivist aspects of leadership, including reference to how it must always be seen in context as inherently relational and collective, as something that cannot be objectively measured but which is entwined in discursive, narrative and rhetorical skills, that are situated and socially defined by day-to-day experience and find emotional expression as well as rational expression.

Capturing data from participants in a leadership development programme, Carroll and colleagues (2008) asked them to reflect on their experiences in the programme. What was evident was their intuitive understanding and articulation of practice as a movement of an idea or insight between different states of awareness, consciousness and identification. The researchers interpreted these movements as occurring across seven areas: habits, process, consciousness, awareness, control, everydayness and identity. What was notable was that the participants did not see themselves as having gained competencies but as having explored their self and learnt in the process. The authors argue that:

> [P]ractitioner talk of practice intuitively draws attention to leadership in 'ordinariness' or an ability to comprehend the subtleties of sophisticated dynamics like unlearning, transition and transformation. It desires leadership to be an embodied, embedded way of being and approaching organizations, contexts and the world. If so, then the translation of much of leadership into competencies does not do them or leadership sufficient justice.

Much of leadership development practice is oriented to trying to develop transformational leaders out of transactional leaders. Transactional leaders are good at setting goals, articulating explicit agreements and providing constructive feedback to keep everybody on task (Bass and Avolio, 1993; Howell and Hall-Merenda, 1999). In contrast, trasnsformational leaders are appreciative of strategy as emergent, as process. Prescriptively, these transformational leaders will seek to be charismatic,

Table 10.4 The adaptive and recursive practices enabling and disabling championing

| | Recursive | | Adaptive | |
	Enabling	Disabling	Enabling	Disabling
Strategy formation	Formal information dissemination practices ensure that individuals hear about strategy Formal feedback channels ensure that champions are able to voice their ideas Clearly operationalized targets and measurements allow for an understanding of strategy and result in feelings of predictability and control	Lack of explicit targets results in strategy being regarded as a platitude or conflicting, and in confusion regarding application Lack of explicit information dissemination and feedback practices result in individuals feeling disrespected, resulting in demotivation	An individual is motivated to champion strategy because it provides a purpose for their work Ownership of the interpretation of proper work practices motivates an individual Interactive communication between strategists and implementers helps the latter implementers find applications for strategy and deepens the former's understanding of implementation issues	Lack of sensegiving support of disseminated information leads to confusion regarding applications Lack of interaction between implementers and strategists leads to unrealistic objectives and demotivation Sensemaking failure concerning strategic direction leads to demotivation and feelings of insecurity and powerlessness
Organizing	Changes in organizational structure transcend talk, directing resources to proper areas Designed career paths based on measurable strategic action motivate championing Explicit task definitions allow for the comprehension of one's role as a part of a greater unity	Ambiguous or dated organizational design leads to strategy being regarded as just talk Overspecialization in strategic tasks undermines the feelings of responsibility of champions, leading to powerlessness and demotivation Task design not reflecting strategy creates conflict in priorities	Continuous negotiation of responsibility leads to ownership of work and flexibility in the application of strategic ideas Cross-organizational development projects challenge the status quo, leading to better cooperation between both implementers and organizational units	An abundance of non-relevant development projects takes time from more crucial activities, leading to frustration Individuals sticking to externally defined roles leads to poor cooperation in strategy implementation
Control	Official participation practices create a feeling of ownership of strategy Performance evaluation based on operationalized strategic targets creates a sense of control over one's success and failure Rewarding based on performance evaluation creates a feeling of championing being valued	Lacking official participation, practices result in a feeling that the strategy is being dictated, or at least in a confusion about whether participation is sought after or not Lack of rewarding of strategic action, in terms of a lacking or a faulty rewarding system, demotivated championing Lack of official practices to secure resources for strategic activities, especially in cross-functional contexts, demotivates championing	Social networks possessed by an individual champion enables them to secure resources and influence the organisation, beyond official structures	Lack of a social networks leaves the champion feeling helpless about this chances of making things happen

Source: Mantere, 2005: 172–174

inspirational, intellectually stimulating and individually considerate, helping individuals to transcend self-interest for the sake of the larger vision of the organization, inspiring others with their vision, creating excitement through their enthusiasm and questioning time-worn assumptions. They will transform existing organizational culture, strategy and structure.

Transformational leadership is particularly relevant in situations of change (Bass, 1985; Avolio et al., 1999) and has been linked positively to motivation and creativity (Burns, 1978; Sosik et al., 1998, 1999; Jung, 2001; Shin and Zhou, 2003), organizational performance (Jung and Avolio, 1999; Jung and Sosik, 2002; Ogbonna and Harris, 2000), innovation (Jung et al., 2003) and effectiveness in different types of organizations (Bass and Avolio, 1997). Transformational leaders are often thought of as *great* leaders – the ones who can take an organization from where it is to where it can be so much better, in terms of its measures of value.

Go Online: One person who outlines what she takes to be the qualities of a great leader, based on a study of 4,000 companies, is Rosalinde Torres in a TED Talk titled 'What it takes to be a great leader'. You can find the video on the TED Talk website, or via a direct link on the companion website for this book: www.edge.sagepub.com/strategy2e.

**Rosalind Torres
TED Talk**

What leaders must do in strategy is to cope, practically, with developing situations as they are strategizing. They need to draw on the resources available to them as strategy practitioners, using socio-material practices at hand. Their strategy must link ends, means and emotions that are appropriate to a particular set of practices. The strategic pattern making that emerges is communicated in narratives and stories. The success of any given strategy depends on an ability of those socially constructing it to anticipate and respond to internal and external opportunities and threats by sharing a common viewpoint. Doing this comprises the chief elements of sensemaking and sensegiving, as we saw in Chapter 9.

In terms of sensemaking, top managers will try to communicate a common viewpoint to middle managers (Balogun and Johnson, 2004) as well as to specialized strategists (Pettigrew 1985; Grant, 2003; Rouleau, 2005), line managers and specialized units (Brown and Eisenhardt, 1997; Orlikowski, 2002; Ahrens and Chapman, 2007), external stakeholders, including customers (Christensen and Bower, 1996), investors (Bower and Gilbert, 2005), strategic partners (Dyer et al., 2001), technology partners (von Hippel and Krogh, 2003), as well as consultants. All these parties can be involved in strategy making.

Next, we turn the spotlight on celebrity. Just as there is celebrity in politics and show business, so there is in business.

How to Become a Celebrity CEOs in Practice?

Increasingly, business people are celebrities and celebrities are business people: Contemporary examples of celebrity in business would include identities such as Victoria Beckham, Richard Branson, Steve Jobs, Donald Trump, Jamie Oliver and Richard Branson, who are all household names, as famous for their celebrity as their business dealings.

> A sign of **celebrity** is when something or someone is known for being well known. Littler (2007: 233) identifies celebrity where the CEO's profile 'extends beyond the financial or business sectors of the media', when the person straddles multiple media sites and genres.

The business and the celebrity seem to hang together as a part of strategy. In this section we ask the question: what is celebrity and what does a **celebrity** strategy mean in practice?

Image 10.4   The Donald Trump brand. Copyright: Leonardo Patrizi

Go Online: The *US Weekly* website recently ran an article on 'Celebrity CEOs: Stars who run their own business empires' looking at celebrities such as Mary-Kate and Ashley Olsen, Giselle Bundchen, Dr Dre and Oprah Winfrey. A direct link to the article can be found on the companion website for this book: www.edge.sagepub.com/strategy2e.

Historically, celebrity CEOs were infamous as much as they were famous: they were the robber barons of late nineteenth century US capitalism – Andrew Carnegie, J.D. Rockefeller, J.P. Morgan and the like. Widely regarded by the turn of the century as parasites, exploiters, fraudsters and corrupters of democratic politics they were widely reviled for their ostentatious wealth and privilege (van Krieken, 2012: 112). By the 1920s they had been transformed into 'industrial statesmen' in a deliberate strategy.

One thing that is notable about each of the cases of business celebrity is that it is a strategy used principally by those with little in the way of initial economic, cultural, social and symbolic capital. It is often an outsider strategy. Victoria Beckham, Richard Branson and Steve Jobs did not start from a position of great wealth: Victoria Beckham was able to leverage having been a Spice Girl and then becoming the wife of a famous footballer (who in turn leveraged that he was her husband); Richard Branson was able to leverage the success of Mike Oldfield's Tubular Bells LP, which was the first release on the Virgin record label that he started, more as an enthusiast than a business person; while Steve Jobs, unlike Branson and Beckham, did get to college – but dropped out to start Apple in a Palo Alto garage with Steve Wozniak. Of course, sometimes celebrity leaders posture as self-made, even when they are not: Donald Trump is an obvious example.

Van Krieken (2012: 120) sees some common elements in the 'celebrification of the entrepreneur'. Amongst these is the creation of a celebrity profile, using a 'hero narrative' (Campbell, 1988) that stresses a rags to riches account of success, their groundedness as a person (think Warren Buffet or Richard Branson), the meritocracy of the story due to the relatively unprivileged origins of the hero and the struggles undergone on the way (think Steve Jobs or Richard Branson) and the role of a supportive wife (think Melinda Gates) who also shares a sense of social responsibility (McCarthy and Hatcher, 2005).

Since the 1970s the celebrity CEO has become an even more important part of the strategy of major firms (Khurana, 2002). Khurana attributes this rise to changes in business strategy that occurred with the rise of 'institutional investor capitalism' since the 1970s (Davis and Steil, 2001). These institutional investors, such as pension funds, are now the major shareowners of contemporary capitalism. Owning considerable shares in organizations they now tend to prefer exercising voice rather than exit when businesses in which they have a large parcel of shares are not performing. Exiting might signal a precipitous decline in stock values in which they can be badly burnt; better to try and appoint some outsider to turn around performance, someone known for 'sharp-bending' (Grinyer and McKiernan, 1998), who can hire and fire the present team more easily than any of them, culpable for poor performance as they are, would be able to do.

If insiders are the problem, then the solution is to go for outsiders; outsiders are recognizable as candidates because of their past success and present celebrity. Khurana (2002: 65) suggests that 'choosing an outsider became a way of demonstrating to Wall Street the board's commitment to change'. Not just any outsider, but one with a successful career, one with celebrity attributes, charismatic leadership qualities, and an ability to promote and communicate a 'can-do' attitude of optimism and confidence in marked contrast to the mediocrity that made this appointment necessary. The ranks of CEO management have extraordinary parallels with the ranks of Premier League Soccer management. Football managers such as Jose Mourinho or Arsene Wenger present cases where the person and the strategy become mythologized and personalized.

How to Become a Celebrity Firm?

There are obviously celebrity corporations. Some companies become celebrity companies in their own right, rather than being founded by an existing celebrity, becoming coterminous with their celebrity CEOs. Some obvious cases would be Apple and Steve Jobs, Microsoft and Bill Gates, Virgin and Richard Branson, and in fashion, Victoria Beckham.

Victoria Beckham's Clothing Line

Celebrity firms' practices seek to 'attract a high level of public attention and generate positive emotional responses from stakeholder audiences' (Rindova et al., 2006: 51). Celebrity is a key intangible asset for a firm. It assures status, legitimacy and reputation, constructing the firm's image and stakeholder recognition of it – it has made Apple one of the most valuable companies on the planet. Rindova et al. see firm celebrity being built around its rare and inimitable qualities of novelty, something that is performatively staged and orchestrated – again, think of Steve Jobs' dramatic product launches or Google and the Googleplex, with its chefs and laid-back lifestyle. These are examples of under-conforming rebels, firms that deliberately broke the rules, and ended up becoming market leaders, institutional entrepreneurs, who redefined the fields that they were engaged in.

As an intangible asset for firm strategy, celebrity is inherently risky. It is invariably transitory, as the very things that made it positively distinctive at one time can, as the times change, become liabilities. A positive case is Enron, lauded by strategists such as Gary Hamel and by magazines such as *Fortune*, only to be exposed subsequently as an accounting house of cards, bringing down Arthur Anderson, its accountants, in its demise. Apple offers a case of this in reverse: initially, its celebrity was a source of an anomaly, not advantage, as it made computers that did not run on industry standards and were more expensive to buy. Only after it focused on a wider range of highly designed objects, especially the iPod, iPhone and iPad, did it become as successful as it is.

Celebrity CEOs are one way of embodying dominant myths about the organization in the consciousness of members, customers and stakeholders. These celebrity CEOs work on the third dimension of power in Lukes' (2005) terms, and the deep structure of culture in Schein's (1997): they embody deep-seated values about the organization, such as steadfastness and acumen with Buffet, fun with Branson or design and innovation with Jobs. Myths can function as a culture, embodying potential unobtrusive control mechanisms, where shared norms and values guide actions. In such circumstances culture may seek to achieve many of the things usually left to rules and structures. Such rules and structure, of course, are equally an embodiment of political relations, shaping the nature of reporting, interactions, duties, responsibilities and so on. Often, the structures and rules that an organization adopts are chosen because they reflect symbolically powerful devices that are well understood in the institutional environment. They help grant legitimacy to an organization because of their respectability.

The Achilles heel of practising a celebrity strategy is what happens when the celebrity CEO dies, retires or is discredited. This is a problem that the sociologist Max Weber (1978) christened as 'the routinization of charisma'. When a charismatic leader has to be succeeded an organization can be rudderless or riven by rivalries that are especially troublesome when an organization's identity is entangled with that of the charismatic leader. By its nature charisma that is projected by and on to a person is ephemeral and transitory. Weber argued that when charisma is superseded it must of necessity move in one of three directions: toward dissolution, toward traditional authority or toward rational-legal authority. Family firms that groom a family member as an heir apparent to the CEO seek to establish tradition; organizations that appoint someone unrelated to any founding family instead usually try to 'normalize' the function of CEO in terms of the accountabilities of office holding. Organizations that were led by a celebrity individual, once they are gone, can no longer rely on the essentially charismatic qualities of that person. Celebrity strategy has to be institutionalized for the organization to survive and thrive in the future.

How to Communicate Celebrity as a Strategy?

Celebrity has to be communicated: this is where the business press comes in. As the advertisement says, 'We live in *Financial Times*'. The significance now given in mainstream broadcast e- and print-media, as well as the specialist press, to the relation between appointments and share valuations, has made celebrities out of previously unknown managerial elites. Success is increasingly attributed to individual narratives in what van Krieken (2012: 124) calls the business information industry, in which business success is explained 'in terms of individual character and personality' (citing Meindl et al., 1985 and Hayward et al., 2004). Having a celebrity CEO such as Branson, Jobs or Buffet is a great way of obtaining free media exposure and publicity – think, especially, of the stunts that Richard Branson regularly practises in promoting the Virgin brand.

The stress on individualism is quite distinct from much of the strategy literature. By contrast, the stress on individualism is anti-determinist, stressing the practices of individual leaders, creating a 'romance of leadership' that attributes complex achievements to individual leaders as stand-alone strategists. As van Krieken (2012) suggests it is much 'easier to explain complex situations and organizations in terms of key individual actors than to comprehend the interaction of an array of cross-cutting processes and mechanisms'. Multivariate explanation, complex networks, contingent events, indeterminate feedback loops, and overall dynamism are not the stuff either of journalism or of everyday understanding.

Khurana (2002: 74) suggests that the public profile of the CEO as celebrity encourages investment decisions. Celebrity becomes a simulacrum for strategy. Celebrity, 'the ability to command attention from the media and stock market analysts in a way that will establish credibility for the firm and inspire confidence in both investors and others', becomes central to the practice of recognizing CEO success, as Khurana (2002: 78) suggests. For such people, 'lifted above the usual competitive anonymity ... hard-won iconicity [can be used] to assert advantages over competitors ... and ... command a market premium' (Sternberg, 1986: 6).

> [O]nce the media have constructed a CEO as a celebrity, this perception will also be resistant to subsequent evidence to the contrary (Chen and Meindl 1991). This results in turn in a greater inclination towards mergers and acquisitions, and inflates the price that CEOs are willing to pay for new acquisitions, because CEOs end up believing their own press, and the resultant CEO hubris (Roll, 1986; Hayward and Hambrick, 1997) inflates a CEO's assessment of their ability to recoup their outlays. (van Krieken, 2012: 125)

How should we best understand this extreme individualization of strategy as celebrity? From a strategy as practice perspective we should focus on the

> [C]lusters of promotional activities, representational practices, and cultural dynamics that revolve around different types of exemplary business personalities – corporate leaders, entrepreneurs, management gurus, investment bankers, traders, marketers, Hollywood agents and producers, and so on. (Guthey et al., 2009: 36)

Go Online: In an article from 2002, *The Economist* suggested that 'big business today has too much in common with show business. When there are no stars, they tend to be created' (see www.economist.com/node/1109770).

The Economist
Article

Stars can sometimes fall the firmament, however, as *The Economist* article discusses.

EXTEND YOUR KNOWLEDGE

If you want to find out more about strategy as practice then the key resource is Golsorkhi, D., Rouleau, L., Seidl, D. and Vaara, E. (2015) *Cambridge Handbook of Strategy as Practice* (2nd edn). Cambridge: Cambridge University Press. Do make sure that you consult the second edition though; it is a greatly expanded and revised version of the earlier edition.

Summary

We now know quite a lot about what occurs in middle management ranks in the development of strategy as a result of strategy-as-practice research. Strategy as practice is one of the most diverse and vibrant fields of current strategy research. The focus is very much on what strategists actually do in doing strategy. In part, the aim is to demystify strategy, to show the tools of strategy as devices that are socially constructed and whose use inheres in a set of practices that enable them to have the effects that they have. Given that strategy as practice research is resolutely non-prescriptive, many traditional strategy researchers, teachers and practitioners are wary of it, dismissing it as merely descriptive. We would be more cautious. Through describing what actually is accomplished through strategy in its various guises, the strategy as practice approach opens up the reality of strategy, doing so in a way that more prescriptive approaches do not. Prescriptive approaches, of which there is a multitude, not surprisingly, are often quite silent about the assumptions that make them possible. Strategy as practice is not.

One weakness of the strategy as practice perspective is that, for reasons of data access and methodology, researcher attention has been paid, mostly, to those elements of strategy that are both accessible and observable. The research initiated under the banner of strategy as practice has one quite evident omission: the elites. For the less observable, less accessible elite locales of strategy, in boardrooms and clubs, different approaches to strategy than those based on direct ethnography are required. We know relatively less about the upper echelons of strategy as a practice and where and how such strategy is conceived and practised. The reasons are obvious: to research the inclusion and exclusion of personnel in strategic practices means entering the citadels of strategic power to see decision-making and non-decision-making at work in the strategy formulation process (see Chapter 11). Usually, great secrecy attends these processes. They are frequently covered up by the rhetoric of commercial-in-confidence. Outsiders, such as researchers, are rarely invited into these citadels of power.

Most strategy formulation is hardly democratic. To see how strategy is conceived and practised means being privy to the elites, their clubs, their boardrooms, their country retreats and country suppers. It is for this reason that the discussion of the relation between elite leadership and strategy is furthest from a practice perspective – we have very little research that takes us into the heart of elite practices and the leadership of strategy that these constitute. It is notable, for instance, that in the largest and most recent compendium of research in the area, the *Cambridge Handbook of Strategy as Practice* (Golsorkhi et al., 2015), there is no specific section or contribution on elites. At this point, short of insider accounts, we may run up against the practical limits of strategy as practice.

In addition, in its emphasis on the practice of strategy, SAP may become overly focused on the process of strategy creation, as opposed both to the content and the need to deal with competitors. In this sense it should be seen as providing foundations about the strategy-making process. It would be interesting to develop a SAP-informed and SAP-shaped approach that also paid attention to that which, in real capitalist business practice, is the essence of the firm's survival: making a profit, to which despite their limitations, Porterian and RBV-based reasoning do make a useful contribution.

TEST YOURSELF

Want to know more about this chapter? Review what you have learnt by visiting www.edge.sagepub.com/strategy2e.

- Test yourself with multiple choice questions
- Revise key terms with interactive flashcards

EXERCISES

1. Having read this chapter, you should be able to say in your own words what each of the following key terms mean. Test yourself or ask a colleague to test you.

   - Strategy as practice
   - Practice as phenomenon
   - Practice as perspective
   - Practice as philosophy
   - Strategy tools
   - SWOT analysis
   - BCG Matrix
   - Storytelling and narrative

   - Institutional logics
   - Strategy consulting
   - Scenario planning
   - Strategic leadership
   - Recursive strategy
   - Adaptive strategy
   - Strategy champions
   - Celebrity strategy

2. Why do organizations need to understand strategy as practice?

3. What are the differences between strategy conceived as phenomenon, perspective and philosophy?

4. How useful do you think strategy as practice is as an approach for practising managers?

5. How do strategy tools figure in the practice of strategy? Illustrate your answer with examples.

6. How is strategy legitimated?

7. What role do narratives and storytelling play in strategy?

8. What are some of the different roles that strategy consultants might play?

9. To what extent can strategy as practice capture top management design as well as middle management implementation of strategy?

10. What happens to practice when celebrity CEOs die? Think of a concrete case such as Steve Jobs being succeeded by Tim Cook at Apple.

CASE STUDY

Articulating vision

TIMOTHY DEVINNEY

Timothy
Devinney Article

In *The Conversation*, in an article called 'All talk, no action: Why company strategy often falls on deaf ears', Professor Timothy Devinney writes about the fact that corporate consultants often say that a company's success depends not only on having a clear vision but also having the ability to articulate it to all levels of staff. Together with colleagues, he researched 20 major corporations in five industries in Australia to see to what extent, if strategies are important to performance, their critical communication to individual employees is achieved. The results were very disappointing.

But how many employees know or understand the overarching strategy of their company? How many know what the priorities are so that they can make the important trade-offs when dealing with their subordinates, customers or other stakeholders?

This issue is made even more important when we consider the need for companies to have multiple strategies: a corporate strategy for the business, for instance, and an environmental/social responsibility strategy for society.

If these strategies are important to performance, then the manner in which they are communicated to individual employees are critical. Timothy Devinney and colleagues decided to investigate this more formally.

All of these companies have clear competitors (competition is oligopolistic) and large market shares. All of these companies have articulated public strategies, and all have an environmental sustainability and social responsibility strategies, publishing reports annually that outline the good that they do. Individuals in the study were presented with six strategy statements and had to indicate which of these fit their firm, as well as their three major competitors. This exercise was repeated with individuals indicating the strategies of firms in an industry in which they did not compete (for example, banking employees were asked to evaluate the strategies of mining companies).

The findings were depressing. Individuals were presented with six different strategy statements, and had a 16.67% chance of getting it right – just by sheer luck. As the table below reveals, this is approximately what is found when the individual is attempting to distinguish amongst different strategies from a random industry.

Table 10.5   The percentage of employees that correctly identified corporate and environmental strategies within and outside their industry of employment

Percentage identified correctly

	Industry of employment	Random industry
Corporate Strategy	29.30%	15.70%
Environmental Strategy	15.80%	16%

Overall, the research found that only 29.3% of employees could correctly match their company to its publicly espoused strategy. 70% of employees could not identify the publicly presented corporate strategy of their employer. When they looked at the environmental strategy of the firm, the numbers are even worse.

At one level, this is a serious indictment on the importance of publicly stated strategies and their value as points of guidance for employees. This is reinforced by the fact that the 20 companies examined all performed well, were leaders locally and/or globally, had won many awards for environmental and social performance, and even touted these in public reports (which all the companies published). Even for the best firms, the 'vision thing' may not matter all that much.

Table 10.6   Questions asked to employees about corporate and environmental strategy within and outside their industry of employment

	Percent of employees saying Yes
Have you seen your company's last annual report?	36.50%
Does your company have an environmental sustainability strategy?	29.20%
Does your company publish a public environmental sustainability report?	17.90%
Does your company have a social responsibility strategy?	16.60%
Does your company have a stakeholder engagement strategy?	7.90%

But we also see some interesting differences and opportunities for improvement.

Some employees do a better job at understanding the differences between their firm and competitors. These individuals are also better at being able to explain their company strategy in words to others. These people may be the key strategic enablers.

It seems that middle managers are better at understanding the strategy than lower-level staff. This may be all that is necessary. Lower-level staff may simply need to understand their tasks and not why those tasks matter. It may be delusional to believe that staff or line workers need to be cognisant about higher-level strategic issues to be effective, although this runs counter to those believing strongly in the value of 'engagement'.

There's no doubt that training matters. Firms with more direct training initiatives seem to have employees who are better able to recognize what the firm views as its goals. What matters most is documentation that outlines clearly how those more vaguely articulated strategies are to be implemented – note that these are not mission statements, statements of value or codes of conduct but actual 'how to' manuals.

Rewards can also play an important role. When the researchers asked individuals about what determines their pay and their performance appraisal, items such as 'meeting the organization's sustainability goals' and 'meeting the company's social responsibility goals' came out last. No wonder that employees spend no time worrying about whether or not they know the company's sustainability strategy.

(Continued)

(Continued)

It's clear that some companies are better at articulating business strategy than others, and some firms might possess employees who are better at recognizing their company's strategies. Yet neither metric seems related to performance.

What are the implications of this? It's important to recognize that the lack of an understanding of the firm's sustainability strategy was more than part of a larger issue. The reality is that employees seem to be more cognisant of the firm's corporate strategy than its environmental strategy, with a random employee being clueless about both. This may imply that most firm's environmental strategies are so loaded with general motherhood statements that there is not much that distinguishes them from the 'feelgood' reports of their competitors.

However, if we are to avoid employee cynicism and truly motivate individuals to do well for both their companies and our society, then managers need to work harder not just in crafting these strategies, but ensuring employees have the enthusiasm and instruction to implement and execute them as well.

QUESTIONS

1. What does this research suggest about the importance of strategy for employees in these major corporations?
2. Why do you think strategy is not well disseminated and understood?
3. Carefully considering the results, and drawing on your understanding of strategy as practice, construct an outline of a programme to improve the enactment of strategy in practice in these corporations.

STRATEGY AND ORGANIZATIONAL POLITICS

POWER, ELITES, INEQUALITY

Learning objectives

By the end of this chapter you will be able to:

1 Grasp the importance of intra-organizational politics and political skill for successful strategic management

2 See the strategy process through the lens of the different dimensions of power

3 Understand what the main contours of micro-politics are likely to be, especially in multinational corporations

4 Analyse the centrality of mandates for strategic politics

5 Appreciate the role that power, legitimacy, resources and centrality play in strategy

6 Appreciate the role of power and elites in strategic decision-making

BEFORE YOU GET STARTED

There is a poem, 'To A Mouse, on Turning Her Up in Her Nest, with the Plough', by the famous Scots poet, Robert Burns, one line of which has passed into folklore, even though for people not familiar with Scots it may not be very clear what he means (which is why the English translation is provided):

The best laid schemes o' mice an' men Gang aft agley, An' lea'e us nought but grief an' pain, For promis'd joy!

The best laid schemes of mice and men Go often askew, And leave us nothing but grief and pain, For promised joy!

Introduction

Like Robert Burn's mouse in the poem, we often devise schemes or strategies that go askew. In this chapter we want to look at how schemes can go awry not just because of unforeseen externalities – the ploughman in Burns' poem – but also because of organizational politics.

An organizational situation where the outcomes that are achieved are driven by organizational politics and self-interest may seem a long way from representations of the cool, calm and rational world of strategy – but it isn't. Strategy is irremediably political. Options get accepted; others are rejected; arguments are made and data marshalled; moves are surreptitiously made and blocked, as a result of which some proposals wither, while others flourish. And behind every proposal stand those making them. And they make these proposals not always from a position of benign neutrality and benevolence but often from a position of knowledge and interest.

In this chapter we begin with a favourite theorist of strategy, Machiavelli, whom we consider the world's first modern strategist. We are not the only ones to think so, as there has been a steady stream of books extolling Machiavelli's usefulness as a strategist for understanding business and politics. A central idea in Machiavelli's thoughts is that CEOs, in his case the Prince, have interests, above all else, and these are what they must serve.

One way of thinking of organizational life is as a site of political games in which various strategies are developed, unfurled and entangled by actors with distinct and sometimes opposing interests. These games sometimes have high stakes; they can be deadly serious. Strategic interests are interests for which some will have a deep commitment. There are likely to be others who feel a strong need to contest these interests, often in their self-interest, but not always. It is different conceptions of interests that give rise to organizational micro-politics. Returning to some of the themes of Chapter 8, in multinational enterprises we often see complex games in play, usually concerning headquarter/subsidiary politics.

It is not possible to discuss organizational politics without discussing organizational elites, if one is to do the topic justice. There is a substantial literature on elites and their strategies and we consider it unfortunate that it rarely makes the pages of strategy texts. For us, strategy without elites is rather like Hamlet without the Prince. Something is missing and that something is the main actor in the plot. Hamlet's resistance to his mother's marriage to his father's brother (and murderer), his uncle Claudius, is the narrative device that drives this most compelling of Shakespeare's plays. In this case, the resistance is futile because, tragically, all the protagonists end up dead, or in Ophelia's case, mad. Resistance is not always so hopeless, as we next elaborate. Resistance can be creative; it can be productive of strategic change (see Chapter 13) rather than merely oppositional and blocking.

Decision-making is the practical expression of power. We begin to discuss decision-making by introducing you to some classic behavioural theories of decision-making associated with Sveriges Riksbank 'Nobel' Laureate, Herbert Simon. To make this abstract concept of decision-making more concrete, we refer to a famous film about a decision-making situation that elapsed over *13 Days* that could have, if the processes and power games had gone otherwise, resulted in nuclear war between the Soviet Union and the Unites States – a Third World War. The decision whether to bomb an opponent is quite concrete; it is a matter, literally, of whether an authorized finger touches a nuclear trigger. Decision-making can sometimes be stark, dramatic and unambiguous.

Of less momentousness than nuclear war but a matter of major regret to those concerned, think of the tennis star Maria Sharapova – when it was announced in March 2016 that she had been using a banned substance several of her multi-million dollar sponsors decided to void her contract, including Porsche and Tag Heuer. The power of the sponsors could not have been more clearly expressed. Decision-making is one of the primary ways that power gets to be translated into action and communicated as strategy.

Thinking about decision-making means not just reflecting on those things that are done, that is, decisions with consequences. It also means thinking about those things that are not done, that are not actions as such, but that still have consequences. Sharapova did not stop taking Meldonium when it appeared on the list of banned substances at the beginning of 2016. She made a decision not to make a decision to stop it.

Wealthy tennis players' woes are a small thing for humanity at large; by contrast, at the time of writing this book, it was recorded that the month just elapsed had the highest global warming recorded since records began. Any politician or businessperson who faces a decision where they might act on the basis of existing scientific knowledge to do something that might cut the amount of carbon being produced – but who chooses *not* to act – is making a *non-decision* that has definite effects. Non-decisions, as much as decisions, have implications, sometimes more severe.

Non-decision-making means that important decisions are not made or that certain issues do not even make it onto the agenda. Sometimes this is because of a decision by the elites, in whom decision-making is vested, not to act. At other times, it is because those that might act against elites do not choose to do so because they consider a latent or manifest challenge to the values or interests of the elite decision-makers. In view of their assessment of the array and distribution of resources, likely dispositions and outcomes, they choose not to act.

Later studies of organizational decision-making, such as the Bradford studies, identified different types of decision-making. Sporadic, fluid and constricted decision-making are characteristic types of decision-making processes encountered in practice.

Finally, by way of demonstrating the interrelatedness of the themes of the book, we return to Machiavelli via a further discussion of paradox and process, complementing that of Chapter 8, concluding this chapter in a way that goes back to the beginning of the book.

Machiavelli

Machiavelli in Context

A theorist who understood power and who still remains an invaluable guide to modern politics was Machiavelli. Niccolò Machiavelli was a Florentine diplomat and author who lived from 1469 to 1527, and is often credited with being one of the founding fathers of strategy. Machiavelli's book *The Prince* (written around 1513) describes the forms and practices of governing a state. The fascination of *The Prince* resides in the fact that Machiavelli did not describe how government *should* work (as many authors before him did) but how it *actually* works. He had little time for noble and normative theories and focused instead on how strategy should be done. Machiavelli, with his concerns with the strategic use of power, as several authors have suggested, was an 'anthropologist of power' (Clegg, 1989; Kuper, 1995; Latour, 1988; von Vacano, 2006). Rather than viewing power normatively or stipulatively, he regarded it much as an ethnographer would: as defined by situated action.

Machiavelli wrote *The Prince* in a situation of great political turmoil, when Italy was divided into many City States that either were conquered or were conquering one another, with shifting support (and success) from the German, the Spanish and the French Kings, as well as from the Vatican. Being involved in negotiations between senior state officials, Machiavelli was less interested in the ceremony of governing than in the reality of politics. As he put it (1961: 40),

> the main foundations of every state … are good laws and good arms; and because you cannot have good laws without good arms, and where there are good arms, good laws inevitably follow, I shall not discuss laws but give my attention to arms.

Implicitly, Machiavelli criticizes theories on governance that are based on contracts, laws and static notions of virtue. For him, it is the power to be able to implement a law that makes the law in the first place: policy follows power.

Machiavelli develops a deep critique of many of the established 'statecraft' texts, books written by ancient philosophers, such as Cicero and Seneca (e.g., Bragues, 2010). Both of these writers were extremely influential, espousing that a leader should rule virtuously. Their influence was found in the advice manuals produced by some of Machiavelli's contemporaries, who also emphasized virtuous and civilized behaviour. Machiavelli did not accord with norms of reciprocity (Gouldner, 1960). He noted a series of paradoxes attaching to virtue. For instance, he pointed out the difficulties of a ruler being generous:

> There is nothing so self-defeating as generosity: in the act of practicing it, you lose the ability to do so, and you become either poor and despised or, seeking to escape poverty, rapacious and hated; and generosity results in your being both. (Machiavelli, 1961: 53)

Machiavelli developed a practical manual of strategic and tactical advice that allows leaders to govern their states effectively. Machiavelli (1961: 12) wrote that *sensing* troubles is the key to successful strategy: 'as the doctors say of a wasting disease, to start with it is easy to cure but difficult to diagnose; after a time … it becomes easy to diagnose but difficult to cure'. (Here we added the emphasis to *sensing* to draw attention to the linkages with the dynamic capabilities perspective that considers sensing as one of the three main functions of DCs.) Hence, one has to take counter-measures as soon as troubles are visible on the horizon. Machiavelli uses the Romans as example: they never avoided war 'because they knew that there is no avoiding of war; it can only be postponed to the advantage of others' (1961: 12). For Machiavelli, power, conflict and war are at the centre of strategy.

Machiavelli portrayed Cesare Borgia, son of the Pope and feared prince of his times, as an example of extraordinary strategic foresight. Borgia was extremely successful in acquiring resources for and enlarging his state through wars. His major ally was his father, Pope Alexander VI. To demonstrate the strategic thinking of Borgia, Machiavelli explains how he guarded against the possibility of a hostile successor to the papacy that would not support him. First, he destroyed all the families of the rulers he had despoiled, so the new Pope could not develop alliances with them against him; second, he made friends with all the patricians in Rome; third, he controlled the College of Cardinals as far as he could (because it controlled the Pope); finally, he acquired enough power to withstand a direct attack. Machiavelli praises Cesare Borgia as strategically focused on exactly those things that allowed him to enlarge and strengthen his empire. In today's strategy parlance, Borgia not only tried to reduce the power of his direct competitors but also his competitors' competitors and supporters, as well as trying to enhance the power of his own supporters/complementors!

Even though he was no sentimentalist, Machiavelli realized that what strategy dictated, prudence might counsel against; yet, *Realpolitik* does not allow for too much pondering. He believed that cruelty could be used well or badly: if it is employed fast, used once and for all, and one's safety depends on it, it is being used well. Machiavelli argued in favour of the 'economy of violence', advocating violence 'to end, not to widen or to open, new conflicts' and 'only to prevent and deter more violence in the interest of political security' (Jackson, 2000: 433). In a similar vein, he argued that it is far better to be feared than loved: 'love is secured by a bond of gratitude which men, wretched creatures that they are, break when it is to their advantage to do so; but fear is strengthened by a dread of punishment which is always effective' (1961: 54).

Machiavelli took a pragmatic approach towards strategy. He acknowledged that it is praiseworthy to honour one's word, yet, he continued, 'nonetheless contemporary experience shows that princes who have achieved great things have been those who have given their word lightly, who have known how to trick men with their cunning, and who, in the end, have overcome those abiding by honest principles' (1961: 56). Therefore, he concluded that a ruler cannot, and must not honour his word, if it places him at a disadvantage and when the reasons for which he made his promise no longer exists (1961: 57). Think of modern politicians – how true is Machiavelli's description!

Machiavelli knew how important it is to display good qualities and hide others. For Machiavelli, the ruler must not let good qualities hinder successful rule. In fact, ethicality can be harmful. A Prince should *appear* to have good qualities, however:

> men in general judge by their eyes rather than by their hands; because everyone is in a position to watch, few are in a position to come in close touch with you. Everyone sees what you appear to be, few experience what you really are. (1961: 58)

Hence representation of what a ruler is doing (in modern terms, press coverage, strategic plans, annual reports, mission statements, spin doctoring, etc.) is more important than reality. Indeed, appearance and rhetoric creates reality; appearance is as important as action. For Machiavelli, power games are the reality of leadership; hence, idle philosophizing about how we ought to act, is in vain.

Machiavelli's narrative posed the all-important dilemma of 'dirty hands'. Machiavelli's prince, if he wants to maintain power, needed to learn how to do good *and* how to do evil – and make a decision about which action, regardless of its moral consequences, will enhance his position. In other words, sometimes you have to accommodate a little evil in order to maintain a position of leadership – from which position one's conception of the good can be fostered. Think of politicians who order the invasion of countries, accepting the civilian casualties that will ensue, using as their rationale the necessity of removing a dictator in order to bring about 'regime change'. Or think about the CEO who sacks employees in the name of a brighter future for those remaining with the firm. Both cases are examples of the 'dirty hand' problematic: in order to achieve what is promulgated and rationalized as a higher good, some ethically questionable activities in the here-and-now are legitimized and authorized. Machiavelli's answer to the dilemma was an amoral one – to remain powerful is the highest priority; doing what others may see as good or evil is determined by that over-arching objective. Outside of power one can do very little; therefore, maintaining those power relations that sustain one's leadership is the central question. One can readily do neither good nor harm without being at the centre of these power relations.

Machiavelli was the world's first modern strategist. Machiavelli did not describe how strategy *should* work (as many authors before him did) but *how it actually works*. Machiavelli's realism resided in the pragmatic rather than normative nature of his strategic advice. Machiavelli provided a practical manual of strategic and tactical advice for governance. For Machiavelli, power and conflict are at the centre of strategy. Machiavelli praised strategists who focused on exactly those things that allowed them to enlarge and strengthen their fortunes. Competition can mean destruction of opponents, as in Porter and the RBV, which is an insight we already find in Machiavelli. We might not agree with the idea of destroying people's lives, as a strategic move to secure power, although it might be necessary, for reasons of state, according to Machiavelli.

The Relevance of Machiavelli Today

Modern management theory rewrote Machiavelli for the modern age of large corporations (Jay, 1967). Even tody, Machiavelli remains very relevant. When Jonathan Powell was Tony Blair's chief of staff in Downing Street from 1995 to 2007 he found that Machiavelli's precepts were still applicable to understanding modern politics and strategy, something that he wrote about in his political memoir and guide to political pragmatics, *The New Machiavelli: How to Wield Power in the Modern World* (Powell, 2010). He noted that Machiavelli is misunderstood. He was not a moral or even an amoral philosopher; rather, he was a pragmatist who sought to describe reality and its practices rather than reform them according to some ideal standards. The focus is on the art of government, a balancing act between individual and collective interests, as well as policy preferences and pragmatics.

Powell found several of Machiavelli's precepts relevant to modern strategy. First, he suggested, leaders need an overall plan, need to choose their targets and then aim high, prudently preparing in the good times for possible futures in which the challenges will be different and considerable. Making a strategy does not mean sticking with it through thick and thin. Events will always transpire that undo the best-laid strategies. There is, as Mintzberg argues, a need for emergence in strategy. Sticking to strategy as the facts change is foolish. J.M. Keynes said, when replying to criticism of him having changed his position on monetary policy, 'When my information changes, I alter my conclusions. What do you do, sir?'[1] (Samuelson, 1986: 275). Inflexible leaders who stick to strategy through changing circumstances are not strong, resolute or tough but foolish; instead, they need to be flexible with their strategies. As circumstances change savvy leaders will change strategy accordingly.

Second, to be able to be reflective about strategy, leaders need space for thought, reflection and conversation, the importance of which is also acceded to by Hamel and colleagues (1999). Many busy CEOs and other strategy leaders fill their time with so many meetings and routines that they leave insufficient time for these vital activities.

Third, if leaders have a strategy then they need to be able to communicate it effectively. This means achieving a degree of conceptual clarity about what is intended and desired. Setting up strategy formulation processes is invaluable to this achievement. At the core of these must be adequate environmental scanning, through media monitoring, demographic updating and critical events planning. These provide essential data and information that can inform discussions about strategy and its recursive revision, so that, as the facts change, so can strategies.

Fourth, strategy is more than just ideas and concepts; it has to be implemented, action plans need enacting, vested interests identified, wooed or defeated – and it is often easier and cheaper to seduce opposition than to overcome it by force especially where those who oppose may be vital to strategic implementation. Strategy should be persuasive; it should persuade others of the soundness of a course of action. Where things have to be deliberated then strategy is invaluable. Strategy stages information, performs selective representations, imagines and marginalizes audiences: it is in every sense of the word, *political*. It creates *strategic interests*.

IN PRACTICE

Major General Mike Smith AO (Ret'd) on politics and strategy

Go Online: Visit the website for this book at https://edge.sagepub.com/strategy2e to watch an interview with Mike Smith conducted by the author team.

Mike Smith is the founding Executive Director of the Asia Pacific Civil-Military Centre of Excellence. A Sword of Honour graduate from the Royal Military College, Duntroon, he served as an Army Officer in the Australian Defense Force for 34 years, seeing active service in Cambodia, East Timor, Kashmir and Papua New Guinea.

(Continued)

Mike Smith
Interview

---

[1]Often this remark is attributed as follows: 'When the facts change, I change my mind. What do you do, sir?'

(Continued)

Mike then pursued a dramatically different path in his career; becoming CEO of Austcare, a non-profit humanitarian aid organization: additionally, he joined the Executive Committee of the Australian Council for International Development. During this time Mike became an author, publishing *Peacekeeping in East Timor: The Path to Independence* and contributing a chapter with Dr Moreen Dee on 'East Timor' in *Twenty-First-Century Peace Operations*, in addition to numerous academic articles.

As a reflection of his broad experience within the military, non-government organizations and academia, Mike takes a very holistic approach to strategy. He notes the need to take a wide view when approaching strategy, looking beyond the immediate influences on your particular situation to assess other factors.

Mike cites the work of the Australian military in Afghanistan as an example of the need for this holistic approach to strategy. As only '20% of the commitment is going to be the shooting war, the other 80% is the whole political, social, cultural and economic situation; they all must be fused together'.

Quite succinct in his approach to the fundamentals of strategy, Mike identifies 'The selection and maintenance of the aim' as the crucial feature for success. This process – the First Principle of War – includes making an accurate assessment of what the aim actually is, showing strong leadership, ensuring clear communication, obtaining necessary buy-in at all levels, from senior management (or the military hierarchy) through to local constituents and, additionally, avoiding heading off on tangents.

The First principle is identified alongside the need to set aside time for reflection, as the most important learning – and one of the greatest challenges – for strategists. After you have watched the video and looked at the associated case material we would like you to think in practice about how you would accommodate power and politics in strategy by answering the following questions, for which you will need to utilize the video interview, the Case Study and the listed reading resources.

Questions

1. How would you describe the relation between power and strategy?

2. From a power perspective, what are the shortcomings of more traditional strategy theories?

3. In what ways is strategy a common term when used in both a military and a business sense?

4. What is distinctive about military strategy as compared with business strategy?

5. Why would the study of social sciences such as anthropology be essential for effective international business strategies?

Organizational politics

Organizational politics, most simply, can be defined as follows on the next page.

Resources, as we saw in Chapter 3, have been seen as a key element in strategy. We have learned from Chapter 3 that the most potent resource is knowledge. As we shall see, power and knowledge play out in a field of forces that is de-centralized, relativistic, ubiquitous and unstable. The assumptions of the centre will never necessarily prevail; any strategic exercise of power is likely to generate its own resistance, and resistance is capable of transforming both power and strategy.

> **Organizational politics** can be defined as the use of organizational resources, such as knowledge, position or networks, to advance a desired position within the organization and/or of the organization itself.

Business involves a relation between interests and actions, connected by strategies formulating actions to realize these interests; thus, Pettigrew (2002) suggested that the strategy process in organizations always entails decisions that will be political. Politics involves the mobilization of support for a position, decision or action (Crick, 2004: 67). A change in strategy can mean a change in politics that can be threatening for existing distributions of organizational resources. What do organizational politics arise from, according to Pettigrew?

1. Structural divisions in the organization between different component elements and identities, and the different values, affective, cognitive and discursive styles associated with these

2. The complexity and the degree of uncertainty attached to the dilemma that strategy seeks to address

3. The salience of issues for different actors and identities in the organization

4. The external pressure coming from stakeholders or other actors or organizations in the environment

5. The history of past politics in the organizations in question.

Consequently, organizational politics are absolutely central to the strategy process, as Buchanan and Badham (2008) argue. Organizations are often lived and experienced as a series of 'turf wars' between different branches, divisions, departments, occupations and cultures located within these: each strategically interested part seeks to protects its own turf and sometimes attacks that of others. Organizations should be conceived as arenas in which many and varied games will be in play, with the rules of the game constantly shifting, frequently being unclear, always overlapping.

According to Pettigrew (2002), organization politics are fundamentally concerned with the management of meaning and is wrapped up in myths, beliefs, language and legend – the stuff of organizational culture. Different actors will seek to legitimate the ideas, values and demands that they espouse while simultaneously denying or decrying those that they seek to oppose. Thus, **power** is ultimately deployed in games of organizational symbolism.

The idea of power *relations* is an essential tool for understanding strategy because power is not something you have or possess. You cannot be pictured with or without it. Power is always relational. You may have the power to do certain things but that power means nothing if it is something that everyone can do. It only begins to be organizationally meaningful when the relations of organizational power enable you to do certain things that others may be restricted from doing. Organizational power involves a relation in which you can get another person not only to do something but to do it in a manner that accords with your expressed intentions as to how it should be done: in a word – organization.

> **Power** characterizes all social relations, as each of us seeks to have others do what we would want them to do, sometimes against their will. In power relations we seek to make some allies and intermediaries against those framed as opponents. Because we are all defined, organizationally, by power relations, we are always potentially both subjects and objects of power.

Organization, conceived as a verb, and organizations, used as a noun, are complex means for stabilizing power relations between people in order to achieve some goal(s). Organization as a verb relates to the day-to-day routinization of activities and processes; as a noun, it is the envelope or crucible in which power is contained and power processes play out. Either way, when we are organized or organize, when we are in organizations, we are, first and foremost, engaged with organizations as tools of and for power, devices for distributing and stabilizing power relations.

Managers in organizations who are not politically skilled will fail. The underlying purpose of politics involves mobilizing support for particular actions by reconciling different interests and values. Thus, skill must be used to influence decisions, agendas and participation in organization politics. Political competence means being a manager who can get things done, despite resistance, because they are skilled at political games (Bacharach, 2005: 93). Only politically skilled managers can be successful strategists.

Skill in politics has much to do with practice. Where power is strongly held and formally codified, rigid strategies tend to result, whereas power differences in Top Management Teams create more fluid strategies, according to Mitsuhashi and Greve's (2004: 125) research on Japanese robotics and shipbuilding firms. Power relations that are relatively stable over long periods of time inhibit politics and impairs 'organizational change as a response to declining performance'. It is those 'Top Management Teams with greater tenure differences among executives [that] are more likely to engage in strategic change overall, and particularly in the face of performance decline' (Mitsuhashi and Greve, 2004: 125).

Mitsuhashi &
Greve

EXTEND YOUR KNOWLEDGE

In Hitoshi Mitsuhashi and Henrich R. Greve's 2004 journal article '**Powerful and free: Intraorganizational power and the dynamics of corporate strategy**', the authors examine the horizontal and vertical dimensions of organizational power structures' influence on the dynamics of corporate strategy. The horizontal dimension is seen to cause inertia, while it is the vertical dimension of power differences in the Top Management Team that is seen to cause strategic change. You can read the journal article on the companion website for this book: www.edge.sagepub.com/strategy2e.

Mitsuhashi, H. and Greve, H.R. (2004) 'Powerful and free: Intraorganizational power and the dynamics of corporate strategy', *Strategic Organization*, 2(2): 107–132.

Strategic interests

That there are different interests at work in any organization is evident. The same person, when she is a young junior manager will have different interests, expressed in terms of different rationalities, from her mature CEO self; production managers will differ in their interests and rationalities from marketing managers, and so on.

Business organizations are complexes of interests; for instance, they are composed of different relations of production, between owners of capital and those hired to maximize returns to capital, managers and the employees hired to deliver services and products that will sell to clients and customers in various markets. Diverse stakeholders have interests in the business and what it does and how, where and for whom it does it, as we saw in Chapter 8. In capitalist enterprises, the key relation is that between the actual owners of capital and those charged with its day-to-day control and application of effort to maximize that capital. Non-business organizations differ only in that the stewardship of their resources is in different hands; the relations of power between different actors and interests are no less significant.

When you act in self-interest in an organization that employs you, be astute enough to realize that the best way to do so is under the guise of a **strategic interest**. To the extent that you can tie your self-interests up with emergent strategic projects then your interests can be presented as entirely legitimate, as something inherently organizationally rational even if, coincidentally, self-interested. Organizational strategies can easily be divisive because they always have the potential to make some winners and others losers.

The main problem with exclusively following self-interest is that if everyone did so, most organizations would soon become unmanageable. They would be a complex story of covert operations, with each individual not being what they seem, with strategic fragmentation, chaos and discord! When different managers have different strategic interests they will deploy these in the opportunities that present themselves, to exercise power over others. In so doing they will maximize their chances of success through the immediate knowledge that they possess or can command. Also, they can draw on networks of social relations and other forms of social capital, a concept that will be discussed later in the chapter.

> A **strategic interest** emerges when there is something at issue regarding the long-term direction of the organization or control of key decisions or resources, which divides opinions and on which people take sides. Dominant interpretations of strategic interests will tend to be represented as those that are legitimate for the organization, even against resistance from other representations.

Political Games and Their Stakes

In business, the rules of the game are neither neutral nor independently arbitrated by a 'referee' with a clear understanding of the rulebook. In business, all actors have strategic interests but some have more strategies at their disposal to further them. As far as the referee goes, the most powerful people can usually blow the whistle, interpret and create the rules, as well as declare others offside. Some of the games that get played in business that Mintzberg identifies include:

1. *Sponsorship games*, when powerful elites in the organization seek to use strategy to sponsor those who are their clients, those who are loyal (or so they think) to them in the organization

2. *Alliance-building games* played amongst peers who implicitly seek reciprocal support

3. *Budgeting games*, where the objective is to secure resources to one's strategic interest and to deny them to the strategic interest of others

4. *Expertise games*, where participants seek to position their expertise as the strategic key to the strategy dilemma – 'it's a marketing issue' says the marketing representative, while the production manager sees the solution in production's terms.

Image 11.1 Rules of the game. Copyright: alphaspirit

What is often at issue in organizational relations of power and politics are struggles either to keep things the same or to change. Usually these are two sides of the same coin: those who want to keep things the same usually do so because the current situation suits their interests; those who want to change believe it is in their interests to do so. Change is expected of new senior appointments for instance; at these times it is not politically healthy for subordinates to be seen as too dedicated to the predecessors' schemes and strategies. They are very likely to be changed. Of course, such politics are usually expressed in terms of organizational rather than sectional interests, in order to appear organizationally legitimate. Legitimacy is aided when contingencies change in the environment that favour one set of interests over another because they are better able to deal with the issues that the new contingencies create.

Intra-organizational power often reflects inter-organizational dependencies, such as reliance on a key supplier or a key financier, and is adjusted, albeit in fits and starts, when environmental changes alter the pattern of interdependence (Hickson et al., 1971; Pfeffer and Salancik, 1974; Boeker, 1989; Donaldson, 1999; Hillman et al., 2000).

New situations require new solutions. In the twentieth century United States the skill and knowledge background of CEOs shifted overwhelmingly from being based in marketing to finance. Once a national market had been established, led by marketing CEOs in the early years of the century, new forms of knowledge, based on budgetary control, became dominant (Fligstein, 1987). Shifts of power usually represent shifts in vested interests, associated strategies and resource allocations. Certain practices, such as financial accounting rather than marketing, become represented in the 'inner circles' (Useem, 1986) of power relations. In this way certain forms of knowledge are positioned at the heart of power relations and agendas become skewed and implicit biases mobilized in characteristic organizational micro-politics.

Organizational Micro-Politics

Where sub-groups such as subsidiaries (see below) or departmental managers play power games within organizations, we may say that **micro-politics** are at work (Dörrenbächer and Gepert, 2009: 200). These micro-political games are sometimes played face-to-face, in the open; sometimes they will be 'refereed,' according to rules, while other times they will be played in ways that are quite covert, deliberately violating the rules.

> **Micro-politics** are strategic attempts to exert a formative influence on social structure and relations in local settings to further sectional interests.

The extent to which micro-politics can be conducted as covert operations depends on the degree to which micro-political actors operate in zones about which elites have little or no knowledge. Where strategy formulation requires the elites to have access to resources and knowledge that they do not have, that they do not know or understand, then those who *do* have detailed knowledge are in a potentially powerful position.

All organizations have micro-politics. Such politics strive to 'secure options, realize interests and to achieve success through efforts that are often but not exclusively motivated by interests or individual career plans of key actors' (Dörrenbächer and Gepert, 2009: 200). Organizations are many things, to many people: for shareholders a source of shareholder value; for rank and file employees a job; for managers an opportunity to build a career, earning substantial salary and options packages, as well as being a springboard to move on, up, or out.

Any strategy, once conceived, is likely to struggle with processes of micro-politics. The process of struggle is one of political change – getting others to do things that they would not otherwise do (Dahl, 1957). It must engage the self-consciousness of those it seeks to change; it must capture their imagination and energies. All strategies see some ideas and their bearers assume more or less importance. These matters of esteem effect relations between people as well as their self-conceptions. Struggles around and over strategy will always be creative, as new identities, self-understandings, social relations and products, goods and services, are created. Strategic struggles occur through communicative action, constructed in terms of plans, documents, models, commands, and reports: there is always a 'discursive' element to strategy and usually many artefacts, such as vision and mission statements. Changes in strategy are a matter of creating categories: think of the BCG's 'cash cows' or 'dogs', or SWOT analysis with its 'strengths', 'weaknesses', 'opportunities' and 'threats'.

Strategy is intended as a road map to success. Ideally, it should coordinate diverse knowledge based in disciplines such as accounting, marketing, production, etc. What happens in practice, when strategy is being formulated, is that those who are repositories of these different types of knowledge will compete to be more compelling in their claims than rivals with different capabilities. Internal 'tournaments' occur in organizations in which proposals are based on specific spheres of competence, functional responsibilities and disciplinary knowledge (Clegg and Courpasson, 2004; Baunsgaard and Clegg, 2013). **Political skill** is an essential prerequisite of the strategic manager's job because mobilizing support is essential if capabilities are to be translated into strategy.

> **Political skill** entails using knowledge, networks and social capital astutely and procedurally, in a manner that best serves the strategic interest one is seeking to advance.

Under the pressure of competitive performance, differences and divisions can sometimes end up being viscerally personal, as failure to perform as expected means loss of position, even if softened by attractive severance packages. Not surprisingly, being in the upper echelons of organizations, where strategy is formulated, is a politically charged environment in which contenders, rivals and incumbents frame strategic interests in their interests. It is often the case that organizations and their strategy are represented as merely the achievement of technical rather than political exercises, a matter of getting the models right, feeding in the right data, and seeing what should be done. Nothing could be further from the truth. Strategy is irremediably political.

In Mintzberg's (1983) terms, business organizations are arenas in which the games that unfold are games of politics. Strategy, therefore, is the sum of all the interconnected games, which have more or less politically skilled players involved in them (Crozier and Friedberg, 1980). The metaphor of a game suggests sports. Sports, as we know, have codes or rules. Rules in business are not quite like those in sport. A sports code is constituted by its rules. You know whether it is a game of soccer or rugby by the shape of the ball, whether it can be handled or not, whether there is a goalkeeper, the design of the posts, and the rules followed and interpreted by the referee. These all shape the arena of action – the game that unfolds on the field of play. Organizational fields of play, especially the more complex the organization, never allow politics to take place on level playing fields but always on terrains already constructed, historically, by the sediment of past struggles, decisions and strategies. Nowhere is this more the case than in complex multinational organizations, especially as they enter into global alliances.

Power relations and alliances

Alliances can engender intense conflicts from which victors and vanquished emerge. Sometimes the combatants, often uneasily, enter into a treaty. Uneasy treaties can often lead to shaky alliances as political forces regroup, perhaps to fight another day. Often, however, the struggles are so vicious that the losers exit or are forced from the organization, such as when a Top Management Team that resisted a takeover is 'let go'. People in organizations that cannot manage their power relations will end up spending more time fighting each other than seeking to find common purpose against competitor organizations. Only very large organizations or those with no competition can survive sustained complex politics for long.

Organizational politics is rarely a question of winner takes all; more usually compromises have to be made and coalitions and alliances formed. Coalitions represent the hitching together of different strategic interests in a form of **alliance** that is specific to particular issues and their extensions.

Alliances are, for everyone involved in them, a means rather than an end. The point of an alliance is to achieve something or other. Negotiations between political coalitions create the ordering of goals in organizations. These negotiations can crisscross organizations: they may occur at the departmental level, around specific strategic projects or over specific strategic issues; they can occur between different organizations, as when different airlines join or leave alliances. For instance, Qantas used to be allied with British Airways (BA) in its flights to Europe; although it still retains an alliance with BA in the Oneworld Alliance, it changed partners on the European leg to Emirates, which is a member of the rival Star Alliance. Interests that might align on one occasion will not necessarily cohere on another.

> An **alliance**, in its broadest sense, is a mechanism that links diverse more or less central and peripheral actors, interests and strategies for mutual gain. Alliances entail a process of convergence of interests (Kalyvas, 2006: 383).

Strategies decided at the centre may order goals but they cannot always ensure their implementation – especially in far-flung corners of the organizational empire. Sometimes the strategic centre of an organization can be at a great distance, in knowledge terms, from those places where implementation occurs: this often happens in organizations that have subsidiaries and strong central direction. The blocking, modifying and avoiding of central directives is sometimes a way of maintaining the discretion to adapt, creatively, what might not otherwise work locally (Sharpe, 2001; Becker-Ritterspach et al., 2002: see Dörrenbächer and Gepert, 2009: 203). Sometimes issues, although seemingly small, can derail much larger strategic projects: for instance, where a subunit is defiantly against adopting some new technology that the company has bought in which they had no hand in developing – sometimes referred to as the *not-invented-here syndrome* (Katz and Allen, 1982).

MNEs are particularly prone to politics. Strategy as it is formulated at the centre entails centripetal controls but we need also to consider centrifugal forces (Morgan, 2001). What is at issue is how certain practices become crucial in determining what is considered to be a strategic interest. Some actors will have micro-political skills that ensure certain positions are blocked, while certain other interests are advanced in terms of the strategic agenda (Johnson et al., 2003).

Microsoft after Bill Gates

MNEs with substantial investments seek to influence host-country government policies to protect earnings, and produce a favourable regulatory environment in legal areas such as immigration, trade and investment through **non-market strategies**. This will especially be the case at a time of initial entry into a country (e.g., Vernon, 1971; Fagre and Wells, 1982; Kim, 1988; Dunning, 1993; Grosse, 1996). At the higest echelons of MNEs central corporate political will often seek to affect the public policy environment in a favourable way (Baysinger, 1984).

> **Non-market strategies** are methods for pursuing strategic goals through attempts to influence actors, such as government, the media and other influential groups.

Multinationals and subsidiary politics

The choice of political strategies depends on the bargaining power of MNE subsidiaries compared to that of the host country (Blumentritt, 2003). For much of the twentieth century the 'Banana Republics' of Central America, of which Guatemala was the most notorious, were countries run by corrupt governments.

Go online: The Guatemalan government worked effectively for the United Fruit Company, often in cahoots with the CIA, early in the twentieth century (see www.mayaparadise.com/ufc1e.htm). You can also find the weblink to this article on the companion website for this book at https://edge.sagepub.com/strategy2e

---

The United Fruit Company

On the whole, government–business relations today tend to be subtler than the Guatemalan case. Today, the means are more likely to be lobbying, funding of parties, sponsorship of representatives, public relations campaigns, sponsoring of legislative initiatives and so on. Canada, for instance, has one of the highest percentages of foreign-owned business inside its borders, mostly US-owned, but given the robustness of Canadian political institutions, the potential for their corruption is very low.

MNEs are inherently political entities. The interests, ideologies, identities and careers of key actors are entangled within the social fabric of the corporation's power relations, as well as reaching outside its formal boundaries (Geppert and Dörrenbächer, 2014). For instance, MNE senior managers in less-developed countries will often meet and mingle extensively with national elites, in prestigious venues, such as the Opera, major sports events and boards of cultural institutions. Power relations and the constitution of interests have a fundamental impact on the transfer of employment practices within MNEs (Morgan and Kristensen, 2006; Ferner et al., 2012; Becker-Ritterspach et al., 2015). For instance, the quality of employment health and safety or sustainability is often improved through the standardization of MNE practices in local subsidiaries or sub-contracting organizations in their value chain.

Other studies point to the crucial role of increased competition and its impact on organizational politics (Becker-Ritterspach and Dörrenbächer, 2011) and conflicts within the MNE (Blazejewski and Becker-Ritterspach, 2011). Where an MNE has been the dominant actor, economically, in a host nation, the entry of new competitors can change the internal politics dramatically. The investment of German supermarket chains, such as Lidl and Aldi, in countries with previously oligopolistic markets is a case in point, as has happened in Australia. Some authors argue that MNEs constitute a fundamentally 'contested terrain' (Edwards and Bélanger, 2009), rather than the unassailable citadels they are sometimes imagined to be. MNEs fail: size and resources are no defence against competition, as companies such as Kodak discovered.

MNEs' primary stakeholders and their dominant external social and economic relations, raise questions about the role of MNE identities and their ideologies. There are many relations of domination and subordination: headquarters over subsidiary; embedded national language over that of the subsidiary hosts; strategy conceived at the centre over improvisations made in peripheries attuned to local contexts; global elites versus national elites, etc. The power of MNEs in relation to the host countries in which their subsidiaries are based are often described as 'asymmetrical' (Clark and Geppert, 2006) or 'hegemonic' (Levy, 2008), notably in the context of emerging economies. Resource-based economies, rich in natural mineral resources, depend on sophisticated MNEs such as Rio Tinto or BP for resource exploitation. The resources available to the MNE are often far in excess of those available to national governments or local organizations in both capital and sophistication.

Newly emerging 'transnational social spaces' (Morgan, 2001) are created by investments from wealthy nations into less developed parts of the world, where indigenous populations exist alongside compounds of global investment. MNEs' (and NGOs') strategy formulation and implementation often occurs in ways that have adverse political effects. Air-conditioned four-wheel drives dash past indigenous people living a wholly different reality from the strategies formulated far away that are reshaping their everyday lives.

MNEs create and distribute systems of governance and control networks of production across regionally dispersed organizational units. Some of these units will be deeply embedded in very different realities to those the strategies emanate from. In such situations strategy becomes the carrier of network relations that lace across the globe, often as global production networks (GPN). As Levy (2008) suggests, GPNs are reflective of an era of transnational development. Not only that which is produced and consumed has become commoditized but also the local organizations engaged in these processes and relations become integrated into global strategy. The socially constructed international division of labour can serve to perpetuate neo-colonial tendencies in which strategic decisions are concentrated in the core cities of the global economy while the decision-takers are spread throughout the 'Third World' and assigned limited roles in global strategies.

The power relations are not just one way, however. Newly insurgent governments sometimes nationalize assets; political 'contests' (Edwards and Bélanger, 2009) emerge between groups of actors occupying various social spaces manifesting the politicization of MNEs at local, national and international levels (Ferner et al., 2012). Contemporary MNEs are divided and politicized on the basis of differential linguistic capabilities (Riad, 2005; Vaara et al., 2005). It matters what language is used in local negotiations, as research on the construction of the new Panama Canal has demonstrated (Van Marrewijk et al., 2016, in press). Joint ventures between different language groups, especially where one is embedded in dominant countries and languages in use, such as the United States, when confronted with a partner thought junior in terms of national sovereignty and experience and whose language is not English, are particularly prone to expressions of 'cultural' politics.

EXTEND YOUR KNOWLEDGE

In a paper in *Organization Studies* that looks at the construction of a megaproject in Panama, the extension of the famous Panama Canal, Alfons van Marrewijk, Sierk Ybema, Karen Smits, Stewart Clegg and Tyrone Pitsis examine the '**Clash of the Titans: Temporal organizing and collaborative dynamics in the Panama Canal Expansion Project**', in which language differences between Spanish and English speakers became constitutive of and constituted as project-based politics. You can download the paper from the website at www.edge.sagepub.com/strategy2e.

van Marrewijk, A., Ybema, S., Smits, K., Clegg, S. and Pitsis, T. (2016) 'Clash of the Titans: Temporal organizing and collaborative dynamics in the Panama Canal Expansion Project, Organization Studies, doi: 10.1177/0170840616655489

Panama Canal Expansion Project

Business elites

MNEs are one of the major mechanisms in creating and leveraging a global business **elite**. Globalization (see Chapter 8) has seen the emergence of a transnational capitalist class that shares a common set of elite interests and is engaged in a regime of global capital accumulation (see, e.g., Carroll, 2010; Murray and Scott, 2012).

Elites maintain their dominant position intergenerationally through elite forms of social reproduction, involving access to honours, titles and education, on the basis of a privileged command of resources of various kinds of capital that creates a series of interlocking elites (Dogan, 2003). While the study of elites is well established from the path-breaking work of C. Wright Mills (1956) onwards, it is only in the last 30 years that a few researchers have begun to trace links

> An **elite** is a social group within a societal hierarchy that claims and/or is accorded power, prestige or command over others, on the basis of a number of criteria, and that seeks to preserve and entrench its status.

between corporate elites as a cohesive group and the types of strategies that they follow. There are guides to such research and examples in the collection edited by Hertz and Imber (1995), particularly the contributions by Thomas (1995) and Useem (1995).[2]

Elites are functionally located; they may be found in business, the military and other institutional areas. In some autocratic contexts little distinction between the different fragments occurs – the military elite is also the political and business elite. In more democratic contexts there are interlocking relations between the different elites with the business elite increasingly being the core elite of developed capitalist societies. They control the most basic resource with which to command other resources – financial capital.

Members of the **business elite** are able to command strategic resources, with the business elite comprising those members of the highest strata in the corporate sphere, usually at the board level, usually as upper tier directors.

> **Business elites** can be identified as that relatively small group within the societal hierarchy that are premised on their command of financial capital in major corporate organizations.

Those elites that enjoy high authority, wide power and substantial control over resources that have consequences for many members of society constitute the '1 per cent', identified in recent manifestations, such as Occupy Wall Street. Command provides resources for social reproduction through education, for instance, whereby the younger generation of any specific elite may have privileged access to commanding positions in the future (Salverda and Abbink, 2013).

Forms of elite capital

Pierre Bourdieu

The writings of Pierre Bourdieu are central to discussions of business elites. He sees these elites as expressions of resource-based and symbolic power. Elites are rooted in what he calls a *habitus*, the sets of assumptions and underlying principles that are reproduced in daily interaction (Bourdieu, 1990). These are manifest in terms of symbolic understandings that function as sources of domination. Elite symbolic understandings frame a coherent 'common sense' for an organization's elite.

In practice, business elites usually have considerable reserves of capital at their disposal. In corporate organizations it is ascension to dominant, board-level positions at the top of major organizations that defines the elite. From these positions they are able to network across other elite social spaces, creating a personal field of power that intersects with others already established. Elite members share a variety of interests arising from similarities of experience, training, public roles or duties, and way of life: they have financial capital and share social capital with other elites, using this capital to command resources such as organizations and their strategies. They are, in Dogan's words (2003), at the apex of power.

Financial or economic capital, in the form of tangible assets, fundamentally defines the elite. The accrual of this capital often occurs through the stock options that are granted as a part of the agency contract. It is this capital that is the main source of power and elite status in business, one of the reasons why executive remuneration is

---

[2]The fields of politics and public administration are better served with ethnographic studies of elites and strategy, as in the work of Powell (2013) and Rhodes (2007); Rhodes et al. (2007), and in anthropology, the work of Lépinay (2011), looking at financial elites' decision-making, as well as the contributions of Ortiz (2013), who investigated the global elite of financial professionals, the kind of people who helped bring on the Global Financial Crisis.

important. Being paid huge amounts attests to the moral worth and legitimacy of the recipient, their rank in the status order.

Social Capital

Bourdieu (1984) regards the knowledge, tastes and cultural dispositions that attach to people assumed to display refinement and status as a form of capital. These are acquired as social capital in the context of the family, its networks and relationships, as well as through education. Social capital is created by experience in school and university, as well as through specific coalitions of interest that are built within and between organizations. As a rule, elite schools and universities build the most valuable social capital.

Social capital aids bridge building of relationships that span 'structural holes', connecting otherwise disconnected realms (Burt, 1992, 2000) as ex-cohorts of students in elite institutions make their separate ways in the world. Some managers, by virtue of their embeddedness in these elite social backgrounds, will have much more valuable social capital to draw on while others, from less-privileged backgrounds, will have to be more skilled at internal coalition building. The greater one's social capital is locally recognized the more one is likely to prevail in debates about strategy formation.

Social capital may be found in kinship and marital ties and connections, as well as in contacts forged within specific milieu in which one is acculturated. Milieu knowledge of how things work, knowing about the relative prestige of institutions, professions and opportunities, is invaluable in this regard. Collective family knowledge can be vital in grasping (or occluding) how these social constructions operate.

Managers deploy social capital to construct networks linking the organizations they work for with others with which they deal (Coleman, 1988). Long tenure grants greater opportunities to build social capital (Barkema and Pennings, 1998; Shen and Cannella, 2002). In the long term, social capital builds power to do things. It intertwines with cultural capital, in the form of both educational qualifications and the general cultural learning that is implicit, embodied and embrained, which is coded in quintessential gestures and modes of speech, dress and deportment.

Symbolic capital attaches to titles, honours and reputation, which explains the attraction of having titled people on boards in those countries that still celebrate noble titles. Clearly, those countries that preserve vestiges of feudalism in their honours systems, with hereditary peerages and titles, are able to contribute peers of the realm to grace Executive Boards. Possession of these forms of capital eases the strategy work of networking and communication between different fractions of the elites, often achieved through multiple interlocking directorships. Indeed, elites in organizations at board level often interconnect different pinnacles of power through holding multiple board positions in different organizations (Palmer, 1983). Such people comprise the 'boundary spanners' (Geletkanycz and Hambrick, 1997), those senior and chief executives with multiple directorships linking different corporate, cultural, civic and political fields, able to learn from and frame strategies across these fields. In Bourdieu's terms, they are 'multi-positional', able to trace common narratives of strategy across multiple domains, creating a common ideology for dominant elites. They share a common frame of reference, a collective business common sense and a shared culture.

Elite Power

Elites are responsible for shaping action at the strategic level that has major effects on the life chances of many stakeholders. These stakeholders include those they employ and unemploy; those whose communities they blight or improve; those whose tax raising capacities they service or avoid. In general, we can say that elite practices have an impact on the generalized interests of the multitude of non-elites in various ways.

Scott (1982, 1991, 1996, 2001, 2008) has made extensive study of elite domination and power in Britain, the USA and elsewhere. In strategy studies, research has focused too infrequently on the extremely powerful, at the pinnacle of very large organizations (Pettigrew, 2002; Pettigrew and McNulty, 1995, 1998). The 'giant firm corporate elite' (Savage and Williams, 2008: 19) and the 'professionals of power' that service them (Clegg et al., 2006: 343) are not so well researched, despite the fact that they are located at the centre of organization power relations closely enmeshing economic and social power (Clegg et al., 2006).

Elite Legitimacy

Social distance is the essential principle of legitimacy of the elites:

> it is by being different, it is by signalling that getting to the top is not possible for everybody, irrespective of their merits, that the elite persuades people that there are impervious worlds and that these worlds are necessary to the balance of societies – and the organization. (Courpasson, 2009: 437)

Elite members of organizations represent inter-generational forms of resilient oligarchical power (McLean and Harvey, 2006) and interlocking inter-organizational circles of socialization and learning (Mizruchi, 1996). They form the inner circle of the business world (Useem, 1986). It is they that set and interpret the rules of the game of corporate strategies and power struggles.

For the vast majority of ordinary organization members, as Clegg and Hardy (1996: 628) observed, it is not that they do not know the rules of elite games of strategy so much as they might not even recognize the games, let alone their rules. Nonetheless, within any field, subordinate organizations and agents strive to find ways to neutralize the advantages of the dominant, and at times discover ways – 'subversion strategies' (Emirbayer and Williams, 2005: 693) – to 'outflank' more capital-rich rivals (Clegg, 1989). Symbolic struggles, Bourdieu argues, possess a degree of autonomy from the structures in which they are embedded.

Elites form an inner circle by virtue of their command of resources, in an echo of the resource-based view. They become dominant by holding a controlling position within an organizational field through command over large, strategically significant resources. Dominant people in society at large tend to be members of dominant organizations. Corporate domination involves control of the economic field by a relatively small number of powerful companies, themselves controlled by a corporate power elite. The corporate power elite operates collectively within *fields of power* that bring together the uppermost strata drawn from distinctive organizational fields. These fields of power are where strategy, at the highest level, is conceived and discussed by the power elites; social spaces that transcend individual organizations and serve as opportunities for different types of social and positional equals to mingle. These are places such as elite clubs, boardrooms of business and cultural institutions, etc., where successful interactions and broader social networks can be constructed. Boardrooms are the ultimate loci of power in organizational settings (Pettigrew and McNulty, 1998) from where broader social networks can be accessed and constructed.

The Social Reproduction of Strategic Elites

The most striking characteristic (Zald and Ash, 1966) of strategic elites is their resilience (Davis et al., 2003). Resilience is not based exclusively on the cohesiveness and closure of inner circles and social networks of competence and acquaintance. Elites are quite capable of social reproduction through new blood. Organizational elites are open oligarchies that, as Courpasson (2009) argues, need elite diversification to be sustained and perpetuated.

New professional groups within organizations, particularly in the areas of strategy, are sub-elites from whom would-be upper elites, or oligarchs, are monitored and recruited. Organizations are contested oligarchies through which elites circulate, perpetuating and refreshing the principal oligarchy (CEOs and major directors). The development of strong and efficient internal elites that owe their election to the leader are favoured by organizational elites. Eventually, these sub-elites, if successful, will become leaders. Elite groups coalesce around issues of strategy – because it is here that major decisions, with big implications, are made.

There is an extended literature on patterns of elite production (Putnam, 1976). Executives' careers can be solidified through the social dynamics of interlocking directorates (Mizruchi, 1996) and the role of specific social networks (Davis et al., 2003). Companies use non-executive directorships as a learning device for those whom they want to groom for leadership and elite roles. The most valuable elite ties are with financial institutions, the purveyors of that most vital ingredient, capital. Sponsored mobility into the right clubs is also important.

Courpasson (2009) suggests that different *paths of social mobility* can lead to the business elite.

- *Embedded mobility* draws on the wealth and prestige that luck in 'being born in the right bed' delivers to many corporate leaders. Such luck in being an heir can, of course, be furthered buttressed by education at elite schools and universities, and by all the social capital and networks delivered by living lives of privilege. Essentially, this fraction of the business elite draws its reproductive ability from fundamental class relations and the condensation and sedimentation of class-based principles. In countries that have a feudal lineage these relations are founded on the basis of an aristocracy and its social devices (the upper-class effect). Caste systems also operate in this way, where to be a Brahmin is an *ascribed status* that attaches to birthright, one that can never be achieved.

- *Network-based mobility* owes its elevation less to birthright and more to social relations through marriage and membership of the right clubs and associations, and through an extensive array of interlocking directorships. This elite fraction often recruits from the ranks of the leading strategists because they have a reputation for being business-savvy and connected. Governance is the mechanism that unites the fraction. Through common exposure and experience in the governance of elite businesses, they acquire cohesion and common learning. They exchange resources between board members, notably information and learning. These exchanges are likely to improve governance decisions and therefore, organizational performance. In his class perspective on interlocks, Zeitlin (1974) stresses how interlocking directorates produce social cohesiveness.

- *Traditional company-based elites* move through fast-track career paths and internal education programmes within one organization. These are the consummate corporate professional bureaucrats – masters of the one company and organization – to which they have devoted a life of service. Here it is intra-organizational mechanisms of career management that enable selection, grooming and conformance, in what can be called an 'organization effect'. M&S used to operate strictly on these principles. The stress is on the capacity of individual organizations to choose and design their own models of authority and legitimacy. Reputational capital attaches to being an organization with attractive career mechanisms; in addition, these help frame a very particular organizational identity.

Maclean and colleagues (2010: 328) observe that in France and Britain there is a 'super-concentration of power in the hands of a small number of dominant agents within the corporate economy.' The empirical foundation of their research was a comparative analysis of the 100 largest French and British companies and their directors between 1998 and 2003 (Maclean et al., 2006).

How elites operate is dependent on specific elements in the national societal context. In Britain and France, the field of power builds and maintains institutional solidarity, with the French cohort being more tightly coupled and endogenous than the British (Kadushin, 1995; Burt, 2000), with strong corporate ties sustained and supported by the state. The British elite is both more open in recruiting talent from outside of dominant social capital networks and more loosely coupled in these networks.

EXTEND YOUR KNOWLEDGE

Maclean, Harvey & Chia

Contemporary studies of power elites and their strategies are unfortunately few and far between; however, you can read an article by Mairi Maclean, Charles Harvey and Robert Chia (2010) on '**Dominant corporate agents and the power elite in France and Britain**' on the companion website for this book: www.edge.sagepub.com/strategy2e.

Maclean, M., Harvey, C. and Chia, R. (2010) 'Dominant corporate agents and the power elite in France and Britain', *Organization Studies*, 31: 327–348.

Resisting elites and changing strategy

If there is not some potential form of resistance, power would be unnecessary. Foucault (1980) suggested that power works in large part through its failures: without some resistance to power there would be no rationale for the constant attempt to impose it.

Elites and top managers cannot expect to exert total control in terms of strategy requirements. Strategy will never be 'perfectly' implemented because power relations in complex organizations entail delegations of authority and discretion, creating a degree of indeterminateness in action. Structures and strategies move through complex circuits of power to be implemented. These 'circuits' constitute how social and system integration occurs in organizations; as electricity flows through an electronic circuit board so does power flow through social and organizational relations. Circuits of power introduce possibilities of discretion, resistance and change (Clegg, 1989; Balogun and Johnson, 2005; Courpasson et al., 2012). Using the discretion available to them, managers can sometimes influence workplace changes and strategies by resisting top-down implementations (Courpasson et al., 2012).

Resistance is inherent to organizational life (Jermier et al., 1994; Thompson and Ackroyd, 1995; Mumby, 2005). Resistance is not necessarily harmful to the organization (Piderit, 2000; Ford et al., 2008; Courpasson et al, 2012). Research has highlighted the creativity of workers in resisting increasing control of the labour process by management (Prasad and Prasad, 2000; Fleming and Sewell, 2002; Spicer and Böhm, 2007). Resisters can sometimes influence top management decisions and produce change through creative resistance (Thomas and Davies, 2005).

Courpasson and colleagues (2012) analysed occasions where resistance became productive. Productive resistance refers to those forms of protest that develop outside of institutional channels; it is concerned with concrete activities that aim to voice claims and interests that are usually not taken into account by management decisions. Its goal is to foster the development of alternative managerial practices likely to benefit the organization as a whole (Courpasson and Dany, 2009).

We often think of resistance to a strategy as something 'dysfunctional', something that is bad for the strategy. However, whatever resistance is organized can only serve to further the categories of the strategy makers, insofar as it must engage with these terms, if only to resist them. Further, resistance can be used by elites to justify a more vigorous application of the strategy being resisted. Resistance serves as a warrant for further strategic application. Failure makes strategy appear even more necessary! Should organization members resist the strategy in ways that suggest that they are not *au fait* with it, such resistance merely serves to demonstrate the necessity of further strategic discipline in order to make them knowledgeable – and powered rather than resistant – subjects.

Elites will invariably represent changes in strategy as a response to a changing environment, or changes in technology; a familiar power strategy is to depersonalize political realities by making them seem merely instrumental. Sometimes the two discourses of a changing technology and a changing business environment get tangled up with each other. Such was the case in the strategy for transforming the public service broadcaster, the Australian Broadcasting Corporation (ABC), in the 1990s, as the case at the end of this chapter elaborates.

One thing is evident from the analysis that Fleming and Spicer make of the ABC: strategy must persuade others; as such there is always a discursive element to any strategy and these discourses are inherently politically unstable. All discourses consist of signifiers that constitute categories that the strategists seek to advance and fix in the organizational or public consciousness. The aim is to make them seem normal, natural or the best way to do things. Consequently, the best way to resist a strategy is not to negate it entirely: it is to leverage some of its meaning and categories away from the positions that the strategists have assumed through posing counter discourses. The politics of strategy most often entails a politics of meaning. Thus, resistance has an impact on strategy to the extent that it wields a degree of power over its determination, as Fleming and Spicer (2007: 6) suggest.

As we have said earlier, the politics of strategy do not take place on a metaphorical level playing field. The strategic centre is invariably more privileged than those who would resist it. Strategy has the potential to change the relations of meaning between organization members For non-elites strategy is both a community-building device when it unites but it can also be a 'white-anting' strategy, something that gnaws away at the grounds of others' legitimacy and respect, dividing organizations. Strategy entails a *power to* get things done but it can only ever achieve this power if it simultaneously is able to exercise *power over* the many others required for its implementation. To each of the methods that a strategist might use to ensure compliance there is always an answer. Strategy might seek to coerce others into compliance but the others can always refuse. There are many ways of refusing ranging from outright non-compliance to puzzled bemusement at one's inability to quite grasp what it is that needs to be done differently.

Strategy is a discipline, as Foucault identifies, argue Knights and Morgan (1991). It bestows world-making powers on certain managers by empowering them with certain skills and strategic responsibilities that legitimate the dimensions of power that they wield. Often these powers are codified in professional discourse. When we enter the sphere of values, traditions, cultures and structures of an institution such as a profession, power can work strategically without consciously seeming to do so. Professions in which strategic knowledge is embedded, such as finance, accounting, supply chain management, while they routinely help create knowledgeable managers, simultaneously introduce specific means of decision and control, such as accounting practices (Whittle and Mueller, 2010). In turn, such practices entail a specific calibration of reporting relations, data collection and analysis, which become powerful and highly unobtrusive ordering devices in businesses and organizations.

Foucault (1979) identifies disciplinary power as being embedded in the taken-for-granted routines that are a normal part of the everyday round of work. Organizationally empowered subjects know how to do and say what is required strategically. Resistant subjects, if they are to be effective, must equally know how to do and say what is required strategically and then use it to advance their strategic interests rather than those enshrined in the official strategy (as did the Friends of the ABC in Fleming and Spicer's (2007) account). Effectively powered people have political skill – a definite prerequisite of managerial success. Successful strategy requires power fused with knowledge, the most indeterminate and intangible of resources with which to inform decision-making.

Strategy and decision-making processes

Making **strategic decisions** is the very stuff of strategy making.

> A **strategic decision** is typically defined as being one that has long-term organizational implications for key success factors such as access and control of resources and effective performance.

Every organizational history is littered with missed opportunities and poor decisions. The process of decision-making has been seen as synonymous with strategy making: as Kathleen Eisenhardt (1999: 1) has noted, 'the ability to make fast, widely supported, and high-quality strategic decisions on a frequent basis is the cornerstone of effective strategy'. Understanding how decisions are made is central to understanding strategy making.

It was the 'Nobel' Laureate, Herbert Simon, who pointed out that perfect decision-making, and so perfect strategy, is simply not possible. Instead, Simon posited that there could only ever be a bounded rationality, as we discussed in Chapter 5. Why is rationality bounded? It is bounded because of the limits that are informational (i.e. perfect information does not exist) and cognitive (the ability of managers to process complex and difficult information). In reality, managers can only review a limited range of factors and possibilities in making their strategic decisions. Charles Lindblom, whose ideas closely aligned with those of Simon's, summarizes it as follows:

> Although such an approach (rational decision-making) can be described, it cannot be practiced except for relatively simple problems and even then in a somewhat modified form. It assumes intellectual capacities and sources of information that men simply do not possess, and it is even more absurd as an approach to policy when the time and money that can be allocated to a policy problem is limited, as is always the case. (Lindblom, 1959: 80)

Decision-makers are thus only able to exercise rationality within the limits of the information that is available to them and their ability to make sense of it. James March argued that '… human beings develop decision procedures that are sensible, given the constraints, however, even though they might not be sensible if the constraints were removed'. As a shorthand term for such procedures, he coined the term **satisficing** (March, 1978: 590).

In reality, strategists usually restrict themselves to a small number of values and consider only a few alternative policies (Lindblom, 1959: 80). For instance, a strategist working in a finance ministry might have the objective of trying to control inflation. There are, of course, many other values that could factor into the objective but, following Lindblom, a strategist 'would quickly admit that he was ignoring many related values' (Lindblom, 1959: 79). Lindblom argued that, in reality, values and policies emerge simultaneously – i.e. talking about a policy necessitates thinking about one's particular position on an issue and vice versa. According to Lindblom a good policy is determined by whether different decision-makers can agree on the policy – as opposed to an alternative

> **Satisficing**: a decision that will both 'satisfy' and 'suffice'. A satisficing decision is where the organization does not strive to make an optimal decision, but instead one that satisfies key actors in the organization and 'does the trick'. A satisficing decision is rarely ideal but it makes do with what is seen to be available and relevant.

EXTEND YOUR KNOWLEDGE

You can read D. Collingridge and J. Douglas' 1984 journal article '**Three models of policymaking: Expert advice in the control of environmental lead**' on the companion website for this book: www.edge.sagepub/strategy2e. It is a good application and discussion of Lindblom's approach.

Collingridge, D. and Douglas, J. (1984) 'Three models of policymaking: Expert advice in the control of environmental lead', *Social Studies of Science*, 14: 343–370.

Collingridge & Douglas

Making decision-making processes more realistic …

The notion that decision-making is not super-rational criteria is pushed further by Cohen and his colleagues (1972). They develop the notion of the garbage can. Their research sought to understand what happened in the decision-making process. Their premise

Image 11.2   Garbage can. Copyright: Skip O'Donnell

was that many organizations are chaotic with loosely defined procedures for making strategic decisions. Seeing decision-making as taking place in situations of ambiguity their results were a startling refutation of rational decision-making processes. Instead of a linear decision-making process what they found was that decision-making was less linear and more random.

The garbage can is a metaphor that seeks to capture the image of problems, solutions, opportunities and decision-makers as adjacent to each other in a purely random fashion. The central premise of the garbage can is that specific decisions do not follow an orderly, linear process, moving seamlessly from problem to solution. Instead, they are the outcomes of several comparatively independent streams of events within the organization. A decision gets made when solutions, problems, participants and choices coincide at a certain point. Like garbage in a can, these adjacencies are often purely random. Therefore, a group of senior strategists might not have strongly developed preferences prior to the decision-making process. Their strategic objectives might derive from the act of actually making a decision in which there might be a very loose connection between strategic means and strategic ends. Any of the many different actors (finance, marketing, HR, etc.) involved in the process might become the focal point for a strategy. In contrast to rational models, the garbage can emphasizes the contingent, anarchic and random nature of decision-making. For the garbage can approach, decisions owe a great deal to luck and politics. Moreover, a decision-making process lacks a clear beginning and a definitive end – it is altogether a fuzzy process.

Organizational decisions entail power and resistance. Some decisions are effortless in implementation; the lack of resistance points to their acceptance as legitimate, as falling within the frontier of control that is deemed to be that of authority. Authoritative organizational power relations are institutionalized into systematic relations of hierarchy and lateral interdependence. Creating a formal structure of authority seeks to stabilize how organizational decision-making structures and procedures are framed (Boeker, 1989; see also Boeker 1992, 1997) by stabilizing decision-making on key offices, roles, responsibilities and relations (Clegg, 1989). Where decisions are more contested in their implementation it suggests that they impinge on what are considered to be borderlines of legitimacy and authority.

Decisions ebb and flow around issues and interests. Legitimacy is assured when power is concentrated and uncontested. Subgroups in organizations form coalitions to try and frame *issues* in decision-making according to their *interests* (Cyert and March, 1963). When critical contingencies of the organization change, so do the *issues* and *interests*. These contingencies will be controlled by particular expertise in the organization, located in different departments, divisions or skills (Hickson et al., 1971; Salancik and Pfeffer, 1977). When News Corp broke the power of the print unions in the 1980s by moving its print production out of Fleet Street to Wapping, it did so by moving out of old-style mechanical typesetting, controlled by the printing union, to the precursor of digital production inputted directly by the journalists. The *interests* of the print unions in controlling the wages and conditions of their members was outflanked by shifting production from being a *collective issue* dominated by unionized skills to an *individual issue* by journalists, who were dominated by the News Corp entities they worked for.

By design, business organizations are hierarchical social systems in which relations of command and domination, obedience and subordination, are normatively framed in ways that seek to establish these relations as authoritative. However, neither authority nor decision-making are guarantees against the instability and dynamism that power relations can sometimes unleash.

Decision-making processes: The Cuban Missile Crisis

Cohen et al. (1972) teach us that decision-making is characterized by uncertainty and ambiguity, which, in turn, intensifies the level of politics associated with the process. This is well illustrated in research into the 1962 Cuban Missile Crisis. The year 1962 is obviously a long time ago but the decisions made then averted what might have been a nuclear war of devastating proportions between the Soviet Union and the United States of America. Kennedy and Schlesinger (1999) and Allison (1971) have documented the processes of decision-making in the crisis and it has also been made into a film, *13 Days*. In the latter, not only the politically but also the emotionally charged nature of the decision-making is especially evident, as the military and diplomatic arguments compete with each other after US spy planes spotted unusual activity in Cuba, ruled by the Communist regime of Fidel Castro. The images demonstrated that the Soviets were installing nuclear missiles with the capacity to hit most places in the USA.

President Kennedy feared an aggressive US response to the missiles being made operational in Cuba would provoke the Soviets into retaliation, probably the invasion of West Berlin, which, in turn, would lead to war. Kennedy was aware of how high the stakes were. He sought to defuse the situation through diplomacy in the estimated 13 days before the missiles became operational. He argued for a blockade to prevent further military components arriving. Using the blockade, he could try and force

Image 11.3   Missile on display at the Parque Historico Militar Morro-Cabana in an exhibit on the 1962 Cuban missile crisis. Copyright: Joel Carillet

negotiation. The military view was that US countervailing power must match Soviet aggression. The Soviets, they thought, could not be appeased as the Allies had done with Hitler prior to the Second World War. The military wanted to bomb the missile site, followed up by an invasion.

Kennedy, and diplomacy, prevailed. What was important about the case is not only its outcome but also the processes. The Cuban missile crisis is a fascinating study into decision-making. You can gain insight into this case by watching the film – *13 Days* (Donaldson, R., 2000).

Power in decision-making

It has been argued that power moves through three levels (Lukes, 1974; Hardy, 1994). The first level is that of formal decision-making. This is where strategy is explicitly made and adopted. At this level strategy is discursively formulated in terms of improving effectiveness (Kumar and Thibodeaux, 1990). The first level of power is where you get others to do what they would not otherwise do (Dahl, 1957). It is just the tip of the strategy iceberg: underlying it is the second level in which non-decision-making occurs.

Non-decision-making occurs where issues are constrained to the legitimate and politically safe, where agendas are constructed with a tacit acknowledgment that certain issues will not be addressed. Often this is a major constraint on strategy making. Everyone knows what are the CEO's 'sacred cows' and 'pet concerns'. No one will openly propose a strategic change that would question these. Hence, they remain non-issues, not matters for decision-making and do not enter on to the agenda. Hence, if the strategy team wants to change these non-issues they have to move very subtly, politically.

Changing the second level power game in strategy is best done by new incumbents in senior roles. Especially when new in post, strategically powerful people, such as CEOs, often create strategic change through changing processes. Marginal or excluded voices are admitted to deliberations; issues left off agendas are instead affirmed and placed there, new members eager for change are placed on committees that in the past have been conservative or resistant. To facilitate these second level changes, new perspectives have to be introduced in ways that legitimate them, which is where new incumbency helps. Another strategy is to get the consultants in to produce a convincing report, one that is able to utter the unutterable and introduce new perspectives.

The third level of power concerns those things that are so fundamentally accepted that they seem just to be the 'existing order of things' (Lukes, 1974: 24), the underlying values, preferences, cognitions and perceptions, the deep assumptions of strategy, that define one as a member in good standing of a particular community of practice or organization. Changing these is difficult *and* politically risky: it entails organization-wide shifts in values and working practices. There have to be interventions into accepted practices, debate about them, definite change proposals for which support must be secured. Agendas will often be covert and people will be manipulated.

While ideological and symbolic bases of power usually function as a tacit resource for the strategically powerful, they can also be leveraged against dominant understandings because symbolic meanings can be seized on, hooked up with projects of resistance and take on quite distinct meanings to those initially taken for granted. The third level of power is associated with attempts to legitimize some claims and delegitimize the claims of others by managing meaning. If strategic elites are successful then they will use these meanings to anchor and secure their positions. However, meanings can always be cut adrift from moorings and used to question and resist the status quo.

Power in non-decision-making

Decisions are crucial to the strategy-making process. Sometimes, however, what is not decided can be of equal importance. Let us explore what we mean by this statement. We can be reasonably certain that a decision tells us something about the organization and the direction it is going in. It might be a decision that quite evidently fudges and satisfices to resolve tensions between competing groups within an organization or, alternatively, it might be a clear statement that one part of a senior management team is in control, setting the direction for the organization. When a strategy proceeds by favouring a dominant group this is known as the 'mobilization of bias'. Paraphrasing

Schattschneider (1960), what the mobilization of bias means is that some issues are organized *into* strategy while others are organized *out* of consideration.

Dominant groups will seek to uphold the status quo, which mobilizes bias to their benefit. According to Bachrach and Baratz, the 'primary method for sustaining a given mobilization of bias is non-decision making' (1970: 44). **Non-decision-making** means that important decisions are not made or do not even make it onto the agenda.

> **Non-decision-making** is when decisions do not get onto the agenda because they have been suppressed, restricted or have not been raised.

Non-decision-making is a means by which demands for change in the existing allocation of benefits and privileges can be silenced, rather than voiced, because opponents of the existing allocations realize that they simply do not have the arguments, given the prevailing rationality, or the numbers, given the balance of power, to make a difference. Non-decision-making keeps opposition covert and disorganized, muted or stilled before it enters the relevant decision-making arena. Should opposition be voiced then it can be slighted, marginalized or dismissed as simply not rational, given 'the way we do things around here'. Anticipating the consequences, the less powerful may see that their grievances and demands will be ignored or dismissed and so do not raise them in the first place. It is the powerful that define which matters are legitimate and discussible, as well as the forums and procedures through which such issues are raised, thus stifling the articulation of some issues and demands, while encouraging 'acceptable' or 'safe' topics and themes (Bachrach and Baratz, 1970).

Matthew Crenson argues for the importance of studying 'political inactivity' (Crenson, 1971: 26) when looking at strategic decisions. Some strategists (see Jarzabkowski and Whittington, 2008) have struggled with the concept of studying things that do not happen. In political science, however, doing this is a well-established approach (see van Iterson and Clegg, 2008). Our view is that constituting zones of strategic inactivity is as important as setting what is strategy. The implication is that by taking non-decision-making seriously, we are compelled to study strategic decisions that are not made, in addition to those that are: 'the proper object of investigation is not political activity [strategic decisions] but political inactivity [strategic non-decisions]' (Crenson, 1971: 26 – insertion in the brackets added by the authors).

Crenson argues that some strategists may have the 'ability to prevent some topics from ever becoming issues and … obstruct the growth of emergent issues' (1971: 177). Often strategists with this ability do not actually need to exercise it because having the reputation for being powerful is often sufficient to keep dominated groups quiescent. Hence, strategic decision-making is 'channelled and restricted by the process of non-decision making' (Crenson, 1971: 178).

Decision-making has reputational effects. Diefenbach (2009: 47 – italics in original) argues that '*strategic decisions are not only made by powerful managers – strategic decisions make managers powerful*'. Managers are made more powerful through making decisions that symbolize them as powerful irrespective of the agendas shaped, non-decisions made, issues included and excluded.

If strategic decisions help make managers powerful, a complete absence from strategic decisions can function in two predictable ways. We can see this in global supply chains that effectively exclude both ends of the supply chain from decision-making. In the core, the multinational companies often have little concrete knowledge of what exactly is happening in the factories in the Third World supplying their products. They can claim decision-making ignorance of local violations of whatever policies they subscribe to. In the Third World periphery, at the bottom of the supply chain, the workers employed are not only excluded from any decision-making but are also often unable to form effective collective organizations, such as trade unions, to provide a strategic force for improving labour conditions.

While denying any role in decision-making by local employees is not always an explicit outcome of strategies in constructing supply chains, it is often a tacit and implicit benefit, rarely questioned at head office until some tragedy puts the Third World workers on the front page of their national metropolitan newspapers.

Go Online: Recent international publicity over the plight of garment workers in Bangladesh provides clear examples that, in the absence of autonomous unions and other legitimate avenues for voice, fundamental labour and democratic rights may be subjugated to the disciplines imposed by the firms at the end of the supply chain. There are numerous articles about this topic, including several articles by Sharif As-Saber listed below from *The Conversation* website, and many others which can be found on the companion website for this book: www.edge.sagepub.com/strategy2e.

Bangladesh Garment Workers

'Bangladesh disaster shows why we must urgently clean up global sweat shops', *The Conversation*.

'Will gains for Bangladesh workers founder on political reality?', *The Conversation*.

'One year on from Rana Plaza collapse, work still to be done', *The Conversation*.

Voice articulates individual dissatisfaction, specific problems or issues with management. It may take the form of collective organization and may function as an input to management decision-making through either positive measures such as quality circles, or through resistance to management initiatives. According to Dundon and colleagues (2004: 152), there are four main ways in which **employee voice** may be given to non-issues, non-strategic actors and the effects of non-decisions.

> **Employee voice** refers to the participation of employees in influencing organizational decision-making. In general, voice concerns *whether* and *how* employees can be heard.

1. The 'articulation of individual dissatisfaction'

2. 'The expression of collective organization'

3. 'Contribution to management decision-making'

4. 'Demonstration of mutuality and cooperative relations'

Management, or other authorities, such as the state, often structure employee voice (Donaghey et al., 2011). It is notable that in the People's Republic of China, although there are trade unions, they are mostly organized by the state rather than representing local workers' interests. Furthermore, the existence of formal structures, such as unions, does not preclude employee silence: if formal channels are not seen as legitimate, or are implemented in an attempt to control dissent, they may actually structure employee awareness of the non-issues and non-decisions (Pinder and Harlos, 2001). One attraction of offshore investment by multinationals in labour intensive processes is that labour costs are much lower than in the core OECD economies. One reason for this is the absence of effective unions.

Types of decision-making

Some decisions can be taken in a considered manner, while others have to be taken rapidly with incomplete and ambiguous information in the face of internal disagreements. As Plato said, it is important to have knowledge as well as numbers to make decisions. All too often, however, information only becomes available in a fragmentary manner. Decisions are rarely the outcome of rational, linear processes but a result of power and politics, negotiations and manipulations, emotions and instincts. If the outcome of these can then be represented in numbers so much the better – a claim of rationality can then be attached to the strategic decisions proposed. In the process, the politics of decision-making can be rationalized (Flyvbjerg, 1998).

Decision-making is a political process in which outcomes evolve out of the processes of power mobilization attempted by different parties in support of their demands (Pettigrew, 1972: 202). This becomes evident in an important study of business decision-making by a team from Bradford University.

In the 1980s, at the University of Bradford, Richard Butler, David Cray, David Hickson, Geoff Mallory and David Wilson conducted a major research study into strategic decision-making in the UK. The study lasted a decade and sought to understand what really happened in the strategy decision-making process. The research was published in a monograph (*Top Decisions*) and a series of articles (some of which are available on this textbook's website). The research produced many important insights into the nature of decision-making that remain as relevant today as when they were first published. While some of the research team have retired, David Wilson (Warwick Business School), together with Susan Miller (Durham University), continue to research decision-making. The *Top Decisions* research studied 150 distinct strategic decision-making episodes in 30 organizations. They were interested in answering the following questions:

- What actually happens in the process of arriving at a strategic decision?
- What differences are there in the process of making decisions?
- Why do these differences exist?

The answers to these seemingly straightforward questions have made a substantial contribution to understanding the way in which decisions are made. They identify independent variables that have an impact on the nature of the decision-making process. These include the type of organizational context, levels of politics associated with a decision, and the complexity of the decision. From this they identify three decision-making types (summarized in Table 11.1):

1. *Sporadic Decisions*: Many decisions are complex and seen as very political. This can 'generate a vortex into which all are swept' (Hickson et al., 1986: 240), something associated with a sporadic decision process, summarized by Butler as follows: 'a sporadic decision involves many interests, it tends to move both horizontally and vertically in the organization and exhibits stops and starts. Where is such a decision made? Not in any once place, but it is made, nevertheless, through a diffuse and complex organizational process ... Sporadic

decisions involve the highest levels in the organization, but the decision is not only made there' (Butler, 1990: 13). Sporadic decisions tended to take longer than other decisions. As Cray et al. put it: 'The decision process lurches from one impasse to the next with individuals and groups debating alternatives in the halls and cafeterias so that the decision process is drawn out' (Cray et al., 1991: 228). Generally, Hickson et al. (1986) found the greater the level of complexity and the greater the political controversy of a decision, the more likely the decision will go back and forwards and be subject to lengthy delays and revision. Topics for sporadic decisions may be complex, definitions problematic, information unavailable and/or difficult to collect, solutions hard to recognize, with the process generating headaches rather than solutions.

2. *Fluid Decisions*: As a decision-making mode, this is characterized by a situation where a decision is strategic and deals with an unusual situation that is not particularly complex or political. Such decisions can be handled formally and quickly.

3. *Constricted Decisions*: As a decision-making mode, these are characterized by Hickson et al. (1986: 240) as 'those matters which bring familiar problems, probably least complex of all, and familiar interests, probably no more than mildly political in nature, they can be processed in a constricted [narrowly channelled] way. This is the *familiar-constricted mode*'. Such decisions are relatively smooth and straightforward and, thus, require little debate.

Table 11.1   Three decision-making types

Decision type	Characterized by:
Sporadic	More delays
	More impediments
	More sources of information
	More variability of information
	More informal interaction
	Some scope for negotiation
	More time to reach a decision
	Decision taken at the highest level
Fluid	Fewer delays
	Fewer impediments
	Fewer sources of information
	Less variability of information
	Some scope for negotiation
	More formal interaction
	Less time to reach a decision
	Decision taken at the highest level
Constricted	More sources of information
	Less effort to acquire information
	Little scope for negotiation
	Less formal interaction
	Decision taken below highest level

Hickson et al. (1986) made the point that decision-making is not necessarily linear but instead can often be iterative and feedback on itself. One of the fascinating parts of the *Top Decisions* book relates to the time a decision takes to make. How long is it reasonable for a strategic decision to take? Hickson et al. (1986) found that there was huge variance over the time a strategic decision took. Some of the strategic decisions they studied were resolved within a month, while others dragged out over a period of four years! In their study, the average time taken for a strategic decision was just over 12 months. Interestingly, there was little difference between public and private sector organizations in this respect. They found that most significant strategic decisions tended to be sporadic ones. Such decisions are characterized by political factions, problemistic search, incremental solutions and dynamic non-linear reiteration and re-definition of almost all the terms in the decision-mix.

EXTEND YOUR KNOWLEDGE

You can read the following journal articles that are relevant to these studies on the companion website for this book at www.edge.sagepub.com/strategy2e.

Kenny, G., Butler, R., Hickson, D., Cray, D., Mallory, G. and Wilson, D. (1987) 'Strategic decision making: Influence patterns in public and private sector organizations', *Human Relations*, 40(9): 613–631.

Wilson, D. (1982) 'Electricity and resistance: A case study of innovation and politics', *Organization Studies*, 3(2): 119–140.

Wilson, D., Butler, R., Cray, D., Hickson, D. and Mallory, G. (1986) 'Breaking the bounds of organization in strategic decision making', *Human Relations*, 39(4): 309–330.

Decision-Making

Paradoxical decision-making

If decision-making occurred in organizations that were straightforward, as a matter of individual actors just making a rational choice, there were would be little need to say a great deal about the process. Get the facts, weigh up the options and make the correct decision. But complex organizational life is not akin to these processes: the facts are often inadequate and difficult to interpret; options are usually unclear; the correct decision can only ever be known in hindsight.

It is not only that organizations and the individual within them are complex but, increasingly, so are their environments. These environments are increasingly characterized by instability, volatility and disruptive change, all of which accentuate the potentiality for paradox, rendering contradictions more salient and persistent (Smith and Lewis, 2011; Küpers and Paullen, 2013).

Traditional decision-making processes, designed to reduce uncertainty (Tsoukas, 2005) have become inadequate, as decisions must be taken in the face of uncertainty in such dynamic environments (Rowley and Gibbs, 2008; Sull and Eisenhardt, 2015). Traditional decision-making is supported by *probability*, which evaluates outcomes that are finite and expected, whereas *possibility* acknowledges inherent uncertainty, implying not only risk but also opportunity (Stamp et al., 2007). Thus, managing *possibility* rather than *probability* may be increasingly relevant (Hays, 2008; Rowley and Gibbs, 2008). In addition, managers must face uncertainty and complexity ethically; recent management scandals express the need for virtue-informed behaviours (Rego et al., 2012).

Paradox was introduced as a framework to deal with the inherent complexity of organizational life (Cameron and Quinn, 1988). The way organizations approach contradiction defines the build-up of dependences that ultimately push them in the direction of either more virtuous or more vicious circles (Smith and Lewis, 2011; Cunha and Tsoukas, 2015). The capacity of leadership to handle contradictions or conflicting demands is key. If approached as dilemmas, i.e. as competing choices that can be weighed on scales, each with its pros and cons, there is the tendency to select one pole or the other, losing the potential of dynamism. In a paradox, contradictions are interdependent: one pole cannot exist without the other. For example, confidence and doubt, and acting as if one knows while one does not know (Ashforth et al., 2014) may be necessary to honour the complexities of the environment and to make more timely and better informed decisions (see the section 'The power of doubt: Finding comfort in discomfort', in Saïd Business School and Heidrick & Struggles, 2015).

An interesting example current at the time of writing, is whether or not the British Government will support major investment in a French designed and built nuclear facility planned for Hinckley Point in Somerset. On the one hand, it will reduce significantly the carbon footprint of electricity generation in the UK; on the other hand, it will saddle electricity consumers in the future with very high costs to pay down the substantial debt. This is a classic contradiction. There are some commentators who argue that the contradiction should not be resolved in its own terms but that a third option, neither 'yes' or 'no' in terms of decision-making, should prevail: green technologies of wind and wave power should be used instead, as the prices of these forms of energy are diminishing rapidly. However, the counter-argument is that these are too contingent on external factors to sustain a base load of electricity that is reliable. Watch this space!

For managers, facing contradiction is not 'a signal of defeat but rather the very lifeblood of human life' (Chia and Holt, 2007: 512) because of the puzzles it poses to ingenuity. It can empower a sense of organizational direction (Chia, 2010; Smith and Lewis, 2011) and facilitate the struggle to thrive in the face of ambiguity, while avoiding preventable errors (Giustiniano et al., 2016). In short, first-rate managers should be able to embrace contradiction and draw insights from them, including the possibility of ignoring them in their expression of wisdom (Farjoun, 2016).

Temporal paradoxes and consistent inconsistency

Patterns of responses to issues are consistently inconsistent, involving frequent shifts. In terms of the Bradford studies, a decision pattern may vary, being sporadic, constricted and fluid over time, as accommodation, choice and acceptance of different decisions are made. Paradoxical decision-making has to be able to handle these classical management problems of differentiation and integration.

Managers need to focus on the pattern of decisions over time and to embrace inconsistencies in decisions, rather than to strive for consistency amongst them; they must accept that decisions evolve with contexts evolving – sticking to the rules rigidly in terms of following past decision precedents may be a recipe for inflexibility and disaster. Key practices for managing paradoxes are *differentiation* and *integration*. *Differentiation* focuses decisions in distinct product and service realms. In the absence of integration, domain-specific advocates can become entrenched in their own position. The likely result is sub-optimality, increased conflict and reluctance to compromise. *Integration* emphasizes synergies between distinct elements. 'Senior leaders who want to sustain commitments to strategic paradoxes can focus on embedding these practices into their top management team' (Smith, 2014: 1618).

As future participants in strategy processes you will need to be prepared for situations which will call for the consideration of multiple and often conflicting interests and dilemmas. In such situations, there is often no 'right' answer, strategy or problem solution. The role of the strategists is then to make, defend and justify decisions and strategic actions and to be aware of choices that will be in the 'grey' area. Many people struggle with the notion of not having the 'right' answer; thinking that if they apply the 'right' strategic tools and processes, and engaged the 'right' people in the organization, they can develop successful strategies.

Strategy can never be wholly successful; its positives will always produce negatives. Strategies can never be successful for everybody on whom organizations have an impact. Strategy entails power and decision-making and power relations cannot always be positive and decision-making cannot always spread satisfaction. As time elapses, the good can be seen as bad; as different stakeholder perspectives are considered the same actions take on many different ethical hues. In many respects, the fundamental insights of Machiavelli are still relevant.

Back to Machiavelli

Familiarity with classics, especially those whose thinking crosses centuries without losing vigour, such as Machiavelli, is a part of the educational canon whose absence management can ill-afford to shed. The education of judgment, once considered essential to diplomatic, political and administrative leadership, used to be central to the curriculum of the classics.

We do not see Machiavelli as a source of 'best practice'. But through the study of Machiavelli, students as well as actual and potential leaders, may better understand the nature of power as a complex social process. We suggest that it is more important to focus on what works in practice rather than on what should work in a given theoretical system, a frequent criticism of the business ethics literature (Locke, 2006).

Machiavelli warned princes against the dangers of *fortuna*: power is sustained with *virtù* and threatened by *fortuna*. As such, princes should invest in *virtù*, and be careful with the desires of fortune. Princes should have strong personal foundations rather than rely on superficial power bases such as networking. Machiavelli's lessons suggested the importance of being flexible in behaviour: respect the ordinary moral values and identify the fundamental rights that must be considered in all decisions (Cavanagh et al., 1981). Stick to these values but be ready to change priorities with regards to the rest. And be aware that others, the 'truly' Machiavellian, may not be doing the same. As one manages with power, one manages others who manage one's managing with power, in an endless circle generating contradictions, resistance and struggles, and sometimes, compliance.

One cautionary note is needed here: most managers are not rule makers, unlike princes. As such, they must negotiate the existing social order and occasionally have to counter its preferences; for example, sacrifices may have to be made for the greater good. Even the best-intentioned manager will have to make hard choices when s/he faces difficult moral dilemmas. Pursuing noble aims often requires less than noble means. That being the case, from a Machiavellian perspective it is better to act swiftly, rather than to execute action in small doses, prolonging the suffering.

Machiavelli (1961: 50) considered 'the gulf between how one should live and how one does live is so wide that the man who neglects what is done for what should be done learns the way to self-destruction'. Following Machiavelli's advice does not imply that the gulf between how we should live and how we do live is fixed (Jackson, 2000). Pursuing noble aims and narrowing the gulf is virtuous – but requires adopting a degree of realism that Machiavelli may help to understand. As Machiavelli suggested, the road to Paradise requires knowing, and avoiding, that to Hell. But avoiding the road to Hell will not necessarily lead to Paradise.

Back to strategy

By reading this chapter you must have by now realized that in real organizational life there is at least as much concern with internal politics and intra-organizational conflict, as with external competition, although Pitelis (2007) tried to analyse what will happen to the use of resources and organizational performance if both are in place. Yet most of the theories discussed in Chapters 2 and 3 all but ignore intra-organizational conflict! In a few words, you should ignore intra-organizational conflict at your peril! Yet this is what most strategy literature and textbooks do.

Summary

To represent strategy as a practice that is entirely rational and without politics is one of the most political forms of representation. It is also one of the most common – and the most fraudulent. The strategy process is always irremediably political, especially when it claims not to be!

Strategy spawns discourses in which interests are paramount and in which politics surround and envelop it: where politics shape what are taken to be the interests of the organization; in which self-interests can be aligned, or others' interests be misaligned, to these strategic interests. Other organizations, such as governments or allied organizations, can be enrolled and translated into strategically interested and aligned partners. Some can be effectively excluded, such as the employees in the local organizations at the end of the supply chains supplying the global organizations.

In all organizations, much of the politics of strategy emerges around the practice of mandate changes, which is especially the case in MNEs as we saw in Chapter 7. Strategy always concerns setting a direction and striving to maintain or trim it against unforeseen resistance and events. Setting a direction and steering it in a complex organization of many different powers and knowledge is always going to be a political activity. This is why strategy, conducted well, is not for the faint-hearted: it produces tough, hard and sometimes robust politics, in which there are winners and losers.

TEST YOURSELF

Want to know more about this chapter? Review what you have learnt by visiting www.edge.sagepub.com/strategy2e.

- Test yourself with multiple choice questions
- Revise key terms with interactive flashcards

EXERCISES

1. Having read this chapter, you should be able to say in your own words what the following key terms mean:

   - Machiavellian
   - Organizational politics
   - Power
   - Strategic interests
   - Political skill
   - Micro-politics
   - Business elites
   - Social capital
   - Resistance
   - Decision-making

   - Satisficing
   - Sporadic decisions
   - Fluid decisions
   - Constricted decisions
   - Garbage can model
   - Non-decision-making
   - Mobilization of bias
   - Employee voice
   - Paradoxical decision-making

2. What can we learn from Machiavelli that is useful for managing power and strategy in contemporary times?

3. What are some of the significant power games and micro-political strategies that occur around the strategy process?

4. How do politics effect headquarter/subsidiary politics in organizations?

5. How do various types of elites differ in their social organization and what are the consequences of elites for power relations?

6. What are some of the major mechanisms for elite formation and reproduction?

7. How are strategic decisions made in practice?

8. What are non-decisions and how do they effect strategy?

9. In what ways can employees resist strategies and articulate voice?

10. In what ways is decision-making less than rational?

CASE STUDY

The Australian Broadcasting Corporation

STEWART CLEGG

Digital technologies and increasing globalization were bundled up together in a number of strategic reforms of the ABC during the 1990s, which were aimed at creating a more entrepreneurial and flexible organization. It was a style of organization that was at some distance from the older, public sector rhetoric of the ABC, with its largely unionized workforce. Not surprisingly, the two main unions resisted the changes but so did a social movement organization known as the Friends of the ABC.

In resisting the newly strategically reformed and refocused ABC, these bodies *creatively appropriated the dominant categories* of global discourses of digital new media that had been used to promulgate strategic change at the ABC. However, they used these new and now dominant categories to oppose elements of the change programme. Not only did they do this, they also identified elements in the new media environment with which they could agree, which they *surfaced as a shared discourse* and sought to demonstrate that other elements of strategy undercut these shared values. Finally, they *revived some old core values* of the ABC that positioned it as safe from the blandishments of commercialism, commercials and a market share mentality. Doing this led to some strategic reverses for the ABC Board as well as a reinvigoration of the very public service ethos that the reforms seemed bent on destroying.

Untangling strategic change at the ABC over the 1990s and into the 2000s requires an analysis of how power relations are constituted as both central strategic initiatives and also as the forces of resistance that confront them. The strategic outcomes represent a negotiated order that is highly contingent on the dynamics of power and resistance (Fleming and Spicer, 2007).

QUESTION

Analyse the impact of digital technologies and increasing globalization on broadcasters in your national domain. (As well as Fleming and Spicers' (2007) work you may also find Castells (2009) *Communication and Power* useful.)

STRATEGY AND STRATEGIC CHANGE

Learning objectives

By the end of this chapter you will be able to:

1 Understand what strategic change is, why and how it occurs

2 Differentiate between different types of change according to their scale and scope

3 Critically evaluate step-based and contingency models of change

4 Understand the processes and practices through which change is implemented and sustained, including the role of symbolism and sensemaking

5 Explain the role played by power, politics and resistance during the change process.

BEFORE YOU GET STARTED

Be the change that you wish to see in the world. (Mahatma Gandhi)

Introduction

Most books on organizational change start by making grand statements about how much *more* change we experience nowadays thanks to increased competition, turbulent markets, globalization and technological innovation. Arguably, though, firms have always had to deal with change; indeed, as well as reacting to exogenous change they have been at the forefront of *creating* change through their own strategic decisions.

Take what is thought to be the world's first multinational corporation – the East India Company. The company was formed in the sixteenth century to trade spices and other goods between England and the Indian subcontinent. The history of the East India Company is one of driving change, not just coping with it. There were changes that the company itself drove (Banerjee, 2006):

- Moves into new markets, often achieved through violent means
- Establishing new trading posts and building new factories, often at the expense of indigenous practices
- Wars fought to establish or retain control over territory and trading routes
- The creation of new labour practices, such as forced cultivation by peasants
- The formation of alliances with often despotic regimes to secure the company's commercial interests
- The use of private armies and changes to ship design, navigation technology and armoury designed to further their power and control over territories

There were also political, economic and social changes that the company faced that challenged their dominance and power:

- Changes in control over territory and trading routes from the Anglo-Dutch Wars (1652–1810)
- A famine in Bengal (1770)
- The infamous Boston Tea Party revolt (1773)
- The legal separation of its political and commercial functions (1784)
- Loss of its monopoly rights on trade with India (1813)
- Changes to ownership and control (1833)
- Nationalization after the Indian Rebellion (1857)

The East India Company was formally dissolved in 1874. In the 247 years the company operated, it would be hard to say that the company did not have to 'manage strategic change'. The ability to manage – or indeed drive – strategic change has therefore *always* been part of strategy, even before the word 'strategy' started to get used in a business context. The (often violent) methods through which the East India Company achieved their global expansion are, clearly, ethically questionable by today's standards, hopefully serving as a reminder of the importance of considering the social values that should underlie strategic change (Banerjee, 2006; Clegg and Cunha, forthcoming).

Nowadays, we take it as given that organizations that do not keep pace with changes in their environment – for example, the development of new technologies, shifts in customer preferences or changing regulatory environments – will experience decline. Moreover, organizations that are proactively *driving* and *leading* change – for example by developing new technologies, driving new customer preferences or actively influencing regulation – thrive and prosper. But strategic change is no easy task. Balogun and Hope Hailey (2008), in their book *Exploring Strategic Change*, cite the alarming statistic that around 70% of organizational change programmes are thought to fail to achieve their aims.

Strategic change involves many challenges and many different stakeholders. Finance might need to be raised to fund the change, such as an acquisition, investment in new technology or entry into a new international market. Investors or shareholders might need to be involved in the change process. Regulators or government bodies might also play a role. Customers and suppliers also might need to be kept informed about what the change involves and how it might affect them.

This chapter will not attempt to cover all the above issues. Textbooks on accounting and finance, marketing and operations management will cover many of the issues involved in managing the role of stakeholders such as investors, shareholders, regulators, customers and suppliers involved in the change process. The focus of this chapter, instead, will be primarily on the *internal* aspects of designing and implementing strategic change. It will focus on how managers – or indeed other 'change agents' who play a role in the change process – manage the *organization* itself through the process of transitioning to a new strategic position.

What is strategic change?

Organizations nowadays seem to be in an almost constant state of change. Organizational systems are one key target for change. New IT systems need to be introduced to keep pace with changes in technology, such as the rise in the use of social media. Organizational structure is another key target for change. Re-structuring exercises seem to be the norm rather than the exception, as departments are restructured to become more integrated and cross functional or hierarchies are delayered to become less bureaucratic and with fewer layers of management. Organizational culture is also a key target for change. Organizations are keen to make sure that a change in strategy becomes deeply embedded in the norms and values of the workforce. Managers therefore seek to change the way employees think about what is right and wrong in order to change their behaviour at work. For example, a firm might want employees to become more risk-taking to enable their strategy of innovation or more customer-focused to match their strategy of differentiation through customer service.

But how does one decide whether any one of these specific changes is *strategic* or not? For some, an objective answer to this question is simple. Strategic change, they would say, is one that involves a change in the 'direction and scope of an organization over the long term' (Johnson et al., 2002: 10) – the classic definition of strategy. Such an answer downplays the power and politics that underlies how strategy is decided, as we have already argued in Chapter 11. This kind of answer underplays the *social and political process* through which organizations decide what their long-term scope and direction is. We know that organizations are not homogenous and unified collectives that harmoniously pursue common goals but rather are *complexes of interests* (see Chapter 11). Organizations are comprised of more or less loose or tight coalitions of heterogeneous actors – these could be individuals or groups such as departments or SBUs – that have both convergent and divergent interests. Decisions about what activities an organization should undertake (its scope) and how it should compete in its markets (its position) and where it should go in the future (its direction) are irremediably political because behind these decisions lay individuals and groups who have a particular stake in them – something to gain or lose.

A case study of a team of management consultants called 'FlexiTeam' by Whittle and Mueller (2010) shows how decisions about strategic scope and direction are the outcome of political systems and power plays – topics covered later in the chapter and that relate back to the previous chapter, Chapter 11. Political tactics are used by various groups to influence the thinking of senior management about which activities have the most value (or potential value) and should therefore receive more investment or which should be divested, downsized or closed down. These political tasks also include the ways in which systems of measurement and 'valuation devices' (Kornberger et al., 2015: 1) – such as accounting systems in Whittle and Mueller's (2010) study – serve to shape how senior management come to view the 'strategic value' of various activities and ideas.

IN PRACTICE

- -

Making ideas into strategies

Whittle and Mueller (2010: 626) ask the question: 'Why do some ideas turn into "strategies" when others do not?' They tell the story from an ethnographic study of a group of management consultants called 'FlexiTeam' (a pseudonym) who worked for a telecommunications firm. The group gave consultancy advice to business customers who were purchasing large volumes of telecoms equipment (e.g. broadband connections or mobile phone packages) about how to implement flexible working arrangements, such as home working, flexi-desks or teleworking arrangements.

The group wanted to convince senior management that a new business-to-business marketing strategy was needed. They believed that the firm was using an outdated 'traditional selling' strategy, where the firm saw themselves as simply 'selling products' and emphasized the features of the product to try to persuade customers to purchase. A better marketing strategy, in their view, was what they called the 'consulting-led selling' approach, which involved viewing the firm not as a seller of a product but as a 'provider of profit'. This meant that the firm must first understand the needs of the business customer, acting more like a management consultant, and offer products that will help the customer to improve their profitability based on this understanding of their business. That way, the seller is no longer selling a product but rather is selling a 'return on investment'. The 'product' is no longer the physical equipment that they sell. The product is the 'profit' their products help the customer to make.

(Continued)

(Continued)

Changing to this new marketing strategy, it was hoped, would mean a bigger role for management consultancy groups such as them. They envisioned having a management consultant embedded into all the sales teams to help them to understand the customer's needs before they tried to 'pitch' to them. However, senior management were not altogether receptive to this idea about changing their marketing strategy. In particular, the biggest problem for the team was that their power and influence in the higher echelons of the organization was limited. It was not because they lacked a charismatic leader or lacked suitable expert knowledge or lacked the right social networks – in fact they had all of these. Rather, their lack of power and influence was rooted in the fact that the value of all business units was measured using a management accounting system that treated all units as independent 'profit centres'. Put simply, each unit had to return a profit, which was calculated by comparing costs (such as staff salaries and company cars, etc.) against revenue.

The only revenue the team could generate was their management consulting fees, which at the time of their study did not even cover their costs. Initial consulting time spent with customers often led to large volume sales later on, but many customers did not want to pay for a full consulting service. Why? Customers seemed to view paying a telecommunications firm for consulting advice about how they could use their telecoms products as a bit like asking a consumer to 'pay extra for the instruction manual that comes with their television' (Whittle and Mueller, 2010: 639). As a result, they often offered 'free' advice to customers to facilitate the big sales deals, but without securing consulting income for themselves. Compounding this difficulty was the fact that it was difficult to identify precisely when their consulting advice had directly influenced the customer's decision to buy the telecoms products. As one consultant explained, the group gave consulting advice to many customers but the sales revenue was 'never be correlated back to us' (2010: 635). As another consultant explained to the ethnographer one day:

> Like with [Client A] ... they only decided to buy the kit after I'd done a vision workshop with them. But how do you put that down tangibly that they only bought it because we gave them the vision? How do you measure that? That's the problem, we are not credited for all the work we do to make things happen. (Consultant Barry, field notes)

Not only did this 'loss making' label affect senior management's perception of their importance and influence in the organization – which led to their ideas about the 'consulting-led selling' strategy falling largely on deaf ears – the group were also worried that their jobs might be on the line if they continued to appear as 'loss-making'. How, then, could they convince senior management of their 'strategic value' and persuade them to take their 'strategic idea' seriously?

Whittle and Mueller describe the political tactics the groups used to manoeuvre and manipulate their 'balance sheet' in order to bolster their claim as to their 'strategic value' of their activities and their ideas about strategy. For example, the group started to charge a small fee for some of the 'free' advice they had previously been giving to various sales teams, thereby instantly boosting their revenue figures. They also convinced the Sales Director to amend their database system to enable a record to be generated of which customers they had given consulting advice to. They hoped to start gathering data to show senior management how many sales deals were facilitated by their consulting advice.

The outcome of the micro-political tactics used by the group had substantial implications for the firm's strategy as well as the group's own employment security. If senior management were not convinced that management consultancy should be offered to their business customers to facilitate sales, even if the consultancy unit itself made a 'loss', they might have decided to shut down the management consultancy unit altogether (altering their strategic *scope*) and pursue a more direct-selling approach in the future that emphasized product features and cost (altering their strategic *direction*). What this case study shows is how decisions about what strategy a firm follows – and crucially which groups have the most power and influence in this decision-making process – is the outcome of *behind-the-scenes political behaviour* directed at constructing or contesting understandings about what sorts of activities have the most 'strategic value'.

Questions

1. How did FitCo evaluate the strategic value of FlexiTeam's activities?

2. What political tactics did FlexiTeam use to influence how their strategic value was understood?

3. What does this case tell us about the social and political processes through which strategic change is managed?

It is clear that any specific organizational change is not inherently a priori more 'strategic' than others. As Whittle and Mueller (2010: 626) put it: 'we cannot assume that certain ideas offer inherently greater value than others'. Rather, whether a particular change is deemed to be strategic is the result of a *socio-political process*. A 'strategic change', then, is simply a change that those in the position of power to decide the firm's strategy have declared is 'strategic' (having themselves been influenced by the perceptions and arguments and actions of the 'other' organizational players). From this perspective, it may be futile debating whether or not a particular new IT system, or a decision to develop a new product line or enter a new market, is (or is not) *inherently* a strategic change. What is important is to understand that this process of defining, categorizing or labelling a particular change as 'strategic' is both an *outcome* of an ongoing political process and is itself a *political act*: one that attempts to position that particular change as more important or valuable to the firm than another.

Not all organizational changes equally attract the label 'strategic'. What kinds of change are typically labelled as strategic? Small adjustments to existing systems or processes typically are not talked about as having strategic importance. As such, these kinds of minor changes are usually not included in documents such as strategic plans or talked about during strategic decision-making activities such as Top Management Team meetings or strategy away-days. This chapter will focus mainly on the kinds of change that typically attract the label 'strategic' in strategy texts and conversations, such as:

- Changes to the competitive position of the firm, such as a move from a focus on cost towards differentiation through superior product or service features (see Chapter 2);

- Changes arising from diversification into selling new products/services to existing customers or selling existing products/services to new customers (see Chapter 2);

- Changes involved in innovation, such as the development of new technologies or capabilities (see Chapter 4);

- Changes to the vertical boundaries of the firm, such as decisions to integrate activities previously done by suppliers or decisions to outsource activities previously done in-house (see Chapter 5);

- Changes arising from mergers or acquisitions, such as the process of restructuring and downsizing departments following a merger (see Chapter 6);

- Changes arising from the creation of new strategic alliances or partnerships (see Chapter 7);

- Changes to the geographical scope of the firm arising from expansion into international markets or retraction through shutdowns (see Chapter 8).

It is important not to forget that smaller, more incremental changes, such as adapting products to meet customer expectations or making small improvements to production techniques – often referred to as 'continuous improvement' – might also have strategic relevance if strategists decide that such small steps can cumulatively contribute to the overall success – or survival – of the firm. In fact, the concept of 'strategic drift' explained below proposes exactly this: failure to make such incremental changes to 'keep pace' with small changes in the environment is a source of organizational failure. Hence, what is important is not the overall size or scale of the change but how strategists *make sense* of, and seek to *influence*, the perceptions of those with power regarding what kinds of changes are important for their long-term future.

Why does strategic change occur?

Rationalistic and functionalistic explanations of why strategic change occurs assume that change is a rational outcome of organizations 'scanning' their environment for signs of changes, such as shifts in customer preferences or the emergence of new technologies, that lead them to adjust their strategy accordingly. The rational story suggests that customers (or other stakeholders) want change – such as new product features or better value for money or the convenience of shopping for products over the Internet rather than in-store. In consequence, it is suggested, firms change their strategy accordingly.

The notion of **strategic drift** mentioned at the start of this chapter is relevant here.

Changes happen all the time, from the development of new technologies or the emergence of new expectations amongst customers, investors or regulators. These changes in the external environment might not be radical or even particularly large. There might be no major technological leap or sudden crisis like a financial crisis or war. Even if the changes are individually quite minor and occur quite gradually, if the firm either fails to notice them, or responds too slowly or doggedly remains wedded to the strategy that has served them well in the past, strategic drift will occur.

Strategic drift is the notion that organizations that fail to keep pace with changes in the external environment will start to 'drift' as the firm's strategy becomes detached from the changing environment.

Blockbuster is a good example of a firm that suffered from strategic drift as it failed to keep pace with technological change in the movie rental business with the advent of Internet-based downloads and streaming. Blockbuster had traditionally rented movies and video games in-store and by mail-order. The firm was slow to adapt to the growing popularity of video-streaming made possible by the development of super-fast fibre optic broadband connections to the consumer's home and the pop-ularity of mobile streaming via smartphones. The environment had changed – new technology enabled customers to seek instant on-demand movies – and yet the firm 'drifted' by failing to keep pace with this change and act fast enough to offer a stream-ing service. Blockbuster lost huge market share to competitors such as Netflix, who were quick to invest in their on-demand streaming service and gain so-called 'first mover advantage', signing people up for monthly subscription plans and building a well-known brand image that consumers instantly associated with movie streaming. Blockbuster filed for bankruptcy protection in 2010 and was subsequently sold for a fraction of its prior valuation. The firm had experienced strategic drift.

To avoid 'strategic drift', it is assumed that organizations need to make regular 'incremental' changes to 'keep pace' (the left hand section of Figure 12.1). If the organ-ization experiences a period of strategic drift (the middle section of Figure 12.1), a more 'radical' or 'transformational' change is needed to realign the organization with its external environment (the right hand section of Figure 12.1).

Strategists, it is assumed, need to ensure they gather the right kind of informa-tion, at the right time and analyse it in the right way in order to ensure they stay in 'fit' with the pace of change in the environment. Popular models abound that are designed to help organizations to map the factors and issues in the external environ-ment that could affect the firm – such as PESTEL analysis (discussed in Chapter 2), Five Forces Analysis (discussed in Chapter 2), SWOT analysis (Strengths, Weaknesses, Opportunities, Threats – the latter two referring to the external environment) and stakeholder analysis (touched on in Chapter 9). These models, it is assumed, will help managers to keep a regular check on what is happening 'out there' in order to decide what needs to change 'in here'.

Underlying such models is a set of assumptions about what the 'environment' is and how managers make sense of this environment. In particular, the models tend to

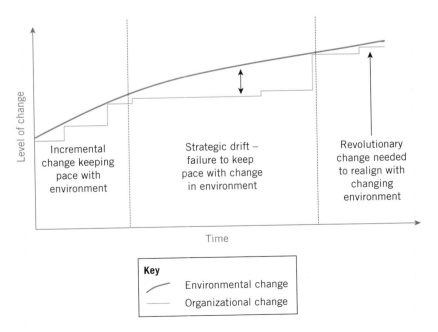

Figure 12.1   Strategic drift

Source: Adapted from Balogun and Hailey (2008: 3) and Johnson et al. (2002: 180).

assume that the environment is 'out there', ready for managers to simply gather more or less accurate and more or less complete information about it. Such assumptions ignore a number of crucial issues.

First, these assumptions that there is an objective external environment ignore the fact that organizations themselves constantly interact with their environment of customers, competitors, investors, shareholders, regulators, etc. As a result, the environment is not just a static entity 'out there' but rather is a *dynamic and interactive process*, in which the signals and moves of the firm itself influences what happens. If the news leaks that there is a new model of a product in the pipeline with enhanced features, then existing models probably have to be discounted or packaged in some way in order to persuade consumers that there is value in purchasing them. Customers do not just have 'needs' or 'preferences' – firms actively try to create these through their marketing communication.

Second, assuming that there is an objective external environment ignores the way in which managers *make sense* of the information they gather about what they take to be the environment, even including what kinds of information they seek to gather in the first place (Pettigrew and Whipp, 1993).

Edith Penrose (1959), whom we discussed in Chapters 1 and 2, made a very important contribution by proposing that the external environment is an 'image' in the mind of its internal human resources, notably the managers. Managerial decisions are therefore based on a 'productive opportunity' that the organization presents, which she defined as the dynamic interaction between the external and internal environments as they are perceived by the organizational actors.

One study that makes this point about the image of the external environment particularly clearly is Meyer's (1982) study of how three Californian hospitals that were facing the same crisis developed different strategies for action.

IN PRACTICE

Making sense of environmental jolts

Meyer (1982) shows how three different hospitals in the San Francisco area made different sense of the same strategic challenge. The challenge was an 'environmental jolt' caused by a sudden sharp increase in insurance prices following a malpractice lawsuit that led to a one-month strike on elective surgery by anaesthesiologists. Elective surgery is typically high-risk and 'optional' for doctors but hugely profitable for the hospital, leading to a major cash flow crisis and drop in hospital admissions.

How did the different hospitals respond to this crisis? One hospital with a history of antagonism with the doctor's union used the crisis as an opportunity to make layoffs it had been planning for years. Another hospital with a good relationship with staff used the crisis to reinforce their no-layoff policy, leading staff to respond with greater loyalty by defining more patients as 'emergency' cases in order to undertake the surgery without breaking the strike. The other hospital used the crisis as an opportunity to attract other non-surgical patients and develop new types of non-surgical procedures to supplement their income stream, helping them to endure the crisis and generate more income once it was over. Each hospital made distinctly different sense of the crisis and the appropriate strategies developed in response.

Questions

1. How did the three hospitals differ in the way they made sense of the crisis?
2. How did these differences in sensemaking shape the strategies they developed to respond to it?

What information is gathered about the external environment, as well as how it is interpreted, is a *social* and *political* process. It is a *social* process because it depends on how managers interpret the information, what information they seek, based on the set of norms, beliefs and assumptions that members of the organization share – and socialize new-comers into – about how the world works and how they should do business (Pettigrew and Whipp, 1993). Tony Grundy, in his book *Implementing Strategic Change*, defines this set of under-lying assumptions about how things should work simply as 'the way we do things around here' (1993: 29). Gerry Johnson (1993: 61) calls it the **paradigm** of the organization.

> An organization's **paradigm** can be defined as the set of core beliefs and assumptions that get embedded in the organization over time, such as beliefs about how they should react to moves by competitors or assumptions about the nature of the customer.

Johnson (1993: 61) explains how this paradigm affects how managers made sense of – and react to – their external environment:

> The various and often confusing signals that the organization faces are made sense of, are filtered, in terms of this paradigm. … It is at one and the same time, a device for interpretation and a formula for action. The strategies organizations follow grow out of this paradigm.

What are the implications of the concept of a dominant paradigm for managing strategic change? One implication is that managers need to be reflexively aware of how the dominant paradigm implicitly shapes strategic change decisions. Paradigms, by their very nature, are often so taken-for-granted and institutionalized that managers don't even realize that these ingrained beliefs and assumptions are guiding their thinking and behaviour and therefore don't take the opportunity to critically reflect on them. Sometimes, strategic change can only be possible when managers start to abandon their paradigm, as difficult and painful as that might be.

For example, imagine you work for a firm that has always held to the belief that customers are driven primarily by price, derived from their long-standing *low-price* position (in the language of Michael Porter's three generic strategies discussed in Chapter 2, this would be a 'cost leadership' strategic position). Holding this belief meant that the managers always worked on the assumption that moves by competi-tors should be met with a 'price war'. These price wars further reinforced the firm's cost cutting and efficiency drives, which in turn drove down operating profits and reduced investment in things like product innovation and customer service – the very things that customers may actually be willing to pay a small price premium for. Being reflexively aware of the implicit paradigm might mean that firm would reflect critically on these beliefs and assumptions in order to break the 'vicious cycle' and the 'race to the bottom' associated with this way of thinking.

What information is gathered, and how it is interpreted is also a deeply *political* process (Pettigrew and Whipp, 1993). As Johnson (1993) points out, any attempts to change a firm's strategy that challenges the taken-for-granted paradigm is likely to have political implications. For example, certain individuals or groups might be symbolically or materially wedded to a particular way of thinking about and acting on the environment. They might gain status and esteem from the current paradigm.

For example, the Operations Director in a cost-focused firm might gain power and influence – and perhaps even a promotion – for being the one credited with enabling greater cost efficiencies that support the firm's low-price strategy. Individuals or groups might also gain materially from the current arrangements. For example, employees of the Operations Department might secure more resources for their department based on this low-price strategy. They might even have performance-related pay tied to this focus on cost efficiency that is linked to the 'cost leadership' strategy. Thus, any change to the paradigm might be interpreted as a threat to the organization's political elites and current power relations. It could also lead to political contests about which of the different interpretations of 'the environment' (e.g. accounts of the changing environment, accounts of what customers want, etc.) put forward by different actors should be used to inform strategy. During these contests, those adept at using power to their advantage are likely to gain ascendance.

The trigger to reflect on – and think about changing – the organization's dominant paradigm could come from a variety of sources. There could be a sudden decline in sales performance. There could be an unexpected innovation by a competitor. There could be a strike amongst employees (as was the case in the studies of hospitals by Meyer (1982) and the study of an orchestra by Glynn (2000) discussed later in this chapter). Critical reflection on the paradigm could also be prompted by negative media coverage – a notion confirmed by research by Michael Bednar of the University of Illinois discussed in the *Conversation*.

Go Online: In an article, Michael Bednar of the University of Illinois explains how important the media can be in shaping the strategic change agenda.

While businesses have typically viewed the news media as a megaphone for publicity, they have not tended to view the media as an influential stakeholder capable of shaping the strategic decisions of key executives.

'As the news media reports negatively about firms, that registers with executives', he said. 'And that, in turn, prompts executives to engage in larger scale strategic change'.

To perform the study, Bednar and co-authors Steven Boivie, a professor of management at the University of Arizona, and Nicholas R. Prince, a doctoral student in business administration at Illinois, used computer-aided content analysis to determine how favourable the media coverage was for 250 firms over the course of five years.

'We analysed approximately 40,000 articles, and were able to quantify how positive or negative the coverage of the firm was', he said. 'After we controlled for performance and several other variables that could affect media coverage, we found evidence for the main effect, that negative media coverage may act as a trigger for strategic change'.

You can read the full article titled 'Bad news can prompt strategic change' via a direct link on the companion website for this book: www.edge.sagepub.com/strategy2e.

Michael Bednar
Article

There are clearly some significant blind spots and weaknesses in the various models of 'fit' with the environment. Similar to Donaldson's SARFIT model ('structural adjustment to regain fit' which we also discuss briefly in Chapter 13), models that assume organizations periodically adjust to their environment assume that ideas about what change is a good idea – or indeed whether change itself is a good idea – are generated, aired and selected in a politically neutral and objective process. Socio-political approaches, on the other hand, point out the role of social, psychological and political factors involved in the reasons why organizations decide to change, such as:

- Departments, functions or business units vying for limited resources seek to monopolize these resources for themselves by bidding for additional investment for their preferred change initiative.

- New leaders join the organization and feel the need to be seen to be 'shaking things up' or 'putting their stamp' on the organization. It is certainly rare to find an example of a large corporation that appointed a new CEO who declared that he or she planned to change nothing significant about the organization because it was well run before by their predecessor. Change is therefore symbolically associated with being a 'strong leader' – regardless of whether or not a steady course already established might be a good idea. The popularity of mergers and acquisitions, despite their persistent failure rate and inability to generate long-term value, is a good example of how strategic change is often driven by hubris, over-confidence and vanity projects – as the article by Andre Spicer in *The Conversation* suggests (see http://theconversation.com/merger-madness-rarely-pays-off-so-why-do-firms-still-make-these-deals-26130) (see also Malmendier and Tate, 2008). This hubris and over-confidence is not just a matter of 'personality'. It is deeply woven into the cultural myths of the 'hero manager' and 'celebrity CEO' and further reinforced by sky-high remuneration packages founded on the belief that 'strong leaders' can single-handedly change a company's fortunes almost overnight – despite all the evidence to the contrary. In fact, research by Sinha and colleagues (2012) shows that the 'cult of celebrity' that emerged around a CEO – and was further reinforced by the media and financial intermediaries – led to an escalation of commitment to the firm's failed acquisition (see the discussion of celebrity in Chapter 10).

- Fads and fashions in management thinking change frequently (Abrahamson, 1991), leading organizations' elites and their managers to fear that they are seen as falling behind the latest ideas and not 'benchmarking' against their competitors, even if these new ideas about how to do business have not been thought through or are not appropriate for that particular firm. Institutional theorists refer to these social forces operating over firms, driving them to look alike and copying each other as they strive for legitimacy, as 'mimetic isomorphism' (DiMaggio and Powell, 1983).

- A whole industry of management consultants, gurus and academics exist to convince managers that existing ways of doing things are outdated. They attempt to persuade firms that innovation is required (see Chapter 4) and 'new' and 'better' ways of doing business are necessary. Of course, these 'new ideas' are what these actors themselves benefit from in the form of book sales, guru talks or consultancy fees (Clark and Fincham, 2002). This 'change industry' has a structural *disincentive* to advise firms that their current strategy is working well, even if it is the case. The change industry also has a structural disinclination to advise organizations that strategic change can be designed and implemented *internally* based on their existing knowledge and competencies – they do not sell their consulting services, books, training or lectures unless managers are convinced that outside 'expert' help and advice is needed to achieve the strategic change.

Go Online: Andre Spicer, writing in *The Conversation*, asks the question: 'If mergers so rarely pay off, why do firms still make these deals?'

Studies repeatedly find that 70% to 90% of mergers fail. Hardly a rational choice, then. Mergers also need to be paid for by cost cutting, which often makes job losses inevitable. Customers, local communities and national governments can also lose out from M&As.

Sometimes the whole of society loses. Consider the M&As behind recent bank failures in the UK: Co-op overreached by taking over Britannia; RBS bought subsidiaries around the world; Halifax and Bank of Scotland became HBOS, which fell victim to the financial crisis; HBOS was bailed out by Lloyds which then in turn ran into difficulties. And when some of these banks had to be bailed out, the taxpayer – and all those affected by the austerity measures that followed – fronted the cost and shouldered the burden.

Even those supposed to be the 'winners' – the shareholders – also lose out. A review of more than 130 studies found that, while on balance M&As created some value for the company selling the assets as well as shareholders, they made no difference to the value of the acquiring company. In other words, acquiring companies often go through painful and expensive processes for absolutely no pay-off.

The real value created by M&As is work for well-paid intermediaries, speculative gains for short-term activist investors and bonuses for senior executives. The costs often end up being carried by downsized employees, abandoned local communities and national governments that can lose their industrial base.

You can find a link to this article on the companion website for this book at www.edge. sagepub.com/strategy2e.

Andre Spicer Article

It is also clear that *sensemaking* is a critical element in the answer to the question 'Why does strategic change occur?' – a concept also discussed in Chapters 9 and 10.

Sensemaking involves the generation of meaning from the often chaotic and ambiguous information and experiences that managers face from their interactions inside the organization and their external environment. Strategic change relies upon individuals and groups first 'sensing' that something needs to change, and then seeking – consensually or otherwise – a collective understanding of what should change and how.

IN PRACTICE

Strategic change in a corporate law firm

**Cindy Carpenter
Interview**

Go Online: Visit the book's website at https://edge.sagepub.com/strategy2e to watch an interview with Cindy Carpenter conducted by the author team.

Cindy Carpenter was the Executive Director of Human Resources and Marketing at law firm Corrs Chambers Westgarth and the Programme Director for the firm's organization-wide change programme, 'Corrs 2010'. Her position within the marketing function of the firm required her to manage the ongoing strategic development of the organization.

Cindy joined Corrs in 2006 after 13 years with the Boston Consulting Group. Her initial role was that of principal consultant before taking internal leadership roles and progressing to General Manager of the Australia and New Zealand offices. Cindy's cross-functional role at Corrs, as well as her extensive experience in leadership makes her an authority on the relationship between culture and strategy.

She provides fascinating examples of using classical strategy theories in a contemporary context. Her theoretical knowledge and extensive experience in management consulting means she is uniquely positioned to lead change and develop strategic competitive advantage in a professional services firm.

Cindy challenges the conventional view that strategy is the means to reach an end. She states that competitive advantage is embedded within the staff and it can only be realized through an integrated strategy between the HR and marketing functions. She focuses on the 'soft stuff', on sensemaking as essentially a process of pattern-making or organizing; fitting clues and cues together and trying to make meaning of them. Therefore, a vital task for a manager is to skilfully lead the pattern of sensemaking by providing those cues, by creating and adapting the frames of reference. Managers become, literally, 'managers of meaning'. Their role is to make and give sense in the organization. Sensemaking by means of manipulation is a process of acting in order to create environments that people can comprehend and manage. Sensemaking creates certainty in an uncertain environment and therefore provides the platform for the manager to become a strong leader or, as others term it, 'Sensegiver'.

In 'pulling the levers of change', Cindy is able to create the appropriate HR environment and concurrently, a suitable brand for the firm by influencing the clients' experience. The integration of the marketing and HR functions is critical as the brand is brought to life through the behaviour of staff. As mentioned in the video, incisive legal advice is a brand promise, so it is pivotal that the staff does, in fact, bring the right skills, capabilities, knowledge and experience to bear in order to provide a service that matches the clients' brand expectation. We interviewed Cindy as a part of the research for this book and made a video with her, which you can find on our website. After you have watched the video and looked at the associated case material we would like you to think in practice about how you would do strategic change of culture by answering the following questions, for which you will need to utilize the video interview, the Case Study and the listed reading resources.

Questions

1. How do Weick's maxims linking sensemaking to the role of the manager apply to this case video?

2. A key concept in sensemaking is the 'enacted environment': how do Corrs enact their environment?

In some cases, those involved in the strategy-making process – such as the Top Management Team (TMT) – can be aligned in their sensemaking about the need for strategic change and the form it should take. However, this is not always the case. Balogun and colleagues (2015) argue that senior managers are not an undifferentiated and homogenous group. TMTs are typically *heterogeneous* – composed of individuals from different professional backgrounds, functional departments and, in multinational corporations in particular, from varied geographical locations. Why would one expect managers to see the same cues as having the same strategic implications when their biographies, interests and experience differ markedly? Balogun and colleagues (2015: 960) propose that shared sensemaking within the TMT about strategic change is affected by the distinct 'interpretive communities' of the different members. The idea that distinct interpretive communities can shape how strategic direction is understood is also evident in Glynn's (2000) study of conflict over strategy in a symphony orchestra.

IN PRACTICE

Strategic crisis in the Atlanta Symphony Orchestra

Glynn (2000) studied a strategic crisis at the Atlanta Symphony Orchestra. The organization had been experiencing years of challenging times: declining attendance, expensive buildings to maintain, a 'graying' audience and decreased opportunities for supplementary revenue generating activities such as touring and recording. Things were brought to a head in 1996 when the musicians went on strike. The administrative managers in charge of finance and operations had sought to impose new contracts that included changes to salary and working conditions. The strike was sparked by management's decision not to offer tenure to six musicians who had successfully met tenure conditions.

Glynn shows how the musicians and managers had different interpretations of who they are and what they do (the organizational identity) and where they should go (strategic direction) that led to competing constructions of the organization's 'core competencies' (a concept discussed in Chapter 3), summarized in the table below.

	View of organizational identity ('who we are')	Resources emphasized	Claims about core capability	Illustrative quote
Musicians	Normative: values of artistry, aesthetics and the musical canon	The aesthetic vitality of the orchestra (requiring more investment for global tours and more tenured musicians)	Producer of high-quality world class classical music	'[Management is] looking at the orchestra like it was a potato chip factory'
Managers	Utilitarian: values of business acumen and fiscal responsibility	Subscribers, consumers, major donors/foundations, recording contracts, volunteers	Low-cost community responsive producer of classical music	'It will take more than great playing to get ASO into financial shape'

Source: Adapted from Glynn, 2000: 291

These two competing interpretations of the 'core competencies' of the organization not only affected the outcome of the strike but actually formed part of the events that triggered it. There were competing claims about what should be considered as the organization's resources and competencies, leading to power struggles between these groups over control of the organization's strategic direction. Two competing strategic change scenarios emerged:

Scenario 1: Investment in artistic excellence through investment in expanding the size of the orchestra and number of tenured positions, investment in musical equipment, global tours, hiring 'star' conductors.

Scenario 2: Fiscal restraint and commercialization though cost cutting, reduction in staff numbers, increasing ticket prices, fund-raising and endowment/sponsorship, improving marketing, focus on local Atlanta customer base (not global expansion).

Questions

1. Based on your analysis of the case, which strategy would you recommend? Justify your answer.

2. What do you think the political implications of your recommendation might be for members of the organization?

3. What would you do in order to manage these political implications? Construct a plan of how you would the power and politics associated with your recommendation.

For Baunsgaard and Clegg (2012, 2013), distinct ways of making sense between different organizational groups are not merely a reflection of idiosyncratic local systems of interpretation, they are deeply power-invested and political systems of thought, what they call *ideological modes of rationality*. In other words, ways of thinking about what is 'rational' and 'logical' are not neutral truths but rather carry with them ideologies: sets of ideas about what is natural or right that systematically benefit certain social groups and disadvantage others. For example, a private equity firm dominated by the ideological mode of rationality of corporate finance might believe that it is 'natural' or 'inevitable' that a profitable manufacturing plant or customer service centre should be shut down, sold off or moved to another country. This ideological mode of rationality tends to lead to practices of asset stripping, mass redundancies and 'social dumping' – the process through which operations are moved to countries with lower labour costs and weaker employment rights in order to increase profits. These practices systematically benefit wealthy investors while having negative effects on individuals, local communities and entire nation-states, furthering social inequality and exploitation.

- -
Go Online: Martin Parker, writing in *The Conversation*, identifies the role of some private equity firms in destroying jobs in order to make profit as just one of the many symptoms of what is wrong with contemporary capitalism – from tax avoidance to the off-shoring of jobs to environmental damage to the forms of 'casino capitalism' responsible for the Global Financial Crisis. A number of scholars calling themselves the 'Corporate Reform Collective' have grouped together to put forward a manifesto for change – published as the book *Fighting Corporate Abuse: Beyond Predatory Capitalism*. You can find out more about this book on the Pluto Books website. You can also read the full *The Conversation* article titled 'How to pull the plug on irresponsible capitalism' via a direct link on the companion website for this book: www.edge.sagepub.com/strategy2e.
- -

Corporate Reform

Particular discourses – forms of language, categories and systems of representation – legitimate certain ways of thinking about strategy as 'natural', 'inevitable' or 'right'. For example, Erkama and Vaara (2010) show how senior managers in a Swedish company used neo-liberal rhetoric to legitimate the shutdown of a manufacturing plant in Finland, despite the fact that the plant was generating profit. To envisage alternative – perhaps more socially, environmentally and ethically responsible – forms of strategic change requires us to reflect critically on these ideological systems of representation that present certain strategic options as *fait accompli*.

Erkama &
Vaara

EXTEND YOUR KNOWLEDGE

You can read a journal article by N. Erkama and E. Vaara called **'Struggles over legitimacy in global organizational restructuring: A rhetorical perspective on legitimation strategies and dynamics in a shutdown case'** on the companion website for this book: www.edge.sagepub.com/strategy2e.

Erkama, N. and Vaara, E. (2010) 'Struggles over legitimacy in global organizational restructuring: A rhetorical perspective on legitimation strategies and dynamics in a shutdown case', *Organization Studies*, 31(7): 813–839.

Types of change

Not all change is the same. A minor tweak to an existing policy or procedure is very different to a fundamental shift in thinking and behaving required by a radical departure in the firm's strategy when it decides to diversify or enter a new market, for example. Strategists therefore need to understand different managerial approaches and challenges associated with different types of change. In fact, many leading thinkers advocate a **contingency** perspective on organizational change (Dunphy and Stace, 1988). The contingency perspective suggests that 'one size fits all' models are wrong. For example, a small, incremental change that is widely supported by employees and is not urgently needed for organizational survival might suit a different change management approach to a more radical, large-scale change that is not widely supported by employees and is urgently needed for organizational survival.

> A **contingency** perspective on change proposes that the 'right' way of managing change depends on – is *contingent* on – the particular context: the type of change, the type of organization or the type of environment the organization is in.

> **Evolutionary change** is change that involves ongoing small adaptations that remain consistent with existing ways of doing things.

> **Revolutionary change** seeks to transform existing ways of doing things in a complete break with the past.

What are the differences in types of change? Dunphy and Stace (1988) and Bartunek and Louis (1988) were some of the first authors to differentiate what Dunphy and Stace (1988) called **evolutionary** and **revolutionary change**.

Other authors refer to evolutionary change as something that is *incremental* or *continuous*. Bartunek and Louis (1988: 100) describe such change as continuing in line with existing 'accepted frameworks' – what Grundy (1993) or

Johnson (1993) might call the organization's *paradigm*, which we discussed earlier in this chapter. For example, a firm might add new product features to existing product lines or launch a new product line that uses existing production equipment. Sometimes this is referred to as 'first order' or 'morphostatic' change because it involves either doing slightly more or less of what the organization already does, or doing these things slightly differently. According to Smith (1982: 318), first-order change involves 'making things look different while remaining basically as they have always been'.

Revolutionary change is *radical* or *discontinuous*. For example, revolutionary change could involve changing the types of products or services the organization provides (e.g. shutdowns, diversification), who it provides them to (e.g. entering new markets) or how it provides them (e.g. move from physical stores to online delivery). Bartunek and Louis (1988: 100) describe these types of change as 'transformational' because they involve 'discontinuous shifts in frameworks' – or *paradigms* as Johnson (1993) calls them. Some people refer to this type of change as 'second order' or 'morphogenetic' change because it involves deciding – or perhaps being forced – to do something fundamentally different to what you have done before. For Levy (1986), second-order change alters the 'core paradigm' of the organization, changing the basic set of assumptions and governing rules through which things are organized. According to Smith (1982: 318), second-order change 'penetrates so deeply into the "genetic code" that all future generations acquire and reflect these changes'. In other words, revolutionary 'second-order' changes alter the (metaphorical) 'DNA' of the organization in such a way that it cannot easily be reversed in the future.

Grundy (1993), in his book *Implementing Strategic Change*, proposes that organizations might go through some periods of incremental change (e.g. small changes in organizational structures or systems) while occasionally experiencing more radical 'discontinuous' change (e.g. a merger, joint venture or shutdown). Moreover, incremental change can occur at different rates. It might occur at a stable or 'smooth' rate – for example an annual review of product features and pricing that occurs every year. Alternatively, incremental change can occur at a more unstable or 'bumpy' rate – for example, where a period of no change to product features and pricing for a number of years is followed by a comprehensive review that results in multiple incremental changes all at once (see Figure 12.2).

Ideas about evolutionary and revolutionary change also relate to some important debates in strategic management about the nature of strategy development

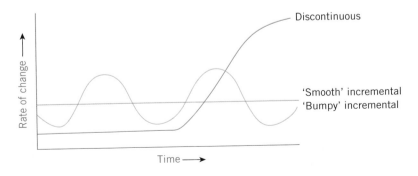

Figure 12.2   Types of change (Grundy, 1993)

processes (see Chapter 9). Against the so-called 'planning school' that was dominant in the early days of strategy development, thinkers such as Quinn (1978) argued that organizations do not develop their strategies through the implementation of long-term plans. Rather, they move forward incrementally, in small but logical steps that are guided by a general idea of where to go but are constantly refined as new information appears and managers reflect on and learn from their actions. This is akin to the 'incremental change' described by Grundy (1993), where organizations make small steps to keep pace with changes in the environment. Those wanting to understand – or manage – radical discontinuous change might, however, argue that such logical incremental steps are only useful for organizations that have the time to let things emerge from this 'trial and error' process. Critics might say that such incremental change is not advisable for organizations facing some kind of discontinuous shift in technology – such as the death of an industry like movie rental with the rise in streaming technology.

Implementing change

The most popular models of change management depict change as a series of steps that an organization undertakes to move from one state to another. One classic early step-based model of change comes from the social psychologist Kurt Lewin (1947). Like many other authors of popular models now found in management textbooks, Lewin was not a management theorist as such. 'Management' was not really a fully fledged subject at the time that he was writing. Lewin was a social psychologist often credited as the 'founding father' of social psychology.

Lewin's abiding interest revolved around group dynamics, including how individuals relate to – and become influenced by – those around them. These social relationships could be with other members of a social group a person is a member of, such as a sports team or a work group, but it could also include more 'distant' and abstract social entities such as the nation-state and ethnic groupings. As an exiled German Jew who fled America when Hitler came to power, he was an outspoken critic of Nazi ideology, fighting also for justice and equality for other disadvantaged minority groups (Cooke, 1999; Burnes, 2004). He was interested in what made a social group – or even a whole society – change for the worse (i.e. the rise of authoritarian, violent and xenophobic regimes) and what could be done to make them change for the better (i.e. democratic, open and peaceful regimes).

Popular versions of Lewin's ideas present a model which proposes that change takes place in three steps or stages (adapted from Burnes, 2004):

Step 1: Un-freezing. First, members of the group need to destabilize the status quo and question existing ways of doing things. This could be achieved through disconfirmation (showing the group the dysfunctional reality of their existing state) or the induction of guilt or anxiety (generating emotional response from revealing the impact of current behaviour). During this 'unfreezing' process, individuals need to be offered psychological safety: reassurance that letting go of existing attitudes and behaviours will not lead to humiliation, loss of status or social networks or inability to cope.

Step 2: Moving. Unfreezing does not itself generate change; it only creates motivation to learn to do things differently. The learning process involves a cycle of gathering information about the new state of affairs, developing viable options, testing out options and learning from these tests in an iterative process of research (thinking) and action (doing).

Step 3: Re-freezing. Without reinforcement, any change developed during the 'moving' stage could be short-lived. Re-freezing is needed to ensure new attitudes and behaviours do not regress back to old ways. For example, group norms and routines could be altered to further reinforce, recognize and reward the new attitudes and behaviours, such as a change to organizational rules, policies, practices and culture – perhaps by introducing elements of the change into the monthly staff meeting or annual performance appraisal process.

EXTEND YOUR KNOWLEDGE

A virtual special issue of the journal *Human Relations* brings together a range of papers on the management of change. The paper by Cummings and colleagues (2016), entitled '**Unfreezing change as three steps**', revisits the famous paper by Lewin (1947), published in the first ever issue of *Human Relations*. The authors argue that many popular understandings of Lewin's work, including the three-step model found in many textbooks, miss much of what Lewin actually said. The virtual special issue also includes many other classic papers on change management, both historical classics and contemporary re-appraisals.

You can also view the "vodcast" about the article by Cummings and colleagues (2016) on YouTube where is it titled 'Unfreezing change as three steps'.

You can read all of the articles in the virtual special issue on this book's companion website: www.edge.sagepub.com/strategy2e.

Go Online: The UK Chartered Institute of Personnel and Development (CIPD) has developed a website full of advice for managers on managing change. This includes a podcast involving experts and practitioners who speak about the challenges of managing organizational change. You can listen to the podcast on the CIPD website. You can also visit the 'Topic page' on Change Management on the CIPD website, which includes many resources such as factsheets, research reports and practical tools. Both links can be accessed via the companion website for this book: www.edge.sagepub.com/strategy2e.

CIPD Resources

The three step model of change has received much criticism – even though, ironically, Lewin never actually articulated any such model in his work (Cummings et al., 2016). Nevertheless, the model that has subsequently been popularised (and is still erroneously attributed to Lewin) is premised on the idea that an organization is a stationary entity until some kind of 'change' comes along to break the status quo.

> Lewin's model was a simple one, with organizational change involving three stages; unfreezing, changing and refreezing … This quaintly linear and static conception – the organization as ice cube – is so wildly inappropriate that it is difficult to see why it has not only survived but prospered. (Kanter et al., 1992: 10)

The problem is that this 'ice cube' metaphor conceptualizes organizations as static entities until some kind of 'change' comes along. If we conceptualize organizations as dynamic and ongoing systems of social interaction – such as interactions between employees, customers, competitors, suppliers and regulators – then viewing the organization as a stable entity is problematic. As Clegg et al. (2016: 377) argue, the 'root metaphor of unfreezing/freezing is profoundly problematic because organizations are always in motion'. That this is the case is a key tenet of the so-called 'processual' perspective on change (see Chapter 9), which seeks to examine the dynamics of change as it happens over time and in a particular context, rather than seeking to measure organizations as if they had stable attributes that could be studied as context-free variables (Dawson, 2003).

The processual view enables us to understand why change can happen without any intention to change amongst top management – for example when employees develop new ways of doing things that deviate from the intended strategic plan, even though management have not officially 'sanctioned' this change in working practices (or might not even be aware of it). Similarly, management might create a strategic plan and put various mechanisms in place to implement it – announcements of the new vision, new policies and procedures, budgets, job descriptions, etc. – yet the interactions between employees lead them to view the change sceptically and therefore that nothing actually changes on the ground.

Mintzberg (1987) highlighted the issue of planned change not always being implemented when he talked about the difference between realized and unrealized strategy (whereby some strategies are realized and others are not), and planned versus emergent strategy (where some strategies are planned and intentional whereas others emerge without any grand plan behind them). Pettigrew's (1985) study of strategic change at ICI also showed that the formal plans of change agents were far removed from what actually happened, shaped as they were by the complex interplay of politics, culture and history. We discuss these approaches in more detail in Chapter 9.

Despite criticism, step-based models of change continue to hold their popularity. According to Cummings and colleagues (2016: 34), ideas that change involves a series of steps – inspired by Lewin's legacy – have become 'regarded both as an objective self-evident truth and an idea with noble provenance.' One influential model that follows in Kurt Lewin's legacy by viewing change as a series of steps is John Kotter's (1996) book *Leading Change*. Here, change is described not as three steps but eight:

Step One: Create Urgency

Develop a sense of urgency around the need for change based on the reality of the marketplace and competition, for example by developing scenarios about future potential threats or opportunities that could be exploited. People must be convinced that the status quo is not sustainable.

Step Two: Form a Powerful Coalition

Create a coalition of change leaders: influential people whose power comes from a variety of sources, including job title, status, expertise and political importance.

Step Three: Create a Vision for Change

Link all the various ideas about what could change together into an overall vision that people can grasp easily and remember and that sounds desirable but viable. A clear vision helps people understand what they are being asked to change and why it is essential.

Step Four: Communicate the Vision

Communicate the vision frequently and consistently. Don't restrict it to just special meetings about the change – embed it into all daily tasks and decision-making to keep it fresh in people's minds, stop other issues drowning it out and ensure all activities tie back to the vision, for example, by embedding the vision in meeting agendas, training and performance reviews.

Step Five: Remove Obstacles

Examine who or what is blocking the change. Why are they resistant to the change? Openly and honestly address peoples' concerns and anxieties. And are there processes or structures that are getting in the way of the change? Look at your organizational structure, job descriptions, and performance and compensation systems to ensure they're in line with your vision.

Step Six: Create Short-term Wins

Give people a taste of success early on. Create short-term targets that are smaller and more achievable – not just one long-term goal. For example, could you pilot the change in one department, or one product line, to show immediate improvements? Could you start with a low-investment and fast-return target for change, so that critics cannot question the justification for the investment?

Step Seven: Build on the Change

Quick wins are only the beginning of a long-term change. After each 'win', analyse what went well and what could be improved. Set longer-term goals to keep the momentum going. Refresh the coalition you created in Step Two, to keep the energy and enthusiasm for the change high. Remind people that the change is not 'finished' but that continuous improvement is the norm.

Step Eight: Anchor the Changes in Corporate Culture

To make the change stick, it should become part of the core values of the organization. Ensure the change is seen in every aspect of your organization – from hiring policies, training for new staff, policies and procedures and informal symbols and stories. For example, make stories of the 'bad old days' of the past and the 'good times' since the change was implemented part of the induction for new staff. Publicly recognize those who have played a key role in championing the change through awards and other symbols of achievement.

Go Online: You can visit the website of John Kotter's consultancy business to learn more about his approach to change management, including his eight-step process and his consultancy firm's strategy consulting activities. The website includes a number of blogs, videos, podcasts and ebook downloads. You can visit the website via a direct link on the companion website for this book: www.edge.sagepub.com/strategy2e.

Kotter Website

Go Online: Professor Rosabeth Moss Kanter is a leading thinker in change management and Professor of Business Administration at Harvard Business School. She is the author of the best-selling book *The Change Masters* (1984) and *The Challenge of Organizational Change* (2003). In a TED Talk, she explains what she thinks are the six success factors that are the keys to positive change in organizations. You can watch Moss Kanter's talk by going to the TED Talk website, or via a direct link on the companion website for this book: www.edge.sagepub.com/strategy2e.

Rosabeth Moss Kanter TED Talk

It is understandable why these kinds of step-based models appeal to managers dealing with major strategic change. Management is a demanding task, with many unforeseen things to deal with on a daily basis. If implementing change is as simple as following a series of predefined stages, such models seem very attractive. They take the uncertainty out of unsettling processes because you have some idea of what you are doing, what to expect and where the impact of change will be registered. The lack of empirical evidence for the efficacy of these step-based models has certainly not dampened practitioners' enthusiasm for them. The value they offer is a sense of security and certainty implying that there is 'one best way' to implement change. If only it were that easy in practice!

With an eye on practice and its complexities rather than on the textbooks and their simplicities, some scholars reject the 'one best way' approach and instead advocate a contingency approach to change management. As we discussed earlier in this chapter, a contingency perspective proposes that the 'right' way of managing change depends on – is *contingent* on – the particular context: such as the type of change, the type of organization or the type of environment in which the organization is situated. Dunphy and Stace (1988) argue that two dimensions should first be considered:

- Scale of change: from small incremental adjustments to major transformations.

- Mode of change: from more collaborative modes to more coercive modes.

Mapping these two dimensions together, Dunphy and Stace (1988) identify four different approaches to change management (see Figure 12.3).

Through this model, Dunphy and Stace (1988) specify four strategic change approaches.

Type 1. Participative evolution: small incremental adjustments achieved by collaborative means.

Type 2. Charismatic transformation: large-scale discontinuous or 'radical' changes achieved through collaborative means. 'Charismatic' here is a reference to the need for charismatic leadership to ensure that those targeted to change seek to follow the vision of the charismatic leader(s).

Type 3. Forced evolution: small incremental adjustments achieved by coercive means, such as the use of power by a legitimate authority.

Type 4. Dictatorial transformation: large-scale discontinuous or 'radical' changes achieved through coercive means.

	Incremental Change Strategies	Transformative Change Strategies
Collaborative Modes	*Type 1* Participative evolution	*Type 2* Charismatic transformation
Coercive Modes	*Type 3* Forced evolution	*Type 4* Dictatorial transformation

Figure 12.3   Four approaches to managing change (Dunphy and Stace, 1988: 337)

Dunphy and Stace (1988, 1993) argue that the approach organizations decide to use depends on – is *contingent* upon – factors such as the volatility of the organization's environment, the degree of strategic drift the organization is experiencing, and the level of support or resistance amongst affected stakeholders for the change. For example:

- Consider an organization that has a fairly stable environment with few changes in customer preferences, infrequent competitive moves by rivals and stable technologies, coupled with a history of keeping pace with any changes, and with broad support amongst employees, suppliers and customers for the change. Here, a participative evolution might be best suited: no radical changes are needed, only minor adjustments. Stakeholders are also broadly supportive and are therefore likely to cooperate or comply with the requirements of the change.

- Consider an organization that has a volatile environment with frequent and significant changes in customer preferences, moves by competitors and changes in technologies, coupled with a history of strategic drift, and with little or no support for the change amongst affected stakeholders. Here, a dictatorial transformation might be necessary: a major and radical change is needed and, given that stakeholders are unlikely to willingly comply, methods of coercion or force (e.g. threats, warnings, etc.) are necessary to push the change through.

While the empirical evidence for a neat categorization such as this is questionable, Dunphy and Stace's model does help to quash one popular myth about change management: namely that change does, or at least ideally should, involve 'consultation' and be designed through 'collaboration' with those the change affects. This myth was promulgated by the popular Organizational Development field – a field of scholars and practitioners interested in how organizations engage in planned change arising from employee participation in decisions about the long-term future, based on principles of empowerment, open communication, collaboration and trust and continuous learning.

Dunphy and Stace (1988, 1993) point out that such situations where change is managed through consultation and collaboration might be an 'ideal' for many theorists but in reality the managerial elites might not have the time to engage in such lengthy consultation processes. Changes that the elites want but need to be implemented quickly (for example, to gain so-called first mover advantage or rescue a failing firm) are unlikely to get off the ground quickly if everyone is involved. The desired change is also more likely to get diluted, or possibly even deviated from, the more people have a say in what happens. Moreover, in situations where there is an incompatibility of interests – a shutdown decision for example – consultation is unlikely to facilitate the change process desired by management. Employees might be viewed as having little knowledge relevant to the desired change; for instance, asking employees in the home country to be involved in strategic decisions about which foreign market to enter. Or employees might simply be outright opposed to the proposed change. For those seeking to impose a change such as a downsizing exercise or a shutdown, there is little to be gained for those in charge by asking employees to be involved in these kinds of decisions – employees are hardly likely to favour and facilitate a decision so detrimental to their immediate interests. In these circumstances, forms of participation and involvement would be either a waste of time or a direct barrier to change, from management's perspective.

Busting this 'myth of consultation' is particularly relevant to major strategic changes, such as decisions about diversification, innovation, internationalization, divestment, mergers and acquisitions, because these decisions are typically either far removed from employees' working lives, or could directly threaten their interests. Diversification threatens investment in existing products or markets which existing employees have self-interest in maintaining. Innovations that involve replacing staff with computers or robots, or replacing retail stores with online shopping, are unlikely to be supported by existing staff. Internationalization strategies are of little interest to those who do not fancy an overseas assignment and whose jobs might actually be on the line. Divestment of an entire business unit is never going to be popular amongst the staff being laid off. Similarly, mergers and acquisitions typically meet with resistance amongst lower level employees fearful of being 'rationalized' out to meet the promised cost savings from the proposed economies of scales or forced to adopt new policies and working practices imported from their new 'partner' organization (see Chapter 5).

From the perspective of those seeking to implement a preferred strategy, what use are lengthy periods of consultation and involvement in situations where the consultation, from the perspective of those setting the agenda, is a waste of time and potentially counter-productive? The agenda setters can sometimes use the privileges afforded by their position in power to convince people that changes not in their apparent interests are something that they do actually desire – what power theorist Steven Lukes (1974) referred to as deploying the 'third dimension' of power (see Chapter 11). For example, Knights and Willmott (2000) show how the discourse of Business Process Reengineering (BPR) involved ideological 'brainwashing' of employees, who were left not only reluctantly complying but *willingly cooperating* in their own exploitation, viewing work intensification and cost cutting through de-layering of management as positive outcomes because of their attachment to the discourse of 'empowerment' and 'employee discretion'.

Leading strategic change: Sensemaking, symbolism, communication

How do strategists lead organizations through a period of strategic change? As we noted at the start of this chapter, major strategic change is likely to affect almost all parts of the organization and those it deals with. Those leading strategic change are likely to have to deal with implications for finance (e.g. raising funds for a new investment), marketing (e.g. communicating to customers about how the change might affect them), as well as operations (e.g. ensuring purchasers, suppliers and distributors act in line with the change). These kinds of issues are covered in textbooks on accounting and finance, marketing and operations management. We will focus in this section mainly on the role of leaders in managing the symbolic aspects of strategic change. First we examine the role of sensemaking and sensegiving in strategic change leadership before moving on to examine the importance of metaphors and stories.

Sensemaking and Sensegiving

Work by Julia Balogun and colleagues (Balogun and Johnson, 2004, 2005; Rouleau and Balogun, 2011; Balogun et al., 2015) shows that *sensemaking* and *sensegiving* are crucial skills required for strategic change – concepts already elaborated in Chapters 9 and 10 and touched upon earlier in this chapter.

EXTEND YOUR KNOWLEDGE

The role of sensemaking in shaping how change recipients make sense of the meaning of change – and how this sensemaking affects intended and unintended strategic change outcomes – is discussed by J. Balogun and G. Johnson in the 2005 journal article '**From intended strategy to unintended outcomes: The impact of change recipient sensemaking**'. You can download the article from our website at www.edge.sagepub. com/strategy2e.

Balogun, J. and Johnson, G. (2005) 'From intended strategy to unintended outcomes: The impact of change recipient sensemaking', *Organization Studies*, 26(11): 1573–1602.

Balogun & Johnson

For example, strategic change relies on managers putting together complex, incomplete and ambiguous cues about the firm's strategic position – including ideas about the firm's internal resources and capabilities and its external environment of customers, competitors, investors and regulators – then piecing them together into a meaningful vision of the future strategic direction the firm should take. Strategists have to persuade employees, investors and customers and other stakeholders that the proposed strategic change is both possible and desirable, so that these important participants start to think in new ways and therefore also act in new ways. A case study of a strategic change initiative in a public university by Gioia and Chittipeddi (1991) shows the important role played by sensemaking and sensegiving during the strategic change process.

IN PRACTICE

Sensemaking and sensegiving in strategic change

Gioia and Chittipeddi (1991) studied the role of a new leader in the first year of a strategic change initiative in a large public US university. The new University President launched the strategic change and appointed a Strategic Planning Task Force (SPTF) to assist with the design and delivery of the change initiative. Gioia and Chittipeddi mapped four distinct phases of the strategic change effort.

1. *Envisioning.* The President began to construct an embryonic strategic vision for the university, even before he formally started the post, based on his conversations with key individuals such as the Deans of the various academic schools and his own prior experience in other institutions. A series of strategic projects called 'presidential initiatives' were launched involving restructuring, growth or retrenchment across various academic and administrative units.

(Continued)

(Continued)

2. *Signalling.* The President signalled to major stakeholders (e.g. academics, administrators, students, etc.) that change was imminent by publicly declaring the start of the strategic change effort in various documents and briefings. He also met with various stakeholders, formalized the vision statement ('A Top-Ten public university') and signalled his intent to break with the past by dismissing a few 'old guard' administrators and restructuring the senior administrative levels. The vision statement was in part *deliberately* ambiguous to allow for multiple interpretations of what it might mean – 'ambiguity-by-design' that was intended to signal the need for change without committing to any specific plans.

3. *Re-visioning.* Some stakeholders began to question the need for change, or for such radical change, and pockets of resistance and opposition emerged. Tension arose within the Top Management Team about how to manage this opposition. The President favoured a more directive process but others favoured a more consultative process, even if that meant compromising some of the ambitions of the change initiative. The President pushed forward with his ambitious plans, while allowing unit heads to engage in some consultation where they felt it was necessary, settling for a somewhat slower pace of change and modifying some of the initiatives based on feedback during the consultation process. The resistance and opposition did not de-rail the entire change initiative, however. Each of the presidential initiatives affected units differently – some were unit specific and had no wider repercussions – meaning resistors failed to generate a united front and power in numbers.

4. *Energizing.* The President sought to energize all those affected by the strategic change by creating a wider circle of consultation and feedback, first with senior members of staff and later with lower-level staff. During these meetings, the President would give the audience an apparently 'hypothetical' scenario – such as the need for consolidation of degree programmes or the need to increase national reputation for research. However, these scenarios were actually derived from his original ideas in the presidential initiatives. The spread of reach of these ideas for change widened ever further, such that all those affected became aware of them and could have input into them, but none of the initial publicly announced initiatives were to be fundamentally altered or abandoned, just fine-tuned. Strategic Study Groups were formed – whose membership was handpicked by the President – to make formal recommendations on the various presidential initiatives.

How did the President design the strategic change? Gioia and Chittipeddi (1991) propose that the two important dimensions involved were *sensemaking* and *sensegiving*, which we introduced earlier. Sensemaking came into play in the ways that various actors constructed (and re-constructed) the meaning of the change. For example, at the early stages – even before he started his role – the President made numerous trips to the university to talk to different stakeholders in order to *make sense* of the strengths and weaknesses of the organization and the opportunities and threats that might exist for the organization. Equally, those affected by the change initiative also had to make sense of the change – what impact it might have on their work and what kind of role they might play in its design or implementation.

Sensegiving related to how certain actors attempted to influence the sensemaking of others by shaping the way they understand an issue or what meaning it has for them. The President did not simply *make sense* of the strategic direction of the organization privately himself, he also actively tried to *give sense* to others by supplying them with his preferred interpretations of where they should go and how they should get there. He did this through his vision briefings, the agenda and charters set for the presidential initiatives and Strategic Study Groups and the scenarios he used at the staff meetings. However, those affected by the change also engaged in sensegiving – not only making sense privately but also communicating their understandings and preferences back to the President and TMT.

Mapped onto the four phases of the strategic change initiative described above, these phases can be understood in light of their focus on sensemaking or sensegiving as follows:

1. *Envisioning*. Sensemaking by President: focused on cognition (understanding).

2. *Signalling*. Sensegiving by President: focused on action (influencing).

3. *Re-visioning*. Sensemaking by affected stakeholders: focused on cognition (understanding).

4. *Energizing*. Sensegiving by President and affected stakeholders: focused on action (influencing). Here the sensegiving by affected stakeholders also led to some modification of the espoused vision and strategic projects in a 'feedback loop'.

Gioia and Chittipeddi (1991) concluded that strategic change is dependent upon leaders not only making sense of the strategy for themselves but crucially also influencing the sensemaking of affected stakeholders so that they start to question the existing interpretive schema (recurrent cognitive patterns of sensemaking) and start to adopt a new interpretive scheme that supports the preferred vision of the future. This process is all the more challenging when there is no immediate crisis looming, making it imperative that leaders first generate a sense of dissatisfaction with the status quo (an idea that links to Lewin's notion of 'unfreezing' discussed earlier in this chapter). Moreover, strategic change is not a one-way process of influence by the leaders to the stakeholders. Strategic change is a negotiated outcome of the interaction of those leading the change and those affected by it, with both attempting to figure out what the change means (sensemaking) and influence the way other parties make sense of the change (sensegiving).

If strategy is a process rather than a planned path, if it is something that is emergent and subject to frequent revision and rationalization, then it is, by definition, never fixed. Under these circumstances of emergence, sensemaking and sensegiving are constantly in play. Via 'sensemaking', managers are able to reach complex understandings of the world that will be communicated via 'sensegiving' to subordinates through coherent messages. These in turn will provide secure and workable ground for actions (Maitlis, 2005; Lüscher and Lewis, 2008). When the targets of the strategists' sensegiving make their own interpretations and communicate these interpretations back to the strategists, this can iteratively affect the strategists' previous sense by changing it or reinforcing it. Changing should trigger a process of reflection, influencing both what is learned and how such learning takes place

(Hays, 2008: 14). Making change happen means learning and improving as the change unfolds (Tichy and Bennis, 2007).

Gioia and Chittipeddi (1991: 433) illustrate how strategy is embedded in cognitive processes. Their argument is that '*strategic* change involves an attempt to change current modes of cognition and action to enable the organization to take advantage of important opportunities or to cope with consequential environmental threats'. The idea of the 'mode of cognition' sounds more complicated than it is: just ask your lecturer how she would describe your university. If she says she is proud of the university's role in educating students, her 'mental model' of what makes a good university is grounded in the idea that teaching is the most valuable activity. However, another lecturer might have a different 'cognitive model': he might say that doing strategy research is the key to help organizations, as research uncovers new ways of doing things. Publishing in journals, the new findings are accessible to literally thousands of managers all over the world. Now imagine if these two lecturers would have to craft a strategy for your university: no doubt these strategies would differ because of the different assumptions both hold dear. They would not even agree on basic questions such as 'what makes a good university?' or 'what is relevant information that should inform the strategy making process?' For the education-oriented lecturer, student evaluations might be important; for the research-driven lecturer, the number of publications in international journals would be a key reference point.

The basic assumption of studies on strategy and sensemaking (see Porac and Thomas (2002), for a good overview) is that organizations are 'interpretation systems' (Daft and Weick, 1984). As such, organizations collect and interpret information, and then act on it. If we follow this perspective, it is crucial to understand how an organization identifies information, how it processes it, and how it relates it to action.

Jane Dutton and Janet Dukerich's (1991) research into how the New York Port Authority reacted to the problem of homelessness in and around its transport hubs in the 1980s provides an example of how strategic change works. First, the organization defined itself as being in the transport business and ignored the problem. When it became too hard to ignore, because there were too many homeless people sleeping and living on their properties, the management team had to re-think the basic identity of the organization. This rethinking exercise resulted in them providing new facilities for homeless people. The organization radically changed how it made sense of its environment, and how it thought of its identity (a point also brought out in Glynn's (2000) study of the Atlanta Symphony Orchestra discussed earlier in this chapter). The Port Authority's managers acted on a mental map of the world in which the only relevant points were stations and travellers, much as in the London tube map. However, neither map features the social tragedies and human comedies that unfold every day in countless stations – the dramas, lost tourists, business people who run late, happy lovers who don't care where they are, and the unfortunates for whom the Tube offers a suicide opportunity. What you make of the tube map depends on the *mental maps* that you bring to bear on it: for the radical Islamist it might be a vehicle for an improvised explosive device while for the anxious lover it is a transport to joy. Meanwhile, more prosaic managers probably see it as a means to the end of getting to an appointment or to work on time.

The importance of sensemaking and sensegiving to the strategic change process applies both to senior managers who are typically tasked with formulating strategy and middle managers who are typically tasked with implementing it. Top Management Teams have the challenge of trying to make a more or less collective and unified sense of the organization's strategic direction. Middle managers also play an important role in translating strategic visions down the organizational hierarchy – as well as influencing strategic sensemaking across functions and upwards as well. Their role in upward, downward and horizontal communication makes 'discursive ability' (Maitlis and Lawrence, 2007; Rouleau and Balogun, 2011) – the ability to use language to influence others – a crucial skill for middle managers.

Rouleau and Balogun (2011) show that middle managers undertake two important activities during strategic change:

1. 'Setting the scene' – this involves bringing people together around a strategic change project to make sense of the future strategic direction and build an alliance who will work towards the change. It involves activities such as:

   i. Knowing who to target, based on identifying whose interests can be related to the change,

   ii. Who to get 'on side' in order to use their position of legitimacy to influence others,

   iii. Setting up the conversations by bringing the right people together (with required skills, experience, knowledge, power, etc.) in the right place, at the right time, with the right information and with the right media (email discussion groups, video conferencing, meetings, etc.),

   iv. Building networks of people they know and trust to be drawn on in future,

   v. Building a personal image and reputation as someone who means business, who should be taken seriously but who also is open to dialogue.

2. 'Performing the conversation' – this involves not just the act of talking (or writing) but drawing on the strategist's knowledge of the socio-cultural context and available symbolic representations to judge things like:

   i. What to say to each stakeholder group,

   ii. Knowing which words and phrases were the 'right' ones to use,

   iii. 'Staging' the conversations in the right way (e.g. following the expected or desired rules and rituals for interactions such as presentations and meetings),

   iv. Using appropriate methods of relating to others (e.g. using first names, putting people at ease, generating a feeling of involvement).

Another important aspect of a strategist's 'discursive ability' (Maitlis and Lawrence, 2007; Rouleau and Balogun, 2011) is their ability to understand and influence the metaphors that are used and the stories that are told about strategic change – two topics we shall consider in the next section.

The role of metaphors and stories in strategic change

The basic function of a story is to organize a series of events and actors into a common, accepted and comprehensible temporal framework (de La Ville and Mounoud, 2010: 185)

We have already touched on the importance of storytelling and narrative for strategy in Chapter 9 on strategy processes and we touched further on the matter in Chapter 10, when we discussed strategy as practice. Stories make sense *for* and *of* us.

From the day we are born, we are immersed in social groups that develop – and reinforce or change – their meaning-systems through the stories that they tell to each other. As children, we learn about the values and social expectations of our culture through the stories that we hear – from our parents or teachers or in books and films. Stories are one of the most fundamental ways in which all human beings develop their understanding of the world around them.

Research suggests that storytelling and narrative play a crucial role in the leadership of strategic change (Barry and Elmes, 1997; de La Ville and Mounoud, 2010; Fenton and Langley, 2011; Brown and Thompson, 2013). To lead stakeholders (employees, customers, investors, suppliers, regulators, etc.) to follow them in their strategic change, strategists have to create compelling stories about the past, present and future. Where have we come from? Where are we now? And where are we going? These stories help these stakeholders to make sense of why the change is necessary, what it involves and what role they want – or perhaps do *not* want – to play in it.

Stories are being told all the time in organizations: colleagues gossiping about their work-mates, old-timers telling new members of staff stories of the good old days, stories about failed or heroic adventures from previous projects (Gabriel, 2000). What makes strategy stories different, according to Barry and Elmes (1997: 430), is that 'strategy must rank as one of the most prominent, influential and costly stories told in organizations'. Stories about strategy are often given more prominence than others because strategy is often deemed more 'important' than other activities. Stories about strategy also tend to have much greater influence inside and outside the organization than other stories – partly because their authors tend to have positions of power. Stories about strategy also tend to incur more costs – both economic, social and symbolic costs – because much 'rides' on how they are viewed by key stakeholders. In fact, research has shown that organizations can prosper or fail on the basis of how legitimate their stories are deemed to be by investors (Jameson, 2000). These stories may be nothing more than a myth; a narrative device designed to appear legitimate in the eyes of investors, as is the case with post-merger earnings forecasts based on a 'comforting tale' of merger optimism for example.

Amel-Zahed Article

Go Online: Research by Amir Amel-Zahed at the University of Cambridge shows that news reports of corporate mergers typically spin an optimistic tale, accompanied by optimistic post-merger earnings forecasts. Yet research has shown that such forecasts are typically over-optimistic and never realized in practice. Stock-financed acquisitions actually tend to be value destructive in the long run. So how can we explain this tendency towards 'rose tinted glasses' in the media reports of mergers? Amir Amel-Zahed thinks these stories are a 'narrative device' that serve to reassure a firm's own shareholders that it is not over-paying, persuading target shareholders that they are not receiving over-valued shares and temper the general investor wariness to stock-based acquisitions. However, shareholders and investors are not that easily fooled and will scrutinize the credibility of such overly cheerful forecasts and heroic narratives of the post-merger future. The full article is titled 'How merger optimism feeds investors a comforting tale of bumper earnings' and can be found on *The Conversation* website, or via a direct link on the companion website for this book: www.edge.sagepub.com/strategy2e.

When strategies come unstuck and organizations have to retreat from them, a narrative has to be produced that explains the retreat. Politicians have to be particularly adept at this strategy but so do CEOs. Mantere and colleagues (2012) describe the efforts of a company to 'backtrack' and return to a previous strategy when a merger attempt failed. This strategic reversal was achieved through re-connecting to pre-existing meaning-systems, emphasizing the role of historical continuity against the accepted wisdom that strategic change involves disconnection with existing meaning-systems.

How do strategists make sense of strategy (sensemaking) – and then influence others to follow their vision of change (sensegiving)? We already know that language and other forms of symbolism – such as symbolic images, artefacts and objects – play an important role in the strategic sensemaking and sensegiving process. Metaphors are also central to the very way we think about business in general (Grant and Oswick, 1996; Morgan, 2006). It is hard to imagine a strategy change announcement being made without some kind of metaphor being used. Strategies are often conceived using some central metaphors, such as:

- Strategy as a *journey* (metaphors of paths, cross-roads, destinations, etc.)
- Strategy as *warfare* (metaphors of battles, fighting, conquering, etc.)
- Strategy as a *game* (metaphors of rules, winners, losers, etc.)
- Strategy as *engineering* (metaphors of toolboxes, reengineering, etc.)
- Strategy as *biological processes* (metaphors of evolution, adaptation, oceans, etc.)

The power of metaphors in framing how people think about strategy should not be under-estimated. Frank Cespedes (2014), writing in *Harvard Business Review*, deplores companies for their use of metaphors such as 'battles' in their strategy statements because it subconsciously leads companies to focus on competitors more than customers.

> **Framing** is the process through which people socially construct the meaning of an event or experience through the use of symbolic constructs, such as words, images or metaphors.

Samra-Fredericks (2003) identifies *deploying metaphors* as one of the six factors defining interpersonal competence in strategy (see Chapter 10). The power of these metaphors in framing – as Fairhurst (2010) suggests – is important for leadership of strategic change because it affects how people make sense of, and act upon, the events and experiences they find themselves involved in during a strategic change process.

Cornelissen and colleagues (2011) suggest that we need to differentiate between whether strategic change is framed as either *additive* or *substitutive*:

- *Additive strategic change* involves adding to or updating an existing organizational template (template is a concept similar to the 'paradigm' discussed earlier in this chapter) – linking to notions of incremental or evolutionary change discussed earlier in this chapter.
- *Substitutive strategic change* entails substituting or replacing the current organizational template – linking to notions of radical or revolutionary change discussed earlier in this chapter.

Cornellisen and colleagues (2011) propose that these two different types of strategic change make a difference to the method used for 'framing' the change, either using analogy or metaphor. Appropriate framing is likely to assist the creation of legitimacy for the change in the eyes of important stakeholders (e.g. employees, customers, investors, etc.). They suggest the following.

> *Additive* changes are more likely to be considered legitimate by stakeholders when they are framed using *analogies* (conjoining of cases from within the same domain), such as the use of references to cases and observations of other business domains, including the organization's own history or examples from its market or industry context. For example: 'We cannot lose our way like IBM have done in the past', 'We must be more like Google in striving for innovation.'

> *Substitutive* changes are more likely to be considered legitimate by stakeholders when they are framed using *metaphors* (cross-category comparisons from different domains), such as the use of references to other domains of experience outside of business such as warfare, sports, art, religion or family. For example: 'We need to beat the competition and win this game', 'We cannot afford to lose this battle for customers.'

Cornelissen,
Holt & Zundel

EXTEND YOUR KNOWLEDGE

You can download the full text of the 2011 article **'The role of analogy and metaphor in the framing and legitimization of strategic change'** by J.P. Cornelissen, R. Holt and M. Zundel from our companion website: www.edge.sagepub.com/strategy2e.

Cornelissen, J.P., Holt, R. and Zundel, M. (2011) 'The role of analogy and metaphor in the framing and legitimization of strategic change', *Organization Studies*, 32(12): 1701–1716.

Strategists not only have to be active in creating symbols such as metaphors or figures of speech in order to intentionally steer stakeholder sensemaking. They also have to be mindful of the unintended consequences of the metaphors and symbols they use. For example, if strategists continuously use metaphors of warfare and fighting in their talk about strategic change, should they be surprised when forms of competitive individualism, low trust and lack of cross-functional teamwork emerges between groups or departments?

Greenberg (1995) tells the story of a restructuring exercise that traces the unintended consequences of a seemingly innocuous and unimportant decision to label the two operational teams created in the restructuring exercise the 'blue' and 'gray' teams. Signifying the two sides in the American civil war, the teams – perhaps unconsciously – started to become more competitive towards each other as they began to enact the presumed underlying analogy. Competition was precisely the opposite of what the strategic change needed because the organization relied on the two teams sharing their knowledge and working closely together.

Strategy storytelling is an art form. The use of the wrong analogies or inappropriate metaphors used off the cuff can be destructive of the best-designed strategy. One of the best examples of this in practice was when Gerald Ratner, a British businessman and motivational speaker, who was formerly chief executive of the major British jewellery company Ratners (now the Signet Group), achieved notoriety after making a speech in which he jokingly denigrated the company's products, which caused the company's near collapse. What he said was 'We also do cut-glass sherry decanters complete with six glasses on a silver-plated tray that your butler can serve you drinks on, all for £4.95. People say, 'How can you sell this for such a low price?' I say, because it's total crap.' He then went on to say that some of the earrings Ratners sold were 'cheaper than an M&S prawn sandwich but probably wouldn't last as long'.

The stories used by strategic change leaders must resonate with the often implicit expectations amongst different stakeholder groups about what a *legitimate* strategy story should look like – such as their understanding of the socially accepted 'template' or 'archetype' of what the plot structure should be (e.g. heroic quest, rags to riches, overcoming the monster, re-birth, etc.) and the roles played by the main characters (e.g. hero, evil villain, mentor, trickster, etc.). These 'story templates' might also be culturally specific. Ng and de Cock (2002) show how senior managers involved in a public takeover in Singapore drew on poetic tropes derived from archetypal Chinese plotlines.

IN PRACTICE

Martin Parker, writing in *The Conversation*, shows how our cultural images of top managers and CEOs is based on a template of the 'evil genius' – reproduced in all kinds of movies including *The Lego Movie*.

This template of 'evil greedy corporate bosses' pursuing their strategies at any cost is widespread:

- Henry J. Waternoose III in *Monsters Inc*;
- Norman Osborne, the CEO of Oscorp who becomes the Green Goblin in *Spiderman*;
- Mr Potter the banker from *It's a Wonderful Life*;
- Kermit the frog fighting the greedy oil baron Tex Richman in *The Muppets*;
- The heroic battle of *Erin Brockovich* against the energy corporation Pacific Gas and Electric Company;
- Jack Sparrow's battles with the evil bosses of the East India Company in the *Pirates of the Caribbean* films.

These story and character templates shape how we come to see what strategists are and should do: the 'selfish, lying, power crazed and determined to smash all opposition to their evil plans', according to Parker. Strategy, therefore, is portrayed as a matter of trampling on any opposition in pursuit of corporate greed, often with means of force and without regard for the implications. Hardly the picture of 'consultation', 'social responsibility' and 'involvement' prescribed in change management textbooks.

The irony, of course, is that these movie characters and plot-lines which are critical of capitalism are also 'big business', grossing millions for the corporations that make them. The popularity of these cultural plot-lines – think of the movies you have seen which portray caring and responsible corporate bosses – may, however, leave students of business, and their teachers, wondering: how can we narrate a different story in future?

(Continued)

Martin Parker
Article

(Continued)

The full article is titled 'Lego Movie CEO is evil because bad bosses sell cinema tickets' (February 2014) and can be found on *The Conversation* website, or via a direct link on the companion website for this book: www.edge.sagepub.com/strategy2e.

Questions

Think of all the movies that you know. Can you outline some in which corporate bosses are the good guys? What is it that makes them good?

The politics of strategic change

Politics of
Strategic Change

The role of power and politics has already been discussed in detail in Chapter 11. Here, we will focus on those aspects most relevant to situations where some kind of *strategic change* is under way. Strategic change is inevitably a political and power-laden process (Pfeffer, 1992). Anything that disrupts the status quo is likely to have winners and losers. People invariably have a stake in the change; something to gain or lose. That something could be a material stake – their job security, their pay or their future promotion prospects. Or it could be a social, symbolic or ideational stake – their close allegiances and friendships, their level of power and influence, their status and reputation, their sense of self-esteem. Therefore, when a change to the current strategy is proposed, some will seek to use power plays and political tactics either to turn it to their advantage, to mitigate its worst effects or even to stop it altogether.

Strategic change therefore relies on strategists first *understanding* what power relations and organizational politics might have an impact upon their proposed strategic change, then *acting through* power plays and political tactics to seek to further their own preferred strategic agenda (Buchanan and Badham, 2008). The Case Study at the end of this chapter describes the power and politics involved in leading strategic change. The Case Study describes how a management consultant, acting as a change leader, implemented a strategic change initiative in a UK subsidiary of a US-owned multinational corporation called 'FitCo' (Mueller et al., 2013; Whittle et al., 2015, 2016). The case reveals the kinds of political tactics and power plays at work when a group of middle managers, led by an external consultant, attempted to change the strategy-making process for the firm's key account customers. The Case Study also shows how important the kinds of 'framing' and 'discursive ability' discussed in the last section are to 'playing the game' of power and politics during periods of strategic change.

EXTEND YOUR KNOWLEDGE

Strategic
Change

You can download the following two articles associated with this Case Study from the companion website for this book: www.edge.sagepub.com/strategy2e.

Whittle, A., Housley, W., Gilchrist, A., Mueller, F. and Lenney, P. (2015) 'Category predication work, discursive leadership and strategic sensemaking', *Human Relations*, 68(3): 377–407.

Whittle, A., Mueller, F., Gilchrist, A. and Lenney, P. (2016) 'Sensemaking, sense-censoring and strategic inaction: The discursive enactment of power and politics in a multinational corporation', *Organization Studies*, 37(9): 1323–51.

Politics is Normal

A survey of 250 managers by Buchanan (2008) confirmed that politics is of vital importance to organizational change initiatives. Of the respondents:

- 60% agreed that 'politics become more important as organizational change becomes more complex'

- 79% agreed that 'politics can be used to initiate and drive useful change initiatives'

- 81% agreed that 'politics can be effective in dealing with resistance to change'

- 93% agreed that 'politics can be used to slow down and block useful change initiatives'

- Only 9% agreed that 'change agents who avoid organization politics are more likely to succeed in their roles.'

What are the political tactics that those trying to implement strategic change should be aware of? Buchanan and Badham's (2008) book *Power, Politics and Organizational Change: Winning the Turf Game* offers one of the most comprehensive and sophisticated overviews of this field. Their summary of all the findings of years of research on power plays and political tactics is summarized in Table 12.1.

Understanding – and possibly being able to undertake – power plays and political tactics is relevant to strategists undertaking strategic change in at least three ways.

1. First, awareness of power and politics enables the strategist to be able to see why ideas about strategic change might be arising – and have a healthy scepticism towards those proposing strategic changes. Are the proposals for strategic change getting to the Top Management Team based on the sectional interests of a specific group or department? Are the criticisms of a proposal for strategic change motivated by self-interest or status more than any legitimate concern with the proposal?

2. Second, being aware of power and politics enables strategists to spot – and therefore try to counter – the power plays and political tactics being used by those who want to block, or fundamentally alter, the proposed change. Who is networking and building alliances behind the scenes to organize resistance to the proposed change? Who is withholding information that is vital for the strategic plan to be formulated as a ploy to derail the initiative?

3. Third and finally, the strategist might want – or need – to engage in these power plays and political tactics in order to drive forward the proposed

change and attempt to overcome inertia, apathy or resistance along the way. What kind of network and alliances will you need to make in order to make the change happen? What kinds of information will you share – or withhold – in order to give the right message to the right people at the right time? What kinds of compromises – or perhaps even dirty tricks – might be necessary to overcome those who seek to de-rail the change?

Table 12.1   Political tactics

image building	we all know people who didn't get the job because they didn't look the part – appearance is a credibility issue
information games	withholding information to make others look foolish, bending the truth, white lies, massaging information, timed release
scapegoating	this is the fault of another department, external factors, my predecessor, a particular individual
alliances	doing secret deals with influential others to form a critical mass, a cabal, to win support for and to progress proposals
networking	lunches, coffees, dinners, sporting events, to get your initiatives onto senior management agendas, to improve visibility
compromise	all right, you win this time, I won't put up a fight and embarrass you in public – If you will back me next time
rule games	I'm sorry, but you have used the wrong form, at the wrong time, with the wrong arguments; we can't set inconsistent precedents
positioning	switching and choosing roles where one is successful and visible; avoiding failing projects; position in the building, in the room
issue selling	packaging, presenting, and promoting plans and ideas in ways that make them more appealing to target audiences
dirty tricks	keeping dirt files for blackmail, spying on others, discrediting and undermining, spreading false rumours, corridor whispers

Source: Buchanan and Badham, 2008: 16

The prescriptive advice in Kotter's (1996) 'eight steps' of managing strategic change described certainly contains many elements of power and politics detailed in Buchanan and Badham's (2008) book – such as Kotter's advice to create a guiding coalition of powerful individuals to lead the change.

Resistance is Normal

In contrast to the rational unitarist perspective, the political perspective views organizations as comprised of more or less loose coalitions of potentially competing interest groups with incompatible goals and agendas. It should be no surprise, therefore, to find that not everyone agrees that a particular change proposal is a good idea – or indeed whether change is needed at all. Resistance to change is part and parcel of any strategic change. If the change generates no resistance at all – not even a little grumble or moan from employees – the chances are that it is so innocuous that it is not going to make much difference to the organization's long-term strategy. Resistance is the necessary corollary to power. If it was not possible to resist and 'do otherwise', there would be no need for power – everyone would simply do as they were instructed.

   Why do people resist change? There can be a variety of underlying reasons why some stakeholders might be cautious, sceptical or simply object to a particular strategic change proposal. As early as the 1930s and 1940s, at a time when the 'human' side of organizations was first being 'discovered' following the infamous Hawthorne studies by Elton Mayo, management scholars began to realize that not all workers would enthusiastically embrace change in the same way as the workers in the Hawthorne factory seemed to. Coch and French (1948) were amongst the first to identify the 'problem' posed to management when workers resist changes to their working practices, in their study of change at the Harwood Manufacturing Corporation:

> This resistance expressed itself in several ways, such as grievances about the piece rate that went with the new methods, high turnover, very low efficiency, restriction of output, and marked aggression against management. (Coch and French, 1948: 512)

Kotter and Schlesinger (1979) were amongst the first to try to differentiate and categorize the various reasons why people might be resistant to change:

1. *Parochial self-interest* – 'I lose out in some way.'

2. *Misunderstanding and lack of trust* – 'They are trying to con me, as usual.'

3. *Low tolerance for change* – 'I hate having to learn new ways of doing things.'

4. *Different assessment arising from access to different knowledge* – 'I know from my experience that this will never work.'

Since then, a plethora of different reasons why people resist change have been identified by research into resistance to change (see Table 12.2).

Go Online: How to deal with resistance to change. Heather Stagl, author of the books *The Irresistible Change Guide* (2014) and *99 Ways to Influence Change* (2015), argues that the underlying reasons why people resist change are not always what change leaders think. She claims that changing the way that we think about the sources of resistance can help us to find new ways to overcome it – or even learn from it. You can view Heather Stagl's TED Talk on the TED Talk website, or via a direct link on the companion website for this book: www.edge.sagepub.com/strategy2e.

Heather Stagl
TED Talk

Table 12.2   Reasons why people resist change

Ignorance	Failure to understand the problem
Comparison	An alternative is preferred
Disbelief	The proposed solution will not work
Loss	Unacceptable personal costs
Inadequacy	Rewards are not sufficient
Anxiety	Fear of being unable to cope
Demolition	Threat to existing social networks
Power cut	Influence and control will be eroded
Contamination	New values and practices are repellent
Inhibition	Willingness to change is low
Mistrust	Management motives are suspicious
Alienation	Other interests are more highly valued
Frustration	Reduction in power base and career opportunities

Source: Adapted from Eccles, T. (1994), cited in Buchanan and Badham (2008: 268)

Understanding the different underlying reasons for resistance is important for those leading strategic change. Leaders need to be cautious about lumping all people who don't enthusiastically embrace their proposed strategy as 'old guard' or 'die hards' who just want to resist the change because of their innate fear of anything new. All too often, leaders impute negative motives such as these onto those who have different views about the future strategy of the organization, dismissing them as 'laggards' or 'blinkered' about the competitive reality the organization faces. Even the very label 'resistance' tends to imply a somewhat negative view of voiced opposition – leading strategists to dismiss their views far too readily.

Yet we know that not all forms of resistance are due to a general 'reluctance to change'. 'Resistors' may have quite reasonable and legitimate causes for concern. They might have superior knowledge of the operational realities of the organization, knowledge that suggests that the proposed change is flawed in some fundamental way. They might have good relationships with customers that lead them to believe that the proposed change is actually the opposite of what the customer wants. They might know what resources are realistically needed to make the change possible – and recognize the dysfunctional side-effects of the change if it is not properly resourced.

In fact, all the 'good reasons' for resisting a proposed strategic change are quite likely to happen for one simple reason: strategies are typically devised by those at senior levels of the organization who are, by definition, far removed from the day-to-day operations. The idea of emergent strategy popularized by Mintzberg and Waters (1985) and Mintzberg (1987) which we encountered in Chapter 9, is relevant here. Where strategies are allowed to emerge from the ground up based on experimentation, learning from doing and trial and error, guided by a more general set of ideas about where to go, rather than being dictated by top-down planning exercises advocated by adherents to the so-called Planning School, employees are probably less likely to want to resist them.

Employees are not the only stakeholders who might resist attempts at strategic change. Two recent examples from the pharmaceutical industry are relevant here. In April 2016, US drug giant Pfizer announced it was abandoning its planned acquisition of Allergen, based in Ireland. The deal had been months in the planning and cost the firm over $150 million. Why did they abandon their strategic plan? President Barack Obama called for 'insidious tax loopholes' to be closed and the US Treasury Department shocked markets with their swift action to clamp down on so-called 'tax efficient' mergers and acquisitions, where firms re-route profits to low-tax countries to lower their corporation tax. In this case, it was *politicians* and *regulators* that were the prime 'resistors', not employees.

In 2014, Pfizer attempted a hostile takeover bid for British-based pharma AstraZeneca, which was rejected by the AstraZeneca board. Here, it was *shareholders* that proved to be the most influential 'resistors' in AstraZeneca. The firm's biggest investors criticized the board's decision to reject Pfizer's deal and lobbied, albeit unsuccessfully, to get the decision reversed. However, divergent interpretations of the takeover were also present, with some big investors speaking in *support* of AstraZeneca Board's decision to reject the deal. Hence, even within the same stakeholder group, it is clear that idiosyncratic *sensemaking* about the change – where some actors make sense of the change as an opportunity and others make sense of it as a threat – can cause some to resist change while others support it.

In Chapter 11 we discussed the work by Courpasson and colleagues (2012) on 'productive resistance'. Rather than think of resistance as something that is 'dysfunctional', resistance can be helpful for the organization as a whole – not just something

Failed Acquisition Attempts

Targeted	Diffuse	
Directed at particular issue or source of threat	General and non-issue specific	
e.g. Refusal to use new IT system	e.g. Absenteeism, shirking, etc.	
Facilitative	**Oppositional**	
Acts of resistance that further legitimate/collective interests	Acts of resistance that serve illegitimate/sectional interests	
e.g. Whistleblowing, voicing problems with a proposal	e.g. Political defending turf, 'stopping the line'.	
Authorized	**Unauthorized**	
Using means that are permitted by the organization	Using means that are not permitted by the organization	
e.g. filing a grievance or complaint, going on strike	e.g. sympathy strikes, blackmail	

Figure 12.4   Types of resistance to change

Source: Adapted from Ashforth and Mael (1998)

designed to protect sectional interests. Resistance, Courpasson and colleagues (2012) argue, should not be seen as a battle between opposing and irreconcilable adversaries. The authors analyse two situations whereby groups of resistors were able to influence top management and bring about a different vision of change.

Not all forms of resistance are the same. Some forms of resistance are more significant for the overall ability of leaders to achieve their desired strategic change. Ashforth and Mael (1998) differentiate six different types of resistance, according to whether the resistance is targeted or diffuse, facilitative or oppositional and authorized or unauthorized (see Figure 12.4).

What do the varieties of resistance mean for leaders of strategic change? Leaders may be more concerned about 'targeted' resistance, for instance, when those who dislike the change for whatever reason voice their concerns strongly to the outside media and potential new recruits. On other occasions, where employee 'buy-in' is absolutely crucial – such as changes that rely on shifts in attitudes and underlying values as well as behaviours – 'diffuse' resistance might be more problematic for leaders. Diffuse resistance that takes the form of a general anti-management attitude, withdrawal of so-called 'citizenship behaviour' and 'discretionary effort' and forms of cynical distancing and mockery of the organization might be major stumbling blocks to some types of strategic change, such as a change to a more customer service orientation as a source of differentiation in the marketplace.

It might also be useful for leaders of strategic change to think about the extent to which the resistance is legitimate, in their eyes at least. Resistance that is facilitative and authorized in Ashforth and Mael's (1998) typology is likely to be treated very differently by top management compared to resistance perceived as oppositional and unauthorized. In fact, the former may even be permitted or even encouraged as part of a 'consultation' process, whereas the latter may be subject to the use of power and politics to quash it, as described in Chapter 11. The strategic change that ultimately emerges, then, can be conceptualized as the outcome of these power battles between those who seek to advance their own preferred change agenda and those who seek to resist them.

Power relations are not only something that those who seek strategic change seek to manipulate to advance their change agenda. Those seeking to *resist* the change agenda must also engage in power relations in their attempts to block, circumvent or alter the change agenda. The same also applies to the notion of 'leadership'. Leadership is not just something that those at the top of the organization do to advance the change agenda. Those involved in resisting change can also seek to 'lead' others in a more coordinated and unified response to the change agenda. In fact, resistance that is more 'organized' and 'led' is, by definition, more likely to succeed in getting its opposing views being heard and alternatives being seriously considered, as compared to disorganized, dispersed and disconnected 'pockets' of resistance.

Zoller and Fairhurst (2007) coined the term 'resistance leadership' to describe the activities of those who seek to 'lead' others in coordinating resistance to change. Leaders can emerge from a group of employees who believe change is somehow bad, or wrong – either to them personally or to the organization as a whole. Resistance leaders inspire others to act on their feelings, turning quiet discontentment into active resistance to change, channelling emotions into a sense of collective purpose and providing a vision of an alternative future. These leaders might emerge spontaneously or they might be informally 'elected' by the group because of their personal strength of character or influence over top management. Sometimes groups of employees start to talk to others in different departments or locations and discover that they too have similar objections to the change, meaning they will have 'strength in numbers' if they join forces and start a collective opposition. Those in power can easily dismiss or marginalize individual complaints, ignoring their concerns, dismissing them as idiosyncratic or picking off the resistors by demoting or transferring them. However, a large number of well-organized resistors led by a 'resistance leader' are certainly a more serious counter-force to be reckoned with.

Summary

Functionalist models of strategic change present it as a rational economic process of scanning the environment for information about changes happening outside the firm that they need to adapt to in order to keep pace and avoid 'strategic drift', coupled with analysis of the internal resources and competencies of the firm which can be leveraged to develop new products or exploit new markets. For advocates of the Planning School, strategic change is simply the final stage in a process of long-term planning. Decisions about the firm's future direction, scope and position are made through analysis of available data during the strategy formulation stage – typically at Top Management Team level. If this strategic plan involves any significant shift in the firm's strategy – diversification, internationalization, acquisitions, divestments, and so on – strategic change is merely the 'strategy implementation' part of the planning process. The organization simply 'follows the plan'. Resources are redirected to where they are now needed. Systems and structures are reconfigured to align with the new strategy. Staff are instructed about what policies and procedures are to be changed to reflect the new strategy. Investors, suppliers and customers are kept informed about how the new strategy affects them. Popular step-based models of change emphasize the view that change is simply a matter of following a logical set of steps to ensure that all those affected are 'on board' with the new strategy.

Departing from this functional and rational view, other perspectives emphasize the role of social, cultural, political and symbolic systems in the strategic change process. In this chapter we have explored the more (purportedly) 'irrational' psychological, symbolic and political processes through which strategic change is triggered – including the political tactics through which various groups vie for influence over what ideas are deemed 'strategic' in the first place. We have differentiated between the different types of change and explored the contingency perspective on change, which rejects the 'one best way' view of many models in favour of understanding the context of the change. We have explored the leadership practices and processes through which strategic change is conceived and implemented, including the role of sensemaking, sensegiving and symbolic aspects (specifically metaphor and storytelling). We examined how important power and politics is for understanding strategic change. Politics acts as as an underlying driver of change, as competing groups battle for influence and resources and push forward their sectional agenda into the strategic decision-making arena. Political tactics and power plays are also ploys that strategists use to push forward their own change agenda and counter resistance and opposition from others. Finally, on the topic of resistance to change, we have explained why resistance to change occurs, what different forms it can take and how it relates to the ongoing struggle for control over the long-term position, scope and direction of the organization.

TEST YOURSELF

Want to know more about this chapter? Review what you have learnt by visiting www. edge.sagepub.com/strategy2e.

- Test yourself with multiple choice questions
- Revise key terms with interactive flashcards

EXERCISES

1. Based on your reading of this chapter, explain in your own words the meaning and significance of these key terms for the management of strategic change:

   - Strategic drift
   - Organizational paradigm
   - Sensemaking
   - Sensegiving
   - Evolutionary change
   - Revolutionary change
   - Contingency perspective on change

   - Three-step model of change
   - Metaphors
   - Storytelling
   - Framing
   - Power
   - Politics
   - Resistance to change

2. Identify a list of potential reasons why a strategic change initiative might fail.

3. If you were a leader embarking upon a strategic change process, what factors would you want to consider before starting the process?

CASE STUDY

Strategic change at FitCo[1]

ANDREA WHITTLE

A key skill for the strategist is the ability to 'read' the organizational power landscape to assess the viability of a proposed strategic change. Another key skill is the ability to 'lead' others by selling them a compelling (and feasible) vision of what needs to change – and how the change will be accomplished.

This case study describes a strategic change initiative that took place in FitCo UK (a pseudonym), the UK subsidiary of an American-owned multinational company in the sportswear industry. The initiative started when the company invited an external consultant, Barry, to help them figure out how to improve their customer relationship with the key account customers. The key account customers were the four major retailers they relied on to sell their products in the absence of their own branded stores. Barry was working on an unpaid basis in return for the opportunity to collect data for his own research project – his own study of strategic change.

Barry started by conducting interviews and observations with all the senior management. He soon started to formulate his own view about what was going wrong with their key account strategies and how it should be changed. He believed that the company was not formulating their key account strategy in the right way. The strategy was supposed to be developed by the Top Management Team – the Board of Directors – but politics, personality clashes and infighting meant this was just not happening. Moreover, he thought that the strategies that did get formulated were not developed in a sufficiently cross-functional way – drawing the expertise of all departments and functions to pool their knowledge and ensure consistency of approach. For example, sales would too readily discount products that marketing had attempted to position as high quality (and therefore with a bigger price tag). Salespeople for the apparel side of the business sometimes pitched their products in direct contradiction to the salespeople for the footwear side. Customer operations would spend a long time developing bespoke in-store displays for one brand, only to find that sales negotiated a better deal on another brand and the whole display was scrapped. The Key Account Plans were cumbersome, far too long (often up to 30 pages) and typically were left on the shelf gathering dust.

Barry has a clear vision of what the key account strategy process should look like. He began by establishing a cross-functional team of middle managers (which he called the 'Steering Group') who were close enough to the 'coal face' to know the issues on the ground and with sufficient seniority to push through their changes but without the history of turf wars at the Board level. The team would develop key account strategies for each of the four key accounts, influencing the account teams who would implement the strategies, while also influencing the Board level to get buy-in for their proposed changes to the four strategies. The strategies themselves would be one A4 page each – summarizing in an easy-to-read format the overall strategic position for each key account

---

[1]This case study is based on research published in Mueller et al. (2013) and Whittle et al. (2015, 2016)

[CUSTOMER X] Key Account Plan

CJ008P

	2002	2003	July YTD 2004	Objectives
US Forecast			9,586,000	• Get in the game – apparel @ 2/3 of footwear value
Sales Bookings			6,859,016	• Sustain double digit growth on footwear @ c. 12%
Billing	16,346,000	19,890,000	8,883,629	• Make [CUSTOMER X] No.1 for [SUB-BRAND] apparel & footwear
Variance			6,158,045	• Improve apparel margin by 3 ppts & footwear by 2ppts

Strategy/Tactics
Leverage [SUB-BRAND] / U.S. Sports Heritage / Classic
- Ride the footwear [SUB-BRAND] success wave with apparel
- Explode range & distribution of [SUB-BRAND] footwear where appropriate
- Capitalise on 'on trend' NFL apparel product
- Capitalise on 'on trend' classic looks e.g. NPC
- Attack [COMPETITOR] where they're weak

[CUSTOMER X] No.1 for [SUB-BRAND]
- Win at point of sale with display & unitary
- Repeat launch success of '04 with Pump launches of '05

Margin
- Re-engineer terms and reflect scale in discount – terms for growth
- Utilise data to drive higher margin ASAP
- Broaden apparel range & land more in line e.g. women's gym
- Get into hot sellers immediately & fuel stock winners

	2002	2003	July YTD 2004
Cust Margin Plan			25.28%
Cust margin Actual	27.74%	29.69%	28.98%
Fallout	4,561,561	5,118,396	1,437,783
% fallout	22%	20%	14%
Average DSO (mean)	19	32	31
FOP trade terms	20.00%	23.00%	23.00%
Settlement terms	2% in 10 days	2% in 10 days	2% in 10 days
Total Co Billing UK and Eire	232,250,000	229,638,000	244,730,000
% Billing	7.04%	8.66%	3.92%
Marketing Spend			
Marketing Spend as % of revenue			
Last revised date = 05.08.04			

Last revised 10th August 2004

[CUSTOMER X] perception of FitCo	Account Profile	FitCo perception of [CUSTOMER X]	Strategy Implementation – Key Actions
Weak Product	No. of stores – 390 rooftops, & fashion	[COMPETITOR] very much in favour and key competitor	
Poor brand image seen as mainstream, poor level of brand investment.	Sq m – 300 per store Demographic profile?	Fashion brands increasing presence Lack of demand for marketing support	
FitCo Position in [CUSTOMER X]	Share by brand?	Eg category across [CUSTOMER X] decreasing	
FitCo in 4th place and share of space	[CUSTOMER X] underperforming at high street, moving to 4 fascias?	as a business focus	
Under attach from puma and non trads	[CUSTOMER X]'s financial restrictions limiting innovation	Consolidation of fascia – future of size?	
[COMPETITOR] attacking on F/W price FW 9%, M&J app 8%, W app 31%	Targeting to be 'the latest and greatest in sports style-progressive, fun and surprising'	Own brand growth and copycatting?	
Decision makers [CUSTOMER X]	Key target 19yr male (15 – 21 male)	Barriers to success in [CUSTOMER X]	
[Name] - founder		Buyers perception of brand	
[Name] - Chairman		Buyers autonomy, unclear hierarchy	
[Name] - CEO		Poor interdepartmental comms and collaboration,	
[Name] – head of B&M Fashion		complex decision making process	
[Name] – Footwear director		Fragmentation of resources and focus	
[Name] – Womens Apparel Director		[CUSTOMER X] performance – budget cuts	
[Name] – Mens Apparel Director		which could influence commercial success.	
[Name] – Mens Plur Buyer		Continual change of internal structure	
[Name] – Distribution Manager			
[Name] – Marketing Director			
[Name] - FD			
Last revised date 07.07.04		Last revised date 07.07.04	Last revised date

[Author 1], [Author 2], [Author 3], [Author 4], [Author 5], [Author 6], [Author 7]

Image 12.1 Key Account Plan

customer (pricing strategy, mix of products, target consumer market, exclusivity deals, relevant financial information, etc.). Each customer was to have a single-page Key Account Plan (see Image 12.1)

Barry had personal experience of developing similar cross-functional teams in his previous career as a senior manager – a 'trick' he himself learnt from a strategy consultancy firm years ago – and with substantial success. The problem was this: how would he convince the Board to let this team of middle managers take control away from them of the key account strategy trial? And how would he convince the middle managers to take on what was, arguably, a politically risky project? In short, there were both superordinate and subordinate politics to handle before he could get his strategic change up and running.

Mueller et al. (2013) describe the discursive 'framing' undertaken by Barry in the first meeting of the new team. Barry tried to construct a 'definition of the situation' for the middle managers, one which sought to persuade them that the strategic change was necessary and that they were the only people who could lead the change. Through a series of accounts, Barry framed the change through a sensemaking process as follows (adapted from Mueller et al., 2013: 1186):

1. There is a problem in this company, and that problem is that politics is stopping the firm from having a clear strategic direction with the key accounts.

2. The Board cannot sort out the problem because they are the source of the political problem.

3. The Steering Group are best placed to sort out the problem because they are not embroiled in politics.

4. To be successful, the Steering Group must be sensitive to the political implications of certain pieces of information, including discussion about politics itself.

(Continued)

(Continued)

5. The Board of Directors already had at their disposal a ready-made political scapegoat, should need one (i.e. the change agent): they could blame Barry is it all went wrong. This should encourage the Board to take a risk and back the initiative.

6. The Steering Group also had a 'leader' (i.e. Barry) who, as an outsider, had no ulterior political motive or allegiances and would therefore support the Steering Group unconditionally.

7. Below the Board of Directors level, the company was actually less political than many others, he advised, which should encourage them to embark upon a change initiative without fear of upsetting the politics of the organization.

Barry's problem was clearly not just about persuading the Board that strategic change was necessary; he also had to convince the team that strategic change was both desirable and possible for them as middle managers. Whittle et al. (2015) show how Barry used his stock of knowledge of the categories of people who had a stake in the change – and the types of rights, roles, responsibilities, obligations, motives, etc. associated with those people (the 'category predicates') to persuade the team to participate in the strategic change project. For example, he reassured the team that their jobs would not be at risk because they were 'stepping on the toes' of the Board – the people typically associated with the role of strategy-formulation. He did this by appealing to the idea that the Board had a motive for wanting change. Also, he tried to persuade the team that they could shift the power balance between the levels of management, thus having the middle managers 'write the agenda' for the Board based on their vision of the key account strategies. A radical shift in power relations was being proposed – strategy formulation was going to be moved from top management to middle management level – something the team partially attempted as the project progressed, with some limited successes.

Barry also tried to convince the team that it was an ideal time to make the change, given the fact that the current UK Sales Director was away in Australia on a business assignment. Here, Barry strategically used their shared stock of social knowledge about what Sales Directors typically want (or don't want) – namely, Sales Directors would be expected to be resistant to any attempt to take control of key account strategy away from them because their own bonus pay rests typically is tied to sales figures. Now was the ideal time to 'make the move', Barry suggested, given the person who would be the most likely to resistant the proposal had his 'eye off the ball'.

According to Whittle et al. (2015) strategic change relies on *discursive leadership* – defined as the process through which leaders, in interaction with followers, use language in interaction in order to manage meaning and influence sensemaking in order to accomplish organizational goals. A crucial part of this discursive leadership, then, is using knowledge of categories of people and their associated predicates to frame the strategic change process to provide a compelling but also realistic vision of the future – what Whittle et al. (2015) call *category predication work*.

Power and politics relating to the subsidiary–headquarters relationship were also important to the success or failure of the strategic change project. Whittle et al. (2016) showed how the group's shared understanding about the power and politics between the UK subsidiary and US parent, an understanding developed during the conversations in their strategy meetings, altered and tempered their strategic plans. Through accounts, stories and metaphors, the team built up a picture of the subsidiary–headquarters relationship as one that was heavily power imbalanced and deeply political.

The group used metaphors of warfare (fighting, standing ground), machinery (steamrollers), social movements (rebellions, alliances) and the animal kingdom (an elephant standing on an ant) to reinforce their existing ideas that any major strategic challenge to the preferred strategy of the US headquarters was politically risky and liable to retaliation from those in power. In particular, the re-telling of the story of a previous manager who, they believed, got sacked for 'standing up to' the headquarters served to further reinforce their sensemaking that the headquarters was a powerful and political adversary to their attempts at strategy-making. This was not 'just talk' – this definition of the situation led them to fundamentally alter their plans for the key account strategies and engage in all sorts of other strategic behaviours, including:

- Deliberately removing information from documents for fear of being perceived as 'critical' of the headquarters, meaning local knowledge was not shared more widely

- Failing to voice their opinions when they saw flaws or problems in centrally determined policies and initiatives

- Scaling back the ambition of their strategic change for fear of political retaliation, including fear of losing their jobs

- Failing to request resources that they felt were needed.

Whittle et al. (2016) described these processes as one of sense-censoring: how actors sometimes consciously 'censor' their sensemaking accounts, due to anticipated reactions or counter-actions by those with power, sometimes even without any official attempts to edit or silence them. This research finding shows how the dominant 'framing' of the headquarters as a powerful and politically hostile 'enemy' led the managers in the subsidiary to hide, dilute or restrict their local sensemaking from the global headquarters through 'sense-censoring', thereby transforming potential strategic change into strategic *in*action.

QUESTIONS

1. How did the consultant, Barry, 'frame' the change to attempt to persuade the managers at FitCo to 'buy in' to his idea? What role did forms of symbolism and discourse play in this process – in particular *stories*, *categories* and *metaphors*?

2. How did the change team's sensemaking about power and politics in the company affect the strategic change initiative? In particular, identify the role that power and politics played in shaping the strategic change initiative in the relationship between:

   - Functional departments?
   - The middle managers and Board of Directors?
   - The subsidiary and parent headquarters?

13

STRATEGY REBOOTED: THE FUTURES OF STRATEGIC MANAGEMENT[1]

Learning objectives

By the end of this chapter you will be able to:

1 Recount the broad outline of the evolution of strategy

2 Grasp the nature of economism and its role in restricting discussion of strategy

3 Know what is irrational about the assumptions of rational strategy

4 Understand the inequities to which strategy has given expression

5 Articulate an agenda of key issues for the future, centred on sustainability

6 Grasp how strategy relates, or might relate, to open sourcing, democracy and hope

[1]Natalia Nikolova, Wal Jarvis, Ace Simpson, Marco Berti, JC Spender, David Weir, Jerry Davis, Daphne Freeder, Ulla Forseth and Peter McKiernan have all provided very useful feedback on successive drafts of this chapter. Thanks to all, with the usual *mea culpa* provisions.

BEFORE YOU GET STARTED

Nothing is more ideological, after all, than the proposition that all affairs and polices, private and public, must turn upon the globalizing economy, its unavoidable laws and its insatiable demands. (Judt, 2015: 308–309)

Introduction

In this chapter we look at the possible futures of strategic management. We begin with a stocktake of the present and recent past; we do so by looking at the milieu of antecedents from which contemporary strategy emerged and flourished. Contemporaneously, we are especially interested in the distributional effects of corporate strategies, as they have been developed in the past 40 years or so. These effects are markedly redistributive; for those who have, more has been taken. This is the case not only in salary differences but also in wealth distribution through stock options. The increasing inequality is, as we shall see, a major impediment to economic growth and development.

These issues do not feature in most discussions of strategy or in discussions of its possible futures. In a representative text, *The Future of Strategy* (Aurik et al., 2015), one finds pretty much more of the same as in the past. In the wake of the Global Financial Crisis this might appear surprising to some; it certainly does to these authors. With a few honourable exceptions the response to the crisis has been largely absent in terms of changed priorities for decision-making in the ranks of strategy practitioners. Outside the ranks of strategy theory, the current crisis was clearly prefigured by two works from the 1970s, one by German social theorist Habermas, the other by American political economist O'Connor. Their work was prescient and we discuss it in the context of the current crisis.

Image 13.1   Wall Street. Copyright: franckreporter

Economic neo-liberalism sees competition as the defining characteristic of human relations. It redefines citizens as consumers, whose democratic choices are best exercised by buying and selling, a process that rewards merit and punishes inefficiency. It maintains that 'the market' delivers benefits that could never be achieved by planning or cooperation (Monbiot, 2016).

The current crisis was exacerbated by the extreme financialization of the economy that had been led by Wall Street. Where Wall Street led the business schools followed; in some instances, even pointing the way. Increasingly, it was apparent that markets were being shaped by struggles of power involving economic actors and nonmarket institutions, particularly the state and the elites of the dominant social class. One of the things that bound these various elites' interests was a discourse of strategy composed of a patchwork of selective inclusions and unacknowledged exclusions. These enabled a common language of business and competitive performance to spread almost everywhere: that of **economic neo-liberalism**.

George Monbiot Article

Go Online: Economic neo-liberalism is identified by George Monbiot as the ideology that is at the root of many contemporary problems in an article that explores the contours of its emergence, thought and impact available: 'Neoliberalism – the ideology at the root of all our problems' (15 April 2016).You can find this article on *The Guardian* website, or via a direct link on the companion website for this book: www.edge.sagepub.com/strategy2e.

The inspiration behind the emergence of economic neo-liberalism was born from an analysis of the conditions that gave rise to Fascism in the 1930s and a determination never to replicate them in the future. To implement this determination the authors of economic neo-liberalism imagined a society conceived in wholly economistic terms, terms that gave rise to an overall 'economism' as a perquisite for thought.[2] In terms of political economy, it was this that gave rise to the doctrines of economic neo-liberalism, first promulgated by an influential group of Austrian economists, notable amongst them the philosopher/economist Friedrich Hayek whose famous book *The Road to Serfdom* was credited by many as a contributor to the fall of central planning.

Parallel to economism, widely accepted in strategy, there is a lack of personalism; people became more or less evicted from strategy as a discourse in favour of reified abstractions: markets, resources, capabilities, etc., although, perversely, the reification on which these were all founded was the fictive personalism of the corporate organization.[3]

Economics has not always been characterized by economism. When Adam Smith first promulgated economics it was as much a theory of moral sentiments as it was of markets. If moral sentiments had remained in the modern economistic frame, then contemporary practices of strategy might be quite different. To make this point we could have chosen any one of a number of cases of a lack of moral sentiments and an excess of economism; we chose to focus on the VW emissions scandal.

Strategy needs rebooting. At the core of this new strategy will be central issues of sustainability and democracy.

---

[2] Economism could be seen most clearly in the Thatcher era's belief that there was no such thing as society, only individuals, firms and families, with the state, at best, a 'night watchman', serving to maintain its boundaries as well as those of personal and property security.

[3] The advantage of these reifications was that, dealing with the abstractions, it could be claimed that there was no alternative to whatever strategy was being implemented, because the abstractions both removed personal responsibility for the plans being implemented while the assumptions, modelling and conclusions of these strategies could be used to foreclose alternatives.

Context

All ideas, all practices, have roots that flourish in a particular ecology, a particular intellectual and practical *terroir*. Strategy is no different. It has a number of possible histories. As we saw in Chapter 1 these possible histories are deeply discontinuous with each other; some are punctuated by nineteenth century West Point engineering, others focus on the changing nature of military strategy, while still others see twentieth century behaviourism as effecting a decisive break. We shall begin with the possible history that focuses on military strategy, particularly in the twentieth century. In this account the Second World War plays a decisive role, or, more accurately, the long-term planning of the US Army Chiefs of Staff does.

The discourses of strategy that flourished from the end of the Second World War through the 1970s, built on the long range planning that the US Army Chiefs of Staff engaged in when planning the campaign to defeat Hitler, starting with the Normandy Landings. War and its management were as essential to the discourse of strategy then as they were in those ancient roots that we canvassed back in Chapter 1 (see Keller, 2009). Not surprisingly, after the war had ended many of the same ideas that had helped to win the war gained traction in 'Civvy Street', particularly as former military officers were recruited into the corporate and governmental sectors.

A natural ecology for strategy was to be found in the very large firms, such as General Motors, firms that dominated predictable and secure markets that they sought to control through long range planning. *Long Range Planning* was also adopted as the name of the first strategy journal. Ironically, at the time that the Soviet bloc engaged in the same practices of long range planning – the Five Year plans – corporate America, the bastion of private enterprise, sought to do the same – albeit based on corporate as opposed to state planning.

In the Soviet case it was the state that sought to plan; in the American case it was left to the corporations. In doing so they were assisted by the facts of post-war corporate life: markets that were largely based in the United States, protection from foreign competition by tariffs, standardization, regulation, subsidies, price supports and government guarantees. Nowhere were these activities more evident than in the Keynesian 'Warfare State' erected, in part, as an essential bastion of the Cold War.[4] Liberal democratic capitalism ran as a planned economy, funded in large part by the state but organized by business, advised by influential bodies such as the RAND Corporation with its provision of 'research services, systematic analysis, and innovative thinking' to government agencies, foundations, and private-sector firms (see www.rand.org/).

Keynesian demand management was not just a feature of the warfare state in the US. In Europe, especially in France with its *plannification*, there was a very explicit linking of centralist state and private sector interests by bureaucrats schooled in the Parisian *Grande Écoles*. Keynesianism was allied with a strong central planning structure in the UK under the Wilson administrations of the 1960s and 1970s. The state, it was believed, could steer the white heat of technological revolution, a belief that died during the terminal stages of the Callaghan administration when the first fluttering of

---

[4]The United States drew on the expertise of German rocket scientists, such as Wernhner von Braun, to develop their military-industrial complex, which was at the heart of the new state. The American Government brought von Braun to Huntsville, Kentucky at the end of the Second World War to help them develop their missile strategy.

the new 'monetarism' emerged to assume full bloom in the Thatcher era of the 1980s, as Keynes was dismissed and Hayek became the new point of reference.

After 1980, with the rise of a new economic liberalism under the sponsorship of President Reagan and Prime Minister Thatcher, new competition was unleashed by the joint forces of creative destruction and liberal economic deregulation. Reich (2007: 68) summarized the situation that resulted as one in which the political system became dominated by the economy of Walmart and Wall Street. It is not surprising that this should be the case: arranging the economy as a market in which the risk is borne by the public while the profits are privatized certainly tilts the playing field in favour of entrepreneurialism and against citizenship (Sandel, 2013). The consequences of these policies came home to roost in the Global Financial Crisis of late 2007 onwards when, in the US, UK and other countries, anyone on any income could obtain – indeed was encouraged to apply for – a mortgage. Loose banking practices, combined with financially ignorant or easily persuaded borrowers who signed up for loans, as well as regulators who did not do their job, led to the subsequent bailout of the failed banks and bankers globally (Koukoulas, 2016). The 2007 crisis is now understood to have been the onset of a financial crisis but in 2007 that this was the case was not so clear. The reaction at the time discussed it as a 'credit crunch' rather than seeing it as a cyclical punctuation of the long waves of capitalism's development, which a generation of scholars schooled in Kondratieff's (1984) wave theory, would have seen (Mandel, 1975, 1980).

Credit Crunch

Go Online: Two comedians called John Bird and John Fortune provide a humorous account of the 'credit crunch', performed before the Global Financial Crisis had reached its denouement with the demise of Lehman Bros, Bear Stearns and other Wall Street Titans. You can find a video titled 'John Bird and John Fortune: The "Credit Crunch"' on the YouTube website, or via a direct link on the companion website for this book: www. edge.sagepub.com/strategy2e.

From the 1980s onward, a new class of managers emerged who were greatly enriched in remuneration relative to all other wage and salary earners. They were so, in part, because of the adoption of agency theory as a strategy widely used in the American corporate world.

Barry Mitnick Paper

Go Online: The origins of agency theory are generally attributed to a 1972 paper by Alchian and Demsetz and a 1976 paper by Jensen and Meckling; however, there are well-documented claims to earlier and alternate points of origin – see the paper by Barry Mitnick on the 'Origin of the theory of agency: An account by one of the theory's originators', available via a link on the companion website for this book: www.edge. sagepub.com/strategy2e.

As Spender (personal communication) points out, Jensen and Meckling's (1976: 318, 345) proposals rest on a fallacy. They deny uncertainty and presume perfect markets. Yet, in perfect markets, all actors are principals so there are no agents. Their assumptions deny the phenomena they are examining. One consequence of this is the extreme abstraction of their models, in which, as Spender (2010: 194) suggests, two classes of individual with idiosyncratic knowledge and interests are presumed, the principal and agent, interacting with rational expectations in efficient markets. The concept of the principal has a dubious status in this theory (Veldman, 2016); on the one hand it represents the individual shareholders; on the other hand, it represents the contracting agency of the corporate form. The manager (agent) is meant to be oriented to profit maximizing objectives. To ensure that they are, their interests need to be aligned with those of shareholders. In reality, however, many shareholders have very little by way of shares, let alone control, while many managers, in part as a result of the adoption of agency theory, are significant shareholders (Pitelis, 1987, 2004c).

The corporate organization, if it is merely an aggregation of individuals, with agency, responsibility and liability, is an agent. However, there is also the notion of a legal personality, that the corporate organization is a fictive collective individual that contracts real individuals to its purposes and is thus presumably the principal with whom these contracts are entered. The executives of the legal fiction are thus both principals and agents. Later developments of the theory by Fama and Jensen (1983a; 1983b), stress that, on the presumption that the firm is a nexus of contracts between individuals, the costs of contract enforcement of always incompletely stipulative contracts will be a perennial problem. These contracts are incomplete because the world of events is, by definition, a world of uncertainty that cannot be predicted and covered by contract; much of this uncertainty is an effect of the different interests that are brought to bear on making sense of those events that do arise.

Jensen and Meckling (1976) have been undoubtedly extraordinarily successful in normal academic terms. Google Scholar attributes over 50,000 citations to Jensen and Meckling's 1976 article. As Davis (2016a: 508) suggests

> The idea that the most important thing about a firm is how stock ownership by its managers aligns incentives with share price is surprising, to put it mildly. Only a tiny proportion of companies list on stock markets, and only a small fraction of those (mostly in the United States) have dispersed ownership. This was a theory about something that almost never happened in nature. A theory of family life would not want to start with the Kardashians; why would a theory of the firm start with managerialist American corporations? Moreover, how is it that a pair of financial economists at the University of Rochester business school, writing in Volume 3 of an anonymous journal published by the University of Rochester business school – which was edited by one of the authors! – managed to create a dominant paradigm for the corporation for the next thirty years? It was as if a self-published novel won its author the Nobel Prize.

As Davis goes on to argue, Jensen and Meckling's influence derived from a quasi-scientific rationale for de-institutionalizing the corporation into nothing but a nexus-of-contracts that existed to create shareholder value. The process was one of wish fulfilment. Corporations that were quite obviously social institutions, with organizational employees treated in the way that social democratic citizens would be, with family health care programmes, decent wages, salaries and pensions, were being invited to deconstruct. '[T]he "nexus" imagery served as a useful provocation, a lever to bust up the unwieldy and shareholder-hostile conglomerates built up over the prior decades. This was a theory perfectly designed to legitimate a bust-up takeover wave' (Davis 2016a: 509). Agency theory was an account that spawned in practice on a grand scale what it theorized in a small and, at the time, seemingly inauspicious paper in an insignificant journal.

The growth and application of agency theory to practice over the last 40 years or so, particularly but not exclusively in the financial sector (Mallaby, 2010), has seen agents become rewarded as principals that don't even have to risk their own capital. In tying their agency to that of the principals, they have voted themselves stock options, thus becoming significant principals in their own right. Recall that in most companies in the United States the CEO tends to enjoy a considerable imbalance of power compared to the nominal authority of the board that appoints the CEO and to which they are legally accountable. Hence, the growing control of CEOs in governance on company boards has vested them with an ability to set, up to a point, their own salaries as well as nominate stock options. The discourse of strategy works to legitimate such practices, amongst many others.

The discourse of strategy

Strategy today is to be found almost everywhere.

> A contemporary organization not styled in the couture of strategy would be regarded as idiosyncratic at best – perhaps run by a self-styled maverick – or, at worst, negligently managed: what well-run organization would not have a strategy? The contrast points to a substantial change in the organization of organizational life over the last 40 years: strategy has become highly institutionalized as a practice across the organizational world, highlighting that strategy is a comparatively recent discourse, even if some may date it back to antiquity. (Carter, 2013: 1047)

A relatively recent discourse it may be, but it is one with many branches, as we have seen. Some, such as the knowledge-based and resource-based views, have close family resemblances; others, such as strategy as practice, seem far distant relatives.

One reason why the discipline of strategy is so difficult to grasp across its different iterations is because its theoretical object is invariably an effect of its discourse. That discourse has as one of its leitmotifs competitive advantage, whether seen in terms of Porterian competitive positioning, Penrosian resource-based theory or Schumpeterian theories of evolution and innovation, all of which we have addressed earlier in the book. From these meta-narratives flow terms that we have encountered earlier, such as efficient markets, transaction costs, principals that are not agents and agents that are not principals, competitive positioning, VRIN resources, etc. These are all products of different strategy theories that are not unified in theory and that do not always mirror practice.

The ramifications are evident. First, the strategy field is a patchwork quilt of different approaches, some seemingly cut from closely related cloth while others are evidently not of the same ilk. Second, these theories are not objective representations of some states of affairs to which they correspond. In fact, they are better thought of as devices that help induce empirical states of affairs that correspond to their theoretical objects. Hence, there is no necessity for correspondence or coherence. Thus, principal/agent theory can aid in producing distributional effects favourable to those that adopt the theory. Third, strategy is communicated through language. To be recognized as a skilled senior executive one has to be able to use chosen terms from strategy with ease and fluency; one has to be able to play in games in which mastery of terms provides the chips. We can think of these as 'language games' (Wittgenstein, 1968). Those who become familiar with contemporary strategy learn a language in which some activities are 'cash cows' and others are 'dogs'; in which there exist Porter's 'diamonds' or Mintzberg's '5Ps'. Strategy develops concepts that are taken up in organizations and become a part of the everyday talk of senior executives; theoretical objects become reified into empirical objects with which they can now correspond. Fourth, strategy talk bestows distinction, it defines the speaker as belonging to a particular tier in the corporate pecking order; thus strategy becomes a shibboleth and being able to 'talk the strategy talk' defines the (executive) credentials of the speaker. Command of strategy is an aspirational and positional good whose exclusivity defines its social capital (Hirsch, 1977).

Introducing strategy discourse into organizations does not merely introduce new language games; it brings a new performative repertoire to bear that demands different actions, different identities and different effects. The point of strategy is to get an organization from where it is to where its senior executives want it be. It is future oriented. It carries a performance-related projection and legitimates performance measures; it implies a 'performativity' (MacKenzie 2008) that negates correspondence in the here and now between theory and practice but presumes a future state of affairs in which the theory creates its own correspondence.

There is an implicit assumption in terms of the conventional philosophy of science that correspondence theory should prevail in analysis of the here and now. The more accurately the workings of the world are captured by theory, the better the theory will be considered. In simple terms, it is presumed that theory about how the world works should mirror, as accurately as possible, the mechanisms involved. Hence, on this account, strategy theory should mirror what strategy practice does. Implicitly, there is a causal relation at work; the practice precedes its theorization. Such a view is incorrect. Strategy does not mirror the world objectively; strategy seeks to *create* a world as an objective mirror of its theory. Strategy is world-making.

The discourse of strategy is not only a patchwork of selective inclusions but also of unacknowledged exclusions. It is a melange of different theoretical objects that are frequently incommensurable, although there are some common features tying these to each other, most notably, a shared economism. Strategy inhabits a world dominated by a 'universal contemporary resort to "economism," the invocation of economics in all discussions of public affairs' (Judt, 2015: 320).

The economist, Tomas Sedlacek, in his book *Economics of Good and Evil* (2011), argues that a defunct economistic view of the world has become a ritual incantation amongst economists and those influenced by them – an inclusion with which the majority of strategy thinkers are easily accommodated.

- -
Go Online: You can watch Tomas Sedlacek speak on the *Economics of Good and Evil* in a video on the Vimeo website. In an excellent opinion piece titled 'If having more no longer satisfies us, perhaps we've reached "peak stuff"'' (January 2016) in *The Guardian*, Will Hutton discusses Sedlacek as he canvasses the view that the economistic approach to analysing the world is now defunct. Links to both can be found via the companion website for this book: www.edge.sagepub.com/strategy2e.

Tomas
Sedlacek

- -

Strategy in an economistic mode has become the Latin – the universal language – of the modern business, political, not-for-profit and non-governmental organizational world. It enables communication amongst peoples of very different backgrounds, providing a common language of the elites.

A common language of the elites is not merely a matter of simple communication; it is also a matter of shared metaphors, images and imaginaries that situate and ground aesthetic sensibilities. The aesthetics of economism is pervasive because it

Tomas
Sedlacek

percolates how we are constantly led to understand we need to make meaning in our lives; is such and such a strategy efficient, economical, profitable? These are the transcendental questions of the strategist and the age created in economism's image.

Creation occurs through co-evolution; as meaning-making systems come to dominate discourse then they produce materialities and realities in their own image. Causal relations between words and deeds blur in the performativity of a co-evolution of ideas and practices, characterized by reciprocal causality, interdependence and recursivity, fuelled by strategic investments that sustain 'a meta-narrative defining our private and public lives and human-nature relationships that privileges an economic reality' (Perey, 2016: 187). The economic reality privileged is similar to a piece of music composed only in one key, a drone, a continuous musical note of low pitch or, to use a visual metaphor, an image devoid of *chiaroscuro*, with no balance and pattern of light and shade. In reality there is no such one-dimensional reality.

A command of strategy discourses enables a common language of business and competitive performance to spread effortlessly across the organizational world, which is to say, everywhere. Barely any organization will be caught short without a strategy in this day and age, whether a school or a political party, a social movement or a multinational enterprise. Strategy is an essential part of any serious senior manager's repertoire. Strategy offers ways of speaking, of thinking, and seeing the world in specific ways. Strategy provides a vocabulary and grammar with which to describe action and think imaginatively. Strategy provides managers with a language and devices with which they can understand and manage organizations (Carter, 2013). Strategy provides focus. Any focus is a matter of inclusion and exclusion. Focus is what privileges inclusions as *figure* and treats other matter as *ground*.[5]

Strategy configures objects as targets for strategic interventions. Strategy has both material and ideational effects. Materially, it produces devices for securing competitive performance; ideationally, it constitutes intellectual apparatuses and devices such as transaction costs and VRIN, which help legitimate the material and social effects produced. For the C-suite, strategy does what few other elements of management theory accomplish: it makes those that speak its discourse and through whom its discourse speaks, indispensable: that is valuable, rare, inimitable and non-substitutable for at least as long as their performance is applauded and measures up according to standard metrics and KPIs. From this perspective the various theories and approaches to strategy are in themselves less interesting than how some people in key relational positions in networks of power are able to use these ideas strategically, to do strategizing with them.

The market for strategy products is highly competitive and there are many different techniques on offer, in part because of their centrality to the consulting processes of the global consulting companies. It is from this market for distinctive theoretical objects that incommensurability, in part, flows. There are several ways that we can interpret the diverse claims of contemporary strategy. One would be to take these claims at face value, to accept them as a set of techniques that simply represent ways of making better sense of the organizational world and its challenges. The other would be to see them as competing ways of representing reality. The latter would be mistaken because strategy tools act to create realities.

The various strategy tools available in the marketplace do not simply represent an existing state of affairs. On the contrary, they are midwife to dreams, imaginaries

---

[5]*Figure–ground* organization is a type of perceptual grouping in vision through which one recognizes objects. The figure is that which is focused on; ground is that to which one's attention, through vision, is not drawn.

and ambition; they deal with what organizations could become, what they might be able to do. Given that the world of organization looks different through different strategy lenses, because different prescriptions follow, we might say that strategy tools are means for trying to produce intended outcomes, make a difference, create possibilities – in other words, they have power effects.

After the war was over

We noted in Chapter 1 that one antecedent of contemporary strategy emerged directly from the discourses of statecraft, while in the introductory remarks to this chapter we noted the importance of its embeddedness in warcraft. Indirectly, another important element in the mix creating contemporary strategy also emerged from the aftermath of warcraft.

After the Second World War some Austrian economists initiated a focus on statecraft that might ensure that war might never ravage Europe again. Powell and colleagues (2010) argue that contemporary economistic accounts of strategy have a common intellectual root in the work of the Austrian economist, Ludwig von Mises, the 'grandfather' (along with Hayek), as Judt (2015) calls him, of the Chicago School of free-market macro economics. Judt notes that the *Weltanschauung*, the worldview, of von Mises and other Austrian contemporaries was embedded in their experience of Fascism. They attributed the rise of Fascism to the introduction of failed state-directed planning, municipal socialism and collectivized economic activity, by Marxists in post-1918 Austria. Fascism arose from the failures of the left in practical politics. From this failure, these Austrian forefathers opined that the best way to ensure a liberal and open society would be by minimizing the state and its role in the economy.

In the immediate post-war era, when Keynesianism was the dominant strand in economic thought, these ideas were not widely supported by political elites. It took 35 years for them to become the basis of a new orthodoxy when the Austrian legacy emerged in the 1980s, as a new strain of politics developed, led by UK Prime Minister Margaret Thatcher and US President Ronald Reagan. In Thatcher's case her economics were inspired very much by the ideas of Austrian economists such as von Mises' contemporary, von Hayek, percolated through her economic advisors.

The new economic liberalism characterized social life not as a matter of citizenship and its rights so much as a matter of satisfying competitive individual consumers. An adjunct of this economization was to elevate forms of impersonal theorizing and abstractions such as markets, financial returns and competitive positioning above all other concerns. In strategy, economics ruled – the objects that economics addressed became central, as did economistic forms of representation and analysis in which social, human and moral considerations were all recast in terms of how business organizations might best prosper in the market by capturing economic rents – returns in excess of the average.

Goods and services are consumed because they are desired by consumers with effective demand: that is, with money in the pocket. Desire is the underlying engine of consumption; that which fuels it is effective demand – which means possessing disposable income. Desire, plus disposability of income, in principle, enables the satisfactions of materiality. In practice, desire may never be sated. Those things desired often owe their attraction to their exclusiveness. Things achieve their status because they are aspirational and positional goods whose exclusivity defines their social capital (Hirsch, 1977). In such circumstances, 'desire's raison d'être is not to realize its goal, to find full satisfaction, but to reproduce itself as desire' (Žižek, 2009: 39).

In the West there are, Hutton (2016) suggests, signs that the engine of desire is dysfunctional. The passion for consumption that fuelled the engines of productivity and growth in money incomes in the west is slowing. The trick of working at jobs that give little satisfaction or meaning to buy 'stuff' that disappoints as soon as the next version is released, is wearing desire down. Hutton, Selacek and Žižek all suggest that this reproduction can no longer be assumed, no longer reproduced with the same hunger. No longer does sacrifice in work provide the increasing marginal returns with which to enjoy more and more stuff. Moreover, for many people the pleasures of mammon diminish as more and more of its fruits are accumulated, till their homes, closets and driveways are stuffed with ever more stuff. Sated on stuff, more stuff just gags. De-cluttering becomes the new mantra. Having stuff doesn't achieve position-ing when everyone is able to buy things signifying the achievement of a position of privilege (Hirsch, 1975). Old money has long known this; that's why aristocratic chic is shabby rather than store bought and fashion led.

It is not only a satiation of stuff; the stuff lacks substance unless it is branded in ways that denote distinction to those audiences receptive to its signalling (Bourdieu, 1984). As Alvesson (2013) argues, the branding is often more crucial than the actual product. Branding is a fickle mistress; as we become more affluent, we become less satisfied with a positional good whose cachet is fading with exposure and aspiration. The illusion of value is not only vested in ever more goods but, as Alvesson states, in ever more people, as their lives become self-managed projects signified in inflated CVs, Facebook pages, likes and Instagram images.

Follow the money: Strategies, salaries and performance

In the US the Keynesian Warfare State created technological innovations in abun-dance. These innovations, such as computers, fibre optics and satellites, creatively destroyed much of the old corporate America, with the rise from the 1980s onwards, of the new economy of digitalization. In tandem with changes in the economy there was a resurgence of market-oriented politics that dismantled many regulatory struc-tures constructed over the past century. Competition became increasingly global and capitalism globally funds-based, led by the US.

Not only did the Keynesian State help create innovations in abundance: it also cre-ated careers in large-scale bureaucracies. These bureaucratic corporations are now in decline. Davis (2016b) charts that the number of American companies listed on the stock market dropped by half between 1996 and 2012. These corporations were, as he says, once an integral part of building the middle class, offering millions of people lifetime employment, a stable career path, health insurance and retirement pensions – the latter two especially important in a non-social democratic society with minimal citizenship rights, such as the United States. Many famous names have become bankrupt and in some cases, such as Borders, the bookshop chain (which the authors particularly miss for fairly obvious reasons), disappeared altogether. Those that survive mostly employ a lot less than in the past. Davis (2016b) argues this is a root cause of contemporary income ine-quality. The businesses that are replacing them employ far fewer people, if they employ many at all: Uber had over 160,000 'driver-partners' in the United States at the time he was writing but recognized only about 2,000 people as actual employees. The sharing economy is not an employing economy – at best it develops self-employment.

In the United States these tendencies have been exacerbated, in part by politics that helped achieve outcomes whose beneficiaries were quite clear: one hardly had to ask '*cui bono*?' Favourable economic policies for the rich, such as low taxation, minimal control of offshore accounts as tax havens, ease of inter-generational wealth transmission through inheritance laws, free mobility of capital and anti-union laws were all implemented as a part of a neo-liberal agenda. The upshot of the political and economic changes that occurred from 1980 onwards was a significant shift in the wages/profits share of the economy. While the increasing inequality produced by business organizations cannot be wholly attributed to the effects of strategy in practice, it is clear that some strategies played a key role, particularly those of principal/agent theory.

Piketty (2014) has addressed the wages/profit share empirically. He relied on tax data to gather new evidence on wealth and income inequality in Britain, France, Germany and the USA since the nineteenth century. Analysing these data, Piketty showed that the rate of return on capital has been higher than economic growth for most of the past two centuries. Given a highly unequal ownership of capital at the starting point of this long duration, growing income inequality and concentration of wealth was structurally assured as a normal part of the rules of the game of a capitalist economy, as the political economist Karl Marx analysed in the third volume of *Capital* (Marx and Engels, 1971). In the following section we shall look more closely at what principal/agent strategies have achieved in financial terms for those who have been their major beneficiaries.

The immediate post-war period saw some equalization across the board in the US, UK, France and elsewhere but, historically, the period proved to be exceptional. During the period from the end of the Second World War to 1980 a number of factors inhibited the tendency to increasing inequality. These included proactive measures such as the progressive taxation of capital income and wealth as well as physical destruction of capital as a result of the war; innovation and economic growth also decreased the concentration of wealth by enriching previously non-wealthy individuals. The post-war period up until the 1980s was an exceptional era in which the rate of return on capital (after tax) was less than economic growth, hence the reduction in income inequality. From the 1980s, things changed.

Drawing on Davis and Mishel (2014), we can see that those earning more than 99.9% of all wage earners, the top 1% of US executives and the top 0.1% of US households saw their income shares double from 1979 to 2007. Since 2007 profits have reached record highs while the wages of most workers (and their families' incomes) have declined since the Global Financial Crisis (Mishel et al., 2012; Mishel, 2013). From 1978 to 2013, CEO compensation, inflation-adjusted, increased 937%, a rise more than double stock market growth that was substantially greater than the 10.2% growth in a typical worker's compensation over the same period. The CEO-to-worker compensation ratio was 20-to-1 in 1965, increasing to 29.9-to-1 in 1978, growing to 122.6-to-1 in 1995, peaking at 383.4-to-1 in 2000 and was 295.9-to-1 in 2013; if Facebook is included, whose executives are extraordinarily well-compensated, the ratio rises to 510.7-to-1.

Over the same period, CEO compensation grew far faster than that of other highly paid workers, so that they were earning more than 99.9% of other wage earners put together. CEO compensation in 2012 was 4.75 times greater than that of the top 0.1% of wage earners, a ratio 1.5 higher than the 3.25 ratio that prevailed over the 1947–1979 period. CEO pay grew far faster than pay of the top 0.1% of wage earners not because of the greater productivity of executives but because of their ability to set the terms of their remuneration: their relative power. That power is easily seen in the outcomes charted in the statistics that Davis and Mishel (2014) provide:

> The modern history of CEO compensation (starting in the 1960s) is as follows. Even though the stock market (as measured by the Dow Jones Industrial Average and S&P 500 Index …) fell by roughly half between 1965 and 1978, CEO pay increased by 78.7 percent. Average worker pay saw relatively strong growth over that period (relative to subsequent periods, not relative to CEO pay or pay for others at the top of the wage distribution). Annual worker compensation grew by 19.5 percent from 1965 to 1978, only about a fourth as fast as CEO compensation growth over that period.

CEO compensation grew strongly throughout the 1980s but exploded in the 1990s and peaked in 2000, increasing by more than 200% between 1995 and 2000. Chief executive pay peaked at around $20 million in 2000, a growth of 1,279% from 1978. This increase even exceeded the growth of the booming stock market, the value of which increased 513% as measured by the S&P 500 or 439% as measured by the Dow Jones Industrial Average from 1978 to 2000. In stark contrast to both the stock market and CEO compensation growth, private-sector worker compensation increased just 1.4% over the same period.

The Top 1 Percent

Go Online: The Economic Policy Institute website has an excellent article on the shifts in the relativities between workers' pay and the pay of the top 1% by Davis and Mishel (2014). If you find this data interesting then you might find the data that is reported in *The Guardian* article of 18th January 2016 titled 'Richest 62 people as wealthy as half of world's population, says Oxfam' by Larry Elliott, the economics editor, also interesting. It reports an Oxfam study that investigates the parameters of global inequality. The 2105 Oxfam report 'Wealth: Having it all and wanting more', prepared from Credit Suisse data, can be accessed here via the website http://policy-practice.oxfam.org.uk. All links can be found on the companion website for this book: www.edge.sagepub.com /strategy2e.

The inequity is not just an effect of increasing salary differentials legitimated by the application of agency theory, important as these are. There are also the effects of what is known as 'shareholder value' – placing emphasis on short-term share value performance as a measure of success and aligning the interests of managerial 'agents' with the 'principals' holding shares, by making stock options a part of the overall remuneration. As Carter wrote

> The share price being used as a performance measure reflected the short-term view held of firm performance by financial markets: what mattered is that a share could be sold at a profit after a short period of time, rather than laying the foundation for sound growth over time. (in Clegg et al., 2011: 365)

The increasing inequality might be best documented in the United States but the effects are wider.

Pay for UK Bosses

The ramifications of these distortions are global, as this excerpt from the January 2015 Oxfam Issue Briefing, *Wealth: Having It All and Wanting More* reports:

In 2014, the richest 1% of people in the world owned 48% of global wealth, leaving just 52% to be shared between the other 99% of adults on the planet. Almost all of that 52% is owned by those included in the richest 20%, leaving just 5.5% for the remaining 80% of people in the world. If this trend continues of an increasing wealth share to the richest, the top 1% will have more wealth than the remaining 99% of people in just two years ... with the wealth share of the top 1% exceeding 50% by 2016 ... The very richest of the top 1%, the billionaires on the Forbes list, have seen their wealth accumulate even faster over this period. In 2010, the richest 80 people in the world had a net wealth of $1.3tn. By 2014, the 80 people who top the Forbes rich list had a collective wealth of $1.9tn; an increase of $600bn in just 4 years, or 50% in nominal terms. Meanwhile, between 2002 and 2010 the total wealth of the poorest half of the world in current US$ had been increasing more or less at the same rate as that of billionaires; however, since 2010, it has been decreasing over this time.

The Guardian Australia's political analyst, Lenore Taylor (2016), suggests that the economic challenges of the 2010s cannot be solved by the 1980s political consensus that saw economic growth being achieved by market deregulation and lower taxes and lower spending. Piketty (2014) argues that rising inequality harms growth, that social expenditures can be a revenue-boosting exercise and that governments need to intervene more not less; in short, Keynes needs to be rediscovered and Hayek and colleagues forgotten. Even the IMF says income distribution matters for growth, linking concentration of income shares at the top of income distribution (the top 20%) with GDP decline and increases in the income share of the bottom 20% with higher GDP growth.

Go Online: The IMF's paper on the 'Causes and consequences of income inequality: A global perspective' can be found on the International Monetary Fund website, or via a link on the companion website for this book: www.edge.sagepub.com/strategy2e.

IMF Paper

The most recent trends from 2015 data reported in 2016 show no shift to a better distribution of incomes in terms of the prospects for growth – in fact, the inequalities are increasing: just 62 people own as much as the poorest half of the world's population, down from 388 in 2010 and 80 in 2015. As the Oxfam (2016) publication, *An Economy for the 1%*, shows

> the wealth of the poorest half of the world's population – that's 3.6 billion people – has fallen by a trillion dollars since 2010. This 38 per cent drop has occurred despite the global population increasing by around 400 million people during that period. Meanwhile the wealth of the richest 62 has increased by more than half a trillion dollars to $1.76tr. Just nine of the '62' are women.

Although world leaders have increasingly talked about the need to tackle inequality, the gap between the richest and the rest has widened dramatically in the past 12 months. Oxfam's prediction – made ahead of the 2015 Davos – that the 1% would soon own more than the rest of us by 2016, actually came true in 2015, a year early.

Oxfam Report

You might wonder where the wealth comes from in the first instance; some of it is inherited, with many of the world's wealthiest being wealthy because of the bed they were born in. Even celebrated entrepreneurial types, such as Rupert Murdoch or Donald Trump, inherited the basis of their wealth from their family. Considerable wealth is derived from inter-generational inheritance of property.

In terms of contemporary wealth generated organizationally in a single lifetime, the sources are usually a combination of innovative entrepreneurialism and tax avoidance on a massive scale, through the creation of complex global tax accounting vehicles, whose major purpose is to reduce tax liability. Executives then share in these rewards through specific strategies of remuneration and motivation lodged in agency theory, as we have discussed previously.

At the centre of organizational wealth generation through tax minimization is the practice known as 'transfer pricing'. Transfer pricing works thus: first, a holding company is established in a tax haven, where little or no corporate tax is charged. Second, complex intercompany contracts are written that transfer valuable, rare, intangible and non-substitutable (VRIN) assets such as software, trademarks and branding to the non-taxed or lightly taxed holding company. Costs are then assigned to these intangible assets. In theory, these costs are supposed to be valued at market prices, as if the company were selling its service to a separate company. The costs are not in any sense of the word 'real' costs; they are whatever clever accounting can inflate them to be, not particularly difficult where one is dealing with hugely oligopolistic companies that can straddle the globe as virtual monopolies, such as Amazon, News Corp International and Google. Unrealistically low values can be assigned to the initial transfer of the intangible assets from the parent company to the holding company established in the favourable tax environment.

Once these intangible assets have been assigned at a low exit value to the holding company in havens such as Luxembourg, Ireland, Bermuda or Singapore, they become intellectual property that can then be licensed and leased back to global subsidiaries established in different national tax authorities such as the US, UK or Australia. In return for using the IP, substantial royalty fees are paid by the subsidiaries. These are tax-deductible. The company in question fixes the transfer prices, often in a context where there is little effective market testing, precisely because it can be claimed that the assets are VRIN – valuable, rare, inimitable and non-substitutable. In this way, nationally accountable taxable income in the authorities' jurisdiction is minimized. Substantial profits accrue in accounting regimes where little or no tax is charged. The holding companies then make payments as a fee for the holding rights to the license back to the country of origin of the business, such as the US, which transaction is charged at a value that seems quite low by comparison to the transactions costs charged in the tax havens.

Seamlessly, contemporary strategy approaches to transactions combine with valuable, rare, inimitable and non-substitutable assets as a part of competitive strategy to make people like Jeff Bezos of Amazon and Rupert Murdoch of News Corp International two of the wealthiest 62 people comprising the 1% that own more than the rest of the 99% of people making up humanity.

Amazon Tax

Go Online: The Amazon case is particularly well documented thanks to investigative reporting by *The Guardian*'s Harry Davies and Simon Mark. Their report may be read in full in *The Guardian* article 'Revealed: How Project Goldcrest helped Amazon avoid huge sums in tax', 18 February 2016, that also contains many useful links to the United States Internal Revenue Services' case against Amazon, one of the major players in these tax-denying schemes. You can read it on *The Guardian* website, or via a direct link on the companion website for this book: www.edge.sagepub.com/strategy2e.

The CEO suite and its incumbents, such as Bezos, have clearly benefited from recent corporate strategies, strategies that are oriented to increasing profits and wealth, maximizing rent seeking and consequently concentrating economic returns through complex manipulation of prices and costs. It should be clear, theoretically, that these transaction costs do not create the corporate structures in question. It is the corporate players and their advisors that create the strategies that create the structures that create the transaction costs. Strategy, in practice, is a bid to fix those objective contours of the future that are of interest to the C-suite and its stakeholders.

What strategy cannot do, however, is ensure its fix of the future as one in which past strategies produce future success.

Crisis, what crisis? The present and recent past of strategy

In the recent past, most notably, in the Global Financial Crisis that began to unfold in the US economy from late 2007, strategies assumed epidemic proportions that unfolded with disastrous consequences. The infusion of epidemiology, literally meaning 'the study of what is upon the people', into strategy seems appropriate.

> In general, the 'epidemic' process can be characterized as one of transition from one state (susceptible) to another (infective) where the transition is caused by exposure to some phenomenon (infectious material). The process need not be restricted to infectious disease but is a more general abstract process that might be applied to many situations. All that is needed is the appropriate interpretation of the process elements, that is, susceptibles, infectives, removals, infectious material, intermediary host, latency period, disease, etc. (Goffman and Newill, 1964: 225)

Image 13.2   Global Financial Crisis headlines. Copyright: kreicher

The *process elements* in the crisis included organizational cultures framed round a tolerance of high risk; complex financial products barely understood by supervisory authorities both intra- and extra-organizational to the financial entities promoting them, encouraging the subsequent failure of regulators to regulate; undisclosed conflicts of interests, as well as credit rating agencies' practices that seemed to compete on how not to minimize the risk but actually to hide it. The upshot was a combination of excessive borrowing, risky investments and lack of transparency by financial institutions, as well as ill preparation and inconsistent action by government. The recent film *The Big Short* (McKay, 2015) that recounts some stories based on reality, is very instructive.

The *susceptibles* were clearly evident in both the ranks of the financial institutions and the regulators. The *removals* included the 1999 repeal of the Glass-Steagall Act, which effectively removed the separation between investment banks and depository banks in the United States. The *infectives* that started the epidemic were the collapsing mortgage-lending standards and the *infectious material* was the mortgage securitization pipeline. The *intermediary host* was the US government: it created a *latency period* by not adjusting its regulatory practices to address twenty-first century financial markets' deregulation of over-the-counter derivatives, especially credit default swaps. The *disease*, or contagion, was the Global Financial Crisis (or GFC) and the *infected* were the people on the receiving end of the results of the poor policies.

The unfolding occurred in a field of activity marked by a lack of knowledge of likely consequences of present actions or of future conjunctures that these actions and that ignorance might create. The inability to envisage the future consequences of present actions in terms of the reactions of others are inherent to the elapsing of future time in any here-and-now we inhabit. The future is always subject to different envisioning of it, with action promoting this envisioning by different actors likely not to correspond or cohere. The future is always indeterminate in terms of the favours it bestows, although as we have noted previously, it helps to have had favour already bestowed on one through inheritance – but there are no guarantees.

Recent and fashionable business school approaches, such as agency theory or transaction cost analysis, favour a focus on atomistic agents – individual shareholders, managers and firms – making choices here-and-now for resource allocation in the future and, depending on the theory, securing future value, competitive positioning, 'VRIN-ness', and so on. The implicit assumptions are that the theory in use is a rational depiction of the way the world works and that the way the world is represented as working now is how it will work in the future.[6]

Assumptions of rational stability can go awry in the socially constructed world of the economy and its organizations. The onset in 2007 of what has become known as the GFC and its aftermath should have rattled the frame of rational assumptions about the futures of strategy. As a rhetorical question, given the flow of ensuing events, ask yourselves how rational were the choices that principals and agents made in assigning the costs of their transactions, given what we now know about the costs of the GFC?

Widespread concerns about equity and ethics surfaced during the 2007 GFC and became endemic in 2008 when there were massive 'bailouts' by governments of

---

[6]Any rational assumption about the world that expects that its objective features today will be its objective features tomorrow is naïve in the extreme, even with reference to the natural world. For instance, the movements of magnetic north and south in the earth's core, as the US National Center for Environmental Information Historical Magnetic Declination charts, varies sharply on an annualized basis (see www.ngdc.noaa.gov/geomag/GeomagneticPoles.shtml). The variation has unfortunate effects for those animals, such as turtles, that use these magnetic forces in their navigation systems, confusing them directionally.

exposed banking institutions, with the UK's Northern Rock and the Icelandic banks being the first dominos to fall. Soon, mighty dominos were being skittled on Wall Street and elsewhere, with some of the pieces being re-arranged by central banks while others were left to rot. The bailout process, directed at institutions that were considered 'too big to fail', has been well covered in historical accounts (Congleton, 2009; Zamagni, 2009). Public perception of a systemic hypocrisy on display in the bailouts crystallized around the capacity to privatize the profits and socialize the losses: seen as a form of socialism for plutocrats (Kates, 2010) and of crony capitalism for the privileged in which taxpayers funded losses. These taxpayers included many made redundant as a result of Wall Street strategies.

Anger at massive imbalances of power and hypocrisy in government economic policy regarding financial regulation and failed recovery became publicly manifest in what became known as the Occupy Movement. Starting in Wall Street on 17 September 2011, the protest was repeated through 60 cities in the US and in 1,500 cities around the world (van Gelder, 2011). The 'movement' was a difficult phenomenon to describe if only because those who took part in it do not easily fit the usual 'movement' characteristics: at first there were no slogans, no list of demands, no press releases and no anointed leaders to front the media. As a result, media outlets were stymied in their search for a catchall reference to depict the protestors' demands or the participants.

At the heart of the protest were local and global moral issues relating to questions of equity and culpability regarding strategies pursued by business over decades. To the extent that these strategies were a result of analytics legitimated by Business Schools (where the same methods of analysis were researched, taught and reproduced) then the legitimacy crisis clearly leached into its knowledge domains, especially those concerned with strategy (Ghoshal, 2005; Khurana, 2007; Locke and Spender, 2011; Morsing and Rovira, 2011).

Spender (2016) argues that Business Schools contain educators' thoughtful responses to particular questions posed by the wider socio-economy. As these change, relevancies and views adapt also. In the most recent period, since the 1980s, the earlier concerns of business educators with phenomena such as human relations, organizational modelling and social purpose were overtaken by a belief in the value of quantitative analysis. The major proponents of such methods were

> [A] cadre of economists … anxious to advance the political impact of their theories that focused on the firm as a purely economic entity. They promoted the view that management education should focus on maximizing shareholder return. Other difficult-to-measure performance criteria were sloughed off, leaving the firm defined by its tangible capital and ROI. But with this step, business educators legitimized the notion that good management might mean dissolving the firm to improve shareholder return, without concern for the social costs to employees who lost their jobs or to communities that lost employers. (Spender, 2016)

Management Education

Strategy is understood today as ideas competing in an arena in which the participants' focus is mostly on how to build capital and achieve wealth accumulation in the face of risk. For firms in key sectors such as finance, risk appeared to be best managed by oligopolistic concentrations of the commanding heights of the economy, something rarely explicitly acknowledged in theory but much practised in fact (for a notable exception see Dawkins et al., 1999).

For a good few years between the dot com collapse of 2002 and late 2007 many finance businesses were making extraordinary amounts of profit. Access to cheap credit fuelled a major investment boom while the credit that was extended to the general public in the major capitalist economies was used to leverage increased consumption, in part of goods whose real price was diminishing as China's export-oriented economy conquered global markets. Behind the credit facility were decisions by the US Treasury Secretary, Alan Greenspan, to maintain a regime of low interest rates to foster economic recovery from the dot com bust of 2001/2. These US rates were shadowed elsewhere by governments and central banks.

While several voices (surveyed in Bezemer, 2009; discussed in Keen, 2012) in governments, universities and even businesses warned against easy credit strategies, they largely fell on deaf ears. The largely post-Keynesian flavour of these warnings hardly chimed with the prevalent neo-classical understandings holding the majority of economic and political institutions and actors in thrall. Expectations and models in which economistic conceptions of rationality held sway characterized conventionally dominant theorizing. One corollary of stressing rationality to such an extent was that heavily mathematized models based on these rational expectations either did not account for or systematically minimized risk and thus increased areas of uncertainty, of non-knowledge; as these risks were minimized conceptually, the areas of ignorance grew practically (Ormerod, 2010: 17).

In practice, as Chakravarty and Downing (2010: 693) argue, it was digital technologies that created and sustained 'the reckless and myopic culture of risk and unhinged speculation associated with global financial markets'. Drawing on Adam's descriptions of digital technology's time reckoning as instantaneous rather than durational, simultaneous rather than sequential, and globally networked rather than globally zoned (Adam, 2004: 128–136; 2007: 41), Hope (2010) shows that the highly condensed experience and expression of time in contemporary financial global capitalism and the emphasis on speedy decision-making and its inter-networked information flows was *the* critical issue in the collapse of the Global Financial Crisis. The instantaneity of flows was a crucial weakness at the core of the global system.

Prompting the Global Financial Crisis, the space and time in which the normal processes of social reflection upon past experience and future implications regarding economic information could occur, disappeared. The absence of real time in which there is pause for reflection created an inherently myopic immediacy bereft of learning capacity. Real time disappeared with the globalization of finance capital through electronic networks composed of satellites, computers, microchip circuitry and the Internet. Digitalization and its carriers extended and accelerated informational and monetary transfers between computer terminals in which processes of human agency diminished.

With the exception of a handful, business academics barely registered that there might be major troubles on the near horizon (Pfeffer and Fong, 2002; Ghoshal, 2005; Pfeffer, 2011; Clinebell and Clinebell, 2008). Part of the reason for this benign indifference resided in the dominance of economic theories of the firm and a neglect of macro social theory. As such we have seen a disinclination to apply conceptions of strategy drawn from a political economy of global finance in favour of analytical recipes drawn from industrial and neo-classical economics. The capacity to manage and understand the social and political implications of macro societal, economic and global trends has consequently not been developed. The belief in a free market, where democracy means people are 'free to choose', together with the unrestricted accumulation and concentration of wealth taken to be the hallmark of capitalism, have come to dominate business and government thought alike (Ghoshal, 2005).

Prefiguring the current crisis[7]

In the broader social science faculties, other than most economics departments, the view of capitalism's freedoms is somewhat less Panglossian than those encountered in the mainstream business literature. For instance, James O'Connor (1972) and Jurgen Habermas (1976) developed two major theories of capitalist crisis in the mid-1970s. For the capitalist state, the crisis is predicated on its inability to bridge a specific structural gap – giving rise to fiscal crisis. There are contradictions inherent in the state's role in capitalism that leads to crisis in capitalism's progress. The state must meet the needs of the monopoly sector, as Marx would have contended, but it also has the role of holding society together. This means that the state must support capital accumulation, in what O'Connor calls the monopoly sector (the large corporations, especially finance capitalism) and promote the legitimization of capitalist society. There are contradictions in the state trying to fulfil these two roles. In short, in the contemporary context, the state is required to privatize the losses incurred through debt financing by the providers of capital while at the same time legitimating its actions in doing so, by maintaining social welfare, benefits and employment.

The state, O'Connor suggested, will find it increasingly difficult to raise enough capital to fulfil its two roles. As the roles become more and more difficult, the state will realize a fiscal crisis characterized by large budget deficits. Where the central provision of capital to the system on the part of monopoly capital fails to occur then the state steps in and bridges the gap between private capital accumulation and circulation. All of this leads to a 'structural gap' between the demands for state activity and the state's ability to raise revenue to pay for these demands. The private crisis of capital accumulation passes into the state sphere. The state now has either to gain more revenues (while its tax base has been shrunk by the crisis of capital accumulation) or to slash expenditures in order to bridge the gap: there is one further alternative, however, and that is a conscious programme of debt deflation through increasing the money supply through a process of 'quantitative easing'. The contours of the present crisis are quite clear in this explication of O'Connor's work: the absence of a Eurozone state only makes the crisis more intractable in that region of the global economy because there is no unified centre of strategic calculation binding the Euro currency member states.

What Habermas (1976) added to this analysis is the realization that crisis tendencies generated in the economic sphere will be displaced, via state action, into the cultural sphere, in turn, creating problems of social integration, undermining many of the resources that the state requires for its ongoing management of the economy. In particular, it creates the possibility of a large-scale loss of legitimacy for government institutions. The loss of legitimacy is attributable to the loss of consultation with the public at large about the economic measures taken. These are seen as questions best addressed through expertise rather than democracy. At its most extreme this sees elected governments placed under the supervision of, or replaced by, technocrats. In such circumstances, especially where it is demanded of the public at large that the costs of economic policies be borne by them, as losses are socialized and profits remain privatized, the social system as a whole begins to suffer a legitimation crisis, manifested in forms of what are conventionally defined as civil disobedience.

---

[7]This section draws from an article by Clegg (2014)

The growing interventions of the state in economic activity need to be rendered as legitimate. The central question is whether the degree of intervention required to avoid some of the dysfunctional effects of the economic market can be made and, simultaneously and subsequently, be justified to the public at large. In the past, remnants of traditions decayed by the growth of capitalism, such as religious belief, deferential attitudes or a work ethic of achievement orientation, acted as forms of civil restraint. Habermas' bet is that, with increasing erosion, the requirements of technocracy and the demands of legitimacy will cease to be aligned.

Neither O'Connor's political economy nor Habermas' political philosophy found much resonance in the strategy literature. In organization theory their concerns, rooted in nineteenth century Marxist analyses, were profoundly unfashionable in the wake of discursive, linguistic and other 'turns'. A weak Marxism struggled to survive in labour process perspectives but these were always strangely disconnected from the broader critique of political economy that was the core of Marx's three volumes of Capital. The labour process perspective became a watered down sociology of work that never gained a major foothold in dominant theoretical approaches. Business Schools as institutions suffered from truncated vision. They lacked a systematic analysis of the crisis, or the tools with which to make one, in large part because of the provenance of these tools in the critique of political economy. Given the typically apocalyptic focus on capitalism's necessary crisis, such political economy hardly suited Business School's rhetorical purposes, except in the limited circles of Critical Management Studies.

'Along with other major stakeholders in the world of commerce and finance, business schools must accept a shared responsibility for the world's current financial mess', says de Onzono (2011: 18), a noted European Business School Dean, echoing earlier commentators such as Mintzberg (2004). His reasoning is that the overly financialized emphasis of many MBA programmes, as well as the aspirations of their best and brightest students to achieve a brilliant career in the high earning finance and consulting sectors, helped to produce the **financialization** of so many areas of business and public life.

> **Financialization** refers to the processes through which the performance of finance capital becomes the key measure of economic worth, characterizing increasing parts of the corporate world, in particular, and civil society, more generally.

Financialization (Sassen, 2005: 18 *et seq*) is usually conceptualized in terms of the emergence of the significance of shareholder value as a principle establishing the dominance of financial over both labour and industrial capital, the increase of volume in financial trading and global financial flows, the production of ever-more sophisticated financial products, and the increasing share of profits produced by the financial industry in comparison to other sectors of the economy (for an overview cf. Krippner, 2005). Put differently, financialization describes an arrangement where financial markets dominate the economy as the central node of economic activity (cf. Aglietta and Breton, 2001: 434). Argitis and Pitelis (2001, 2006) have documented the tendency of financial capital to increase its share over both labour and industrial capital. They argued that this tendency, alongside restrictive monetary policies, was deleterious to economic performance, something that they established econometrically. Yet, despite the articles preceding and anticipating the crisis, they were basically ignored, much as were many others that pointed to the evident contradictions and tensions. Economism does not understand crisis; anything about crisis, therefore, is simply expunged from its reasoning.

Beyond these purely economic terms, financialization also entails that ordinary people have to manage increasing access to and knowledge about financial markets in everyday life, due to the tendency to switch provision of education, housing, health and aged care to private, credit-based schemes. Crouch (2009) describes such schemes as 'privatized Keynesianism' by which the state is replaced as a provider of means to fulfil basic needs by the financial markets. This diffusion of 'finance' from the economic to the private produces new forms of subjectivity and sociality, which revolve around the management of (financial) risk as a problem of culture and social integration (e.g. Martin, 2002; Lazzarato, 2011). Financialization can therefore be simultaneously understood as an economic, political, social and cultural phenomenon.

The absences of accounts such as those of Habermas and O'Connor that offer structural and non-individualist accounts of crisis in the contemporary strategy literature are particularly important. These authors stress that markets are shaped by struggles of power 'that involve[s] economic actors and nonmarket institutions, particularly the state and social classes' (Zukin and DiMaggio, 1990: 20), which seek to alter and influence shared cognitive structures and cultural norms, while simultaneously creating new ones prioritizing consumers and markets. Little of this concern with power registers explicitly in the discourse of strategy, even those explicitly oriented to the future.

The future of strategy: Old wine in a new bottle?

What is a typical view of the possible futures of strategy? Approaches to strategy as the creation and capture of value consider what might be the best, if not perfect, environment in which these objectives can be attained. The disadvantage is that the futures envisaged seem remarkably similar to the pasts experienced.

A simple example of envisaged futures will suffice, in terms of a recent book on *The Future of Strategy* by Aurik and colleagues (2015), one closely tied to practice, in this case that of A.T. Kearney, the strategy consulting firm, of which Aurik is a principal. The advantage of such work is that it is explicitly oriented to the effects that it might possibly create in the future.

The Future of Strategy begins with three principles:

1. *Draw inspiration from the future* – look to fundamental trends, collect data in the form of facts, figures and stories.

2. *Be organizationally inclusive* – the authors argue good strategy does not cascade from the apex of the authority structure to its base. It should be organizationally comprehensive, inclusive, engaged and multidisciplinary.

3. *Take a portfolio approach* – the focus is competitive advantage but such advantage never lasts long; rather than a single strategy that unfolds, a portfolio of competitive opportunities should be continuously under revision in terms of goals and environments.

These are fairly bland ways of approaching the future; the first, with respect to those things we can be reasonably certain about, such as demographic trends, is pretty obvious. Being organizationally inclusive is a good thing but we suspect most organizations have very little idea how to be so; certainly, many Chief Strategy Officers will find it challenging. Their expertise and position is based upon holding esoteric and uncodifiable knowledge – wisdom drawn from the masses often does not sit easily with the grand designs sketched in the eyrie of the organization or its consultants. As for the portfolio approach, well it is a truism not to put all your eggs in one basket. Moreover, on the down side, a portfolio approach is a perfect way of dissipating focus and building sectional commitments and interests as sub-goals become formulated, heavily promoted and protected in the ensuing turf wars.

Aurik and colleagues' (2015) main concern is with 'creating and capturing value' for the corporation. To achieve this, they recommend that a successful strategy should rest on the following:

- A portfolio of competitive opportunities inclusively developed

- Strategic guidance and operational commitment

- A 'fit' between (1) strategic guidance and the current situation; (2) the constraints facing the organization; (3) evolving future events whose unfolding determines resource allocations

- A culture of trust and respect

There are so many things one could say about these generalizations. Briefly:

1. Opportunities both exist already and are created and co-created (Pitelis and Teece, 2010), sometimes for serendipitous reasons. Hence developing a portfolio of opportunities basically assumes uncertainty and serendipity away.

2. A portfolio of cooks will not necessarily create a better broth – it might but it can as easily dissipate energies as focus them.

3. Strategic guidance is often wrong; operational commitment is fragile, often cynical, and little stronger than the cash nexus: they cite VW as an exemplar organization – hardly, after the emissions scandal, which we will address later in the chapter. The scandal is an example of bad strategic guidance and poor operational commitment as well as a focus on short-term economic gains.

4. Achieving 'fit' is something that can only ever be known retrospectively – as Donaldson (2001) has argued with his 'strategic adjustment to regain fit' (SARFIT) model. As the here-and-now unfolds in an ever-changing present there is plenty of opportunity for drift from past-envisaged fit to occur; for instance, constraints are not always known – they depend in large part on competitor strategies. The world of strategy is a complex experimental situation in which nearly every party is seeking to control the standing conditions so that they act in their favour – it is pretty obvious not all can do this in a zero-sum game, in which wins for some foreshadow losses to others. As for events, well they can never be known in advance and their meaning is always problematic because of this. Arab Springs turn into deadly civil wars; wars against terror create new enemies more fearsome than those initially fought, while the old enemies are not defeated but merely more patient than their adversaries.

5. As for a culture of trust and respect, this is hard to achieve in organizations where the salaries and benefits of the elites are clearly much more respected than those of middle managers and the shop floor. That there is such a thing as 'a culture', a single unifying, unique and homogenizing life world abroad in an organization – well, consultants may even believe this and may even find paying customers prepared to buy into creating these conditions, but wishful thinking is rarely the mother of invention.

The focus on competitive strategy informed by the nostrums in circulation at A.T. Kearney is hardly likely to change the trajectory of strategy that much. There is little or no concern for any implications that pursuit of such a strategy might entail in terms of issues of sustainability, ethics and so on. Strategy, as a field, seems somewhat sociologically retarded with respect to any reflexive consideration of the social construction of its ideas.

IN PRACTICE

Imagine that you are explaining what strategy is to someone who has never read any strategy books or done any strategy courses. This might not be as easy as you assume because many people believe that the only reason a business exists is to make profits and that how they make these profits and the externalities that are caused in doing so are of little consequence for shareholders. Your job is to be an advocate for a more sustainable approach.

Considering what you have learned from this book and the other reading that you have done please try and answer the following questions.

Questions

1. What would be the key points that you would want to communicate about which approaches to strategy are important?

2. Provide reasons for why the approaches that you have chosen are most appropriate.

3. In your own words, how would you characterize the discourse of strategy that you considered most appropriate?

In contemporary economics, mathematics trumps understanding and algebra is presumed capable of rendering all that is thought intellectually worthwhile. It was not always the case that economics was so narrow, so sociologically challenged. Adam Smith is invariably acknowledged as the grandfather of modern economics. Smith, while today known as an economist, always saw himself as primarily a moral philosopher, and in some ways was equally a founding father of empirical workplace sociology. For him, a theory of moral sentiments was the necessary corollary to a theory of the economy.

Moral sentiments and strategy

Traditionally, in its eighteenth century origins, economics discourse was as much a theory of moral sentiments as it was of markets and efficiency, centred on *The Theory of Moral Sentiments* (Smith, 1759/2010; also see the discussions in Clarke, 2016; Hanley, 2016). Today the moral sentiments have shifted decisively, as Judt (2015) indicates.

Go Online: You can gain considerable insight into Smith's arguments by watching a BBC documentary on the *History of Scotland*, particularly Episode 3, 'Scottish enlightenment', which tells the story of Adam Smith and how he became increasingly critical of the capitalist practices of Scottish merchants.

As Judt (2015) noted, there has been a break with traditions of liberal theorizing, albeit one that is relatively recent. Nearly 150 years after Adam Smith, the critical sentiment in modern economics was still strong. Even as late as the end of the nineteenth century economists were still concerned with what Smith termed moral sentiments and we might call ethics. Hobson, a contemporary of Lenin's and fellow analyst of imperialism, produced a critical account of rent-seeking behaviour:

> Under present conditions it appears that the apportionment (of rents) is ruled by forces social, political, economic, which assign various and shifting amounts of monopolistic power to the owners of the requisites of production, and that the operation of these forces is to no appreciable extent affected by considerations drawn from any estimate of the subjective surplus or net gain of human welfare. (Hobson, 1893: 401)

Powell notes that Hobson asked questions such as:

- Is competitive advantage immoral?
- What are the non-financial consequences of competitive advantage?
- Is it right to encourage firms to achieve competitive advantage?
- Is it right to teach executives how to achieve it?
- What are the alternatives to competitive advantage?

Judt, in a more critical and historical vein, advises us of the moral consequences of ritual incantations to the idol of economism, the goal of competitive advantage and the icons of productivity, efficiency and growth:

> For the last thirty years, in much of the English-speaking world (though less so in continental Europe and elsewhere), when asking ourselves whether we support a proposal or an initiative, we have not asked, is it good or bad? Instead we enquire: Is it efficient? Is it productive? Would it benefit gross domestic product? Will it contribute to growth? This propensity to avoid moral considerations, to restrict ourselves to issues of profit and loss – economic questions in the narrowest sense – is not an instinctive human condition. It is an acquired taste. (Judt, 2015: 320)

The propensity to avoid moral considerations may be an acquired taste but it is one that has become deeply embedded and embrained in the discourse of strategy. In fact, in an intellectual division of labour, these moral sentiments pop up elsewhere outside the *cordon sanitaire* that strategy erects around its performative discourse because an emphasis on performativity opens for consideration not so much the ends being targeted but the means for their accomplishment.

It is largely the case that strategy rarely lifts its gaze beyond fairly mid-term market concerns and the need to produce more profits more efficiently. Strategy's goal is to increase profits using whatever it takes. A corollary of this is that the market has pushed out society. Where the market rather than collective provision in whatever shape can provide a good or a service, there is a profit to be made. Metaphorically, what this means is that the discourse of the market has become dominant in public life and public spaces; that the way we are able to view the world is increasingly shaped by the rhetoric and discourse that privileges 'the market'. Readers that listen to the financial news of the day will be familiar with the fact that some days the market is reported as having had a good day; other days it has reportedly had a bad day. When an abstract concept takes on seemingly lifelike properties we can refer to it as reification (Berger and Pullberg, 1966). The concept has life attributed to it. It performs.

Performance is managed through indicators, in which market performance, or some surrogate for it, is key to organizational success. From the early 1980s excellence literature onwards (Peters and Waterman, 1982), through the critique of public sector management that it partly nurtured (Osborne and Gaebler, 1993), this idea spread far and wide. Performance targets enable individual accountability to be determined easily: an individual either meets or does not meet their specific performance targets. How it is done, the means, are of less concern than that the targets be met, the ends achieved.

It is, perhaps, no coincidence that Rhodes and Wray-Bliss (2013) note that the *Business Ethics Quarterly* was first published in 1991, *Business Ethics: A European Review* in 1992 and *The Journal of Business Ethics* in 1997. The timing is significant: if we recall that the Reagan/Thatcher era of the 1980s saw the first full-flowering of the new economic liberalism, the crucible from which financialization emerged, then the turn to ethics followed hard on the heels of this flowering. Ethics arose as a phoenix from the ashes of moral sentiments sundered from and cremated by the disciplines first of 'positive' then neo-classical economics in co-evolution with the rise of neo-liberalism (Kinderman, 2012).

If there is something rotten in the state of business conceived as the expression of the interests of atomistic subjects through individual behaviours, then the remedy to behaviour conceived in individualistic terms must be the reform of individuals. Business Ethics as either a standalone subject or a field of knowledge could be integrated into the curriculum (Sims, 2002; Rich, 2006; Ulrich, 2008; Melé, 2012) as a form of inoculation, rather as one might prescribe a vaccine, individual by individual, to stop a contagion. Business ethics, with its concerns with the individual, sits separately but alongside strategy in the curriculum. Strategy, traditionally conceived, does not focus on individual people. It is composed of resources (albeit some are 'human resources'), competitive pressures, drivers, alignments, capabilities, transaction costs, clusters and value chains. By contrast, Powell suggests strategic management 'is a very human activity, conducted by people, through people, and for people. People define the problems, solve the problems, and research the problems, and nearly all of the problems involve people as their subject matter in one way or another' (Powell, 2014: 201).

Powell draws on Bowne's (1908) contrast between mechanical and organic theorizing, which in the former case excludes the person and in the latter binds all perception of objects and things to being embodied in the experiencing human being, which Bowne called personalism. It takes a person to make a physical observation or perform an objectification; what people do effects the objects that they interact with, most notably in terms of phenomena such as climate change; only people can make sense of the patterns of relations between mechanically conceived variables – their patterning does not disclose nature's message except to those whose ways of seeing, their paradigms, enable them to yield the secrets hidden in the relations; finally, the patterns created are always a matter of human interest – for example, prioritizing economism over people serves some interests just as prioritizing citizens over consumers serves some other interests.

Embedding an impersonal approach in theorizing creates more impersonalism in practice, suggests Powell (2014: 203):

> [T]he downward spiral of impersonalism becomes problematic in phenomena that are fundamentally about people, yet amenable to impersonal theory and method – social sciences like economics, sociology, and strategic management. Here, Bowne warns that impersonal theories and methods tend to colonize, mutate, and crowd-out the personal, and scholars may unwittingly lose their way and eliminate their own subject matter – namely, people.

Jarzabkowski and colleagues (2015) also argue for bringing the person back in to the picture, through the practice perspective, which we discussed in Chapter 10. How practices are interpreted, manipulated and improvised in many different ways by socially skilled actors (Jarzabkowski, 2008; Paroutis and Heracleous, 2013) depends in part on their relative position in the organization (Balogun and Johnson, 2004; Mantere and Vaara, 2008; Rouleau and Balogun, 2011). It is not sensible to focus merely on the strategy as a disembodied logic that ignores *who* enacts *what* practices as well as *how* they are enacted. Who is doing the strategizing, why and how they do it shapes what patterns become defined as formal deliberate strategy. Moreover, this deliberate strategy will constantly be glossed in different ways, as a result of the ways it is enacted: emergence and deliberate determination are in constant interplay in specific contexts of action.

Who, how and what questions are best addressed through research that pays close attention to local contexts if only because what is espoused and what is actually done can differ considerably, as we shall see subsequently when we come to discuss VW and the emissions scandal. Local adjustments of strategy in context may deviate from deliberate corporate strategy in ways that may be positive as well as negative for competitive strategies. Local improvisations may better position organizations in terms of key strategic markets, branding and skills (Balogun et al., 2011), creating innovations that subsequently can have a radical effect on strategy (Regnér, 2003; Courpasson et al., 2012). Without local contextual improvisations dependent on key personnel the complexities of delivering strategy in multiple contexts with diverse stakeholders would be insurmountable (Rouleau and Balogun, 2011).

Rangan Video

Go Online: In a fairly short video Professor Subramanian Rangan introduces some firms that he thinks might be doing the right things. The video is linked to the contributions to *Performance and Progress: Essays on Capitalism, Business, and Society*, edited by Rangan (2015). Reasons to be cheerful? Perhaps. You can find the video on the YouTube website, or via a direct link on the companion website for this book: www.edge.sagepub.com/strategy2e.

Sociologically, the ways in which individual subjects and the invisible hand that steers their actions towards a collective rationality are conceptualized in strategy is a matter more of myth than empirical analysis. The new economic sociology (Swedberg and Granovetter, 2011), formulated as a critique of neoclassical economics, rather than seeing markets as anonymous interactions of exchange, through which actors exercise rational choice so as to maximize their utility, focuses instead on the socially embedded structural, cultural and cognitive dimensions of economic exchange (Granovetter, 1985: 495; Zukin and DiMaggio, 1990). For instance, pricing on financial markets is highly dependent on shared understandings of social processes, as is demonstrated, for instance, by Montagna (1990) for accounting, and Zaloom (2007) for price finding in stock trading. All these activities produce collective rationality through specifically socialized calculative practices by the dominant actors.

In order for any market to function properly, market actors must embed the market in a network structure that produces the necessary trust amongst market participants for them to engage in economic exchange. Trust in markets can be earned, institutionalized or bought in rational legal practices. To be earned, experience of reciprocal normativity in expectations and actions is necessary. To be institutionalized, there must exist some rational legal coding that is stipulative of appropriate norms and actions with the power of effective sanction to back up transgression. To be bought – well, that is the sphere of corruption. Corrupt capitalism has re-invented a new form of certainty: the bribe, as the recent FIFA, Unaoil and other scandals reminds us.

Trust is essentially an offshoot of legitimate expectations that certain actions will have certain consequences. Of late the focus has increasingly been on developing the need for political narratives to be pro-business, in shaping expectations. Every aspiring politician has to be seen to be pro-business. But as Hayek, the guru himself had argued, the mantra should be pro-competition. For Hayek, being pro-competition is always pro-market and pro-business (as it favours the efficient and best). Pro-market orientations need not be pro-competition and being pro-business need not be pro-market, let alone pro-competition. In today's phase of deconstructed and corrupt capitalism, Hayek sounds echoes of Karl Marx! Being pro-business is such a broad category that it encompasses the power to pollute and to despoil, to be pro-emissions, as the VW case shows. Seen this way markets are less a natural outcome of rational choice and instead would be better described as social structures or fields. Markets are dependent on shared collective understandings in the form of a common culture, which proscribes or limits market exchange and sustains a shared rationality anchored in the cognitive structure of the market actors.

A recent scandal is instructive in canvassing the role of moral sentiments and shared cognitive structures in contemporary strategy.

Strategy and the VW emissions scandal

The VW emissions scandal broke as a news event on 18 September 2015 when the United States Environmental Protection Agency (EPA) issued a Notice of Violation of the Clean Air Act to German automaker Volkswagen Group. The event was caused by a group of five scientists at West Virginia University who carried out live road tests on three diesel cars (VW Passat, a VW Jetta and a BMW X5) while conducting testing for the International Council on Clean Transportation (ICCT). They discovered that nitrogen oxide emissions were up to 40 times higher on the VWs than the posted laboratory emissions test results. The reason, they discovered, was that the cars were fitted with a piece of software that functioned as a defeat device, something prohibited by the Clean Air Act. VW had programmed their 2009 through 2015 turbocharged direct injection (TDI) diesel engine so that US standards nitrogen oxides emissions were met only during laboratory emissions testing. One of the testers reported that 'someone had to take these vehicles out, test them on the standard test cycle, make sure that the emission controls are supposed to be working when they're supposed to be working': in other words, a deliberate fraud had been perpetrated.

An estimated eleven million cars worldwide, and 500,000 in the United States, included the programming. Volkswagen's stock price plunged in value by a third

Volkswagon
Scandal

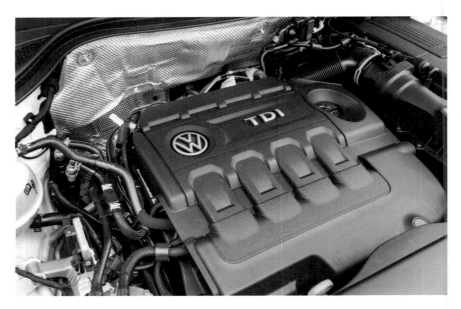

Image 13.3   VW engine. Copyright: ollo

in the days immediately after the news. Volkswagen Group CEO Martin Winterkorn resigned, and the head of brand development Heinz-Jakob Neusser, Audi research and development head Ulrich Hackenberg, and Porsche research and development head Wolfgang Hatz were suspended. *Süddeutsche Zeitung* reported that Neusser had ignored at least one engineer's warnings over 'possibly illegal' practices in 2011 (Fromm et al., 2015). Volkswagen announced plans to spend US$7.3 billion on rectifying the emissions issues and planned to refit the affected vehicles as part of a recall campaign.

Contrition followed a year of denial by VW, arguing that the discrepancies in testing were mere technical glitches. The company stressed repeatedly its unawareness of its coding the data that the tests had introduced; it continued to proclaim an official lack of comprehension of this data. Communication stayed within the bounds of a second order rationalized discourse of company rhetoric that did not recognize the claims being made. It was only after being confronted with evidence regarding the programming of the software that the deception was acknowledged on 3 September 2015, an admission that came after the EPA threatened to withhold approval for the company's 2016 Volkswagen and Audi diesel models (Gardner et al., 2015). The time reckoning system in play in VW appears to have been based on toughing it out and not acknowledging liability, something not yet formally done at the time of writing.

The firm is under intense political pressure from German President Merkel who has suggested that if VW fully discloses what happened and changes its corporate structures in a way that ensures that something like this can never happen again it can put the scandal behind it (Boston, 2015). VW is still maintaining, communicatively, that the issue was not systemic but the result of a few people's decisions. The history of the VW scandal is still in progress. The crisis was caused by an unexpected event, with the testing in non-laboratory conditions. According to official information released by Bosch, the car parts manufacturer provided the software that has materialized as the object of the scandal. However, in 2007, Bosch advised VW's management that this software was only designed for testing vehicles' performances and was not to be implemented as a standard setting for all vehicles. On the same date, according to the German newspaper *Bild Am Sonntag* (27 September 2015) and the French TV channel BFM TV, Bosch warned about a potential fraudulent use of the software. Given the fact that this knowledge from Bosch has now entered the public domain we might conclude that the management of VW decided to ignore fraudulent use of the software for eight years.

Originally, in 2005, VW discussed purchasing a system from Mercedes for reducing pollution but the idea was rejected in preference to developing a proprietary system. The system developed by VW failed to combine good fuel economy with compliant emissions. VW, faced with this contingency, then programmed the engine control to switch from good fuel economy and high emissions to low-emission compliant mode when an emissions test was detected. This caused the engine to pollute in daily operation while appearing to be compliant with regulations when tested (Ewing, 2015). The low emissions levels of Volkswagen vehicles when laboratory tested enabled the company to receive green car subsidies and tax exemptions in the US and many other countries.

The newspaper *Die Frankfurter Allgemeine Zeitung* in its edition of 6 October 2015 reported that, according to the newly appointed CEO who has replaced the former CEO, Martin Wirkenhorn, only a small circle of engineers was involved in the fraud and that they kept the secret of this manipulation to themselves. In its edition of 7 October 2015, *Le Monde* advanced a still slightly modified version borrowed from reports in *Bild Zeitung*. According to this article, fear and even terror characterized the organizational culture of the VW group, a culture inflicting conditions of work reportedly comparable to the 'North Korean regime'. The existence of fear might explain deviant behaviours. The engineers in charge knew that the objectives of simultaneously reducing gas emissions, gas consumption and increasing the power of engines were unreachable without substantially modifying the architecture of the engines. Nonetheless, the impossibility of the matter was discursively excluded, because to raise it ran the risk of their immediately being threatened with termination. Given these conditions, the very top management might not have known what was occurring, with the scandal going no higher than Neusser, Hackenberg and Hatz. Only the coming inquiry will deliver evidence on what is the most believable scenario.

The scandal at VW illustrates that fear became one of the main norms of the VW culture. Paradoxically, it could explain the temporal stability of the group while proceeding to acquire several automakers (Audi, Seat, Skoda) and restructuring them. Fear stimulated talents and eroded any apparent and disputable contest. If fear helped construct VW's stability it has also differentiated and fragmented the group, driving ingenuity underground, stimulating the emergence of hidden resistance with hidden means to cope with the fear of not being able to deliver the objectives required for competitive strategy. Fear also legitimated the top management in ignoring the warnings coming from outside the VW system, as taking them into account would have meant jeopardizing the assigned objectives. In this case, cheating the test control was considered as a non-event for the organization. Exposing the inability to meet the objectives, overcoming fear, would have been an event that would have begun to address the situation.

The time reckoning that revealed the fraud was significant. The three American researchers inadvertently selected an event that had occurred in the past within the VW system (the decision taken to use the software to cheat) by checking the level of emissions from their diesel vehicles. Doing so, comparing the expected results to the actual ones, they used experimental research, seeking either confirmation or disconfirmation of the hypothesized level predicted by VW. Experimentally, they noted an anomaly with the emission figures formally posted by VW – these figures were magnified up to 40 times – hence, the formal figures were disconfirmed. The institutionalized features of VW as a technologically sophisticated and trustworthy auto manufacturer (*Das Auto*) were transformed by testing initially registered only through scientific discourse but that has now percolated into the legal system.

Businesses that are subject to regulation by standards had better try to achieve these standards because their failure to do so can become the story. If the story becomes the arrogance of the management, the duplicity of the engineers, and the hubris of the CEO, heads will roll. In a world where social media is ubiquitous it is no longer as easy to channel or control media relations. The VW case is but one example of an organization that tried to manage communications in a way that was better suited to the pre-digital age; in the post-digital age enhanced transparency is imposed by the absence of barriers to communication and trying to restore these barriers through hierarchy, control of central information dissemination or abrogation of responsibility is not as easy as when information was broadcast from the few to the many, now that the many can address each other directly. The VW case is but one example of how an organization came to grief on the basis of external analysis that was rapidly disseminated through social media (see Rhodes, 2016). It will not be the last.

All organizations can learn simple lessons from the VW scandal: the most important is to be honest about saying what you are doing – don't say something different; if you do something different, make the doings and the sayings aligned, and make them aligned from the outset. It is called integrity, an old-fashioned and simple idea.

Rebooting strategy

'The future is uncertain and the end is always near', as poet Jim Morrison (1970), late of The Doors, wrote a year before his death. We do not know what will happen; we can only tell you what we think the scenarios for the future might be. One scenario is positive; we think that with a combination of technology and its affordances, coupled with the democracy of open sources and regulation for sustainability, the future of strategy will not be dismal. By the same token, to the extent that strategy continues its mechanistic impersonalization, its fetishization of outmoded models of science and its reluctance to attend to what it is that strategists do in practice, we think a scenario in which strategy becomes more than ever remote, conservative and essentially socially destructive is not unlikely.

Strategy oriented to competitive advantage, Porterian competitive positioning and transactions and the analysis of their costs, can only incidentally serve society and stakeholders at large. Penrosian resource-based theory, Schumpeterian theories of evolution and innovation, Nelson and Winter's (1982) evolutionary theories and Cyert and March's (1963) behavioural views hold more promise but they are also often interpreted in ways that deprive them of their potential, in the process turning them in to just another way of gaining static competitive advantage.

Digital Futures

Whittington et al. (2011) point out that information technology plays a major role in transforming what strategy and strategy making might become in the future; it certainly played a major enabling role in the Global Financial Crisis. In a weightless economy that is digitally designed, people will increasingly do strategy through devices, artefacts and affordances offered by technology rather than through the strategy models of the past. As Plesner and Gulbrandsen (2015: 154) note,

> despite a focus on technologies as co-constitutive of strategy practices, only relatively little attention has been given to the role of new media, such as social media (software), smartphones (hardware) and Big Data (informational phenomena).

The digitalization of information and the democratic distribution of it amongst the many that can afford its devices mean that citizens and other stakeholders not 'interior' to the organization can increasingly interact with and direct its operations. Plesner and Gulbrandsen (2015) use the examples of Rue89, a French news organization, which allows anyone that is digitally connected to contribute to the production and dissemination of news (Raviola and Boczkowski, 2012). Production, dissemination, consumption and markets become entangled and intertwined, blended in 'open-sourced strategy' (Dobusch, 2012).

Organizations increasingly use 'Big Data', the aggregations of behavioural traces that people continuously leave using programs such as Twitter or browsers such as Google. For instance, the World Bank increasingly relies on such data (World Bank, 2014). The organization's strategies do not depend on internal proprietary information or inimitable knowledge but widely available outside data sources not designed for the purposes to which they are put when developing strategy based on data mining.

New media generate sharing, idea creation, participation and criticism that dissolve distinctions between organizations with their strategies and environments as objectively external determinants. The boundaries of the firm dissolve. Strategy morphs into a co-produced socio-technical phenomenon where local practices transform globally available resources.

Increasing reliance on input and meta-data from users and customers means that organizations must handle the blowback that comes with the ability of critics and opponents to ironize or critique strategic choices made with marketing strategies. Managerial fiat can be widely and easily challenged. New media can enable both discerning customers and ardent critics to become involved in co-producing management's strategic choices. When we couple this capability to the agenda shortly to be discussed – the issue of sustainability – then it affords a powerful source of pressure for different conceptions of good strategy that can directly reach customers, users, employees and suppliers.

Control is increasingly distributed across a network of actors, including new media and their users. It is a diminishingly private sphere of management control alone. Hackers can seize the company's social media projections; they can critique, ridicule and ironize them, they can disrupt them through sabotage; they can work together, provided there is trust, empathy and commitment on all sides. Again, in light of sustainability issues, this is significant strategically. Organizations such as the World Bank or United Nations can reuse data from existing communicative infrastructures to examine policy and programme effectiveness. They do not need to do traditional evaluations. Control over such data as they do use 'will be distributed across complex socio-material networks that include interested organizations, automated algorithms, analysts and privately controlled meta-data systems' (Plesner and Gulbrandsen, 2015: 157).

Boundaries, choices and control are all shifting in the direction of increasing fluidity and plurality. Moreover, the new media modify the personalism of strategy futures: it is evident that, in these days, if we are bereft of our digital devices and their affordances, we are less than fully human – McLuhan's (1964) hypothesis that the media become extensions of our nervous systems holds. Additionally, technology is being used as a means of distraction and appeasement. People become so wedded to their devices and the voyeurism of looking into other people's lives that nervous systems are adapted to the erosion of long-term ethicality as the digital carnival unfolds its tropes. We need to see socio-technology as more than human, as a space in which human choices interact with technological structuration of the strategic uses that can be made of the technologies: Google rankings, for instance. Devices make us members of those communities we co-create and share; they network our proclivities, interests and desires. New possibilities of network formation are central to strategy as these networks evolve communities over time (Fosfuri et al., 2011). Once again time is of the essence: gadgets and devices change rapidly; Filofax users become Palm Pilot users; Palm Pilot users morph into Blackberry users, who in turn become iPhone acolytes – the only constant is change.

Increasingly, change has to include a concern with strategies of sustainability, a topic that even sophisticated writers on strategy tend to overlook as a part of strategy's future (Vaara and Whittington, 2012) although, to be fair, in another context, Vaara has noted a brief concern with environmental destruction (Vaara and Durand, 2012: 249).

Sustainable Futures

What is sustainability? For firms, sustainability is often interpreted as having a 'triple bottom line', which is usually taken to mean auditing and managing environmental and social as well as financial/economic outcomes (Savitz and Weber, 2006; Boulouta and Pitelis, 2013). More generally it is commonly defined as development that 'meets the needs of the present without compromising the ability of future generations to meet their own needs' (World Commission on Environment and Development (WCED), 1987); thus, sustainability seeks to balance the interests of the present generation in a good life lived well with the possibilities for future generations to do likewise: the meaning of intergenerational equity.

There are limitations to the UN definition. By focusing on intergenerational 'needs', it begs the question whether sustainability can be attainable merely by monitoring the needs of future (not just present) generations. Surely this is not the intention, raising doubts about the wisdom of referring to 'needs' in general and across generations in particular. In addition, sustainability need not necessarily be linked to an objective such as 'development'. Ideally the term should be defined generically and then be applied to particular cases.

Essentially, as Perrey (2016: 164) argues, sustainable economic growth 'must be tempered so that organizational actions do not degrade or damage the environment in ways that would inhibit future generations being able to share those same environmental resources'. There are economic dimensions to such sustainable growth.

In strategy terms, **sustainability** can be defined as shown here.

Sustainability is the condition under which the satisfaction of a particular objective by economic agents in the short term is not pernicious to the satisfaction of the same objective in the longer term, and/or when the satisfaction of the objective of an economic agent does not prejudice the satisfaction of the objectives of other economic and social agents.

Business sustainability, suggest Bansal and DesJardine (2014: 71), can be defined as the ability of firms to respond to their short-term financial needs without compromising their (or others') ability to meet their future needs; translated into less economistic terms this entails not depleting or damaging current resources in pursuit of future profits or in denial of future liabilities such pursuit might incur. Of course, it is

Image 13.4   Sustainability. Copyright: Petmal

impossible to know if any action here-and-now will have these effects there-and-then. Pointers are, as Bansal and DesJardine (2014: 73) suggest, that:

> [F]irms that can manage the long term and the short term are more likely to invest strategically in research and development for new product and process innovations, train employees for higher productivity and lower turnover, and build enduring relationships with the community to ensure that resources are developed responsibly (Slawinski and Bansal, 2012).

Think of these safeguards against short-termism as possible indices of sustainability. Current theories of strategic management often constitute such short-termism through their focus on immediate returns and decision-making that neglects temporal impacts of present actions.

IN PRACTICE

Strategy, ethics and sustainability in practice

Go Online: Visit the book's website at https://edge.sagepub.com/strategy2e to watch an interview with Maria Atkinson conducted by the author team.'

Maria Atkinson is a sustainability strategist and experienced in advising and engaging with governments as well as non-government organizations, academic and research

Maria Atkinson
Interview

(Continued)

(Continued)

institutions. She is an internationally recognized leader in sustainability, green building, corporate responsibility and impact investment. Maria sits on the City of Sydney's Design Advisory Panel, playing a strategic role in the public and private development that shapes the city. She also co-founded the Green Building Council of Australia in 2002 and was founding CEO until 2006.

As Maria states in the video, 'You can't have a strategic direction for an organization just based on economics alone. Strategies that do not respond to the community in which you operate, as well as the environmental impacts that you obviously have, aren't really strategies'. In practice, it is important to consider there may be differing fundamental reasons why sustainability would be incorporated into an organization's strategy. The core motivational context may be related to one, or a combination, of three key drivers.

The organization might identify that sustainability provides a unique market opportunity, either as a response to or, pre-emption of, consumer trends. For example, a firm operating in a highly regulated domestic market may be able to promote their sustainable goods in other international markets where such practices are less prevalent and therefore achieve first-mover advantage. Alternatively, the shift towards a sustainability-driven strategy might be due to future or current regulation and legislation. By becoming an early adopter, the organization may, at best, strategically develop ahead of their competition or, at worst, avoid costly fines or operating restrictions, such as Royal Dutch Shell experienced with the Brent Spar controversy in 1995.

The third driver for sustainable development is that of a values-based organization, one that incorporates sustainability into their 'eco-enterprise strategy' by placing the issue at the very core of its values network. They may be founded to create environmentally friendly goods or services, such as The Body Shop, or progressively evolve through the integration of ecologically and ethically sound practices into their strategic planning structures.

Questions

1. How does Maria approach potential resistance to sustainability thinking within the organization?

2. What are the skills and experiences that a strategist should possess when dealing with issues of sustainability?

3. What are some sound business reasons for an environmentally sustainable approach to business?

4. How does sustainable and social responsible behaviour impact on the various business functions? Maria gives some examples of implications for IT, HR or Marketing. How can other areas within an organization incorporate sustainable and social responsible behaviours?

5. Why do sustainable strategies sometimes fail? What are the risks and how can organizations make sure they are successful?

An example of non-sustainable practices could involve a car company that pursues profits here-and-now without regard for regulatory or customer demands for less polluting vehicles and then systematically misleads regulators and customers as to the levels of emission that its vehicles create. It compromises its ability to keep making profits in the future as a result of both subsequent regulatory pressures and not pursuing emerging cleaner methods of production as well as producing employees who, in disillusionment, move to other companies or engage in resistance to the culpable management. Concerning economic sustainability, the focus of the company in question on 'exploitation' at the expense of 'exploration' (March, 1991), for example, may lead to its eventual failure, as a result of the appearance of disruptive, more innovative competitors.

Non-sustainability becomes more complex when one focuses on the impact of one's actions on the 'peer group', namely others who share similar (or the same) objectives or activities. For example, in the VW case, non-sustainability would involve over-exploiting the environment. The use of restrictive practices that defeat regulatory surveillance would serve to stymie competition and innovation and potentially damage the reputation of the sector for customers. Customers, disillusioned with the strategic practice of the firm and the sector may well shift to other sectors, such as cycling or using public transport (economic non-sustainability). Those employees exploited by their duplicitous enrolment in covert practices may well strike or revolt, creating social non-sustainability.

It is widely accepted in strategic management that the objective of firms is to obtain sustainable competitive advantage (SCA). Conceptual perspectives, such as reduction of rivalry through 'positioning' (Porter, 1980), minimization of transaction costs (Williamson, 1975b, 1985), resource-based (Penrose, 1959; Barney, 1991), evolutionary (Nelson and Winter, 1982), and/or (dynamic) capabilities-based (Teece et al., 1997) views all provide explanations and prescriptions for how SCA can be achieved. However, without exception, the 'S' (sustainable) in SCA is limited to the sustainability of advantage vis-à-vis one's 'competitors', without much regard to wider sustainability issues, such as those of environmental, social or economic sustainability intra-nationally, let alone internationally. That this should be the case is not surprising if strategy is taken to be about outperforming 'rivals'. However, unless wider sustainability issues are considered, the word 'sustainable' in SCA becomes suspect, or only applicable in the short term.

Returning to the focus on sustainability, the critical question is sustainability of what? The 'sustainability of development' concept adopted by the UN is too broad and contested. The debate in development and growth economics concerning the definition of development, its relationship to growth, the means of measurement, etc., is endless (see, for example Frynas, 2008; Todaro and Smith, 2009). Indicatively, do we refer to sustainability of development in terms of GDP per capita, or the Human Development Index (HDI), or another index, and do these lead to the same results? Because alternative measures exist, the answer is probably that they do not produce the same results otherwise there would be no need for alternatives to be devised. Ideally, an appropriate index should balance at least four measures, according to the United Nations (2010) *Teaching and Learning for a Sustainable Future*, as Perey (2016: 165) reports. These are social, ecological, economic and political dimensions of sustainability.

How do we measure sustainable development? It is arguable that a more generic, history- and theory-founded, and potentially operationalizable concept is that of inter-temporal and sustainable worldwide value creation. Such a concept differs from an economic focus on Pareto efficiency, defined as a condition where one cannot be made better off without someone else becoming worse off, as a result of a change (Varian, 1992). Pareto efficiency is intra-nationally focused and ignores distributional inequities between nations. Today, these have become pervasive enough to be considered by many scholars as a major contributor to current ecological crisis (Argitis and Pitelis, 2006; Stiglitz, 2012). The focus on sustainable worldwide value creation avoids both intra-national and distributional limitations to provide a better benchmark for business ethics scholarship (Mahoney et al., 2009).

These questions of sustainability as essentially temporal, ongoing and enduring have yet been barely integrated into strategy other than through discourses of CSR which, with their focus on the firm's performance here-and-now, do not address the broader issues of sustainability. It is impossible to do so without bringing politics into the picture.

Some elements of politics entail the actions of states. Giddens (2008) argues that the state has a prime function in tackling climate change, especially in terms of negotiating international treaties and enforcing them. Noting the litany of failures associated with state planning, Giddens suggests that this does not necessarily absolve states of responsibility. Broadly speaking, he advocates the creation of the 'ensuring state':

> A return to planning cannot mean going back to heavy-handed state intervention, with all the problems that it brought in its train. The role of the state (national and local) should be to provide an appropriate regulatory framework that will steer the social and economic forces needed to mobilise action against climate change. I prefer the concept of the 'ensuring state' to that of the 'enabling state'. The idea of the enabling state suggests that the role of the state is confined to stimulating others to action and then letting them get on with it. The ensuring state is an enabling state, but one that is expected or obligated to make sure such processes achieve certain defined outcomes – in the case of climate change the bottom line is meeting set targets for emissions reductions. (Giddens, 2008: 8–9)

For Giddens (2009: 68–69),

> In the case of 'development', we should focus on the contrast between the developed and developing societies. In so far as the rich countries are concerned, the problems created by affluence have to be put alongside the benefits of economic growth.

Banerjee, paralleling Giddens, argues that sustainable development is little more than an oxymoron (Giddens, 2009: 68). In particular, Banerjee suggests that many of the assumptions underpinning sustainable development share family resemblances with older development discourses. Sustainable development, he argues,

> is very much subsumed under the dominant economic paradigm. As with development, the meanings, practices, and policies of sustainable development continue to be informed by colonial thought, resulting in disempowerment of a majority of the world's populations, especially rural populations in the Third World. (Banerjee, 2003: 144)

As he says, 'environmental destruction is not egalitarian' (Banerjee, 2003: 173), in that it delivers 'economic unfreedoms to a marginalized majority of the world's poor' (ibid.), lacks a strong sense of local empowerment, and inscribes indigenous populations as the 'passive objects of western history' (ibid. p. 174). Banerjee concludes that sustainable development may be little more than the legitimation of markets and transnational capital.

Whatever the limitations (Giddens, 2009) or dangers of sustainable development (Banerjee, 2003), any attempt to change the balance of the economy that will have practical import involves power relations that redefine conventional carbon economy-based conceptions of acceptable behaviour. Only the state has the regulatory reach and powers to be able to do this. At base, what people take to be their interests in material goods such as cheap energy will need to be reframed.

The state and sustainable strategies

Carbon Tax

The politics of climate change mean that those with interests in a fossil-fuelled economy, such as mineral extraction companies and the trade unions that represent workers in these industries, will have to accept actions that run counter to their immediate interests in the development of an extractive economy. A carbon tax that builds a future fund for sustainable enterprise investments seems the only feasible way for the state to shift the behavioural parameters of enterprise.

A carbon tax is a tax on pollution and despoliation. Carbon taxes are often grouped with two other economic policy instruments: tradable pollution permits/credits and subsidies – policy instruments built upon a foundation of state regulation that sets a price for carbon dioxide emissions. The price should serve not just as a compensation for the externalities of pollution accounted here-and-now but should have a significant deterrent effect in order to shift behaviours from polluting to non-polluting technologies. Future costs, as well as present costs, need to be accounted.

Future strategy will need to build temporal accounting into strategic models premised on eliminating future costs in terms of pollution and climate change that will serve behaviourally to modify corporate actions; we need a *proper* resource-based view alert to issues of the sustainability of resources, one that regards resources in more than merely economistic terms (see Williams, 2016).

Regulation ...

As we had already noted however, governance by the state, as well as by international organizations, faces limitations in terms of the degree of monitoring required and the possibility of collusive behaviour by the leading private sector players to thwart regulation. These are well rehearsed in the literature on regulatory capture (Pitelis, 1991).

The present conjuncture is loosely orchestrated by the global climate summits organized by the United Nations Climate Change Conferences. These need to foster plural and diverse national and international activities oriented to sustainable worldwide value creation. As a type of governance it is not without limitations but could well be better than current systemic failures to limit emissions. We elaborate on this idea below.

In all countries, there exist a host of organizations and institutions, such as the family, the church, NGOs, state-owned enterprises, that can have an impact on the ability of firms' and governments' incentives and capabilities to foster value and wealth creation. These are usually referred to as the 'third sector', albeit in our view a better description would be the term 'polity'. In the context of the polity, value is in effect co-created by complementary and co-specialized economic agents (Pitelis and Teece, 2009).

It is arguable that firms do relatively 'better' in terms of commercialization in markets in which, in exchange for the realization of profit, there is involvement of states in policy-making, ideology formation and legitimacy creation and in which the 'polity' contributes to social capital and sustainability. Within the corporate sector, small firms can have advantages in flexibility and large ones in unit cost economies. Inter-firm cooperation, for example, in clusters, can benefit from 'external economies' and foster innovation, productivity and value creation (Porter, 1990). The identification of the respective advantages and capabilities of the co-creating agents as well as the specialization and division of labour between them becomes critical. Competition, together with cooperation (coopetition), self-interest and altruism, can all help foster value creation.

For strategy and corporate governance to help foster sustainable worldwide value creation, they should be aligned with the directions of public and supra-national governance. Corporations and all economic agents should be expected and required to internalize potentially negative externalities from their operations, that would diminish the value of the environment and the society as a whole. For this to happen, internal and external controls may be required, including national and supra-national incentives and sanctions. Concentrated and embedded power structures, with associated corruption, should be the target for elimination at all levels: intra-firm, intra-country (regulatory capture), between host governments and multinationals, and supra-nationally.

... Moral Sentiments

The interplay, pluralism and diversity of institutions, organizations, individuals, ideas, cultures, religions, norms, customs and civilisations, can in part, play the role of a 'steward' and 'monitor' for each other, hence also promoting the realization and pursuit of enlightened self-interest by all, notably the most powerful stakeholders. There is a role for Smith's 'moral sentiments': 'at a deep level the adoption of ecological sustainability is a moral action' (Perey, 2016: 169).

Moral action can be imposed but it is better deliberated. Inclusive democracy is a precondition for what may be termed a de-growth economy and society (Fotopoulos, 2010); deliberative democracy inclusive of stakeholders needs to characterize strategy formulation. There are also, as Perey (2016: 175) stresses, aesthetic dimensions to consider as well, because moral action is in large part formed through aesthetic sensibilities. Rampant economic exploitation, which despoils, devours and degrades the environment and the lives of those in it, is ugly, nasty and brutal.

A model of economic and ecological sustainability and resilience that encompasses moral and aesthetic dimensions is required. It is important that the process is 'managed', 'guided' and 'moulded' through informed, motivated and (self) monitored agency, so that 'deliberative democracy' is aligned to performance-sustainable value creation.

A representative supra-national organization with economic sustainability as its core agenda and mission could help serve this purpose. Such an organization could be fashioned on the model of the 'third party' (the Board of Directors) of the corporation, as in the work of Blair and Stout (1999). Similar considerations, relating the need to sustain the investments of actors with co-specialized and complementary capabilities for value creation apply at the supra-national level, as they do to the corporate and national ones. Allocating the role of the guardian of economic sustainability to bodies composed of representatives from the private–public–polity nexus, aimed at fostering a systemic interest in sustainable worldwide value creation, might appear utopian but it could be one way through which crises, such as the Global Financial Crisis and its aftermath, may be anticipated and their strength and impact at least moderated. With sufficient early warning systems in place from academic and policy research the signals might well be recognized in time to take remedial action.

The times may be changing. The Panama Papers are merely the latest despatch from the frontlines of a global economy that is increasingly being exposed as corrupted. It is a fascinating feature of the recent European crisis that so much attention is paid to corrupt politicians as receivers of bribes and so little to their paymasters, yet all know that it takes two to tango (Pitelis, 2012).

Go Online: The Panama Papers suggest that deceit and corruption in the market may well be a default position for many in the global elite of companies and individuals. Improving upon this lack of concern requires situations of trust, building social capital, emphasizing the 'ethical dimension'. Go to *The Guardian* website and search 'Panama Papers' to find a wealth of news articles.

Panama Papers

The power of corporations to act as sovereign agents in the context of the free market jeopardizes democracy that depends on deliberation and equivalence of powers between individuals (Barley, 2007). Corporate sovereignty – conceived on the model of the individual legal personality – is now so dominant and so corruptive of the politics of democracy that we are once again experiencing populist revolt of the least privileged orchestrated by authoritarian leaders against the political processes of corrupted democracy: The Trump, Le Pen and Farage agenda recalls the earliest years of the rise of Fascism. The context is important: market failures in the twenty-first century, together with the institutional delegitimation of major pillars of society, by revelations concerning corrupt media, police, politicians, banks, etc. (in particular but not at all exclusively in the UK) has, together with capitalism's extended crisis, further delegitimated economistic models of neo-liberalism as well as serving to demonstrate that equally ethical standards of behaviour are not expected across all strata of society. Corporate sovereignty rigs the rules – as *The Big Short* (McKay, 2015) notes.

Go Online: Anatole Kaletsky suggests 'rejecting the theories that have dominated economics since the 1980s, together with the institutional arrangements based upon them' in a short but provocative article on the *Project Syndicate* website. You can also find a direct link to this article on the companion website for this book: www.edge.sagepub. com/strategy2e.

Anatole Kaletsky

Increasingly, neo-liberalism cannot guarantee prosperity in the future without an active state to direct its preferences. The crisis has destabilized two pillars of the economistic consensus. The first element destabilizing the consensus is that the version of capitalism favoured by the elites is broken. In 2016, the current crisis assumed the length of the global depressions of the 1890s and 1930s. The second pillar destabilized is the boundedness of the crisis: it has shifted from the American housing market and Wall Street to Europe and the state, with every indication that it will engulf emerging markets such as Turkey, Brazil, Malaysia and possibly even China.

Will Hutton Article

Go Online: Will Hutton charts the shifting contours of the global crisis that have spread from the US, through Europe and into emerging markets in an 11 October 2015 *The Guardian* article 'The world economic order is collapsing and this time there seems no way out'. You can find the article on *The Guardian* website, or via the companion website for this book: www.edge.sagepub.com/strategy2e.

Exclusive focus on self-interest may well be the biggest foe of economic sustainability as the recent crisis attests (Hart and Zingales, 2011). Fostering pluralism, diversity, the polity and representative and self-monitored bodies with oversight, serves as a move in the right direction, although, as Fisse and Braithwaite (1993: 37) note, the difficulties are many;

> Prosecutors are confronted with what amounts to a network of complexities: tortuous legislation, intricate accounting practices, convoluted organizational accountability, amnesia among witnesses, and jurisdictional complications.

Nonetheless, further discussion on the need, prerequisites and mechanisms for supra-national governance for worldwide economic sustainability is a topic worthy of further investigation. It is as unfortunate as it is self evident that strategy scholarship and textbooks currently serve more as consolidators of the status quo than pioneers of sustainable futures. We hope the present text makes a small contribution towards opening up the debate in and, indeed, the subject of strategy.

Imagine what strategy might be and do if re-regulated, democratically accountable and sustainable criteria became its norm.

> When we hope for something grand, we draw from the beauty of the goal the courage to brave all obstacles. If the chance of reaching it diminishes, the desire grows proportionally. The farther from reality lies the goal, the more desirable it is, and since desire is the supreme force it has the greatest amount of force at its service. The vulgar goods of life are so small, a thing that in comparison the ideal conceived must appear immense: all of our petty joys are shattered before that of realizing an elevated idea. This idea, even if it amounts to almost nothing in the realm of nature and even of science can, in relation to us, be everything: it's the offering of the poor. To seek the truth: this act offers nothing of the conditional, the doubtful, the fragile. We have something in our hands, not the truth perhaps (who will ever hold it?), but at least the spirit that wants to discover it. When you stubbornly halt before some too narrow doctrine, it's a chimera that flees from your fingers; but carry on, keep seeking, keep hoping: this alone is not a chimera. The truth is found in movement, in hope, and it is with reason that we have proposed as a complement to positive morality a 'philosophy of hope'. (Guyau, 1895)

Strategy's 'philosophy of hope' has centred largely on rent seeking and profits, even when, as we have seen in the VW case, it means malfeasance creating widespread deceit in the market, dissonance in the organization and lack of trust amongst consumers. Anomie is usually taken to mean a state of normlessness, detachment and non-solidarity created by a mismatch between personal or group standards and wider social standards.[8]

---

[8]The term is ineluctably associated with the sociologist Emile Durkheim but was, in fact, coined by Jean-Marie Guyau (1886; see Orru, 1983).

The gap occurs because of the lack of social ethics integrating individuals into broader moral sentiments. When competitive strategy engenders indifference through the behavioural norms that it spreads, as in the case of VW's fabrication of emissions levels, anomie is escalated in corporate ranks, along with resentment in its publics and in its customers, a sense of having been duped.

Summary

This chapter has canvassed openly normative views of possible futures of strategy. Unashamedly, because strategy is an essentially normative discourse, largely skewed to the interests of capital and the doctrines of economic liberalism. In this chapter we have sought to rebalance the ledger. We have criticized strategy as a discourse that is economistic. We have identified the ways that corporate governance models and agency theory, in combination, in the United States, have greatly enriched the 1% relative to the remaining 99%. We have criticized conventional views of the future of strategy, which, we suggest do nothing more than to reproduce the present vices of strategy rather than reposition it in terms of virtues. The future, we argue, belongs to those who can think outside of the limited frames of tropes such as competitive strategy and its vice-like grip on the imagination. To do so requires developing a reflexive relation to the discourse of strategy, registering its reifications, thinking in different ways. We have called for a strategy that is future oriented in sustainable ways; we have considered the ways in which digital affordances might make it a more democratic exercise than at present.

There is also the matter of the curriculum. Who now dares to be interested in political economy in teaching strategy in Business Schools? Marxism is dead and even though the heavily financialized market economy does not seem to be doing too well for most people, either in Europe or in the United States, there is, today, no clear alternative to what it has to offer, no historical subjects waiting in the wings to ascend to power, no alternative strategy scenarios. In such a conjuncture it is worth reflecting how we might have arrived at the current impasse and that is the main reason why social theory is useful. There is excellent social theory that speaks directly to current Business School issues but it seems to be barely recognized. On reflection, it should be.

At the outset of this book we proposed that power + knowledge = strategy. The proportions matter; too much power and too little knowledge, or the wrong knowledge, are a doleful combination, even dangerous.[9] Strategy needs to be made less elite, more democratic, with more distribution of power and thus more sharing of more knowledge. We need strategy to serve more stakeholders, not just the interests

---

[9] Although not a business case, well, not directly, the strategy of the George W. Bush administration in Iraq provides an object lesson of too much power and too little knowledge. Here the knowledge required was quite clearly that of excluded sensemaking capable of providing *awareness*, or maybe *intelligence*, which implies both *understanding* (based on the integration of tacit and explicit knowledge and the integration of multiple sources in a coherent frame, which enables action) and *judgment* (which in turn requires ethical assessment and responsibility). The Bush administration's problem was not so much a lack of knowledge but the lack of awareness and intelligence in making sense of that knowledge they did have as well as an awareness of what they did not have: detailed anthropological, sociological and theological knowledge of Shia/Sunni rivalries and how they were likely to play out in practice. Assuming that the state could be destroyed and that democracy and markets would fill the vacuum proved to be disastrously naïve.

of the super wealthy of hyper capitalism and to be informed by knowledge other than simply the dogmas of enhanced profit, economic rents, competitive advantage and growth in productivity. Not only is more distributed knowledge required; we also need more distributed power. Elite power, even when informed by distributed knowledge, is still narrow and usually authoritarian. Distributed power means that distributed knowledges can be engaged in more strategic conversations that are not merely gestural, rhetorical and illusionary.

Strategy is a social construct, a particular assemblage of power and knowledge relations that does not have to be as it has become; this book is a contribution to changing how we might think and teach strategy.

TEST YOURSELF

Want to know more about this chapter? Review what you have learnt by visiting www.edge.sagepub.com/strategy2e.

- Test yourself with multiple choice questions
- Revise key terms with interactive flashcards

EXERCISES

1. Having read this chapter, you should be able to say in your own words what the following key terms mean:

   - Economism
   - Sustainability
   - Personalism
   - Impersonalism
   - Ensuring state
   - Enabling state

   - Carbon tax
   - Financialization
   - Shareholder value
   - Income share
   - Anomie
   - Integrity

2. How might strategy that reflects broad-based stakeholder interests be developed?

3. Is sustainability the most significant strategic issue of our times? Elaborate the reasons for your conclusions.

4. What are the major ethical implications of the VW scandal? What lessons do they teach strategy?

CASE STUDY

Australian coal mining

Joshua Robertson Article

STEWART CLEGG

A report written by Joshua Robertson in *The Guardian Online* Australian edition entitled 'Coal giants abandon unprofitable mines, leaving rehabilitation under threat' (January 2016) poses some interesting strategy issues.

Robertson's report tells the story of how a global resource company, Anglo American, divested itself of the open cut Callide coal mine in Queensland, selling it on to a bunch of Queensland investors who formed Batchfire Resources, with three quarters of a million dollars equity. The mine has liabilities for the future that now pass to the new owners. These liabilities are such that Batchfire must produce a site rehabilitation bond of more than $121m, either in cash or a bank guarantee, to be held by the Queensland Government. In the story it is reported that:

> Tim Buckley, of the Institute for Energy Economics and Financial Analysis (IEEFA), said the emergence of private miners willing to exist on smaller profit margins but with reduced ability to cover rehabilitation costs would be an 'absolutely reoccurring theme for coal in Australia this year'.

Go the book's website at www.edge.sagepub.com/strategy2e to read the article, then answer the question below.

QUESTION

You are employed as a strategy consultant to government. Government's concern is that they are worried about situations where there is future divestment by major multinational companies of ageing coalmines by selling the mine on to new entities, where, on the surface, the new entities appear unable financially to meet statutory sustainability requirements for remediation. What strategic advice do you proffer to government? Elaborate your reasons for the advice that you deliver and indicate what you are drawing on that you have learned from this book.

GLOSSARY

Agency cost Where owners of capital lack information about how the organization in which they have invested is organized they are potentially at the mercy of the managers, the agents, leading to the problem of monitoring those agents. The cost of this monitoring is called agency cost.

Agency theory Agency theory is concerned with resolving problems that can exist in agency relationships between principals (such as shareholders) and agents of the principals (for example, senior executives and top managers).

Agile Agile organizations have 'the capacity (1) to sense and shape opportunities and threats, (2) to seize opportunities and (3) to maintain competitiveness through enhancing, combining, protecting, and, when necessary, reconfiguring the business enterprise's intangible and tangible assets' (Teece, 2009: 4).

Alliance An alliance, in its broadest sense, is a mechanism that links diverse more or less central and peripheral actors, interests and strategies. Alliances entail a process of convergence of interests (Kalyvas, 2006: 383).

Alliance governance Alliance governance concerns the way an alliance is co-governed by the partners, in particular with regard to the integration of their interests, the use of combined resources and their relationship.

Ambidextrous organizations Ambidextrous organizations create specialist subunits with unique processes, structures and cultures that are specifically intended to support early stage innovation, comprised of one or more innovation teams *within* the larger parent organization. They are set up to support those unique approaches, activities and behaviours required when launching a new business or product.

Arbitrage Arbitrage is the practice of profiting from differences in costs and processes across borders – basically buying where prices are lowest, selling where prices are greatest, and using international operations as a means of reducing tax liabilities in countries with high tax regimes and concentrating profits in low tax regimes and losses in high tax regimes.

Asset specificity Asset specificity is the degree to which an asset is specific to use or user.

Born global Born global businesses may be defined as organizations that, from or near their founding, seek superior international business performance from the application of knowledge-based resources to the sale of outputs in multiple countries (Knight and Cavusgil, 2005: 24).

Bounded rationality Taken from March and Simon (1958) bounded rationality captures the fact that we never have perfect knowledge and hence can never be perfectly rational. Because rationality is always bounded it leads to parties not being able to foresee all the possible consequences of a contract.

Business elites Business elites can be identified as that relatively small group within the societal hierarchy that are premised on their command of financial capital in major corporate organizations.

Business model A business model is the complete system that firms use to create, deliver and capture value.

Business unit strategies Business unit strategies respond to 'How do we compete in this business?'

Celebrity A sign of celebrity is when something or someone is known for being well known. Littler (2007: 233) identifies celebrity existing where the CEO's profile 'extends beyond the financial or business sectors of the media', when the person straddles multiple media sites and genres.

Clusters Clusters are geographical agglomerations of firms in particular, related, and/or complementary, activities, sharing a common vision, and exhibiting horizontal, vertical intra- and/or inter-sectoral linkages, embedded in a supportive socio-institutional setting, and cooperating and competing in national and international markets (Pitelis, 2012: 1361).

Codes of ethics A major aspect of governance is the rules and norms through which governance occurs. These are usually referred to as 'codes of ethics'

Competency traps Competency traps lead firms to fall unconsciously into adherence to routines and deny the need for change. They lead them to rely on past successful processes that may no longer be optimal.

Contingency A contingency perspective on change proposes that the 'right' way of managing change depends on – is *contingent* on – the particular context: the type of change, the type of organization or the type of environment the organization is in.

Coopetition Coopetition refers to cooperation designed to provide mutual gain between businesses that have previously seen each other as competitors.

Core competencies Prahalad and Hamel (1990) introduced and popularised the term core competencies, which may be defined as an assemblage of multiple resources, skills and capabilities located at the organization level that work together effectively to achieve the collective learning necessary to maintain a competitive edge.

Corporate governance Cioffi (2000: 574) sees the context of corporate governance as including a 'nexus of institutions defined by company law, financial market regulation, and labor law'.

Corporate-level strategy Corporate-level strategy responds to 'What business should we be in?'

Corporate social responsibility (CSR) Corporate social responsibility has been defined by the European Commission (2005) as existing when companies integrate 'social and environmental concerns in their business operations and in their interactions with their stakeholders on a voluntary basis'.

Cost leadership To implement a cost leadership strategy successfully a firm has to develop efficiencies in regards to the use of facilities and production processes to create the same benefit for customers at a much lower cost than competitors.

Creative destruction Creative destruction involves the replacement of older less efficient processes, products, services or organizational practices with newer more efficient ones. It is destruction because it annihilates the old and inefficient but it is creative because it replaces it with the new and more efficient.

Cultural integration Cultural integration is said to occur when changes are made in two different cultural systems because particular elements of culture have spread from one system to the other, in both directions (Berry, 1980: 215).

Culture Culture represents the taken for granted ways an organization perceives its environment and itself.

Deliberate strategy Deliberate strategy may be what the strategy team intentionally designs as they integrate data and scan the environment.

Design thinking Tim Brown defines design thinking as innovation that is 'powered by a thorough understanding, through direct observation, of what people want and need in their lives and what they like or dislike about the way particular products are made, packaged, marketed, sold, and supported' (Brown, 2008: 86).

Deutero-learning Deutero-learning is continuous, behavioural-communicative and largely unconscious learning that is a form of triple loop learning. It encompasses and transcends both single and double loop learning by focusing on transforming organizational members by helping them learn how to learn and to recognize when learning is needed.

Differentiation In a differentiation strategy a firm seeks to be unique in its industry by offering products or services that stand out from the competition based on features or components that customers value most and are willing to pay for.

Double loop learning Double loop learning means changing the frame of reference that normally guides behaviour, teach you how to change the rules of the game. It implies rethinking the task at hand and considering whether its accomplishment is beneficial or not.

Dynamic capabilities Dynamic capabilities are the firm's capacities to integrate, build and reconfigure internal and external resources/competences to address and shape rapidly changing business environments (Teece et al., 1997).

Ecological modernization strategies Ecological modernization strategies suggest that economic and technological win–win solutions – gaining less pollution and more profits through more efficient use of resources – can ameliorate harmful environmental effects.

Economic neo-liberalism Economic neo-liberalism sees competition as the defining characteristic of human relations. It redefines citizens as consumers, whose democratic choices are best exercised by buying and selling, a process that rewards merit and punishes inefficiency. It maintains that 'the market' delivers benefits that could never be achieved by planning or cooperation (after Monbiot, 2016).

Economic rent Economic rent may be defined as the situation where an organization earns above average industry returns. It can be a measure of market power or differential efficiency.

Efficiency Economists focus on allocative efficiency defined as a matter of the optimal allocation of resources that are scarce (in short supply), such as land, labour and capital, by mechanisms such as markets and hierarchies (the corporation and the state).

Elite An elite is a social group within a societal hierarchy that claims and/or is accorded power, prestige or command over others, on the basis of a number of criteria, and that seeks to preserve and entrench its status.

Emergent strategies Emergent strategy originates in the interaction of the organization with its environment. As events unfold and ideas about them coalesce emergent strategies tend to converge as ideas and actions from multiple sources integrate into a pattern.

Employee voice Employee voice refers to the participation of employees in influencing organizational decision-making. In general, voice concerns *whether* and *how* employees can be heard.

Evolutionary change Evolutionary change is change that involves ongoing small adaptations that remain consistent with existing ways of doing things.

Explicit knowledge Explicit knowledge is easily absorbed, and can be transferred to various uses immediately by media such as writing or video.

Financialization Financialization refers to the processes through which the performance of finance capital becomes the key measure of economic worth, characterizing increasing parts of the corporate world, in particular, and civil society, more generally.

Foreign Direct Investment (FDI) Foreign Direct Investment (FDI) involves ownership and/or control of production capabilities and facilities cross-border. It often involves participation in management, joint venturing and transfer of technology, branding and expertise. It can take place through mergers and acquisitions, building new facilities, reinvesting profits earned from overseas operations and intra-company loans.

Framing Framing is the process through which people socially construct the meaning of an event or experience through the use of symbolic constructs, such as words, images or metaphors.

Functional-level strategies Functional-level strategies are concerned with the methods of implementing the decisions that are made at the corporate and/or business-unit strategy.

Globalization Globalization can be thought of as worldwide integration in virtually every sphere, achieved principally through international movement of diverse goods, services and processes across the borders of global regions and countries into different geographic locations or markets.

Glocalization Glocalization as a term is a hybridization of the global and the local, of globalization and localization. It is intended to describe how regional tendencies and local cultures intersect with the proliferation of global corporations. Glocalization means the simultaneous presence of both universalizing and particularizing tendencies.

High-velocity environment A high-velocity environment is characterized by 'rapid, discontinuous and simultaneous change in demand, competitors, technology and regulation' (Wirtz et al., 2007: 297).

Horizontal integration Horizontal integration occurs when a firm acquires or merges with another.

Industrial organization (IO) Industrial organization takes an external perspective, that of the industry or sector, and is concerned with the industry settings within which firms operate and behave as producers, sellers and buyers of goods and services.

Innovation Innovation refers to the development and introduction of new products, services, processes or business models. In business this means successful commercialization but innovation can also occur in a non-commercial context, when new practices are developed and adopted.

Innovation and resource-value creation The innovation and resource-value creation variant draws on Penrose's focus on endogenous firm growth through knowledge-learning-induced slack resources, sometimes combined with a more dynamic variant of transaction costs theorizing (Teece, 1982).

Innovators' dilemma The innovators' dilemma describes companies whose successes and capabilities can become obstacles in the face of changing markets and technologies.

Institutional entrepreneurs Institutional entrepreneurs not only play the role of traditional entrepreneurs but also help establish new (and sometimes challenge old) institutions in the process of their activities. They do so by leveraging resources to create new institutions or to transform existing ones (Maguire et al., 2004: 657).

Institutional logic The idea of institutional logic is quite simple. Organizations are arenas in which there are many different kinds of members and stakeholders. People draw on well-regarded ideas from professional developers, consultants and so on to try and make their sense of the situations they are in. Highly legitimated sensemaking forms an institutional logic.

Inter-firm Cooperation (IFC) Inter-firm cooperation is quasi-stable and durable, formal or informal arrangements between two or more independent firms, aiming to further the perceived interests of the parties involved (Pitelis, 2012).

Intranet An Intranet is a privately controlled and maintained computer system that is very similar to the World Wide Web, except it is normally restricted to use by employees inside the organization. It seeks to store knowledge but also to generate an electronic forum in which knowledge can be shared, communities created and problems solved.

Isolating mechanism An isolating mechanism is an entry barrier or a mobility barrier to a market that can limit market entry. Unique firm characteristics make competitive positions stable and defensible.

Joint venture A joint venture is an entity owned by multiple parent firms that is legally distinct from the parent firms. The joint venture is undertaken to share the cost and profit of a specific business project.

Knowledge Management (KM) A simple definition of Knowledge Management is that it is a managerial practice that seeks to identify, leverage, control and create knowledge in an organization.

Knowledge-based organization A knowledge-based organization attends to two related processes that underlie its everyday processes: the effective application of existing knowledge and the creation of new knowledge.

Learning organizations Learning organizations facilitate learning by all their members in order to improve continuously and transform *what* they do, *how* they do it and *why* it is done.

Legitimacy Legitimacy has been defined as 'a recognized perception or assumption that the actions of an entity are desirable, proper, or appropriate within some socially constructed system of norms, values, beliefs and definitions' (Suchman, 1995: 574).

Mandates Mandates are tasks that are assigned to subsidiaries by headquarters or that are acquired independently by the subsidiary, which have a specific time and content limitation placed on them, and which frame the internal division of labour within a MNE.

Market A market is the group of buyers and sellers, where buyers determine demand and sellers determine supply, together with the means whereby both exchange their goods or services.

Micro-politics Micro-politics are strategic attempts to exert a formative influence on social structure and relations in local settings to further sectional interests.

Mobility barriers Mobility barriers are similar to barriers to entry, but act as barriers for a group within an industry rather than for the industry as a whole. Firm specific sources of mobility barriers include organizational structure and control systems, management skills and capabilities, the nature and extent of diversification and of vertical integration, and the nature of the firm's ownership and its connections with powerful groups such as unions, consumer groups and state regulators.

Multinational enterprises (MNEs) Multinational enterprises (MNEs), defined as companies with facilities and other assets in at least one country other than its home country, own and control production facilities in different countries and usually have a centralized head office where they coordinate their global operations.

Multinational organization A multinational organization is one with facilities and other assets in at least one country other than its home country. Such companies have offices and/or factories in different countries and usually have a centralized head office where they coordinate global management.

National innovation systems National innovation systems are composed of different patterns of institutions and organizational relationships (Coriat and Weinstein, 2002).

Network form of organization The network form of organization can be defined as a collection of two or more actors engaged in repeated and enduring exchange relations with one another but that lacks a legitimate organizational authority to resolve disputes that may arise during exchange (Podolny and Page, 1998: 59).

Non-decision A non-decision is a decision that results in suppression, thwarting or otherwise not raising a latent or manifest challenge to the values or interests of the decision maker.

Non-market strategies Non-market strategies are methods for pursuing strategic goals through attempts to influence actors, such as government, the media and other influential groups.

Opportunism Opportunism prevails when actors try to gain advantage by being economical with, or even distorting, 'the truth'; the possibility of opportunism ensures that there is also the possibility of uncertainty about agreements being maintained.

Organizational boundary decisions According to TCE, the boundary of the firm is a result of economic considerations concerning whether to make or buy, internalize or externalize activities.

Organizational capability An organizational capability is an organizationally embedded and firm-specific resource that is hard to transfer and/or imitate.

Organizational improvisation Kamoche and Cunha (2001: 96) define organizational improvisation as 'the conception of action as it unfolds, by an organization and/or its members, drawing on available material, cognitive, affective and social resources'.

Organizational politics Organizational politics can be defined as the use of organizational resources, such as knowledge, position or networks, to advance a desired position within the organization and/or of the organization itself.

Outsourcing Outsourcing involves moving activities that were previously undertaken by the organization to outside suppliers as contractors.

Paradigm An organization's paradigm can be defined as the set of core beliefs and assumptions that get embedded in the organization over time, such as beliefs about how they should react to moves by competitors or assumptions about the nature of the customer.

Platform A platform is a base upon which other applications, processes or technologies can be developed. It is an evolving ecosystem that is created from many interconnected pieces.

Political skill entails using knowledge, networks and social capital astutely and procedurally, in a manner that best serves the strategic interest one is seeking to advance.

Power Power characterizes all social relations as each of us seeks to have others do what we would want them to do. In doing so we seek to make some others allies and intermediaries against those framed as opponents. Because we are all engaged in these power relations we are always potentially both subjects and objects of power.

Product and **Process innovation** While product innovation involves creating new things, process innovation means making the same product or offering the same service in a different way. Of course, the two are not independent but can be related.

Radical or **Incremental innovation** Radical innovation fundamentally changes what is being offered. Incremental innovation makes small or continuous improvements to an existing offering. Introducing difference is the key ingredient.

Resources Resources are stocks of tangible and intangible assets that can generate value. There are four major types – capital, labour/human, land and knowledge/organization.

Revolutionary change Revolutionary change seeks to transform existing ways of doing things in a complete break with existing ways of doing things.

Satisficing Satisificing is a decision that will both 'satisfy' and 'suffice'. A satisficing decision is where the organization does not strive to make an optimal decision, but instead one that satisfies key actors in the organization and 'does the trick'. A satisficing decision is rarely ideal but it makes do with what is seen to be available and relevant.

Sensegiving Sensegiving involves the attempt to influence the sensemaking of others towards the preferred version of reality of the sensegiver.

Sensemaking Sensemaking is the subjective and inter-subjective process through which people give meaning to their experiences.

Services Services are 'the application of specialized competencies (knowledge and skills) through deeds, processes, and performances for the benefit of another entity or the entity itself' (Vargo and Lusch, 2004: 2).

Shanzhai Shanzhai refers to a part of China's informal industry that is known for fast product cycles as well as the tendency to seek inspiration in, or simply copy, successful products.

Single loop learning Single loop learning optimizes its knowledge of a given problem by using skills, refining abilities and acquiring knowledge that is necessary to achieve resolution of that problem.

Strategic alliances Strategic alliances are commonly defined as purposive linkages between organizations that cover collaborations involving an exchange, a co-development or a sharing relationship (Gulati, 1995).

Strategic decision A strategic decision is typically defined as being one that has long-term organizational implications for key success factors such as access and control of resources and effective performance.

Strategic drift Strategic drift is the notion that organizations that fail to keep pace with changes in the external environment will start to 'drift' as the firm becomes detached from the changing environment.

Strategic group Porter (1980) defined a strategic group as a group of firms in the same industry that follow the same or similar strategies.

Strategic interest A strategic interest emerges when there is something at issue regarding the long-term direction of the organization or control of key decisions or resources, which divides opinions, on which people take sides. Dominant interpretations of strategic interests will tend to be represented as those that are legitimate for the organization, even against resistance from other representations.

Strategic management Strategic management involves the 'major intended and emergent initiatives taken by general managers on behalf of owners involving utilization of resources to enhance the performance of firms in their external environments' (Nag et al., 2007: 942–943).

Sustainability Sustainability is the condition under which the satisfaction of a particular objective by economic agents in the short term is not pernicious to the satisfaction of the same objective in the longer term, and/or when the satisfaction of the objective of an economic agent does not prejudice the satisfaction of the objectives of other economic and social agents.

Sustainable competitive advantage (SCA) Sustainable competitive advantage is what allows a business to maintain and improve its competitive position in a market against competitors in the long term. Achieving SCA is the purpose of strategic management since it allows a firm to make a profit in a sustained way. Strategists have diverging ideas about how SCA can best be achieved as it is embodied, embrained and taken for granted. A manual for how to ride a bike would not be equivalent to the realization that you *can* do it.

Tacit knowledge The learner cannot appropriate tacit knowledge immediately because it cannot be explicitly conveyed sufficiently quickly.

Transaction frequency Transaction frequency refers to the repeatability of transactions.

Uncertainty Uncertainty is associated with the unfolding of events relevant to contracts, the contingencies of which cannot necessarily be controlled. Uncertainty is positively related to hierarchical governance, due to the power of managerial fiat.

Value Value is perceived worthiness of a subject matter to a socio-economic agent that is exposed to and/or can make use of the subject matter in question.

Value appropriation/capture The value appropriation/capture variant emphasizes the ability of firms to capture above-average rents by virtue of differential resource bases.

Value chain A value chain is a set of activities that an organization carries out to create value for its customers by delivering a product or service that the market values and is prepared to buy at a price that affords the organization a profit margin.

Vertical integration Vertical integration involves moving into activities that were previously an input into the firm undertaken by one's suppliers 'downstream' (backward integration) or part of the post-production process undertaken by customers 'upstream' (forward integration).

Wicked problem A wicked problem is a problem that is hard to describe, has many interrelated causes, no criteria for evaluating potential solutions, where actions to address the problem tend to cause more unanticipated problems and where defining the problem itself is as difficult as identifying potential solutions.

REFERENCES

Abo, T. (1994) *Hybrid Factory*. New York: Oxford University Press.

Abrahamson, E. (1991) 'Managerial fads and fashions: The diffusion and rejection of innovations', *Academy of Management Review*, 16(2): 586–612.

Abrahamson, E. and Freedman, D.H. (2006) *A Perfect Mess: The Hidden Benefits of Disorder. How Crammed Closets, Cluttered Offices, and On-the-Fly Planning Make the World a Better Place*. London: Weidenfeld & Nicolson.

Abrahamsson, B. and Broström, A. (1980) *The Rights of Labor*. Beverly Hills, CA: Sage.

Acedo, F.J., Barroso, C. and Galan, J.L. (2006) 'The resource-based theory: Dissemination and main trends', *Strategic Management Journal*, 27: 621–636.

Acemoglu, D., Johnson, S. and Robinson, J.A. (2001) 'The colonial origins of comparative development: An empirical investigation', *American Economic Review*, 91(5): 1369–1401.

Adam, B. (2004) *Time*. Cambridge, UK: Polity.

Adam, B. (2007) 'Foreword', in R. Hassan and R. Purser (eds), *24/7 Time and Temporality in the Network Society*. Stanford, CA: Stanford University Press. pp. ix–xi.

Adams, R., Bessant, J. and Phelps, R. (2006) 'Innovation management measurement: A review', *International Journal of Management Reviews*, 8(1): 21–47.

Adelstein, J. and Clegg, S.R. (2015) 'Code of ethics: a stratified vehicle for compliance', *Journal of Business Ethics*, 138(1): 1–14.

Adler, P. and Kwon, S. (2002) 'Social capital, prospects for a new concept', *Academy of Management Review*, 27: 17–40.

Agarwal, R. and Selen, W. (2009) 'Dynamic capability building in service value networks for achieving service innovation, *Decision Sciences*, 40(3): 431–475.

Aglietta, M. and Breton, R. (2001) 'Financial systems, corporate control and capital accumulation', *Economy and Society*, 30(4): 433–466.

Ahrens, T. and Chapman, C.S. (2007) 'Management accounting as practice', *Accounting, Organizations and Society*, 32: 1–27.

Ahuja, G., Soda, G. and Zaheer, A. (2012) 'The genesis and dynamics of organizational networks', *Organization Science*, 23: 434–448.

Albrow, M. (1997) *Do Organizations Have Feelings?* London: Routledge.

Alchian, A A. and Demsetz, H. (1972) 'Production, information costs, and economic organization', *The American Economic Review*, 62(5): 777–795.

Allison, G. (1971) *Essence of Decision: Explaining the Cuban Missile Crisis*. Boston: Little Brown.

Almeida, P., Grant, R. and Phene, A. (2002) 'Knowledge transfer through alliances: The role of culture', in M. Gannon and K. Newman (eds), *Handbook of Cross Cultural Management*. Oxford: Blackwell.

Alvarez, S.A. and Barney, J.B. (2007) 'Discovery and creation: Alternative theories of entrepreneurial action', *Strategic Entrepreneurship Journal*, 1/1–2: 11–26.

Alvaro, C.C. (2006) 'Who cares about corruption?', *Journal of International Business Studies*, 37(6): 807–822.

Alvesson, M. (2013) *The Triumph of Emptiness: Consumption, Higher Education, and Work Organization*. Oxford: Oxford University Press.

Alvesson, M. and Willmott, H. (1995) 'Strategic management as domination and emancipation: From planning and process to communication and praxis', in P. Shrivastava and C. Stubbart (eds), *Advances in Strategic Management: Challenges from Outside the Mainstream*. Greenwich, CT: JAI Press.

Amabile, T. and Conti, R. (1999) 'Changes in the work environment for creativity during downsizing', *Academy of Management Journal*, 42(6): 616–629.

Amit, R. and Schoemaker, P.J.H. (1993) 'Strategic assets and organizational rent', *Strategic Management Journal*, 14: 33–46.

Amit, R. and Zott, C. (2001) 'Value creation in e-business', *Strategic Management Journal*, 22: 493–520.

Amsden, A. (2001) *The Rise of 'The Rest': Challenges to the West from Late-Industrializing Economies*. Oxford: Oxford University Press.

Andersson, U. and Pahlberg, C. (1997) 'Subsidiary influence on strategic behaviour in MNEs: An empirical study', *International Business Review*, 6(3): 319–334.

Andersson, U., Forsgren, M. and Holm, U. (2007) 'Balancing subsidiary influence in the federative MNC: A business network view', *Journal of International Business Studies*, 38(5): 802–818.

Andrews, K.R. (1971) *The Concept of Corporate Strategy*. New York: Dow Jones-Irwin.

Andrews, K. (1989) 'Ethics in practice', *Harvard Business Review*, September–October: 99–104.

Anguera, R. (2006) The Channel Tunnel—an ex post economic evaluation, *Transportation Research Part A: Policy and Practice*, 40(4): 291–315.

Ansoff, H.I. (1965) *Corporate Strategy: An Analytic Approach to Business Policy for Growth and Expansion*. New York: McGraw-Hill.

Ansoff, H.I. (1991) 'Critique of Henry Mintzberg's "The design school: reconsidering the basic premises of strategic management"', *Strategic Management Journal,* 12(6): 449–461.

Aoki, M. (2004) 'An organizational architecture of T-form: Silicon Valley clustering and its institutional coherence', *Industrial and Corporate Change*, 13(6): 967–981.

Argitis, G. and Pitelis, C. (2006) 'Global finance, income distribution and capital accumulation', *Contributions to Political Economy*, 25(1): 63–81.

Argitis, G. and Pitelis, C.N. (2001) 'Monetary policy and the distribution of income: Evidence for the United States and the United Kingdom', *Journal of Post Keynesian Economics*, 23(4): 617–638.

Argyris, C. (1990) *Overcoming Organizational Defences*. Boston, MA: Allyn and Bacon.

Argyris, C. (1991) 'Teaching smart people how to learn', *Harvard Business Review*, 69(3): 99–109.

Argyris, C. and Schön, D. (1978) *Organizational Learning: A Theory of Action Perspective*. Reading, MA: Addison Wesley.

Ariño, A.and Reuer, G.G. (2006) *Strategic Alliances: Governance and Contracts*. London: Palgrave Macmillan.

Ariño, A., De la Torre, J. and Smith Ring, P. (2001) 'Relational quality: Managing trust in corporate alliances', *California Management Review*, 44(1): 109–131.

Arrow, K.J. (1962) 'The economic implications of learning by doing', *Review of Economic Studies*, 29: 155–173.

Arrow, K.J. (1974) *The Limits of Organization*. New York: WW Norton.

Ashforth, B.E. and Mael, F.A. (1998) 'The power of resistance: Sustaining valued identities', in R.M. Kramer and M.A. Neale (eds), *Power and Influence in Organizations*. London: Sage. pp. 89–120.

Ashforth, B.E., Rogers, K.M., Pratt, M.G. and Pradies, C. (2014) 'Ambivalence in organizations: A multilevel approach', *Organization Science*, 25(5): 1453–1478.

Ashwell, R. (2015) *The World of Shabby Chic*. New York: Riizzoli.

Augier, M. and Sarasvathy, S.D. (2004) 'Integrating evolution, cognition and design: Extending Simonian perspectives to strategic organization', *Strategic Organization*, 2(2): 169–204.

Augier, M. and Teece, D.J. (2007) 'Dynamic capabilities and multinational enterprise: Penrosean insights and omissions', *Management International Review*, 47/2: 175–192.

Augier, M. and Teece, D.J. (2008) 'Strategy as evolution with design: Dynamic capabilities and the design and evolution of the business enterprise', *Organization Studies*, 29: 1187–1208.

Aurik, J., Fabel, M. and Jonk, G. (2015) *The Future of Strategy*. New York, NY: McGraw Hill.

Avolio, B.J., Bass, B.M. and Jung, D.I. (1999) 'Re-examining the components of transformational and transactional leadership using the Multifactor Leadership Questionnaire', *Journal of Occupational and Organizational Psychology*, 72(4): 441–462.

Axelrod, R. (1984) *The Evolution of Cooperation*. New York, NY: Basic Books.

Axelrod, R. (1997) *The Complexity of Cooperation: Agent-Based Models of Competition and Collaboration*. Princeton, NJ: Princeton University Press.

Bacharach, S. (2005) *Get Them on Your Side: Win Support, Convert Skeptics, Get Results*. Avon, MA: Platinum.

Bachrach, P. and Baratz, M. (1970) *Poverty and Power: Theory and Practice*, Oxford: Oxford University Press.

Baden-Fuller, C. and Morgan, M. (2010) 'Business models', *Long Range Planning*, 43: 156–217.

Bahrami, H. and Evans, S. (1995) 'Flexible re-cycling and high-technology entrepreneurship', *California Management Review*, 37(3): 62–89.

Bailey, B. and Peck, S. (2011) 'Board processes, climate and the impact on board task performance', proceedings of the *First International Conference on Engaged Management Scholarship*.

Bain, J.S. (1956) *Barriers to New Competition: Their Character and Consequences for Manufacturing Industries*. Boston, MA: Harvard University Press.

Bain, J. S. (1968) *Industrial organization*. London: John Wiley & Sons.

Balakrishnan, S. and Koza, M. (1993) 'Information asymmetry, adverse selection and joint ventures', *Journal of Economic Behaviour and Organization*, 20(1): 99–118.

Balogun, J. and Hailey, V.H. (2008) *Exploring Strategic Change*. London: Pearson Education.

Balogun, J. and Johnson, G. (2004) 'Organizational restructuring and middle manager sensemaking', *Academy of Management Journal*, 47(4): 523–549.

Balogun, J. and Johnson, G. (2005) 'From intended strategy to unintended outcomes: The impact of change recipient sensemaking', *Organization Studies*, 26(11): 1573–1602.

Balogun, J., Bartunek, J.M. and Do, B. (2015) 'Senior managers' sensemaking and responses to strategic change', *Organization Science*, 26(4): 960–979.

Balogun, J., Jarzabkowski, P. and Vaara, E. (2011) 'Selling, resistance and reconciliation: A critical discursive approach to subsidiary role evolution in MNEs', *Journal of International Business Studies*, 42(6): 765–786.

Bamford, J., Ernst, D. and Fubini, D. (2004) 'Launching a world-class joint venture', *Harvard Business Review*, 82(2): 90–100.

Banerjee, S.B. (2003) 'Who sustains whose development? Sustainable development and the reinvention of nature', *Organization Studies*, 24(1): 143–180.

Banerjee, S.B. (2006) 'The problem with corporate social responsibility', in S. Clegg and C. Rhodes (eds), *Management Ethics: Contemporary Contexts*. London: Palgrave. pp. 55–76.

Banerjee, S.B. (2007) *Corporate Social Responsibility: The Good, The Bad and The Ugly*. Cheltenham: Edward Elgar.

Banerjee, S.B., Carter, C. and Clegg, S.R. (2009) 'Managing globalization', in M. Alvesson, T. Bridgman and H. Wilmott (eds), *The Oxford Handbook of Critical Management Studies*. Oxford: Oxford University Press. pp. 186–212.

Bansal, P. and DesJardine, M. (2014) 'Business sustainability: It's about time', *Strategic Organization*, 12(1): 70–78.

Barkema, H.G. and Pennings, J.M. (1998) 'Top management pay: Impact of overt and covert power', *Organization Studies*, 19(6): 975–1003.

Barley, S. (2007) 'Corporations, democracy, and the public good', *Journal of Management Inquiry*, 16(3): 201–215.

Barley, S. and Kunda, G. (2004) *Gurus, Hired Guns and Warm Bodies: Itinerant Experts in a Knowledge Economy*. Princeton, NJ: Princeton University Press.

Barnett, W. and McKendrick, D. (2004) 'Why are some organizations more competitive than others? Evidence from a changing global market', *Administrative Science Quarterly*, 49(4): 535–571.

Barney, J.B. (1986) 'Strategic factor markets: Expectations, lucks and business strategy', *Management Science*, 32: 1231–1241.

Barney, J. (1991) 'Firm resources and sustained competitive advantage', *Journal of Management*, 17(1): 99–120.

Barney, J. B. (1995) 'Looking inside for competitive advantage', *The Academy of Management Executive*, 9(4): 49–61.

Barney, J.B. (2001) 'Is the resource-based theory a useful perspective for strategic management research? Yes', *Academy of Management Review*, 26: 41–56.

Barney, J.B. and Hesterly, W.S. (1996) 'Organizational economics: Understanding the relationship between organizations and economic analysis', in S.R. Clegg, C. Hardy and W.R. Nord, *Handbook of Organization Studies*. London: Sage Publications.

Barry, D. and Elmes, M. (1997) 'Strategy retold: Toward a narrative view of strategic discourse', *Academy of Management Review*, 22(2): 429–452.

Barthelemy, J. (2001) 'The hidden costs of IT outsourcing', *Sloan Management Review* (Spring): 60–69.

Bartlett, A. and Preston, D. (2000) 'Can ethical behaviour really exist in business?', *Journal of Business Ethics*, 23(2): 199–209.

Bartlett, C.A. and Ghoshal, S. (1987) Managing across borders: new strategic requirements.

Bartlett, C.A. and Ghoshal, S. (1989) 'The transnational corporation.' New York.

Bartlett, C.A. and Ghoshal, S. (1995) *Managing Across Borders: The Transnational Solution*. Boston, MA: Harvard Business School Press.

Bartunek, J.M. and Louis, M.R. (1988) 'The interplay of organization development and organizational transformation', *Research in Organizational Change and Development*, 2: 97–134.

Bass, B.M. (1985) *Leadership and Performance Beyond Expectation*. New York: Free Press.

Bass, B.M. and Avolio, B.J. (1993) 'Transformational leadership: A response to critiques', in M.M. Chemers and R. Ayman (eds), *Leadership Theory and Research: Perspectives and Directions*. New York: Academic Press. pp. 49–80.

Bass, B.M. and Avolio, B.J. (1997) *Full-range of Leadership Development: Manual for the Multifactor Leadership Questionnaire*. Palo Alto, CA: Mind Garden.

Basu, K. and Palazzo, G. (2008) 'Corporate social responsibility: A process model of sensemaking', *Academy of Management Review*, (33)1: 122–136.

Bateson, G. (1958) *Naven* (2nd edn). Stanford, CA: Stanford University Press.

Bateson, G. (1963) 'Exchange of information about patterns of human behavior', in W.S. Fields and W. Abbott (eds), *Information Storage and Neural Control*. Spring-field, IL: Thomas Books. pp. 173–186.

Bateson, G. (1972) *Steps to an Ecology of Mind*. San Francisco: Chandler.

Battilana, J. and Dorado, S. (2010) 'Building sustainable hybrid organizations: The case of commercial microfinance organizations', *Academy of Management Journal*, 53(6): 1419–1440.

Bauerschmidt, A. and Chrisman, J.J. (1993) 'Strategies for survival in the microcomputer industry: 1985–1989', *Journal of Management Inquiry*, 2(1): 63–82.

Baunsgaard, V.V. and Clegg, S.R. (2012) 'Dominant ideological modes of rationality: Organizations as arenas of struggle over members' categorization devices', in D.Courpasson, D. Golsorkhi and J.J. Sallaz (eds), *Rethinking Power in Organizations, Institutions and Markets,* Research in the Sociology of Organizations, Vol. 34. Bingley: Emerald. pp. 199–232.

Baunsgaard, V. and Clegg, S.R. (2013) '"Walls and boxes": The effects of professional identity, power and rationality on strategies for cross-functional integration', *Organization Studies*, 34(9): 1299–1325.

Baysinger, B. (1984) 'Domain maintenance as an objective of business political activity: An expanded typology', *Academy of Management Review*, 9(2): 248–258.

Beamish, P. (1994) 'Joint ventures in LDCs: Partner selection and performance', *Management International Review*, 34: 60–75.

Bechky, B.A. (2003) 'Sharing meaning across occupational communities: The transformation of understanding on a production floor', *Organization Science*, 14(3): 312–330.

Bechky, B.A. (2006) 'Gaffers, goffers, and grips: Role-based coordination in temporary organizations', *Organization Science*, 17: 3–21.

Becker, B.E. and Huselid, M.A. (2006) 'Strategic human resources management: Where do we go from here?', *Journal of Management*, 32/6: 898–925.

Becker-Ritterspach, F. and Dörrenbächer, C. (2011) 'An organizational politics perspective on intra-firm competition in multinational corporations', *Management International Review*, 51(4): 533–559.

Becker-Ritterspach, F., Lange, K. and Lohr, K. (2002) 'Control mechanisms and patterns of reorganization in MNCs', in M. Geppert, D. Matten and K. Williams (eds), *Challenges for European Management in a Global Context – Experiences from Britain and Germany*. Basingstoke: Palgrave. pp. 68–95.

Becker-Ritterspach, F., Blazejewski, S., Dörrenbächer, C. and Geppert, M. (2015) *Micropolitics in the Multinational Corporation: Foundations, Applications and New Directions*. Cambridge: Cambridge University Press.

Beckman, S.L. and Barry, M. (2007) 'Innovation as a learning process: Embedding design thinking', *California Management Review*, 50(1): 25–56.

Belliveau, M.A., O'Reilly III, C.A. and Wade, J.B. (1996) 'Social capital at the top: Effects of social similarity and status on CEO compensation', *Academy of Management Journal*, 39(6): 1568–1593.

Bendix, R. (1956) *Work and Authority in Industry: Ideologies of Management in the Course of Industrialisation*. Berkley: University of California Berkley.

Benson, J. and Ieronimo, N. (1996) 'Outsourcing decisions: Evidence from Australia-based enterprises', *International Labour Review*, 135(1): 59–73.

Benson, J. and Littler, C. (2002) 'Outsourcing and workforce reductions: An empirical study of Australian organisations', *Asia Pacific Business Review*, 8(3): 16–30.

Berfield, S. and Bagiorri, M. (2013) *Zara's Fast-Fashion Edge*. Available at: www.businessweek.com/articles/2013-11-14/2014-outlook-zaras-fashion-supply-chain-edge (accessed 20 January 2015).

Berger, P. and Pullberg, S. (1966) 'Reification and the sociological critique of consciousness', *New Left Review*, 35: 56–71.

Berglund, J. and Werr, A. (2000) 'The invincible character of management consulting rhetoric: How one blends incommensurates while keeping them apart', *Organization*, 7(4): 633–655.

Berkowitz, D., Pistor, K. and Richard, J. (2003) 'Economic development, legality, and the transplant effect', *European Economic Review*, 47: 165–195.

Berle, A.J. and Means, C.G. (1932) *The Modern Corporation and Private Property*. New York: Harcourt Brace

Berliner, D., Regan Greenleaf, A., Lake, M., Levie, M. and Noveck, J (2015) *Labor Standards in International Supply Chains*. Cheltenham: Edward Elgar.

Berrone, P. (2008) 'Current global financial crisis: An incentive problem', IESE Business School Occasional Paper (OP-158), University of Navarra.

Berry, J.W. (1980) 'Social and cultural change', in H.C. Triandis and R.W. Brislin (eds), *Handbook of Cross-Cultural Psychology*. Boston, MA: Allyn & Bacon. pp. 211–279.

Berry, J.W. (1983) 'Acculturation: A comparative analysis of alternative forms', in R.J. Samadu and S.L. Woods (eds), *Perspectives in Immigrant and Minority Education*. Lanham, MD: University Press of America. pp. 66–77.

Bessant, J. and Tsekouras, G. (2001) 'Developing learning networks', *AI and Society*, 15(2): 82–98.

Bessant, J., Kaplinsky, R. and Morris, M. (2003) 'Learning networks', *International Journal of Technology Management and Sustainable Development*, 2(1): 19–28.

Bezemer, D.J. (2009) *'No One Saw This Coming': Understanding Financial Crisis Through Accounting Models*. Groningen, The Netherlands: Faculty of Economics University of Groningen.

Bezemer, P. and Nicholson, G. (2014) 'Inside the boardroom: Exploring board member interactions', *Qualitative Research in Accounting and Management*, 11(3): 238–259.

Bezemer, P., Peij, S., de Kruijs, L. and Maassen, G. (2014) 'How two-tier boards can be more effective', *Corporate Governance: The International Journal of Business in Society*, 14(1): 15–31.

Biggart, N. (1991) 'Explaining Asian Economic Organization: Towards a Weberian economic perspective', *Theory and Society*, 20(2): 199–232.

Biggart, N. and Guillén, M.F. (1999) 'Developing social organization and the rise of the auto industries of South Korea, Taiwan, Spain, and Argentina', *American Sociological Review*, 64(5): 722–747.

Birkinshaw, J. (1999) 'The determinants and consequences of subsidiary initiative in multinational corporations', *Entrepreneurship theory and practice*, 24(1): 9–36.

Birkinshaw, J. and Hood, H. (eds) (1998) *Multinational Corporate Evolution and Subsidiary Development*. Basingstoke: Macmillan.

Birkinshaw, J. and Lingblad, M. (2005) 'Intrafirm competition and charter evolution in the multibusiness firm', *Organization Science*, 16(6): 674–686.

Birkinshaw, J. and Ridderstråle, J. (1999) 'Fighting the corporate immune system: A process study of subsidiary initiatives in multinational corporations', *International Business Review*, 8(2): 149–80.

Birkinshaw, J., Bessant, J. and Delbridge, R. (2007) 'Finding, forming and reforming: Creating networks for continuous innovation', *California Management Review*, 49(3): 67–84.

Birkinshaw, J., Hamel, G. and Mol, M.J. (2008) 'Management innovation', *Academy of Management Review*, 33(4): 825–845.

Bitner, M.J., Ostrom, L. and Morgan, F.N. (2008) 'Service blueprinting: A practical technique for service innovation', *California Management Review*, 50(3): 66–94.

Blair, M. and Stout, L. (1999) 'A team production theory of corporate law', *Virginia Law Review*, 85(2): 248–328.

Blasco, M. and Zølner, M. (2010) 'Corporate social responsibility in Mexico and France: Exploring the role of normative institutions', *Business and Society*, 49(2): 216–251.

Blazejewski, S. and Becker-Ritterspach, F. (2011) 'Conflict in headquarter-subsidiary relations: A critical literature review and new directions', in M. Geppert and C. Dörrenbächer (eds), *Politics and Power in the Multinational Corporation: The Role of Interests, Identities, and Institution*s. Cambridge: Cambridge University Press. pp. 139–190.

Blazevic, V. and Lievens, A. (2008) 'Managing innovation through customer coproduced knowledge in electronic services: An exploratory study', *Journal of the Academy of Marketing Science*, 36: 138–151.

Bleeke, J. and Ernst, D. (1991) 'The way to win in cross-border alliances', *Harvard Business Review*, 69: 127–135.

Blumentritt, T.P. (2003) 'Foreign subsidiaries' government affairs activities: The influence of managers and resources', *Business and Society*, 42(2): 202–233.

Boddewyn, J. (1975) *Corporate External Affairs: Blueprint for Survival*. New York: Business International Corporation.

Boddewyn, J. (1988) 'Political aspects of MNE theory' *Journal of International Business Studies*, 19(3): 341–363.

Boddewyn, J. (1993) 'Political resources and markets in international business: Beyond Porter's generic strategies', *Research in Global Strategic Management*, 4: 83–99.

Boddewyn, J. and Brewer, T.L. (1994) 'International-business political behavior: New theoretical directions', *Academy of Management Review*, 19(1): 119–143.

Boeker, W. (1989) 'The development and institutionalization of subunit power in organizations', *Administrative Science Quarterly*, 34(3): 388–410.

Boeker, W. (1992) 'Power and managerial dismissal: Scapegoating at the top', *Administrative Science Quarterly*, 37(3): 400–421.

Boeker, W. (1997) 'Strategic change: The influence of managerial characteristics and organizational growth', *Academy of Management Journal*, 40(1): 152–170.

Boje, D.M. (1991) 'The storytelling organization: A study of story performance in an office-supply firm', *Administrative Science Quarterly*, 36(1): 106–126.

Boje, D.M. (1996) 'Lessons from premodern and modern for postmodern management', in G. Palmer and S. Clegg (eds), *Constituting Management: Markets, Meanings and Identities*. Berlin: de Gruyter. pp. 329–345.

Boje, D.M. (2008) 'Storytelling', in S.R. Clegg and J.R. Bailey (eds), *International Encyclopaedia of Organization Studies*, Vol. 4. Sage: London. pp. 1454–1458.

Boland, R.J. and Collopy, F. (2004) *Developing Capability: Managing and Designing*. Palo Alto, CA: Stanford University Press.

Bolman, L.G. and Deal, T.E. (2001) *Leading with the Soul*. San Francisco, CA: Jossey-Bass.

Boltanski, L. and Thévenot, L. (1991) *De la justification*. Paris: Gallimard.

Borgatti, S.P., Mehra, A., Brass, D.J. and Labianca, G. (2009) 'Network analysis in the social sciences', *Science*, 323: 892–895.

Borys, B. and Jemison, D.B. (1989) 'Hybrid arrangements as strategic alliances: Theoretical issues in organizational combinations', *Academy of Management Review*, 14: 234–249.

Boston, W. (2015) 'Merkel urges volkswagen to make full disclosure in emissions scandal', *Wall Street Journal*, 31 October. Available at: www.wsj.com/articles/merkel-urges-volkswagen-to-make-full-disclosure-in-emissions-scandal-1446290032 (accessed 1 November 2015).

Boulouta, I. and Pitelis, C. (2013) 'Who needs CSR? The impact of corporate social responsibility on national competitiveness', *Journal of Business Ethics*, 119(3): 1–16.

Bouquet, C. and Birkinshaw, J. (2008) 'Managing power in the multinational corporation: How low-power actors gain influence', *Journal of Management*, 34(3): 477–508.

Bourantas, D. (2008) 'Phronesis: A strategic leadership virtue', unpublished article, Athens University of Economics and Business. Available at: www.mbaexecutive.gr/vdata/File/bibli othiki/Arthra/PHRONESIS%202008.pdf.

Bourdieu, P. (1977) *Outline of a Theory of Practice*. (trans. R. Nice). Cambridge: Cambridge University Press.

Bourdieu, P. (1984) *Distinction: A Social Critique of the Judgment of Taste*. Cambridge, MA: Harvard University Press.

Bourdieu, P. (1990) *The Logic of Practice*, trans. R. Nice.Stanford, CA: Stanford University Press.

Bourdieu, P. (2002) *Outline of a Theory of Practice*. Cambridge: Cambridge University Press.

Bower, J.L. and Gilbert, C.G. (2005) *From Resource Allocation to Strategy*. Oxford: Oxford University Press.

Bowman, C. and Swart, J. (2007) 'Whose human capital? The challenge of value capture when capital is embedded', *Journal of Management Studies*, 44/4: 488–505.

Bowne, B. (1908) *Personalism*. Cambridge, MA: Houghton Mifflin.

Bradach, J.L. and Eccles, R.G. (1989) 'Price, authority, and trust: From ideal types to plural forms', *Annual Review of Sociology*, 15: 97–118.

Bragues, G. (2010) 'Profiting with honor: Cicero's vision of leadership', *Journal of Business Ethics*, 97: 21–33.

Brandenburger, A. and Nalebuff, B.J. (1995) 'The right game: Use game theory to shape strategy', *Harvard Business Review*, 73/4: 57–71.

Brass, D.J., Galaskiewicz, J., Greve, H.R. and Tsai, W. (2004) 'Taking stock of networks and organizations: A multilevel perspective', *Academy of Management Journal*, 47: 795–819.

Brodie, R.J., Pels, J. and Saren, M. (2006) 'Toward a new dominant logic: A service centered perspective', in S.L. Vargo and R.F. Lusch (eds), *The Service Dominant Logic of Marketing: Dialog, Debate, and Directions*. Armonk, NY: ME Sharpe. pp. 307–319.

Brouwer, E., Budil-Nadvornikova, H. and Kleinknecht, A. (1999) 'Are urban agglomerations a better breeding place for product innovation? An analysis of new product announcements', *Regional Studies*, 33(6): 541–549.

Brown, A. (2008) 'A materialist development of some recent contributions to the labour theory of value', *Cambridge Journal of Economics*, 32: 125–146.

Brown, A.D. and Starkey, K. (2000) 'Organizational identity and organizational learning: A psychodynamic perspective', *Academy of Management Review*, 25(1): 102–120.

Brown, A.D. and Thompson, E.R. (2013) 'A narrative approach to strategy-as-practice', *Business History*, 55(7): 1143–1167.

Brown, J S. (2004) 'Minding and mining the periphery', *Long Range Planning*, 37(2): 143–151.

Brown, S.L. and Eisenhardt, K.M. (1997) 'The art of continuous change: Linking complexity theory and time-paced evolution in relentlessly shifting organisations', *Administrative Science Quarterly*, 42: 1–34.

Brown, T. and Pitoski, M. (2003) 'Managing contract performance: A transaction costs approach', *Journal of Policy Analysis and Management*, 22(2): 275–297.

Brum, E. (2016) 'Brazil is going through an identity crisis, not just an impeachment', *The Guardian*, 18 April. Available at: www.theguardian.com/commentisfree/2016/apr/18/brazil-impeachment-identity-crisis-dilma-rousseff-workers-party (accessed 19 April 2016).

Brundin, E. and Melin, L. (2006) 'Unfolding the dynamics of emotions: how emotion drives or counteracts strategizing', *The International Journal of Work Organisation and Emotion*, 1(3): 277–302.

Bruno, K. and Karliner, J. (2002) *Earth Summit Biz: The Corporate Take-over of Sustainable Development*. Oakland, CA: Food First Books.

Brunsson, N. (1994) *The Organization of Hypocrisy: Talk, Decisions and Actions*. Chichester: Wiley.

Brunsson, N. and Jacobsson, B. (2001) *A World of Standards*. New York: Oxford University Press.

Brynjolffson, E. (2004) 'Productivity's technology iceberg', *MIT Technology Review*. Available at: www.technologyreview.com/articles/print_version/wo_brynjolfsson031004.asp (accessed 10 March 2004).

Buck, T. and Shahrim, A. (2005) 'The translation of corporate governance change across nations: The case of Germany', *Journal of International Business Studies*, 36(1): 42–61.

Buckley, P. (2003) 'Globalization and multinational enterprise' in D. Faulkner and A. Campbell (eds), *The Oxford Handbook of Strategy*. Oxford: Oxford University Press.

Buckley, P.J. and Casson, M.C. (1976) *The Future of Multinational Enterprise*. London: Macmillan.

Buchanan, D.A. (2008) 'You stab my back, I'll stab yours: Management experience and perceptions of organization political behaviour', *British Journal of Management*, 19(1): 49–64.

Buchanan, D. and Badham, R. (2008) *Power, Politics, and Organizational Change: Winning the Turf Game*. London: Sage.

Bunch, D. S. and Smiley, R. (1992) Who deters entry? Evidence on the use of strategic entry deterrents, *The Review of Economics and Statistics*, 74(3): 509–521.

Buono, A.F. and Bowditch, J.L. (1989) *The Human Side of Mergers and Acquisitions: Managing Collisions between People, Cultures and Organizations*. London: Jossey-Bass.

Buono, A.F., Bowditch, J.L. and Lewis III, J.W. (1985) 'When cultures collide: The anatomy of a merger', *Human Relations*, 38: 477–500.

Burgelman, R.A. (1991) 'Intraorganizational ecology of strategy making and organizational adaptation: Theory and field research, *Organization Science*, 2(3): 239–262.

Burnes, B. (2004) 'Kurt Lewin and the planned approach to change: A re-appraisal', *Journal of Management Studies*, 41(6): 977–1002.

Burns, J.M. (1978) *Leadership*. New York: Harper and Row.

Burns, L.D. and Wholey, D.R. (1993) 'Adoption and abandonment of matrix management programs', *Academy of Management Journal*, 36: 106–138.

Burt, R.S. (1992) *Structural Holes: The Social Structure of Competition*. Cambridge, MA: Harvard University Press.

Burt, R.S. (2000) 'The network structure of social capital' in B.M. Staw and R.I. Sutton (eds), *Research in Organizational Behavior*. New York: Elsevier. pp. 345–423.

Butler, R. (1990) 'Decision-making research: Its uses and misuses, a comment on Mintzberg and Waters: Does decision get in the way?', *Organization Studies*, 11(1): 11–16.

Cameron, K. and Quinn, R. (1998) 'Organizational paradox and transformation', in R. Quinn and K. Cameron (eds), *Paradox and Transformation: Toward a Theory of Change in Organization and Management*. Cambridge, MA: Ballinger. pp. 1–18.

Camillus, J.C. (2008) 'Strategy as a wicked problem', *Harvard Business Review*, 86(5): 98–106.

Campbell, J. (1988) *The Power of Myth*. New York, NY: Doubleday.

Cantwell, J.A. (1989) *Technological Innovation and Multinational Corporations*. Oxford: Blackwell.

Carlin, W. and Mayer, C. (2003) 'Finance, investment, and growth', *Journal of Financial Economics*, 69: 191–226.

Capelli, P. (2009) 'The future of the US business model and the rise of the competitors', *Academy of Management Perspectives*, 23(2): 5–10.

Cappelli, P., Singh, H., Singh, J. and Useem, M. (2011) *The India Way: How India's Top Business Leaders are Revolutionizing Management*. Cambridge, MA: Harvard Business School Press.

Carlile, P.R. (2002) 'A pragmatic view of knowledge and boundaries: Boundary objects in new product development', *Organization Science*, 13(4): 442–455.

Carlile, P.R. (2004) 'Transferring, translating, and transforming: An integrative framework for managing knowledge across boundaries', *Organization Science*, 15(5): 555–568.

Carlsen, A., Clegg, S.R. and Gjersvik, R. (2012) *Idea Work*. Oslo: Cappellen Damm.

Carney, M. (1998) 'A management capacity constraint? Obstacles to the development of the overseas Chinese family business', *Asia Pacific Journal of Management*, 15: 137–162.

Carrillo, P. (2004) 'Managing knowledge: Lessons from the oil and gas sector', *Construction Management and Economics*, 22: 631–642.

Carroll, B., Levy, L. and Richmond, D. (2008) 'Leadership as practice: Challenging the competency paradigm', *Leadership*, 4: 363–380.

Carroll, L. (1946) *Through the Looking Glass*. New York, NY: Random House.

Carroll, W.K. (2010) *The Making of a Transnational Capitalist Class: Corporate Power in the 21st Century*. London: Zed Books.

Carter, C. (2013) 'The age of strategy: Strategy, organizations and society', *Business History*, 55(7): 1046–1057.

Carter, C., Clegg, S.R., Hogan, J. and Kornberger, M. (2003) 'The polyphonic spree: The case of the Liverpool dockers', *Industrial Relations*. 34(4): 290–304.

Carter, C., Clegg, S. and Kornberger, M. (2008) 'Strategy as practice', *Strategic Organization*, 6(1): 83–99.

Cartwright, S. and Cooper, C.L. (1993) 'The role of culture compatibility in successful organizational marriage', *Academy of Management Executive*, 7: 57–70.

Casciaro, T. and Piskorski, M.J. (2005) 'Power imbalance, mutual dependence, and constraint absorption: A closer look at resource dependence theory', *Administrative Science Quarterly*, 50(2): 167–199.

Casper, S. (2007) 'How do technology clusters emerge and become sustainable? Social network formation and inter-firm mobility within the San Diego biotechnology cluster', *Research Policy*, 36(4): 438–455.

Casson, M. (2005) 'Entrepreneurship and the theory of the firm', *Journal of Economic Behavior and Organization*, 58(2): 327–348.

Casson, M., Yeung, B., Basu, A. and Wadeson, N. (2006) *The Oxford Handbook of Entrepreneurship*. New York: Oxford University Press.

Castells, M. (1996) *The Rise of the Network Society. The Information Age: Economy, society and culture*, Vol. I. Cambridge, MA: Blackwell.

Castells, M. (2000) 'Materials for an exploratory theory of the network society', *British Journal of Sociology*, 51: 5–24.

Castells, M. (2009) *Communication Power*. Oxford: Oxford University Press.

Cavanagh, G.F., Moberg, D.J. and Velasquez, M. (1981) 'The ethics of organizational politics', *Academy of Management Review*, 6: 363–374.

Cespedes, F.V. (2014) 'Stop using battle metaphors in your company strategy', *Harvard Business Review*. Available at: https://hbr.org/2014/12/stop-using-battle-metaphors-in-your-company-strategy.

Chakravartty, P. and Downing, J.H.H. (2010) 'Media, technology, and the global financial crisis', *International Journal of Communication*, 4: 693–695.

Chamberlin, E.H. (1933) *The Differentiation of the Product: The Theory of Monopolistic Competition: A Re-orientation of the Theory of Value*. Cambridge, MA: Harvard University Press.

Chan, K.B. and Ng, B.K. (2000) 'Myths and misperceptions of ethnic Chinese capitalism', in K.B. Chan (ed.), *Chinese Business Networks: State Economy and Culture*. Singapore: Prentice Hall. pp. 286–302.

Chandler, A.D. (1962) *Strategy and Structure: Chapters in the History of the Industrial Enterprise*. Cambridge, MA: MIT Press.

Channon, D. (1973) *The Strategy and Structure of British Enterprise*. London: Macmillan.

Chappell, C., Rhodes, C., Tennant, M., Solomon, N. and Yates, L. (2003) *Reconstructing the Lifelong Learner*. London: Routledge.

Charan, R. and Tichy, N.M. (1998) *Every Business is a Growth Business*. New York: Times Books/Random House.

Charkham, J. (1994) *Keeping Good Company: A Study of Corporate Governance in Five Countries*. Oxford: Oxford University Press.

Chen, C.C. and Meindl, J.R. (1991) 'The construction of leadership images in the popular press: The case of Donald Burr and People Express', *Administrative Science Quarterly*, 36(4): 521–555.

Chesbrough, H.W. (2003) 'The era of open innovation', *Sloan Management Review*, 44: 35–41.

Chesbrough, H.W. (2006) *Open Business Models: How to Thrive in the New Innovation Landscape*. Boston, MA: Harvard Business School Press Books.

Chesbrough, H.W. and Appleyard, M.M. (2007) 'Open Innovation and Strategy', *California Management Review*, 50(1): 57–76.

Chesbourgh, H.W. and Rosenbloom, R.S. (2002) 'The role of the business model in capturing value from innovation: Evidence from Xerox corporation's technology spin-off companies', *Industrial and Corporate Change*, 11/3: 529–555.

Chesbrough, H.W. and Teece, D.J. (1996) 'When is virtual virtuous? Organizing for innovation', *Harvard Business Review*, 74(1): 65–73.

Chia, R. (2010) 'Rediscovering becoming: Insights from an oriental perspective on process organization studies', in T. Hernes and S. Maitlis (eds), *Process, Sensemaking, and Organizing*. Oxford: Oxford University Press. pp. 112–139.

Chia, R. and Holt, R. (2007) 'Wisdom as learned ignorance', in E.H. Kessler and J.R. Bailey (eds), *Handbook of Organizational and Managerial Wisdom*. Thousand Oaks: Sage. pp. 505–526.

Chia, R. and Holt, R. (2009) *Strategy without Design: The Silent Efficacy of Indirect Action*. Cambridge: Cambridge University Press.

Chia, R. and Mackay, B. (2007) 'Post-processual challenges for the emerging strategy-as-practice perspectives; Discovering strategy in the logic of practice', *Human Relations*, 60(1): 217–242.

Child, J. (1972) 'Organizational structure, environment, and performance: The role of strategic choice', *Sociology*, 6: 1–22.

Child, J. (2009) 'Context, comparison, and methodology in Chinese management research', *Management and Organization Review*, 5(1): 57–73.

Child, J. and Faulkner, D. (1998) *Strategies of Co-operation: Managing Alliances, Networks, and Joint Ventures*. New York: Oxford University.

Child, J. and Yan, Y. (1999) 'Investment and control in international joint ventures: The case of China,' *Journal of World Business*, 34(1): 3–15.

Child, J., Faulkner, D. and Tallman, S. (2005) *Cooperative Strategy: Managing Alliances, Networks and Joint Ventures*. Oxford, UK: Oxford University Press.

Christensen, C. (1997) *The Innovator's Dilemma*. Boston, MA: Harvard Business School Press.

Christensen, C.M. and Bower, J.L. (1996) 'Customer power, strategic investment, and the failure of leading firms', *Strategic Management Journal*, 17: 197–218.

Christensen, S.L. (2008) 'The role of law in models of ethical behaviour', *Journal of Business Ethics*, 77(4): 451–461.

Cialdini, R., Trost, M. and Newsom, J. (1995) 'Preference for consistency: The development of a valid measure and the discovery of surprising behavioral implications', *Journal of Personality and Social Psychology*, 69: 318–328.

Cioffi, J.W. (2000) 'Governing globalization? The state, law, and structural change in corporate governance', *Journal of Law and Society*, 27(4): 572–600.

Clark, D.N. (1997) 'Strategic management tool usage: A comparative study', *Strategic Change*, 6(7): 417–427.

Clark, E. and Geppert, M. (2006) 'Socio-political processes in international management in post-socialist contexts: Knowledge, learning and transnational institution building', *Journal of International Management*, 12(3): 340–357.

Clark, K.B. and Fujimoto, T. (1991) *Product Development Performance*. Boston, MA: Harvard Business School Press.

Clark, T. and Fincham, R. (2002) *Critical Consulting: New Perspectives on the Management Advice Industry*. Oxford: Blackwell.

Clarke, C. (2016) *Ethics and Economic Governance: Using Adam Smith to Understand the Global Financial Crisis*. London: Routledge.

Clarke, T. (2007) *International Corporate Governance: A Comparative Approach*, Vol. 1. London: Routledge.

Clarke, T. and Boersma, M. (2015) 'The governance of global value chains: Unresolved human rights, environmental and ethical dilemmas in the apple supply chain', *Journal of Business Ethics*, 122(1): 1–21.

Clausewitz, C.V. (1943) *On War* (trans. O. Jolles). Chicago: University of Chicago Press. Available at: www.clausewitz.com/readings/OnWar1873/TOC.htm

Clegg, S.R. (1989) *Frameworks of Power*. London: Sage.

Clegg, S.R. (1990) *Modern Organizations: Organization Studies in the Postmodern World*. London: Sage.

Clegg, S. (2011) 'Under reconstruction: Modern bureaucracies', in S. Clegg, M. Harris and H.Hopfl (eds), *Managing Modernity: Beyond Bureaucracy*. Oxford: Oxford University Press. pp. 202–229.

Clegg, S.R. (2014) 'Reflections: Why old social theory might still be useful', *Journal of Change Management*, 15(1): 8–18.

Clegg, S.R. and Carter, C. (2009) 'Globalization and macro-organizational behaviour', in S.R. Clegg and C. Cooper (eds), *Handbook of Macro-Organizational Behaviour*. London: Sage. pp. 496–508.

Clegg, S.R. and Courpasson, D. (2004) 'Political hybrids: Tocquevillean views on project organizations', *Journal of Management Studies*, 41: 525–547.

Clegg, S.R. and Cunha, M.P. (forthcoming) 'Organizational dialectics', in M.W. Lewis, W.K. Smith, P. Jarzabkowski and A. Langley (eds), *The Oxford Handbook of Organizational Paradox: Approaches to Plurality, Tensions, and Contradictions*. Oxford: Oxford University Press.

Clegg, S.R. and Hardy, C. (1996) 'Representations', in S.R. Clegg, C. Hardy and W. Nord (eds), *Handbook of Organization Studies*. London: Sage. pp. 676–708.

Clegg, S.R. and Pitelis, C.N. (2016) 'An efficiency/power view and co-creating strategy practices', *Social Science Research Network*, 17 March. Available at: http://papers.ssrn.com/sol3/papers.cfm?abstract_id=2749160.

Clegg, S.R., Pitsis, T., Rura-Polley, T. and Marosszeky, M. (2002a) 'Governmentality matters: Designing an alliance culture of inter-organizational collaboration for managing projects', *Organization Studies*, 23(3): 317–337.

Clegg, S.R., Cunha, J.V. and Cunha, M.P. (2002b) 'Management paradoxes: A relational view', *Human Relations*, 55(5): 483–503.

Clegg, S., Courpasson, D. and Phillips, N. (2006) *Power and Organizations*. London: Sage.

Clegg S.R., Kornberger, M. and Rhodes, C. (2007) 'Business Ethics as Practice', *British Journal of Management*, 18(2): 107–122.

Clegg, S.R., Carter, C., Kornberger, M. and Schweitzer, J. (2011) *Strategy: Theory and Practice* (1st edn) London: Sage.

Clegg, S.R., Flyvbjerg, B. and Haugaard, M. (2014) 'Reflections on phronetic social science: A dialogue between Stewart Clegg, Bent Flyvbjerg and Mark Haugaard', *Journal of Political Power*, 6(2): 341–347.

Clegg, S.R., Kornberger, M. and Pitsis, T.S. (2015) *Managing and Organizations: An Introduction to Theory and Practice*. London: Sage.

Clinebell, S.K. and Clinebell, J.M. (2008) 'The tension in business education between academic rigor and real-world relevance: The role of executive professors', *The Academy of Management Learning and Education*, 7(1): 99–107.

Coase, R. (1937) 'The nature of the firm', *Economica*, 4: 386–405.

Coase, R. (1991) 'The nature of the firm: Influence', in O. Williamson and S.Winter (eds), *The Nature of the Firm: Origins, Evolution and Development*. Oxford: Oxford University Press.

Coch, L. and French, J.R. (1948) 'Overcoming resistance to change', *Human Relations*, 1(4): 512–532.

Coff, R.W. (1997) 'Human assets and management dilemmas: Coping with hazards on the road to resource-based theory', *Academy of Management Review*, 22/2: 374–402.

Coff, R.W. (1999) 'When competitive advantage doesn't lead to performance: The resource-based view and stakeholder bargaining power', *Organization Science*, 10/2: 119–131.

Coffee, J.C. Jr. (2001) 'Do norms matter? A crosscountry evaluation', *University of Pennsylvania Law Review*, 149(6): 2151–2177.

Cohen, M.D., March, J.G. and Olsen, J.P. (1972) 'A garbage can model of organizational choice', *Administrative Science Quarterly*, 17(1): 1–25.

Cohen, M.D., Burkhart, R., Dosi, G., Egidi, M., Marengo, L., Warglien, M. and Winter, S. (1996) 'Routines and other recurring action patterns of organizations: Contemporary research issues', *Industrial and Corporate Change*, 5(3): 653–698.

Coleman, J.S. (1988) 'Social capital in the creation of human capital', *American Journal of Sociology*, 94 (Supplement): S95–S120.

Collier, J. and Esteban, R. (2007) 'Corporate social responsibility and employee commitment', *Business Ethics: A European Review*, 16(1): 19–33.

Collinbridge, D. and Douglas, G. (1984) 'Three models of policy making: Expert advice in the control of environmental lead', *Social Studies of Science*, 14(3): 343–370.

Collinson, D.L. (2003) 'Identities and insecurities: Selves at work', *Organization*, (10)3: 527–547.

Collinson, D.L. and Ackroyd, S. (2005) 'Resistance, misbehaviour and dissent', in S. Ackroyd, P. Thompson, R. Batt and P.S. Tolbert (eds), *The Oxford Handbook of Work and Organization*. Oxford, UK: Oxford University Press. pp. 305–326.

Collis, D.J. and Montgomery, C. (1998) 'Creating corporate advantage', *Harvard Business Review*, 76/3: 70–83.

Congleton, R.D. (2009) 'On the political economy of the financial crisis and bailout of 2008–2009', *Public Choice*, 140 (3–4): 287–317.

Cook, J. and Brown, J.S. (2002) 'Bridging epistemologies: The generative dance between organizational knowledge and organizational knowing', in S. Little, P. Quintas and T. Ray (eds), *Managing Knowledge*. London: Sage. pp. 68–101.

Cooke, B. (1999) 'Writing the left out of management theory: The historiography of the management of change', *Organization*, 6(1): 81–105.

Cool, K., Dierickx, I. and Jemison, D. (1989) 'Business strategy, market structure and risk-return relationships: A structural approach', *Strategic Management Journal*, 10(6): 507–522.

Coombs, R. and Miles, I. (2000)' Innovation, measurement and services: The new problematique', in S.J. Metcalf and I. Miles (eds), *Innovation Systems in the Service Sectors: Measurement and Case Study Analysis*. Boston, MA: Kluwer. pp. 85–104.

Contractor, F.J. and Lorange, P. (1988) 'Why should firms cooperate? The strategy and economics basis for cooperative ventures', *Cooperative strategies in international business*, pp 3–30.

Coriat, B. and Weinstein, O. (2002) 'Organizations, firms, and institutions in the generation of innovation', *Research Policy*, 32(2): 273–290.

Cornelissen, J.P., Holt, R. and Zundel, M. (2011) 'The role of analogy and metaphor in the framing and legitimization of strategic change', *Organization Studies*, 32(12): 1701–1716.

Courpasson, D. (2000) 'Managerial strategies of domination; Power in soft bureaucracies', *Organization Studies*, 21(1): 141–161.

Courpasson, D. and Clegg, S. (2012) 'The polyarchic bureaucracy: Cooperative resistance in the construction of a new political structure of organizations', in D. Courpasson, D. Golsorki and J. Sallaz (eds), *Rethinking Power in Organizations, Institutions and Markets*, Research in the Sociology of Organizations, 34: 55–80.

Courpasson, D. and Dany, F. (2009) 'Cultures of resistance', in S.R. Clegg and M. Haugaard (eds), *The Sage Handbook on Power*. London: Sage. pp. 332–348.

Courpasson, D., Dany, F. and Clegg, S.R. (2012) 'Resisters at work: Generating productive resistance in the workplace', *Organization Science*, 23(3): 801–819.

Cowling, K. and Waterson, M. (1976) 'Price-cost margins and market structure', *Economica, New Series*, 43(171): 267–274.

Cray, D., Mallory, G., Butler, R., Hickson, D. and Wilson, D. (1991) 'Explaining decision processes', *Journal of Management Studies*, 28(3): 207–322.

Crenson, M. (1971) *The Un-Politics of Air Pollution*. London: Johns Hopkins University Press.

Crick, B. (2004) *Essays on Citizenship*. New York: Continuum Books.

Crombie, N.A. and Geekie, T.J. (2010) 'The levers of control in the boardroom', 6th Asia Pacific Interdisciplinary Research in Accounting Conference (APIRA 2010), Sydney, Australia.

Crouch, C. (2009) 'Privatised Keynesianism: An unacknowledged policy regime', *British Journal of Politics and International Relations*, 11(3): 382–399.

Crozier, M. and Friedberg, E. (1980) *Actors and Systems: The Politics of Collective Action*. Chicago: University of Chicago Press.

Cummings, S. and Daellenbach, U. (2009) 'A guide to the future of strategy? The history of long range planning', *Long Range Planning*, 42: 234–263.

Cummings, S., Bridgman, T. and Brown, K.G. (2016) 'Unfreezing change as three steps: Rethinking Kurt Lewin's legacy for change management', *Human Relations*, 69(1): 33–60.

Cummins, E. (2000) The Pakistan soccer ball stitching industry (Public Document). Islamabad: Save the Children Fund.

Cunha, M.P. (2004) 'Time traveling: Organizational foresight as temporal reflexivity', in H. Tsoukas and J. Shepherd (eds), *Managing the Future: Foresight in the Knowledge Economy*. Malden, MA: Blackwell. pp. 133–150.

Cunha, M.P. and Da Cunha, J.V. (2008) 'Managing improvisation in cross cultural virtuous teams', *International Journal of Cross Cultural Management*, 1(2): 187–208.

Cunha, M.P. and Tsoukas, H. (2015) 'Reforming the State: Understanding the vicious circles of reform', *European Management Journal*, 33(4): 225–229.

Cunha, M.P., Fortes, A., Rego, A., Gomes, E. and Rodrigues, F. (2015) 'Leadership, paradox, and contingency', presented at the *31st EGOS Colloquium*, Athens, 2–4 July.

Cunha, M.P., Clegg, S.R., Costa, C., Leite, A.P., Rego, A., Simpson, A.V., de Sousa, M.O., and Sousa, M. (2016) 'Gemeinschaft in the midst of Gesellschaft? Love as an organizational virtue', *Journal of Management, Spirituality & Religion*, DOI:10.1080/14766086.2016.1184100.

Cusamano, M.A. and Gawer, A. (2002) 'The elements of platform leadership', *Sloan Management Review*, 43: 51–58.

Cyert, R.M. and March, J.G. (eds) (1963) *A Behavioral Theory of the Firm* (2nd edn, 1992). Englewood Cliffs, NJ: Prentice Hall.

Czarniawska, B. (1997) *Narrating the Organization*. Chicago: Chicago University Press.

Czarniawska, B. and Sevón, G. (2005) *Global Ideas: How Ideas, Objects, and Practices Travel in the Global Economy*. Copenhagen, Denmark: CBS Press.

Czarniawska-Joerges, B. and Sevón, G. (1996) *Translating Organizational Change*. Berlin: de Gruyter.

D'Aveni, R. (1994) *Hypercompetition*. New York: Free Press.

Daft, R.L. and Lewin, A.Y. (1993) 'Where are the theories for the "new" organizational forms? An editorial essay', *Organization Science*, 16: 332–343.

Daft, R.L. and Weick, K.E. (1984) 'Towards a model of organizations as interpretation systems', *Academy of Management Review*, 9(2): 284–295.

Dahl, R.A. (1957) 'The concept of power', *Behavioral Science*, 2(3): 201–215.

Damanpour, F. (1991) 'Organizational innovation: A meta-analysis of effects of determinants and moderators', *Academy of Management Journal*, 34(3): 555–590.

Danneels, E. (2002) 'The dynamics of product innovation and firm competences', *Strategic Management Journal*, 23(12): 1095–1122.

Darwin, J. (2007) *After Tamerlane: The Rise and Fall of Global Empires 1400–2000*. London: Penguin.

Das, T. and Teng, B. (1999) 'Managing risks in strategic alliances', *Academy of Management Executive*, 13(4): 50–62.

David, R.J. and Han, S-K. (2004) 'A systematic assessment of the empirical support for transaction cost economics', *Strategic Management Journal*, 25: 39–58.

Davies, J. (2009) *Managed by the Markets: How Finance Re-shaped America*. Oxford: Oxford University Press.

Davis, A. and Mishel, L. (2014) 'CEO pay continues to rise as typical workers are paid less', *Economic Policy Institute*, 12 June. Available at: www.epi.org/publication/ceo-pay-continues-to-rise/ (accessed 17 May 2016).

Davis, E.P. and Steil, B. (2001) *Institutional Investors*. Cambridge, MA: MIT Press.

Davis, G.F. (1991) 'Agents without principles? The spread of the poison pill through the inter-corporate network', *Administrative Science Quarterly*, 36: 583–590.

Davis, G.F. (2016a) 'What might replace the modern corporation? Uberization and the web page enterprise', *Seattle University Law Review*, 39: 501–515.

Davis, G.F. (2016b) *The Vanishing American Corporation*. Oakland, CA: Berrett-Koehler Publications.

Davis, G.F. and Useem, M. (2002) 'top management, company directors, and corporate control', in A. Pettigrew, H. Thomas and R. Whittington (eds), *Handbook of Strategy and Management*. London: Sage. pp. 233–259.

Davis, G.F., Yoo, M. and. Baker, W.E. (2003) 'The small world of the American corporate elite, 1982–2001', *Strategic Organization*, 1(3): 301–326.

Davis, M. with Troupe, Q. (1989) *Miles: The Autobiography*. New York, NY: Simon & Schuster.

Davis, S.M. and Lawrence, J. (1977) *Matrix*. Reading, MA: Addison-Wesley.

Dawkins, P., Harris, M. and King, S. (eds) with a foreword by P.K. Ruthven (1999) *How Big Business Performs: Private Performance and Public Policy*. Allen and Unwin, in association with the Melbourne Institute of Applied Economics and Social Research.

Dawley, S. (2007) 'Fluctuating Rounds of inward investment in peripheral regions: Semiconductors in the North East of England', *Economic Geography*, 83(1): 51–73.

Dawson, P. (2003) *Understanding Organizational Change: The Contemporary Experience of People at Work*. London: Sage.

de La Ville, V.I. and Mounoud, E. (2010) 'A narrative approach to strategy as practice: Strategy making from texts and narratives', in D. Golsorkhi et al. (eds), *Cambridge Handbook of Strategy as Practice*. Cambridge: Cambridge University Press. pp. 183–198.

de Onzoño, S.I. (2011) *The Learning Curve: How Business Schools are Re-inventing Education*. London: Palgrave.

de Rond, M. (2003) *Strategic Alliances as Social Facts: Business, Biotechnology, and Intellectual History*. Cambridge University Press: Cambridge, UK.

Deal, T.E. and Kennedy, A.A. (1982) *Corporate Cultures: The Rites and Rituals of Corporate Life*. Reading, MA: Addison-Wesley.

Deegan, C. (2002) 'The legitimising effect of social and environmental disclosures – A theoretical foundation', *Accounting, Auditing and Accountability Journal*, 15(3): 282–311.

Deegan, C., Rankin, M. and Tobin, J. (2002) 'An examination of the corporate social and environmental disclosures of BHP from 1983–1997: A test of legitimacy theory', *Accounting, Auditing and Accountability Journal*, 15(3): 312–343.

Delgado-Gomez, J., Ramirez-Aleson, M. and Espitia-Escuer, M. (2004) 'Intangible resources as a key factor in the internationalisation of Spanish firms', *Journal of Economic Behavior and Organization*, 53(4): 477–487.

Demil, B. and Lecocq, X. (2006) 'Neither market nor hierarchy nor network: The emergence of bazaar governance', *Organization Studies*, 27: 1447–1466.

Demsetz, H. (1973) 'Industry structure, market rivalry, and public policy', *Journal of Law and Economics*, 16: 1–9.

Denis, J.-L., Lamothe, L. and Langley, A. (2001) 'The dynamics of collective leadership and strategic change in pluralistic organizations', *The Academy of Management Journal*, 44(4): 809–837.

Denis, J.-L., Langley, A. and Rouleau, L. (2007) 'Strategizing in pluralistic contexts: Rethinking theoretical frames', *Human Relations*, 60(1): 179–215.

DeSarbo, W.S. and Grewal, R. (2007) 'An alternative efficient representation of demand-based competitive asymmetry', *Strategic Management Journal*, 28(7): 755–766.

DeSarbo, W.S. and Grewal, R. (2008) 'Hybrid strategic groups', *Strategic Management Journal*, 29(3): 293–317.

DeSarbo, W.S., Grewal, R. and Wang, R. (2009) 'Dynamic strategic groups: Deriving spatial evolutionary paths', *Strategic Management Journal*, 30(13): 1420–1439.

De Onzono, S. I. (2011) *The learning curve: How business schools are re-inventing education.* Springer.

Diani, M. (2000) 'Social movement networks virtual and real', *Information, Communication and Society*, 3(3): 386–401.

Dicken, P. (2007a) 'Economic globalization: Corporations', in G. Ritzer (ed, *The Blackwell Companion to Globalization*. Oxford: Blackwell. pp. 291–306.

Dicken, P. (2007b) *Global Shift: Mapping the Changing Contours of the World Economy*, 5th edn. Thousand Oaks, CA:Sage.

Diefenbach, T. (2009) *Management and the Dominance of Managers: An Inquiry into Why and How Managers Rule Our Organizations*. London: Routledge.

Dierickx, I. and Cool, K. (1989) 'Asset stock accumulation and the sustainability of competitive advantage: reply', *Management Science,* 35(12).

DiMaggio, P. and Powell, W. (1983) 'The iron cage revisited: Institutional isomorphism and collective rationality in organizational fields', *American Sociological Review*, 48: 147–160.

Djelic, M.-L. (1998) *Exporting the American Model: The Post-war Transformation of European Business*. Oxford: Oxford University Press.

Dobb, M. (1973) *Theories of Value and Distribution since Adam Smith: Ideology and Economic Theory*. Cambridge: Cambridge University Press.

Dobbs, R., Koller, T., Ramaswamy, S., Woetzel, J., Manyika, J., Krishnan, R. and Andreula, N. (2015) 'Playing to win: The new global competition for corporate profits', *McKinsey Global Institute*, September. Available at: www.mckinsey.com/business-functions/strategy-and-corporate-finance/our-insights/the-new-global-competition-for-corporate-profits (accessed 12 March 2016).

Dobusch, L. (2012) 'The digital public domain: relevance and regulation', *Information & Communications Technology Law*, 21(2): 179–202.

Dogan, M. (2003) *Elite Configurations at the Apex of Power*. Leiden-Boston: Brill.

Doh, J.P., Rodriguez, P., Uhlenbruck, K., Collins, J. and Eden, L. (2003) 'Coping with corruption in foreign markets', *Academy of Management Executive*, 17(3): 114–127.

Doig, S J., Ritter, R.C., Speckhals, K. and Woodson, D. (2001) 'Has outsourcing gone too far?', *The McKinsey Quarterly*, 4: 24–37.

Donaghey, J., Reinecke, J., Niforou, C. and Lawson, B. (2013) 'From employment relations to consumption relations: Balancing labor governance in global supply chains', *Human Resource Management*, 53(2): 229–252.

Donaghey, J., Cullinane, N., Dundon, T. and Wilkinson, A. (2011) 'Reconceptualising employee silence: Problems and prognosis', *Work, Employment and Society*, 25: 51–67.

Donaldson, L. (1987) 'Strategy and structural adjustment to regain fit and performance: In defence of contingency theory', *Journal of Management Studies*, 24(1): 1–24.

Donaldson, L. (1999) *Performance-driven Organizational Change: The Organizational Portfolio*. Thousand Oaks, CA: Sage.

Donaldson, L. (2000) 'Design strategy to fit strategy', in E. Locke (ed.), *Handbook of Principles of Organizational Behaviour*. Oxford: Blackwell. pp. 291–303.

Donaldson, L. (2001) *The Contingency Theory of Organizations*. Thousand Oaks, CA: Sage.

Donaldson, R. (2000) *13 Days* [Film]. Hollywood, Los Angeles CA: New Line Cinema, Tig Productions and Beacon Pictures.

Donaldson, T. and Dunfee, T.W. (1995) 'Towards a unified conception of business ethics: Integrative social contracts theory', *Academy of Management Review*, 19(2): 252–275.

Dörrenbächer, C. and Gammelgaard, J. (2006) 'Subsidiary role development: The effect of micro-political headquarters subsidiary negotiations on the product, market and value-added scope of foreign owned subsidiaries', *Journal of International Management*, 12(3): 266–268.

Dörrenbächer, C. and Gepert, M. (2009) 'Micro-political strategies and strategizing in multinational corporations: The case of subsidiary mandate change', in L.A. Costannzo and R.B. MacKay (eds), *Handbook of Research on Strategy and Foresight*. Cheltenham: Edward Elgar. pp. 200–218.

Dorst, K. (2015) *Frame Innovation*. Boston: MIT Press.

Dosi, G. (1982) 'Technological paradigms and technological trajectories. A suggested interpretation of the determinants and directions of technical change', *Research Policy*, 11(3): 147–162.

Dosi, G. (1995) 'Hierarchies, markets and power: Some foundational issues on the nature of contemporary economic organisations', *Industrial and Corporate Change*, 4(1): 1–19.

Dosi, G. and Marengo, L. (2007) 'On the evolutionary and behavioral theories of organizations: A tentative roadmap', *Organization Science*, 18(3): 491–502.

Dosi, G., Faillo, M. and Marengo, L. (2008) 'Organizational capabilities, patterns of knowledge accumulation and governance structures in business firms: An introduction', *Organization Studies*, 29(8/9): 1165–1185.

Dosi, G., Nelson, R. and Winter, S. (eds) (2000) *The Nature and Dynamics of Organizational Capabilities*. Oxford: Oxford University Press.

Dosi, G., Nelson, R. and Winter, S. (eds) (2010) *The Nature and Dynamics of Organizational Capabilities*. Oxford: Oxford University Press.

Dougherty, D. (2004) 'Organizing practices in services: Capturing practice-based knowledge for innovation', *Strategic Organization*, 2(1): 35–64.

Dougherty, D. (2006) 'Organizing for innovation in the 21st Century', in S.R. Clegg, C. Hardy, T.B. Lawrence and W.R. Nord (eds), *Handbook of Organization Studies* (2nd edn). London: Sage. pp. 598–617.

Dougherty, D. and Hardy, C. (1996) 'Sustained product innovation in large, mature organizations: Overcoming innovation-to-organization problems', *Academy of Management Journal*, 39(5): 1120–1153.

Dougherty, P. (2008) 'Bridging social constraint and social action to design organizations for innovation', *Organization Studies*, 29(3): 415–434.

Doz, Y.L. (1996) 'The evolution of cooperation in strategic alliances: Initial conditions or learning processes', *Strategic Management Journal*, 17(1): 55–83.

Doz, Y.L. and Hamel, G. (1998) Alliance advantage: The art of creating value through partnering. Harvard Business Press.

Drejer, I. (2004) 'Identifying innovation in surveys of services: A Schumpeterian perspective', *Research Policy*, 33(3): 551–562.

Dundon, T., Wilkinson, A., Marchington, M. and Ackers, P. (2004) 'The meanings and purpose of employee voice', *International Journal of Human Resource Management* 15(6): 1149–1170.

Dunning, J.H. (1980) 'Toward an eclectic theory of international production: Some empirical tests', *Journal of International Business Studies*, 11(1): 9–31.

Dunning, J.H. (1981) *International Production and the Multinational Enterprise*. London: Allen & Unwin.

Dunning, J. (1993) *Multinational Enterprises and the Global Economy*. Wokingham: Addison-Wesley.

Dunning, J.H. (1997) *Alliance Capitalism and Global Business*. Routledge: London.

Dunning, J.H. (2001) 'The eclectic (OLI) paradigm of international production: Past, present and future', *Int. J. Econ. Bus.*, 8(2): 173–190.

Dunning, J.H. and Lundan, S.M. (2009) 'The MNE as a creator, fashioner and respondent to institutional change', in S. Collinson and G. Morgan (eds), *The Multinational Firm*. Oxford: Blackwell. pp. 93–115.

Dunning, J.H. and Narula, R. (eds) (1996) *Foreign Direct Investment and Governments: Catalysts for Economic Restructuring*. London: Routledge.

Dunphy, D.C. and Stace, D.A. (1988) 'Transformational and coercive strategies for planned organizational change: Beyond the OD model', *Organization Studies*, 9(3): 317–334.

Dunphy, D. and Stace, D. (1993) The strategic management of corporate change, *Human relations*, 46(8): 905–920.

Durcikova, A. and Gray, P. (2009) 'How knowledge validation processes affect knowledge contribution', *Journal of Management Information Systems*, 25/4: 81–107.

Durisin, B. and Puzone, F. (2009) 'Maturation of corporate governance research, 1993–2007: An assessment', *Corporate Governance: An International Review*, 17(3): 266–291.

Dussauge, P. and Garrette, B. (1999) *Cooperative Strategy: Competing Successfully through Strategic Alliances*. Chichester, UK: Wiley.

Dutton, J. E. and Dukerich, J. E. (1991) Keeping an Eye on the Mirror: Image and Identity in Organizational Adaptation, *Academy of Management Journal*. 34(3): 517–44.

Drucker, P. F. (1988) The Coming of the New Organization, *Harvard Business Review*, 66(1): 45–53.

Dyas, G. and Thanheiser, H. (1976) *The Emerging European Enterprise*. London: Macmillan.

Dyer, J.H. and Nobeoka, K. (2000) 'Creating and managing a high-performance knowledge-sharing network: The Toyota case', *Strategic Management Journal*, 21: 345–367.

Dyer, J.H. and Singh, H. (1998) 'The relational view: Cooperative strategies and sources of interorganizational competitive advantage', *Academy of Management Review*, 23(4),: 660–679.

Dyer, J.H., Kale, P. and Singh, H. (2001) 'How to make strategic alliances work', *Sloan Management Review*, 42(4): 37–43.

Dylan, B. (1966) Absolutely Sweet Marie on *Blonde on Blonde* [LP]. Columbia Records.

Easterly, W. and Levine R. (1997) 'Africa's growth tragedy: Policies and ethnic divisions', *Quarterly Journal of Economics*, 112(4): 1203–1250.

Eccles, R.G. (1985) *The Transfer Pricing Problem: A Theory for Practice*. New York: Lexington Books.

Eccles, R.G. and Crane, D.B. (1987) 'Managing through networks in investment banking', *California Management Review*, 30(1): 176–195.

Eccles, T. (1994) *Succeeding with Change: Implementing Action-driven Strategies*. London: McGraw-Hill.

Economist, The (2015) 'Schumpeter: Death and transfiguration: The golden age of the Western corporation may be coming to an end', 19 September. Available at: www.economist.com/news/business/21665073-golden-age-western-corporation-may-be-coming-end-death-and-transfiguration?cid1=cust/ednew/n/n/n/20160312n/owned/n/n/nwl/n/n/n/email (accessed 12 March 2016).

Eden, L. and Molot, M.A. (2002) 'Insiders, outsiders and host country bargains', *Journal of International Management*, 8(4): 359–388.

Edwards, P.K. and Bélanger, J. (2009) 'The MNC as a contested terrain', in S. Collinson and G. Morgan (eds), *Images of the Multinational*. Oxford: Wiley. pp. 193–216.

Edwards, R. (1979) *Contested Terrain: The Transformation of the Workplace in the Twentieth Century*. New York: Basic Books.

Eisenberg, H. (1997) 'Reengineering and dumbsizing: Mismanagement of the knowledge resource', *Quality Progress*, 30(5): 57–64.

Eisenhardt, K. (1999) 'Strategy as decision-making', *Sloan Management Review*, 40(30): 65–92.

Eisenhardt, K. and Martin, J.A. (2000) 'Dynamic capabilities: What are they?', *Strategic Management Journal*, 21(10–11): 1105–1121.

Eisenhardt, K.M. and Schoonhoven, C.B. (1996) 'Resource-based view of strategic alliance formation: Strategic and social effects in entrepreneurial firms', *Organization Science*, 7: 136–150.

Eisenhardt, K. and Zbaracki, M. (1992) 'Strategic decision-making', *Strategic Management Journal*, 13(Special Issue): 17–37.

Elger, T. and Smith, C. (1994) 'Global Japanization? Convergence and competition in the organization of the labour process', *Global japanization*, pp. 31–59.

Ellis, C. (1996) 'Making strategic alliances succeed', *Harvard Business Review*, 74(4): 8–9.

Emirbayer, M. and Williams, E.M. (2005) 'Bourdieu and social work', *Social Service Review*, 79(4): 689–724.

Eriksson, P. and Lehtimäki, H. (2001) 'Strategy rhetoric in city management: How the presumptions of classic strategic management live on?', *Scandinavian Journal of Management*, 17(2): 201–223.

Erkama, N. and Vaara, E. (2010) 'Struggles over legitimacy in global organizational restructuring: A rhetorical perspective on legitimation strategies and dynamics in a shutdown case', *Organization Studies*, 31(7): 813–839.

Espeland, W. and Saunder, M. (2007) Rankings and Reactivity: How Public Measures Recreate Social Worlds, *American Journal of Sociology*, 113(1): 1–40.

Estabrooks, M. (1995) *Electronic Technology, Corporate Strategy, and World Transformation*. Westport, CT: Quorum

Ethisphere (2014) *World's Most Ethical Companies Ranking*. Available at: http://ethisphere.com/worlds-most-ethical/wme-honorees (accessed 22 April 2014).

Evans, P. (1995) *Embedded Autonomy: States and Industrial Transformation*. Princeton, NJ: Princeton University Press.

Evans, P. and Rauch, R. (1999) 'Bureaucracy and growth: A cross-national analysis of the effects of "Weberian" state structures on economic growth', *American Sociological Review*, 64(5): 748–765.

Evans, P. (2000) 'International flavour – Noma', 11 May [online] http://www.lifestylefood.com.au/articles/international-flavour-noma.aspx, (accessed 27 October 2016).

Ewing, J. (2015) *Volkswagen Says 11 Million Cars Worldwide are Affected in Diesel Deception*. Available at: www.nytimes.com/2015/09/23/business/international/volkswagen-diesel-car-scandal.html?_r=0 (accessed 14 October 2015).

Ezzamel, M. and Burns, J. (2005) 'Professional competition, economic value added and management control strategies', *Organization Studies*, 26(5): 755–777.

Ezzamel, M. and Willmott, H. (2004) 'Rethinking strategy: Contemporary perspectives and debates', *European Management Review*, 1(1): 43–48.

Ezzamel, M. and Willmott, H. (2008) 'Strategy as discourse in a global retailer: A supplement to rationalist and interpretive accounts', *Organization Studies*, 29(2): 191–217.

Fagerberg, J. (2005) 'Innovation: A guide to the literature', in J. Fagerberg, D.C. Mowery and R.R. Nelson (eds), *The Oxford Handbook of Innovation*. Oxford: Oxford University Press. pp. 1–28.

Fagre, N. and Wells, L.T. (1982) 'Bargaining power of multinations and host governments', *Journal of International Business Studies*, 13(2): 9–24.

Fairhurst, G.T. (2010) *The Power of Framing: Creating the Language of Leadership*. London: John Wiley & Sons.

Fama, E.F. (1980) 'Agency problems and the theory of the firm', *Journal of Political Economy*, 88: 288–307.

Fama, E.F. and Jensen, M.C. (1983a) 'Agency problems and residual claims', *Journal of Law and Economics*, 26: 327–349.

Fama, E F. and Jensen, M.C. (1983b) 'Separation of ownership and control', *Journal of Law and Economics*, 26: 301–325.

Farjoun, M. (2016) 'Contradictions, dialectics and paradoxes', in A. Langley and H. Tsoukas (eds), *The Sage Handbook of Process Organization Studies*. London: Sage.

Faulkes, S. (2009) *A Week in December*. London: Hutchinson.

Faulkner, D. (1988) 'Portfolio matrices', in V. Ambrosini, G. Johnson and K. Scholes (eds), *Exploring Techniques of Analysis and Evolution in Strategic Management*. Harlow: Pearson. pp. 205–218.

Faulkner, D. and Campbell, A. (eds) (2003) *The Oxford Handbook of Strategy*. Oxford: Oxford University Press.

Fauré, B. and Rouleau, L. (2011) 'The strategic competence of accountants and middle managers in budget making', *Accounting, Organizations and Society*, 36: 167–182.

Fei, X.T. (1992) *From the Soil: The Foundations of Chinese Society* (trans., introduction and epilogue, G.G. Hamilton and W. Zheng). Berkeley, CA: University of California Press.

Feldman, M.S. and Orlikowski, W.J. (2011) 'Theorizing practice and practicing theory', *Organization Science*, 22(5): 1240–1253.

Felin, T. and Hesterly, W.S. (2007) 'The knowledge-based view, nested heterogeneity, and new value creation: Philosophical considerations on the locus of knowledge', *Academy of Management Review*, 32/1: 195–218.

Fenton, C. and Langley, A. (2011) 'Strategy as practice and the narrative turn', *Organization Studies*, 32(9): 1171–1196.

Ferner, A., Edwards, T. and Tempel, A. (2012) 'Power, institutions and the cross-national transfer of employment practices in multinationals', *Human Relations*, 65(2): 163–187.

Ferrill, A. (1966) 'Herodotus and the strategy and tactics of the invasion of Xerxes', *The American Historical Review*, 72(1): 102–115.

Fiegenbaum, A. and Thomas, H. (1990) 'Strategic groups and performance: The US insurance industry, 1970–1984', *Strategic Management Journal*, 11(3): 197–215.

Financial Times, 17 May 2000.

Fincham, R. (1999) 'The consultant–client relationship: Critical perspectives on the management of organizational change', *Journal of Management Studies*, 36(3): 335–351.

Fincher, D. (2010) *The Social Network* [Film]. New York: Columbia.

Fineman, S. (1996) 'Emotion and organizing', in S. Clegg, C. Hardy and W. Nord (eds), *Handbook of Organization Studies*. London: Sage. pp. 543–564.

Fiol, C.M. and Lyles, M.A. (1985) 'Organizational learning', *Academy of Management Review*, 10: 803–813.

Fischer, K. and Schot, J. (1993) *Environmental Strategies for Industry: International Perspectives on Research Needs and Policy Implications*. Washington DC: Island Press.

Fischli, I. (1996) 'Outsourcing: A new management tool or just a fad?', *Bulletin of the American Society for Information Science*, 22(4): 20–21.

Fisher, S.L., Graham, M.E., Vachon, S. and Vereecke, A. (2010) 'Guest editors' note: Don't miss the boat: Research on HRM and supply chains', *Human Resource Management*, 49: 813–828.

Fisse, B. and Braithwaite, J. (1993) *Corporations, Crimes and Accountability*. Cambridge: Cambridge University Press.

Fitzgerald, M., Kruschwitz, N., Bonnet, D. and Welch, M. (2013) 'Embracing digital technology: A new strategic imperative', Research Report 2013, *MIT Sloan Management Review.*

Fleming, A. and Spicer, A. (2002) 'Workers playtime: Cynicism, irony and humour in organisation studies', in S. Clegg (ed.), *Management and Organization Paradoxes*. Amsterdam: Benjamins. pp. 65–86.

Fleming, A. and Spicer, A. (2003) 'Working at a cynical distance: Implications for power, subjectivity and resistance', *Organization*, (10)1: 157–179.

Fleming, P. and Sewell, G. (2002) 'Looking for the good soldier, Švejk: Alternative modalities of resistance in the contemporary workplace', *Sociology*, 36(4): 857–873.

Fleming, P. and Spicer, A. (2007) *Contesting the Corporation*. Cambridge: Cambridge University Press.

Fligstein, N. (1985) 'The spread of the multidivisional form among large firms, 1919–1979', *American Sociological Review*, 50: 377–391.

Fligstein, N. (1987) 'The intraorganizational power struggle: Rise of finance personnel to top leadership in large corporations, 1919–1979', *American Sociological Review*, 52(1): 44–58.

Fligstein, N. (2001) *The Architecture of Markets: An Economic Sociology of Capitalist Societies*. Princeton, NJ:Princeton University Press.

Fligstein, N. and Choo, J. (2005) 'Law and corporate governance', *Annual Review of Law and Social Science*, 1: 61–84.

Fligstein, N. and Freeland, R. (1995) 'Theoretical and comparative perspectives on corporate organization', *Annual Review of Sociology*, 21: 21–40.

Flyvbjerg, B. (1998) *Rationality and Power: Democracy in Practice*. Chicago: University of Chicago Press.

Flyvbjerg, B., Bruzelius, N., & Rothengatter, W. (2003) *Megaprojects and risk: An anatomy of ambition*. Cambridge University Press.

Fombrun, C.J. (2005) 'The leadership challenge: Building resilient corporate reputations', in J.P. Doh and S.A. Stumpf (eds), *Handbook on Responsible Leadership and Governance in Global Business*. Cheltenham: Edward Elgar. pp. 54–68.

Fombrun, C.J., Gardberg, N.A. and Barnett, M.L. (2000) 'Opportunity platforms and safety nets: Corporate citizenship and reputational risk', *Business and Society Review* (105)1: 85–106.

Ford, J.D. Ford, L.W. and D'amelio, A. (2008) 'Resistance to change: The rest of the story', *Academy of Management Review*, 33(2): 362–377.

Forsgren, M., Holm, U. and Johanson, J. (1995) 'Division headquarters go abroad: A step in the internationalization of the multinational corporation', *Journal of Management Studies*, 32(4): 475–491.

Fosfuri, A., Giarratana, M.S. and Roca, E. (2011) 'Community-focused strategies', *Strategic Organization*, 9(3): 222–239.

Foss, N.J. (1999) 'Networks, capabilities, and competitive advantage', *Scandinavian Journal of Management*, 15: 1–15.

Foss, N.J., Klein, P.G., Kor, Y.Y.and Mahoney, J.T. (2008) 'Entrepreneurship, subjectivism, and the resource-based view: Toward a new synthesis', *Strategic Entrepreneurship Journal*, 2/1: 73–94.

Fotopoulos, T. (2010) 'The de-growth utopia: The incompatibility of de-growth within an internationalised market economy', in H. Quingzhi (ed.), *Eco-socialism as Politics*. Amsterdam: Springer. pp. 103–121.

Foucault, M. (1972) *The Archaeology of Knowledge* (trans., A.M. Sheriden-Smith). London: Tavistock.

Foucault, M. (1979) *Discipline and Punish*. Harmondsworth, UK: Penguin Books.

Foucault, M. (1980) in C. Gordon (ed.), *Power/Knowledge: Selected Interviews and Other Writings by Michel Foucault, 1972–77*. Harvester: Brighton, UK.

Foucault, M. (1986) 'Of other spaces: Utopias and heterotopias', *Diacritics*, 16: 22–27.

Foucault, M. (1991) 'Governmentality' (trans., R. Braidotti), in G. Burchell, C. Gordon and P. Miller (eds), *The Foucault Effect: Studies in Governmentality*. Chicago, IL: University of Chicago Press. pp. 87–104.

Freeman, L.C. (2011) 'The development of social network analysis – with an emphasis on recent events', in J. Scott and P.J. Carrington (eds), *The Sage Handbook of Social Network Analysis*. London: Sage. pp. 26–39.

Freeman, R.E. (1984) 'Stakeholder management: framework and philosophy'. Pitman, Mansfield, MA.

Freeman, R.E. (2004) 'The stakeholder approach revisited', *Zeitschrift für Wirtschafts-und Unternehmensethik*, 5(3): 228.

Frenkel, M. (2005) 'The politics of translation: How state-level political relations affect the cross-national travel of management ideas', *Organization*, 12(2): 275–301.

Frenkel, M. and Shenhav, Y. (2004) 'From Americanization to colonization: The diffusion of productivity models revisited', *Organization Studies*, 24(9): 1537–1561.

Friedman, M. (1970) 'The social responsibility of business is to increase its profits', *New York Times Magazine*, 13 September: 33.

Friedman, T. (2005) *The World is Flat: A Brief History of the Twenty-First Century*. New York: Farrar, Straus and Giroux.

Fromm, T., Hägler, M. and Ott, K. (2015) *VW-Topmanager schwer belastet*. Available at: www.sueddeutsche.de/politik/abgas-affaere-vw-topmanager-schwer-belastet-1.2669920 (accessed 14 October 2015).

Frost, P.J., Moore, L.F., Reis Louis, M., Lundberg, C.C. and Martin, J. (1991) *Reframing Organizational Culture*. Newbury Park, CA: Sage.

Frynas, J.G. (2008) 'Corporate social responsibility and international development: Critical assessment', *Corporate Governance: An International Review*, 16 (4): 274–281.

Furrer, O., Thomas, H. and Goussevskaia, A. (2008) 'The structure and evolution of the strategic management field: A content analysis of 26 years of strategic management', *Research International Journal of Management Reviews*, 10(1): 1–23.

Gabriel, Y. (2000) *Storytelling in Organizations: Facts, Fictions, and Fantasies: Facts, Fictions, and Fantasies*. Oxford: Oxford University Press.

Galbraith, J. (1971) 'Matrix organization designs', *Business Horizons*, 14(1): 29–40.

Gallagher, M.E. (2007) *Contagious Capitalism: Globalization and the Politics of Labor in China*. Princeton: Princeton University Press.

Gallouj, F. and Weinstein, O. (1997) 'Innovation in services', *Research Policy*, 26: 537–556.

Galunic, D.C. and Eisenhardt, K.M. (1996) 'The evolution of intracorporate domains: Divisional charter losses in high-technology, multidivisional corporations', *Organization Science*, 7(3): 255–282.

Gamble, J. (2010) 'Transferring organizational practices and the dynamics of hybridization: Japanese retail multinationals in China', *Journal of Management Studies*, 47(4): 705–732.

Ganley, J. and Grahl, J. (1988) 'Competition and efficiency in refuse collection: A critical comment', *Fiscal Studies*, 9(1): 80–85.

Gardner, N. (2009) 'Resurrecting the "Icon": The enduring relevance of Clausewitz's *On War*', *Strategic Studies Quarterly*, 3(1): 119–133.

Gardner, T., Lienert, P. and Morgan, D. (2015) 'After year of stonewalling, VW stunned US regulators with confession', *Reuters*. Available at: www.reuters.com/article/2015/09/24/usa-volkswagen-deception-idUSL1N11U1OB20150924.

Garfinkel, H. (1967) *Studies in Ethnomethodology*, Englewood cliffs, NJ: Prentice-Hall.

Garfinkel, H. (1967) *Studies in Ethnomethodology*. New Jersey: Prentice-Hall.

Garg, S. and Eisenhardt, K. (2014) 'Unpacking the CEO-board relationship: Board-level strategic decision making in entrepreneurial firms', Working paper.

Garrett, G. (1998a) *Partisan Politics in the Global Economy*. New York: Cambridge University Press.

Garrett, G. (1998b) 'Global markets and national politics: Collision course or virtuous circle?', *International Organization*, 52 (4): 787–824.

Geisler, C. (2001) 'Textual objects: Accounting for the role of texts in the everyday life of complex organizations', *Written Communication*, 18: 296–325.

Geletkanycz, M.A. and Hambrick, D.C. (1997) 'The external ties of top executives', *Administrative Science Quarterly*, 42: 654–681.

Geppert, M. (2002) 'Change management approaches in MNCs: A comparison of sensemaking and politics in British and German subsidiaries', *Management Research News*, 25(8–10): 58.

Geppert, M. and Dörrenbächer, C. (2014) 'Politics and power within multinational corporations: Mainstream studies, emerging critical approaches and suggestions for future research', *International Journal of Management Reviews*, 16(2): 226–244.

Geppert, M. and Matten, D. (2006) 'Institutional influences on manufacturing organization in multinational corporations: The cherrypicking approach', *Organization Studies*, 27(4): 491–515.

Geppert, M. and Williams, K. (2006) 'Global, national and local practices in multinational corporations: Towards a sociopolitical framework', *International Journal of Human Resource Management*, 17(1): 49–69.

Geppert, M., Williams, K. and Matten, D. (2003) 'The social construction of contextual rationalities in MNCs: An Anglo-German comparison of subsidiary choice', *Journal of Management Studies*, 40(3): 617–641.

Geringer, M. (1991) 'Strategic determinants of partner selection criteria in international joint venture', *Journal of International Business Studies*, 22(1): 41–63.

Geroski, P.A. (1995) 'What do we know about entry?', *International Journal of Industrial Organization*, 13(4): 421–440.

Geyskens, I., Steenkamp, J-B.E.M. and Kumar, N. (2006) 'Make, buy, or ally: A transaction cost theory meta-analysis', *Academy of Management Journal*, 49(3): 519–543.

Ghemawat, P. (2002) 'Competition and business strategy in historical perspective', *Business History Review*, 76(Spring): 37–74.

Ghoshal, S. (2005) 'Bad emanagement theories are destroying good management practice', *Academy of Management Learning and Education*, 4(1): 75–91.

Ghoshal, S. and Bartlett, C.A. (1990) 'The multinational corporation as an interorganizational network', *Academy of Management Review*, 15(4): 603–625.

Ghoshal, S. and Moran, P. (1996) 'Bad for practice: A critique of transaction cost theory', *Academy of Management Review*, 21: 13–47.

Ghoshal, S., Hahn, M. and Moran, P. (2002) 'Management competence, firm growth and economic progress' in C. Pitelis (ed.), *The Growth of the Firm: The Legacy of Edith Penrose*. Oxford and New York: Oxford University Press.

Giddens, A. (1984) *The Constitution of Society*. Cambridge: Polity.

Giddens, A. (1990) *The Consequences of Modernity*. Oxford: Polity Press.

Giddens, A. (1991) *Modernity and Self-identity: Self and Society in the Late Modern Age*. Cambridge: Polity.

Giddens, A. (2008) 'The politics of climate change: National responses to the challenge of global warming', *Policy Network paper*. Available at: www.policy-network.net.

Giddens, A. (2009) *The Politics of Climate Change*. Cambridge: Polity Press.

Gilley, M. and Rasheed, A. (2000) 'Making more by doing less: An analysis of outsourcing and its effects on firm performance', *Journal of Management*, 26(4): 763–790.

Gioia, D.A. and Chittipeddi, K. (1991) 'Sensemaking and sensegiving in strategic change initiation', *Strategic Management Journal*, 12(6): 433–448.

Giustiniano, L, Cunha, M.P, and Clegg, S.R. (2016) 'Organizational zemblanity', *European Management Review*, 34(1): 7–21.

Glaser, B. and Strauss, A. (1967) The discovery of grounded theory. London: Weidenfeld and Nicholson, 24(25): 288–304.

Glasersfeld, E. von (2002) *Radical Constructivism: A Way of Knowing and Learning*. London: Routledge Falmer.

Glynn, M.A. (2000) 'When cymbals become symbols: Conflict over organizational identity within a symphony orchestra', *Organization Science*, 11(3): 285–298.

Gnan, L., Hinna, A. and Scarozza, D. (2013) 'Leading organisational changes in public sector building blocks in understanding boards behaviour', in L. Gnan, A. Hinna and F. Monteduro (eds), *Conceptualizing and Researching Governance in Public and Non-Profit Organizations,* Studies in Public and Non-Profit Governance, Vol. 1 (1st edn). Bingley: Emerald Group. pp. 57–89.

Gnyawali, D.R., He, J. and Madhavan, R. (2006) 'Impact of co-operation on firm competitive behavior: An empirical examination', *Journal of Management*, 32: 507–530.

Goffman, W. and Newill, V.A. (1964) 'Generalization of epidemic theory. An application to the transmission of ideas', *Nature*, 204: 225–228.

Golsorkhi, D., Rouleau, L., Seidl, D. and Vaara, E. (2015) *Cambridge Handbook of Strategy as Practice* (2nd edn). Cambridge: Cambridge University Press.

Gomes-Casseres, B. (2001) 'Inter-firm alliances', in *Routledge Encyclopedia of International Political Economy.* London: Routledge.

Gomez, P.Y. and Korine, H. (2008) *Entrepreneurs and Democracy: A Political Theory of Corporate Governance*. Cambridge: Cambridge University Press.

Gonzales, L. (2003) *Deep Survival: Who Lives, Who Dies, and Why: True Stories of Miraculous Endurance and Sudden Death*. New York: WW Norton.

Goodrick, E. and Reay, T. (2011) 'Constellations of institutional logics', *Work and Occupations*, 38(3): 372–416.

Gordon, R., Clegg, S. and Kornberger, M. (2009a) 'Embedded ethics: Discourse and power in the New South Wales Police Service', *Organization Studies*, (30)1: 73–99.

Gordon, R., Clegg, S. and Kornberger, M. (2009b) 'Power, rationality and legitimacy in public organizations', *Public Administration: An International Quarterly*, (27)1: 15–34.

Gottfredson, M., Puryear, R. and Phillipos, S. (2005) 'Strategic sourcing: From periphery to core', *Harvard Business Review*, 83(2): 132–139.

Gouldner, A.W. (1954) *Patterns of Industrial Bureaucracy*. New York: Free Press.

Gouldner, A.W. (1960) 'The norm of reciprocity: A preliminary statement', *American Sociological Review*, 25(2): 161–178.

Grand, S., Rüegg-Stürm, J. and Arx, W. von (2010) 'Constructivist epistemologies in strategy as practice research' in D. Golsorkhi, L. Rouleau, D. Seidl and E. Vaara (eds), *Cambridge Handbook of Strategy as Practice*. Cambridge: Cambridge University Press. pp. 63–78.

Grandy, G. and Mills, A.J. (2004) 'Strategy as simulacra? A radical reflexive look at the discipline and practice of strategy', *Journal of Management Studies*, 41(7): 1153–1170.

Granovetter, M. (1985) 'Economic action and social structure: The problem of embeddedness', *American Journal of Sociology*, 91(3): 481–510.

Granovetter, M. (1995) 'Coase revisited: Business groups in the modern economy', *Industrial and Corporate Change*, 4(1): 93–130.

Grant, R.M. (1996) 'Toward a knowledge-based theory of the firm', *Strategic Management Journal*, 17: 109–122.

Grant, R.M. (2003) 'Strategic planning in a turbulent environment: Evidence from the oil majors, *Strategic Management Journal*, 24(6): 491–517.

Grant, D. and Oswick, C. (eds) (1996) *Metaphor and Organizations*. London: Sage.

Green, J. (2010) 'The management secrets of the Grateful Dead', *The Atlantic*, March. Available at: www.theatlantic.com/magazine/archive/2010/03/management-secrets-of-the-grateful-dead/307918/.

Green, R., Agarwal, R. and Logue, D. (2015) 'Innovation', in J.D. Wright (ed.), *International Encyclopedia of the Social and Behavioral Sciences*, Volume 12 (2nd edn). Oxford: Elsevier. pp. 145–151.

Greenberg, D.N. (1995) 'Blue versus gray: A metaphor constraining sensemaking around a restructuring', *Group and Organization Management*, 20(2): 183–209.

Greif, A. (2008) 'Coercion and exchange: How did markets evolve,' SSRN Working Paper, No. 1304204.

Griffin, A. and Hauser, J.R. (1992) 'Patterns of communication among marketing, engineering and manufacturing—a comparison between two new product teams', *Management Science*, 38: 360–373.

Grint, K. and Case, P. (1998) 'The violent rhetoric of re-engineering: Management consultancy on the offensive', *Journal of Management Studies*, 35(5): 557–577.

Grinyer, P. and McKiernan, P. (1988) *Sharpbenders: The Secrets of Unleashing Corporate Potential*. Oxford: Blackwell.

Grönroos, C. (2008) 'Service logic revisited: Who creates value? And who co-creates?', *European Business Review*, 20(4): 298–314.

Grosse, R. (1996) 'International technology transfer in services', *Journal of International Business Studies*, 27(4): 781–800.

Grossman, S. and Hart, O. (1986) 'The costs and benefits of ownership: A theory of vertical and lateral integration', *Journal of Political Economy*, 94(4): 691–719.

Grundy, T. (1993) *Implementing Strategic Change*. London: Kogan Page.

Guillén, M.F. (1994) *Models of management: Work, authority, and organization in a comparative perspective*. University of Chicago Press.

Guillién, M.F. (2001a) *The Limits of Convergence: Globalization and Organizational Change in Argentina, South Korea, and Spain*. Princeton, NJ: Princeton University Press.

Guillén, M.F. (2001b) 'Is globalization civilizing, destructive or feeble? A critique of five key debates in the social science literature', *Annual review of sociology*, pp. 235–260.

Gulati, R. (1995) 'Social structure and alliance formation pattern: A longitudinal analysis', *Administrative Science Quarterly*, 40(4): 619–642.

Gulati, R. (1998) 'Alliances and networks', *Strategic Management Journal*, 19(4): 293–317.

Gulati, R. and Singh, H. (1998) 'The architecture of cooperation: Managing coordination costs and appropriation concerns in strategic alliances', *Administrative Science Quarterly*, 43(4): 781–814.

Gulati, R., Nohria, N. and Zaheer, A. (2000) 'Strategic networks', *Strategic Management Journal*, 21(3): 203–215.

Gummesson, E. (2006) 'Many-to-many marketing as grand theory', in R.F. Lusch and S.L. Vargo (eds), *The Service-dominant Logic of Marketing: Dialog, Debate, and Directions*. Armonk, NY: M.E. Sharpe. pp. 339–353.

Guthey, E., Clark, T. and Jackson, B. (2009) *Demystifying Business Celebrity*. London: Routledge.

Gutierrez, I. and Surroca, J. (2014) 'Revisiting corporate governance through the lens of the Spanish evidence', *Journal of Management and Governance*, 18(4): 989–1017.

Guyau, J-M. (1886) *L'Irréligion de l'avenir: Etude Sociologique*. Paris: F. Alcan.

Guyau, J-M. (1895) *Pages Choisies des Grands Écrivains*. Paris: A. Colin.

Habermas, J. (1971) *Knowledge and Human Interests*. London: Heinemann.

Habermas, J. (1976) *Legitimation Crisis*. London: Heinemann.

Hagedoorn, J., Roijakkers, N. and Van Kranenburg, H. (2006) 'Inter-firm R&D networks: The importance of strategic network capabilities for high-tech partnership formation', *British Journal of Management*, 17: 39–53.

Hagel, J. (1999) 'The coming battle for customer information', in D. Tapscott (ed.), *Creating Value in the Network Economy*. Boston, MA: Harvard Business School Press. pp. 159–171.

Hall, P. and Soskice, D. (2001) *Varieties of Capitalism: The Institutional Foundations of Comparative Advantage*. Oxford: Oxford University Press.

Hall, P. and Soskice, D. (2003) 'Varieties of capitalism and institutional complementarities', *Institutional Conflicts and Complementarities*. Springer US, pp. 43–76.

Hall, R. (1993) 'A framework linking intangible resources and capabilities to sustainable competitive advantage', *Strategic Management Journal*, 14(8): 607–618.

Hamel, G. (1991) 'Competition for competence and inter-partner learning within international strategic alliances', *Strategic Management Journal*, 12: 83–103.

Hamel, G. (2006) 'The why, what and how of management innovation', *Harvard Business Review*, 84(2): 72–83.

Hamel, G., Prahalad, C.K., Thomas, H. and O'Neal, D. (1999) *Strategic Flexibility: Managing in a Turbulent Environment*. London: Wiley.

Hamilton, G.G. (1996) *Asian Business Networks*. Berlin: de Gruyter.

Hamilton, G. and Biggart, N.W. (1988) 'Market, culture, and authority: A comparative analysis of management and organization in the Far East, *American Journal of Sociology*, 94(Supplement): 52–94.

Hanley, R. (ed.) (2016) *Adam Smith: His Life, Thought and Legacy*. Princeton, NJ: Princeton University Press.

Hansen, F. (2005) 'International business machine', *Workforce Management*, July: 37–46.

Hansmann, H. (1996) *The Ownership of Enterprise*. Cambridge, MA: Belknap.

Hansmann H. and Kraakman, R. (2001) 'The end of history for corporate law', *Georgetown Law Journal*, 89: 439–468.

Harbeson, J. (1995) 'Africa in world politics: Amid renewal, deepening crisis', in J. Harbeson and D. Rothchild (eds), *Africa in World Politics: Post-cold War Challenges*. Boulder, CO: Westview. pp. 3–20.

Hardy, C. (1994) *Managing Strategic Action: Mobilizing Change: Concepts, Readings, and Cases*. London: Sage.

Hardy, C., Palmer, I., & Phillips, N. (2000) Discourse as a strategic resource. *Human relations*, 53(9): 1227–1248.

Hardy, C. and Thomas, R. (2014) 'Strategy, discourse and practice: The intensification of power', *Journal of Management Studies*, 51 (2): 320–348.

Hart, J. (1982) *Herodotus and Greek History*. London: Croom Helm.

Hart, O. and Moore, J. (1990) 'Property rights and the nature of the firm', *Journal of Political Economy*, 98(6): 1119–1158.

Hart, O. and Zingales, L. (2011) 'A new capital regulation for large financial institutions', *American Law and Economics Review*, 13(2): 453–90.

Harzing, A.W. (1999) *Managing the Multinationals: An International Study of Control Mechanisms*. Cheltenham: Edward Elgar.

Harzing, A.W. and Noorderhaven, N. (2006) 'Geographical distance and the role and management of subsidiaries: The case of subsidiaries down-under', *Asia Pacific Journal of Management*, 23(2): 167–185.

Haspeslagh, P.C. and Jemison, D.B. (1991) *Managing Acquisitions: Creating Value through Corporate Renewal*. New York: Free Press.

Hatch, M.J. (1993) 'The dynamics of organizational culture', *Academy of Management Review*, 18: 657–693.

Hatch, M.J. (1999) 'Exploring the empty spaces of organizing: How improvisational jazz helps redescribe organizational structure', *Organization Studies*, 20(1): 75–100.

Hatch, N. and Mowery, D. (1998) 'Process innovation and learning by doing in semiconductor manufacturing', *Management Science*, 44(11): 1461–1477.

Hawken, P. (1993) *The Ecology of Commerce: A Declaration of Sustainability*. New York, NY: HarperCollins.

Hawken, P., Lovins, A. and Lovins, L.H. (1999) *Natural Capitalism: Creating the Next Industrial Revolution*. Boston: Little, Brown.

Hays, J. (2008) 'Dynamics of organizational wisdom', working paper series, School of Management, Marketing and International Business, Australian National University.

Hayward, M.L.A. and Hambrick, D.C. (1997) 'Explaining the premiums paid for large acquisitions: Evidence of CEO hubris', *Administrative Science Quarterly*, 42(1): 103–127.

Hayward, M.L.A., Rindova, V.L. and Pollock, T.G. (2004) 'Believing one's own press: The causes and consequences of CEO celebrity', *Strategic Management Journal*, 25: 637–653.

He, D. and Nickerson, J. (2006) 'Why do firms make and buy? Efficiency, appropriability, and competition in the trucking industry', *Strategic Organization*, 4(1): 43–69.

Heberer, T. (2003) *Private Entrepreneurs in China and Vietnam. Social and Political Functioning of Strategic Groups*, China Studies published for the Institute for Chinese Studies, University of Oxford. Leiden: Brill.

Hecker, A. and Kretschmer, T. (2010) 'Outsourcing decisions: The effect of scale economies and market structure', *Strategic Organization*, 8(2): 155–175.

Hedlund, G. (1986) 'The hypermodern MNC: A heterarchy?', *Human Resource Management*, 25: 9–36.

Hedlund, G. (1994) 'A model of knowledge management and the N-form corporation', *Strategic Management Journal*, 15: 454–461.

Heery, E. (2009) 'The representation gap and the future of worker representation', *Industrial Relations Journal*, 40(4): 324–336.

Heide, J.B. and John, G. (1990) 'Alliances in industrial purchasing: The determinants of joint action in buyer-supplier relationships', *Journal of Marketing Research*, 27: 24–36.

Heimeriks, K.H., Duysters, G. and Vanhaverbeke, W. (2007) 'Learning mechanisms and differential performance in alliance portfolios', *Strategic Organization*, 5: 373–408.

Helfat, C., Finkelstein, S., Mitchell, W., Peteraf, M., Singh, H., Teece, D. and Winter, S. (2007) *Dynamic Capabilities: Understanding Strategic Change in Organizations*. Blackwell, MA: Malden.

Henderson, B.D. (1970) 'The product portfolio', *The Boston Consulting Group*, Perspectives No. 66, Boston, MA.

Henderson, B.D. (1973) 'The experience curve reviewed, IV. The growth share matrix of the product portfolio', *The Boston Consulting Group*, Perspectives No. 135, Boston, MA.

Henderson, V.J. (2005) *New Economic Geography*. Northampton, MA: Elgar.

Hendry, J. (2000) 'Strategic decision-making, discourse, and strategy as social practice', *Journal of Management Studies*, 37(7): 955–977.

Hendry, K., Kiel, G. and Nicholson, G. (2010) 'How boards strategise: A strategy as practice view', *Long Range Planning*, 43(1): 33–56.

Henisz, W.J. (2000) 'The institutional environment for multinational investment', *Journal of Law Economics and Organization*, 16(2): 334–364.

Hennart, J.F. (1982) *A Theory of Multinational Enterprise*. Ann Arbor, MI: University of Michigan Press.

Hennart, J.F. (1988) 'A transaction cost theory of equity joint ventures', *Strategic Management Journal*, 9(4): 361–374.

Hennart, J.F. (1991) 'The transaction costs theory of joint ventures: An empirical study of Japanese subsidiaries in the USA', *Management Science*, 37: 483–497.

Hennart, J.F., Kim, D.J. and Zeng, M. (1998) 'The impact of joint venture status on the longevity of Japanese stakes in US manufacturing affiliates', *Organization Science*, 9(3): 382–395.

Heracleous, L. and Jacobs, C. (2008) 'Crafting strategy: The role of embodied metaphors', *Long Range Planning*, 41(3): 309–325.

Herrmann, P. and Datta, D. (2005) 'Relationships between top management team characteristics and international diversification: An empirical investigation', *British Journal of Management*, 16(1): 69–78.

Hertz, R. and Imber, J.B. (eds) (1995) *Studying Élites Using Qualitative Methods*. Thousand Oaks, CA: Sage.

Hickman, M. (2010) 'Concern over human cost overshadows iPad launch', *The Independent*, 27 May: 2.

Hicks A.M. (1999) *Social Democracy and Welfare Capitalism: A Century of Income Security Politics*. Ithaca, NY: Cornell University Press.

Hickson, D.J., Hinings, C.R., Lee, C.A., Schneck, R.E. and Pennings, J.M. (1971) 'A strategic contingencies theory of intra-organizational power', *Administrative Science Quarterly*, 16(2): 216–229.

Hickson, D.J., Butler, R.J., Cray, D., Mallory, G.R. and Wilson, D C. (1986) *Top Decisions: Strategic Decision-Making in Organizations*. San Francisco: Jossey-Bass.

Higgins, J.W. and Hallström, K. (2007) 'Standardization, globalization and rationalities of government', *Organization*, 14(5): 685–704.

Hill, S. and Rifkin, G. (2000) *Radical Marketing: From Harvard to Harley, Lessons from Ten that Broke the Rules and Made it Big*. New York: HarperCollins.

Hill, T. and Westbrook, R. (1997) 'SWOT analysis: It's time for a product recall', *Long Range Planning*, 30(1): 46–52.

Hillman, A.J., Cannella, A.A. and Paetzold, R.L. (2000) 'The resource dependence role of corporate directors: Strategic adaptation of board composition in response to environmental change', *Journal of Management Studies*, 37(2): 235–256.

Hillman, A.J., Withers, M.C. and Collins, B.J. (2009) 'Resource dependence theory: A review', *Journal of Management*, 35(6): 1404–1427.

Hirsch, F. (1975) *The Social Limits to Growth*. London: Routledge.

Hirschman, A.O. (1970) *Exit, Voice, and Loyalty: Responses to Decline in Firms, Organizations, and States*. Cambridge, MA: Harvard University Press.

Hirst, P. and Thompson, G. (1996) *Globalization in Question: The International Economy and the Possibilities of Governance*. Cambridge: Polity.

Hislop, D. (2013) *Knowledge Management in Organisations: A Critical Introduction*, Oxford University Press: Oxford.

Hitt, A.M., Dacin, M.T., Levitas, E., Arregle, J.-L. and Borza, A. (2000) 'Partner selection in emerging and developed market contexts: Resource-based and organizational learning perspectives', *Academy of Management Journal*, 43(3): 449–467.

Hitt, M., Tihanyi, L., Miller, T. and Connelly, B. (2006) 'International diversification: Antecedents, outcomes, and moderators', *Journal of Management*, 32(6): 831–867.

Hobbes, T. (1651/1968) *Leviathan*, ed. CB Macpherson. London: Penguin.

Hobson, J.A. (1893) 'The subjective and the objective view of distribution', *Annals of the American Academy of Political and Social Science*, 4: 42–67.

Hodge, G. (1999) 'Competitive tendering and contracting out: Rhetoric or reality?', *Public Productivity & Management Review*, 22(4): 455–469.

Hodgkinson, G. and Wright, G. (2002) 'Confronting strategic inertia in a top management team: Learning from failure', *Organization Studies*, 23(6): 949–977.

Hodgkinson, G., Whittington, R., Johnson, G. and Schwartz, M. (2006) 'The role of strategy workshops in strategy development processes: Formality, communication, coordination and inclusion', *Long Range Planning*, 39: 479–496.

Holcombe, R. (1991) 'Privatisation of municipal wastewater treatment', *Public Budgeting and Finance*, 11(3): 28–42.

Holmes, J., Burdon, S. and Terrill, D. (2003) *Productivity and organizational transformation: Optimising investment in ICT*. Canberra: National Office of Information Economy.

Hope, W. (2010) 'Time, communication, and financial collapse', *International Journal of Communication*, 4: 649–669.

Hoskin, K., Macve, R. and Stone, J. (1997) 'The historical genesis of modern business and military strategy: 1850–1950', *Interdisciplinary Perspectives on Accounting Conference*, Manchester, 7–9 July. Available at: http://laisumedu.org/DESIN_Ibarra/salon/apoyo/hoskin. PDF (accessed 19 March 2016).

Howell, J. and Hall-Merenda, K. (1999) 'The ties that bind: The impact of leader–member exchange, transformational and transactional leadership, and distance on predicting follower performance', *Journal of Applied Psychology*, 84(5): 680–694.

Huber, G.P. (1991) 'Organizational learning: The contributing processes and the literatures', *Organization Science*, 2: 88–115.

Huczynski, A.A. (1993) 'Explaining the succession of management fads', *The International Journal of Human Resource Management*, 4(2): 443–463.

Hult, G.T.M., Hurley, R.F. and Knight, G.A. (2004) 'Innovativeness: Its antecedents and impact on business performance', *Industrial Marketing Management*, 33(5):429–438.

Human, S.E. (2009) 'Emergent theory', in S.R. Clegg and J.R. Bailey (eds), *International Encyclopaedia of Organization Studies*. London: Sage. pp. 425–426.

Hunt, M.S. (1972) 'Competition in the major home appliance industry', PhD. dissertation, Harvard University.

Hunter, J D. and Cooksey, R.W. (2004) 'The decision to outsource: A case study of the complex interplay between strategic wisdom and behavioural reality', *Journal of the Australian and New Zealand Academy of Management*, 10(2): 26–40.

Hunter, J.D. and Gates, G.R. (1998) 'Outsourcing: Functional, fashionable, or foolish?', in G. Griffin (ed.), *Management Theory and Practice: Moving to a New Era*. Melbourne: Macmillan. pp. 133–144.

Hurley, R. and Hult, G.T.M. (1998) 'Innovation, market orientation, and organizational learning: An integration and empirical examination', *Journal of Marketing*, 62(3): 42–54.

Huse, M., Hoskisson, R., Zattoni, A. and Viganò, R. (2011) 'New perspectives on board research: Changing the research agenda', *Journal of Management and Governance*, 15(1): 5–28.

Husted, B. (2005) 'Risk management, real options, and corporate social responsibility', *Journal of Business Ethics*, 60(2): 175–183.

Hutt, M.D., Stafford, E.R., Walker, B.A. and Reingen, P.H. (2000) 'Case study: defining the social network of a strategic alliance', MIT Sloan Management Review, 41(2): 51.

Hutt, M. D., Stafford, E. R., Walker, B. A. and Reingen, P. H. (2000). Case study: defining the social network of a strategic alliance. *MIT Sloan Management Review*, 41(2): 5–62.

Hutton, W. (2007a) *The Writing on the Wall: China and the West in the 21st Century*. London: Little, Brown.

Hutton, W. (2007b) 'New China, New Crisis', *The Observer*, 7 January: 4.

Hutton, W. (2016) 'If having more no longer satisfies us, perhaps we've reached "peak stuff"', *The Guardian,* 31 January. Available at: /www.theguardian.com/commentisfree/2016/jan/31/consumerism-reached-peak-stuff-search-for-happiness.

Huy, Q.N. (2012) 'Emotions in strategic organization: Opportunities for impactful research', *Strategic Organization*, 10(2): 240–247.

Hymer, S.H. (1960/1976) *The International Operations of National Firms: A Study of Foreign Direct Investment*. Cambridge, MA: MIT Press.

Iansiti, M. and Levien, R. (2004) 'Strategy as ecology', *Harvard Business Review*, 82(3): 68–78.

Ibarra-Colado, E.I. (2008) 'Neoliberalism and organization', in S.R. Clegg and J.R. Bailey (eds), *International Encyclopedia of Organization Studies*, Vol. 3. London: Sage. pp. 959–963.

ILO (International Labour Organization) (2008) *Meeting the Challenge: Proven Practices for Human Trafficking Prevention in the Greater Mekong Sub-region*. Bangkok: ILO.

Inkpen, A.C. (1998) 'Learning and knowledge acquisition through international strategic alliances', *Academy of Management Executive*, 12(4): 69–80.

Ireland, R.D. (2007) 'Strategy vs. entrepreneurship', *Strategic Entrepreneurship Journal*, 1(1–2): 7–10.

Isaacson, W. (2011) *Steve Jobs: The Exclusive Biography*. New York: Simon & Schuster.

Jackall, R. (1988) *Moral Mazes: The World of Corporate Managers*. New York: Oxford University Press.

Jackson, M. (2000) 'Imagined republics: Machiavelli, utopia, and utopia', *Journal of Value Inquiry*, 34(4): 427–437.

Jackson, R. and Howe, N. with Strauss, R. and Nakashima, K. (2008) *The Graying of the Great Powers: Demography and Geopolitics in the 21st Century*. Washington: Center for Strategic and International Studies.

Jackson, T. (2000) 'Management ethics and corporate policy: A cross-cultural comparison', *Journal of Management Studies*, 37(3): 349–369.

Jacobs, R. (2014) 'On top of the world: This could be the start of a century of German success', *Newsweek*, 17 July. Available at: www.newsweek.com/2014/07/25/top-world-could-be-start-century-german-success-259410.html (accessed 4 January 2016).

Jacques, M. (2009) *When China Rules the World: The Rise of the Middle Kingdom and the End of the Western World*. Harmondsworth: Allen Lane.

Jacques, M. and Hutton, W. (2009) 'Is western supremacy but a blip as China rises to the global summit', *The Guardian*, 23 June: 29.

James, P., Johnstone, R., Quinlan, M. and Walters, D. (2007) 'Regulating supply chains to improve health and safety', *Industrial Law Journal*, 36(2): 163–187.

Jameson, D.A. (2000) 'Telling the investment story: A narrative analysis of shareholder reports', *Journal of Business Communication*, 37(1): 7–38.

Jarillo, J.C. (1988) 'On strategic networks', *Strategic Management Journal*, 9: 31–41.

Jarzabkowski, P. (2003) 'An activity theory perspective on continuity and change', *Journal of Management Studies*, 40(1): 23–56.

Jarzabkowski, P. (2004) 'Strategy as practice: Recursiveness, adaptation and practices-in-use', *Organization Studies*, 25(4): 529–560.

Jarzabkowski, P. (2005) *Strategy as Practice: An Activity-based Approach*. London: Sage.

Jarzabkowski, P. (2008) 'Shaping strategy as a structuration process', *Academy of Management Journal*, 51(4): 621–650.

Jarzabkowski, P. and Seidl, D. (2008) 'The role of meetings in the social practice of strategy', *Organization Studies*, 29(11): 1391–1426.

Jarzabkowski, P. and Spee, A.P. (2009) 'Strategy as practice: A review and future directions for the field', *International Journal of Management Reviews*, 11(1): 69–95.

Jarzabkowski, P. and Whittington, R. (2008) 'Hard to disagree, mostly', *Strategic Organization*, 6(1): 101–106.

Jarzabkowski, P. and Wilson, D.C. (2006) 'Actionable strategy knowledge', *European Management Journal*, 24(5): 348–367.

Jarzabkowski, P., Matthiesen, J. and Van de Ven (2009) 'Doing which work? A practice approach to institutional pluralism', in T.B. Lawrence, R. Suddaby and B. Leca (eds), *Institutional Work: Actors and Agency in Institutional Studies of Organizations*. Cambridge: Cambridge University Press. pp. 284–316.

Jarzabkowski, P., Spee, A.P. and Smets, M. (2013a) 'Material artifacts: Practices for doing strategy with "stuff"', *European Management Journal*, 31(1): 41–54.

Jarzabkowski, P., Lê, J.K. and Van de Ven, A.H. (2013b) 'Responding to competing strategic demand: How organizing, belonging, and performing paradoxes coevolve', *Strategic Organization*, 11(3): 245–280.

Jarzabkowski, P., Kaplan, S., Seidl, D. and Whittington, R. (2015) 'On the risk of studying practices in isolation: Linking what, who and how in strategy research', *Strategic Organization*, 14(3): 270–4.

Jay, A. (1967) *Machiavelli and Management*. Harmondsworth: Penguin.

Jay, A. (1994) *Management and Machiavelli: Discovering a New Science of Management in the Timeless Principles of Statecraft*. San Diego, CA: Pfeiffer.

Jay, J. (2013) 'Navigating paradox as a mechanism of change and innovation in hybrid organizations', *Academy of Management Journal*, 56(1): 137–159.

Jensen, M.C. and Meckling, W.H. (1976) 'Theory of the firm: Managerial behavior, agency costs and ownership structure', *Journal of Financial Economics*, 3(4): 305–360.

Jensen, T., Sandström, J. and Helin, S. (2009) 'Corporate codes of ethics and the bending of moral space', *Organization*, 16(4): 529–545.

Jermier, J.M., Knights, D. and Nord, W.R. (1994) 'Resistance and power in organizations: Agency, subjectivity and the labour process', in J.M. Jermier, D. Knights and W.R. Nord (eds), *Resistance and Power in Organizations*. New York: Routledge. pp. 1–24.

Johanson, J. and Vahlne, J. (1977) 'The internationalization process of the firm – A model of knowledge development and increasing foreign market commitments', *Journal of International Business Studies*, 8(1): 23–32.

Johanson, J. and Vahlne, J.E. (2009) 'The Uppsala internationalization model revisited: From liability of foreignness to liability of outsidership', *Journal of International Business Studies*, 40 (9): 1411–1433.

Johnson, G. (1987) *An 'Organization Action' Approach to Strategic Management*. Manchester: Manchester Business School.

Johnson, G. (1993) 'Processes of managing strategic change', in C. Mabey and B. Mayon-White (eds), *Managing Change* (2nd edn). London: Open University/Paul Chapman Publishing. pp. 59–64.

Johnson, G., Scholes, K. and Whittington, R. (2002) *Exploring Corporate Strategy.*, Harlow: Financial Times-Prentice Hall.

Johnson, G., Melin, L. and Whittington, R. (2003) 'Micro-strategy and strategising', *Journal of Management Studies*, 40(1): 3–22.

Johnson, G., Scholes, K., and Whittington, R. (2007) *Exploring Corporate Strategy* (8th edition) London: Pearson Education Limited.

Jones, C. and Lichtenstein, B. (2008) 'Temporary inter-organizational projects: How temporal and social embeddedness enhance coordination and manage uncertainty', in S. Cropper, M. Ebers, C. Huxham and P. Smith Ring (eds), *The Oxford Handbook of Inter-organizational Relations*. Oxford: Oxford University Press. pp. 231–255.

Jones, G. and Pitelis, C. (2015) 'Entrepreneurial imagination and a demand and supply-side perspective on the MNE and cross-border organization', *Journal of International Management*, 21(4): 309–321.

Jones, L.B. (1996) *Jesus CEO: Using Ancient Wisdom for Visionary Leadership*. New York: Hyperion.

Jordan, T. and Taylor, P. (1998) 'A sociology of hackers', *Sociological Review*, 46: 757–780.

Josserand, E. (2004) *The Network Organization: The Experience of Leading French Multinationals*. Cheltenham, UK: Edward Elgar.

Josserand, E., Teo, S. and Clegg, S. (2006) 'From bureaucratic to post-bureaucratic: The difficulties of transition', *Journal of Organizational Change Management*, 19: 54–64.

Judge, T.A., Piccolo, R.F. and Kosalka, T. (2009) 'The bright and dark sides of leader traits: A review and theoretical extension of the leader trait paradigm', *Leadership Quarterly*, 20: 855–875.

Judt, T. (2005) *Postwar: A History of Europe since 1945*. London: Heinemann.

Judt, T. (2015) *When the Facts Change: Essays, 1995–210*. New York, NY: Penguin.

Jung, D.I. (2001) 'Transformational and transactional leadership and their effects on creativity in groups', *Creativity Research Journal*, 13(2): 185–197.

Jung, D.I. and Avolio, B.J. (1999) 'Effects of leadership style and followers' cultural orientation on performance in group and individual task conditions', *Academy of Management Journal*, 42(2): 208–219.

Jung, D.I. and Sosik, J.J. (2002) 'Transformational leadership in work groups: The role of empowerment, cohesiveness, and collective-efficacy on perceived group performance', *Small Group Research*, 33(3): 313–337.

Jung, D.I., Chow, C. and Wu, A. (2003) 'The role of transformational leadership in enhancing organizational innovation: Hypotheses and some preliminary findings', *Leadership Quarterly*, 14(4–5): 525–544.

Kadushin, C. (1995) 'Friendship among the French financial elite', *American Sociological Review*, 60: 202–221.

Kahn, K.B. (2013) *The PDMA Handbook of New Product Development* (3rd edn). New York: Wiley.

Kaine, S. and Wright, C.F. (2013) 'Conceptualising CSR in the context of the shifting contours of Australian employment regulation'. *Labour and Industry*, 23(1): 54–68.

Kaldor, N. (1970) 'The case for regional policies', *Scottish Journal of Political Economy*, 17/3: 337–348.

Kale, P., Singh, H. and Perlmutter, H. (2000) 'Learning and protection of proprietary assets in strategic alliances: Business relational capital', *Strategic Management Journal*, 21: 217–237.

Kale, P., Dyer, J.H. and Singh, H. (2001) 'Value creation and success in strategic alliances: Alliancing skills and the role of alliance structure and systems', *European Management Journal*, 17(5): 463–471.

Kale, P., Dyer, J.H. and Singh, H. (2002) 'Alliance capability, stock market response, and long-term alliance success: The role of the alliance function', *Strategic Management Journal*, 23: 747–767.

Kalyvas, S.N. (2006) *The Logic of Civil War*. Cambridge: Cambridge University Press.

Kamoche, K. and Cunha, M.P.E (2001) 'Minimal structure: From jazz improvisation to product innovation', *Organization Studies*, 22(5): 733–764.

Kang, S.C., Morris, S.S. and Snell, S.A. (2007) 'Relational archetypes, organizational learning, and value creation: Extending the human resource architecture', *Academy of Management Review,* 32/1: 236–256.

Kanter, R. M. (1984) *The Change Masters*. London: George Allen & Unwin.

Kanter, R.M. (1988) 'When a thousand flowers bloom: Structural, collective and social conditions for innovation in organizations', in B.M. Staw and L.L. Cummings (eds), *Research in Organizational Behavior*, Vol. 10. Greenwich, CT: Jai Press. pp. 123–167.

Kanter, R.M. (1992) *The Challenge of Organization Change: How Companies Experience It and Leaders Guide It*. New York: Free Press.

Kanter, R.M., Stein, B. A. and Jick, T.D (1992) *The Challenge of Organizational Change*. New York: The Free Press.

Kanter, R.M. (2002) 'Strategy as improvisational theatre', *Sloan Management Review*, 43(2): 76–81.

Kanter, R.M., Stein, B. and Jick, T. (1992) *The challenge of organizational change: How companies experience it and leaders guide it*. New York: Free Press.

Kaplan, S. (2011) 'Strategy and PowerPoint: An inquiry into the epistemic culture and machinery of strategy making', *Organization Science*, 22(2): 320–346.

Kates, S. (2010) *Macroeconomic Theory and its Failings: Alternative Perspectives on the Global Financial Crisis.* Massachusetts: Edward Elgar.

Katkalo, V.S., Pitelis, C.N. and Teece, D J (2010) 'Introduction: On the nature and scope of dynamic capabilities', *Industrial and Corporate Change,* 19(4): 1175–1186.

Katz, M.L. and Shapiro, C. (1994) 'Systems competition and network effects', *Journal of Economic Perspectives,* 8(2): 93–115.

Katz, R.S. and Allen, T. (1982) 'Investigating the Not Invented Here syndrome: A look at the performance, tenure and communication patterns of 50 R&D project groups, *R&D Management,* 12(1): 7–19.

Kauffman, S. (1995) *At Home in the Universe.* New York: Oxford University Press.

Kay, J. (1995) *Foundations of Corporate Success: How Business Strategies add Value.* Oxford: Oxford University Press.

Kellaway, L. (2010) 'Why insensitive bosses make so much sense', *Financial Times,* 15 February: 12.

Keller, G.F. (2009) 'The influence of military strategies on business planning', *International Journal of Business and Management,* 3(5): 129–135.

Keen, A. (2015) *The Internet is not the Answer.* New York, NY: Atlantic Books.

Keen, S. (2012) *Predicting the 'Global Financial Crisis': Post Keynesian Macroeconomics.* Available at: www.debtdeflation.com/blogs/2012/05/22/predicting-the-global-financial-crisis-post-keynesian-macroeconomics-2/#_ENREF_31 (accessed 5 March 2016).

Kennedy, R. and Schlesinger, A. (1999) *Thirteen Days: A Memoir of the Cuban Missile Crisis.* New York: WW Norton.

Kenny, G., Butler, R., Hickson, D.G., Cray, D., Mallory, G. and Wilson, D. (1987) 'Strategic decision making: Influence patterns in public and private sector organization', *Human Relations,* 40(9): 613–631.

Kessing, S.G., Konrad, K.A. and Kotsogiannis, C. (2007) 'Foreign direct investment and the dark side of decentralization', *Economic Policy,* 49: 6–70.

Ketchen, J.D.J., Combs, J.G., Russell, C.J., Shook, C., Dean, M.A., Runge, J., Lohrke, F.T., Naumann, S.E., Haptonstahl, D.E., Baker, R., Beckstein, B.A., Handler, C., Honig, H. and Lamoureux, S. (1997) 'Organizational configurations and performance: A meta-analysis', *Academy of Management Journal,* 40: 223–240.

Kets de Vries, F.R. (1991) *Organizations on the Couch: Handbook of Psychoanalysis and Management.* New York: Jossey-Bass.

Keupp, M.M., Palmie, M. and Gassman, O. (2012) 'The strategic management of innovation: A systematic review and paths for future research', *International Journal of Management Reviews,* 14(4): 367–390.

Khan, F.R., Munir, K.A. and Willmott, H. (2007) 'A dark side of institutional entrepreneurship: Soccer balls, child labour and postcolonial impoverishment', *Organization Studies,* 28: 1055–1077.

Khandwalla, P. (1977) *The Design of Organizations.* New York: Harcourt Brace Jovanovich.

Khurana, R. (2002) *Searching for a Corporate Savior: The Irrational Quest for Charismatic CEOs.* Princeton: Princeton University Press.

Khurana, R. (2007) *From Higher Aims to Hired Hands: The Social Transformation of American Business Schools and the Unfulfilled Promise of Management Education.* Princeton: Princeton University Press.

Kilduff, M. and Brass, D.J. (2010) 'Organizational social network research: Core ideas and key debates', *Academy of Management Annals,* 4: 317–357.

Kim, B., Burns, M. and Prescott, J. (2009) 'The strategic role of the board: The impact of board structure on top management team strategic action capability', *Corporate Governance: An International Review,* 17(6): 728–743.

Kim, J.and Mahoney, J.T. (2002) 'Resource-based and property rights perspectives on value creation: The case of oil field unitization', *Managerial and Decision Economics* 23/4: 225–245.

Kim, W. (1988) 'The effects of competition and corporate political responsiveness on multinational bargaining power', *Strategic Management Journal,* 9(3): 289–295.

Kim, W. C. and Mauborgne, R. (2004) Blue ocean strategy, *Harvard Business Review*, 82(10): 76–84, 71.

Kim, W.C. and Mauborgne, R. (2005) *Blue Ocean Strategy: How to Create Uncontested Market Space and Make the Competition Irrelevant*. Boston: Harvard Business School Press.

Kinderman, D. (2012) 'Free us up so we can be responsible! The co-evolution of corporate social responsibility and neo-liberalism in the UK, 1977–2010', *Socio-Economic Review*, 10(1): 29–57.

Kinzer, S. (2011) 'America and the rise of middle power', *The Guardian*, 11 January. Available at: www.theguardian.com/commentisfree/cifamerica/2011/jan/10/usa-usforeignpolicy (accessed 10 May 2016).

Kjonstad, B. and Willmott, H. (1995) 'Business ethics: Restrictive or empowering?', *Journal of Business Ethics*, 14(6): 445–644.

Klein, B., Crawford, R.G. and Alchian, A.A. (1978) 'Vertical integration, appropriable rents and the competitive contracting process', *Journal of Law and Economics*, XXI: 297–326.

Klein, N. (2007) *The Shock Doctrine: The Rise of Disaster Capitalism*. New York: Metropolitan Books.

Klein, N. (2014) *This Changes Everything*. New York: Penguin.

Klein, P.G., Mahoney, J.T., McGahan, A.M. and Pitelis, C.N. (2012) 'Who is in charge? A property rights perspective on stakeholder governance', *Strategic Organization*, 10(3): 304–315.

Knight, G.A. and Cavusgil, S.T. (2005) 'A taxonomy of born global firms', *Management International Review*, 45: 15–35.

Knights, D. (1992) 'Changing spaces: The disruptive impact of a new epistemological location for the study of management', *The Academy of Management Review*, 17(3): 514–536.

Knights, D. and Morgan, G. (1991) 'Corporate strategy, organizations, and subjectivity: A critique', *Organization Studies*, 12(2): 251–273.

Knights, D. and Morgan, G. (1996) 'Selling oneself: Subjectivity and the labour process in selling life insurance', in C. Smith, D. Knights and H. Willmott (eds), *White-Collar Work. The Non-Manual Labour Process*. Basingstoke: Macmillan.

Knights, D. and Willmott, H. (eds) (2000) *The Reengineering Revolution: Critical Studies of Corporate Change*. London: Sage.

Kogut, B. (1988) 'Joint ventures: Theoretical and empirical perspectives', *Strategic Management Journal*, 9(4): 319–332.

Kogut, B. (2000) 'The network as knowledge: Generative rules and the emergence of structure', *Strategic Management Journal*, 21: 405–425.

Kogut, B. (2002) 'International management and strategy', in A. Pettigrew, H. Thomas and R. Whittington (eds), *Handbook of Strategy and Management*. London: Sage.

Kogut, B. and Zander, U. (1992) 'Knowledge of the firm, combinative capabilities and the replication of technology', *Organization Science*, 3: 383–397.

Kogut, B. and Zander, U. (1993) 'Knowledge of the firm and the evolutionary theory of the multinational corporation', *Journal of International Business Studies*, 24(4): 625–645.

Kondratieff, N. (1984) *Long Wave Cycle* (trans., Guy Daniels). London: E P Dutton.

Kono, T. and Clegg, S.R. (1998) *Transformations of Corporate Culture: Experiences of Japanese Enterprises*, De Gruyter Studies in Organization, No. 83. Berlin and New York: de Gruyter.

Kono, T. and Clegg, S.R. (2001) *Trends in Japanese Management*. London: Palgrave.

Kor, Y.Y. and Mahoney, J.T. (2000) 'Penrose's resource-based approach: The process and product of research creativity', *Journal of Management Studies*, 37(1): 99–139.

Kor, Y.Y. and Mahoney, J.T. (2004) 'Penrose's resource-based approach: The process and product of research activity', *Journal of Management Studies*, 41(1): 109–139.

Kornberger, M. (2013) 'Clausewitz: On strategy', *Business History*, 55(7): 1058–1073.

Kornberger, M. and Carter, C. (2010) 'Manufacturing competition: How accounting practices shape strategy making in cities', *Accounting, Auditing and Accountability Journal*, 23(3): 325–349.

Kornberger, M. and Clegg, S.R. (2011) 'Strategy as performative practice: The case study of Sydney 2030', *Strategic Organization*, 9: 136–162.

Kornberger, M., Justesen, L., Madsen, A.K. and Mouritsen, J. (eds) (2015) *Making Things Valuable*. Oxford: Oxford University Press.

Kostova, T. and Zaheer, S. (1999) 'Organizational legitimacy under conditions of complexity: The case of the multinational enterprise', *Academy of Management Review*, 24(1): 64–81.

Kotter, J.P. (1996) *Leading Change*. Harvard: Harvard Business Press.

Kotter, J.P. and Schlesinger, L.A. (1979) 'Choosing strategies for change', *Harvard Business Review*, 57(2): 106–114.

Koukoulas, S. (2016) 'The doomsayers are wrong – our debt is well-regulated, and sound', *The Guardian* (Australian edition), 17 March. Available at: www.theguardian.com/business/com mentisfree/2016/mar/18/the-doomsayers-are-wrong-our-debt-is-well-regulated-and-sound.

Kraaijenbrink, J., Spender J.C. and Groen, A.J. (2010) 'The resource-based view: A review and assessment of its critiques', *Journal of Management*, 36(1): 349–372.

Krippner, G.R. (2005)' The financialization of the American economy', *Socio-Economic Review*, 3(2): 173–208.

Krugman, P.R. (1991) *Geography and Trade*. Boston, MA: MIT Press.

Krugman, P. (1996) 'Making sense of the competitiveness debate', *Oxford Review of Economic Policy*, 12/3: 17–25.

Kuhn, T.S. (1962) *The Structure of Scientific Revolutions*. Chicago: University of Chicago Press.

Kühne, K and Dieaiter, S. (2011) 'Scandalous co-determination', in A. Brink (ed.), *Corporate Governance and Business Ethics*. Berlin: Springer. pp. 75–87.

Kühne, K. and Sadowski, D. (2011) Scandalous co-determination, *Corporate Governance and Business Ethics*. Netherlands: Springer, pp. 75–87.

Kumar, K. and Thibodeaux, M. (1990) 'Organizational politics and planned organizational change', *Group and Organizational Studies*, 15(4): 357–365.

Kuper, A. (1995) 'Machiavelli in precolonial Southern Africa', *Social Anthropology* 3(1): 1–13.

Küpers, W. and Paullen, D. (2013) *A Handbook of Practical Wisdom. Leadership, Organization and Integral Business Practice*. London: Gower.

La Porta, R.., Lopez-de-Silanes, F., Shleifer, A. and Vishny, R.W. (1997a) 'Legal determinants of external finance', *Journal of Finance*, 52(3): 1131–1150.

La Porta, R., Lopez-de-Silanes, F., Shleifer, A. and Vishny R.W. (1997b) 'Trust in large organizations', *American Economic Review*, 87(2): 333–338.

La Porta, R., Lopez-de-Silanes, F., Shleifer, A. and Vishny, R.W. (1998) 'Law and finance', *Journal of Political Economy*, 106(6): 1113–1155.

La Porta, R., Lopez-de-Silanes, F. and Shleifer, A. (1999) 'Corporate ownership around the world', *Journal of Finance*, 54(2): 471–517.

La Porta, R., Lopez-de-Silanes, F. and Shleifer, A. (2002) 'Government ownership of banks', *Journal of Finance* 57(1): 265–301.

Laine, P.-M. and Vaara, E. (2007) 'Struggling over subjectivity: A discursive analysis of strategic development in an engineering group', *Human Relations*, 60(1): 29–58.

Lakhani, T., Kuruvilla, S. and Avgar, A. (2011) 'From the firm to the network: Global value chains and employment relations theory', *British Journal of Industrial Relations* 51(3): 440–472.

Langlois, R.N. (1992) 'Transaction cost economics in real time', *Industrial and Corporate Change*, 1(1): 99–127.

Langlois, R.N. and Robertson, P.L. (1995) *Firms, Markets, and Economic Change: A Dynamic Theory of Business Institutions*. Abingdon, UK, and New York, NY: Routledge.

Lanzara, D.F. (2016) *Shifting Practices: Reflections on Technology, Practice, and Innovation*. Boston, MA: MIT Press.

Larsson, R. and Lubatkin, M. (2001) 'Achieving acculturation in mergers and acquisitions: An international case survey', *Human Relations*, 54: 1573–1607.

Latour, B. (1988) 'How to write "The Prince" for machines as well as for machinations', in B. Elliott (ed.), *Technology and Social Change*. Edinburgh: Edinburgh University Press. pp. 20–43.

Law, J. and Urry, J. (2004) 'Enacting the social', *Economy and Society*, 33(3): 390–410.

Lawrence, T., Phillips, N. and Hardy, C. (1999) 'Watching whale-watching: Exploring the discursive foundations of collaborative relationships', *Journal of Applied Behavioral Science*, 35: 479–502.

Lazonick, W. and O'Sullivan, M. (2000) 'Maximizing shareholder value: A new ideology for corporate governance', *Economy and Society*, 29(1): 13–35.

Lazzarato, M. (2011) *La fabrique de l'homme endetté: Essai sur la condition néolibérale*. Paris: Editions Amsterdam.

Learned, E.P., Christensen, C.P., Andrews, K.P. and Guth, W. (1969) *Business Policy*. Homewood, IL: Irwin.

Leblebici, H., Salancik, G.R., Copay, A. and King, T. (1991) 'Institutional change and the transformation of interorganizational fields: An organizational history of the US radio broadcasting industry', *Administrative Science Quarterly*, 36: 333–363.

Lee, S-Y. (2016) 'Responsible supply chain management in the Asian context: The effects of on relationshop commitment and supplier performance', *Asia Pacific Business Review*, 22(2): 325–342.

Lee, S.M., Olson, D.L. and Trimi, S. (2010) 'Strategic innovation in the convergence era', *International Journal of Management and Enterprise Development*, 9 (1): 1–12.

Lenz, R.T. and Lyles, M. (1985) 'Paralysis by analysis: Is your planning system becoming too rational?', *Long Range Planning*, 18(4): 64–72.

Lepak, D.P., Smith, K.G. and Taylor, M.S. (2007) 'Value creation and value capture: A multilevel perspective', *Academy of Management Review*, 32/1: 180–194.

Lépinay, V.A. (2011) *Codes of Finance: Engineering Derivatives in a Global Bank*. Princeton: Princeton University Press.

Levine, R. (1997) 'Financial development and economic growth: Views and agenda', *Journal of Economic Literature*, 35(2): 688–726.

Levy, A. (1986) 'Second-order planned change: Definition and conceptualization', *Organizational Dynamics*, 15(1): 5–23.

Levy, D.L. (1994) 'Chaos theory and strategy: Theory, application, and managerial implications', *Strategic Management Journal*, 15(Special Issue): 167–178.

Levy, D.L. (2008) 'Political contestation in global production networks', *Academy of Management Review*, 33(4): 943–962.

Lewin, K. (1947) 'Frontiers in group dynamics', in D. Cartwright (ed.), *Field Theory in Social Science*. London: Social Science Paperbacks. pp. 301–336.

Liebeskind, J.P. (1996) 'Knowledge, strategy, and the theory of the firm', *Strategic Management Journal*, 7(5): 502–518.

Liebeskind, J.P., Oliver, A.L., Zucker, L. and Brewer, M. (1996) 'Social networks, learning, and flexibility: Sourcing scientific knowledge in new biotechnology firms', *Organization Science*, 7: 428–443.

Lindblom, C. (1959) 'The science of muddling through', *Public Administration Review*, 19(2): 79–88.

Lippman, S.A. and Rumelt, R.P. (2003a) 'The payments perspective: Micro-foundations of resource analysis', *Strategic Management Journal*, 24: 903–927.

Lippman, S.A. and Rumelt, R.P. (2003b) 'A bargaining perspective on resource advantage', *Strategic Management Journal*, 24: 1069–1086.

Littler, J. (2007) 'Celebrity CEOs and the cultural economy of tabloid intimacy', in S. Redmond and S. Holmes (eds), *Stardom and Celebrity: A Reader*. London: Sage. pp. 230–243.

Loasby, B.J. (1998) 'The concept of capabilities' in N.J. Foss and B.J. Loasby (eds), *Economic Organization, Capabilities and Co-ordination: Essays in Honour of G. B. Richardson*. London and New York: Routledge.

Loasby, B.J. (1999) 'The significance of Penrose's theory for the development of economics', *Contributions to Political Economy*, 18: 31–45.

Loasby, B.J. (2010) 'Capabilities and strategy: Problems and prospects', *Industrial and Corporate Change*, 19(4): 1301–1316.

Locke, R. and Spender, J.C. (2011) *Confronting Managerialism*. London: Zed Books.

Locke, E.A (2006) 'Business ethics: A way out of the morass', *Academy of Management Learning and Education*, 5: 324–332.

Locke, R. (1995) *Remaking the Italian Economy*. Ithaca, NY: Cornell University Press.

Logue, D., Jarvis, W.P., Clegg, S.R. and Hermens, A. (2015) 'Translating models of organization: Can the Mittlestand move from Bavaria to Geelong?', *Journal of Management and Organization*, 21(1): 17–36.

Long, B.S. and Driscoll, C. (2008) 'Codes of ethics and the pursuit of organizational legitimacy: Theoretical and empirical contributions', *Journal of Business Ethics*, (77)2: 173–189.

Lonsdale, C. and Cox, A. (2000) 'The historical development of outsourcing: The latest fad?', *Industrial Management and Data Systems*, 100: 444–450.

Lorenzoni, G. and Ornati, O. (1988) 'Constellations of firms and new ventures', *Journal of Business Venturing*, 88(1): 41–57.

Lorsch, J. (1997) 'Corporate governance', in M. Warner (ed.), *The Concise International Encyclopaedia of Business and Management*. London: Thomson. pp. 96–106.

Lounsbury, M. (2007) 'A tale of two cities: Competing logics and practice variation in the professionalizing of mutual funds', *Academy of Management Journal*, 50(2): 289–307.

Lounsbury, M. and Boxenbaum, E. (eds) (2013) *Institutional Logics in Action,* Vol. 39A/B. Bingley: Emerald.

Lui, S. and Ngo, H.Y. (2005) 'The role of trust and contractual safeguards on cooperation in nonequity', *Alliance Journal of Management*, 30(4): 471–485.

Lukes, S. (1974) *Power: A Radical View*. London: Macmillan.

Lukes, S. (2005) *Power: A Radical View* (2nd edn). London: Palgrave Macmillan.

Lundvall, B-Å. (ed.) (1992) *National Systems of Innovation: Towards a Theory of Innovation and Interactive Learning*. London: Pinter Publishers.

Lüscher, L. and Lewis, M. (2008) 'Organizational change and managerial sensemaking: Working through paradox', *Academy of Management Journal*, 51(2): 221–240.

Macaulay, S. (1966) *Law and the Balance of Power. The Automobile Manufacturers and their Dealers*. New York: Russell Sage Foundation.

MacDonald, G.and Ryall, M.D. (2004) 'How do value creation and competition determine whether a firm appropriates value?', *Management Science* 50/10: 1319–1333.

MacDuffie, J. (1995) 'human resource bundles and manufacturing performance — organizational logics and flexible production systems in the world auto industry', *Industrial and Labour Relations Review*, 48(2): 197–221.

Machiavelli, N. (1961) *The Prince*, London: Penguin.

Machiavelli, N. (1995) *The Prince* (trans. and ed. S.J. Milner; intro, notes and other critical apparatus, J.M. Dent). London: Everyman.

Machold, S. and Farquhar, S. (2013) 'Board task evolution: A longitudinal field study in the UK', *Corporate Governance: An International Review*, 21(2): 147–164.

MacKenzie, D. (2008) *An engine, not a camera: How financial models shape markets*. Mit Press.

Maclean, M., Harvey, C. and Press, J. (2006) *Business Elites and Corporate Governance in France and the UK*. London: Palgrave Macmillan.

Madhok, A. and Tallman, S.B. (1998) 'Resources, transactions and rents: Managing value through interfirm collaborative relationships', *Organization Science*, 9(3):326–339.

Magnus, G. (2016) 'Should we be worried by economic warnings of a bear in the China shop?', *The Guardian*, 20 January. Available at: www.theguardian.com/commentisfree/2016/jan/20/china-economy-policymaker-warnings-dark-global-outlook (accessed 21 January 2016).

Magretta, J. (2002) 'Why business models matter', *Harvard Business Review*, 80(5): 86–92.

Maguire, S., Hardy, C. and Lawrence, T. (2004) 'Institutional entrepreneurship and emerging fields: HIV/AIDS treatment advocacy in Canada', *Academy of Management Journal*, 47(5): 657–679.

Mahan, A.T. (1890) *The Influence of Sea Power upon History, 1660–1783*. Boston: Little Brown. Available at: https://archive.org/details/influenceseapow05mahagoog, (accessed 19 March 2016).

Mahmood, I. P. and Rufin, C. (2005) Government's dilemma: The role of government in imitation and innovation, *Academy of Management Review*, 30(2): 338–360.

Mahoney, J.T. (2005) *Economic Foundations of Strategy*. Thousand Oaks, CA: Sage Publications.

Mahoney, J.T. and Pandian, J.R. (1992) 'The resource-based view within the conversation of strategic management', *Strategic Management Journal*, 13: 363–380.

Mahoney, J.T., McGahan, A. and Pitelis, C (2009) 'The interdependence of private and public interests', *Organization Science*, 20(6): 1034–1052.

Maitlis, S. (2005) 'The social processes of organizational sensemaking', *Academy of Management Journal*, 48: 21–49.

Maitlis, S. and Lawrence, T.B. (2003) 'Orchestral manoeuvres in the dark: Understanding failure in organizational strategizing', *Journal of Management Studies*, 40(1): 109–140.

Maitlis, S. and Lawrence, T.B. (2007) 'Triggers and enablers of sensegiving in organizations', *Academy of Management Journal*, 50(1): 57–84.

Makadok, R. (2001) 'Toward a synthesis of the resourcebased and dynamic-capability views of rent creation', *Strategic Management Journal*, 22: 387–401.

Malerba, F. (2002) S'ectoral systems of innovation and production', *Research Policy*, 31(2): 247–264.

Mallaby, S. (2010) *More Money than God: Hedge Funds and the Making of a New Elite*. London: Bloomsbury.

Malmendier, U. and Tate, G. (2008) 'Who makes acquisitions? CEO overconfidence and the market's reaction', *Journal of Financial Economics*, 89(1): 20–43. Mandel, E. (1975) *Late Capitalism*. London: New Left Books.

Mandel, E. (1975) *Late Capitalism*. London: New Left Books.

Mandel, E. (1980) *Long Waves of Capitalist Development: The Interpretation*. New York: Cambridge University Press.

Manne, H.G. (1965) 'Mergers and the market for corporate control', *The Journal of Political Economy*, 73(2): 110–120.

Mantere, S. (2005) 'Strategic practices as enablers and disablers of championing activity', *Strategic Organization*, 3(2): 157–284.

Mantere, S. (2013) 'What is organizational strategy? A language-based view', *Journal of Management Studies*, 50(8): 1408–1426.

Mantere, S., Schildt, H.A. and Sillince, J.A. (2012) 'Reversal of strategic change', *Academy of Management Journal*, 55(1): 172–196.

Mantere, S. and Vaara, E. (2008) 'On the problem of participation in strategy: A critical discursive perspective', *Organization Science*, 19(2): 341–358.

Marceau, J. (2008) 'Innovation' in SR. Clegg and JR. Bailey (eds), *The International Encyclopaedia of Organizations*. Thousand Oaks, CA: Sage. pp. 670–673.

March, J.G. (1976) 'The technology of foolishness', Ambiguity and choice in organizations, 69 (81).

March, J.G. (1991) 'Exploration and exploitation in organizational learning', *Organization Science*, 2(1): 71–87.

March, J.G (1978) 'Bounded rationality, ambiguity, and the engineering of choice', *Bell Journal of Economics*, 9(2): 587–608.

March, J.G. and Olsen, J.P. (1976) *Ambiguity and choice in organisations*. Bergen: Universitetsforlaget 37.

March, J.G. and Simon, H.A. (1958) *Organizations*. New York: Wiley.

Markides, C. (2000) *All the Right Moves: A Guide to Crafting Breakthrough Strategy*, Vol. 1. Boston, MA: Harvard Business School Press.

Marris, R. (1968) *The Economic Theory of Managerial Capitalism*. New York: Basic Books.

Marshall, A. (1920) *Principles of Economics* (9th edn, 1961, Guillebaud edn). London: Macmillan.

Martin, J. (2001) *Organizational Culture: Mapping the Terrain*. Thousand Oaks, CA: Sage.

Martin, J. (2002) *Organizational Culture: Mapping the Terrain*. Thousand Oaks, CA: Sage.

Martin, R. (2002) *Financialization of Daily Life*. Philadelphia: Temple University Press.

Martinuzzi, A. and Krumay, B. (2013) 'The good, the bad, and the successful – How corporate social responsibility leads to competitive advantage and organizational transformation', *Journal of Change Management*, 13(4): 424–443.

Marx, A., Wouters, J., Rayp, G. and Beke, L. (eds) (2015) *Global Governance of Labour Rights*. Cheltenham: Edward Elgar.

Marx, K. (1959) *Capital*. London: Lawrence and Wishart.

Marx, K. and Engels, F. (1971) *Capital*, Vol. 3. Moscow: Progress.

Marx, T. (1991) 'Removing the obstacles to effective strategic planning', *Long Range Planning*, 24(4): 21–28.

Mason, E. (1939) 'Price and production policies of large-scale enterprise', *American Economic Review*, 29(1): 61–74.

Mason, E. (1949) 'The current state of the monopoly problem in the US', *Harvard Law Review*, 62: 1265–1285.

Mason, P. (2015) *Post Capitalism*. London, UK: Allen Lane.

Matthews, J.A. (2002) 'Competitive advantages of the latecomer firm: A resource-based account of industrial catch-up strategies', *Asia Pacific Journal of Management*, 19(4): 467–488.

Matthews, J.A. (2010*)* 'The Hsinchu Model: Collective efficiency, increasing returns and higher-order capabilities in the Hsinchu Science-based Industry Park', Keynote Address, Chinese Society for Management of Technology (CSMOT) 20th anniversary conference. Tsinghua University, Hsinchu, Taiwan.

Mayer, M. and Whittington, R. (1999) 'Euro-elites: Top British, French and German managers in the 1980s and 1990s', *European Management Journal*, 17(4): 403–408.

Mayrhofer, U. and Prange, C. (2015) 'Multinational Corporations (MNCs) and Enterprises (MNEs)', *Wiley Encyclopedia of Management*, London: Wiley.

McAdam, R. and McCreedy, S. (2000) 'A critique of knowledge management: Using a social constructivist model', *New Technology, Work and Employment*, 15(2): 155–168.

McCarthy, P. and Hatcher, C. (2005) 'Branding Branson: A case study of celebrity entrepreneurship', *Australian Journal of Communication*, 32(3): 45–61.

McDougall, P.P., Shane, S. and Oviatt, B.M. (1994) 'Explaining the formation of international new ventures', *Journal of Business Venturing*, 9(6): 469–487.

McEntee, G. (1985) 'City services: Can free enterprise outperform the public sector?', *Business and Society Review* (Fall): 43–47.

McGee, J. and Thomas, H. (1986) 'Strategic groups: Theory, research and taxonomy', *Strategic Management Journal*, 7(2): 141–160.

McGuire, D. and Hutchings, K. (2006) 'A Machiavellian analysis of organizational change', *Journal of Organizational Change Management*, 19(2): 192–209.

McKay, A. (2015) *The Big Short* [Film, director]. Hollywood, CA: Paramount.

McKinlay, A. (2002) 'The limits of knowledge management', *New Technology, Work and Employment*, 17(2): 76–88.

McLean, M. and Harvey, C. (2006) *Business Elites and Corporate Governance in France and the UK*. Basingstoke: Palgrave Macmillan.

McLuhan, M. (1964) *Understanding Media*. Mentor, New York.

McNamara, G., Deephouse, D.L. and Luce, R.A. (2003) 'Competitive positioning within and across a strategic group structure: The performance of core, secondary, and solitary firms', *Strategic Management Journal*, 24(2): 161–181.

McNulty, T. and Pettigrew, A. (1999) 'Strategists on the board', *Organization Studies*, 20(1): 47–74.

McNulty, T. and Pettigrew, A. (1995) Power and influence in and around the boardroom', *Human Relations*, 48(6): 845–873.

McPherson, C.M. and Sauder, M. (2013) 'Logics in action: Managing institutional complexity in a drug court', *Administrative Science Quarterly*, 58(2): 165–196.

Meacham, J.A. (1983) 'Wisdom and the context of knowledge: Knowing that one doesn't know', in D. Kuhn and A. Meachan (eds), *On the Development of Developmental Psychology*. Basel: Karger. pp. 111–134.

Meardi, G. and Marginson, P (2013) 'Global labour governance: Potential and limits of an emerging perspective', paper for the 2013 Work, Employment and Society Conference, Warwick, 3–5 September.

Meindl, J.R., Ehrlich, S.B, Dukerich, J.M. (1985) 'The romance of leadership', *Administrative Science Quarterly*, 30: 78–102.

Melé, D. (2012) *Management Ethics: Placing Ethics at the Core of Good Management*. New York: Palgrave Macmillan.

Ménard, C. (1995) 'Markets as institutions versus organizations as markets?: Disentangling some fundamental concepts', *Journal of Economic Behavior and Organization*, 28(2): 161–182.

Ménard, C. (2004) 'The economics of hybrid organizations', *Journal of Institutional and Theoretical Economics*, 160(3): 345–376.

Merali, Y. (2000) 'Individual and collective congruence in the knowledge management process', *Journal of Strategic Information Systems*, 9: 213–234.

Merton, R.K. and Barber, E. (2004) *The Travels and Adventures of Serendipity*. Princeton, NJ: Princeton University Press.

Meyer, A.D. (1982) 'Adapting to environmental jolts', *Administrative Science Quarterly*, 27(4): 515–537.

Meyer, J. and Rowan, B. (1977) 'Institutionalized organizations: Formal structure as myth and ceremony', *American Journal of Sociology*, 83(2): 340–363.

Meyer, J.W. and Rowan, B. (1983) 'The structure of educational educations', in J.W. Meyer and W.R. Scott (eds), *Organizational Environments: Ritual and Rationality*. Thousand Oaks, CA: Sage. pp. 71–97.

Meyer, J., John, B., George, M. and Francisco, O. (1997) 'World society and the nation state', *American Journal of Sociology*, 103(1): 144–148.

Micklethwaite, J. and A. Wooldridge (1996) *The Witch Doctors: Making Sense of the Management Gurus*. New York: Times Books.

Micklethwaite, J. and Wooldridge, A. (2000) *A Future Perfect: The Challenge and Hidden Promise of Globalization*. London: Crown Business.

Microsoft (2014a) *Microsoft Finance Code of Professional Conduct*. Available at: www.micro soft.com/investor/CorporateGovernance/BoardOfDirectors/Contacts/MSFinanceCode.aspx (accessed 22 April 2014).

Microsoft (2014b) *Microsoft Values*. Available at: www.microsoft.com/en-us/legal/compliance/ Buscond/default.aspx#values (accessed 22 April 2014).

Microsoft (2014c) *Microsoft Standards of Business Conduct*. Available at: www.microsoft.com/ about/legal/buscond/default.mspx (accessed 22 April 2014).

Middell, M. and Naumann, K. (2010) 'Global history and the spatial turn: From the impact of area studies to the study of critical junctures of globalization', *Journal of Global History*, 5: 149–170.

Milgrom, P. and Roberts, J. (1988) 'An economic approach to influence activities in organizations', *American Journal of Sociology*, Vol. 94, Supplement: S154-S179.

Mintzberg, H. (1973) The nature of managerial work.

Mintzberg, H. (1973) *The Nature of Managerial Work*. New York: Harper & Row.

Mintzberg, H. (1978) 'Patterns in strategy formation', *Management Science*, 24(9): 934–948.

Mintzberg, H. (1980) 'Structure in 5's: A synthesis of the research on organization design', *Management Science*, 26: 322–341.

Mintzberg, H. (1983) *Power in and around organizations*. Vol. 142. Englewood Cliffs, NJ: Prentice-Hall.

Mintzberg, H. (1987) *Crafting Strategy*. Boston, MA: Harvard Business School Press.

Mintzberg, H. (1989) *Mintzberg on Management: Inside our Strange World of Organizations*. New York: Free Press.

Mintzberg, H. (1990) 'The design school: reconsidering the basic premises of strategic management', *Strategic Management Journal*, 11(3): 171–195.

Mintzberg, H. (1993) 'The pitfalls of strategic planning', *California Management Review*, 36(1): 32–47.

Mintzberg, H. (1994) 'The fall and rise of strategic planning', *Harvard Business Review*, 72(1): 107–114.

Mintzberg, H. (2004) *Managers not MBAs: A Hard Look at the Soft Practice of Managing and Management Development*. San Francisco: Berrett-Koehler.

Mintzberg, H. and McHugh, A. (1985) 'Strategy formation in an adhocracy', *Administrative Science Quarter*, 30(2): 160–197.

Mintzberg, H. and Waters, J.A. (1985) 'Of strategies, deliberate and emergent', *Strategic Management Journal*, 6: 257–272.

Mishel, L. (2013) 'Working as designed: High profits and stagnant wages', *Working Economics* (Economic Policy Institute blog), 28 March. Available at: www.epi.org/blog/working-designed-high-profits-stagnant-wages/.

Mishel, L., Bivens, J., Gould, E. and Shierholz, H. (2012) *The State of Working America* (12th edn), an Economic Policy Institute book. Ithaca, NY: Cornell University Press.

Mitchell, R.K., Agle, B.R. and Wood, D.J. (1997) 'Toward a theory of stakeholder identification and salience: Defining the principle of who and what really counts', *Academy of Management Review*, 22(4): 853–886.

Mitchell, W. and Singh, K. (1996) 'Survival of businesses using collaborative relationships to commercialize complex goods', *Strategic Management Journal*, 17(3): 169–196.

Mitroff, I.I. and Denton, E. (1999) *A Spiritual Audit of Corporate America*. San Francisco: Jossey-Bass.

Mitsuhashi, H. and Greve, H.R. (2004) 'Powerful and free: Intraorganizational power and the dynamics of corporate strategy', *Strategic Organization*, 2(2): 107–132.

Mizik, N. and Jacobson, R. (2003) 'Trading off between value creation and value appropriation: The financial implications of shifts in strategic emphasis', *Journal of Marketing*, 67/January: 63–76.

Mizruchi, M.S. (1992) *The Structure of Corporate Political Action: Interfirm Relations and their Consequences*. Cambridge, MA: Harvard University Press.

Mizruchi, M.S. (1996) 'What do interlocks do? An analysis, critique, and reassessment of research on interlocking directorates', *Annual Review of Sociology*, 22(4): 271–298.

Modigliani, F. (1958) 'New developments on the oligopoly front', *Journal of Political Economy*, 66/3: 215–232.

Mockler, J.R. (1999) *Multinational Strategic Alliances*. New York, NY: Wiley.

Mol, A.P.J. (1995) *The Refinement of Production: Ecological Modernization Theory and the Chemical Industry*. Utrecht: Van Arkel.

Mol, A.P.J. and Spaargaren, G. (1993)' Environment, modernity and the risk-society: The apocalyptic horizon of environmental reform', *International Sociology*, 8(4): 429–459.

Monbiot, G. (2016) 'Neoliberalism – the ideology at the root of all our problems', *The Guardian*, 15 April. Available at: www.theguardian.com/books/2016/apr/15/neoliberalism-ideology-problem-george-monbiot?CMP=share_btn_link (accessed on 19 April 2016).

Moran, T. (1985) 'Multinational corporations and the developing countries: An analytical overview', in T. Moran (ed.), *Multinational Corporations: The Political Economy of Foreign Direct Investment*. Lexington, MA: D.C. Heath. pp. 3–24.

Montagna, P. (1990) 'Accounting rationality and financial legitimation', in S. Zukin and P. DiMaggio (eds), *Structures of Capital: The Social Organization of the Economy*. Cambridge, MA: Cambridge University Press. pp. 227–261.

Monteverde, K. and Teece, D.J. (1982) 'Supplier switching costs and vertical integration in the automobile industry', *Bell Journal of Economics*, 13: 206–213.

Morgan, G. (2001) 'The multinational firm: Organizing across institutional and national divides', in G. Morgan, P.H. Kristensen and R. Whitley (eds), *The Multinational Firm: Organizing Across Institutional and National Divides*. Oxford: Oxford University Press. pp. 1–24.

Morgan, G. (2006) *Images of Organization*. London: Sage.

Morgan, G. (2009) 'Globalization, multinationals and institutional diversity', *Economy and Society*, 38(4): 580–605.

Morgan, G. and Kristensen, P.H. (2006) 'The contested space of multinationals: Varieties of institutionalism, varieties of capitalism', *Human Relations*, 59(11): 1467–1490.

Morrison, J. (1970) 'Roadhouse blues' (recorded by The Doors). On *Roadhouse Blues* [LP]: CA: Elektra Records.

Morsing, M. and Rovira, A.S. (eds) (2011) *Business Schools and their Contribution to Society*. London: Sage.

Mueller, F., Whittle, A., Gilchrist, A. and Lenney, P. (2013) 'Politics and strategy practice: An ethnomethodologically-informed discourse analysis perspective', *Business History*, 55(7): 1168–1199.

Mumby, D.K. (1987) 'The political function of narrative in organizations', *Communications Monographs*, 54 (2): 113–127.

Mumby, D.K. (2005) 'Theorizing resistance in organization studies: A dialectical approach', *Management Communication Quarterly* (19)1: 1–26.

Munro, I. (1992) 'Codes of ethics. Some uses and abuses', in P. Davies (ed.), *Current Issues in Business Ethics*. London: Routledge. pp. 97–106.

Murray, G. and Scott, J. (2012) *Financial Elites and Transnational Business: Who Rules the World?* Cheltenham: Edward Elgar.

Murray, R., Caulier-Grice, J. and Mulgan, G. (2010) *The Open Book of Social Innovation*. London: NESTA.

Naar, L. and Clegg, S.R. (2015) *Gehry in Sydney*. Sydney: Images Press.

Nachum, L. and Zaheer, A. (2005) 'The persistence of distance? The impact of technology on MNE motivations for foreign investment', *Strategic Management Journal*, 26(8): 747–767.

Nag, R., Hambrick, D.C. and Chen, M.J. (2007) 'What is strategic management, really? Empirical induction of a consensus definition of the field', *Strategic Management Journal*, 28(9): 935–955.

Nahapiet, J. and Ghoshal, S. (1998) 'Social capital, intellectual capital, and the organizational advantage', *Academy of Management Review*, 23: 242–266.

Nahavandi, A. and Malekzadeh, A.R. (1988) 'Acculturation in mergers and acquisitions', *Academy of Management Review*, 13: 79–90.

Nath, D. and Gruca, T.S. (1997) 'Convergence across alternative methods for forming strategic groups', *Strategic Management Journal*, 18(9): 745–760.

Nelson, R.R. (1993) (ed.) *National Innovation Systems: A comparative analysis*. New York: Oxford University Press.

Nelson, R. (2005) *Technology, Institutions, and Economic Growth*. Cambridge, MA: Harvard University Press.

Nelson, R.R. and Winter, S.G. (1982) *An Evolutionary Theory of Economic Change*. Cambridge, MA: Harvard University Press.

Nelson, R.R. and Winter, S.G. (2002) 'Evolutionary theorizing in economics', *The Journal of Economic Perspectives*, 16(2): 23–46.

Newbury, W. and Zeira, Y. (1997) 'Generic differences between equity international joint ventures (EIJVs), international acquisitions (IAs) and international greenfield investment (IGIs): Implications for parent companies', *Journal of World Business*, 32(2): 87–102.

Newton, T. (2002) 'Creating the new ecological order?', *Academy of Management Review*, 27(4): 523–540.

Nicolini, D. (2102) *Practice Theory, Work, and Organization: An Introduction*. Oxford: Oxford University Press.

Nielsen, S. and Huse, M. (2010) 'The contribution of women on boards of directors: Going beyond the surface', *Corporate Governance: An International Review*, 18(2): 136–148.

Ng, W. and de Cock, C. (2002) 'Battle in the boardroom: A discursive perspective', *Journal of Management Studies*, 39(1): 23–49.

Nohria, N. and Eccles, R.G. (eds) (1992) *Networks and Organizations*. Boston, MA: Harvard Business School Press.

Nonaka, I. and Takeuchi, H. (1995) *The Knowledge-Creating Company: How Japanese Companies Create the Dynamics of Innovation*. Oxford: Oxford University Press.

Nonaka, I. and Toyama, R. (2007) 'Strategic management as distributed practical wisdom (phronesis)', *Industrial and Corporate Change*, 16(3): 371–394.

Nooteboom, B. (2004) *Inter-Firm Collaboration, Networks and Strategy: An Integrated Approach*. New York, NY: Routledge.

Nooteboom, B. (2008) 'Learning and innovation in inter-organizational relationships', in M. Ebers and P. Smith Ring (eds), *Handbook of Inter-organizational Relationships*. Oxford, UK: Oxford University Press. pp. 607–634.

Nordberg, D. (2010) 'Unfettered agents? The role of ethics in corporate governance. Corporate Governance: A synthesis of theory', *Research and Practice*, 17: 5–191.

Nordqvist, M. and Melin, L. (2008) 'Strategic planning champions: Social craftspersons, artful interpreters and known strangers', *Long Range Planning*, 41(3): 326–344.

Normann, R. (2001) *Reframing Business: When the Map Changes the Landscape*. Chichester: John Wiley & Co.

North, D.C. (1990) *Institutions, Institutional Change, and Economic Performance*. Cambridge: Cambridge University Press.

O'Connor, J. (1972) *The Fiscal Crisis of the State*. New York: St Martins Press.

O'Reilly, C.A. and Tushman, M.L. (2004) 'The ambidextrous organization', *Harvard Business Review*, 82(40): 74–81.

O'Rourke, D. (2006) 'Multi-stakeholder regulation: Privatizing or socializing global labor standards?', *World Development*, 34: 899–918.

Oakes, L.S., Townley, B. and Cooper, D.J. (1998) 'Business planning as pedagogy: Language and control in a changing institutional field', *Administrative Science Quarterly*, 43(2): 257–292.

OECD (1997) *OECD Jobs Report*. Paris: OECD.

Ogbonna, E. and Harris, L.C. (2000) 'Leadership style, organizational culture and performance', *International Journal of Human Resource Management*, 11(4): 766–788.

Offe, C. and Wiesenthal, H. (1985) 'Two logics of collective action: Theoretical notes on social class and organizational form', *Political Power and Social Theory*, 1: 67–115.

Ohmae, K. (1990) *The Borderless World*. London: Collins.

Ohmae, K. (1995) *The End of the Nation State*. New York: Free Press.

Oliver, C. (1992) 'The antecedents of deinstitutionalization', *Organization Studies*, 13(4): 563–588.

Orlikowski, W.J. (2002) 'Knowing in practice: Enacting a collective capability in distributive organizing', *Organization Science*, 13: 249–273.

Orlikowski, W. (2015) 'Practice in research: Phenomenon, perspective and philosophy', in D. Golsorkhi, L. Rouleau, D. Seidl and E. Vaara (eds), *Cambridge Handbook of Strategy as Practice* (2nd edn). Cambridge: Cambridge University Press.

Orlikowski, W.J. and Iacono, C.S. (2001) 'Desperately seeking the "IT" in IT research—A call to theorizing the IT artifact', *Information Systems Research*, 12(2): 121–134.

Ormerod, P. (2010) 'The current crisis and the culpability of macroeconomic theory', *21st Century Society*, 5(1): 5–18.

Orr, J.E. (1996) *Talking about Machines: An Ethnography of a Modern Job*. Cornell: Cornell University – ILR Press.

Orru, M. (1983) 'The ethics of anomie: Jean Marie Guyau and Emile Durkheim', *British Journal of Sociology*, 34(4): 499–518.

Ortiz, H. (2013) 'Financial professionals as a global elite', in J. Abbink and T. Salverda (eds), *The Anthropology of Elites: Power, Culture, and the Complexities of Distinction*. London: Palgrave. pp. 185–206.

Orwell, G. (2003) *Homage to Catalonia*. London: Penguin Classic.

Osborne, D. and Gaebler, T. (1993) *Reinventing Government: How the Entrepreneurial Spirit is Transforming the Public Sector*. New York: Penguin.

Osterwalder, A. and Pigneur, Y. (2010) *Business Model Generation: A Handbook for Visionaries, Game Changers, and Challengers*, eBook, Kindle edn. John Wiley & Sons.

Ouchi, W.G. (1979) 'A conceptual framework for the design of organizational control mechanisms', *Management Science*, 25(9): 833–847.

Ouchi, W.G. (1980) *Markets, Bureaucracies, and Clans*. Ithaca, NY: Cornell University Press.

Oviatt, B.M. and McDougall, P.P. (1994) 'Toward a theory of international new ventures', *Journal of International Business Studies*, 25(1): 45–64.

Owen, D.L., Swift, T.A., Humphrey, C. and Bowerman, M. (2000) 'The new social audits: Accountability, managerial capture or the agenda of social champions', *European Accounting Review*, 9(1): 81–90.

Owen, D.L., Swift, T. and Hunt, K. (2001) 'Questioning the role of stakeholder engagement in social and ethical accounting, auditing and reporting', *Accounting Forum*, 25(3): 264–282.

Owen-Smith, J. and Powell, W.W. (2008) 'Networks and institutions', in R. Greenwood, C. Oliver, K. Sahlin and R. Suddaby (eds), *The Sage Handbook of Organizational Institutionalism*. Thousand Oaks, CA: Sage Publications. pp. 295–336.

Oxfam Briefing paper (2016) An Economy for the 1%, 18 January 2016. Available at: www.oxfam.org/sites/www.oxfam.org/files/file_attachments/bp210-economy-one-percent-tax-havens-180116-en_0.pdf (Accessed 29 July 2016).

Oxley, J.E. (1997) 'Appropriability hazards and governance in strategic alliances: A transaction cost approach', *Journal of Law, Economics, and Organization*, 13: 387–409.

Ozcan, P. and Eisenhardt, K.M. (2009) 'Origin of alliance portfolios: Entrepreneurs, network strategies, and firm performance', *Academy of Management Journal*, 52(2): 246–279.

Pache, A. and Santos, F. (2013) 'Inside the hybrid organization: Selective coupling as a response to conflicting institutional logics', *Academy of Management Journal*, 56(4): 972–1001.

Paddon, M. (1991) 'The real costs of contracting out: Re-assessing the Australian debate from UK experience', Discussion Paper No 21, Public Sector Research Centre, University of New South Wales, Sydney.

Paddon, M. (1993) 'Competitive tendering and contracting out in British local government 1979–1992', Discussion Paper No 30, Public Sector Research Centre, University of New South Wales, Sydney.

Paddon, M. and Thanki, R. (1995) 'Submission from Public Sector Research Centre UNSW', in M. Paddon and R. Thanki (eds), *Australia's Contracting Public Services: Critical Views of Contracting-out by the Public Sector*, Public Sector Research Centre Collected Papers No 2, University of New South Wales, Sydney.

Paine, L.S. (1994) 'Managing for organizational integrity', *Harvard Business Review* (72)2: 106–117.

Paine, L.S. (2003) *Value Shift: Why Companies Must Merge Social and Financial Imperatives to Achieve Superior Performance*. New York: McGraw-Hill.

Pälli, P., Vaara, E. and Sorsa, V. (2009) 'Strategy as text and discursive practice: A genre-based approach to strategizing in city administration', *Discourse and Communication*, 3(3): 303–318.

Palmer, D. (1983) 'Broken ties: Interlocking directorates and intercorporate coordination', *Administrative Science Quarterly*, 28(1): 40–55.

Palmer, D.A. and Barber, B. (2001) 'Challengers, elites and owning families: A social class theory of corporate acquisitions in the 1960s', *Administrative Science Quarterly*, 46(1): 87–120.

Papanastassiou, M. and Pearce, R. D. (2009) *The Strategic Development of Multinationals*. Palgrave Macmillan: Basingstoke, UK.

Park, S.H. and Ungson, G. (2001) 'Interfirm rivalry and managerial complexity: A conceptual framework of alliance failure', *Organization Science*, 12(1): 37–53.

Parker, B. and Clegg, S.R. (2006) 'Globalization', in S.R. Clegg, C. Hardy, W. Nord and T. Lawrence, *Handbook of Organization Studies*. London: Sage. pp. 651–674.

Parker, C. and Nielsen, V.L. (2009) 'Corporate compliance systems: Could they make any difference?', *Administration and Society*, 41(1): 3–37.

Parker, H. (2002) 'Governing the corporation', in *Business: The Ultimate Resource*. Cambridge, MA: Perseus. pp. 239–240.

Parkhe, A. (1991) 'Interfirm diversity, organizational learning, and longevity in global strategic alliances', *Journal of International Business Studies*, 22(40): 579–601.

Parkhe, A. (1993) 'Strategic alliance structuring: A game theoretic and transaction cost examination of inter-firm cooperation', *Academy of Management Journal*, 36(4): 794–829.

Parkhe, A. (1996) 'International joint ventures', in B.J. Punnett and O. Shenkar (eds), *Handbook for International Management Research*. Cambridge, MA: Blackwell.

Parmigiani, A. (2007) 'Why do firms both make and buy? An investigation of concurrent sourcing', *Strategic Management Journal*, 28(3): 285–311.

Paroutis, S. and Heracleous, L. (2013) 'Discourse revisited: Dimensions and employment of first-order strategy discourse during institutional adoption', *Strategic Management Journal*, 34(8): 935–956.

Pascale, R.T. (1990) *Managing on the Edge*. London, UK: Penguin Books.

Pascale, R.T. (1984) 'Perspectives on strategy: The real story behind Honda's success', *California Management Review*, 26(3): 47–72.

Pearce, R.J. (1997) 'Toward understanding joint venture performance and survival: A bargaining and influence approach to transaction cost theory', *Academy of Management Review*, 22(1): 203–225.

Pearce, J.A. and Zahra, S.A. (1991) 'The relative power of CEOs and boards of directors: Associations with corporate performance', *Strategic Management Journal*, 12(2): 135–153.

Pearce, J. A. and Zahra, S. A. (1991) The relative power of CEOs and boards of directors: Associations with corporate performance, *Strategic Management Journal*, 12(2): 135–153.

Pels, J. and Saren, M. (2006) 'The role of assumptions in the choice of marketing strategy', *Finanza, Marketing e Produzione*, 23(3): 71–77.

Penrose, E.T. (1959) *The Theory of the Growth of the Firm*. Oxford: Oxford University Press.

Penrose, E.T. (1995) 'Foreword', in *The Theory of the Growth of the Firm* (3rd edn). Oxford, UK: Oxford University Press. pp. i–xxi.

Penrose, E.T. (2008) 'Strategy/organization and the metamorphosis of the large firm', *Organization Studies*, 29(8/9): 1117–1124.

Penrose, E.T. (2009) *The Theory of the Growth of the Firm* (4th edn), with an introduction by C.N. Pitelis. New York: John Wiley and Sons.

Perey, R. (2016) *Ecological Imaginaries Reframing Organization*. Copenhagen: CBS Press.

Perkins, A. (2015) 'We all love Marks & Spencer – but not enough to buy its clothes', *The Guardian*. Available at: www.theguardian.com/commentisfree/2014/dec/29/marks-and-spencer-clothes-customers-value-for-money (accessed 20 January 2015).

Perrow, C. (1984) *Normal Accidents: Living with High Risk Technologies*. New York: Basic Books.

Perrow, C. (2011) *The Next Catastrophe: Replacing our Vulnerabilities to Natural, Industrial and Terrorist Disasters*. Princeton: Princeton University Press.

Perrey, R. (2016) *Ecological Imaginaries Reframing Organizations*. Copenhagen: Copenhagen Business School Press.

Peteraf, M.A (1993) 'The cornerstone of competitive advantage, *Strategic Management Journal*, 14: 179–191.

Peteraf, M.A. (2006) 'New domains and directions for research in organizational identity', presentation at the IIB Organizational Organizational Identity Workshop, Stockholm.

Peteraf, M.A. and Barney, J.B. (2003) 'Unravelling the resource based tangle', *Managerial and Decision Economics*, 24(4): 309–323.

Peteraf, M.A. and Shanley, M. (1997) 'Getting to know you: A theory of strategic group identity', *Strategic Management Journal*, 18(summer special issue): 165–186.

Peters, T. (2005) *Design: Innovate, Differentiate, Communicate*. New York, Dorling Kindersley.

Peters, T. and Waterman, R. (1982) *In Search of Excellence: Lessons from America's Best Run Companies*. New York: Harper & Row/Watertown, MA: Harvard Business School Press.

Pettigrew, A. (1972) 'Information control as a power resource', Sociology, 6(2): 187–204.

Pettigrew, A. (1985) *The Awakening Giant. Continuity and change at ICI*. New York: Basil Blackwell.

Pettigrew, A. (1987) 'Context and action in the transformation of the firm', Journal of management studies, 24(6): 649–670.

Pettigrew, A. M. (1987) Context and action in the transformation of the firm, *Journal of management studies*, 24(6): 649–670.

Pettigrew, A. (2002) Strategy Formulation as a Political Process. In S. R. Clegg (ed.), Central Currents in Organization Studies II: Contemporary Trends, London: Sage, pp. 43–9 (originally published in (1977) *International Studies of Management and Organization*. 1: 78–87).

Pettigrew, A. and McNulty, T. (1995) 'Power and influence in and around the boardroom', *Human Relations*, 48(8): 845–873.

Pettigrew, A. and McNulty, T. (1998) 'Control and creativity in the boardroom', *Navigating change: How CEOs, top teams and boards steer transformation*, pp. 226–255.

Pettigrew, A. and Whipp, R. (1993) 'Understanding the environment', in C. Mabey and B. Mayon-White (eds), *Managing Change* (2nd edn). London: Open University/Paul Chapman Publishing. pp. 5–19.

Pettigrew, A., Thomas, H. and Whittington, R. (2002) Strategic management: the strengths and limitations of a field, *Handbook of Strategy and Management*, London: Sage, pp. 3–30.

Pettigrew, A., Thomas, H. and Whittington, R. (2002) 'Strategic management: the strengths and limitations of a field', *Handbook of Strategy and Management*, 3.

Pfeffer, J. (1972) 'Size and composition of corporate boards of directors: The organization and its environment', *Administrative Science Quarterly*, pp. 218–228.

Pfeffer, J. (1992) *Managing with Power: Politics and Influence in Organizations*. Harvard: Harvard Business Press.

Pfeffer, J. (1998) *The Human Equation: Building Profits by Putting People First*. Harvard: Harvard Business School Press.

Pfeffer, J. (2010) 'Building sustainable organizations: The human factor', *The Academy of Management Perspectives*, 24: 34–45.

Pfeffer, J. (2011) 'Management a profession? Where's the Proof?', *Harvard Business Review*, 89 (September): 38. Available at: http://hbr.org/2011/09/management-a-profession-wheres-the-proof/ar/1 (accessed 3 March 2012).

Pfeffer, J. and Fong, C.T. (2002) 'The end of business schools? Less success than meets the eye', *Academy of Management Learning and Education*, 1(1): 78–95.

Pfeffer, J. and Salancik, G.R. (1974) 'Organizational decision-making as a political process: The case of a university budget', *Administrative Science Quarterly*, 19(2): 135–151.

Phillips, N., Sewell, G. and Jaynes, S. (2008) 'Applying critical discourse analysis in strategic management research', *Organizational Research Methods*, 11(4): 770–789.

Phillips, W., Lamming, R., Bessent, J. and Noke, H. (2006) 'Discontinuous innovation and supply relationships – Strategic dalliances', *R&D Management*, 36(4): 451–461.

Piderit, S.K. (2000) 'Rethinking resistance and recognizing ambivalence: A multidimensional view of attitudes toward an organizational change', *Academy of Management Review*, 25(4): 783–794.

Pieke, F. (2004) 'Contours of an anthropology of the Chinese state: Political structure, agency, and economic development in rural China', *Journal of the Royal Anthropological institute* (N.S.), 10: 517–538.

Piketty, T. (2014) *Capital in the Twenty First Century*. Cambridge: Harvard University Press.

Pinder, C.P. and Harlos, K.P. (2001) 'Employee silence: Quiescence and acquiescence as responses to perceived injustice', *Research in Personnel and Human Resources Management*, 20: 331–370.

Pisano, G. (1989) 'Using equity participation to support exchange: Evidence from the biotechnology industry', *Journal of Law, Economics and Organization*, 5(1): 109–126.

Pitelis, C.N. (1987) *Corporate Capital: Control, Ownership, Saving and Crisis*. New York: Cambridge University Press.

Pitelis, C.N. (1991) *Market and Non-market Hierarchies: Theory of Institutional Failure*. Oxford: Basil Blackwell.

Pitelis, C.N. (ed.) (2002) *The Growth of the Firm: The legacy of Edith Penrose*. Oxford: Oxford University Press.

Pitelis, C.N. (2004a) 'Edith Penrose and the resource-based view of (international) business strategy', *International Business Review*, 13/4: 523–532.

Pitelis, C.N. (2004b) '(Corporate) governance, (shareholder) value and (sustainable) economic performance', *Corporate Governance: An International Review*, 12/2: 210–223.

Pitelis, C.N. (2004c) *Corporate capital: Control, ownership, saving and crisis*. Cambridge University Press.

Pitelis, C.N. (2007) 'A behavioral resource-based view of the firm: The synergy of Cyert and March (1963) and Penrose (1959)', *Organization Science*, 18/3: 478–490.

Pitelis, C.N. (2009a) 'The sustainable competitive advantage and catching-up of nations: FDI, clusters and liability (asset) of smallness', *Management International Review*, 49/3–4: 95–119.

Pitelis, C.N. (2009b) 'The co-evolution of organizational value capture, value creation and sustainable advantage', *Organization Studies*, 30(10): 1115–1139.

Pitelis, C.N. (2012) 'Clusters, entrepreneurial ecosystem co-creation, and appropriability: A conceptual framework', *Industrial and Corporate Change*, 21(6): 1359–1388.

Pitelis, C. (2013) 'Towards a more "ethically correct" governance for economic sustainability', *Journal of Business Ethics*, 118(3): 655–665.

Pitelis, C. and Sugden, R. (1986) 'The separation of ownership and control in the theory of the firm: A reappraisal', *International Journal of Industrial Organization*, 4(1): 69–86.

Pitelis, C.N. and Taylor, C. (1996) 'From generic strategies to value for money in hypercompetitive environments', *Journal of General Management*, 21/4: 45–61.

Pitelis, C.N. and Teece, D.J. (2009) 'The (new) nature and essence of the firm', *European Management Review*, 6(1): 5–15.

Pitelis, C.N. and Teece, D.J. (2010) 'Cross-border market co-creation, dynamic capabilities and the entrepreneurial theory of the multinational enterprise', *Industrial and Corporate Change*, 19(4): 1247–1270.

Pitelis, C.N. and Wahl, M.W. (1998) 'Edith Penrose: Pioneer of stakeholder theory', *Long Range Planning*, 31/2: 252–261.

Pitsis, T., Clegg, S.R., Marosszeky, M. and Rura-Polley, T. (2003) 'Constructing the Olympic Dream: Managing innovation through the future perfect', *Organization Science*, 14(5): 574–590.

Plesner, U. and Gulbrandsen, I.T. (2015) 'Strategy and new media: A research agenda', *Strategic Organization*, 13(2): 153–162.

Podolny, J.M. and Page, K.L. (1998) 'Network forms of organization', *American Review of Sociology*, 24: 57–76.

Polanyi, M. (1969) *Knowing and Being: Essays by Michael Polanyi* (ed., M. Greene). Chicago: University of Chicago Press.

Polanyi, M. (1983) *The Tacit Dimension*. Garden City, New York: Doubleday. (Originally published 1966.)

Pondy, L.R. and Mitroff, I.I. (1979) 'Beyond open systems models of organizations', in B.M. Staw (ed.), *Research in Organizational Behavior*. Greenwich, CT: JAI Press. pp. 3–39.

Poppo, L. and Zenger, T. (2002) 'Do formal contracts and relational governance function as substitutes or complements?', *Strategic Management Journal*, 23(8): 707–725.

Porac, J.F. and Thomas, H. (1994) 'Cognitive categorization and subjective rivalry among retailers in a small city', *Journal of Applied Psychology*, 79(1): 54–66.

Porac, J.F. and Thomas, H. (2002) 'Managing cognition and strategy: Issues, trends and future decision', in T. H. Pettigrew and R. Whittington (eds), *Handbook of Strategy and Management*. London: Sage. Pp. 165–181.

Porac, J.F., Thomas, H., Wilson, F., Paton, D. and Kamfer, A. (1995) 'Rivalry and the Scottish knitwear producers', *Administrative Science Quarterly*, 40(2): 202–227.

Porter, M. (1980) *Competitive Strategy: Techniques for Analyzing Industries and Competitors*. New York: The Free Press.

Porter, M.E. (1985) *Competitive Advantage: Creating and Sustaining Superior Performance*. New York, NY: Simon & Schuster.

Porter, M. (1987) 'From competitive advantage to corporate strategy', *Harvard Business Review*, 65(3): 43–59.

Porter, M.E. (1990) *The Competitive Advantage of Nations*. New York, NY: The Free Press.

Porter, M.E. (1996) 'What is strategy?', *Harvard Business Review*, 74(6): 61–78.

Porter, M.E. (2008) *On Competition*. Cambridge, MA: Harvard Business School Press.

Porter, M.E. and Heppelmann, J.E. (2014) 'How smart, connected products are transforming competition', *Harvard Business Review*, 92(11): 64–88.

Porter, M.E. and Kramer, M.R. (2011) 'Creating shared value', *Harvard Business Review*, 89: 62–77.

Powell, F. (2013) *The politics of civil society*. Policy Press.

Powell, J. (2010) *The New Machiavelli: How to Wield Power in the Modern World*. London: Vintage.

Powell, T.C. (2001) 'Competitive advantage: Logical and philosophical considerations', *Strategic Management Journal*, 22(9): 857–888.

Powell, T.C. (2014) 'Strategic management and the person', *Strategic Organization*, 12(3): 200–207.

Powell, T.C., Rahman, N. and Starbuck, W.H. (2010) 'European and American origins of competitive advantage', *Advances in Strategic Management*, 27: 313–351.

Powell, W.W. (1990) 'Neither market nor hierarchy: Network forms of organization', in L.L. Cummings and B. Staw (eds), *Research in Organizational Behavior*, Vol. 12. Greenwich, CT: JAI Press. pp. 295–336.

Powell, W.W. and DiMaggio, P.J. (1983) 'The iron-cage revisited: Institutional isomorphism and collective rationality in organizational fields', *American Sociological Review*, 48: 147–160.

Powell, W.W., Koput, K.W. and Smith-Doerr, L. (1996) 'Interorganizational collaboration and the locus of innovation: Networks of learning in biotechnology', *Administrative Science Quarterly*, 41: 116–145.

Powell, J. (2010) *The New Machiavelli: How to Wield Power in the Modern World*. Random House.

Power, M. (2009) *Organized Uncertainty: Designing a World of Risk Management*. Oxford: Oxford University Press.

Prahalad, C.K. (2004) 'The blinders of dominant logic', *Long Range Planning*, 37(2): 171–179.

Prahalad, C.K. and Doz, Y.L. (1987) *The Multinational Mission*. New York: Free Press.

Prahalad, C.K. and Hamel, G. (1990) 'The core competence of the corporation', *Harvard Business Review*, 68(3): 79–91.

Prahalad, C.K. and Ramaswamy, V. (2004) 'The new frontier of experience innovation', *Sloan Management Review*, 44(2): 12–18.

Prasad, P. and Prasad, A. (2000) 'Stretching the Iron Cage: The constitution and implications of routine workplace resistance', *Organization Science*, 11(4): 387–403.

Pugliese, A., Bezemer, P., Zattoni, A., Huse, M., Van den Bosch, F.A.J. and Volberda, H. (2009) 'Boards of Directors' contribution to strategy: A literature review and research agenda. *Corporate Governance: An International Review*, 17(3): 292–306.

Pugliese, A., Nicholson, G. and Bezemer, P.J. (2015) 'An observational analysis of the impact of board dynamics and directors' participation on perceived board effectiveness', *British Journal of Management*, 26(1): 1–25.

Puranam, P., Singh, H. and Zollo, M. (2006) 'Organizing for innovation: Managing the coordination–autonomy dilemma in technology acquisitions', *Academy of Management Journal*, 49: 263–280.

Putnam, R. D. (1976) *The Comparative Study of Political Elites*. Englewood Cliffs, NJ: Prentice Hall.

Quiggin, J. (1994) 'The fiscal gains from contracting out: Transfers of efficiency improvements', *Australian Economic Review*, 3rd quarter: 97–102.

Quiggin, J. (1996) 'Competitive tendering and contracting in the Australian public sector', *Australian Journal of Public Administration*, 55(3): 49–58.

Quinn Mills, D. and Friesen, B. (1992) 'The learning organization', *European Management Journal*, 10: 146–156.

Quinn, J.B. (1978) 'Strategic change: "Logical incrementalism"', *Sloan Management Review*, 20(1): 7–19.

Rahrami, H. (1992) 'The emerging flexible organization: Perspectives from Silicon Valley', *California Management Review*, 34(4): 33–52.

Rajan, R. and Zingales, L. (1998) 'Power in the theory of the firm', *The Quarterly Journal of Economics*, 113(2): 387–432.

Ramirez, R. (1999) 'Value co-production: Intellectual origins and implications for practice and research', *Strategic Management Journal*, 20: 49–65.

Ranft, A.L. and Lord, M.D. (2002) 'Acquiring new technologies and capabilities: A grounded model of acquisition implementation', *Organization Science*, 13: 420–441.

Rangan, S. (2015) *Performance and Progress: Essays on Capitalism, Business, and Society*. Oxford: Oxford University Press.

Rao, K. and Tilt, C. (2015) 'Board composition and corporate social responsibility: The role of diversity, gender, strategy and decision making', *Journal of Business Ethics*:1–21.

Rasche, A. and Esser, D.E. (2007) 'Managing for compliance and integrity in practice', in C. Carter, S. Clegg, M. Kornberger, S. Laske and M. Messner (eds.), *Business Ethics as Practice: Representation, Reflexivity and Performance.*, Cheltenham UK and Northhampton, MA: Edward Elgar.

Ravenscraft D. J. and Scherer, F. M. (1987) *Mergers, Sell-Offs and Economic Efficiency*. Berkeley, CA: The Brookings Institution.

Raviola, E. and Boczkowski, P. (2012) 'Newsroom meets community in journalism: An account of institutional innovation in a French news site', paper presented at Organization Studies Winter Conference, Steamboat Springs, CO, 7–10 February.

Rea, A. (2004) *The CFO's Perspective on Alliances: Growth, Risk, and Measurement*. Boston, MA: CFO Publishing Corp.

Reay, T. and Hinings, C.R. (2009) 'Managing the rivalry of competing institutional logics', *Organization Studies*, 30(6): 629–652.

Regnér, P. (2003) 'Strategy creation in the periphery: Inductive versus deductive strategy making', *Journal of Management Studies*, 40(1): 57–82.

Rego, A., Cunha, M.P. and Clegg, S. (2012) *The Virtues of Leadership: Contemporary Challenge for Global Managers*. Oxford: Oxford University Press.

Reich, R. (2007) *Supercapitalism: The Transformation of Capitalism, Business and Everyday Life*. New York, NY: Vintage.

Ren, H., Gray, B. and Kim, K. (2009) 'Performance of international joint ventures: What factors really make a difference and how?', *Journal of Management*, 35(3): 805–883.

Rennie, M.W. (1993) 'Global competitiveness: Born global', *McKinsey Quarterly*, 4(1): 45–52.

Reuer, J.J. (2005) 'Avoiding lemons in M&A deals', *MIT Sloan Management Review*, 46(3): 15–17.

Reuer, J.J. and Ariño, A. (2002) 'Contractual heterogeneity in strategic alliances', IESE Working Paper No. D/482. Available at: http://ssrn.com/abstract=462302 or doi:10.2139/ssrn.462302 (accessed 29 April 2010).

Reuer, J.J., Zollo, M. and Singh, H. (2002) 'Post-formation dynamics in strategic alliances', *Strategic Management Journal*, 23: 135–151.

Rhodes, C. (2016) 'Democratic business ethics: Volkswagen's emissions scandal and the disruption of corporate sovereignty', *Organization Studies*, doi: 10.1177/0170840616641984.

Rhodes, C. and Wray-Bliss, E. (2013) 'The ethical difference of *Organization*', *Organization*, 20(1): 39–50.

Rhodes, R.A.W. (2007) 'The everyday life of a minister: A confessional and impressionist tale', in R.A.W. Rhodes, P. 't Hart and M. Noordegraaf (eds), *The Ethnography of Government Elites: Up Close and Personal*. Houndmills, Basingstoke: Palgrave-Macmillan. pp. 21–50.

Rhodes, R.A.W., 't Hart, P. and Noordegraaf, M. (eds) (2007) *The Ethnography of Government Elites: Up Close and Personal*. Houndmills, Basingstoke: Palgrave-Macmillan.

Riad, S. (2005) 'The power of "organisational culture" as a discursive formation in merger integration', *Organization Studies*, 26(10): 1529–1554.

Rich, A. (2006) *Business and Economic Ethics: The Ethics of Economic Systems*. Leuven: Peeters.

Richardson, G. (1972) 'The organisation of industry', *The Economic Journal*, 82(327): 883–896.

Riisgaard, L. and Hammer, N. (2011) 'Prospects for labour in global value chains: Labour standards in the cut flower and banana industries', *British Journal of Industrial Relations*, 49(1): 168–190.

Rindova, V., Dalpiaz, E. and Ravasi, D. (2011) 'A cultural quest: A study of organizational use of new cultural resources in strategy formation', *Organization Science*, 22(2): 413–431.

Rindova, V.P., Pollock, T.G. and Hayward, M.L.A. (2006) 'Celebrity firms: The social construction of market popularity', *Academy of Management Review*, 31(1): 50–71.

Ring, P. and Van de Ven, A. (1994) 'Developmental processes of cooperative interorganizational relationships', *Academy of Management Review*, 19(1): 90–118.

Ringland, G. (1998) *Scenario Planning: Managing for the Future*, John Wiley & Sons, Chichester.

Ritzer, G. (2004) *The Globalization of Nothing*. Thousand Oaks, CA: Pine Forge Press.

Robertson, R. (1982) *Globalization: Social Theory and Global Culture*. London: Sage.

Robins, J.A., Tallman, S. and Fladmoe-Lindquist, K. (2002) 'Autonomy and dependence of international cooperative ventures', *Strategic Management Journal*, 23: 881–902.

Rodrigues, S.B. (2006) 'The political dynamics of organizational culture in an institutionalized environment', *Organization Studies*, 27: 537–557.

Rodriguez, P., Uhlenbruck, K. and Eden, L. (2005) 'Government corruption and the entry strategies of multinationals', *Academy of Management Review*, 30(2): 383–396.

Rodrik, D. (ed.) (2003) *In Search of Prosperity: Analytic Narratives on Economic Growth*. Princeton, NJ: Princeton University Press.

Roe, M.J. (1994) *Strong Managers, Weak Owners: The Political Roots of American Corporate Finance*. Princeton, NJ: Princeton University Press.

Roe, M. J. (2003) *Political determinants of corporate governance: Political context, corporate impact*. Oxford University Press on Demand.

Roll, R. (1986) 'The hubris hypothesis of corporate takeovers', *Journal of Business* 59(2): 197–216.

Romme, A.G.L. (2003) 'Making a difference: Organization as design', *Organization Science*, 14(5): 558–573.

Romme, A.G.L. and Endenburg, G. (2006) 'Construction principles and design rules in the case of circular design', *Organization Science*, 17(2): 287–297.

Romme, G., Zollo, M and Berends, P. (2010) 'Dynamic capabilities, deliberate learning and environmental dynamism: A simulation model,' *Industrial and Corporate Change*, 19(4): 1271–1299.

Roos, J. and Victor, B. (1999) 'Towards a new model of strategy-making as serious play', *European Management Journal*, 17(4): 348–355.

Rose, N. and Miller, P. (1992) 'Political power beyond the state problematics of government', *British Journal of Sociology*, 43(2): 173–205.

Rosenzweig, P.M. and Nohria, N. (1994) 'Influences on human resource management practices in multinational corporations', *Journal of International Business Studies*, 25(2): 229–251.

Rothery, B. and Roberts, L. (1995) *The Truth about Outsourcing*. Aldershot: Gower.

Rouleau, L. (2005) 'Micro-practices of strategic sensemaking and sensegiving: How middle managers interpret and sell change everyday', *Journal of Management Studies*, 42(7): 1413–1441.

Rouleau, L. and Balogun, J. (2011) 'Middle managers, strategic sensemaking and discursive competence', *Journal of Management Studies*, 48(5): 953–983.

Rowley, J. and Gibbs, P. (2008) 'From learning organization to practically wise organization', *The Learning Organization*, 15(5): 356–372.

Rugman, A.M. and Verbeke, A. (1993) 'Generic strategies in global competition', in A.M. Rugman and A. Verbeke (eds), *Research in Global Strategic Management: Global Competition Beyond the Three Generics*, Vol. 4. Greenwich, CT: JAI Press. pp. 3–15.

Rumelt, R.P. (1991) 'How much does industry matter?', *Strategic Management Journal*, 12(3): 167–185.

Rumelt, R.P., Schendel, D.E. and Teece, D.J. (1994) *Fundamental Issues in Strategy: A Research Agenda*. Boston: Harvard Business School Press.

Sacks, H. and Jefferson, G. (1992) *Lectures on Conversation*. Oxford, UK/ Cambridge, MA: Blackwell.

Saïd Business School and Heidrick & Struggles (2015) *The CEO Report: Embracing the Paradoxes of Leadership and the Power of Doubt*. London: Saïd Business School and Heidrick & Struggles.

Salancik, G. and Pfeffer, J. (1977) 'Who gets power – and how they hold on to it: A strategic-contingency model of power', *Organizational Dynamics*, 5(3): 3–21.

Saloner, G., Shephard, A. and Podolny, J. (2001) *Strategic Management*. New York: John Wiley and Sons.

Salverda, T. and Abbink, J. (2013) 'Introduction: An anthropological perspective on elite power and the cultural politics of elites', in J. Abbink and T. Salverda (eds), *The Anthropology of Elites: Power, Culture and the Complexities of Distinction*. London: Palgrave Macmillan. pp. 1–28.

Sambharya, R. (1996) 'Foreign experience of top management teams and international diversification strategies of US multinational corporations', *Strategic Management Journal*, 17(9): 739–746.

Sampson, R.C. (2005) 'Experience effects and collaborative returns in R&D alliances', *Strategic Management Journal*, 26(11): 1009–1031.

Samra-Fredericks, D. (2003) 'Strategizing as lived experience and strategists' everyday efforts to shape strategic direction', *Journal of Management Studies*, 40(1): 141–174.

Samra-Fredericks, D. (2004a) 'Managerial elites making rhetorical and linguistic 'moves' for a moving (emotional) display', *Human Relations*, 57(9): 1103–1143.

Samra-Fredericks, D. (2004b) 'Understanding the production of "strategy" and "organization" through talk amongst managerial elites', *Culture and Organization*, 10(2): 125–141.

Samra-Fredericks, D. (2005) 'Strategic practice, "discourse" and the everyday interactional constitution of "power effects"', *Organization*, 12(6): 803–841.

Samuelson, P. (1986) *The Collected Scientific Papers of Paul Samuelson*, Vol. 5. Boston, MA: MIT Press.

Sánchez-Fernández, R. and Iniesta-Bonillo, M.Á. (2007) 'The concept of perceived value: A systematic review of the research', *Marketing Theory*, 7: 427–451.

Sánchez-Fernández, R., Iniesta-Bonillo, M.Á. and Holbrook, M.B. (2009) 'The conceptualisation and measurement of consumer value in services', *International Journal of Market Research*, 51(1): 93–113.

Sandel, M.J. (2013) *What Money Can't Buy: The Moral Limits of Markets*. New York, NY: Farrer, Strauss and Giroux.

Sarala, R.M. (2010) 'The impact of cultural differences and acculturation factors on post-acquisition conflict', *Scandinavian Journal of Management*, 26: 38–56.

Sassen, S. (2005) 'The embeddedness of electronic markets: The case of global capital markets', in K. Knorr-Cetina and A. Preda (eds), *The Sociology of Financial Markets*. Oxford: Oxford University Press. pp. 17–37.

Sauermann, H. and Stephan, P. (2013) 'Conflicting logics? A multidimensional view of industrial and academic science', *Organization Science*, 24(3): 889–909.

Savage, M. and Williams, K. (2008) 'Elites: Remembered in capitalism and forgotten by social sciences', in M. Savage and K. Williams (eds), *Remembering Elites*. Oxford: Blackwell. pp. 1–24.

Savitz, A. and Weber, K. (2006) *The Triple Bottom Line: How Today's Best-Run Companies are Achieving Economic, Social and Environmental Success – and How You Can Too*. San Francisco, CA: Jossey-Bass.

Sawyer, R.D. (1994) *The Art of War*. Boulder, CO: Westview Press.

Saxenian, A. (1994) *Regional Advantage: Culture and Competition in Silicon Valley and Route 128*. Cambridge, MA: Harvard University Press.

Sayles, L.R. (1976) 'Matrix management: The structure with a future', *Organizational Dynamics*, 5(2): 2–17.

Schattschneider, E. (1960) *The Semi-Sovereign People*. New York: Holt, Rinehart and Winston.

Schatzki, T.R. (1996) *Social Practices: A Wittgensteinian Approach to Human Activity and the Social*. Cambridge, MA: Cambridge University Press.

Schatzki, T. (2001) 'Introduction: Practice theory', in T. Schatzki, K. Knorr Cetina and E. von Savigny (eds), *The Practice Turn in Contemporary Theory*. London: Routledge. pp. 1–14.

Schatzki, T.R. (2002) *The Site of the Social: A Philosophical Account of the Constitution of Social Life and Change*. University Park, PA: Pennsylvania State University Press.

Schein, E.H. (1997) *Organizational Culture and Leadership* (2nd edn). San Francisco: Jossey Bass.

Schein, E. (1988) *Process Consultation, Volume I: Its Role in Organization Development*. Reading, MA: Addison-Wesley.

Schein, E. (1999) *Process Consultation Revisited: Building the Helping Relationship*. Reading, MA: Addison-Wesley.

Scherer, F.M. and Ross, D.R. (eds) (1990) *Industrial Market Structure and Economic Performance* (3rd edn). Boston, MA: Houghton Mifflin.

Schmalensee, R. (1982) 'Antitrust and the new industrial economics', *American Economic Review*, 72 (May): 24–28.

Schrage, M. (2000) *Serious Play: How the Worlds Best Companies Simulate to Innovate*. Boston: Harvard Business Press.

Schumpeter, J.A. (1934/2008) *The Theory of Economic Development: An Inquiry into Profits, Capital, Credit, Interest and the Business Cycle* (trans. Redvers Opie). London: Transaction Publishers.

Schumpeter, J. (1942) *Capitalism, Socialism and Democracy* (1987, 5th edn). London: Unwin Hyman.

Schütz, A. (1967) *The Phenomenology of the Social World*. Evanston, IL: Northwestern University Press.

Schweizer, L. (2005) 'Organizational integration of acquired biotechnology companies into pharmaceutical companies: The need for a hybrid approach', *Academy of Management Journal*, 48: 1051–1074.

Scott, J. (1982) *The Upper Classes: Property and Privilege in Britain*. London: Macmillan.

Scott, J. (1991) 'Networks of corporate power: A comparative assessment', *Annual Review of Sociology*, 17: 181–203.

Scott, J. (1996) *Stratification and Power: Structures of Class, Status and Command*. Cambridge: Polity Press.

Scott, J. (2001) *Power*. Cambridge: Polity Press.

Scott, J. (2008) 'Modes of power and the re-conceptualization of elites', in M. Savage and K. Williams (eds), *Remembering Elites*. Oxford: Blackwell, pp. 27–43.

Scott, R.W. (1995) *Institutions and Organizations*. Thousand Oaks, CA: Sage.

Scott, R.W. and Davis, G.F. (2007) *Organizations and Organizing: Rational, Natural, and Open System Perspectives*. Upper Saddle Valley, NJ: Pearson Prentice Hall.

Scott, W.R. (2014) *Institutions and Organizations: Ideas, Interests, and Identities* (4th edn). Thousand Oaks, CA: Sage.

Sedlacek, T. (2011) *Economics of Good and Evil: The Quest for Economic Meaning from Gilgamesh to Wall Street*. Oxford: Oxford University Press.

Seidl, D. (2007) 'General strategy concepts and the ecology of strategy discourses: A systemic-discursive perspective', *Organization Studies*, 28(2): 197–218.

Senge, P. (1990) *The Fifth Discipline: The Art and Practise of the Learning Organization*. New York, NY: Currency Doubleday.

Serapio, M. and Cascio, W. (1996) 'End games in international alliances', *Academy of Management Executive*, 10(1): 62–74.

Servan-Schreiber, J. (1967) *The American Challenge*. New York: Scribner.

Sewell, G. and Barker, J.R. (2006) 'Coercion versus care: Using irony to make sense of organizational surveillance', *Academy of Management Review*, 31(4): 934–961.

Sharpe, D.R. (2001) 'Globalization and change: Organizational continuity and change within a Japanese multinational in the UK', in G. Morgan, P. Kristensen and R. Whitley (eds), *The Multinational Firm: Organizing across Institutional and National Divides*. Oxford: Oxford University Press. pp. 196–222.

Shaw, G., Brom, R., and Bromley, P. (1998) 'Strategic stories: How 3M is rewriting business planning', *Harvard Business Review*, 76(5): 41–50.

Shelanski, H.A. and Klein, P.G. (1995) 'Empirical research in transaction cost economics: A review and assessment', *Journal of Law, Economics, and Organization*, 11: 335–361.

Shen, W. and Cannella, A. Jr. (2002) 'Power dynamics within top management and their impacts on ceo dismissal followed by inside succession', *Academy of Management Journal*, 45(6): 1195–1206.

Shenhav, Y. (2003) 'The historical and epistemological foundations of organization theory, fusing sociological theory with engineering discourse', in H. Tsoukas and C. Knudsen (eds), *The Oxford Handbook of Organization Theory*. Oxford: Oxford University Press. pp. 183–209.

Shin, S.J. and Zhou, J. (2003) 'Transformational leadership, conservation and creativity: Evidence from Korea', *Academy of Management Journal*, 46(6): 703–715.

Shotter, J. and Tsoukas, H. (2014) 'In search of phronesis: Leadership and the art of judgment', *Academy of Management Learning and Education*, 13(2): 224–243.

Shrivastava, P. and Schneider, S.C. (1984) 'Organizational frames of reference', *Human Relations*, 37(10): 795–807.

Siguaw, J.A., Simpson, P.M. and Enz, C.A. (2006) 'Conceptualizing innovation orientation: A framework for study and integration of innovation research', *Journal of Product Innovation Management*, 23(6): 556–574.

Sillince, J. (2006) 'The effect and rhetoric on competitive advantage: Knowledge, rhetoric and resource-based theory', in S. Clegg et al. (eds), *The Sage Handbook of Soma Organization Studies* (2nd edn). London: Sage.

Sillince, J.A.A. and Jarzabkowski, P. (2012) 'Shaping strategic action through the rhetorical construction and exploitation of ambiguity', *Organization Science*, 23: 630–650.

Sillince, J.A.A. and Mueller, F. (2007) 'Switching strategic perspective: The reframing of accounts of responsibility', *Organization Studies*, 28(2): 155–176.

Silvia, S. (2013) *Holding the Shop Together: German Industrial Relations in the Postwar Era*. Ithaca: Cornell University Press.

Simoes, E. (2016) 'Brazilian prosecutors charge former president Lula in money-laundering probe', *Sydney Morning Herald*, 10 March. Available at: www.smh.com.au/world/brazilian-prosecutors-charge-brazils-lula-in-money-laundering-probe-20160310-gnf8ir.html#ixzz42eroGIGu.

Simon, H.A. (1947) *Administrative Behavior*. Macmillan: New York.

Simon, H.A. (1951) 'A formal theory of the employment relationship', *Econometrica*, 19(3): 293–305.

Simon, H.A. (1969) *The Sciences of the Artificial*. Cambridge, MA: MIT Press.

Simon, H.A. (1972) 'Theories of Bounded Rationality', in C.B. McGuire and R. Radner (eds), *Decision and Organization*. Amsterdam: North-Holland Publishing Company. pp. 161–176.

Simon, H. A. (1978) Rationality as process and as product of thought, *The American Economic Review*, 68(2): 1–16.

Simon, H.A. (1995) 'Organisations and markets', *Journal of Public Administration, Research and Theory* (Transaction), 5(3): 273–295.

Simonin, B.L. (1999) 'Ambiguity and the process of knowledge transfer in strategic alliances', *Strategic Management Journal*, 20(7): 595–623.

Simpson, P.M., Siguaw, J.A. and Enz, C.A. (2006) 'Innovation orientation outcomes: The good and the bad', *Journal of Business Research*. 59(10): 1133–1141.

Sims, R.R. (2002) *Teaching Business Ethics for Effective Learning*. Westport, CN: Quorum Books.

Sinha, P.N., Inkson, K. and Barker, J.R. (2012) 'Committed to a failing strategy: Celebrity CEO, intermediaries, media and stakeholders in a co-created drama', *Organization Studies*, 33(2): 223–245.

Slawinski, N. and Bansal, P. (2012) 'A matter of time: The temporal perspectives of organizational responses to climate change', *Organization Studies*, 33(11): 1537–1563.

Smets, M., Morris, T. and Greenwood, R. (2012) 'From practice to field: A multilevel model of practice-driven institutional change', *Academy of Management Journal*, 55(4): 877–904.

Smircich, L. (1983) 'Concepts of culture and organization analysis', *Administrative Science Quarterly*, 28: 339–358.

Smith, A. (1759/2010) *The Theory of Moral Sentiments*. London: Penguin.

Smith, A. (1776/1937) *An Inquiry into the Nature and Causes of the Wealth of Nations*. New York: Random House.

Smith, K.K. (1982) 'Philosophical problems in thinking about organizational change', in P.S. Goodman et al. (eds), *Change in Organizations*. San Francisco, CA: Jossey-Bass. pp. 316–374.

Smith, W.K. (2014) 'Dynamic decision making: A model of senior leaders managing strategic paradoxes', *Academy of Management Journal*, 57(6): 1592–1623.

Smith, W.K. and Lewis, M.W. (2011) 'Toward a theory of paradox: A dynamic equilibrium model of organizing', *Academy of Management Review*, 36: 381–403.

Sol, C.T. (2014) *Practically Investing: Smart Investment Techniques your Neighbour Doesn't Know*. Bloomington, IN: iUniverse.

Sosik, J.J., Kahai, S.S. and Avolio, B.J. (1998) 'Transformational leadership and dimensions of creativity: Motivating idea generation in computer mediated groups', *Creativity Research Journal*, 11(2): 111–122.

Sosik, J.J., Kahai, S.S. and Avolio, B.J. (1999) 'Leadership style, anonymity, and creativity in group decision support systems', *Journal of Creative Behavior*, 33(4): 227–257.

Spaargaren, G. and Mol, A. (1992) 'Sociology, environment and modernity: Ecological modernization as a theory of social change', *Society and Natural Resources*, 5(4): 323–344.

Spee, A.P. and Jarzabkowski, P. (2009) 'Strategy tools as boundary objects', *Strategic Organization*, 7(2): 223–232.

Spee, P. and Jarzabkowski, P. (2011) 'Strategic planning as communicative process', *Organization Studies*, 2(9): 1217–1245.

Spekman, R., Forbes, T.M., Isabella, L.A. and Magavoy, T.C. (1998) 'Alliance management: A view from the past and a look to the future', *Journal of Management Studies*, 35(6): 747–772.

Spence, M. (1977) 'Entry, capacity, investment and oligopolistic pricing', *Bell Journal of Economics*, 8: 534–544.

Spencer, B., Peyrefitte, J. and Churchman, R. (2003) 'Consensus and divergence in perceptions of cognitive strategic groups: Evidence from the health care industry', *Strategic Organization*, 1(2): 203–230.

Spender, J-C. (1996) 'Organisational knowledge, learning and memory: Three concepts in search of theory', *Journal of Organisational Change Management*, 9(1): 63–78.

Spender, J-C. (2010) 'Human capital and agency theory', in A. Burton-Jones and J-C. Spender (eds), *Oxford Handbook of Human Capital*. Oxford: Oxford University Press.

Spender, J-C. (2016) 'How management education's past shapes its present', *BizEd*. Available at: www.bizedmagazine.com/archives/2016/2/features/how-management-education-past-shapes-present (accessed 16 March 2016).

Spice, A. and Böhm, S. (2007) 'Moving management: Theorizing struggles against the hegemony of management', *Organization Studies*, 28(11): 1667–1698.

Spicer, A. (2006) 'Beyond the convergence–divergence debate: The role of spatial scales in transforming organization logic', *Organization Studies*, 27(10): 1467–1483.

Spicer, A., Dunfee, T. and Bailey, W. (2004) 'Does national context matter in ethical decision-making? An empirical test of integrative social contracts theory', *Academy of Management Journal*, 47(4): 610–622.

Stagl, H. (2014) *Irresistible Change Guide: Design and Influence Change Without Getting Stuck*. Alpharetta, GA: Enclaria.

Stamp, G., Burridge, B. and Thomas, P. (2007) 'Strategic leadership: An exchange of letters', *Leadership*, 3: 479–496.

Starbuck, W.H. (1983) 'Organizations as action generators', *American Sociological Review*, 48(1): 91–102.

Starbuck, W.H. (1992) 'Learning by knowledge-intensive firms', *Journal of Management Studies*, 29(6): 713–740.

Starbuck, W.H. (1993) 'Keeping a butterfly and an elephant in a house of cards: The elements of exceptional success', *Journal of Management Studies*, 30(6): 885–921.

Stark, D. and Paravel, V. (2008) 'PowerPoint in Public Digital Technologies and the New Morphology of Demonstration', *Theory, Culture & Society,* 25(5): 30–55.

Steinfield, C., Bauer, J. and Caby, L. (1994) *Telecommunications in Transition. Policies, Services and Technologies in the European Community*. London: Sage.

Sternberg, E. (1986) 'Phantasmagoric labor: The new economics of self-presentation', *Futures*, 30(1): 3–21.

Stevens, B. (1994) 'An analysis of corporate ethical code studies: "Where do we go from here?"', *Journal of Business Ethics*, 13(1): 63–69.

Stiglitz, J.A. (2012) *The Price of Inequality: How Today's Divided Society Endangers Our Future*. New York: Norton.

Stiles, R.M. and Oliver, M. (1998) 'Anecdotes from alliancing', New Zealand Petroleum Conference Proceedings. Available at: www.med.govt.nz/crown_minerals/1998_pet_conference/stiles/index. html (accessed 14 September 2000).

Stinchcombe, A. L. (1985) 'Project administration in the North Sea', in A. L. Stinchcombe and C. A. Heimer (eds*), Organization Theory and Project Management: Administering Uncertainty in Norwegian Offshore Oil*. Norway: Norwegian University Press.

Stonehouse, G. and Snowdon, B. (2007) 'Competitive advantage revisited: Michael Porter on strategy and competitiveness', *Journal of Management Inquiry*, 16(3):256–273.

Storper, M. and Salais, R. (1997) *Worlds of Production: The Action Frameworks of the Economy*. Cambridge, MA: Harvard University Press.

Strange, S. (1996) *The retreat of the state: The diffusion of power in the world economy*. Cambridge: Cambridge University Press.

Stulz, R.M. and Williamson, R. (2003) 'Culture, openness, and finance', *Journal of Financial Economics*, 70(3): 313–349.

Sturdy, A. (1997a) 'The consulting process: An insecure business?', *Journal of Management Studies*, 34(3): 389–413.

Sturdy, A. (1997b) 'The dialectics of consultancy', *Critical Perspectives on Accounting*, 8(5): 511–535.

Sturdy, A., Clark, T., Fincham, R. and Handley, K. (2004) 'Silence, procrustes and colonization: A response to Clegg et al.'s "Noise, parasites and translation: Theory and practice in management consulting"', *Management Learning*, 35(3): 337–340.

Suchman, M.C. (1995) 'Managing legitimacy: Strategic and institutional approaches', *Academy of management review*, 20(3): 571–610.

Sull, D. (1999) 'Why good companies go bad', *Harvard Business Review*, July–August: 42–52.

Sull, D. and Eisenhardt, K.M. (2015) *Simple Rules*. New York: Houghton-Mifflin.

Swedberg, R. and Granovetter, M.S. (eds) (2011) *The Sociology of Economic Life* (3rd edn). New York: Westview Press.

Tanev, S. (2012) 'Global from the start: The characteristics of born-global firms in the technology sector', *Technology Innovation Management Review*, March: 5–8.

Tapscott, D. and Williams, A.D. (2008) *Wikinomics: How Mass Collaboration Changes Everything*. New York: Portfolio Trade.

Taylor, J.R. and Van Every, E.J. (1999) *The emergent organization: Communication as its site and surface*. Routledge.

Taylor, L. (2016) 'A shift in political thinking is giving Labor a sense of purpose', *Guardian Australia*. Available at: www.theguardian.com/australia-news/2016/mar/18/a-shift-in-political-thinking-is-giving-labor-a-sense-of-purpose (accessed 19 March 2016).

Teece, D.J. (1976) *Multinational Corporation and the Resource Cost of International Technology Transfer*. Cambridge, MA: Ballinger.

Teece, D.J. (1981) 'The market for know-how and the efficient international transfer of technology', *Annals of the Academy of Political and Social Science*, 458(1): 81–96.

Teece, D.J. (1982) 'Towards an economic theory of the multiproduct firm', *Journal of Economic Behavior and Organization*, 3: 39–63.

Teece, D.J. (1984) 'Economic analysis and strategic management', *California Management Review*, 26(3): 87–110.

Teece, D.J. (1986) 'Profiting from technological innovation: Implications for integration, collaboration, licensing and public policy', *Research Policy*, 15(6): 285–305.

Teece, D.J. (1996) 'Profiting from technological innovation: Implications for integration, collaboration, licensing and public policy', *Research Policy*, 15(6): 285–305

Teece, D.J. (1998) 'Capturing value from knowledge assets', *California Management Review*, 40: 55–79.

Teece, D.J. (2006) 'Reflections on the Hymer Thesis and the multinational enterprise', *International Business Review*, 15(2): 124–139.

Teece, D.J. (2007a) 'Explicating dynamic capabilities: The nature and microfoundations of (sustainable) enterprise performance', *Strategic Management Journal*, 28(13): 1319–1350.

Teece, D.J. (2007b) 'Managers, markets, and dynamic capabilities', in C. Helfat, S. Finkelstein, W. Mitchell, M. Peteraf, D.J. Singh, D.J. Teece and S. Winter (eds), *Dynamic Capabilities: Understanding Strategic Change in Organizations*. Blackwell: Oxford. pp. 19–29.

Teece, D.J. (2009) *Dynamic Capabilities and Strategic Management: Organizing for Innovation and Growth*. Oxford: Oxford University Press.

Teece, D.J. (2010) 'Technological innovation and the theory of the firm: The role of enterprise-level knowledge, complementarities, and (dynamic) capabilities', in N. Rosenberg and B. Hall (eds), *Handbook of the Economics of Innovation*, Vol. 1. Amsterdam: North-Holland.

Teece D.J. and Pisano, G. (1994) 'The dynamic capabilities of firms: An introduction', *Industrial and Corporate Change*, 3(3): 537–556.

Teece, D.J. Rummelt, R., Dosi, G. and Winter, S. (1994) 'Understanding corporate coherence: Theory and evidence', *Journal of Economic Behavior and Organization*, 23(1): 1–30.

Teece, D.J., Pisano, G. and Shuen, A. (1997) 'Dynamic capabilities and strategic management', *Strategic Management Journal*, 18(7): 509–533.

Teerikangas, S. and Véry, P. (2006) 'The culture–performance relationship in M&A: From yes/no to how', *British Journal of Management*, 17(S1): S31–S48.

Teerikangas, S. and Véry, P. (2012) 'Culture in M&A: A critical synthesis', in D. Faulkner, S. Teerikangas and R. Joseph (eds), *The Handbook of Mergers and Acquisitions*. Oxford: Oxford University Press. pp. 392–430.

Tempel, A., Edwards, T., Ferner, A., Muller-Camen, M. and Wachter, H. (2006) 'Subsidiary responses to institutional duality: Collective representation practices of U.S multinationals in Britain and Germany', *Human Relations*, 59(11): 1543–1570.

ten Bos, R. (1997) 'Business ethics and Bauman ethics', *Organization Studies*, 18(6): 997–1014.

ten Bos, R. (2000) *Fashion and Utopia in Management Thinking*. Amsterdam and Philadelphia: John Benjamin.

Tether, B. (2005) 'Do services innovate (differently)? Insights from the European innobarometer survey', *Industry and Innovation*, 12(2): 153–184.

Thomas, L.G. and D'Aveni, R. (2009) 'The changing nature of competition in the US manufacturing sector, 1950–2002', *Strategic Organization*, 7(4): 387–431.

Thomas, R.J. (1995) 'Interviewing important people in big companies', in R. Hertz, and J.B. Imber (eds), *Studying Élites using Qualitative Methods*. Thousand Oaks, CA: Sage. pp. 3–17.

Thomas, R. and Davies, A. (2005) 'Theorizing the micro-politics of resistance: New public management and managerial identities in the UK public services', *Organization Studies*, 26(5): 683–706.

Thomas, R., Sargent, L.D. and Hardy, C. (2011) 'Managing organizational change: Negotiating meaning and power-resistance relations', *Organization Science*, 22(1): 22–41.

Thompson, P. and Ackroyd, S. (1995) 'All quiet on the workplace front? A critique of recent trends in British industrial sociology', *Sociology*, 29(4): 615–633.

Thomsen, S. (2006) 'The hidden meaning of codes: Corporate governance and investor rent seeking', *European Business Organization Law Review*, 7(4): 845–861.

Thornton, P.H. (2004) *Markets from Culture: Institutional Logics and Organizational Decisions in Higher Educational Publishing*. Stanford, CA: Stanford University Press.

Thornton, P.H., Ocasio, W. and Lounsbury, M. (2012) *The Institutional Logics Perspective: A New Approach to Culture, Structure and Process*. Oxford: Oxford University Press.

Tichy, N.M. (1997) *The Leadership Engine: How Winning Companies Build Leaders at Every Level*. New York: Harper Business.

Tichy, N.M. and Bennis, W.G. (2007) *Judgment: How Winning Leaders make Great Calls*. New York: Penguin.

Tidd, J. and Bessant, J. (2009) *Managing Innovation: Integrating Technological, Market and Organizational Change*. Chichester: Wiley.

Tihanyi, L., Ellstrand, A., Daily, C. and Dalton, D. (2000) 'Composition of the top management team and firm international diversification', *Journal of Management*, 26(6):1157–1167.

Tirole, J. (1988) *The Theory of Industrial Organization*. Cambridge, MA: MIT Press.

Tiwana, A., Konsynski, B. and Bush, A.A. (2010) 'Research commentary—platform evolution: Coevolution of platform architecture, governance, and environmental dynamics', *Information Systems Research*, 21(4): 675–687.

Todaro, M.P. and Smith, S.C. (2009) *Economic Development*. New York: Pearson Addison Wesley.

Torchia, M., Calabro, A. and Huse, M. (2011) 'Women directors on corporate boards: From tokenism to critical mass', *Journal of Business Ethics*, 102(2): 299–317.

Townley, B. (1997) 'The institutional logic of performance appraisal', *Organization Studies*, 18(2): 261–285.

Townley, B., Beech, N. and McKinlay, A. (2009) 'Managing the motley crew: Managing in the creative industries', *Human Relations*, 62: 639–662.

Tracey, P., Phillips, N. and Jarvis, O. (2011) 'Bridging institutional entrepreneurship and the creation of new organizational forms: A multilevel model', *Organization Science*, 22(1): 60–80.

Treacy, M. and Wiersema, F. (1995) *The Discipline of Market Leaders*. Reading, MA: Addison-Wesley.

Trevino, L.K. (1986) 'Ethical decision making in organizations: A person-situation interactionist model', *Academy of Management Review* (11)3: 607–617.

Trevino, L.K. and Nelson, K.A. (2011) *Managing Business Ethics* (5th edn). Hoboken, NJ: John Wiley and Sons.

Trevino, L.K., Weaver, G.R., Toffler, D.G. and Ley, B. (1999) 'Managing ethics and legal compliance: What works and what hurts', *California Management Review* (41)2: 131–151.

Trice, M.T. and Beyer, J.M. (1993) *The Cultures of Work Organizations*. Englewood Cliffs, NJ: Prentice Hall.

Tsai, W. (2002) 'Social structure of "coopetition" within a multiunit organization: Coordination, competition, and intraorganizational knowledge sharing', *Organization Science*, 13: 179–190.

Tsoukas, H. (1994) 'From social engineering to reflective action in organizational behaviour', in H. Tsoukas (ed.), *New Thinking in Organizational Behavior*. Oxford: Butterworth–Heinemann. pp. 1–22.

Tsoukas, H. (1996) 'The firm as a distributed knowledge system: A constructionist approach', *Strategic Management Journal*, 5(4): 289–301.

Tsoukas, H. (1998) 'The word and the world: A critique of representationalism in management research', *International Journal of Public Administration*, 21(5): 781–817.

Tsoukas, H. (2003) 'Do we really understand tacit knowledge?', in M. Easterby-Smith and M.A. Lyles (eds), *The Blackwell Handbook of Organisational Knowledge Management*. Oxford: Blackwell. pp. 410–427.

Tsoukas, H. (2005) *Complex Knowledge*. Oxford: Oxford University Press.

Tsui, A. (2006) 'Contextualization in Chinese management research', *Management and Organization Review*, 2(1): 1–13.

Turner, S. (1994) *The Social Theory of Practices. Tradition, Tacit Knowledge, and Presuppositions*. Chicago: The University of Chicago Press.

Tushman, M.L. and O'Reilly, C. (1996) 'Ambidextrous organizations: Managing evolutions and revolutionary change', *California Management Review*, 38(4): 8–30.

Uhlenbruck, K., Hitt, M.A. and Semaden, M. (2006a) 'Market value effects of acquisitions involving internet firms: A resource-based analysis', *Strategic Management Journal*, 27: 899–913.

Uhlenbruck, K., Rodriguez, P., Doh, J. and Eden, L. (2006b) 'The impact of corruption on entry strategy: Evidence from telecommunication projects in emerging economies', *Organization Science*, 17(3): 402–414.

Ulrich, P. (2008) *Integrative Economic Ethics: Foundations of a Civilized Market Economy*. Cambridge: Cambridge University Press.

USA Today (2013) 'EU launches legal action against Microsoft', *USA Today*, 26 July: 1. Available at: www.abcnews.go.com/Technology/story?id=6668756&page=1 (accessed 30 July 2013).

Useem, M. (1986) *The Inner Circle: Large Corporations and the Rise of Business Political Activity in the US and UK*. Oxford: Oxford University Press.

Useem, M. (1995) 'Reaching corporate executives', in R. Hertz and J.B. Imber (eds), *Studying Élites using Qualitative Methods*. Thousand Oaks, CA: Sage. pp. 18–39.

Useem, M. and Karabel, J. (1986) 'Pathways to top corporate management', *American Sociological Review*, 51(2): 184–200.

Uzzi, B. (1997) 'Social structure and competition in interfirm networks: The paradox of embeddedness', *Administrative Science Quarterly*, 42: 35–67.

Vaara, E. (2000) 'Construction of cultural differences in post-merger change processes: A sensmaking perspective on Finnish–Swedish cases', *M@n@gement*, 3: 81–110.

Vaara, E. (2002) 'On the discursive construction of success/failure in narratives of post-merger integration', *Organization Studies*, 23(2): 213–250.

Vaara, E. (2003) 'Post-acquisition integration as sensemaking: Glimpses of ambiguity, confusion, hypocrisy, and politicization', *Journal of Management Studies*, 40(4): 859–894.

Vaara, E. and Durand, R. (2012) 'How to connect strategy research with broader issues that matter?', *Strategic Organization*, 10(3): 248–255.

Vaara, E. and Faÿ, E. (2012) 'Reproduction and change on the global scale: A Bourdieusian perspective on management education', *Journal of Management Studies*, 49(6): 1023–1051.

Vaara, E. and Pedersen, A.R. (2014) 'Strategy and chronotopes: A Bakhtinian perspective on the construction of strategy narratives', *M@n@gement*, 16(5): 93–604.

Vaara, E. and Whittington, R. (2012) 'Strategy-as-practice: Taking social practices seriously', *Academy of Management Annals*, 6: 285–336.

Vaara, E., Tienari, J., Piekkari, R. and Santti, R. (2005) 'Language and the circuits of power in a merging multinational corporation', *Journal of Management Studies*, 42(3): 595–623.

Vaara, E., Sorsa, V. and Pälli, P. (2010) 'On the force potential of strategy texts: A critical discourse analysis of a strategic plan and its power effects in a city organization', *Organization*, 17(6): 685–702.

Vaccaro, I., Jansen, J., Van Den Bosch, F. and Volberda, H. (2012) 'Management innovation and leadership: The moderating role of organizational size', *Journal of Management Studies*, 49(1): 28–51.

van der Heijden, K. (2005) *Scenarios: The Art of Strategic Conversation* (2nd edn). Chichester: Wiley.

van der Panne, G., van Beers, C. and Kleinknecht, A. (2003) 'Success and failure of innovation: A literature review', *International Journal of Innovation Management*, 7(3): 309–338.

van der Windt, H., Abma, A-J., Gerkema, M. and Wieringa, N. (2009) *The New Asian Innovation Dynamics: China and India in Perspective*. London: Palgrave MacMillan.

van Gelder, S. (2011) *This Changes Everything: Occupy Wall Street and the 99% Movement*. San Francisco: Berrett-Koehler.

van Iterson, A. and Clegg, S.R. (2008) 'The politics of gossip and denial in inter-organizational relations', *Human Relations*, 61(8): 1117–1137.

van Krieken, R. (2012) *Celebrity Society*. London: Routledge.

Van Marrewijk, A. (2016) 'Conflicting subcultures in mergers and acquisitions: A longitudinal study of integrating a radical internet firm into a bureaucratic telecoms firm', *British Journal of Management*, 27(2): 338–54.

Van Marrewijk, A.Y.S., Smits, K., Pitsis, T. and Clegg, S.R. (2016) 'Clash of the Titans: Temporal organizing and collaborative dynamics in the Panama Canal Megaproject', *Organization Studies*. ISSN 0170-8406 (In Press).

Vanhaverbeke, W. and Noorderhaven, N.G. (2002) 'Competition between alliance blocks: The case of the RISC microprocessor technology', *Organization Science*, 22(1): 1–30.

Vargo, S.L. and Lusch, R.F. (2008) 'Service dominant logic: Continuing the evolution', *Journal of the Academy of Marketing Science*, 36(1): 1–10.

Vargo, S.L. and Lusch, R.H. (2004) 'Evolving to a new dominant logic for marketing', *Journal of Marketing*, 68(1): 1–17.

Vargo, S.L., Maglio, P.P. and Akaka, M.A. (2008) 'On value and value co-creation: A service systems and service logic perspective', *European Management Journal*, 26(3): 145–152.

Varian, H.P. (1992) *Microeconomic Analysis*. New York: Norton.

Veldman, J. (2016) 'Corporation: Reification of the corporate form', in M. Greenwood, R. Mir and H. Willmott (eds), *Routledge Companion to Philosophy in Organization Studies*. New York: Routledge; pp. 333–42.

Verganti, R. (2006) 'Innovating through design', *Harvard Business Review*, 84(12): 114–122.

Vernon, R. (1971) *Sovereignty at Bay*. New York: Basic Books.

Victor, B. and Cullen, J. (1988) 'The organizational bases of ethical work climate', *Administrative Science Quarterly*, 33(1): 101–125.

Victor, B. and Stephens, C. (1994) 'The dark side of the new organizational forms: An editorial essay', *Organization Science*, 5: 479–482.

Vidal, M. (2016) 'What's behind the rise in income inequality? Technology or class struggle?', *CounterPunch*. Available at: www.counterpunch.org/ (accessed 18 March 2016).

Vince, R. and Broussine, M. (1996) 'Paradox, defense and attachment: Accessing and working with emotions and relations underlying organizational change', *Organization Studies*, 17(1): 1–21.

Visser, M. (2007) 'Deutero-learning in organizations: A review and a reformulation', *Academy of Management Review*, 32(2): 659–667.

Vitols, S. (2001) 'Varieties of corporate governance: Comparing Germany and the UK', in P. Hall and D. Soskice (eds), *Varieties of Capitalism: The Institutional Foundations of Comparative Advantage*. Oxford: Oxford University Press. pp. 337–60.

Vitt, G. (2013) *The Risk in Risk Management*. London: Routledge

von Hippel, E. and von Krogh, G. (2003) 'Open source software and the "private-collective" innovation model: Issues for organization science', *Organization Science*, 14: 209–223.

von Vacano, D. (2006) *The Art of Power: Machiavelli, Nietzsche and the Making of Aesthetic Political Theory*. Lanham, MD: Lexington Books/Rowman & Littlefield.

Wade R. (1990a) *Governing the Market: Economic Theory and the Role of Government in East Asian Industrialization.* Princeton, NJ: Princeton University Press.

Wade, R. (1990b) 'Financial regime change', *New Left Review*, 53(5): 5–21.

Walker, R. and Walker, B. (2000) *Privatisation: Sell off or Sell out: The Australian Experience.* ABC Books: Sydney.

Walker, G., and Weber, D. (1984) 'A transaction cost approach in Make-or-Buy decisions', *Administrative Science Quarterly*, 29(3): 373–391.

Wally, S. and Becerra, M. (2001) 'Top management team characteristics and strategic changes in international diversification: The case of US Multinationals in the European Community', *Group and Organization Management*, 26(2): 165–175.

Wang, Y. and Nicholas, S. (2005) 'Knowledge transfer, replication and learning in non-equity alliances: Operating joint ventures in China', *Management International Review*, 1: 45.

Warglien, M. and Masuch, M. (1995) *The Logic of Organizational Disorder.* Berlin: de Gruyter.

Warren, R. (1993) 'Codes of ethics: Bricks without straw', *Business Ethics: A European Review*, 2(4):185–191.

Watkins, M.D. and Bazerman, M.H. (2003) 'Predictable surprises: The disasters you should have seen coming', *Harvard Business Review*, 81(3): 72–80.

Watzlawick, P., Bavelas, J.B. and Jackson, D.D. (1967) *Pragmatics of Human Communication: A Study of Interactional Patterns, Pathologies and Paradoxes.* New York: Norton.

Weaver, G.R., Treviño, L.K. and Cochran, P.L. (1999a) 'Integrated and decoupled corporate social performance: Management commitments, external pressures, and corporate ethics practices', *Academy of Management Journal*, 42(5): 539–553.

Weaver, G.R., Treviño, L.K. and Cochran, P.L. (1999b) 'Corporate ethics practices in the mid-1990s: An empirical study of the Fortune 1000', *Journal of Business Ethics*, 18(3): 283–294.

Weber, M. (1978) *Economy and Society.* Berkeley, CA: University of California Press.

Weber, Y. (1996) 'Corporate cultural fit and performance in mergers and acquisitions', *Human Relations*, 49: 1181–1202.

Weber, Y., Shenkar, O. and Raveh, A. (1996) 'National and corporate cultural fit in mergers/acquisitions: An exploratory study', *Management Science*, 42: 1215–1227.

Weick, K.E. (1979) *The Social Psychology of Organizing* (2nd edn). New York: Addison-Wesley.

Weick, K.E. (1993) 'The collapse of sensemaking in organizations: The Mann Gulch disaster', *Administrative Science Quarterly*, 38(4): 628–652.

Weick, K.E. (1995a) 'South Canyon revisited: Lessons from high reliability organizations', *Wildfire*, 4(4): 54–68.

Weick, K.E. (1995b) *Sensemaking in Organizations.* Thousand Oaks, CA: Sage.

Weick, K.E. (2001) *Making Sense of the Organization.* Malden, MA: Blackwett.

Weick, K.E., Sutcliffe, K.M. and Obstfeld, D. (2005) 'Organizing and the process of sensemaking', *Organization Science*, 16(4): 409–421.

Weick, K.E. (2007) 'Foreword', in E.H. Kessler and J.R. Bailey (eds), *Handbook of Organizational and Managerial Wisdom.* Thousand Oaks: Sage. pp. ix-xiii.

Weill, P. and Ross, J.W. (2013) *IT Governance: How Top Performers Manage IT Decision Rights for Superior Results* [eBook, Kindle edn]. Harvard Business Review Press.

Weiss, L. (1998) *The Myth of the Powerless State.* Ithaca, NY: Cornell University Press.

Weizsäcker, E., Lovins, A.B. and Lovins, L.H. (1997) *Factor Four: Doubling Wealth – Halving Resource Use.* Sydney: Allen & Unwin.

Wellman, B. and Berkowitz, S.D. (eds) (1988) 'Social structures: A network approach', *Contemporary Studies in Sociology*, Vol. 15. Cambridge, UK: Cambridge University Press.

Wernerfelt, B. (1984) 'The resource-based view of the firm', *Strategic Management Journal*, 5: 171–180.

Werr, A., Stjernberg, S. and Docherty, P. (1997) 'The functions of methods of change in management consulting', *Journal of Organizational Change Management*, 10(4): 288–307.

Westley, F. (1990) 'Middle managers and strategy: Micro-dynamics of inclusion', *Strategic Management Journal*, 11(5): 337–351.

Westney, E. (1993) 'Institutionalization theory and the MNE', in S. Ghoshal and E. Westney (eds), *Organization Theory and the Multinational Corporation*. New York: St. Martin's Press. pp. 53–76.

Westphal, J.D. and Zajac, E.J. (1997) 'Defections from the inner circle: Social exchange, reciprocity, and the diffusion of board independence in U.S. corporations', *Administrative Science Quarterly*, 42: 161–183.

Whetten, D.A. (2009) 'An examination of the interface between context and theory applied to the study of Chinese organizations', *Management and Organization Review*, 5(1): 29–55.

Whitt, A. (1982) *Urban Elites and Mass Transportation: The Dialectics of Power*. Princeton, N.J.: Princeton University Press.

Whitley, R. (1991) 'The social construction of business systems in East Asia', *Organization Studies*, 12(1): 1–28.

Whitley, R. (1992) *European Business Systems: Firms and Markets in their National Contexts*. London: Sage.

Whitley, R. (1994a) 'Dominant forms of economic organization in market economies', *Organisation Studies*, 15(2): 153–182.

Whitley, R. (1994b) 'The internationalization of firms and markets: Its significance and institutional structuring, *Organization*, 1: 101–124.

Whitley, R. (1999) *Divergent Capitalisms: The Social Structuring and Change of Business Systems*. Oxford: Oxford University Press.

Whittington, R. (1993) *What is Strategy – and Does it Matter?* London: Routledge.

Whittington, R. (1996) 'Strategy as practice', *Long Range Planning*, 29(5): 731–735.

Whittington, R. (2002) 'Corporate structure: From policy to practice', in A. Pettigrew, H. Thomas and R. Whittington (eds), *Handbook of Strategy and Management*. London: Sage. pp. 113–128.

Whittington, R. (2003) 'The work of strategizing and organizing: for a practice perspective', *Strategic Organization*, 1(1): 117–126.

Whittington, R. (2004) 'Strategy after modernism: Recovering practice', *European Management Review*, 1(1): 62–68.

Whittington, R. and Mayer, M. (2000) *The European Corporation: Strategy, Structure, and Social Science*. Oxford: Oxford University Press.

Whittington, R., Jarzabkowski, P., Mayer, M., Mounoud, E., Nahapiet, J. and Rouleau, L. (2003) 'Taking strategy seriously: Responsibility and reform for an important social practice', *Journal of Management Inquiry*, 12: 396–409.

Whittington, R., Molloy, E., Mayer, M. and Smith, A. (2006) 'Practices of strategising/organising: Broadening strategy work and skills', *Long Range Planning*, 39(6): 615–629.

Whittington, R., Cailluet, L. and Yakis-Douglas, B. (2011) 'Opening strategy: Evolution of a precarious profession', *British Journal of Management*, 22(3): 531–544.

Whittle, A. and Mueller, F. (2010) 'Strategy, enrolment and accounting: The politics of strategic ideas', *Accounting, Auditing and Accountability Journal*, 23(5): 626–646.

Whittle, A., Housley, W., Gilchrist, A., Mueller, F. and Lenney, P. (2015) 'Category predication work, discursive leadership and strategic sensemaking', *Human Relations*, 68(3): 377–407.

Whittle, A., Mueller, F., Gilchrist, A. and Lenney, P. (2016) 'Sensemaking, sense-censoring and strategic inaction: The discursive enactment of power and politics in a multinational corporation', *Organization Studies*, 37(9): 1323–51.

Whyte, W.H. (1956) *The Organization Man*. Philadelphia, PA: University of Pennsylvania Press.

Whyte, W.H. (2013) *The Organization Man* (foreword by Joseph Nocera).: University of Pennsylvania Press. Available at: https://muse.jhu.edu/book/23676 (accessed 14 May 2016).

Williams, T. (2016) 'Future-work: Agency and emergence in sustainability strategy as practice', submitted for the degree of Doctor of Philosophy, University of Technology, Sydney, January.

Williamson, O.E. (1968) 'Economics as an anti-trust defense: The welfare trade-offs', *American Economic Review*, 58/1: 18–36.

Williamson, O.E. (1975a) 'The economics of governance: Framework and implications', *Journal of Theoretical Economics*, 140: 195–223.

Williamson, O.E. (1975b) *Markets and Hierarchies: Analysis and Antitrust Implications. A Study in the Economics of Internal Organization*. New York: The Free Press.

Williamson, O.E. (1981a) 'The modern corporation: Origins, evolution, attributes', *Journal of Economic Literature*, 19/4: 1537–1569.

Williamson, O.E. (1981b) 'The economics of organizations: The transaction cost approach', *American Journal of Sociology*, 87(3): 548–577.

Williamson, O.E. (1985) *The Economic Institutions of Capitalism*. New York: Free Press.

Williamson, O.E. (1991a) 'Comparative economic organization: The analysis of discrete structural alternatives', *Administrative Science Quarterly*, 36(2): 269–296.

Williamson, O.E. (1991b) 'Strategizing, economizing, and economic organization', *Strategic Management Journal*, 12: 75–94.

Williamson, O.E. (1996a) *The Mechanisms of Governance*. Oxford, UK: Oxford University Press.

Williamson, O.E. (1996b) 'Efficiency, power, authority and economic organization', in J. Groenewegen (ed.), *Transaction Cost Economics and Beyond*. Boston, MA and London, UK: Kluwer Academic Publishers. pp. 11–42.

Williamson, O.E. (1998) 'Transaction cost economics: How it works; where it is headed', *Economist*, 146: 23–58.

Williamson, O.E. (2005) 'The economics of governance', *American Economic Review*, 95(2): 1–18.

Williamson, O.E. (2008) 'Outsourcing: Transaction cost economics and supply chain management', *Journal of Supply Chain Management*, 44(2): 5–16.

Wilson, D. (1982) 'Electricity and resistance: A case study of innovation and politics', *Organization Studies*, 3(1): 119–140.

Wilson, D., Butler, R., Cray, D., Hickson, D.J. and Mallory, G. (1986) 'Breaking the bounds of organization in strategic decision making', *Human Relations*, 39(2): 309–332.

Winter, S.G. (1988) 'On Coase, competence, and the corporation', *Journal of Law, Economics, and Organization*, 1(4): 163–180.

Winter, S.G. (1993) *On Coase, Competence, and the Corporation: The Nature of the Firm*. Oxford, UK: Oxford University Press.

Winter, S.G. (2003) 'Understanding dynamic capabilities', *Strategic Management Journal*, 24: 991–995.

Wirtz, B.W. (2001) 'Reconfiguration of value chains in converging media and communications markets', *Long Range Planning*, 34: 489–506.

Wirtz, B.W., Mathieu, A. and Schilke, O. (2007) 'Strategy in high velocity environments', *Long Range Planning*, 40: 295–313.

Wissema, H. (2002) 'Driving through red lights: How warning signals are missed or ignored', *Long Range Planning*, 35(5): 521–539.

Wit, B. and Meyer, R. (2010) *Strategy Synthesis: Resolving Strategy Paradoxes to Create Competitive Advantage*. London: Thomson.

Wittgenstein, L. (1968) *Philosophical Investigations*. Oxford: Blackwell.

Wolin, S.S. (1960) *Politics and Vision*. Boston: Little Brown & Co

Woods, J., Dalziel, T. and Barton, S. (2012) 'Escalation of commitment in private family businesses: The influence of outside board members', *Journal of Family Business Strategy*, 3(1): 18–27.

Worenklein, J.J. (2003) 'The global crisis in power and infrastructure: Lessons learned and new directions', *The Journal of Structured and Project Finance*, 9(1): 7–11.

World Bank (2014) *New Report: Big Data in Action for Development*, 30 October. Available at: http://data. worldbank.org/news/big-data-in-action-for-development (accessed 21 November 2014).

World Commission on Environment and Development (WCED) (1987) *Our Common Future*. New York: Oxford University Press.

Wright, C.F. (2011) *Beyond the Employment Relationship: Collective Bargaining and Supply Chain Coordination*. London: Trade Union Congress.

Wright, C. and Nyberg, D. (2015) *Climate Change, Capitalism, and Corporations: Processes of Creative Self-Destruction*. Cambridge: Cambridge University Press.

Wright, R., Paroutis, S. and Blettner, D. (2013) 'How useful are the strategic tools we teach in business schools?', *Journal of Management Studies*, 50(1): 92–125.

Wright Mills, C. (1956) The Power Elite. Oxford: Oxford University Press.

Xu, D. and Shenkar, O. (2002) 'Institutional distance and the multinational enterprise', *Academy of Management Review*, 27(4): 608–618.

Yanagisako, S.J. (2002) *Producing Culture and Capital: Family Firms in Italy*. Princeton: Princeton University Press.

Yearley, S. (2007) 'Globalization and the environment', in G. Ritzer (ed.), *Blackwell Companion to Globalization*. Oxford: Blackwell, pp. 393–453.

Yeung, H.W-C. (2000) 'The dynamics of globalization of Chinese business firms', in H.W.C. Yeung and K. Olds (eds), *Globalization of Chinese Business Firms*. Basingstoke: Macmillan. pp. 75–104.

Yinan, H. (2010) 'Suicides at China's Foxconn reveal woes', *China Daily*, 26 May. Available at: www.asianewsnet.net/home/news.php?id=12141&sec=1 (accessed 6 April 2015).

Yoo, Y., Boland, R.J. and Lyytinen, K. (2006) 'From organization design to organization designing', *Organization Science*, 17(2): 215–229.

Young, G., Smith, K.G. and Grimm, C.M. (1996) 'Austrian and industrial organization perspectives on firm-level activity and performance', *Organization Science*, 7(3): 243–254.

Zack, M.H. (1999) 'Managing codified knowledge', *Sloan Management Review*, 40(4): 45–58.

Zahra, S. and Pearce, J. (1989) 'Boards of directors and corporate financial performance: A review and integrative model', *Journal of Management*, 15: 291–334.

Zajac, E.J. and Olsen, C.P. (1993) 'From transaction cost to transactional value analysis: Implications for the study of interorganizational strategies', *The Journal of Management Studies*, 30(1): 131–145.

Zald, M.N. and Ash, R. (1966) 'Social movements organizations: Growth, decay, and change', *Social Forces*, 44(3): 327–341.

Zaloom, C. (2007) 'Ambiguous numbers: Trading technologies and interpretation in financial markets', *American Anthropologist*, 30(2): 258–272.

Zamagni, S. (2009) 'The lesson and warning of a crisis foretold: A political economy approach', *International Review of Economics*, 56(3): 315–334.

Zander, I. and Zander, U. (2005) 'The inside track: On the important (but neglected) role of customers in the resource-based view of strategy and firm growth', *Journal of Management Studies*, 42(8): 1519–1648.

Zeitlin, M. (1974) 'Corporate ownership and control: the large corporations and the capitalist class', *American Journal of Sociology*, 79(5): 1073–1119.

Zhang, G., An, X., Lu, J. and Zhang, G. (2010) 'China's IP system comes of age', *Managing Intellectual Property*, Supplement. Available at: www.managingip.com/Article.aspx?ArticleID=2460070 (accessed 6 April 2015).

Zhang, H. and van den Bulcke, D. (2000) 'Internationalization of ethnic Chinese-owned enterprises: A network approach', in H.W.C. Yeung and K. Olds (eds), *Globalization of Chinese Business Firms*. Basingstoke: Macmillan. pp. 126–149.

Zhang, P. (2010) 'Board information and strategic tasks performance', *Corporate Governance: An International Review*, 18(5): 473–487.

Zietsma, C. and Lawrence, T.B. (2010) 'Institutional work in the transformation of an organizational field: The interplay of boundary work and practice work', *Administrative Science Quarterly*, 55(2): 189–221.

Zilber, T.B. (2011) 'Institutional multiplicity in practice: A tale of two high-tech conferences in Israel', *Organization Science*, 22(6): 1539–1559.

Žižek, S. (2009) *The Plague of Fantasies*. London: Verso.

Zola, E. (1883) *Au Bonheur des Dames*. Paris: Charpentier.

Zoller, H.M. and Fairhurst, G.T. (2007) 'Resistance leadership: The overlooked potential in critical organization and leadership studies', *Human Relations*, 60(9): 1331–1360.

Zollo, M. and Singh, H. (2004) 'Deliberate learning in corporate acquisitions: Post-acquisition strategies and integration capability in U.S. bank mergers', *Strategic Management Journal*, 25: 1233–1256.

Zollo, M. and Winter, S.G. (2002) 'Deliberate learning and the evolution of dynamic capabilitie', *Organization Science*, 13(3): 339–351.

Zollo, M., Reuer, J.J. and Singh, H. (2002) 'Interorganizational routines and performance in strategic alliances', *Organization Science*, 13(6): 701–713.

Zueva-Owens, A., Fotaki, M. and Pervez Ghauri, P. (2012) 'Cultural evaluations in acquired companies: Focusing on subjectivities', *British Journal of Management*, 23: 272–290.

Zukin, S. and DiMaggio, P. (eds) (1990) *Structures of Capital: The Social Organization of the Economy*. Cambridge, MA: Cambridge University Press.

INDEX